REFORM IN THE OTTOMAN
EMPIRE, 1856-1876

REFORM IN THE
OTTOMAN EMPIRE
1856-1876

By RODERIC H. DAVISON

PRINCETON, NEW JERSEY
PRINCETON UNIVERSITY PRESS
1963

For Louise

and John and Richard

ꙮ PREFACE ꙮ

The study of the Tanzimat period—that crucial time of attempted reform and westernization in the nineteenth-century Ottoman Empire —is still in its infancy. We are many years and scores of monographs away from a definitive history, which will be possible only after full exploitation of the Turkish archives and of other widely scattered materials in over a dozen languages. Much still remains to be known simply of what happened and how and when, not to speak of why. This, therefore, is a preliminary attempt to recount and assess the major reform developments and to put them in their historical context. The focal period is the climactic two decades of the Tanzimat which led up to the promulgation of the first Ottoman constitution in 1876.

Social scientists interested in the impact of the West on a nonwestern area may find points of useful comparison in this analysis of the later Tanzimat period. It deals in large measure with westernization, particularly in the political sphere, and may be considered to bear also on the even more slippery concept of modernization. Yet I am reluctant to call this a case study. I have attempted no comparisons with other areas where the political and cultural impact of the West has been strong. There are parallels to be drawn, but also sharp contrasts. And as will, I hope, be obvious to the reader, individual personalities and the pure concatenation of historical events exercised a major influence on efforts made in this period to reform and revitalize the Ottoman Empire. The genesis of the constitution of 1876, for example, is otherwise inexplicable. It can be asserted with more confidence that this essay in a key period of modern Turkish history will provide some of the background necessary to an understanding of later reform efforts and of aspects of the growth of the Turkish Republic. I have tried, however, not to focus only on those developments which adumbrate the emergence of the modern Turkish nation, but rather to look at the problems of the vast and heterogeneous Ottoman Empire as it then was.

My debt to the contemporaries who recorded events and currents of that time, and to modern scholars who have dug back into various aspects of the Tanzimat, will be evident on almost every page. I am further indebted to the many scholars who have given me suggestions

on one point or another, or help in locating materials. Among them
are William L. Langer, with whose encouragement this study was
begun, Halil İnalcık, Lewis V. Thomas, Niyazi Berkes, George C.
Miles, Aydın Sayili, Sevinç Dıblan Carlson, Stanford Shaw, and the
late Michael Karpovich and Chester W. Clark. I am also grateful to
four others, now gone from us, who many years ago read critically
parts or all of the original dissertation from which this book took its
start: Abdülhak Adnan-Adıvar, J. Kingsley Birge, Walter L. Wright,
Jr., and Daniel C. Dennett, Jr. Dankwart Rustow furnished very helpful criticism at a later stage. Three other friends—A. O. Sarkissian,
Jakob Saper, and Elie Salem—have helped me to use materials in
Armenian, Polish, and Arabic. My brother, W. Phillips Davison, assisted me in using materials in the Scandinavian languages, and also
copied some documents in the Swedish archives. Howard A. Reed,
Robert Devereux, and Albertine Jwaideh kindly allowed me to consult their unpublished dissertations.

The staffs of many libraries have been very helpful. Among them
are the Harvard College Library, the Princeton University Library,
the New York Public Library, the Library of Congress, the British
Museum, the Bibliothèque Nationale, the Centralbibliothek in Zürich,
the George Washington University Library, the State Department
Library, and the Middle East Institute Library. I have received many
courtesies also from the staffs of the Public Record Office in London,
the Archives des Affaires Etrangères in Paris, the Haus- Hof- und
Staatsarchiv in Vienna, and the National Archives in Washington.
The American Board of Commissioners for Foreign Missions gen-
erously granted permission for use of their manuscript records.

In its initial stages the work was made possible by a fellowship
from the Social Science Research Council. I am also much indebted
to Sir Hamilton Gibb, Derwood Lockard, and others of the Center for
Middle Eastern Studies at Harvard who in the spring of 1960 provided a research fellowship that greatly helped to bring this study
along toward completion. At the same time, a light teaching load was
kindly arranged by Robert Lee Wolff and Myron P. Gilmore of
Harvard's History Department. The Committee on Research of the
George Washington University has also given assistance. On several
occasions Nancy Hull Keiser, of the Keiser Foundation, and the
Middle East Institute have provided a haven for research and writ-

PREFACE

ing. Carolyn Cross, Brenda Sens, and Bonnie Pugh did meticulous typing. Miriam Brokaw and Mary Tozer have provided sound editorial advice. What I owe to my wife and sons for their tolerance for research cannot adequately be expressed. The book is dedicated to them.

Washington
August, 1962   R. H. D.

Anyone who has read at all widely on the Near East will be familiar with the confusion among systems of transliteration from the Arabic alphabet, which was, in any case, unsuited to the Turkish language. When one writes Turkey's history the problem is complicated by the change made there in 1928 from Arabic to Latin characters. The modern spelling of Turkish words is not yet in all cases standardized. Yet it is phonetic, and seems to offer the most sensible base on which to build. There is, further, a rapidly increasing literature of historical scholarship in modern Turkish. I have, therefore, followed modern Turkish usage except for a preference for "b" and "d" rather than "p" and "t" where there is an option.

The Turkish alphabet includes only a few letters which present any problem to the reader of English. These are:

c — pronounced like the "j" in "job"
ç — pronounced like the "ch" in "child"
ğ — a very soft and sometimes guttural "gh"
ı — pronounced roughly like the "i" in "bird," or something
    between the "i" in "will" and the "u" in "bug"
ö — pronounced like the "eu" in French "peu"
ş — pronounced like the "sh" in "shall"
ü — pronounced like the "u" in French "tu"

A circumflex over a vowel indicates a broadened pronunciation. Thus "Âli" was formerly written "Aali" by western Europeans.

Many Turkish common nouns are so close to their Anglicized forms as to create no difficulty either for pronunciation or comprehension, and the Turkish spelling is more accurate. Thus, though the eye of the English reader may at first be offended, "vezir" will be used for the English form "vizier," "ferman" for "firman," "sipahi" for "spahi," et cetera. The same is true of other common Turkish words, also close to the Anglicized form, which use one of the new Turkish letters not found in English—thus "kadı" for "cadi," "meclis" for "mejlis," "şeriat" for "sheriat." For such common words the Turkish spelling will be used as if it were already accepted in English (as no doubt in many cases it soon will be), without italics. Less common Turkish terms will be italicized. The plurals for the latter category of words, since they are treated as Turkish, should properly vary with the vowel form. But for convenience in reading, and to avoid complications, I have abandoned the Turkish plurals for an " 's"—thus "*âyan*'s" instead of "*âyanlar*," "*kariye*'s" instead of "*kariyeler*."

In the case of proper nouns, I have used "İstanbul" for "Constantinople," "Edirne" for "Adrianople," "İzmir" for "Smyrna," and so on, despite Churchill's haughty wartime dictum that "İstanbul" was a form for stupid people, and that "foreign names were made for Englishmen, not Englishmen for foreign names." In a study designed to treat Turks not as foreigners, but as central figures in their own historical development, it seems suitable to use the Turkish names at least for places within the borders of modern Turkey. Names of places outside modern Turkey will be put in the ordinary English form, with an occasional parenthetical equivalent for the Turkish or local form where this will help to locate the particular place on a map. For the names of people I have followed a similar principle. Thus "Âli Paşa" will appear for "Aali Pasha," "Sultan Abdülaziz" for "Sultan Abdul Aziz," "Cevdet Efendi" for "Djevdet Effendi," and so on. Armenian, Greek, and other names have been put in English rather than Turkish equivalents.

All dates given in the text are in Gregorian style, although Old Style (Julian) was in common use in the Ottoman Empire, running twelve days behind the Gregorian in the period here discussed. Years given in the bibliographical citations which are in the 1200's or 1300's are, almost without exception, Hicrî (Hegira) dates, with the "A.H." omitted. A very few are Malî (Turkish financial year) dates, which in the period here discussed were about one year in advance of the Hicrî date. The divergence fifty years later was about three years.

Titles in other than the major western languages are translated in the bibliography, but not in the footnotes.

Abbreviations used in the footnotes are:

ABCFM — Archives of the American Board of Commissioners for Foreign Missions on deposit at Houghton Library, Harvard University

AAE — Correspondance Politique, Archives des Affaires Etrangères, Paris

FO — Foreign Office Archives, Public Record Office, London

HHS — Politisches Archiv, Haus- Hof- und Staatsarchiv, Vienna

SRA — Diplomatica Samlingen, Svenska Riksarkivet, Stockholm

USNA — Department of State Records, United States National Archives, Washington

CONTENTS

CONTENTS

REFORM IN THE OTTOMAN

EMPIRE, 1856-1876

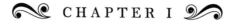

CHAPTER I

INTRODUCTION: DECLINE AND REFORM
TO 1856

At three o'clock in the afternoon of February 18, 1856, a crowd of several thousands gathered at the Sublime Porte in İstanbul to hear the solemn reading of a Hatt-ı Hümayun, an imperial edict on the organizational reform of his empire addressed by Sultan Abdülmecid to his grand vezir Âli Paşa. Not only were the ministers of the Ottoman Empire and many Turkish notables present, but also the Greek and Armenian patriarchs, the grand rabbi, and other dignitaries of the various non-Muslim peoples of the empire. The edict concerned all the subjects of the sultan, Muslim or not.

In a sentence as complex as the question of reform itself, the sultan's edict began thus: "Wishing today to renew and enlarge yet more the new regulations instituted for the purpose of obtaining a state of affairs in conformity with the dignity of my empire and the position which it occupies among civilized nations, . . . I desire to increase well-being and prosperity, to obtain the happiness of all my subjects who, in my eyes, are all equal and are equally dear to me, and who are united among themselves by cordial bonds of patriotism, and to assure the means of making the prosperity of my empire grow from day to day." To these ends, Abdülmecid continued, he directed his grand vezir to elaborate and execute various projects of reorganization. The edict laid particular stress on the equality of all peoples of the empire—Muslims, Christians, and Jews—and singled out for specific mention a number of ways in which the equal rights of non-Muslims should be guaranteed. The Hatt-ı Hümayun thus heralded, in its own phrase, "the beginning of a new era."

But when, the reading of the edict finished, the customary invocation of God's blessing was offered by a preacher well known in the mosques of İstanbul, his prayer contained no mention at all of reforms, of non-Muslims, or of equality. "O God," he beseeched, "have mercy on the people of Muhammad. O God, preserve the people of Muhammad." A chill fell on the assemblage. The minister of war whispered in the ear of his neighbor that he felt like a man whose evening-long labors on a manuscript were ruined through careless

3

upsetting of the inkpot.[1] Printed copies of the edict were then distributed to those in attendance, and the momentous occasion was over.

Just a week later representatives of the European powers, the grand vezir Âli Paşa among them, gathered in Paris to draw up the treaty which ended the Crimean War. Russia had been defeated by a coalition of Britain, France, Piedmont, and the Ottoman Empire, with Austria as a nonbelligerent ally. Now, a victor, the Ottoman Empire was formally admitted to the concert of Europe by the treaty signed on March 30.[2] Her independence and integrity were guaranteed by the treaty. Further, article 9 took note of the Hatt-ı Hümayun: the powers "recognized the high value" of the edict which the sultan had communicated to them and declared that this communication gave them no right of intervention in the internal affairs of the empire. Finally, on April 15, 1856, the representatives of Britain, France, and Austria signed a tripartite treaty guaranteeing joint and several defense of Ottoman independence and integrity.[3] The Turks, victorious in war and protected by three great powers, were thus given a respite to work out their own salvation.

But there were dangers ahead, symbolically foreshadowed at a huge banquet given by Sultan Abdülmecid to celebrate the treaty of Paris. As one of the guests described it: "A minute or two after the Sultan had retired we were startled by two frightful claps of thunder followed by a storm of wind and hail. The whole building seemed to shake, and in a moment the gas went out and we were in total darkness. The band dropped their instruments with a clash and fled. For some moments no one spoke, and then a thin, shrill voice was heard in French saying, 'It wants but the handwriting on the wall and the words "Mene, Tekel, Upharsin" to make of this a second feast of Belshazzar.' "[4]

[1] Cevdet Paşa, *Tezâkir 1-12*, ed. by Cavid Baysun (Ankara, 1953), pp. 67-69, most of which is reproduced in Ahmet Refik, "Türkiyede ıslahat fermanı," *Tarih-i osmanî encümeni mecmuası* 14:81 (1340), 195-197. Descriptions of the ceremony also in F. Eichmann, *Die Reformen des Osmanischen Reiches* (Berlin, 1858), p. 240, and in Prokesch-Osten's report, HHS, XII/56, 21 February 1856.

[2] Treaty text in Gabriel Noradounghian, *Recueil d'actes internationaux de l'Empire ottoman* (Paris, 1897-1903), III, 70-79.

[3] Text in Thomas E. Holland, *The European Concert in the Eastern Question* (Oxford, 1885), pp. 259-260.

[4] Edmund Hornby, *Autobiography* (London, 1928), p. 83. Similar accounts in Lady Hornby, *Constantinople During the Crimean War* (London, 1863), pp. 407-410, and in C. S. de Gobineau, ed., *Correspondance entre le Comte de Gobineau et le Comte de Prokesch-Osten (1854-1876)* (Paris, 1933), p. 97.

In this somewhat ominous fashion the Ottoman Empire entered upon the second and crucial phase of its mid-nineteenth-century attempts at reorganization and westernization, a period known in Turkish history as the Tanzimat. During the succeeding two decades, when the western powers were occupied with the wars attendant upon the creation of Italy and Germany as modern nation-states, and when tsarist Russia was healing her Crimean wounds and attempting far-reaching internal reform, events in Europe seemed to confirm the respite accorded the Ottomans. But the great powers did not stick to their promise of nonintervention, nor did the three guarantors protect the Ottoman Empire when a crisis finally arose. And Ottoman efforts to reorganize and strengthen the empire by creating a genuine equality among all its subjects met many obstacles, among which the mentality evident in the prayer after the Hatt-ı Hümayun was not least in importance.

The fundamental problem confronting Ottoman statesmen was how to prevent their empire's being weighed in the balance and found wanting, how to postpone the time when its days would be numbered. All major projects which they undertook in the succeeding two decades of reform,[5] up to and including the constitution of 1876, were aimed at preserving the empire. Whether the heterogeneous empire had a right to exist is a question that need not be argued here; obviously for the Ottoman statesmen it had. They were struggling to keep the empire together as a going administrative concern and as a territorial unit; looking for some centripetal force or form of organization, as also was the similarly heterogeneous Habsburg Empire in the same years; hoping to prevent the breaking away of further provinces through rebellion or through the diplomatic and military action of the great powers of Europe. To preserve the Ottoman heritage, the Tanzimat statesmen crushed rebellion wherever they

---

[5] It is argued by Lewis V. Thomas in *The United States and Turkey and Iran* (Cambridge, Mass., 1951), p. 51, that "reform" is incorrect as a term to apply to the measures of westernization adopted in the nineteenth-century Ottoman Empire, since the word implies the conviction of westerners of those days that their ways were morally superior to Ottoman ways; hence the Ottomans should "reform." The argument has merit, since the word "reform" often was used with such implications. But it is a convenient term, more inclusive than "westernization," and, if understood in its basic sense of reform, reshape, may perhaps be used without qualms. The word *ıslahat* (sing., *ıslah*) was used by Turks in this same sense, as the equivalent of the French *réformes*, and applied to the measures of the Tanzimat period, whether western-influenced or not, including the Hatt-ı Hümayun of 1856 itself. *Islah* means "improving, reforming, putting defective things into more perfect condition."

could, played off one great power against another when possible, and instituted measures of domestic reorganization. Whether the task was hopeless from the start, or whether the statesmen tried too little and did it too late, are questions that must wait for an answer until the years 1856 to 1876 have been surveyed. But it was plain that no Ottoman statesman took office in order to preside over the liquidation of empire. The 1876 constitution, culmination of this period of reform, significantly proclaimed this objective of self-preservation in its first article: the empire "cannot be divided at any time whatsoever for any cause whatsoever."

Reforms were, therefore, undertaken to revitalize the empire and so to preserve it in a world increasingly ordered by European power and civilization. There was no aspect of Ottoman life that did not require change if this objective were to be attained. Advance was most obviously needed in military strength, to meet the challenge of Europe. But, to undergird this, economic progress was necessary; so also was improvement in the educational system, in the administration of justice, in the revamping of law to meet the needs of modern life, and in the organization and efficiency of public administration. These requirements for change were intertwined; each affected the other. One cannot, as many writers on nineteenth-century Turkey have done, isolate one requirement of reform as the sole key to progress and specify that all other advance depended on it alone. The finances of the central government, the corrupted method of tax collection, the system of land tenure, the manner in which justice was administered, have all been singled out in this fashion. The liberal-humanitarian writers of Europe in the last century frequently picked on the treatment of Christians in the empire as the key to reform, proclaiming that satisfaction of the desires of minorities was the central issue. But all such assertions were oversimplifications, though each pointed to an important problem. No more in Ottoman than in any other field of history is a monistic explanation either adequate or accurate. The causes for the difficult situation in which the Ottoman Empire found itself were many. The needs for reform were also many—military, economic, social, intellectual, legal, and political. The Ottoman statesmen undertook projects of reform touching all these areas in the twenty years after 1856. Sometimes their proclamations of reform measures were used tactically to ward off intervention on the part of the European powers. Sometimes the proclamations themselves were

6

hypocritical. But the basic drive behind the reform movement was not to throw dust in the eyes of Europe. Rather it was to revitalize the empire through measures of domestic reorganization which should include the adoption or adaptation of some western ideas and institutions in these several fields.

Although reforms in the various segments of Ottoman life were interdependent, and progress in each was necessary to insure progress in the others, it is nevertheless true that the government stood at the center of the reforming process and, therefore, that reform in governmental structure and in the efficiency of administration controlled to a large degree what might be achieved in the other fields. Of course, the improvement or reorganization of government itself depended on many other changes, such as educational reform, to produce better bureaucrats and a more reform-minded climate of opinion, or economic progress, to produce a larger national income and augmented revenues for the government. But in this cyclical process, wherein each change depended on other changes, the government itself was the planner and executive agent of reforms in all fields. It could not be otherwise, given the autocratic Ottoman tradition and the character of nineteenth-century Ottoman society. The decay of the old administrative system from the later sixteenth century onward, and its inadequacies in meeting the internal pressures on the structure of the empire thereafter, had been one of the primary reasons for Ottoman weakness. "The fish begins to stink at the head" was a proverb frequently quoted by Ottoman subjects in the nineteenth century. Reform also had to come from the head. Reform from the top down was characteristic of the Tanzimat period no less than of other periods in Turkish history, both earlier and later.[6] The initiative came from the central government; it did not spring from the people. Since the government was the reforming institution, what was done to improve governmental structure and administrative practice deserves particular attention.

In the years from 1856 to 1876 the Tanzimat statesmen worked not only at the traditional task of rooting out administrative abuses, but also at the job of adapting western ideas which laid the basis for representative government and the ultimate secularization of govern-

---

[6] Equally characteristic, of course, was reform from the outside in, which began with externals such as dress and military organization before it tackled fundamentals like education and agriculture.

ment. They spoke of the equality of all Ottoman subjects and tried to create something of a concept of common citizenship (*Osmanlılık*, or Ottomanism), initiated the rudiments of a representative system in provincial and in national councils, and finally put together in 1876 the first written constitution in Ottoman history. The trend in governmental reorganization was away from the classical Islamic concept that the status, rights, and duties of an individual were rooted in his membership in a religious community, be it Muslim, Christian, or Jewish, and toward the western secular concept that his status derived from his citizenship in the Ottoman Empire and from his allegiance to the government of that empire. But the constitution with its embryonic representative principle did not, as in western countries, spring from the pressures of an economically prosperous bourgeoisie demanding political rights. It came from the top down, and specifically from a few statesmen seeking answers to the problems of the day.

The government was also the agency which had to hold the peoples of the empire together, not only by maintenance of sufficient prestige to command their respect and allegiance, but by evolving an administrative system with enough flexibility of local government under central control to be workable. Therefore reforms were undertaken in the manner of provincial administration and in the structure of the non-Muslim communities; and at one point in this period a plan for a federalized empire was broached. These efforts were intended not only to produce more honest and efficient administration, but to prevent the breaking away of more provinces or the creation of further "twilight zones" of sovereignty such as Serbia and the Danubian principalities, Egypt and the Lebanon, already represented in varying degrees. No more for this question than for the others that faced the reformers was a fully satisfactory solution arrived at. But the efforts were important in themselves, and laid a base for future efforts.

Western writers have frequently dealt with the attempts at reforming Ottoman government, and with the reform measures instituted by that government, as if the only important force behind the Tanzimat were the diplomatic pressures exerted by the great powers. Such pressure was highly significant. The Ottoman statesmen were painfully aware of it. But the Tanzimat period cannot be considered simply as a phase of the Eastern Question, and examined from the outside looking in. The changes made within the empire cannot be measured solely in terms of the amount of prodding from European powers. Indeed, the constant interference of Europe in Ottoman affairs often hampered reform and helped to render it ineffectual. And great power diplomacy had, of course, on several occasions led to the territorial diminution of the empire. Such intervention was never disinterested. There was more than a little truth in Fuad Paşa's acid jest to a western diplomat: "Our state is the strongest state. For you are trying to cause its collapse from the outside, and we from the inside, but still it does not collapse."[7]

But, important as European diplomacy was both in prompting and in hindering reform, the detail of great-power maneuvering will be slighted here; other writers have dealt with it extensively. Instead, the reform question will be examined as a domestic problem, on which the diplomatic pressure was but one of many influences. Among the others were Islamic tradition, the previous efforts at reform in the empire, the varying viewpoints of the most important Ottoman statesmen of the time, and a small but vocal public opinion which developed as contact with the West brought the telegraph, journalism, and the start of a new movement in literature. It is impossible to be scientifically precise about the climate of opinion in the Ottoman Empire of 1856 to 1876, but the successes and failures of the Tanzimat period cannot be understood without some reference to it. The term "public opinion" (*efkâr-ı umumiye*) was increasingly used by Turkish writers in these years, and this opinion was the product of converging and competing influences ranging from the oldest Muslim tradition to the latest Parisian secular thought. By 1876 this public opinion had to be reckoned with.

The following pages, then, do not attempt to reconstruct the entire history of the Ottoman Empire, but try to analyze the historical process of governmental reform, to outline the nature of reform instituted by government, from the Hatt-ı Hümayun of 1856 to the constitution of 1876, and to inquire into the influences and pressures which converged on the statesmen in İstanbul. Among the strongest influences was, as has been remarked, the legacy of reform efforts before 1856. A brief review of the necessity for such measures, and of their character, will clarify the situation as it existed when the Hatt-ı Hümayun of 1856 was proclaimed.

[7] Abdurrahman Şeref, *Tarih musahabeleri* (İstanbul, 1339), p. 104.

About the year 1300 the empire of the Ottoman sultans had sprung from humble origins in northwest Anatolia. At first it expanded slowly, but by the later fifteenth century it controlled the Balkan provinces of the former Byzantine Empire up to the Danube and in places beyond, as well as most of Anatolia. The territorial growth of the Ottoman state continued into the seventeenth century, even after the first signs of internal decay could be noticed. From his capital of İstanbul the sultan could survey one of the greatest empires of the day—great not only in lands, but in power, as compared to its neighbors—stretching from Budapest to Basra, and from Algiers to Armenia.

This achievement in empire-building had many causes, among which the weaknesses of neighboring states and pure good fortune were not inconsiderable. In the early days Ottoman expansion also owed much to the gazi spirit—the spirit of warriors conquering for the true Muslim faith. By the sixteenth century, however, when the empire attained its period of greatest grandeur even though it had by then lost some of its elementary vigor, the cement which held it together was not the gazi spirit, but the governmental system which had been built up over the previous two hundred years.

At the apex of the system was the sultan, an autocrat whose authority was limited only by the şeriat, the Islamic law under which he as well as his subjects stood, by the innate conservatism and tradition-mindedness of his people, and by the threat of rebellion. The sultan had traditionally the prerogative of legislating, which he often did, since the religious law did not begin to meet the needs of a complex organization like the Ottoman state. In his hands the sultan held all the reins of government, and until the sixteenth century he attended personally to many details of its business. The efficiency of government depended on his character and ability. Fortunately the Ottoman dynasty had produced a series of ten sultans who until the middle of that century were relatively or conspicuously able men. The sons of sultans usually had experience as provincial governors and as commanders of troops before accession.

The civil and military officials, and the standing army, made up the Ruling Institution.[8] All of them were personal slaves of the sultan. Their slavery was not at all a condition of peonage or penal servitude, but a legal fact designed to give the sultan complete control over his

[8] A convenient descriptive term invented by Albert H. Lybyer, *The Government of the Ottoman Empire in the Time of Suleiman the Magnificent* (Cambridge, Mass., 1913).

officials, including the power of life and death. Since under the religious law the sultan could have no such arbitrary power over his free-born Muslim subjects, his slave officials were born Christians who, through capture in war, purchase in the slave market, or the systematic requisition of boys from Christian families of the empire, were taken into the sultan's service. Through a careful selection process, followed by years of education and training in schools maintained in the imperial palaces, the cream of the crop were prepared to assume the burdens of various offices in the imperial household and central administration, in the government of provinces, and as commanders of various bodies of troops. They became Muslims, but remained slaves. The way was open to them for advance to the highest post of the empire—that of grand vezir. Slave recruits weeded out during the selection process underwent other training to emerge as members of the standing armed forces, chief among which was the corps of Janissaries. Sons of the members of the Ruling Institution could not, because they were free-born Muslims, enter the privileged slave hierarchy. Consequently the growth of a hereditary aristocracy of officials was prevented.

Other soldiers were provided when necessary through the system of land grants made by the sultans to their sipahis, or free-born Muslim cavalrymen. As the Ottoman armies advanced into the Christian areas, the state had taken title to most of the conquered land. This land was granted in fiefs of varying sizes to the sipahis, each of whom was obliged to rally to the standard of a provincial governor at need and provide a stipulated number of armed men. As salary, the cavalryman collected the tithe owed by peasants within his fief. Fiefs could be and often were granted to the sons of cavalrymen, so that the position sometimes became in effect hereditary in one family, but land title and the right of grant remained with the state. In addition to providing for troops, this system of land tenure gave the state sufficient control to prevent the rise of a permanent landed aristocracy with vested interests opposed to those of the central government; forestalled the growth of oversize personal estates; and gave to the peasantry a local lord who was unlikely to grind them down through exactions both because he was controlled by the state and because his long-range interests were linked to their continuing prosperity. The sipahis were not slaves. Some auxiliary naval forces were provided, to supplement the standing navy, on a similar basis by local lords whose fiefs lay on the Aegean littoral.

Parallel to the Ruling Institution was the Muslim Institution,[9] which was open to all free-born Muslims. Their training was in Islamic religion and law. This class of ulema, or learned men of Islam, provided candidates for such jobs as teachers in schools of all levels and preachers in the mosques, but in the state hierarchy its chief function was to staff the legal and judicial posts, from the lowest to the highest. One who advanced to the top of the judicial hierarchy might become the chief judge of Anatolia or Rumelia. At the apex of the hierarchy of juriconsults, or müftis, was the şeyhülislâm, the müfti of İstanbul, who represented the highest legal and religious authority.

Both the Ruling Institution and the Muslim Institution were represented in the sultan's divan, his privy council. At its meetings the grand vezir, the commanders of the Janissaries and of the navy, the chancellor, the treasurer, and the two chief judges, often with other dignitaries in attendance, discussed affairs of state. Until the fifteenth century the sultan himself presided over the sessions of the divan. Later he listened from behind a screen.

Provincial administration was in the hands of members of the sultan's slave hierarchy, the sancak beys or governors, who themselves were subordinate to governors-general, originally two in number, although later there came to be more. Each governor was at the same time head of the civil administration of his province and commander of the troops stationed or levied there. He presided over a divan which in composition reflected the divan in İstanbul, each functionary in it a representative on a lower level of his chief in the capital. In the same administrative divisions of the empire were judges and müftis subordinate to those of the central government.

To this outline of Ottoman government one addition of considerable importance must be made, for the non-Muslim subjects of the empire were organized in semiautonomous bodies which in some ways replaced the direct authority of the sultan's government, even though the locus of ultimate authority was never in doubt. The principal groups of these non-Muslim subjects were Greek Orthodox, Gregorian Armenian, and Jewish. Although many conquered peoples, particularly in the earliest days of Ottoman expansion, had accepted Islam, many had not; and others, especially Jews fleeing from per-

[9] This is also Lybyer's term.

secution in Christian Europe, had immigrated after the empire had nearly reached the limits of its expansion. In the tradition of Islam, the Turks were tolerant of non-Muslims who possessed recognized books of divine revelation—"people of the book" (*ehl-i kitab*), as they were called. People of the book were absorbed into the empire, and granted protection and toleration of their forms of worship, provided they accepted the domination of the Ottoman Turks and paid special taxes. Though they did not live in completely segregated or compact groups, but were scattered about the empire, for administrative convenience an organization of each group under its ecclesiastical heads was recognized by the Ottomans from the time of Mehmed the Conqueror. Each group constituted a millet within the empire; membership in the millet automatically followed lines of religious allegiance.[10]

Each non-Muslim millet was headed by a patriarch (or, in the case of the Jews, by a grand rabbi) who was confirmed in office by the Ottoman government. In addition to his spiritual powers and the supervision of his own ecclesiastical subordinates the patriarch had a fairly extensive civil authority over matters of internal millet administration. This authority rested on the assumption once current in the West, and still current in the nineteenth-century Near East, that law was personal rather than territorial in its basis and that religion rather than domicile or political allegiance determined the law under which an individual lived. Hence the chiefs of the millets controlled not only the clerical, ritual, and charitable affairs of their flocks, but also education and the regulation of matters of personal status like marriage, divorce, guardianship, and inheritance. The ecclesiastical hierarchy had jurisdiction over legal cases between members of the millet except in criminal matters, which the Ottoman government reserved for its own courts. Even some taxes due the sultan's government from the non-Muslims were collected through the millet organization, as well as the taxes imposed by the hierarchy on its own people for its own support. The patriarch was recognized by the Ottoman government

[10] "Millet" by the second half of the nineteenth century began to be used by a few Turks to mean "nation," in the sense of the whole people, rather than to denote a specific religious group. Traditionally, however, the millet denoted a religious community such as those described above, and it continued throughout the Tanzimat period to have this primary meaning. For references on the minority millets and their development see below, chapter IV. The Muslim millet was, of course, under the direct rule of its own sultan and bureaucracy.

13

as the voice of his millet, and his decisions were backed by its authority; on his part, the patriarch found it advisable to listen to and cooperate with the Ottoman government which was the ultimate sanction for his civil authority, and with which his interests were usually closely allied.

This governmental framework served the Ottoman Empire well. But the empire never stood poised at a peak of development within a perfected framework. Its history, like the history of other states, is a series of ages of transition. If the Ottoman Empire achieved brilliance and grandeur in the sixteenth century under Süleyman the Lawgiver, it is also true that the seeds of Ottoman decline can be discerned in this age. Some irregularities in the administration which demanded correction were apparent even to Süleyman: for instance, confusion and corruption in the distribution of military fiefs by provincial governors led him to take back into his own hands the allocation of all sizable tımars. But the weakening of the empire in relation to the rising power and culture of western Europe was not evident to Ottoman Turks of that day. Nor, indeed, was this weakening made manifest in any reduction of its territory. The failure of the Ottoman army before Vienna in 1529 was not disastrous; the empire continued to expand into the seventeenth century and began to wane in earnest only with the military defeats culminating in the Treaty of Carlowitz in 1699. Nevertheless, during the seventeenth century a number of Ottoman statesmen became fully aware of some of the evils in the administration of empire which threatened to weaken the whole structure, and felt also the superior progress of Europe at least in military equipment and organization. But neither they nor their eighteenth-century successors were aware of the total explanation for the gradual weakening of the Ottoman state, which continued progressively down to the Tanzimat period both in relation to Europe and in relation to the golden age of the Ottoman system.

European superiority was becoming apparent on the battlefield, but this was only an outward result of the general intellectual, economic, and political development in the West in which the Ottoman dominions did not participate and which the Ottomans for long did not comprehend. The Islamic world experienced no period of renaissance and reformation. It saw no release of individual energies comparable to that in the West—no burst of technological invention, no general scientific and rational development in thought, no far-flung oceanic

voyages of discovery, no upsurge in business and industry. To employ
the usual capsule terms of western history, the ages of humanism and
of reason, the commercial revolution, the industrial revolution, and
the agricultural revolution did not spread into the Ottoman dominions. This comparative disadvantage of the Ottoman Empire arose
in part from the lack of intimate contact with western life and in part
from innate scorn of things non-Muslim. This attitude in its turn came
not only from the tradition-mindedness and conservatism which was
perhaps more characteristic of the Near East than the West—though
all peoples have throughout history shared these qualities—but also
from traditional religious views and practices. Islam, which was not
only a way of worship but a way of life, a total outlook, and the basis
of the law, had ceased to develop and change as rapidly as the times
required. Ottoman tradition and Islamic conservatism had their effect
also on political organization. Whereas the strong, centralized national monarchy was becoming dominant in the West and over the
seas, led more and more by a bourgeois class which produced new
political ideas and demands, the sprawling and heterogeneous Ottoman Empire remained what it was, but therefore at an increasing
disadvantage in competition of all sorts. "The Ottomans' traditional
methods and techniques, the total Ottoman synthesis of Faith, State,
and Way, had become no longer good to hold its own against its
foes."[11]

Though the Ottoman system of government remained what it was
in outward structure down to the beginning of the nineteenth century,
its workings became corrupted. The administration suffered at all
levels, beginning significantly with the sultan himself. After Süleyman, the tenth in a line of able rulers, the vigor and general personal
quality of the sultans was markedly less, though Osman II and
Murad IV were brief seventeenth-century exceptions. After A.D. 1603,
princes ceased to have practical experience in provincial government
before accession to the throne. Instead, they were kept in luxurious
but debilitating confinement in one of the imperial palaces, in private
apartments known as the *kafes* ("lattice" or "cage"). Any prince who
inherited the throne emerged from such confinement not only inex-
perienced, but often a mental case and with debauched tastes. Their
urge to luxury and grandeur, which had shown itself even before the
kafes became an institution, increased; the sultans became oriental

[11] Thomas, *United States and Turkey*, p. 49.

potentates, no longer leading their armies in battle, but interested in the hunt, the harem, or the bottle. Their lavish spending on themselves and their favorites led them to make inroads on the state treasury and to countenance bribery and simony. Often the sultans were strongly influenced by the women of their harem, especially the sultan-mothers or the mothers of princes ambitious for their sons; in the seventeenth century the empire was for a time ruled, in fact, by women of the harem.

The whole Ruling Institution became corrupted as well. The system was weakened as early as the sixteenth century by arbitrary promotion to the highest posts of imperial favorites who had not worked up through the ranks by merit. Venality also crept into the administration. The purchase and sale of public office both corrupted the officials involved and replaced merit with other less desirable criteria for appointment. The method of recruitment of slaves broke down and was eventually abandoned, so that the posts were filled by freeborn Muslims with family connections and interests, which increased the possibilities of favoritism, faction, and intrigue. A rapid turnover of officeholders, accompanied by the giving and taking of bribes, resulted. The corruption of the bureaucracy had a greater effect since, from the fifteenth century on, the sultans ceased to preside in person over the divan and to coordinate state affairs; the job fell to the grand vezir and his subordinates, who ran the state from their offices in the Sublime Porte. The divan met infrequently, and mostly for ceremonial purposes. A parallel corruption enveloped the Muslim Institution, as kadıs grew avaricious for fees and bribes. It became one of the familiar complaints among Turks that justice was bought and sold.

The Janissary corps, earlier the flower of the Ottoman armies, gradually became valueless in war and, instead, a danger to the state. Members of the corps became accustomed to largesse distributed on the accession of each new sultan, which constituted in effect the purchase of Janissary approval. They could exercise considerable power by the threat of rebellion, and were often hard to control. Those Janissaries stationed in the farther provinces became oppressive and highhanded, taking without payment what they wanted from the populations. Not only were the Janissaries becoming dangerous in their conduct, but the whole system of their organization fell to pieces. Once the rule against marriage while on active service was relaxed,

Janissaries began to have family connections, and sons who were free-born Muslims rather than the sultan's slaves were accepted into the corps, followed by other Muslims. As the combat effectiveness of the corps declined, its size increased to unwieldy proportions. The pay ticket which each Janissary possessed became an object of commerce, like a stock certificate: there were numerous instances of important men who were not Janissaries holding many such certificates and receiving commensurate unearned pay. Large numbers of Janissaries became essentially artisans of various sorts in the cities, drawing military pay but otherwise leading a civilian life. On occasions when Janissary units were mustered in Istanbul to go on campaign, the column of men would mysteriously melt to half its size before it had gone far from the capital.

In like manner the system for providing sipahis from military fiefs became corrupted, with serious results not only for Ottoman military strength but also for the whole system of land tenure and for the peasantry at the base of the system. Many of the fiefs were allocated not to fighting men, but to imperial favorites, including women of the harem and officials of the bureaucracy, some of whom acquired plural holdings and enjoyed the income but produced no soldiers. "Sword fiefs" became "shoe money" for the women of the palace. Although such fiefs were still legally state-owned, they came to be treated more and more as outright personal property. At the same time both the state and fief holders began to use the system of tax farming, whereby the concession to collect taxes in a given area was sold to the highest bidder. The tax farmer then squeezed the peasantry to recoup his purchase price and to make a profit over and above the sum due the state for taxes. In many localities a landed aristocracy of âyan's, or notables, grew up. These notables, in addition to securing quasi-permanent title to lands, arrogated to themselves a considerable measure of local political authority. Some became strong enough to defy the central government.

All these developments had serious consequences for the system of provincial administration. The provinces, now known as eyalets, into which the empire was divided in the later sixteenth century, were governed by valis who purchased the office and then set out through exactions from the inhabitants to indemnify themselves and to secure funds for periods of future unemployment. So long as they could hold office, many of the valis disregarded orders from Istanbul. This centrifugal process was increased in the eighteenth century, especially in the farther provinces, by the rise of local landholders to governorships which they were able to make hereditary in their family and relatively independent of İstanbul. These *derebeyi*'s ("lords of the valley") were not infrequently less oppressive than short-term governors, since their interest was bound to the continuing prosperity of the peasantry within their domains, but their rise was disastrous for integrated imperial policy and the cohesion of empire.

The diversion of revenues to the pockets of landholders, officials, or spendthrift sultans naturally weakened the financial condition of the empire. So also did the series of unsuccessful wars from the seventeenth century on, which brought no booty but cost a great deal. So also did the necessity for meeting the pay tickets of Janissaries. A good deal of land also ceased to produce revenue for the state because it was illegally made into *vakıf*, or property in perpetual trust. The income from this property should properly have gone for pious and charitable works, but often accrued to the benefit of individuals only. Fieflands so illegally converted into *vakıf* escaped reassignment by the state. The influx of cheap American silver brought inflation. Financial distress led the government on several occasions to resort to debasement of the coinage; the short-term advantage was, however, wiped out by the renewed inflationary process thus induced.

The system of millet administration did not collapse, but was sapped by venality in the ecclesiastical hierarchies, especially the Greek, and by the financial squeezing of the people by the higher clergy for their own purposes.[12] Often the upper clergy of a minority millet and Ottoman officials were in league together in bleeding the people. More disastrous ultimately for the preservation of the Ottoman state than corruption within the millets was the simple fact that the continued existence of these distinct religious communities offered convenient opportunity to the great powers of Europe for agitation and intrigue among the minorities—for fifth-column activity in time of war and diplomatic intervention in time of peace. By the early nineteenth century the modern doctrine of nationalism began to seize the imagina-

---

[12] There is a running and presumably irresolvable argument between Greeks and Turks as to whether the Turks learned bribery and corruption from Byzantine and Greek Orthodox example, or whether the Greeks learned corruption from the Ottomans through example and through the hypocritical subservience toward which their subordinate role in the empire urged them.

tion of some minority millets and result in separatist movements in which the great powers also aided.

The picture of corruption and decay that has been sketched here, although truthful, is not quite true; otherwise the Ottoman Empire would have collapsed far sooner than it did. Several mitigating factors operating within the empire, as well as counterbalancing rivalries among the great powers on the outside, gave the Ottoman Empire enough strength to survive for three centuries after the first signs of internal decay appeared. First, there were a few sultans of comparative ability. Second, the administrative system, corrupted as it became, still included men of integrity and threw to the top every so often grand vezirs of remarkable ability, among whom members of the Köprülü family in the seventeenth century rank high. Third, the corrupted system seems to have produced some equilibriums of its own. Officials who exploited the populace and manipulated the sultan, and powerful cliques or individuals in the shadows behind the officials, had a vested interest in the system which made them seek to preserve the empire, not to destroy it;[13] the weapon of confiscation could be used to wipe out the ill-gotten gains of pashas, though the funds thus recouped for the imperial treasury again trickled into illegal channels; and a sort of balance emerged—among officials of Palace and Porte, Janissaries who occasionally spoke as the voice of the people, and paternalistic *derebeyi*'s—which prevented any one group from driving the empire to immediate ruin. Finally, well before the Tanzimat there were reformers and reform efforts. Many of these reform efforts came to nothing, but all served to provide a background for the reforms of the nineteenth century.

The background was in one way negative, for the tendency of the early reformers was simply to identify the elements of corruption in the administrative system and to advise a return to honesty and efficiency. They looked back to the golden age of the empire for their model. This tradition of backward-looking reform was still important in the nineteenth century as a countervailing force to the efforts of other reformers who wanted westernization; it can be noticed in the phraseology of the reform decree of Gülhane in 1839 and in the

[13] This is the thesis of Walter L. Wright, Jr., *Ottoman Statecraft* (Princeton, 1935), pp. 56-60.

thinking of various statesmen. Among those who sounded the alarm, and insisted on high standards among the bureaucracy, was Ayni Ali who in 1607 wrote, at the command of the then grand vezir Kuyucu Murad Paşa, a fairly extensive review of the abuses in the administration, pointing out particularly corruption in the system of fief-holding.[14] Some two decades later Mustafa Koçi Bey produced a broad investigation of abuses within the empire, together with detailed suggestions on reform.[15] Kâtib Çelebî, usually known in the West as Hadji Khalifa, again a few years later examined provincial government and the financial and military situations in a brief treatise.[16] Early in the eighteenth century Sarı Mehmed Paşa the Defterdar, or Treasurer, wrote a book of counsel for vezirs and governors which once more indicted the bureaucracy for abuses and recommended remedies.[17] These men, and others who wrote in similar vein, knew what they were talking about. Usually they had held varied and important administrative positions, and could compare the corruption they saw about them with their idealized picture of the great age of Süleyman. Officials who were also poets likewise wrote devastating indictments of the bribery and general lack of morality prevalent in both the Ruling Institution and the Muslim Institution. Veysi, a judge of the early seventeenth century, spoke like an Old Testament prophet: "The great men do the purse adore"; the vezirs are "foes to Faith and State."[18] Toward the end of the same century Yusuf Nabi painted an equally gloomy picture in a poem of counsel to his son, advising him that the bribery, corruption, and oppression involved in provincial governorships, as well as in the legal hierarchy, made the life of an official a constant nightmare.[19]

When in the eighteenth century the first glimmer of westernizing reform made its appearance, it was quite naturally concerned with the armed forces. The corruption and unruliness of the Janissaries turned the thoughts of a number of sultans to reform of this arm of the service. Murad IV as far back as the early seventeenth century had

---

[14] Trans. in P. A. von Tischendorf, *Das Lehnswesen in den moslemischen Staaten insbesondere im osmanischen Reiche* (Leipzig, 1872), pp. 57-103.

[15] Trans. by W. F. Behrnauer in *Zeitschrift der Deutschen Morgenländischen Gesellschaft*, 15 (1861), 272-332.

[16] Trans. by Behrnauer, *ibid.* 11 (1857), 111-132.

[17] Trans. in Wright, *Ottoman Statecraft*, pp. 61-158.

[18] His *kaside* is partially translated in E. J. W. Gibb, *History of Ottoman Poetry* (London, 1900-1909), III, 214-218.

[19] Partial translation in *ibid.*, pp. 343-345.

curbed the Janissaries somewhat, and apparently harbored designs of abolishing the corps and building up a new regular army; but even his ruthless use of the old-fashioned reformer's weapons of death and confiscation was not equal to the task. To the obvious need for reform or abolition of the Janissary corps were added the equally obvious lessons learned from the increasing European military superiority in the century of warfare following the Ottoman retreat from the second siege of Vienna in 1683.[20] Sultans and grand vezirs turned to western military science for help. In the 1730's the French adventurer Bonneval, who presented himself to the sultan as an expert in many military lines, turned Turk and, as Ahmed Paşa, was employed to reorganize the Ottoman corps of bombardiers. His efforts produced only ephemeral results; they represent, however, one of the first instances of official sanction for any type of westernization in the Ottoman system.[21] Three decades later Baron de Tott, a Hungarian formerly in French employ, served in the Ottoman Empire as instructor in artillery and as teacher in a school of mathematics for naval personnel.[22] The treaty of Küçük Kaynarca, concluding a disastrous war with Russia in 1774, drove home again the need for military reform, and under Sultan Abdülhamid I (1774-1789) the grand vezir Halil Hamid Paşa made renewed efforts at conscious westernization of artillery, sapper, and bombardier corps with the guidance of French specialists, and a school for army engineers was founded soon thereafter. French was taught in this school, along with scientific subjects. But none of these efforts at military reform attempted more than a thin veneer of westernization. None was informed by an understanding of the cultural background out of which western military superiority arose. Their importance was that they represented the thin edge of the wedge of westernized reform.

For the military reforms helped to increase the channels of communication with Europe and to swell the trickle of information about western ways. Such channels there had always been, through wars, diplomatic missions, Greeks and Armenians and Jews of the empire,

[20] A document of 1717 gives an early example of the realization of European superiority in some matters; Faik R. Unat, "Ahmet III. devrine ait bir ıslahat takriri," *Tarih vesikaları*, 1:2 (August 1941), 107-121, cited in Niyazi Berkes, "Historical Background of Turkish Secularism," in Richard N. Frye, ed., *Islam and the West* (The Hague, 1956), p. 49.

[21] See Albert Vandal, *Le pacha Bonneval* (Paris, 1883); Osman Ergin, *Türkiye maarif tarihi* (İstanbul, 1939-1943), I, 44-50.

[22] See François Baron de Tott, *Mémoires*, 3 vols. (Amsterdam, 1785).

European travellers and traders, and European renegades who turned Muslim. As early as 1720 Yirmi Sekiz Çelebi Mehmed, sent on embassy to Paris and instructed to survey aspects of western manufacture and knowledge which would be applicable to the empire, had reported favorably on the West.[23] But in general even the educated men of the Ottoman Empire were little touched by European knowledge or example until the nineteenth century. The first press in the empire, for instance, was established in 1493 by Jews fled from Spain; Armenian and Greek presses followed during the next two centuries. But the first press in the empire to print books in Turkish was authorized by the Ottoman government only in 1726, and was established not by a Turk but by İbrâhim Müteferrika, a Magyar captive who turned Muslim. The *fetva* of authorization limited the output to scientific and historical works and dictionaries, since the ulema would not permit printing of works on theology or law.[24] This attitude was to remain typical of the large body of ulema who, until the demands of military science began to open the way for westernized education, were the chief educated class; but the ulema were defending their vested interests and most of them were vastly ignorant about their times and their world. By distinguishing between sacred and secular works, and in effect abdicating their authority to control the latter, the ulema protected their own peculiar sphere but made it easier for a new group, educated along secular lines, to arise.[25]

The needs of military reform opened the way not only to the employment of foreign specialists, but to the founding of the naval and military engineering schools, to the translation and printing of western mathematical and other scientific works, to medical education required for the army, and then to similar undertakings in nonmilitary fields. Some Turks began to learn French, a language which opened up to them new vistas, either while on missions abroad or by study at home. Sometimes the western knowledge arrived by devious routes. Raif Mahmud Efendi was at the end of the eighteenth century a secretary in the Ottoman embassy in London. There, using somewhat

[23] E. Z. Karal in *Tanzimat*, I (İstanbul, 1940), 19; Berkes, "Historical Background," p. 50 and n.3.

[24] Abdülhak Adnan-Adıvar, *Osmanlı Türklerinde ilim* (İstanbul, 1943), pp. 146-148; Franz Babinger, *Stambuler Buchwesen im 18ten Jahrhundert* (Leipzig, 1919), pp. 10ff; Avram Galanti Bodrumlu, *Türkler ve Yahudiler*, 2nd ed. (İstanbul, 1947), p. 100; Berkes, "Historical Background," pp. 50-51; T. Halasi-Kun, "İbrâhim Müteferrika," *İslâm ansiklopedisi*, v, 898-899.

[25] Berkes, "Historical Background," pp. 50-51.

outdated western sources, he wrote a geography in French which was translated into Turkish by a Greek in the Ottoman diplomatic service in Vienna and was printed in Turkish at the press established in Üsküdar under the direction of the recently founded military engineering school.[26] One of the best-educated men of his day, Hoca İshak Efendi, a Muslim of Jewish ancestry, was a teacher at the military engineering school and its second director, early in the nineteenth century. He employed his wide linguistic knowledge to utilize western sources for his writing, particularly in a four-volume work on the natural sciences and mathematics.[27] Some of the coming leaders in reform owed their westernizing outlook at least in part to their military education.

The beginnings of westernized military education and the corollary importation of knowledge from Europe were augmented in the time of Sultan Selim III (1789-1807), during whose reign occurred some of the innovations mentioned above. The French Revolution, with its tremendous upheaval in political ideas as well as in the territorial status quo and European balance of power, also came in his reign to touch the Ottoman Empire. The most dramatic event was Napoleon's invasion of Egypt, which again demonstrated the military superiority of Europe and provided French example and inspiration for the westernizing process which was soon thereafter begun in Egypt by Mehmed Ali. The vicissitudes of the revolutionary period brought to İstanbul a larger number of Frenchmen, who spread new ideas of liberty and provided military assistance to the Turks. Some of the reaction among Ottoman Turks was decidedly unfavorable, both to the French political doctrine of the right of revolution against kings and to the atmosphere of secularism and godlessness which came from eighteenth-century France. The foreign minister (*reis ül küttab*) in 1798 condemned events in France as the product of atheists like Voltaire and Rousseau, and defended religion and holy law as the only sound basis for state and society.[28] French influence in Turkey went up and down, and for a time reactionary sentiment triumphed; nevertheless, new

---

[26] *Tanzimat*, I, 525; Adnan-Adıvar, *Osmanlı Türklerinde ilim*, pp. 188-189.

[27] *Ibid.*, pp. 196-197; Bodrumlu, *Türkler ve Yahudiler*, p. 130; *idem, Histoire des juifs d'Istanbul* (İstanbul, 1941), I, 28.

[28] Atıf Efendi's memorandum to the Divan, 1798, cited from an appendix in vol. VI of *Tarih-i Cevdet* by Adnan-Adıvar, *Osmanlı Türklerinde ilim*, p. 192, and translated in part in Bernard Lewis, "The Impact of the French Revolution on Turkey," *Journal of World History*, I:I (July 1953), 121-122. Cf. Sıddık S. Onar, *İdare hukukunun umumî esasları* (İstanbul, 1952), pp. 539-540, n.2, quoting the same memorandum.

and unconventional ideas spread among some of the younger Turks, even in the Porte and Palace. As the Ottoman historian of the period, a conservative opponent of the new ideas, wrote, the French "were able to insinuate Frankish customs in the hearts and endear their modes of thought to the minds of some people of weak mind and shallow faith."[29] At least a few Turks thus came to know the politically explosive principles embodied in the Declaration of the Rights of Man and the Citizen.

Selim III was among the liberals. Although upset by the execution of Louis XVI, his impulse was in the direction of westernization, particularly in the military sphere. By all accounts he was a man of great enlightenment for his time and position; his vision went beyond the mere correction of abuses, with which he was, of course, vitally concerned, to a "New Deal" for the Ottoman state, expressed as the *nizam-i cedid*, or new order. Prior to his accession Selim had enjoyed more freedom from the *kafes* than the princes before him, and had been in correspondence with Louis XVI. His edicts from the start of his reign reveal his concern for reform. In recognition of the demands of the times he encouraged educational measures, especially the military schools, established regular Ottoman embassies in several European capitals, confiscated a number of fiefs whose holders provided no troops and used the proceeds to further his reform projects, and proposed to regularize appointments to provincial governorships and to abolish tax-farming. He favored establishing a consultative assembly (*meclis-i meşveret*) of leading officials. Such an assembly actually met under Selim's chairmanship at the start of his reign, to discuss reform measures.[30] He sought written recommendations on such measures from many of the leading officials. Selim's most courageous project, and the one which brought about his downfall, was the establishment of a new regular army in embryo, trained and dressed along European lines. But the forces of reaction, encouraged by a majority of the ulema, who feared innovation and French influence, and spearheaded by a revolt of the Janissaries, whose special position was obviously threatened, deposed him in 1807 and killed him in the fol-

[29] Lewis, "Impact of the French Revolution," p. 125, translating a passage from *Asim tarihi*; see also Adnan-Adıvar, *Osmanlı Türklerinde ilim*, p. 192.

[30] Recai G. Okandan, *Umumî amme hukukumuzun ana hatları* (İstanbul, 1948), I, 53-55 and n.1; Ahmet Rasim, *İstibdaddan hakimiyeti milliyeye* (İstanbul, 1342), I, 33-36. Both are based on *Tarihi Cevdet*, IV, 289, the account of the assembly of 20 Şaban 1203.

lowing year. A number of the young westernizers, including graduates of the new military schools, also fell martyr to this reaction against Selim.

Mahmud II, who came to the throne in 1808, had himself escaped the fate of Selim III only by hiding on the palace roof. His situation at this point was precarious, since the ulema and Janissaries were strong potential opponents in the capital and his authority in the provinces was practically nonexistent. But Mahmud, as the last of the direct Osmanli line, was for the moment personally safe. During the year before his accession he had imbibed from Selim III some of the latter's zeal for reform, and therefore appeared to be cast in the role of avenger of Selim's death and continuer of his program. But Mahmud had to go slowly. His first and major efforts had to be directed simply to becoming master in his own house. In this he was hampered by a series of wars and revolts which sapped the remaining Ottoman strength. The Napoleonic wars had brought on a renewed Serbian rebellion and a war with Russia which lasted until 1812; the Wahhabi power had risen in Arabia, and Mahmud had to call on his Egyptian vassal Mehmed Ali to proceed against it; the Greek revolt broke out in 1821, bringing in its wake Anglo-French support for the Greeks and another Russo-Turkish war in 1828-1829; thereupon, while the conditions of Greek independence from the Ottoman Empire were still being settled by the great powers, Mehmed Ali marched against Mahmud in 1832, threatened to approach İstanbul itself, and was bought off only by renewed intervention of the great powers, which left him in control of Syria until 1840. Russia, as her reward for services rendered on this occasion, exacted of Mahmud the treaty of Hünkâr İskelesi, which made the Ottoman Empire essentially a junior partner in alliance with Russia. In 1839 war again broke out between Mehmed Ali and Mahmud II; the sultan died just before details of the destruction of his army reached the capital, and also just before his fleet surrendered to the Egyptians without firing a shot. In view of the circumstances, it was remarkable that Mahmud II was able to accomplish anything in the way of reform. Yet the circumstances, as well as his own inclinations, pushed him toward reform which was a combination of the rooting out of abuses, repression of rival authority in the empire, and westernization.

All three of these aspects of reform were involved in Mahmud's master stroke—the abolition of the Janissary corps in 1826. Mahmud's original intention was not to exterminate the Janissaries, but to create a new westernized army into which members of the various Janissary messes would be incorporated piecemeal. Thus he would eliminate the Janissary corps as a threat to his own power, root out at the same time the traffic in pay certificates, and continue the westernization of the armed forces along lines attempted by Selim III and more successfully adopted by Mehmed Ali in Egypt during the preceding few years. Although Mahmud made careful preparations over several years, obtaining the pledged support of members of the ulema, of civil and military officials, and of a group of notables convened in the capital, a Janissary rebellion broke out on June 14, 1826, two days after a handful of officers outfitted in new European-style uniforms began to drill. The counterattack by loyal forces killed several thousand Janissaries. Others were hunted down, many more were exiled, and two days later the corps was formally abolished. New troops, the "Triumphant Soldiers of Muhammad," soon began to drill under the eye of the sultan, who asked for French engineer officers and German military musicians to supplement his instructors. It was years before the new army achieved military effectiveness, but at least the Janissaries were no longer an organized force in being to oppose further reform. The "auspicious event," as this carnage became known to the Turks, had seen to that.[31] The new army kept the way open for the penetration of further western influence. A military academy was established in 1834, and some of its graduates were sent to European capitals for further study. New army instructors were obtained from Prussia, including the elder Moltke, who was then at the start of his famous military career.

Mahmud's arm also reached out into the provinces. Military expeditions brought such regions as Kurdistan and Iraq once more under the control of İstanbul. By a combination of diplomacy and force the might of the derebeyi's was largely crushed. The most famous rebel, Ali Paşa of Yanina, was killed, and his head displayed on a dish set out in the first court of the palace. Some derebeyi's were kept away from their lands and under the imperial eye by means of forced residence in various towns.[32] Greece and Egypt were too much for Mah-

---

[31] Basis for the above summary is Howard A. Reed, *The Destruction of the Janissaries by Mahmud II in June, 1826* (Princeton, unpublished dissertation, 1951).

[32] Some examples of what happened to derebeyi's in Abdolonyme Ubicini, *La Turquie actuelle* (Paris, 1855), pp. 261-264; Frederick Millingen, *Wild Life Among the Koords* (London, 1870), pp. 56-58; H. F. Tozer, *Turkish Armenia and Eastern*

mud to handle, and with Serbia an arrangement of semiautonomy was reached. But in most of the provinces, which were slightly rearranged in size and number, the governors now appointed paid more heed to İstanbul than had their predecessors. The power of life and death was formally taken away from these valis. Mahmud himself made trips of inspection in some provinces. At least two of these tours were devoted in part to an investigation of the treatment of his Christian subjects.[33] Mahmud attempted no general westernization in the methods of provincial government, but his concern for just administration for the minorities was apparent in his occasional expressions about the equality of all his subjects. Muslims and non-Muslims, he admonished various provincial notables, should be treated alike.[34]

In other matters, often superficial and external, Mahmud copied the West. The fez, a red headdress of Moroccan origin, was made compulsory for all officials except the ulema in place of the turban; so also was the stambouline, a black frock coat, which with the fez became the uniform of the Ottoman bureaucracy. Mahmud founded a medical school where strong western influences prevailed in the subject matter, in the staff of teachers, and in the language of instruction, which was French; this school, unlike its predecessors, had a long life. Small groups of students, medical as well as military, were sporadically sent to study in Paris, London, and Vienna from 1834 on.[35] Mahmud had a census taken, abolished the remaining military fiefs, created a quarantine system, increased the sending of regular diplomatic missions abroad, and founded the first official newspaper, the *Moniteur Ottomane*, which was soon followed by its counterpart in Turkish, the *Takvim-i vekayi*. The latter paper represents the start of Turkish journalism, which grew rapidly in importance in the next half century.

The fez, the stambouline, and the official gazette, in which new

---

Asia Minor (London, 1881), pp. 175-176; Robert Walsh, *A Residence at Constantinople* (London, 1836), I, 394.

[33] Helmuth von Moltke, *Briefe über Zustände und Begebenheiten in der Türkei*, 3rd ed. (Berlin, 1877), pp. 124-144. (Moltke accompanied Mahmud on an inspection tour in 1837.) See also Felix Kanitz, *Donau-Bulgarien und der Balkan* (Leipzig, 1875-1879), I, 84.

[34] See the various statements recorded in Harold Temperley, *England and the Near East: The Crimea* (London, 1936), pp. 40-41.

[35] Ergin, *Maarif tarihi*, II, 278-279, 297, 306. Bernard Lewis, *The Emergence of Modern Turkey* (London, 1961), dates the first student mission abroad as 1827. These were four slave boys educated in Husrev Paşa's household. Cf. İ. A. Gövsa, *Türk meşhurları ansiklopedisi* (İstanbul, n.d.), p. 125, s.v. "Ethem Paşa."

regulations and appointments were now printed, were the outward signs of a reformed and slowly westernized bureaucracy which sprang essentially from the work of Mahmud II. Some of the traditional positions, among them palace sinecures, were abolished. The hierarchy of civilian officials was reclassified.[36] Mahmud announced that no longer would there be arbitrary confiscation of the estates of deceased officials. He tried to discourage bribery and to pay salaries regularly. Toward the end of his reign he changed the titles of some of his ministers to conform to European usages, creating ministries of foreign affairs, of the interior, and of the treasury. These and other ministers composed the ministerial council (*meclis-i has*, "privy council"), which was intended to resemble a European cabinet more than the old divan. Each minister was responsible for the administration of his department. The council, however, did not take office as a unit, since the sultan could reshuffle ministers at will without necessarily affecting the position of the grand vezir, who presided over the ministerial council. The title of grand vezir (*sadr-ı âzam* or *vezir-i âzam*) was itself abolished briefly in favor of "prime minister" (*baş vekil*), but the old title was restored in 1839.[37] Early in 1838 Mahmud established also the Supreme Council of Judicial Ordinances (*meclis-i vâlâ-yı ahkâm-ı adliye*, usually called in the West "Grand Council of Justice"), which was charged with the thorough discussion and preparation of new regulations.[38] It was this council which, going through a series of transformations in the next thirty years, was to be the first organ of central government to embody the representative principle by including selected individuals from the non-Muslim minorities. It was this council also which emerged in 1868 as the Council of State (*şûra-yı devlet*), quite on the European model of the times.

One of Mahmud II's innovations, born of the practical problem of carrying on increased diplomatic business with the western powers, had results far beyond what might at the moment have been foreseen. This was the establishment of the *tercüme odası*, or translation bureau, in the department which became the ministry of foreign affairs. For

[36] Changes as of 1834 are listed in Joseph von Hammer-Purgstall, *Geschichte des Osmanischen Reiches* (Pest, 1827-1835), X, 695-712.

[37] Abdurrahman Şeref, *Tarih musahabeleri*, pp. 264-266, on this and two similar changes in title later in the century.

[38] The Supreme Council first sat in the palace. Mahmud created also a council at the Porte, to deliberate on administrative policy (*Dar-ı şura-yı Babıâli*); this was, however, less important for the future.

centuries the imperial divan had had an interpreter, who in the course of time acquired assistants. These interpreters had generally been Christians, or Christian converts to Islam, since few Turks knew any western language, and in the eighteenth century the office of chief interpreter had become in effect a monopoly of a few of the prominent Phanariote Greek families of the capital. But Greeks were generally unwelcome in official positions after the Greek revolt of 1821; hence the establishment of the *tercüme odası*, where the routine of work was supplemented by training in French, history, arithmetic, and other subjects. This office, an arrangement of administrative convenience, soon became the nursery for some of the most prominent Ottoman officials of the nineteenth century. From it emerged young Ottoman bureaucrats who rose to important posts both in the foreign ministry and in other departments; some became grand vezirs. Two secretaries taken from the *tercüme odası* helped to establish the first telegraph system in the Ottoman Empire in the 1850's; two other alumni of the same bureau were among the original instructors in a school set up in 1859 to train provincial administrators. Among the alumni of the translation office were Âli Paşa, Fuad Paşa, Ahmed Vefik Paşa, Münif Paşa, Mehmed Raşid Paşa, Safvet Paşa, and Namık Kemal Bey. In the translation office they learned or perfected their French. The diplomatic affairs with which they dealt put them in touch with European developments, but the language itself was even more of an open sesame to western ideas. A good many of the *tercüme odası* employees had additional experience in the diplomatic service in European capitals. In the translation bureau itself westerners were also employed—the great English orientalist Redhouse was for a time its head; a Prussian or Austrian renegade, Emin Efendi, taught European languages in it and was also librarian of the foreign ministry. "Frank influence and thrift" were said to prevail there.[39] Some Ottoman Christians were also employed there, probably fewer Greeks and more Armenians, and some Jews.[40] The *tercüme odası* offered an in-

---

[39] ABCFM, Armenian Mission VIII, #81, 8 April 1859.

[40] The author knows of no detailed study of the *tercüme odası* and its effect on Ottoman reform. It is mentioned in the biographies of many statesmen. For bits of information see Ergin, *Maarif tarihi*, I, 52, 56-60; II, 499, 518-519, 533; III, 900-902; Mustafa Nihat, *Metinlerle Türk muasır edebiyatı tarihi* (İstanbul, 1934), p. 8; Ahmed H. Tanpınar, *Ondokuzuncu asır Türk edebiyatı tarihi* (İstanbul, 1942), pp. 66, 98; Sommerville Story, ed., *The Memoirs of Ismail Kemal Bey* (London, 1920), p. 21; Andreas D. Mordtmann, *Stambul und das moderne Türkenthum* (Leipzig, 1877-1878), I, 129-131, 141, 177, 179; Murad Efendi (Franz von Werner), *Türk-*

teresting parallel in the civil administration to the westernized professional schools in the military establishment. In each case European
pressures, military and diplomatic, resulted in new institutions which
encouraged the study of French and opened up new channels for the
transmission of western ideas, with important results for the future.
A few years after the *tercüme odası* was founded the old practice of
providing a teacher of Persian and Arabic for the secretaries at the
Sublime Porte was discontinued.[41]

It has sometimes been asserted that Mahmud II was interested in
creating a constitution for his empire, and that during his reign a
plan for two-chamber parliamentary government was drawn up.[42]
But no scheme for a western-style constitution could have prospered
then, and it seems quite unlikely that Mahmud II would have considered this a serious possibility. References to constitutional ideas in
his reign probably arise from the fact that the Supreme Council of
Judicial Ordinances which he established was a deliberative body and
was later to include members to represent the non-Muslim minorities.[43]

The true significance of Mahmud's reign for the development of
reform and westernization in the Ottoman Empire lies in a number
of beginnings which opened up possibilities for the future, rather than
in reforms effectively achieved by 1839. Many of Mahmud's efforts
were comparatively ineffectual. He failed, in reality, to abolish bribery
and confiscation and to pay salaries regularly. His new army and new
schools were rudimentary. There is also justice in the charge that he
began at the wrong end, with externals like the enforced changes in
dress, though he may have realized that this was psychological preparation for more fundamental changes, as did Mustafa Kemal Atatürk
with his hat reform a century later. Ibrahim Paşa, the able son of

---

ische Skizzen (Leipzig, 1877), II, 72; Abdolonyme Ubicini and Pavet de Courteille,
Etat présent de l'Empire ottoman (Paris, 1876), p. 87; *Tanzimat*, I, 448; Walsh,
Residence, II, 33-34.

[41] Tayyib Gökbilgin, "Babıâli," *İslâm ansiklopedisi*, II, 177.

[42] Benoît Brunswik, *La réforme et les garanties* (Paris, 1877), p. 21, asserts without
proof that the constitutional idea was born in 1834. Gad Franco, *Développements
constitutionnels en Turquie* (Paris, 1925), pp. 12-13, refers to unnamed "writers" as
his authority, and says "he is assured" that a copy of the constitutional project was in
one of the İstanbul libraries, though he could not find it.

[43] At the start of his reign Mahmud entered into a contract with an assembly of
provincial notables, putting limits on the central government, but this was soon disregarded: Okandan, *Umumî âmme hukukumuz*, I, 56-58. This was no constitution, but
at least one authority regards it as the start of the principle of the state under law:
Sıddık S. Onar, "Les transformations de la structure administrative et juridique de la
Turquie," *Revue internationale des sciences administratives*, IV (1955), 771.

Mehmed Ali of Egypt, was severe in his judgment of Mahmud. "The Porte have taken civilization by the wrong side;—it is not by giving epaulettes and tight trousers to a nation that you begin the task of regeneration;—instead of beginning by their dress . . . they should endeavor to enlighten the minds of their people."[44] Innate popular conservatism was aroused by measures such as these that defied tradition. The dervish who seized the reins of Mahmud's horse and shouted: "Infidel sultan, God will demand an accounting for your blasphemy. You are destroying Islam and drawing down upon us all the curse of the Prophet," symbolized the opposition.[45] In a sense, Mahmud's reforms antagonized many of his people just as Peter the Great by his innovations had "cleft the soul of Muscovy." Mahmud's arbitrary methods, like Peter's, had a similar effect.

The channels for the penetration of western ideas had, nevertheless, been kept open and enlarged. Further, Mahmud's desire to ensure equal treatment for his subjects of whatever creed paved the way for the official proclamation of the doctrine of Ottoman equality in the years 1839 and after. "I distinguish among my subjects," Mahmud is reported to have said, "Muslims in the mosque, Christians in the church, Jews in the synagogue, but there is no difference among them in any other way."[46]

More significant than these beginnings in constructive achievement were Mahmud's works of destruction, in which he was more immediately effective. By exterminating the Janissaries and by crushing the

---

[44] Memorandum of Alexander Pisani's report of interview with Ibrahim, 10 March 1833 (sic), enclosed in Canning to Palmerston, #12, 7 March 1832 (sic), FO 78/209, as cited in Frank E. Bailey, *British Policy and the Turkish Reform Movement* (Cambridge, Mass., 1942), p. 172, n.153. The dates here are obviously garbled. Moltke mocked not only the western externals, but their hybrid nature in the 1830's: "The most unfortunate creation was that of an army on the European model with Russian jackets, French regulations, Belgian weapons, Turkish caps, Hungarian saddles, English swords, and instructors from all nations. . . ." Moltke, *Briefe*, p. 418.

[45] Ahmed Rasim, *Istibdaddan hakimiyeti milliyeye*, I, 179, cited in Okandan, *Umumî âmme hukukumuz*, pp. 61-62; cf. A. de la Jonquière, *Histoire de l'Empire ottoman* (Paris, 1881), pp. 481-482.

[46] Abdurrahman Şeref, *Tarih musahabeleri*, p. 65; cf. Reşat Kaynar, *Mustafa Reşit Paşa ve Tanzimat* (Ankara, 1954), p. 100. Reed, *Destruction of the Janissaries*, p. 247, finds the seeds of this doctrine of equality in the 1826 decree abolishing the Janissaries, in which Mahmud preached brotherhood to his Muslim subjects alone. The ferman exhorts: "Let all the congregation of the Muslim people, and the small and great officials of Islam and the ulema, and members of other military formations, and all the common folk be as one body. Let them look upon each other as brethren in the faith. . . ." But this may be no more than a reemphasis of the doctrine of brotherhood of the faithful and the equality of all believers pronounced by the Prophet in the seventh century.

power of the *derebeyi*'s he had contributed much to the preservation of unity and central control in the empire—a primary objective of all the reformers. But by the same token Mahmud had removed two of the real checks on the arbitrary exercise of authority by the central government.[47] The old equilibrium, corrupt though it had been, was upset. Power now lay with the Palace and the Porte, and the possibilities of direct oppression of the people by the central government were thereby increased. The power of the central government could be for good as well as evil; how it would be exercised now depended on the character of the sultans and the officials. When the sultan was strong, or the bureaucracy feeble, he would now run the government and find support among cliques of officials. Thus Mahmud II's deeds prepared the way for the disastrous periods of personal rule by Abdülaziz after 1871 and by Abdülhamid II after 1878. When, on the other hand, the bureaucracy produced strong men who could control weak or indifferent sultans, or could curb arbitrary sultans, officialdom was supreme. This was generally the case from the time of Mahmud's death in 1839 to 1871, and also during the year 1876. Significantly, the Supreme Council established by Mahmud moved, after his death, from the Palace to the Porte. The modernized bureaucracy which Mahmud began to create assumed a leading role in the Tanzimat period.

There was, of course, no sharp break with the past; changes in the bureaucracy came slowly. It still represented, as it had in the glorious days of the Ruling Institution as well as during its decline, a ruling class, which was, however, an aristocracy of office rather than of blood. The tendency grew for sons of officials to follow their fathers' calling, but birth was in itself no guarantee of official position, and the ruling group was replenished by additions from below. Officialdom was, however, sharply set off against the mass of the peasantry by position, by pride in position and scorn of the common man, and by education.

Education meant for the bureaucrats of the middle nineteenth century essentially the ability to read and write. Those who had mastered these arts were commonly entitled "efendi." Reading and writing were no mean achievements, considering the difficulty of the language and the calligraphic system, and especially the complexity of the official

---

[47] Mahmud had also begun to curb some of the autonomy of the ulema, weakening though not destroying their influence: see Bernard Lewis in *Encyclopaedia of Islam*, new ed., I, 837-838 and 972-973, s.vv. "Baladiyya" and "Bāb-ı mashīkhat."

style, which was loaded with Arabic and Persian terminology and often sought elegance of expression at the expense of clarity. The efendi's education, after his early boyhood days in the harem were over, began with his learning the elements of reading and writing in primary (and, after the 1840's, secondary) school, together with a smattering of other subjects. In his early teens he then became a *kâtib*, or secretary, in one of the government offices, where he continued to learn on the job. The best educated of the efendis were essentially self-educated; they absorbed knowledge from their own reading and experience and from discussions in some of the intellectual salons of İstanbul. After Selim III, and particularly after the reforms of Mahmud II, more and more of the efendis began to learn French and to adopt various western customs. At the very end of Mahmud's reign, in 1838, a school designed specifically to train employees for government offices, the Mekteb-i Maarif-i Adliye, was founded. Here French was taught, as well as geography, mathematics, and other subjects.[48]

What passed for westernization was, however, usually no more than skin-deep. By mid-century the efendi of İstanbul was a curious mixture of East and West. He wore the stambouline and the fez. His French might be quite indifferent. Some of the efendis picked up western ways from contact with the Levantines of Pera (Beyoğlu), the most Europeanized quarter of the capital. Others had actual experience in the West. In both cases the best of the efendis acquired new ideas without losing character or ability. The new ideas ranged from western literary tastes through concepts of new economic development to thoughts of limiting the sultan's powers. Other efendis, however, acquired only a veneer of phrases, manners, and vices. Kıbrıslı Mehmed Paşa, who had spent several years in Paris and London and was three times grand vezir, was said by his wife to have acquired only a veneer of knowledge over a mass of ignorance, like "the greater number of those who have been sent to Europe to be educated."[49] Some returned from the West as reformers, while others were rendered only disillusioned and cynical by the contrasts they observed. The *alafranga* efendi, the westernized efendi, was often a contemptible person, sometimes a Levantine in outlook if not in blood because of the unassimilated elements of East and West in his training. At his worst, the

[48] Ergin, *Maarif tarihi*, II, 330-341.
[49] Melek Hanum, *Thirty Years in the Harem* (London, 1872), pp. 277-278. Melek was a Levantine, and was divorced by Kıbrıslı Mehmed Paşa, so perhaps she was unduly bitter.

alafranga efendi appeared thus: "The same black frock coat, black trousers, generally unbuttoned where European ideas would most rigorously exact buttoning, the same padded underclothes, shiny boots, and slight red cap, the same shuffling gait and lack-lustre eye, characterize every man of the tribe."[50] Turks of the old school often despised him. "I would rather see my son a really good Christian and an honest man," said one pasha, "than a Constantinople Turk *alla Franca* and a Pasha."[51] Cevdet Paşa, one of the most learned and intelligent of the ulema, referred sarcastically to the *"alafranga çelebiler,"* the "westernized gentlemen."[52] Turks who knew Europe and French quite well were also critical of the common run of Ottoman bureaucrat as the uneducated product of a bad school system.[53] Yet these were the officials on whom the progress of westernized reform depended.

Some of the officials were competent and industrious, whatever their degree of westernization. But the majority were not, and many looked only for sinecures, of which there were never enough to go around. It was estimated that half the people in İstanbul lived off the state in some way. Many, both in İstanbul and in the provincial capitals, became unsalaried hangers-on of pashas, hoping that position or graft would come their way. The crowd of relatives and parasites in the anterooms of every high official was one of the great curses of Ottoman administration, leading to favoritism, inefficiency, and bribery. Mahmud had been unable to exterminate bribery, which was still often necessary to secure a post and led to the traditional extortion or embezzlement then necessary to pay back debts and care for an uncertain future. It is hard to condemn the giving and taking of gifts on purely moral grounds, since the practice had entered so deeply into Ottoman custom.[54] It was, nevertheless, a tremendous obstacle to good

[50] William G. Palgrave, *Essays on Eastern Questions* (London, 1872), p. 14.

[51] G. G. B. St. Clair and C. A. Brophy, *Twelve Years' Study of the Eastern Question in Bulgaria* (London, 1877), p. 310. St. Clair was a Turcophil who would be happy to report and endorse the sentiment.

[52] Cevdet Paşa, *Tezâkir*, p. 68; cf. Fatma Aliye, *Ahmed Cevdet Paşa ve zamanı* (İstanbul, 1332), p. 84.

[53] See Ziya Paşa's strictures in *Hürriyet*, #5 (7 rebiülâhir 1285), reproduced in İhsan Sungu, "Tanzimat ve Yeni Osmanlılar," *Tanzimat*, I, 840-41; also Süleyman Paşa, *Hiss-i inkılâb* (İstanbul, 1326), pp. 3-4, where he condemns officials of the 1870's as so ignorant as not to know arithmetic, geography, or the three kingdoms of nature as taught in primary and secondary schools.

[54] Friedrich Hellwald, *Der Islam* (Augsburg, 1877), p. 37, makes the interesting comment that the United States and Turkey were on the same plane as regards pur-

government. Officials were caught in the toils of the system. "I have no inducement to be honest," said the governor of Diyarbekir. "If I attempt to rule justly all of the other pashas will combine against me and I shall soon be turned out of my place, and unless I take bribes I shall be too poor to purchase another."[55] So the higher officials in general remained open to monetary argument and surrounded by parasites and servants who were eavesdroppers, retailers of information to rival officials and foreign embassies, and the means of approach to favor-seekers who crossed their palms.[56]

At the center of Ottoman officialdom stood the Sublime Porte (Babıâli). Although by the nineteenth century this term was commonly used to designate the whole Ottoman government, it referred more particularly to the building which in mid-century housed the offices of the grand vezir, the ministries of foreign affairs and of the interior, and the Supreme Council of Judicial Ordinances and its successor councils. The great brick building, finished in yellow and rose plaster, had been constructed anew after a disastrous fire in 1839. From that date until the death of Âli Paşa in 1871 it was the effective center of government, dominant over the sultans and the Palace, controlled by the bureaucracy which Mahmud II had begun to create. Most of the offices in the Porte now bore European labels, but the confusion in the bureaus was still oriental. Offices and corridors

---

chase of government office; Hornby, for ten years a judge in the British consular court in İstanbul, found Canadians just as rabid for *bahşiş* as Turks: *Autobiography*, p. 90.

[55] ABCFM, Assyrian Mission #61, 15 August 1859.

[56] On the Ottoman bureaucracy from Mahmud's time to 1876 there are many scattered observations: Frederick Millingen (Osman-Seify Bey), *La Turquie sous le règne d'Abdul Aziz, 1862-1867* (Paris, 1868), pp. 255-257; Melek Hanum, *Thirty Years*, pp. 93, 278-283, 374-375; Mordtmann, *Stambul*, I, 131-137, 196-206, and II, 242; Orhan F. Köprülü, "Efendi," *İslâm ansiklopedisi*, IV, 132-133; Murad, *Türkische Skizzen*, I, 26, and II, 42-52, 62-79; Henry J. Van Lennep, *Travels in Little-Known Parts of Asia Minor* (London, 1870), I, 5, 223, and II, 29-30; Hermann Vambéry, *Der Islam im neunzehnten Jahrhundert* (Leipzig, 1875), pp. 80-85; Hermann Vambéry, *Sittenbilder aus dem Morgenlande* (Berlin, 1876), pp. 196-203; Nassau W. Senior, *A Journal Kept in Turkey and Greece* (London, 1859), pp. 121, 143-144; Abdolonyme Ubicini, *La Turquie actuelle* (Paris, 1855), pp. 189-208; Uriel Heyd, *Foundations of Turkish Nationalism* (London, 1950), p. 75. Thomas, *United States and Turkey*, pp. 46-47, describes the traditional Ottoman ruling class. Ahmed Midhat, *Üss-i inkılâb* (İstanbul, 1294-1295), I, 97-99, describes officialdom and hangers-on in the provinces. Gibb, *Ottoman Poetry*, V, 42-52, reproduces Ziya Bey's own story of his youth and training; Fatma Aliye, *Ahmed Cevdet Paşa*, gives an account of the formal and extracurricular education of one of the ulema who later became a civil official, together with a description, on pp. 82-85, of İstanbul officialdom and its financial embarrassments just before the Crimean War; Ergin, *Maarif tarihi*, I, 51-55, and II, 315-321, on the general education of officials.

swarmed with officials, secretaries, petitioners, servants, vendors, and professional storytellers. These sat on divans or stood about while state business was transacted before their eyes. Secretaries wrote on low tables or on their knees. Superior officials spent infinite time on detail. Every official had the famous *torba*, a silk or linen bag in which important documents were kept—and often buried for weeks. The archives were likewise housed in *torba*'s hung on pegs in the wall. On a smaller scale this scene was reproduced in each seat of provincial administration. It was possible, and sometimes happened, that even in this setting business was efficiently conducted. More often, it was not.[57]

When Mahmud II died in 1839, his work of reform only begun and his empire threatened by the new victories of Mehmed Ali of Egypt, he was succeeded by his son Abdülmecid, a boy of sixteen. The reign of the new sultan was characterized by increased efforts at reform and westernization along many lines. But Abdülmecid was, in contrast to his father, not the moving spirit behind the new efforts. His youth and inexperience when he ascended the throne of Osman, as well as his rather mild character, contributed to the dominance of the Sublime Porte. The great reform edict of November 3, 1839, which marked the opening of Abdülmecid's reign, was issued in his name as a formal imperial rescript, or Hatt-ı Hümayun. It was not, however, promulgated on the sultan's initiative, but was the work of a brilliant statesman, Mustafa Reşid Paşa, minister of foreign affairs.

Reşid was still a young man, not yet forty, whose political star had been rising since he entered on a government career in his teens. Periods of employment in various of the Sublime Porte secretariats had been followed by ambassadorships in Paris and London, which furnished him with the knowledge of the West that informed his subsequent career, and with command of fluent French. In Paris, Reşid's

[57] The aspect of the Porte did not change much until 1878, when fire again damaged it. For descriptions see Tayyib Gökbilgin, "Babıâli," *İslâm ansiklopedisi*, II, 174-177; Jean Deny, "Bab-i ali," *Encyclopaedia of Islam*, Supplement I, xi-xii, 35; Murad, *Türkische Skizzen*, I, 31, and II, 70-77; Vambéry, *Sittenbilder*, pp. 191-193, 203-209; Antonio Gallenga, *Two Years of the Eastern Question* (London, 1877), II, 330-338; Charles de Moüy, *Lettres du Bosphore* (Paris, 1879), pp. 57, 180; Van Lennep, *Travels*, I, 223; Ergin, *Maarif tarihi*, I, 51, n.1, and 52, n.1. On fires, Abdurrahman Şeref, "Babıâli harikleri," *Tarih-i osmanî encümeni mecmuası*, II:7 (1327), 446-450. On efficiency, Vambéry, *Der Islam im neunzehnten Jahrhundert*, pp. 80-85; V. Hoskiær, *Et Besøg i Grækenland, Ægypten og Tyrkiet* (Copenhagen, 1879), p. 154.

short, stocky figure and intelligent face, framed in a coal-black beard, had been familiar in the salons, at the theatre, and among litterateurs. French journalists described him as "M. Thiers transformed into a pasha and with a fez on his head."[58] His knowledge of western ways was not thorough, but it was probably more than superficial, despite the criticisms often directed at him. Some of his apparent shallowness came from his undoubted vanity; he sought the praise of the European journals. The fact that he had to go slowly in attempted reforms, in view of the opposition aroused by even the most modest introduction of western institutions, helps to explain further Reşid's apparent superficiality. Yet he was a sincere reformer, the first in the line of those who became known as Tanzimatçı's, or men of the Tanzimat, and one of those often called a gâvur pasha, an unbeliever of a pasha, by the populace. He gained this appellation not only because of his personal westernisms, but because of his belief in the need to treat with equality people of all creeds within the empire.[59] A part of his drive was also, of course, the simple desire to put order into government, to enhance the role of the ministers, and to safeguard the bureaucracy against the arbitrary whims of the sultan. Sincere reformer though he was, Reşid was also a good politician and an opportunist. He recognized talent in others and raised up a group of disciples among whom Âli and Fuad became the most prominent, but he wanted to keep the direction of affairs in his own hands. His actions were sometimes guided by fear, sometimes perhaps by cupidity. But usually they were guided by the maxim that politics is the art of the possible. Reşid aimed at the possible in westernization whenever the opportunity offered.[60]

[58] C. Hippolyte Castille, Réchid-pacha (Paris, 1857), p. 23.
[59] See quotation from one of his memoranda in Halil İnalcık, Tanzimat ve Bulgar meselesi (Ankara, 1943), p. 3, n.1; also F. S. Rodkey, "Reshid Pasha's Memorandum of August 12, 1839," Journal of Modern History, II:2 (June 1930), 251-257, reprinted as well in Bailey, British Policy, pp. 271-276.
[60] For various pictures of Reşid see Abdurrahman Şeref, Tarih musahabeleri, pp. 75-79; Ali Fuad, Rical-i mühimme-i siyasiye (İstanbul, 1928), pp. 6-55; Castille, Réchid-pacha; Cavit Baysun, "Mustafa Reşit Paşa," in Tanzimat, I, 723-726; Melek Hanum, Thirty Years, pp. 164-170; Ubicini, La Turquie actuelle, pp. 153-168; Vambéry, Der Islam, pp. 148-150; Mordtmann, Stambul, I, 10, and II, 268; Nassau W. Senior, A Journal Kept in Turkey and Greece (London, 1859), pp. 55-58; L. Thouvenel, Trois années de la Question d'Orient (Paris, 1897), pp. 222-225; Durand de Fontmagne, Un séjour à l'ambassade de France (Paris, 1902), p. 139; Murad Efendi, Türkische Skizzen, II, 153-156; Temperley, England and the Near East, pp. 158-159; Stanley Lane-Poole, The Life of . . . Stratford Canning (London, 1888), II, 104-107; Nicholas Milev, "Réchid pacha et la réforme ottomane," Zeit-

Such was the case when Reşid secured the proclamation of the Hatt-ı Şerif of Gülhane in 1839.[61] In the face of Mehmed Ali's serious threat to the integrity of the Ottoman Empire, it was imperative that Reşid secure some outside help. Given the diplomatic situation of the time, this was most likely to be forthcoming from England. But the Ottoman Empire had to appear to be worth saving, to be reforming itself, and to be as liberal as the Egypt of Mehmed Ali. Reşid had earlier, while on diplomatic mission in London, conferred with Palmerston, the British foreign minister, outlining his ideas on reform and seeking European support. Now, as foreign minister in his own capital, Reşid moved the young sultan to issue his reform decree just four months after his accession. The time of issuance was certainly determined by the circumstances and the Hatt-ı Şerif was used as a diplomatic weapon. But it is equally true that Reşid used the diplomatic crisis as a means of getting support among otherwise conservative ministers for a liberal decree. The Hatt-ı Şerif was, then, not a work of hypocrisy on Reşid's part, and remains a remarkable document for its time and place.[62] Nor was it dictated or inspired by the British government; it was Reşid's creation.[63]

---

schrift für Osteuropäische Geschichte, II (1912), 382-398; Kaynar, Mustafa Reşit, pp. 41-223, passim (mostly documents); Mehmed Selaheddin, Bir türk diplomatının evrak-ı siyasiyesi (İstanbul, 1306), pp. 5-37; Cevdet, Tezâkir, pp. 13, 16-17.

[61] A Hatt-ı şerif (Illustrious rescript) or Hatt-ı hümayun (Imperial rescript) was a formal edict of the sultan preceded by a line in his own hand saying, "Let it be done accordingly." This was an exercise of the historic prerogative of sultans to legislate in matters outside the şeriat, although, in fact, this sort of imperial legislation sometimes trespassed on the province of the religious law. By the nineteenth century these terms came to be applied simply to the sultan's published commands on basic reforms. See the article by İ. H. Uzunçarşılı in İslâm ansiklopedisi, V, 373-375. Western writers have ordinarily referred to the edict of 1839 as the Hatt-ı Şerif, which was its title in the official French translation distributed by the Sublime Porte to foreign diplomats at the time of its proclamation. See the facsimiles of French and Turkish texts in Yavuz Abadan, "Tanzimat fermanın tahlili," Tanzimat, I, following p. 48. But this name is not generally used by Turkish writers, who use either Hatt-ı hümayun, as in the Turkish text of 1839, or else Gülhane fermanı or Tanzimat fermanı. The author shall, nevertheless, follow the customary western terminology in order to avoid confusion and to provide a convenient distinction from the Hatt-ı Hümayun of 1856, on which see chapter II.

Gülhane is the name given to a part of the gardens next to the old Top Kapu palace in İstanbul, alongside the Sea of Marmora, where the 1839 edict was publicly proclaimed.

[62] Texts of the edict are available in many places: in Turkish in the Ottoman histories of Abdurrahman Şeref (II, 355-360) and Ahmed Rasim (IV, 1865-1877), as well as in the Düstur, I (İstanbul, 1289), 4-7. A modern Turkish transliteration is in Enver Ziya Karal, Nizam-ı Cedit ve Tanzimat devirleri (Ankara, 1947), pp. 263-266. Thomas X. Bianchi, Nouveau guide de la conversation en français et en

To modern ears the whole Hatt-ı Şerif of Gülhane sounds naïve, partly owing to its laborious justification of the obvious. But principally the ingenuous tone arises from the effort to reconcile the old with the new, absolute equality of all Ottoman subjects with the sacred law, and new departures with a return to the happiness and prosperity of "the early times of the Ottoman monarchy." The whole decline of the empire for a century and a half is laid to the nonobservance of "the precepts of the glorious Koran and the laws of the Empire." But the remedy is presented not simply as a return to respect for the law, but also in terms of "new institutions" and "an alteration and complete renovation of the ancient usages."[64] At the same time these innovations are to prosper "with the aid of the Most High" and "with the assistance of our Prophet." It is impossible to dismiss the references to religion, law, and the glorious past as mere window dressing to make the promised new institutions palatable to conservatives or fanatics. Certainly Reşid was concerned to make reforms palatable to Muslim conservatives, but the dual personality of the Hatt-ı Şerif in fact reflects the dual personality of the whole Tanzimat period: new and westernized institutions were created to meet the challenges of the times, while traditional institutions of faith and state were preserved and also, to a degree, reformed. It is hard to see how this dualism could have been avoided, since no people can break sharply with its own past; yet the inherent difficulties are obvious.

---

turc, 2nd ed. (Paris, 1852), pp. 37-40, 296-299, gives Turkish text and French translation. Belin, "Charte des Turcs," *Journal asiatique*, Series III: 9 (January 1840), 5-29, gives his own translation into French, more literal than the official translation, on pages facing the Osmanli text. The official French texts are not literal translations of the Turkish, but follow the sense closely. These official texts are identical except that Grégoire Aristarchi Bey, *Législation ottomane*, II (Constantinople, 1874), 7-14, omits the last three paragraphs and adds a ferman that accompanied the *hat*. George Young, *Corps de droit ottoman* (Oxford, 1905-1906), I, 29-33, runs the text of the *hat* into the ferman that follows, 33-36. French texts may also conveniently be found in Edouard Engelhardt, *La Turquie et le Tanzimat* (Paris, 1882-1884), I, 257-261, and Abdolonyme Ubicini and Pavet de Courteille, *Etat présent de l'Empire ottoman* (Paris, 1876), pp. 231-234. An English translation is in J. C. Hurewitz, *Diplomacy in the Near and Middle East* (Princeton, 1956), II, 113-116.

[63] Bailey, *British Policy*, pp. 184-190, investigates this question; but see Okandan, *Umumî âmme hukukumuz*, pp. 88-89, n.1, on the likelihood of foreign inspiration. Palmerston, British foreign minister, writing to his ambassador Ponsonby in İstanbul said, "Your Hathi Sheriff was a grand stroke of policy." C. K. Webster, *The Foreign Policy of Palmerston, 1830-1841* (London, 1951), II, 657.

[64] These phrases do not sound quite so radical in the Turkish text as in the official French text. "New institutions" is, in the Turkish, "some new laws"; "alteration and complete renovation" is, in the Turkish, "complete alteration and delimitation."

The specific promises made in the edict were, in fact, not now made for the first time, but recalled earlier promises and reform efforts.[65] Three broad points were made in particular: (1) There must be guarantees for the security of life, honor, and property of all subjects; trials must be public and according to regulations, and confiscation abolished. (2) An orderly system of fixed taxes must be created to replace tax farming. (3) A regular system of military conscription must be established, with the term of service reduced from lifetime to four or five years. The details of the "good administration" which the *hat* promised were not otherwise spelled out, except for stipulations that the military expenditures must be limited, that adequate fixed salaries be paid to officials and bribery eliminated, and that a penal code be compiled which should apply to ulema and vezirs, great and small, alike. Since similar promises had been made before, their restatement was a confession of past failure, but also a formal declaration on which to build for the future.

The most remarkable promise of the Hatt-ı Şerif was, however, the affirmation, "These imperial concessions are extended to all our subjects, of whatever religion or sect they may be."[66] In this fashion equality before the law among all Ottoman subjects became for the first time solemnly announced official policy. Phrases of this sort on equality without distinction as to religion recur like a leitmotif throughout the Tanzimat period. The ultimate implication was that millet barriers would be broken down, that the creation of a multinational brotherhood of all Ottoman subjects was the official aim, and, therefore, that the concepts of state and citizenship would become increasingly western and secularized. The hope was, as Reşid had argued and as the Gülhane *hat* also hinted, that such general guarantees of equal protection under law would strengthen the independence and integrity of the Ottoman Empire by increasing the loyalty of its subjects, Christian as well as Muslim, and by diminishing separatist

[65] The most recent effort had been only in the previous year, when the ministers and the Supreme Council had approved a reform program adumbrating that of 1839. The 1838 attempt, however, fizzled out into a pilot project of property registration for the sancaks of Bursa and Gelibolu: Baysun in *Tanzimat*, I, 731-732, citing *Takvim-i Vekayi*, #169 (1838); Kaynar, *Mustafa Reşit*, pp. 115-120; Bailey, *British Policy*, pp. 197-198.

[66] The Turkish text gave special mention to Muslims in this promise of equality: "The objects of our imperial favors are without exception the people of Islam and other peoples among the subjects of our imperial sultanate." One wonders whether the Turkish and French texts were prepared with their respective domestic and foreign audiences in mind.

tendencies. Reşid apparently did not realize the full implications of the growing nationalism among the various Balkan Christian peoples, and may be called naïve on this score.

The Hatt-ı Şerif of Gülhane has sometimes been described as a sort of constitution.[67] It was not, of course. There were no effective limits, or sanctions to enforce limits, on the power of the sultan; at best, he was included among those on whom his edict called down the curse of God in case they violated its provisions. The edict did echo the eighteenth-century principles of "life, liberty, and property" of the American and French revolutions, and as a charter of civil liberties and equality did lay the basis for future reform and for the constitution of 1876. But the edict of 1839 did not reflect the further progress of the French and American revolutions toward constitutional government, except in one particular. This was the setting up of a parliamentary procedure in the Supreme Council of Judicial Ordinances which was to discuss and elaborate needed specific measures to carry out the rather general promises of the Hatt-ı Şerif. That edict itself provided that the Supreme Council, augmented as necessary by additional members, should elaborate the new laws on civil rights and taxation by free discussion. The sultan engaged himself to accord his imperial sanction to "all measures which shall be decided by a majority of votes" in working out the principles laid down in the Hatt-ı Şerif.[68] In the following month procedural rules for the Supreme Council, obviously borrowed from western practice, were formulated. It was provided that all members should speak freely, that speaking should be in the order of inscription, that agenda should be drawn up in advance, that ministers might be interpellated, that minutes were to be kept, and that decisions should be taken by a majority of votes.[69] The imperial sanction of course remained crucial. The process amounted to parliamentary procedure without representative or responsible government. Reşid himself, in a memorandum written two years later, denied that he was trying to imitate western constitu-

[67] As in Osman Nuri, *Abdülhamid-i Sani ve devr-i saltanatı* (İstanbul, 1327), I, 35; Amand von Schweiger-Lerchenfeld, *Bosnien*, 2nd ed. (Vienna, 1879), p. 25; Friedrich Hellwald, *Der Islam, Türken und Slaven* (Augsburg, 1877), p. 34; or Ahmed Midhat, *Üss-i inkılâb*, I, 60, n., though Ahmed Midhat makes it plain he knows this was not a genuine constitution. Cf. Yavuz Abadan's arguments in *Tanzimat*, I, 39-44.
[68] Ferman to the provincial pashas: Aristarchi, *Législation*, II, 12.
[69] Text in Freiherr Friedrich Wilhelm von Reden, *Die Türkei und Griechenland in ihrer Entwicklungsfähigkeit* (Frankfurt a.M., 1856), pp. 288-290.

tionalism. "It would be quite impossible," he wrote, "to govern by constitutional methods a people as ignorant and as incapable of understanding its true interests as ours."[70] The sultan had not abdicated his law-making authority; he had only delegated it in part, and within the limits of the promises in the Hatt-ı Şerif, to a council which was appointed rather than elected. At the opening session of the Supreme Council in 1840, Abdülmecid made a sort of speech from the throne, stressing the value of free debate and promising to appear annually before the council to present a legislative program.

Thus was inaugurated in 1839 the period of the Tanzimat. The term "Tanzimat," derived from a root meaning "order," carries the implication of reorganized or reformed institutions, of fundamental regulations; by usage it has become nearly the equivalent for "reform movement" in the years from the Hatt-ı Şerif to the constitution of 1876.[71] And this reform moved in the direction of westernization, building on the initial efforts of Selim III and Mahmud II. Many of the attempted reforms were destined to be half measures, partial successes, total failures, or to remain on paper only. Yet the cumulative effect of the years 1839 to 1876 on Turkish history is impressive, particularly in the gradual development of administrative institutions reflecting the concepts of the equality of all Ottoman subjects, of the representative principle in local and national government, and of secularization. This meant in fact a breaking away, however gradual, from ancient usages, and the end of serious attempts to go back to the glorious days of Süleyman, much as some of the Ottoman statesmen and people would have liked to do so.

It is small wonder that the principles of the Hatt-ı Şerif were hard to work out in practice and that the *hat* itself, especially in its emphasis on equality, was far from meeting with general approbation in the empire. Abdülmecid had sworn before God to uphold the principles enunciated in his *hat*, and had caused the high officials and ulema to take the same oath in the room where the mantle of the Prophet was preserved. He ordered it to be read and observed in all the provincial seats of government. But Reşid and reform had doughty opponents among the more conservative ministers and the bulk of ordinary officials, while the ulema were not, as a body, prepared to see radical

[70] Milev, "Réchid pacha," p. 389.
[71] Sometimes the term *tanzimat-i hayriyye* was used even in the years preceding 1839. This means, approximately, "beneficent legislation."

departures toward equality and secularization. In the Supreme Council itself there were many who either did not understand or did not appreciate the projects Reşid laid before it, although the council was capable at times of such declarations as this: "The real aim of the Tanzimat . . . is to abolish tyranny and abuses, and to give to people and subjects security and comfort."[72] Among the Turkish population an initial reaction which was favorable to the promises of security of life and property, of tax reform and of conscription reform, was followed by an opposite reaction directed primarily against the doctrine of equality. The sacred law of Islam, they said, was being subverted. "The bigots regarded Reşid as careless in matters of religion and were dissatisfied with him because of his increased intercourse with Europeans."[73] Muslim objections took the form of public disturbances in some Anatolian cities, of hopes voiced in İstanbul that Mehmed Ali would deliver the Ottoman government from European influence and the control of the *gâvur* pasha Reşid, and of expressions that equality was simply against the natural order of things. A Muslim, haled to the police station by a Christian for having insulted the latter with the epithet *gâvur*, was told by the police captain: "O my son, didn't we explain? Now there is the Tanzimat; a *gâvur* is not to be called a *gâvur*."[74] How could the new dispensation be acceptable if the plain truth, as Muslims saw it, could not be spoken openly?

There was also naturally opposition to the application of the *hat* from those other than the ulema who had a vested interest in the status quo. Among them were provincial governors who feared closer supervision, tax farmers, and even the Greek clergy, who suspected that the traditional position of the Greek millet as first among the subject peoples of the empire would be threatened by the doctrine of equality.[75] Some of the opposition to turning the promises of the Hatt-ı Şerif into actuality arose from the speed with which Reşid began; he had a sense of urgency, feeling that the occasion for reforms must be seized before it vanished. Reşid's sense of urgency was justified by

[72] From the minutes of the Supreme Council on the situation in Bosnia in the late 1840's, 29 rebiyyülevvel 1265, Başvekâlet Arşiv 14/1, 1.46, quoted in İnalcık, *Tanzimat ve Bulgar meselesi*, p. 9, n.3.

[73] Cevdet, *Tezâkir*, p. 8.

[74] Abdurrahman Şeref, *Tarih musahabeleri*, p. 73.

[75] On general reactions to the 1839 edict, *ibid.*, pp. 67-74; some of his information reappears in Karal, *Nizam-ı Cedit ve Tanzimat devirleri*, pp. 189-192; see also Edouard Driault, *L'Egypte et l'Europe, la crise de 1839-41* (Cairo, 1930-1934), I, letter 79; II, letters 9, 57, 95; and III, letters 38, 39, 46.

the diplomatic situation, since it was the Egyptian threat to Ottoman integrity which had in 1839 and early 1840 rallied an unstable support of other statesmen behind Reşid's program. When the intervention of all the powers except France had driven Mehmed Ali out of Syria and back into the confines of Egypt, and reform was not so immediately needed as a diplomatic weapon, opposition to it became more open and active.[76] Reşid did not shrink from the struggle with his adversaries, who on occasion went so far as to accuse him, as the later reformer Midhat Paşa was also to be accused, of harboring sentiments of republicanism.[77] But Reşid was up against formidable opposition, which periodically checked the reform efforts as he went in and out of office.

Despite the difficulties, some important beginnings were made between 1840 and the outbreak of the Crimean War. In certain matters of law the principle of equality was restated and partially applied, and the influence of western procedures and secular codes began to be felt. Some Christians were admitted to the military medical school after 1839. The Supreme Council completed the promised revised penal code in 1840, which reaffirmed the equality of all Ottoman subjects.[78] Mixed tribunals, composed of Muslims and non-Muslims, were established to deal with commercial cases involving foreigners; mixed police courts soon followed. It was a further step toward equality that Christian testimony against Muslims was admitted in these tribunals. The first wholesale borrowing of western law came with the commercial code of 1850, largely copied from the French. Tax farming was, as promised in the Hatt-ı Şerif, actually abolished in 1840. The leading sarraf's, the Christian bankers and moneylenders who either bought the farm of taxes themselves or advanced funds to Ottoman officials for the purchase, were called together in İstanbul and told that their contracts were cancelled. Though in some districts the direct collection of taxes by administrative officials lessened the exactions on the peasantry, the new system itself became involved in corruption and also failed to produce sufficient revenue, so that within two years tax farming was reintroduced. In the 1840's also an attack was made on the fundamental problem of providing a more modern, and therefore secular, education than was possible in the grammar schools (mekteb's)

[76] Cf. Cevdet, Tezâkir, p. 7.
[77] Ibid., p. 13; Baysun in Tanzimat, I, 738-739; Ergin, Maarif tarihi, II, 353.
[78] This was a nonwestern code both in 1840 and in its revision of 1851.

and theological schools (medreses) controlled by the ulema. The commission appointed to examine this question included Âli and Fuad, Reşid's disciples. Its report of 1846 recommended not the total reform or abolition of the Muslim schools, but the creation of a parallel educational system from primary schools, through secondary, to a university. Though a council on public instruction and a ministry of education were established, progress was slow: the university failed to develop after its founding, and very few secondary schools (*rüşdiye*'s) were started. Modern secular education began, nevertheless, to take root, and an Academy of Learning (Encümen-i Daniş) was founded to prepare textbooks.

The concept of equality of all Ottomans, Christian and Muslim, was implicit in the adoption of western law, mixed tribunals, and secular education. After the Hatt-ı Şerif public statements on equality became more common. "Muslims, Christians, Jews, all of you, are subjects of one ruler and you are children of one father," said Riza Paşa to a visiting delegation of non-Muslim millet leaders.[79] Such statements made for public and foreign consumption were often not followed by action, and were sometimes hypocritical. But these utterances were not always insincere. The difficulty was that the leaders were in advance of popular opinion, and could proceed only with caution. The very touchy subject of equality in conversion from Islam to Christianity and vice versa was long avoided by the Porte, but under great pressure from Stratford Canning, the British ambassador, an imperial declaration was given him in 1844 that the death penalty for apostasy from Islam would no longer be applied to Muslims, converts from Christianity, who wished to revert to their original faith. The Supreme Council in 1850 debated the similarly ticklish proposition that Christians should serve equally with Muslims in the armed forces, something that contravened Ottoman tradition. The Muslims could not, however, bring themselves to accept Christians as officers, and the Christians, further, were reluctant to serve, preferring to pay the traditional exemption tax.[80] Only a few Greek sailors were taken into the navy. The principle of equality continued to be accepted, but the application to be deferred.

[79] Karal, *Nizam-ı Cedit ve Tanzimat devirleri*, p. 175. Cf. a similar allocution by Reşid in Engelhardt, *La Turquie*, I, 81.
[80] On this tax cf. H. A. R. Gibb and Harold Bowen, *Islamic Society and the West*, I, part 2 (London, 1957), 16 and n.1, 251-252 and n.3.

Aside from the redefinition of the legislative function of the Supreme Council, the most significant reforms touching the administrative structure of the empire were concerned with provincial government. The problem here was more complex than simply how to secure honesty and efficiency, important though this was. The Porte was trying to devise a system whereby the central control over the eyalets and their governors, reestablished by Mahmud II, could be combined with a certain administrative flexibility giving to the inhabitants of each locality at least a minimal voice in local government and a modest control over the actions of the governors. In the years between the Hatt-ı Şerif and the Crimean War three methods were used by the Porte to oversee the provincial officials and content the governed. One was to call delegates from the provinces to the capital; another, to send out commissioners from İstanbul to inspect the provinces; and the third, to attach to each provincial governor a council somewhat representative of the local population. All three methods were destined to serve as precedents for the further development of administrative reform; they also broadened the application of the principle of equality of Ottomans and first established the principle of representation in government councils. The makers of the constitution of 1876 could look back to these precedents.

It was not unusual for the Ottoman government in times of stress to convene in the capital gatherings of notables to discuss policy and strengthen the hand of the administration. This sort of general assembly (*meclis-i umumî*) was an established custom and, until the mid-nineteenth century, still a working institution. But it was not a representative national assembly with delegates from the provinces; those called together were the civil, religious, and military notables, both in and out of office, who were usually already in İstanbul and represented officialdom only.[81] The general assembly considered matters of war and peace, or of basic administrative policy and reform. It also happened occasionally that delegations from provinces came to İstanbul to lay grievances before the Porte.[82] Being built perhaps on

---

[81]There had been a gathering of provincial notables in 1808; cf. Okandan, *Umumî âmme hukukumuz*, pp. 56-58. But this was not the usual *meclis-i umumî* of the type described above. Âli and Fuad Paşas after 1856 neglected this traditional *meclis-i umumî*, for which Reşid criticized them: Cevdet, *Tezâkir*, p. 80.

[82] See two instances of Cypriote delegations in George Hill, *A History of Cyprus* (Cambridge, 1940-1952), IV, 153 and 170; also a delegation of Bulgars in İnalcık, *Tanzimat ve Bulgar meselesi*, pp. 75 and 80. The Bulgars were actually sent by one of the Porte's special commissioners investigating causes of unrest in the province in 1850.

these precedents, a serious experiment in convening an assembly of provincial notables was made in 1845 when two representatives, Christian and Muslim, of each province were called together to consider the state of agriculture, taxes, and roads. The Porte's optimistic description of the delegates' function was that they were to discuss administrative conditions and improvements, enrich one anothers' minds with this exchange of views, and then return to their provinces to spread their new ideas and assist in improving the state of affairs.[83] The delegates stayed more than two months in the capital, and expressed their wishes on tax and economic reforms at a meeting which Abdülmecid attended, concealed behind a screen. Some years later one of the delegates said that the sultan promised all they asked, but that only one promise was fulfilled—that the tithe be collected in kind and not in coin. Although the men of the provinces made known some basic desires for economic improvement, they were evidently afraid both of offending the sultan and of suffering reprisals from the provincial officials who had sent them, if they were too outspoken.[84]

No further assembly of provincial delegates was convened until the national parliament of 1877. But the assembly of 1845 gave impetus to the use of commissions of provincial inspection. The commissioner on inspection (*müfettiş*) was already familiar in the empire, sent out from the capital as a trouble shooter with powers sometimes almost as extensive as those of Charlemagne's *missi*.[85] Two members of the ulema had been sent on tours of provincial inspection as recently as 1840.[86] Now, after the delegates from the assembly of 1845 returned home, the function of inspection was enlarged. Ten "commissions of improvement" (*mecalis-i imariye*) were sent out, five to Europe and five to Asia, to inspect the provinces and oversee economic improvements. Each commission was composed of one army officer,

[83] Text of circular of 13 April 1845 in Louis Antoine Léouzon le Duc, *Midhat Pacha* (Paris, 1877), pp. 12-14, and Benoît Brunswik, *La Turquie, ses créanciers et la diplomatie* (Paris, 1877), pp. 124-129.

[84] Ubicini, *Letters*, I, 321-322; Okandan, *Umumî âmme hukukumuz*, pp. 72-73, 106; Engelhardt, *La Turquie*, I, 75-76; Senior, *Journal*, pp. 177-178; Kanitz, *Donau-Bulgarien*, I, 92; Berhard Stern, *Jungtürken und Verschwörer*, 2nd ed. (Leipzig, 1901), p. 85. Mehmed Ali experimented with somewhat analogous gatherings in Egypt and Syria in the 1830's; cf. Henry Dodwell, *The Founder of Modern Egypt* (Cambridge, 1931), p. 205.

[85] Mouradgea D'Ohsson, *Tableau générale de l'Empire othoman* (Paris, 1788-1824), VII, 289, comments that in the eighteenth century the inspectors themselves often became party to venality and oppression.

[86] Engelhardt, *La Turquie*, I, 42.

one civil official, and one member of the ulema. The future provincial administrator Midhat Paşa here gained some of his earliest experience, as secretary to two of the commissions. It is not apparent that much resulted from these commissions except for the increased knowledge in the capital of provincial problems. But the tactic of improving provincial government and rectifying abuses through commissions of inspection became now almost standard procedure. Other inspectors went out in 1850 and 1851, and again on a fairly wide scale in 1860 and the years following—events which paved the way for the complete reorganization of provincial administration in the vilayet law of 1864.[87] Abdülmecid also followed the example of Mahmud II and himself made trips of inspection in his provinces, on one occasion taking with him the future sultans Abdülaziz and Murad V.[88]

The real innovation of the 1840's in provincial government was to attach to each governor a *meclis*, or council, in which the non-Muslim communities were represented, and to give this council a check on the actions of the governor. The new system was tried experimentally in 1845 in three eyalets in Europe and two in Asia, and then extended to the others. The council was so constituted that it contained a majority of Muslims, most of them officials; the non-Muslim members were the chief local ecclesiastical authorities and the elected heads (*kocabaşı*'s) of the local non-Muslim communities. The council was given the right to discuss freely civil, financial, and judicial questions, and was intended to give broad supervision to the execution of the promises made in the Hatt-ı Şerif. The governor, whose powers had already been shorn by Mahmud II, was now required to secure from this council a *mazbata*, or written and sealed protocol, endorsing his actions.

Considered in the abstract, this system represented an intelligent attempt at combining centralization with decentralization, balancing officials appointed from İstanbul with representatives of the local population. In actuality, it failed to work smoothly. It often happened that the governor simply hid behind the *mazbata* to avoid assuming re-

---

[87] On 1845 commissions, Ubicini, *Letters*, I, 322; Léouzon, *Midhat*, pp. 12, 14; Brunswik, *La Turquie, ses créanciers*, pp. 124-129. On later inspectors, Temperley, *England and the Near East*, p. 236; Charles Thomas Newton, *Travels and Discoveries in the Levant* (London, 1865), I, 113-114. See below, chapter III, for commissions in the 1860's.

[88] İnalcık, *Tanzimat ve Bulgar meselesi*, p. 81; Nassif Mallouf, *Précis de l'histoire ottomane* (İzmir, 1852), p. 53; Ubicini, *Turquie actuelle*, p. 110.

sponsibility. The council, further, was usually controlled by the Muslim majority, in which influential local landowners became dominant; therefore, they could control the vali. Local Christian notables, who had a similar interest in preserving a status quo favorable to themselves, often cooperated with the dominant group to oppose any fundamental reforms proposed by the governor. The council, it is obvious, was not representative of the common people, either Christian or Muslim. The Porte, swinging back toward more centralized control, tried to remedy this situation in 1852 with a ferman which again broadened the administrative authority of the vali, who was more likely than the local notables or minor officials to have a reforming tendency. But, as is obvious from contemporary descriptions of provincial administration up to the time of the Crimean War, the situation was not essentially improved. Local vested interests, and complaisant or inefficient governors, hindered progress, and only the most energetic of governors could accomplish anything. The residue of the experiment was, in fact, that the principle of popular representation, however deficient in application, was introduced into the governmental structure of the empire by way of the provincial councils.[89]

Down to the outbreak of the Crimean War the fruits of reform were disappointingly few. Reşid, who had since 1839 been foreign minister twice and grand vezir three times, bemoaned the indolence and prejudice which slowed down progress when haste was necessary.[90] He himself apparently lost some of his reforming zeal toward the

---

[89] The provinces as of 1847 are listed in the first imperial yearbook (*salname*), largely reproduced in Thomas X. Bianchi, "Notice sur le premier annuaire . . . de l'Empire ottoman . . . ," *Journal asiatique*, 11 (1848), 12-21. For the provincial council organization see İnalcık, *Tanzimat ve Bulgar meselesi*, p. 6; Ubicini, *Letters*, I, 45-46; Karal, *Nizam-ı Cedit ve Tanzimat devirleri*, pp. 195-196. There is possible precedent for the provincial council in some areas of the empire which had special privileges, though the author has found no direct connection: see, for example, the organization of Samos in 1832 in Aristarchi, *Législation*, II, 145-146, and Young, *Corps de droit*, I, 115-116. Syria and Crete, when under Egyptian rule in the 1830's, also had local councils in which non-Muslims were represented: M. Sabry, *L'Empire égyptien sous Mohamed-Ali et la Question d'Orient* (Paris, 1930), pp. 346, 398. For 1852 ferman, Engelhardt, *La Turquie*, I, 105-110. Criticism of the system is abundant, especially useful in the case studies of Cyprus by Hill, *History of Cyprus*, IV, 177-182, and of Bulgaria by İnalcık, *Tanzimat*, pp. 75-77; see also John Barker, *Syria and Egypt Under the Last Five Sultans of Turkey* (London, 1876), I, 145-148; the later criticism by New Ottomans in *Tanzimat*, I, 821-822; and the rather cynical account by Melek Hanum in *Thirty Years*, pp. 52-134 passim, of the term of office of her husband, Kıbrıslı Mehmed Paşa, as governor of Jerusalem in the 1840's.

[90] Engelhardt, *La Turquie*, II, 235.

end of this period.[91] The crisis of 1852 and 1853, which arose over the Holy Places and then led to broad Russian demands for protection of the Greek Orthodox subjects in the Ottoman Empire, seems to have aroused not only a popular anti-Russian spirit, but an increased Muslim resentment against equality, Ottoman brotherhood, and reforms in general.[92] There had, however, been some significant change in the preceding decade and a half, even apart from the beginnings in administrative, legal, and educational institutions mentioned above. The tone of life in the Ottoman Empire was a little different, especially with the increase of security of life, honor, and property which the Hatt-ı Şerif had promised. Justice was, on the whole, more evenhanded, confiscations a thing of the past. "Until the accession of Abdul Medjid," wrote a European who for some years lived near Ankara, "neither the Armenian merchant nor the Turkish pasha dared put panes of glass in his house, for fear of attracting to him the jealousy of the authorities and of losing his life along with his treasures."[93] The Tanzimat had become known in the farthest villages of Anatolia, where the wry comments on it made by a local official and a predatory Kurd indicate some degree of effectiveness in the Porte's efforts to foster government according to law and to enforce public order.[94] Some of the outward marks of Christian and Jewish second-class status were being discarded without opposition—marks such as the strip of black cloth which formerly had to be attached to the fez, or the requirement that non-Muslims dismount when riding past a Muslim.[95] There was even some emigration from independent Greece into the Ottoman dominions, where Greeks had found the demands of government less oppressive.[96] Similarly, Armenians who had migrated to the Caucasus, forced to do so or lured by the Russians after the Russo-Turkish War of 1828-1829, were filtering back into the Ottoman Empire when they could, in search of the greater freedom they enjoyed

[91] So Stratford thought: Temperley, *England and the Near East*, p. 244.

[92] Engelhardt, *La Turquie*, I, 102; Andreas D. Mordtmann, *Anatolien: Skizzen und Reisebriefe* (Hannover, 1925), p. 39.

[93] Christine la Princesse de Belgiojoso, *Asie Mineure et Syrie* (Paris, 1858), p. 226.

[94] H. A. Layard, *Discoveries in the Ruins of Nineveh and Babylon* (New York, 1853), pp. 16, 20.

[95] Cyrus Hamlin, *Among the Turks* (New York, 1878), p. 334; Edmund Spencer, *Travels in European Turkey in 1850* . . . (London, 1851), I, 244-245, cited in Barbara Jelavich, "The British Traveller in the Balkans," *Slavonic and East European Review*, 33:81 (June 1955), 398.

[96] Charles Albert A. E. Dumont, *Le Balkan et l'Adriatique* (Paris, 1874), pp. 381-382.

under Turkish rule.[97] In short, a beginning toward equality, Ottomanism, orderly administration, representative government, and general westernization had been made; but the course of future development was quite uncertain.

[97] Layard, *Discoveries*, pp. 13-16. Undoubtedly a part of this freedom was owing not only to traditional Turkish toleration, but to administrative laxity as compared with Russian practice.

CHAPTER II

THE HATT-I HÜMAYUN OF 1856 AND THE CLIMATE OF ITS RECEPTION

The lull which overtook the reform movement in the early 1850's was soon broken by the impact of the Crimean War. In the wake of the English and French armies that swarmed into the Bosporus and went on to the Black Sea came new western influences, good and bad. Britain and France used their status as allies of the Ottoman Empire to urge the Turks toward further westernization and more effective application of the doctrine of equality.[1] At the end of the war, their pressure culminated in a new edict, the Hatt-ı Hümayun of 1856, which inaugurated the second and final phase of the Tanzimat.

Already during the war period the British ambassador Stratford Canning, now become Lord Stratford de Redcliffe, had been instrumental in securing the proclamation of a ferman which removed one of the distinctions among Ottoman subjects by allowing the admission of Christian testimony in some criminal actions.[2] Secular police courts were set up to take cognizance of these mixed criminal cases,[3] in an effort to avoid the prejudice of the Muslim kadı against Christian testimony; the courts, however, were filled with nominees of the Muslim governors. In the same year the establishment of a new council of reforms was probably hastened by the presence if not the direct pressure of the allies. This was the Tanzimat Council (*Meclis-i âli-i Tanzimat*), which took over the function of drafting reform legislation formerly exercised by the Supreme Council of Judicial Ordinances.[4] The council was also, significantly, charged with investigating ministers and with general oversight of the administration of law and order. It was, in fact, to be a sort of watchdog for the grand vezir over the bureaucracy, and instances of corruption were among the events that impelled Reşid to establish the council.[5] Âli Paşa was its

---

[1] The French and English influence and pressure appear clearly throughout Cevdet Paşa, *Tezâkir 1-12*, ed. by Cavid Baysun (Ankara, 1953); cf. Fatma Aliye, *Ahmed Cevdet Paşa ve zamanı* (İstanbul, 1336), pp. 118-119.

[2] Text of regulations in F. Eichmann, *Die Reformen des osmanischen Reiches* (Berlin, 1858), pp. 429-432.

[3] Text of ferman in *ibid.*, pp. 426-428.

[4] Text of edict in Friedrich Wilhelm von Reden, *Die Türkei und Griechenland* (Frankfurt a.M., 1856), pp. 298-300.

[5] Cevdet, *Tezâkir*, pp. 27, 36; Fatma Aliye, *Cevdet*, pp. 119-122.

first president, and among the members were Fuad Efendi (later Paşa) and Mütercim Mehmed Rüşdi, with whom Âli often worked closely. The council could draft new laws on subjects referred to it, or could take the initiative in proposing new legislation. During the war the Tanzimat Council, again under allied pressure, prepared another measure to remove one of the important inequalities between Muslims and non-Muslims. This abolished the *haraç*, or tax paid by non-Muslims in place of military service, and permitted them to do such service thereafter.[6] But it proved impossible to render this measure effective because of antagonism on both sides.

The allies' initiative in these measures was symptomatic of their concern throughout the war for a more general reform in the Ottoman Empire. Their original intention of securing guarantees for the rights of Christians in particular brought strong objections from Âli Paşa that this was unnecessary and would infringe the sovereign rights of the sultan.[7] So the diplomats turned to discussion of more thoroughgoing reform which should affect equally all the sultan's subjects. From this discussion resulted the Hatt-ı Hümayun of 1856, which was in many ways the magnum opus of Lord Stratford. Throughout the month of January 1856 he met regularly with Thouvenel, the French ambassador, and Prokesch, the Austrian internuncio to the Porte. Âli Paşa and Fuad Paşa, now grand vezir and foreign minister respectively, and Prince Kallimaki, an Ottoman Greek, met with the three ambassadors to discuss their project.[8] The three powers were pushing the Turks to complete the decree before the Paris peace conference opened, so that Russia would have no hand in Turkish reform, but would be presented with a fait accompli. In this they were successful; but Turkish resentment of what was essentially foreign dictation of a reform program shows through accounts of the negotiation, even though Âli and Fuad were prepared to admit the validity of almost all the points made in the *hat*. Stratford did not obtain all he wished,

---

[6] Text in Eichmann, *Reformen*, pp. 436-440. Cf. Felix Bamberg, *Geschichte der orientalischen Angelegenheit* (Berlin, 1892), p. 263; Eichmann, *Reformen*, pp. 226-232; Edouard Engelhardt, *La Turquie et le Tanzimat* (Paris, 1882-1884), I, 126-127. The terms *haraç* and *cizye* were used interchangeably in the nineteenth century to mean a head tax paid by the non-Muslim peoples of the book, with the understanding that this was in lieu of military service, although neither term originally had this meaning.

[7] Memorandum of December 28, 1854, and Âli's argument in Eichmann, *Reformen*, pp. 214, 374-381.

[8] Kallimaki kept records of the discussions: Cevdet, *Tezâkir*, p. 73.

since the Turks found French and Austrian support for softening some of the demands, but the resultant Hatt-ı Hümayun of 1856 was, in contrast to the Hatt-ı Şerif of 1839, essentially made in Europe, and autochthonous in form alone. Turkish face was saved because the edict was proclaimed as a spontaneous act of the sultan, and because the Treaty of Paris included a provision that the *hat* was not to lay the basis for foreign interference.[9]

Although the Hatt-ı Hümayun[10] sprang from foreign dictation, while the Hatt-ı Şerif of Gülhane did not, in a number of ways the two documents were alike. Each was promulgated when the Ottoman Empire was deeply involved in international complications, and each was aimed at European opinion as well as at domestic reform.[11] Each

[9] On negotiations see Great Britain, *Parliamentary Papers*, 1856, vol. 61, *Accounts and Papers*, vol. 24, Eastern Papers (part 18); Prokesch's report of 24 January 1856 in HHS, XII/56 and enclosure; Bamberg, *Geschichte*, pp. 263-265; Stanley Lane-Poole, *Life of . . . Stratford Canning* (London, 1888), II, 439-443; Harold Temperley, "The Last Phase of Stratford de Redcliffe," *English Historical Review*, 47 (1932), 226-231; Enver Ziya Karal, *Nizam-ı cedit ve Tanzimat devirleri* (Ankara, 1947), pp. 257-258. Cevdet, *Tezâkir*, p. 67, says that the şeyhülislâm Ârif Efendi was also on the drafting commission. Stratford's efforts to urge the Turks to solemn proclamation, and his regrets that the *hat* was not more explicit and inclusive, are clear from his dispatches in FO 78/1173, #176, 13 February 1856, and #213, 21 February 1856.

[10] Westerners have always called this edict the Hatt-ı Hümayun, following the title as officially communicated by the Porte to the Paris peace conference of 1856 and as written on the Turkish texts distributed just after the proclamation. But Turks almost always call it the "Islahat Fermanı," the "reform ferman," as it is referred to in *Düstur*, I (İstanbul, 1289), I and 7, or popularly the "imtiyaz fermanı," the ferman of privileges or concessions. To avoid confusion with the edict of 1839, the author will use the common western form.

Well-preserved copies of the original edict as distributed in 1856 may be seen in both the Turkish and French versions in Stratford to Clarendon, #213, 21 February 1856, enclosures, FO 78/1173, and in Prokesch to Buol, #16A-G, 21 February 1856, HHS, XII/56; a facsimile of the Turkish text of 1856 is in *Tanzimat*, I, following p. 56. The Turkish text in printed form is available in many places: as in Ahmed Rasim, *Resimli ve haritalı osmanlı tarihi*, IV (İstanbul, 1328-1330), 2048-2062; and most usefully with transliteration and comments in Thomas Xavier Bianchi, *Khaththy Humaïoun . . . en français et en turc* (Paris, 1856). A transliteration in modern Turkish is in Karal, *Nizam-ı cedit ve Tanzimat devirleri*, pp. 266-272. The Turkish text was not numbered by articles; hence the various French versions differ in paragraphing. The official French text may be found in many places, for instance: George Young, *Corps de droit ottoman* (Oxford, 1905-1906), II, 3-9; Eichmann, *Reformen*, pp. 353-360; Engelhardt, *La Turquie*, II, 263-270. Grégoire Aristarchi Bey gives an independent translation from the Turkish in *Législation ottomane* (Constantinople, 1873-1888), II, 14-22. An English translation is in J. C. Hurewitz, *Diplomacy in the Near and Middle East* (Princeton, 1956), I, 149-153.

[11] This point, that the edict of 1856 was made to assuage European opinion, is made specifically in the report of a special meeting of Ottoman statesmen to consider ways of applying some of its promises: Mehmet Selâheddin, *Bir türk diplomatının evrak-ı siyasiyesi* (İstanbul, 1306), p. 149.

was cast in the most solemn form of imperial decree, and made promises which required implementation by more specific regulations. The
guarantees of 1839 were logically repeated and extended in the edict
of 1856. But there were also significant differences. The edict of 1856
was more meticulous than its predecessor in enumerating the changes
to be made; it started with a confirmation of the promises of 1839,
but went far beyond. And the edict of 1856, unlike that of 1839, did
not have a split personality. Not only were its tone and language more
modern and western, to the point of clarity and conciseness unusual
for Ottoman documents of those days, but it contained not one mention of the sacred law, the Koran, or the ancient laws and glories of
the empire. Psychologically, this was dangerous. But the whole decree
looked ahead, not back.

This remains true despite the fact that some of the pledges of
1856 had been made before. The abolition of tax farming was again
promised; likewise the abolition of bribery. The equal liability of
Muslims and non-Muslims to military service was reiterated. A note
annexed to the *hat* repeated the affirmation of 1844 that apostasy
from Islam would not be punished by death.[12] But other stipulations
of the Hatt-ı Hümayun went beyond the promises of 1839: strict
observance of annual budgets, the establishment of banks, the employment of European capital and skills for economic improvement, the
codification of penal and commercial law and reform of the prison
system, and the establishment of mixed courts to take care of a greater
proportion of cases involving Muslims and non-Muslims.

These and other reforms were to be for the benefit of all the sultan's subjects, of whatever creed or class. Although this reaffirmation
of the principle of equality again echoed the Hatt-ı Şerif of Gülhane,
equality received considerably greater emphasis in 1856. The implications of Osmanlılık were elaborated in some detail: Muslims and non-
Muslims should be equal in matters of military service, in the administration of justice, in taxation, in admission to civil and military
schools, in public employment, and in social respect. A special anti-
defamation clause banned the use by officials or private persons of
deprecatory epithets[13] "tending to make any class whatever of the sub-

---

[12] The text of the Hatt-ı Hümayun itself did not go so far on this touchy subject,
stating only, "No one shall be compelled to change his religion"—perhaps an echo
of Sura, 11:257 (Bell's translation), "There is no compulsion in religion."

[13] This presumably included not only the popular term for infidel, *gâvur*, and its
literary equivalent *kâfir*, but also *reaya*, which from its original meaning of "flocks"

jects of my empire inferior to another class on account of religion, language or race." Before mixed tribunals, witnesses of all creeds were to have equal status, and to be sworn according to their own formulae. The whole edict implied the removal of millet barriers and the substitution of a common citizenship for all peoples of the empire. Throughout the *hat* recur phrases innocent of religious distinction— "imperial subjects," "subjects of the sublime sultanate," and "subjects of the Exalted [Ottoman] State."[14] In the preamble of the Hatt-ı Hümayun was introduced the concept of patriotism or "compatriotism" as the bond among all the subjects of the empire.[15] This was a step toward a secular, western concept of nationality. Yet there was a dualism implicit in the fact that the Hatt-ı Hümayun, with all its emphasis on equality without distinction as to religion, was in part devoted to enumerating the rights of the Christian and other non-Muslim communities, and specifically retained the millet organizations, although prescribing their reform. Millet boundaries were to be blurred, but they were still there. Complete equality, egalitarian Ottomanism, was yet to come, even in theory.

The Hatt-ı Hümayun promised also an extension of the principle of representation in government, in three separate provisions. The

---

had come to designate the mass of the sultan's peasant subjects, but in the nineteenth century was commonly used only to refer to the non-Muslim subjects of the empire. Cf. Bianchi, *Khaththy Humaïoun*, p. 12, n.1, and H. A. R. Gibb and Harold Bowen, *Islamic Society and the West*, I, part 1 (London, 1950), 237. Joseph von Hammer-Purgstall, *Des osmanischen Reichs Staatsverfassung und Staatsverwaltung* (Vienna, 1815), I, 181, makes clear the bitter connotations of the term *reaya*.

[14] *tebaa-yı şahane, tebaa-yı saltanat-ı seniye, tebaa-yı Devlet-i Aliyye*. In the 1839 Hatt-ı Şerif the expression *tebaa-yı saltanat-ı seniye* had been used once, and was evidently coined for the occasion: see T. X. Bianchi, *Le Nouveau Guide de la conversation . . .* , 2nd ed. (Paris, 1852), p. 296, n.2.

[15] Bianchi, *Khaththy Humaïoun*, p. 4, n.1, says the term *vatandaş*, here used for the French *patriotisme*, was a new form. The word *vatan*, which down to the nineteenth century meant "place of birth or residence," was by mid-century equated to "fatherland," the French *patrie*, both in popular and official usage. Cf. Reşid's use of *vatan* in 1856 in Cevdet, *Tezâkir*, p. 75. Curiously, the official French text of the 1839 Hatt-ı Şerif twice translated *vatan*, which appeared in the Turkish text, as *pays*, while rendering *millet* as *patrie*. See comments on the evolution of the word in Bernard Lewis, "The Impact of the French Revolution on Turkey," *Journal of World History*, 1:1 (July 1953), 107-108; cf. Sylvia G. Haim, "Islam and the Theory of Arab Nationalism," *Die Welt des Islams*, n.s. IV:2/3 (1955), 132-135, on the evolution of the term in Arabic. *Vatandaş* came to be used for "citizen," and "patriotism" to be translated by *vatanperverlik*, as illustrated, for instance, in the Turkish translation of French terms in Mustafa Fazıl Paşa's letter to the sultan in 1867. *Vatan* continued to be used for "fatherland," but gathered most of its emotional content from the manner in which the New Ottomans used it, especially Namık Kemal in his play of 1873, also called *Vatan*, on which see below, chapter VIII.

provincial and communal councils, which already embodied this principle, were to be reconstituted to ensure the fair choice of Muslim and non-Muslim delegates and the freedom of their discussion in the councils. The Supreme Council of Judicial Ordinances was henceforth to include representatives of the non-Muslim millets. And the millet structures themselves were to be recast so that temporal affairs of the non-Muslim communities would be supervised not by the clergy alone, but by councils including lay delegates. In the Supreme Council and the millet organizations the representative principle was thus introduced on an empire-wide scale.

Reaction to the proclamation of the Hatt-ı Hümayun was mixed, but in general it aroused more opposition than enthusiasm. This was above all true among the Muslim Turks. Many of them, particularly in the capital, were resentful of the foreign pressures which led to the edict. The *şeyhülislâm* referred pointedly to the fact that not only English and French fleets, but also land armies of both nations, were in the environs of İstanbul. Reşid openly criticized the *hat*, referring to it as the ferman of concessions. In a lengthy memorandum he argued that Âli and Fuad were going too far too fast in giving political privileges to Christians. To be sure, Christians could no longer be treated as they were a hundred or even twenty years ago, but all change must be gradual and without foreign interference. The complete equality promised in the ferman, he said, will give the Ottoman Empire a color completely different from that of the past six centuries, eliminating the distinction between the ruling millet and the ruled. Muslim opinion will object to this; minds must be prepared. Reşid predicted troubles in various parts of the empire. He also objected strongly to the manner in which the ferman was drafted and to its mention in the Treaty of Paris. These matters seriously affected the honor, independence, and integrity of the state and sultan. Yet, continued Reşid, the ministers and a few slavish followers acted hastily, without summoning the time-honored general assembly of notables for discussion.[16]

Reşid was moved by personal pique at the fact that his pupils now controlled the government while he was out of office, but his criticisms were not without weight and were echoed by other Turks, who re-

---

[16] Reşid's memorandum is in Cevdet, *Tezâkir*, pp. 76-82. At the same time, however, Reşid was evidently telling his European friends that the Hatt-ı Hümayun did not go far enough! Prokesch to Buol, #16D, 21 February 1856, HHS XII/56.

sented the emphasis on equality and could, of course, not be legislated into giving up the term *gâvur*. The ruling position of the Muslim millet won by the blood of their forefathers was being abandoned, they said; "it was a day of weeping for the people of Islam."[17] A few of the young half-westernized efendis took the *hat* cheerfully, and some were reported to rejoice that with the increased mingling of Muslim and non-Muslim in Ottoman society the Muslims would realize an increase in the value of their real estate. But these were exceptions. Turks who were in favor of reform resented not only the foreign dictation but the sweeping nature of the Hatt-ı Hümayun, which was sure to arouse opposition. "I have no patience with the authors of the *Hatt-i-Humayoon*," said one. "We were going on rapidly with our reforms, and now comes this silly false move, and, perhaps, spoils the game of the improvers for twenty years. . . . The people who sent it to us from Paris know nothing of our institutions."[18] From the interior of Anatolia it was reported that "the remaining bigotry of the Musulman race has been aroused by the late *Hatti Humayoon*, and they hate the Europeans to whom they ascribe it, and the Rayas for whose benefit it has been granted. . . ."[19] In Maraş and some Syrian centers there were outbursts.[20]

Among Christian subjects of the Porte, reaction to the Hatt-ı Hümayun was still mixed, though on the whole more favorable. What the Christians thought depended on their particular situation. Probably the most enthusiastic were the Bulgars, who saw a chance to throw off the detested yoke of the Greek Orthodox hierarchy in the provisions of the *hat* that enjoined a reorganization of the millets and supplanted elastic ecclesiastical revenues by fixed salaries for clergy.[21] Among the ordinary Christians of whatever sect there was approval for the prospect that laymen should have greater voice in the control

[17] Cevdet, *Tezâkir*, pp. 67-68.
[18] Nassau Senior, *A Journal Kept in Turkey and Greece* (London, 1859), p. 72.
[19] Van Lennep, 12 June 1858, #386, ABCFM, Armenian Mission VIII.
[20] On Muslim Turkish reactions to the Hatt-ı Hümayun see Cevdet, *Tezâkir*, pp. 66-89, which includes Reşid's lengthy memorandum; Ahmed Refik, "Türkiyede Islahat Fermanı," *Tarih-i osmanî encümeni mecmuası*, 14:81 (1340), 195ff., largely plagiarizing Cevdet's information; Karal, *Nizam-ı cedit ve Tanzimat devirleri*, pp. 258-259; Karal, *Islahat fermanı devri* (Ankara, 1956), pp. 7-11, largely Cevdet simplified; George Hill, *A History of Cyprus* (Cambridge, 1940-1952), IV, 177, 201-203; Andreas D. Mordtmann, *Anatolien; Skizzen und Reisebriefe* (Hannover, 1925), pp. 252, 255-256, 262.
[21] Alois Hajek, *Bulgarien unter der Türkenherrschaft* (Stuttgart, 1925), p. 188; William W. Hall, *Puritans in the Balkans* (Sofia, 1938), p. 15.

of millet affairs, as well as general enthusiasm for most of the provisions on equality. But they resented the prospect of equality in military service, and it was foolish to suppose that this burden, disliked
and evaded when possible by Turks, should be gladly accepted by
Christians. The experiment tried during the Crimean War had turned
out so badly that the Hatt-ı Hümayun itself had to admit the principle
of buying off from military service, which now theoretically was the
equal privilege of both Muslim and Christian.[22] The higher Christian
clergy were generally opposed to the Hatt-ı Hümayun, because it
struck at their power over the millets, especially at their ability to
fleece their spiritual subjects. The Greek hierarchy, fearing the loss of
their primacy among the non-Muslims, disliked not only this invasion
of traditional prerogative, but also the general emphasis on equality.
"The state puts us together with the Jews," some of the Greeks were
reported to have said. "We were content with the superiority of Islam."[23] It is quite probable that the Greek metropolitan of İzmit
uttered the wish attributed to him as the Hatt-ı Hümayun was put
back into its red satin pouch after the ceremonial reading at the Porte:
"*İnşallah*—God grant that it not be taken out of this bag again."[24]
The Greeks had good reason to worry about the *hat*'s indication of
creeping equality, though, in fact, the precedence of Greek clerics over
other non-Muslim ecclesiastics was to some degree preserved throughout the Tanzimat era.[25]

The promulgation of the Hatt-ı Hümayun was, in sum, a mixed
blessing, although it stands as one of the great documents of the Tanzimat period. Âli and Fuad had obviously made the best of a bad job,
and had consented to the decree in order to stave off more active for-

[22] Prokesch to Buol, #39 A-E, 16 May 1856, HHS, XII/56. Benoît Brunswik,
Etudes pratiques sur la question d'Orient (Paris, 1869), pp. 148-149, claims that
the Porte, fearful of arming Christians, ordered the Christian patriarchs to object
to this point. But it is clear that the Christian peoples had their own grounds for
objection, and that the patriarchs had independent reasons for disliking the Hatt-ı
Hümayun.

[23] Cevdet, *Tezâkir*, p. 68.

[24] Engelhardt, *La Turquie*, I, 142; Karal, *Islahat fermanı devri*, p. 11. Karal, in
Nizam-ı cedit ve Tanzimat devirleri, p. 191, attributes the same remark to the Greek
Orthodox patriarch at the reading of the 1839 edict, which is probably an error.
See, further, Engelhardt, *La Turquie*, I, 140, 147-148; Senior, *Journal*, p. 152.
Cevdet, *Tezâkir*, pp. 82-83, summarizes and quotes from a memorandum by Stephen
Vogorides, a Greek completely devoted to the service of the Porte, which argues that
the grant of equality is too sudden and runs counter to ancestral customs and values.

[25] Cf. Article 2 of 1869 (?) regulations on precedence in provincial councils:
Düstur, I, 719; Aristarchi, *Législation*, II, 297.

eign intervention and keep the initiative in their own hands.[26] The clause in the Paris peace treaty forbidding outside interference seemed to confirm the wisdom of their course.[27] But the foreign origin of the Hatt-ı Hümayun was well known; this created not only resentment among Turks, but a tendency among the Christian minorities to look to Europe for support in securing the promised equality rather than to an Ottoman government which had issued the decree only under pressure. The Ottoman ministers tried to explain the Hatt-ı Hümayun as all things to all men: to represent it to the European powers and to their non-Muslim subjects as an important concession, and to their Muslim subjects as containing nothing particularly new or injurious to their prestige.[28] It is likely that a series of smaller measures would have accomplished more, and occasioned less resentment, than a Hatt-ı Hümayun issued with such fanfare, for the mere existence of the Hatt-ı Hümayun laid the basis for Muslim complaints about its concessions and Christian and European complaints about nonfulfillment. It remained, nevertheless, a mark to shoot at. It was not self-enforcing, but required future legislation and administrative action.

What success would attend these efforts depended on the improvement of officialdom and of the educational level within the empire—subjects on which the *hat* was largely silent. It depended also on the general climate of opinion in the empire in 1856. "You can give good advice, but not good customs," says the Turkish proverb. Fuad Paşa, reviewing the accomplishments of the reform program a decade after the Hatt-ı Hümayun, echoed this: "L'on ne saurait improviser la réforme des moeurs."[29] Baron Prokesch, the Austrian internuncio, agreed. It would take time, he said, to change ideas, and then to achieve social changes; reform cannot be rushed.[30] What the obstacles to the implementation of the Hatt-ı Hümayun were can be understood only in the light of the situation of the Ottoman Empire and the outlook of its peoples at the end of the Crimean War period.

[26] Fuad argued that issuance of the *hat* had prevented the powers from inserting details on Ottoman reform into the peace treaty: Cevdet, *Tezâkir*, p. 85.

[27] See appendix A on interpretation of this clause.

[28] See Fuad Paşa's rather specious argument—but one justified by the literal text of the Hatt-ı Hümayun—to Muslims, that the *hat* did not really say Christians would be members of the Supreme Council, but only that they should be summoned to its discussions: Cevdet, *Tezâkir*, p. 71.

[29] Considérations sur l'exécution du Firman Impérial du 18 février 1856," in Aristarchi, *Législation*, II, 26.

[30] Prokesch to Buol, #41C, 20 May 1856, HHS XII/56.

In 1856 the Ottoman Empire was still a sprawling conglomeration of territories, which any government could have administered only with difficulty. To introduce effective reform over such an area would be harder yet. Serbia, Moldavia, Wallachia, Egypt, and Tunis enjoyed varying degrees of autonomy; except for Tunis, which in the succeeding two decades snuggled closer to the Porte in an attempt to ward off French domination, all were moving rapidly in the direction of independence. The control of the central government over the Arab provinces in Asia, though firmer than it had been fifty years before, was still tenuous. Tribal groups frequently escaped the Porte's control almost completely. Often the central government not only had little control over some areas, but little knowledge about many regions. A discussion in the Crimean War period of regrouping villages on the Greek frontier revealed, on Sultan Abdülmecid's questioning, that there was no map of the region. At the end of the Tanzimat period the Turks still needed to buy maps of their own Balkan territories from the Austro-Hungarian general staff.[31]

Something like thirty-six million people lived in the empire.[32] Muslims were an absolute majority, numbering about twenty-one million, but the Turks were a minority of perhaps ten to twelve million. Only in Anatolia did they live in a compact mass. The other principal elements in the empire were some six million Slavs, including the Bulgars, two million Greeks, four million Roumanians, two and a half million Armenians, perhaps six to eight million Arabs, a million and a half Albanians, and a million Kurds. Jews and other peoples formed smaller groups. Except for the Armenians, most of whom were in the Gregorian church, the bulk of the non-Muslims were Greek Orthodox. This heterogeneity presented the reformers with a formidable task in their efforts to knit together a reorganized empire based on Osmanlılık. It is true that over the centuries there had been various types of racial mixtures, and a remarkable degree of religious syncretism among the common people of all creeds. But the millet bar-

[31] Cevdet, *Tezâkir*, pp. 50-51; Alexander Novotny, *Quellen und Studien zur Geschichte des Berliner Kongresses 1878*, I (Graz-Köln, 1957), 183. On the geographical work done in this period, most of it by Europeans, see İ. H. Aykol, "Tanzimat devrinde bizde coğrafya ve jeoloji," *Tanzimat*, I, 527-548.

[32] The most problematic figures here are for Arabs and Turks. Ubicini counts only 4,700,000 Arabs, including those in Egypt and Tunis. This seems low, but Egypt toward the end of Mehmed Ali's rule had only a little over 2,000,000 people: Helen Rivlin, *The Agricultural Policy of Muhammad 'Ali in Egypt* (Cambridge, Mass., 1961), pp. 263, 278-280. See Appendix B on census and population sources.

riers still remained, reinforced by the interests of their respective ecclesiastical hierarchies. The millets emphasized not only the distinction
between Muslim and non-Muslim, but the antagonisms among non-
Muslim sects, which in the nineteenth century caused the Porte endless
trouble: Christian contempt for Jew, Greek opposition to Armenian,
and the squabbles of Gregorian, Roman, and Protestant Armenians.
It was true also that there was a partial linguistic amalgam of the
peoples in the empire. Many Greeks and Armenians did not know their
national languages and spoke Turkish alone, though they wrote it in
Greek and Armenian characters.[33] But by mid-century the western
concept of nationalism was becoming stronger among the minority
peoples, who put greater emphasis on their vernaculars. They were
driven toward separatism rather than Ottomanism. Serbs, Roumanians, and Greeks were already infected; Bulgarians and Armenians
were beginning to be. Turks and Arabs were the last of the Ottoman
peoples to turn into the path of nationalism.

Over this mélange the Turk still ruled. He was the mediator among
the diverse peoples, best fitted for the job by temperament and situation, as Turkish ministers liked to point out to Europeans.[34] The symbol of Turkish government was the Turkish soldier stationed at the
Church of the Holy Sepulchre in Jerusalem to keep order among the
quarreling Christians. The Turk, though his government might be
inefficient and corrupt, also had considerable ability as a governor.
Thundering condemnations of the Turk as an untutored barbarian,
unfit for administration, which issued from Europe in mid-century
must be taken as symptoms of a bad case of moral superiority.

But in fact there was no such person as "the Turk." There was the
ruling Ottoman group, now largely concentrated in the bureaucracy
centered on the Sublime Porte, and the mass of the people, mostly
peasants. The efendi looked down on "the Turk," which was a term
of opprobrium indicating boorishness, and preferred to think of himself as an Osmanli. His country was not Turkey, but the Ottoman
State.[35] His language was also "Ottoman"; though he might also call

[33] An American missionary working among them estimated that "fully half" of the
Greeks and Armenians did not know their own tongues: ABCFM, Western Turkey
Mission III, #21, 11 August 1874.

[34] Cf. Fuad to a French visitor: P. Challemel-Lacour, "Les hommes d'état de la
Turquie," *Revue des deux mondes*, 2nd period, 73 (15 February 1868), 922.

[35] Many terms were used to designate the Ottoman Empire, but "Turkey" was not
among them, until Turkish national consciousness began to develop later in the

it "Turkish," in such a case he distinguished it from *kaba türkçe*, or coarse Turkish, the common speech. His writing included a minimum of Turkish words, except for particles and auxiliary verbs. The maligned Turkish peasant, at the other end of the social scale, was generally no better off than the ordinary non-Muslim and as much oppressed by maladministration. In addition, the ordinary Turk had to bear the burden of the five-year military service instituted after 1839. He was as much in need of reformed government as the Christian, but be had neither treaty, foreign power, nor patriarch to protect him, and his lot was generally unknown to Europe.

The line of basic demarcation ran, therefore, not between Muslim and Christian, Turk and non-Turk, but between ruler and ruled, oppressor and oppressed.[36] Those on top—whether Ottoman civil servants or army officers, Greek or Armenian bankers or merchants or higher ecclesiastics—looked down on the masses.[37] Sometimes this scorn represented the opposition of urban populations to the provincials or peasantry. But, though there is truth in this dichotomy, the mass of townsmen were ruled, not ruling; the line still ran between rulers and ruled. There was no extensive urban middle class to bridge the gap, particularly among the Turks, since so many of the businessmen were non-Muslims. The artisan gilds (*esnaf*'s) were feebler in the nineteenth century than before, and although they exerted influence toward reform in some of the millets, especially among Bulgars and Armenians, they did not constitute a national middle class.[38] In

---

century. *Memalik-i osmaniye, devlet-i aliye, devlet-i osmaniye* were among the more common terms. The 1876 constitution used *Memalik-i Devlet-i Osmaniye*.

[36] Mustafa Fazıl Paşa pointed this out forcefully in his *Lettre adressée à S. M. le Sultan* (n.p., n.d., but Paris either late 1866 or early 1867).

[37] Melek-Hanum, *Thirty Years in the Harem* (London, 1872), provides a good, because apparently unconscious, composite example. She was a Levantine—half French, one quarter Greek, and one quarter Armenian—married to Kıbrıslı Mehmed Paşa, an important Turkish statesman. Throughout her autobiography she exhibits occasional sympathy for peasants, but a general attitude of looking down her nose at the ruled.

[38] On background of gilds see Gibb and Bowen, *Islamic Society*, I, part 1, 288-299. For the nineteenth century: H. G. O. Dwight, *Christianity Revived in the East* (New York, 1850), pp. 184-185; Salaheddin, *La Turquie à l'exposition universelle* (Paris, 1867), pp. 163-168; Great Britain, *Parliamentary Papers*, 1870, vol. 66, *Accounts and Papers*, vol. 26, pp. 231-235, 247, and 1871, vol. 68, *Accounts and Papers*, vol. 32, pp. 729, 766-770, 826-827. Süleyman Paşa, ardent reformer of 1876, discounted the *esnaf*'s of İstanbul as having neither interest in, nor effect on, political reform: *Süleyman Paşa muhakemesi* (İstanbul, 1328), p. 76. On Armenian gildsmen see below, chapter IV; on Bulgar gilds, C. E. Black, *The Establishment of Constitutional Government in Bulgaria* (Princeton, 1943), pp. 13-15.

the provinces the gap between large landowners and the peasantry continued to exist. The provincial notables did not fill the role of a progressive rural middle class, as had the smaller landed gentry in some other societies, but they resisted reform, because they profited from disorganization and inefficiency in the central government to maintain their political and financial control. Among the notables were Christians as well as Muslims; both oppressed the peasantry.[39] These social and economic gaps in Ottoman society, as well as the religious and linguistic differences, were serious obstacles to any reform program that aimed at equality of rights, security of all life and property and honor, and representative political institutions.

Given this situation as it existed in 1856, and the lack of organized pressures from below, the ruling group had to be the reforming group. But the ruling group was far from united on either objectives or methods of reform, and some were opponents of any change in the status quo. There were important men—true and intelligent conservatives—who conscientiously opposed any radical break with the past. They wanted to reform abuses, perhaps to change things slowly, but to continue to serve faith and state much as their forefathers had done. There were also those who were conservative solely because of vested interest in what the status quo gave them, who were less interested in serving faith and state than in serving themselves. There were also those of the efendis, described in the preceding chapter, whose superficial westernisms did not make them serious reformers. In time there came to be radical reformers as well—young men in a hurry, who were influenced by their knowledge of western intellectual, political, and economic patterns, as well as by their interpretation of Islam, who spent most of their energies criticizing the government of the day.[40] Thus there was only a comparative handful of men among the ruling

[39] On the dominant position of provincial notables and depression of peasantry see especially Halil İnalcık, *Tanzimat ve Bulgar meselesi* (Ankara, 1943), passim, and, in particular, pp. 10-11, 75-81, 135-142; *idem*, "Tanzimat nedir?" *Tarih araştırmaları, 1940-1941* (İstanbul, 1941), pp. 245-251, 259-260; Abdolonyme Ubicini, *Letters on Turkey*, trans. by Lady Easthope (London, 1856), I, 266-283, on the taxes imposed on the peasantry; Black, *Constitutional Government in Bulgaria*, pp. 10-12, on the local *çorbacı*'s or Bulgar notables; T. W. Riker, *The Making of Roumania* (London, 1931), pp. 3-7, 292-294, on parallel conditions in Moldavia and Wallachia; Wayne S. Vucinich, "The Yugoslav Lands in the Ottoman Period," *Journal of Modern History*, 27:3 (September 1955), pp. 287-305, on a number of significant recent studies on this question by Yugoslav scholars, in particular by Bogićević, Hadžibegić, Elezović, and Djurdjev.
[40] Principally the New Ottomans; see below, chapter VI.

64

group who were seriously interested in carrying out the promises of the Tanzimat—individuals of the cast of Âli and Fuad, with a sense of urgency born of external and internal pressures, dedicated to preservation of the state, with the vision to walk toward distant goals by a succession of small steps, with some knowledge of western ways and the demands of modern life, and with an appreciation of the past and a sense of responsibility in government. These men also had their flaws, among them vanity, the love of high office, and at times a too-casual disregard for the Islamic past, but they were the leaders in reform. The obstacles they faced were imposing.

Among the obstacles was the all-enveloping effect of traditional Islam. Turkish Muslims were generally tolerant of adherents of other revealed religions; they were not given to persecution of Christians and Jews, and were quite likely to say to them, "Your faith is a faith, and my faith is a faith." But there did remain among Muslim Turks an intensity of feeling which, at times of political crisis, was capable of producing fanatic outbursts. Even more important as an obstacle to reform based on equality of all Ottoman subjects was the innate pride, the conviction of superiority, which Muslim Turks possessed. They assumed without question that they were the ruling millet (*millet-i hâkime*).[41] The pride was evident among the most learned of the ulema.[42] It was evident also among the mass of Turks who, whatever the degree of pagan or mystic sufi admixture in their beliefs, still conceived of Islam as the true faith. Christianity and Judaism were partial revelations of the truth, not the whole. Therefore, Christians and Jews were inevitably considered second-class citizens in the light of religious revelation, as well as by reason of the plain fact that they had been conquered and were ruled by the Ottomans. The common term for the infidel, *gâvur*, carried this implication of Muslim superiority.

Islam embodied also a strong prejudice against innovation (*bid'at*). Reform along the lines of Osmanlılık might encounter this prejudice not only among Muslim theologians and among those of the ruling group who still conscientiously served faith as well as state, but also

---

[41] Count Léon Ostrorog, one of the most knowledgeable westerners, observed simply, "Islam is not fanatical, it is proud." *The Turkish Problem*, trans. by Winifred Stephens (London, 1919), p. 17.

[42] See Cevdet Paşa's account of his conversation on Islam and Christianity with M. Mottier, the French ambassador, in Ebül'ulâ Mardin, *Medenî hukuk cephesinden Ahmed Cevdet Paşa* (İstanbul, 1946), pp. 291-294; cf. also Cevdet, *Tezâkir*, p. 79.

in the popular mind, which would assimilate the religious suspicion of innovation to the usual conservatism of inertia. It is true that Muslim doctrine included also the concept of "good" or acceptable innovation, as well as of ijma, or consensus, which modernists attempt to use in justification of accepting changes in institutions and customs. But the doctrine of consensus was meant to note common acceptance of a change already made and to link it with the past, rather than to create innovation. Ijma could with difficulty cover broad reform. The fundamental conservatism of Islam and its prejudice against innovation were particularly important in the Tanzimat period in the field of law. Since Islam was not only a way of worship, but a way of life prescribing man's relations to man and to the state, as well as to God, the sacred law stood as the basis for society and for government, even though it was an ideal, not a law code, and actually covered few aspects of public law. Ottoman sultans had never hesitated to legislate in their own right, but the şeriat and the religious courts still stood alongside the sultan's *kanun*'s and his secular courts. Western law had by 1856 started to come into the Ottoman Empire through commercial law, and its reception grew with time. But the şeriat principles remained dominant in some fields of law until the twentieth century, notably in family and inheritance law. The sacred law had grown inflexible after the Gate of Interpretation was shut following the tenth century; the rigidity was not absolute, particularly in the Ottoman Empire, but was characteristic.[43] The şeriat remained also a symbol or shibboleth, by which new measures should be tested. Ottoman reformers had to build, in fact, on the traditional legislative powers of the sultan, but to convince their critics that proposed measures were in conformity with, or at least not in contravention of, the sacred law. Even under the constitution of 1876, the regulations of the senate gave to that body the duty of seeing that all legislation conformed to the şeriat.[44] It may have been to their advantage that some of the Tanzimat statesmen were, in the words of a modern critic, "unbelievably ignorant of the juridical traditions of the country,"[45] and so unconscious of contravening Islamic law in some of their measures.

It was possible to argue that Islam was no barrier to modernization, westernization, equality, and representative government. Such

---

[43] See Léon Ostrorog, *The Angora Reform* (London, 1927), chapters 1 and 2.
[44] Aristarchi, *Législation*, V, 313.
[45] Fuad Köprülü, "L'institution du Vakouf," *Vakıflar dergisi*, II (1942), 32.

arguments were advanced in the Tanzimat period, both by Turks and by foreigners. Ubicini maintained at mid-century that in the teachings of the Koran were to be found "all the essentials of modern democracy."[46] Within a few years the New Ottomans, and then Midhat Paşa, were to argue the fundamental democracy of Islam, that the Muslim community was originally a sort of republic, and that the elective principle was basic in the faith. This is not the place to begin an investigation of what political views can or cannot be justified on the basis of Koranic texts, the traditions of the Prophet, and early Muslim practice, but it is important to note that in the Tanzimat period such modernist arguments did not represent the view of Muslim teaching and tradition common among Ottoman Turks. They were conditioned to regard the sacred law, as they knew it, as supreme and to regard the sultan also as caliph; they were unconcerned with historical debate about the validity or invalidity of his using such a title.

Muslim tradition and Muslim learning were upheld by the ulema, who naturally supported the system which was their life and bread. As a class, the ulema were conservative and an obstacle to reform, though there were individual exceptions. It is difficult to describe the ulema as fanatic, though they retained the capacity to inspire fanatic sentiment among the population if times of stress presented the appropriate occasion. Many of the ulema apparently put on a show of fanatic devoutness for the sake of maintaining influence among the faithful and of inspiring donations from the wealthy.[47] A few among them, on the other hand, read the Christian scriptures and inquired into Christianity. Despite the lack of open fanaticism, however, the ulema as a group maintained an innate pride in their faith, as well as a pride in their position in the society established in that faith, and knew no other way except that of defending established tradition. Thus they opposed innovation. Cevdet Efendi (later Paşa), who began to learn French in 1846, had to do so secretly for fear of criticism; to learn such a language was considered incompatible with his character as one of the ulema.[48] Selim Sabit Efendi, another member of

[46] *Letters*, I, 57. Cf. p. 132, where he maintains that Islamic law "formally sets forth the sovereignty of the nation, universal suffrage, the principle of election extended to all, even to the governing power, equality between all members of the body politic. . . ."

[47] Henry J. Van Lennep, *Travels in Little-Known Parts of Asia Minor* (London, 1870), I, 118-119.

[48] Fatma Aliye, *Cevdet Paşa*, pp. 33-34.

the ulema, who had had the unusual advantage of a stay in Paris, was vigorously opposed by his colleagues when he tried to introduce into a school in İstanbul such modern aids as maps; such practices were incompatible with faith and religion, they charged.[49] Of course, the ulema also opposed innovations by the civilian bureaucrats, as, for instance, the adoption of any principles of non-Muslim law.[50]

Related to the opposition to innovation, and probably more important than this blind stubbornness as a bar to progress, was the ignorance of the majority of the ulema. In the eighteenth century apparently there had been a perceptible decline in their learning and integrity.[51] In the nineteenth century most of the ulema were not really learned in Islam and knew even less of the outside world. "Seek knowledge even in China" was generally accepted as one of the sayings of the Prophet, but the majority of the ulema knew nothing of China or even of the Europe of which the Ottoman Empire was physically a part. "Why," asked a molla within Moltke's hearing, "should even today ten thousand Osmanlis not rise and with firm belief in Allah and sharp swords ride to Moscow?"[52] These were the men who were the teachers in Ottoman schools. Since the educational reforms begun in the 1840's had by 1856 borne little fruit, the ulema still taught the bulk of those Muslim Turks who had any schooling, whether in the traditional grammar school or in the medrese.[53] The subject matter of instruction had changed little for centuries. In the earliest years reading, calligraphy, arithmetic, the Koran, and the principles of religion and morality were taught. Higher education resembled, in many respects, the medieval trivium and quadrivium,

[49] Osman Ergin, Türkiye maarif tarihi (İstanbul, 1939-1943), II, 384. Significantly, the şeyhülislâm supported the ulema's protests, while the ministry of education allowed Selim Efendi to introduce such changes provided they be gradual and with due regard for public opinion.

[50] Cevdet, Tezâkir, p. 63. A new school to train kadıs, established in 1854, and granting its first diplomas in the year of the Hatt-ı Hümayun, evidently touched on western-influenced law only slightly. After 1869 elements of the newly codified civil law, the Mecelle, were studied there. But the Mecelle was religious law except in its classification principles, and the major study of western-influenced law had to be carried on in a separate law school set up in 1869: Ergin, Maarif tarihi, I, 135.

[51] Gibb and Bowen, Islamic Society, I, part 2 (London, 1957), 104-113.

[52] "Why not," answered a Turkish army officer, "if their passports are visaed by the Russian legation?" But the officer was European in education, and he replied in French: Helmuth von Moltke, Briefe über Zustände und Begebenheiten in der Türkei, 3rd ed. (Berlin, 1877), pp. 313-314.

[53] Ergin, Maarif tarihi, II, 383ff., on grammar schools and ignorance of the teachers.

within an Islamic framework.[54] Most Turks, of course, had little or no schooling. Ziya Bey in 1868 estimated that only about two per cent of the Muslim population were literate.[55] Ahmed Midhat, writing at the close of the Tanzimat period, thought that illiteracy ran from ninety to ninety-five per cent, and lamented that the rest were "without pen and without tongue."[56] Süleyman Paşa at the same period guessed that in the capital itself only twenty thousand Muslims could read a newspaper.[57] And even literate Turks of the higher classes spent their early years in the harem where, despite the fact that some upper-class women enjoyed considerable acquaintance with the arts and with French culture, ignorance and superstition also made their home. Thus the generally low educational level of the Turks of the empire and the traditional attitudes of Islam must be considered along with the extent of the empire, its heterogeneity, and its social structure as important obstacles to reform based on egalitarian Ottomanism.

To these considerations must be added another which, especially in the period after the Crimean War and the Hatt-ı Hümayun, assumed added importance—the impression made on the Turks by Christian Europe. Since many of the reforms were borrowed or adapted from the West, the reception accorded them would depend in part on the nature of the contacts with Europe. By 1856, and continuing in the years following, these contacts were greatly increased. Western influence was observable in the advent of telegraphic connection between İstanbul and western Europe; the first message to Paris and London announced the entry of the Allied forces into Sebastopol in 1855.[58] The age of concessions for railway-building in the empire started with the war, while European shipping interests helped to prompt the construction of the first series of modern lighthouses along the Ottoman coasts. In more superficial matters western influence was immediately felt—as shown, for instance, by the startling increase in the use of knives, forks, chairs, and bedsteads in the seaboard cities. Parisian or *alafranga* modes and manners, which had already found imitators before the Crimean War, now caught on more rapidly. Such imitation did not necessarily indicate any increased un-

[54] *Ibid.*, I, 82-102, 115-117; Ubicini, *Letters*, I, letter 9; Arminius Vambéry, *Sittenbilder aus dem Morgenlande* (Berlin, 1876), pp. 120-127; Gibb and Bowen, *Islamic Society*, I, part 2, chapter 11.
[55] *Hürriyet*, #5, quoted in *Tanzimat*, I, 841.
[56] *Üss-i inkılâb* (İstanbul, 1294-1295), I, 122.
[57] *Süleyman Paşa muhakemesi*, p. 76.   [58] Young, *Corps de droit*, IV, 345.

derstanding of the West, or any predisposition to reform. Some of the most intelligent reformers were, in fact, antagonistic to *alafranga* costume and manners.[59] But the western influences increased apace. Symbolic of the times was the precedent-shattering attendance of Sultan Abdülmecid at a ball given by Lord Stratford in İstanbul. The grand vezir, the Christian patriarchs, and the grand rabbi also graced this western gathering with their presence, though the *şeyhülislâm* made his excuses.[60] Aside from the temporary presence of allied soldiers, the channels of communication were the traditional ones: diplomats, travellers, businessmen, missionaries, adventurers, students, refugees, and native Christians of the empire. The volume of communication was now sharply increased in the numbers of Europeans coming to the Ottoman Empire.[61] The total impact of Europe on the Ottoman Turks was obviously not uniformly good. At best, it was mixed.

This was true in the case of those Turks who went to Europe, either in the diplomatic service or as civilian or military students. They learned French and acquired new ideas. Some, like İbrahim Şinasi Efendi, who had been to Paris even before the Crimean War, became well acquainted with French literature.[62] Others, like some of those who had gone to Europe before the war, returned discouraged or embittered by the contrasts they found. İngiliz Mehmed Said Paşa, an army officer who owed his nickname to his education in Edinburgh, said later, "I had lived abroad till I fancied I had made myself a man, and when I came back to my country I saw about me merely brutes. . . ."[63] Still others acquired only western manners and sometimes debauched habits.[64]

[59] Süleyman Paşa, *Hiss-i inkılâb* (İstanbul, 1326), p. 11; Ziya Paşa in *Hürriyet*, #35, quoted in *Tanzimat*, I, 815. On the spread of European modes and manners see, further, ABCFM, Armenian Mission VIII, #394, 2 September 1857; Spence to Marcy, 28 November 1856, USNA, Turkey 14. As usual, the Christians in the empire adopted these fashions more quickly. But just before the Crimean War French modes had affected upper-class women in İstanbul and even penetrated the palace, a process assisted by an influx of free-spending members of the Egyptian ruling family: Fatma Aliye, *Cevdet*, p. 84; Cevdet, *Tezâkir*, p. 20. The fork and the individual dinner plate came into use in the palace about 1860; Leila Hanoum, *Le Harem impérial* (Paris, 1925), p. 139. On the 1860's see Dumont, *Le Balkan*, pp. 120ff.

[60] Cevdet, *Tezâkir*, pp. 61-62.

[61] Cevdet makes a particular point of increased trade and the results for Ottoman law: *Tezâkir*, pp. 63-64.

[62] On Şinasi see below, chapter VI. The new literary movement which he began was in the end the most important result of these mid-century contacts.

[63] Antonio Gallenga, *Two Years of the Eastern Question* (London, 1877), I, 134.

[64] For various examples see Vambéry, *Der Islam*, pp. 100, 108-109; Durand de Fontmagne, *Un séjour à l'ambassade de France* (Paris, 1902), p. 305; Dumont, *Le*

Most of the contacts flowed the other way. Among the Europeans in the empire, diplomats were the most prominent. Russian diplomats were in a category apart, generally suspect to Turks because of their demands for special privileges for the Balkan Slavs, which would in the end lead to a partition of the empire; Ottoman literature on this period is full of complaints about Russian intrigues. But even French and English diplomats, who represented powers that had just sustained the Ottoman Empire in war, were often disliked because of their frequent and highhanded interference in Ottoman affairs. They used Turks as pawns in their own diplomatic games, and sometimes made and unmade grand vezirs. If Britain supported Reşid, France supported Âli and Fuad.[65] The British ambassador in 1856, Lord Stratford de Redcliffe, had in many ways done great service for the Ottoman Empire, but Âli three times asked London to recall him. Stratford would not allow the sultan to reign as coequal with himself, the British ambassador, charged Âli; further, said Âli, Stratford demanded influence for himself "so paramount and notorious" that the Porte lost prestige in the eyes of its own public.[66] Years later Âli still spoke of Stratford with real hatred.[67] Fuad, whose easy European manners put him on good terms with foreign diplomats, nevertheless voiced almost the identical criticism of a sympathetic French ambassador, M. Bourée, because "the French will never be satisfied with giving friendly advice in an unassuming way; . . . whatever good thing was done must be advertised as a benefit conferred by France. . . ."[68] Aside from the natural resentment of Ottoman statesmen at

Balkan, pp. 57-58; Hoskiær, *Et Besøy-i Grækenland, Ægypten og Tyrkiet* (Copenhagen, 1879), p. 116. It is hard to determine in what numbers Turks went to Europe. From 1855 to 1874 the Porte maintained a small school in Paris for about sixty Ottoman military students: Ergin, *Maarif tarihi,* II, 379-381. In 1856 ten government clerks were to be sent to Europe to study sciences: Cevdet, *Tezâkir,* p. 62. In 1857 about two hundred young Turks went to Paris, as well as a number of Ottoman Greeks and Armenians: ABCFM, Armenian Mission V, #269, n.d., 1857. The *Levant Herald,* 17 September 1862, mentions fifteen technical students going to Paris. The biographical dictionaries mention periods of service abroad in sketches of a fair number of Ottoman statesmen.

[65] Cf. the comments by İbnülemin Mahmud Kemal İnal, *Osmanlı devrinde son sadrıâzamlar* (İstanbul, 1940-1953), I, 15.

[66] Clarendon to Stratford, 4 January 1856, Private Stratford Mss., FO 352/44, quoted in Temperley, "The Last Phase of Stratford," p. 218. Âli at this period, of course, resented the interference even more because his own backing was French; that of his rival Reşid, English.

[67] L. Raschdau, ed., "Diplomatenleben am Bosporus. Aus dem literarischen Nachlass . . . Dr. Busch," *Deutsche Rundschau,* 138 (1909), 384.

[68] Elliot to Stanley, #68 confidential, 17 December 1867, FO 78/1965.

outside interference, accompanied though it might be by valid suggestions on reform, the consequent debasement of the Porte in the eyes of its own subjects presented a significant obstacle to general acceptance of a government-ordered reform program. "The foreigners, after having rendered the Turkish Government hateful, try to render it contemptible," said an Armenian resident of İstanbul in 1857.[69] The Tanzimat statesmen were acutely aware of this. "The Porte considers itself a great Power," wrote the Austrian internuncio, "and in their confidential effusions the Turkish ministers complain that the Powers who claim to be interested in its consolidation reduce it to the level of a second-rate state."[70] Leading Turks also complained that the diplomats who pressed advice on them did not really know Turkey. Cevdet Paşa told a French ambassador: "You have been living in Beyoğlu [i.e., Pera, the most Europeanized quarter of the capital, where the embassies were]. You have not learned properly the spirit of the Ottoman state or even the circumstances of İstanbul. Beyoğlu is an isthmus between Europe and the Islamic world. From there you see İstanbul through a telescope."[71]

The conduct of foreign consuls was likely to make an even worse impression on the Turks. They tended to quarrel endlessly with the local Turkish governors, to drag national honor into their personal arguments with Turks, and often to conduct themselves like little lords. "The consuls in each region became independent rulers," said Süleyman Paşa.[72] A good many consular agents were not nationals of the countries they represented, but Levantines, who put on airs and grew rich on fees charged to those who sought their protection. Sometimes they used their privileges to personal advantage in shady transactions.[73]

Interference by diplomats and consuls rankled particularly when it

[69] Senior, *Journal*, p. 152.

[70] Prokesch to Buol, #41B, 30 May 1856, HHS, XII/56.

[71] Quoted in Mardin, *Cevdet Paşa*, p. 294. Süleyman Paşa criticized the Europeans of Beyoğlu for associating only with Greeks and Armenians, not with Turks: *Hiss-i inkılâb*, p. 5.

[72] *Ibid.*, p. 4.

[73] See examples in Bulwer to Russell, #177, 27 September 1859, enclosing Bulwer to C. Alison of same date, FO 78/1435; Edmund Hornby, *Autobiography* (London, 1928), pp. 97-100, 131-139; Dr. K. [Joseph Koetschet], *Erinnerungen aus dem Leben des Serdar Ekrem Omer Pascha* (Sarajevo, 1885), pp. 69-71; Hill, *History of Cyprus*, IV, 62, n.2. The New Ottomans of the 1860's complained much about diplomatic and consular interference of all sorts: see, for example, Ziya in *Hürriyet*, #48, quoted in *Tanzimat*, I, 787-789.

was based on the extraterritorial rights secured to individual foreigners under the capitulations. The special privileges accorded the foreign national in Turkish courts, the benefit of consular courts, and the various sorts of tax exemption were stretched and abused by the representatives of the great powers.[74] Among the greatest abuses was the extension of protection to thousands, largely Ottoman Christians, who had never left the empire and had never seen the protecting country. Numbers of these protégés were given not only berats of protection, but even foreign nationality and foreign passports. The capitulatory privileges helped them to a new prosperity in business. Also among the protégés were many who came from outside the Ottoman dominions, but were only pseudo-westerners: Maltese and Ionian Greeks under British protection, Algerians under the French, Croats and Dalmatians under the Austrian. Especially during and just after the Crimean War the major seacoast cities of the empire were filled with this rabble, often of a shady or even criminal type. Many of these, together with a number of genuine nationals of western European countries, were engaged in the concessions racket, again profiting by the protection of the capitulations. They sought concessions ostensibly to develop Turkish economic resources—mines, agricultural products, or communications. But the real object was to turn a quick profit through commissions, guarantees, operations on European stock markets, or litigation against the Porte. The respectable Europeans in the empire were ashamed of a situation that caused the West to stink in Turkish nostrils, but the embassies continued to accord protection to all manner of people for the sake of their prestige in the East. If such persons were, after the Crimean War, numerically the most representative of the West, western-rooted reform was hardly likely to find a favorable reception. Baron Prokesch was cynical in his comment: "There are no respectable people, at least in appearance, except the Turks, whom we are going to civilize and initiate into the mysteries of our progress."[75]

---

[74] On capitulatory privileges see especially G. Pelissié de Rausas, *Le régime des capitulations dans l'Empire ottoman*, 2 vols. (Paris, 1902-1905); Young, *Corps de droit ottoman*, I, 251-278; P. M. Brown, *Foreigners in Turkey: their juridical status* (Princeton, 1914); Nasim Sousa, *The Capitulatory Regime of Turkey* (Baltimore, 1933).

[75] Prokesch to Buol, 10 January 1856, HHS, XII/56. On the system of protection see Brown, *Foreigners*, pp. 93-95; Sousa, *Capitulatory Regime*, pp. 89-101; E. C. Grenville Murray, *Turkey*, rev. ed. (London, 1877), pp. 353-359; Hornby, *Autobiography*, pp. 92-94, where he estimates that the number of "so-called British pro-

There were, of course, some respectable westerners in the Ottoman Empire. Their conduct might elicit Turkish approval, but might also arouse resentment. Missionaries were prominent among them. Both Roman and Protestant missions from France, England, Germany, Italy, and America were fairly widely distributed over the empire.[76] Although the missionaries were moral and God-fearing people, and might be respected as individuals by the Turks, their evangelistic activities could easily cause trouble. In the view of a British consular court judge, missionaries were, "next to habitual criminals, the most troublesome people in the world to deal with." He cited the extreme case of two English missionaries who one day affixed a poster to the mosque of St. Sophia advertising that on the morrow from its steps they would denounce the prophet Muhammad as an impostor.[77] Although in the post-Crimean period a few Turks were converted from Islam to Christianity,[78] most of the missionary work was among the native Christians of the empire. Even so, by encouraging sectarianism and helping such peoples as Bulgars, Arabs, and Armenians regain their vernacular and national consciousness, the missionary labors often

tected subjects" about 1856 was "I should think little short of a million" (p. 93); Senior, *Journal*, pp. 42, 46-50, 113, 119, 131; Charles T. Newton, *Travels and Discoveries in the Levant* (London, 1865), I, 76ff.; Spence to Marcy, #50, 15 October 1857, USNA, Turkey 14; Williams to Cass, #98, 17 September 1860, USNA, Turkey 16, estimating the number of Ottoman-born subjects in İstanbul actually enjoying foreign nationality as fifty thousand; Morris to Seward, #74, 7 January 1864, USNA, Turkey 18, with a list of American protégés; Bulwer to Russell, #222, enclosing Dalzell (Erzurum) to Bulwer, #16, 30 September 1859, FO 78/1436, on Russian sale of passports to Ottoman Armenians. Some of the protégés were, of course, legitimate employees of foreign embassies, like the dragomans: Franz von Werner, *Türkische Skizzen* (Leipzig, 1877), I, 74-75.

On the crime among the İstanbul rabble see Prokesch to Buol, #56 B, 25 July 1856, HHS, XII/57; Senior, *Journal*, pp. 72-73; *Augsburger Allgemeine Zeitung*, 27 May 1857 (Ausserord. Beilage); (Marco Antonio) Canini, *Vingt ans d'exil* (Paris, 1868), pp. 111-142, a picture of Galata and Pera by a political refugee who was there; Lady Hornby, *Constantinople During the Crimean War* (London, 1863), pp. 92, 118-119.

On concessions see Hornby, *Autobiography*, pp. 113-114; Mordtmann, *Anatolien*, pp. 521-525; Charles Mismer, *Souvenirs du monde musulman* (Paris, 1892), pp. 98-100; Prokesch to Buol, 10 January 1856, HHS/56. The quest for concessions led also to bribing of Ottoman civil servants: Mardin, *Cevdet Paşa*, pp. 88-89, n.99.

[76] Noel Verney and George Dambmann, *Les puissances étrangères dans le Levant* (Paris, 1900), pp. 31-145, assesses European influences of all sorts in Turkey. The ABCFM records indicate the wide activities of the American Congregationalists. Ubicini, *Letters*, II, 206-208; Ergin, *Maarif tarihi*, II, 637-648; Hilaire, *La France Catholique en Orient* (Paris, 1902), passim, deal with Catholic schools.

[77] Hornby, *Autobiography*, pp. 124-125.

[78] ABCFM, Armenian Mission VIII, #56, 12 February 1857; #79, 11 March 1859; #82, 9 April 1859; #87, 31 October 1859.

went counter to Ottoman interests. The mission-founded schools were frequented mostly by Christians, and affected the Muslims only later. Perhaps the chief immediate profit derived by Muslims from the missionaries was in matters of technology rather than religion. The Yankee ingenuity of Cyrus Hamlin, for instance, contrived a tin shop, a steam bakery, and a laundry in Istanbul at the time of the Crimean War.[79] American missionaries in Syria introduced the potato, kerosene lamps, wire nails, sewing machines, and similar useful gadgets.[80]

Other Europeans were distributed over the empire, usually in the cities; most were merchants, skilled workmen, or experts in the employ of the Porte. Some of them obviously were respected by Muslims. It is reported, for example, that when a Muslim of Beirut wanted to use an oath stronger than "by the beard of Muhammad," he swore "by the word of Black, the Englishman," who was a Beirut merchant.[81] Dr. Josef Koetschet, a Swiss physician, spent his entire adult life in Turkish service, and obviously enjoyed the confidence of most Turks.[82] There were a good many such individuals. But it is hard to assess their influence as a group on the Turks; most of the merchants lived somewhat apart in Europeanized suburbs, and often dealt more closely with Levantines, sometimes intermarrying, so that the ordinary Turk may have assimilated them to Levantines in his thinking. There were also small colonies of Europeans in various places. One in Ankara, composed of English, French, and Dutch merchants, had existed from 1650 to 1800 but had left no trace of influence fifty years later.[83] At one point during the reign of Abdülaziz there was a colony of some four hundred English workmen at the Hasköy dockyards; they taught the Turks some skills, but lived generally apart.[84] In Amasya a fair-sized colony of German Swiss worked in a silk factory owned by a Strasbourg entrepreneur named Metz. Metz was also an idealist who thought to spread Protestantism among the Turks. As an influence among Turks the Amasya colony was not a success, religiously or otherwise, probably because the Swiss considered themselves better than the native inhabitants and failed to understand their

[79] Cyrus Hamlin, *Among the Turks* (New York, 1878), pp. 212-243.
[80] Henry Harris Jessup, *Fifty-three Years in Syria* (New York, 1910), I, 360-361.
[81] *Ibid.*, I, 49; II, 465.
[82] Cf. his works cited in the bibliography, and his biography in the preface to *Aus Bosniens letzter Türkenzeit* (Vienna, 1905), pp. v-vii.
[83] Van Lennep, *Travels*, II, 177-178.
[84] Gallenga, *Two Years*, II, 247-252.

customs.[85] Some Turkish officials were eager for European colonists in order to raise the economic level of the country, and at the end of the Crimean War an edict was issued, promising to prospective colonists free lands and six to twelve years' exemption from taxes and military service.[86] Abdülmecid and Reşid Paşa provided funds for the founding of a Polish colony at the foot of Mount Olympus in Thessaly immediately after the Crimean War, but epidemic and emigration destroyed the community within two years.[87] A more successful Polish colony had been established in the 1840's on the Asiatic side of the Bosporus by Prince Adam Czartoryski, but again it is hard to discover how great an influence it exerted on the surrounding population.[88]

The Polish and Hungarian refugees who came into the Ottoman Empire in considerable numbers after the revolutions of 1830, 1848, and 1863 were undoubtedly more favorably viewed by Turks in general than were other westerners. Because of their bitterness against Russia, the Poles and Hungarians were often more Turkish than the Turks.[89] A number of them, for various personal or political reasons, adopted Islam, took Turkish names, and married Turkish wives. As a group they served no great power, although hoping for the restoration of freedom to their own countries. Among them were many with a professional education, who entered the employ of the Porte as doctors, engineers, and army officers. They helped to build roads,

[85] Van Lennep, *Travels*, I, 94-102; Mordtmann, *Anatolien*, pp. 94, 472, 559, n.65; ABCFM, Western Turkey Mission II, #301, 17 September 1861; Great Britain, *Parliamentary Papers*, 1871, vol. 68, *Accounts and Papers*, vol. 32, p. 733.

[86] Text in B. C. Collas, *La Turquie en 1864* (Paris, 1864), pp. 456-458. See also expressions of local officials in Mordtmann, *Anatolien*, pp. 512, 539. Edhem Paşa, foreign minister in 1857, tried with no success to attract German, Irish, and Scandinavian immigrants: Mordtmann, *Stambul*, II, 310.

[87] Adam Lewak, *Dzieje emigracji polskiej w Turcji (1831-1878)* (Warsaw, 1935), pp. 144-145.

[88] Lewak, *Emigracji polskiej*, pp. 50-51, describes the colony, which served also as an asylum for Polish nationalist agents and was protected by the French consul. Variously referred to as "Adampol" and "Adamköy," the Turks call the settlement "Polonezköy." Cf. also Ubicini, *Letters*, I, 325.

[89] Particularly in the view of Balkan Slavs, who could regard Russia as a liberator rather than an oppressor: G. Muir Mackenzie and A. P. Irby, *Travels in the Slavonic Provinces of Turkey in Europe* (London, 1866), pp. 236-237. On the anti-Russian policy of the Polish exiles see Marceli Handelsman, *Czartoryski, Nicolas Ier et la question du Proche-Orient* (Paris, 1934), passim; and M. Kukiel, *Czartoryski and European Unity, 1770-1861* (Princeton, 1955), pp. 229-250, 273-305. On Kossuth's somewhat parallel, and also anti-Austrian, efforts see Dénes Jánossy, "Die ungarische Emigration und der Krieg im Orient," *Archivum Europae Centro-Orientalis*, V:1-4 (1939), 113-275.

railroads, forts, telegraph lines, and to man the telegraph offices.[90] "Here in Turkey we enjoy the greatest freedom that a political emigrant can have," wrote one of the Poles, "and at the same time we have access to everything. We are valued here as useful and superior beings."[91] One of the most remarkable individuals of this sort was an Austrian Croat, Michel Lattas, who as Ömer Lûtfi Paşa achieved a distinguished career as army officer and provincial governor and became commander in chief of the Turkish armies. Sometimes known as "Macar" or as "Frenk" Ömer Paşa, his foreign origin was not forgotten, and yet the impression he made on Turks was generally of the best.[92] It was characteristic that, as governor of Baghdad in 1857, Ömer had on his staff five Poles, one Hungarian, and two Croats.[93]

Given this background of contact with westerners, the reception accorded western ideas and institutions was bound to be mixed. The mass of Turks had, of course, occasional rather than sustained contact with westerners, even though the number who visited the empire was greatly increased after 1856 through tourist travel, as well as in other ways.[94] To ordinary Turks such travellers might be the objects of curiosity or suspicion—even regarded as sorcerers.[95] Some peasants feared westerners as intolerant and conquerors; some believed them to be tolerant and just.[96] The western technology which began to ap-

[90] Lewak, *Emigracji polskiej*, chapter 4 and pp. 86-88 on Poles in the Turkish army; *ibid.*, pp. 108, 190-192, on other professional men and technicians. Jánossy, "Die ungarische Emigration," pp. 260-263, gives an Austrian list from 1854 of over a hundred Magyars in the Ottoman Empire, with their occupations. There were two Polish regiments in the Ottoman army in 1854: Werner (Murad), *Skizzen*, II, 125-127. "Murad" was a member of one of them. See also, for instance, references to Poles and Hungarians in Ottoman service in Fred Burnaby, *On Horseback Through Asia Minor* (London, 1877), I, 180, and II, 120, 169, 231, 262; Avram Galanti (Bodrumlu), *Türkler ve Yahudiler* (İstanbul, 1947), p. 129. Âli Paşa seems to have used some of the Poles as agents to watch pan-Slavic activity: Josef Koetschet, *Osman Pascha* (Sarajevo, 1909), pp. 50-51.
[91] Lewak, *Emigracji polskiej*, p. 191.
[92] Cf. biographies in Abdurrahman Şeref, *Tarih musahabeleri*, pp. 235-237, Mehmed Süreyya, *Sicill-i osmanî* (İstanbul, 1308-1311), III, 602-603, and İbrahim A. Gövsa, *Türk meşhurları ansiklopedisi* (İstanbul, 1946), p. 301; also Koetschet, *Erinnerungen aus dem Leben des Serdar Ekrem Omer Pascha* (Sarajevo, 1885), and J. F. Scheltema, ed., *The Lebanon in Turmoil* (New Haven, 1920), p. 21 and n.32.
[93] Koetschet, *Erinnerungen*, pp. 51-54.
[94] Tours to the Holy Land especially became fashionable. Cook's tourists became familiar to the Arabs as "Kukiyye." Lesley Blanch, *The Wilder Shores of Love* (New York, 1954), p. 71.
[95] F. W. Hasluck, *Christianity and Islam Under the Sultans* (London, 1929), II, 641-645.
[96] Melek Hanum, *Thirty Years*, pp. 263-264.

pear, especially through the telegraph and a few small railroad lines, in the post-1856 period was greeted with as much superstitious criticism as with favor. Mechanical skill and invention sometimes aroused fear and were typically attributed to Satan. Cyrus Hamlin, who understood and propagated such things, was introduced by one Turk to another as "the most *Satanic* man in the empire."[97] Even road building appeared to many Turks not so much a useful economic device as a path for tax collectors, invading armies, foreign spies, or just an aid to Christian merchants.[98] A small group of educated Turks, of course, understood the usefulness if not the scientific basis of such improvements, but even in this group knowledge of western ways was limited. To take a small example, when in the 1877 parliament it was proposed that sessions begin at 11 a.m., western time, in order to avoid the vagaries of Turkish time, the idea was rejected on the argument that most of the deputies did not understand western time and owned no watches.[99] It is also obvious that western vices spread in equal measure with more acceptable western ways.[100]

Though western technology might meet with fear, superstition, or ignorance, longer acquaintance with it could remove the Turkish suspicion. This was not so easy in the case of the fundamental aims of the Tanzimat, which dealt with political institutions and public philosophy. Changes in this realm ran into the imponderable but immense opposition to change, to hurry, to abandoning the ways of the forefathers. Hurry was a characteristic of the devil. Dignity was the characteristic of the Ottoman Turks: their proverbs commonly accorded wealth to India, intelligence to the West, but dignity or majesty to the family of Osman.[101] Dignity and revulsion against hurry and change shaded off into passiveness and fatalism. In a sense

[97] Hamlin, *Among the Turks*, p. 58. Hamlin says the term was used seriously, and demonstrated superstition. But it can also mean "ingenious, cunning, devilishly clever." Cf. also on superstitious reactions Mordtmann, *Anatolien*, p. 383; Van Lennep, *Travels*, I, 85.

[98] Dumont, *Le Balkan*, pp. 262-264.

[99] Hakkı Tarık Us, *Meclis-i meb'usân 1293:1877 zabıt ceridesi* (İstanbul, 1940-1954), II, 40, cited in Robert Devereux, *A Study of the First Ottoman Parliament of 1877-1878* (George Washington University, unpublished M.A. thesis, 1956), p. 120. Turkish time varied according to the hour of sunrise and sunset.

[100] Cf. Jessup, *Fifty-three Years*, I, 234-235; idem, *The Women of the Arabs* (New York, 1873), pp. 191-195; G. G. B. St. Clair and C. A. Brophy, *Twelve Years' Study of the Eastern Question in Bulgaria* (London, 1877), pp. 183-193.

[101] Hammer, *Staatsverfassung*, II, 431; David Urquhart, *Fragments on Politeness* (London, 1870), p. 2.

this was the strength of the Muslim Turk, giving him patience to endure almost any tribulation. But reform ran head on into this imponderable too.[102] The psychological block to change in the Tanzimat period came not only from the natural aversion to change, plus the natural reluctance to admit defects in the Turkish way of life and to copy the institutions of an alien western society; it came also from the practical fact that this meant also copying the ways of the second-class subjects of the empire, the Christian minorities, who because of their religious and commercial affiliations with the West were sometimes ahead of Turks in their assimilation of western ideas and patterns of life, even if much of this assimilation was superficial only. Religious belief, the simple pride in Islam, reinforced this reluctance to change. The proposed reforms of the Tanzimat period, therefore, represented a threat to the established order, to the Muslim way, and to the integrity and cohesiveness of Turkish society. The challenge was especially strong if the doctrine of equality, or Osmanlılık, were to be worked out in practical political institutions. Even many of the most advanced Turks were only half-convinced of the desirability of the changes they professed to sponsor.

If this was the climate of opinion in the empire after the Crimean War, complete success for the measures proposed in the Hatt-ı Hümayun could hardly be expected, except over a long period of slow change. Immediate success could not even be contemplated. Yet the situation of the empire demanded immediate action, and so did some of the European diplomats who had fathered the Hatt-ı Hümayun. "Admitting that the whole scheme of reform could not be accomplished in a week," said Stratford, "I urged the rapid movement of human society in the present age, the favouring circumstances of the time. . . ."[103] But Stratford was urging the impossible. Fuad Paşa some years later put the difficulty concisely, even though his memorandum was a justification and an apology:

"The execution of so complex a program, embracing all the branches of administration and touching the largest problems of the social order, presented difficulties of various kinds, of which the most serious lay in the national prejudices and in the condition of public mores.

[102] Cf. Gibb and Bowen, *Islamic Society*, I, part 2, 205-206, who blame sufi and dervish influence.

[103] Great Britain, *Parliamentary Papers*, 1856, vol. 61, *Accounts and Papers*, vol. 24, Eastern Papers (part 18), #34, Stratford to Clarendon, 9 January 1856.

Each one of the reforms thus required a double effort commensurate with the double obstacle to be surmounted."[104]

Application of the Hatt-ı Hümayun was made no easier by the general situation of the empire after the Crimean War. There was physical as well as mental uneasiness. Minor incidents of Muslim fanaticism occurred in Anatolia and the Arab provinces, and instances of Christian provocation in the Balkans. There was ephemeral rising or disorder in Kurdistan, Bosnia, Herzegovina, Albania, and Tripoli in Africa. Border clashes occurred over territorial disputes with Montenegro. Six thousand Tatar refugees fled Russian dominion and required settlement in the empire. More serious were the deeds of violence and theft perpetrated not only by the western-protected rabble in the cities, but by soldiers mustered out of the Ottoman army, especially irregulars who had been attached to English units. These men, whose pay was often grossly in arrears, were given a few piasters and left to beg or rob their way home. Deserters, of whom there were many, dared not settle down for fear of detection, and so lived by plunder. The war had also dislocated Ottoman economy, fields had remained untilled, and in some regions the price level was by 1856 triple that of two years before.[105]

Though the obstacles appeared formidable, changes were made in the half decade following the Crimean War. It was a period of groping. But out of it emerged a new political leadership—the team of Âli Paşa and Fuad Paşa.

[104] Fuad's memorandum of 1867, in Ubicini, *Etat présent*, p. 244.

[105] The conditions of 1856 are described in Prokesch's despatches to Buol in HHS XII/56 and XII/57 throughout the year; in ABCFM, Armenian Mission VIII, #386, 12 June 1856, #390, 2 February 1857, #393, 21 June 1857. On soldiers see also Senior, *Journal*, pp. 140-141, and Mordtmann, *Anatolien*, p. 432.

CHAPTER III

REFORM AND CONSPIRACY, 1856-1861: ÂLI, FUAD, AND KIBRISLI MEHMED

In the period of slightly more than five years between the proclamation of the Hatt-ı Hümayun and the death of Sultan Abdülmecid there were no far-reaching changes in the administrative structure of the empire. But there were attempts to carry out promises made in the *hat* and to widen the area of effective equality among all Ottoman subjects. These efforts were impeded by a number of provincial disturbances and by the Kuleli affair—an incipient revolt in the capital based on an ill-defined sentiment of objection to Ottoman equality. Political rivalries among leading Ottoman statesmen also interfered with reform. Though there were many contenders for high state office, four men dominated the government during this half decade: Reşid Paşa, Âli Paşa, Fuad Paşa, and Kıbrıslı Mehmed Paşa. They did not represent political parties, of which there were none, but viewpoints and interest groups which contended for control. Kıbrıslı Mehmed was the conservative; the others were more favorable to westernization. But the triumvirate of westernizers split. Âli and Fuad began to prevail over Reşid, and after Reşid's death in 1858 they were left without rivals as reform leaders. By 1861, with the accession of a new sultan, they had emerged supreme in Ottoman politics.

The rivalry between Reşid and his former disciples Âli and Fuad reflected not only a divergence of views on reforms, but also the clash of personalities, the conflict of ambitions, and the direct pressure of foreign ambassadors that characterized Ottoman political life of these years.[1] Âli as grand vezir and Fuad as foreign minister were responsible for the Hatt-ı Hümayun and the Treaty of Paris. Reşid had objections to both. In addition, he was apparently resentful at being eclipsed by his pupils, and was perhaps in need of the financial emoluments of office. But he was unable to oust Âli until November 1, 1856, when Lord Stratford, seeking to thwart the French plan to unite the

---

[1] Cevdet Paşa was caustic about the politicians of the post-Crimean period working for their personal interests: *Tezâkir 1-12*, ed. Cavid Baysun (Ankara, 1953), p. 87. The rivalry of Reşid and his disciples had begun before the war, and was sharpened at its close: *ibid.*, p. 16; Fatma Aliye, *Ahmed Cevdet Paşa ve zamanı* (İstanbul, 1336), pp. 88-90, 109; Ali Fuad, *Rical-i mühimme-i siyasiye* (İstanbul, 1928), pp. 63, 68.

Danubian principalities and highly annoyed at the close relations of Âli and Fuad with the French ambassador Thouvenel, brought his influence to bear on Sultan Abdülmecid. It is more than coincidental that Reşid was appointed to the grand vezirate on the same day that Stratford invested the sultan with the Order of the Garter. British warships were at the same time conspicuous in the harbor of İstanbul.[2] Fuad resigned, along with Âli, and neither would take a ministry under Reşid, though both accepted nomination to the Supreme Council.[3] Reşid's ministerial colleagues were a heterogeneous lot, and the appointment of his own son Ali Gâlib as minister of foreign affairs in the spring of 1857 made the combination even stranger. Since Ali Gâlib was married to the sultan's oldest living daughter, Fatma, and since another of Reşid's sons, Mehmed Cecil, was the Ottoman ambassador in Paris, comment on the family grip on government was aroused. Fuad furnished, as usual, the most biting: "It is clear that we are in the process of becoming Christians. We have the Father Reşid, the Son Ali Gâlib who proceeds from the Father, and Lord Stratford who reveals to us the Holy Spirit through the medium of his first dragoman, M. Revelaki, who is, however, no dove."[4]

Reşid fell from office on July 31, 1857, over the same Roumanian question which had brought him to power. This time it was Thouvenel's pressure on the sultan that caused the change.[5] Âli now became foreign minister, during the short grand vezirate of Mustafa Naili Paşa, and when Reşid again was reappointed to the highest office on October 22, apparently on the sultan's own initiative, Âli con-

---

[2] See, on the change in posts, Harold Temperley, "The Last Phase of Stratford de Redcliffe, 1855-58," *English Historical Review*, 47 (1932), 237-238; W. E. Mosse, "The Return of Reschid Pasha," *English Historical Review*, 68 (1953), 546-573, correcting some errors in Temperley's article; Prokesch to Buol, #83C Vertraulich, 24 October 1856, #84B Vertraulich, 29 October 1856, and #86A-D, 5 November 1856, in HHS, XII/57; A. H. Ongunsu, "Âli Paşa," *İslâm ansiklopedisi*, I, 337; Ali Fuad, *Rical-i mühimme*, pp. 35-36. T. W. Riker, *The Making of Roumania* (London, 1931), deals with the shift as an incident in the development of Moldavia and Wallachia.

[3] Ali Fuad, *Rical-i mühimme*, pp. 71-72, 102-103. Âli Paşa seems to have been quite exercised by Reşid's criticisms.

[4] L. Thouvenel, *Trois années de la question d'Orient* (Paris, 1897), p. 102; İbnülemin Mahmud Kemal İnal, *Osmanlı devrinde son sadrıâzamlar* (İstanbul, 1940-1953), II, 188, gives a variant of the story.

[5] İnal, *Son sadrıâzamlar*, I, 17; Temperley, "Last Phase," p. 246; Riker, *Roumania*, p. 127; Ongunsu, "Âli Paşa," p. 337; Ali Fuad, *Rical-i mühimme*, pp. 37-38; Nassau Senior, *A Journal Kept in Turkey and Greece* (London, 1859), pp. 125-126. The question in the principalities this time was the annulment of fraudulent elections which produced a majority opposed to union.

sented to stay on at his post.[6] But Reşid was nearing his end. On January 7, 1858, he died, not yet sixty years old, in the third month of his sixth grand vezirate.[7]

Reşid, an astute politician, had been the originator of the Tanzimat, and by some was regarded as the elder statesman of the empire, whose advice was to be sought on all major questions.[8] Yet his death at this point was no great loss to the empire. His energy and mental acuteness declined in his later years, and he was less able to deal with Abdülmecid.[9] He had made his contribution, which was not only to initiate the reform program of the Gülhane edict, but to raise up a generation of disciples. Reşid seems to have had the quality of attracting to himself young men of ability, and he interested himself in furthering their education and public careers. It is hard to say what the nineteenth-century empire would have been like without Reşid. Among his protégés were men of views as varied as the scholar Ahmed Vefik, the learned member of the ulema Ahmed Cevdet, and Âli and Fuad. It was the latter two who inherited Reşid's political mantle, but by the time of his death the pupils had run before the master. Until Fuad's death in 1869, and Âli's in 1871, they were with brief interruptions the personification of Ottoman administration. One was frequently grand vezir while the other was foreign minister or president of the Tanzimat Council. In these positions they were responsible for foreign relations and for domestic reform. Though quite unlike as persons, they worked well together. Fuad tended to be more advanced and to furnish the éclat; Âli was more conservative, more meticulous, and less obtrusive. Together they sought to stave off European intervention, to preserve Ottoman integrity, to solve each problem as it arose, and gradually to elaborate and introduce reforms. Benevolent critics said that their maxim was

---

[6] Temperley, "Last Phase," pp. 249-251; Riker, *Roumania*, p. 150; *Tanzimat*, I (İstanbul, 1940), p. 745.

[7] Reşid's sudden death was unexpected, and gave rise to suspicions, apparently quite without foundation, that his rivals, perhaps Fuad or Âli or Kıbrıslı Mehmed, were implicated in the death. See Frederick Millingen, *La Turquie sous le règne d'Abdul Aziz* (Paris, 1868), pp. 276-278, n.; Lady Hornby, *Constantinople During the Crimean War* (London, 1863), pp. 499-500; C. S. de Gobineau, ed., *Correspondance entre le Comte de Gobineau et le Comte de Prokesch-Osten* (Paris, 1933), p. 169. Physicians of the foreign legations were invited to Reşid's house to establish the fact of death: *Presse d'Orient*, 8 January 1858.

[8] See the comment of the *şeyhülislâm* Arif Efendi in 1856: Cevdet, *Tezâkir*, p. 72.

[9] Abdurrahman Şeref, *Tarih musahabeleri* (İstanbul, 1339), p. 107.

"sufficient unto the day is the evil thereof."[10] Opponents charged them with operating on the principle of "après moi, le déluge."[11] Their characters and viewpoints set the tone for reform down to 1871.

Mehmed Emin Âli Paşa was forty-three years old at the time of Reşid's death. Of humble origins, Âli had become a government clerk at fifteen, an employee of the translation bureau at eighteen, and then had risen with astonishing rapidity as the result of hard work, native ability, and Reşid's patronage. At twenty-six he had been ambassador to London, at thirty-one foreign minister, and in 1852 for the first time grand vezir, when he was only thirty-seven. He then held two provincial governorships, served as the first president of the Tanzimat Council during the Crimean War, became foreign minister for the third time, and in the spring of 1855 rose for the second time to the grand vezirate. Upon Reşid's death in 1858, Âli was again advanced to the highest administrative post in the empire.

This career had given Âli a fairly good knowledge of Europe, since he had also served in the Vienna embassy as a secretary, had travelled briefly to St. Petersburg, and had been the first Ottoman plenipotentiary at the Paris peace congress of 1856. It had given him also a mastery of Turkish official style and a good knowledge of French. Because his formal education had been slim, Âli owed these achievements to hard work and occasional private lessons. French he studied for long hours in the embassy garden in Vienna. He always regretted that he had never really learned Arabic, though he had studied it with Cevdet Paşa, and even once apologized to Cevdet for writing to him in *kaba Türkçe* ("vulgar Turkish") rather than using Arabic expressions.[12] By 1858 Âli had also the reputation of a first-rate diplomat, though many who knew him, including Fuad, said that his tendency was to avoid or postpone problems instead of forging ahead toward a solution. He had also acquired a reputation for honesty, which went generally unchallenged, although later he was censured by Cevdet for having accepted a sizable gift from the governor of Egypt.[13]

Âli was physically a small, frail man, "so delicate that a piece of

[10] Charles Mismer, *Souvenirs du monde musulman* (Paris, 1892), pp. 192-194.
[11] Franz von Werner, *Türkische Skizzen* (Leipzig, 1877), II, 172. Clician Vassif, *Son Altesse Midhat Pacha* (Paris, 1909), p. 17, says this of Âli alone.
[12] Fatma Aliye, *Cevdet*, pp. 91-92 and 97-98. The reference to *kaba Türkçe* is humorous; Âli's style was hardly "boorish."
[13] İnal, *Son sadrıâzamlar*, I, 36-37, quoting Cevdet's *Maruzat*.

sponge falling from a shelf would hurt him."[14] He spoke haltingly in a voice that was almost a whisper, his step was hesitant, and only his eyes were lively. But his mind was perpetually alert, seizing upon and storing up information extracted from all whom he met. He could be obsequious and pliant to the sultan, polite but immensely stubborn to all others who crossed him. His self-control was tremendous; his ability to hear the gravest news without a flicker in his expression was well known, as was his capacity for knowing when to keep silent. Some of these qualities are reflected in his admiration for Lord Chesterfield's letters to his son, and in his apparent fondness for Machiavelli's *Prince*. Âli was a firm believer in official formalities, which seem to have been for him not only a refuge but a creed. He demanded obedience from subordinates, required that all their administrative relations with the Palace be channeled through him, and became even more autocratic in manner toward the end of his life. In part, this was calculated policy, for Âli made a determined effort to keep the administrative hierarchy free from interference by the sultan and palace coterie; he was defending the independence of the Sublime Porte. In part, this was Âli's jealousy of his position: he could brook no rivals and trained no successors. Abdülaziz chafed under this curb in the later 1860's, but felt impotent to dismiss the statesman who had made himself indispensable. "Whom will I bring in instead?" asked Abdülaziz of a palace official who urged Âli's dismissal.[15]

Âli's split with his patron Reşid, which developed only gradually and involuntarily after Âli first became grand vezir and as malicious tongues tried to set the two men against each other, did not indicate that he abandoned Reşid's reforming ideals. Âli continued to be a conservative reformer, or a moderate liberal. He did not believe in radical departures. While to some of his critics he appeared to be too much of an innovator, to others of his contemporaries, both Turks and Europeans, he seemed reactionary because he made haste slowly. This again was a calculated policy. "Our speed is limited by the fear of making the boilers burst," he said. "Our metamorphosis must be cautious, gradual, internal, and not accomplished by flashes of lightning."[16] He believed that the Ottoman Turks were best fitted to govern the heterogeneous empire and that the prestige of Islam must

---

[14] Abdurrahman Şeref, *Tarih musahabeleri*, p. 91.

[15] İnal, *Son sadrâzamlar*, I, 27.

[16] Durand de Fontmagne, *Un séjour à l'ambassade de France* (Paris, 1902), p. 45.

not be undermined by allowing freedom of proselytism throughout the dominions. The Ottomans and Islam were the foundations of government, and Âli was deeply concerned that the prestige of government not be diminished by thoughtless reform or foreign intervention. "To maintain good order in the country," he wrote, "to introduce the necessary reforms, and to assure the prosperity of the subjects, it is necessary above all that the government be feared at the same time as it is respected and loved." Though this was said to influence Thouvenel and to rebuke the French press for stirring up discontent among the minorities of the empire, it was none the less true.[17] Christian minorities, Âli pointed out cogently, were not the only ones who suffered under misrule. Âli also had some doubts as to the wisdom of over-educating an upper class in the then condition of the empire. "What will become of all these people? Will they all become lawyers and idlers as in Greece?"[18] Sometimes Âli appeared to be a Metternich, trying to hold together the empire for the house of Osman, as Metternich tried to prop up his "worm-eaten" Habsburg house. To the editor of *La Turquie* Âli remarked: "All we can do is live from day to day. The future is God's."[19]

Despite these doubts and hesitations, Âli was still a reformer, though sometimes it was hard to fathom his real opinions on any given subject; his ability at dissimulation evidently led him to yield to great pressure from Europe for reforms which he deemed as yet inopportune, or to prepare measures which he really approved and to pretend that these were imposed on him by Europe, in order that he might fend off attacks from conservative opinion. He tended also, like Metternich, to be overfond of subtlety and intrigue—to play off foreign embassies against the sultan, the ulema against foreign embassies, and one official against another. But he really believed in a gradual adaptation of western institutions, in small steps instead of sweeping measures, as well as in the traditional reformer's task of putting the Ottoman house in order. He was willing to change established ways in such matters as secularizing the lands which were *vakıf*, "in trust for charitable purposes," or in taking over a degree of secular western justice and instituting mixed nonsectarian courts. These reforms he proposed when again president of the Tanzimat Council in 1859-

[17] Âli to Thouvenel, 25 November 1858, in Thouvenel, *Trois années*, p. 316.
[18] Sommerville Story, ed., *The Memoirs of Ismail Kemal Bey* (London, 1920), p. 57.
[19] Mismer, *Souvenirs*, p. 93.

1860. In the year of Reşid's death he asserted that his object was to inculcate a doctrine of equality and brotherhood of all peoples.[20]

In the course of time Âli's views on the gradualness of change underwent something of a metamorphosis. What he believed in the last years of his life is best expressed in a remarkable memorandum written in 1867 in Crete, where he was engaged in pacification of a rebellion.[21] Aroused by the dangers which external intervention and domestic revolt offered to the integrity of the empire, Âli declared that now was no time for half measures, that some cargo must be jettisoned to save the ship. His major proposal was that all public offices be open to all Ottoman subjects, including the Christian minorities. This would arouse Muslim resentment, he conceded, especially since the Christians were often better educated and so better fitted for office than Muslims. Âli emphasized also the need for improved schools to help Turks catch up with Christians as quickly as possible, and for mixed schools in which both Muslim and Christian would study together as Ottomans. This, he felt, should help to prevent the minorities from sending their children to schools in Greece or Russia, where anti-Turkish feelings were inculcated. Finally, a new civil law code on the western model, such as Egypt was inaugurating, should be drawn up, together with plans for more mixed tribunals for mixed cases. This, said Âli, would not contravene the sacred law of Islam.

It is obvious that Âli was pushed to these conclusions by the rush of events, and not by thinking in a vacuum about the virtues of equality for all Ottoman subjects. The first half of his memorandum delineated the internationally isolated and internally dangerous condition of the empire. Âli believed that Ottoman integrity could be preserved only if Christian-Muslim equality were a fact; then the minorities would lose their enthusiasm for separatism. They would no longer heed the siren call of foreign propagandists and, instead, would regard themselves not as held in subjection by a Muslim state, but as subjects of a monarch who protected all equally. Clearly, Âli failed to understand the irrational and emotional character of modern nationalism, which in the end would be satisfied not with mere equality, but with

[20] Thouvenel, *Trois années*, p. 316.
[21] Ali Fuad, *Rical-i mühimme*, pp. 118-127, gives the text. Mahmud Celaleddin, *Mirât-ı hakikat* (İstanbul, 1326-1327), I, 30, gives a summary. A. D. Mordtmann published a German translation in the *Augsburger Allgemeine Zeitung* of 18 September 1876, and reprinted it in his *Stambul und das moderne Türkenthum* (Leipzig, 1877-1878), I, 75-88.

nothing short of independence. But there can be little question of Âli's sincerity, even though his views on equality were dictated by Ottoman self-interest. It was an enlightened self-interest. Âli's conclusion was this: the only salvation of the empire was the fusion of all its subjects, except in purely religious matters. But, it must be noted, he stopped short of advising parliamentary government, and to this view he adhered until his death, believing that the empire's peoples were insufficiently educated for it. Ottoman equality and brotherhood, yes; constitution, no.[22]

Âli's colleague, Keçecizade Mehmed Fuad Paşa, was so unlike him that one may well wonder how they got along together. Yet they complemented each other beautifully, and were recognized as a team by friend and foe alike.[23] Âli was small and frail, Fuad tall and handsome; Âli was self-contained and silent, Fuad expansive and loquacious; Âli was meticulous, Fuad sometimes sloppy in attention to detail; Âli was circumspect and hesitant about new departures, Fuad more enterprising and rather less cautious; Âli was flexible and tact-

---

[22] It is a commentary on the nature of materials for Ottoman history that there is no full-scale biography of a man as prominent as Âli, whose public career approaches those of Bismarck, Thiers, or Disraeli in importance; there is neither an authorized life and letters nor a later scholarly volume. The best picture now is A. H. Ongunsu, "Âli Paşa," *Islâm ansiklopedisi*, I, 335-340; fuller but somewhat old-fashioned biographical portraits are in Ali Fuad, *Rical-i mühimme*, pp. 56-140, and in İnal, *Son sadrıâzamlar*, I, 1-58; an excellent anecdotal account in Abdurrahman Şeref, *Tarih musahabeleri*, pp. 88-97. Cevdet's writings, many still unpublished, are sprinkled with comment on Âli, often unfriendly. Âli's statement on religious toleration and Islam is in his dispatch of 30 November 1864 to Musurus (London), encl. in Morris to Seward, #108, 29 March 1865, USNA, Turkey 18. Sketches of Âli by contemporaries include the following: Mordtmann, *Stambul*, I, 59-71; Werner, *Türkische Skizzen*, II, 156-166; Hermann Vambéry, *Der Islam im neunzehnten Jahrhundert* (Leipzig, 1875), pp. 153-154; Amand von Schweiger-Lerchenfeld, *Serail und Hohe Pforte* (Vienna, 1879), pp. 39-40; L. Raschdau, ed., "Diplomatenleben am Bosporus," *Deutsche Rundschau*, 138 (1909), 404; Melek-Hanum, *Thirty Years in the Harem* (London, 1872), pp. 165-166, 419; *Levant Herald*, *Levant Times*, and *La Turquie*, each of 7 September 1871; Mismer, *Souvenirs*, pp. 23-27, 53-55; Durand de Fontmagne, *Séjour*, p. 42; Abdolonyme Ubicini, *La Turquie actuelle* (Paris, 1855), pp. 168-170; P. Challemel-Lacour, "Les hommes d'état de la Turquie, Aali Pacha et Fuad Pacha," *Revue des deux mondes*, 2nd series, 73 (15 February 1868), 913-917. The New Ottomans wrote a great deal about Âli, usually in bitter criticism; though what they say is based in truth, their picture of Âli is unfair. See references in chapter VI for New Ottoman sources. Their style of criticism has an echo in some modern criticisms of Âli, as by Afet İnan, *Aperçu général sur l'histoire économique de l'Empire turc-ottoman* (İstanbul, 1941), p. 16, where she refers to Âli's concept of reforms as the jettisoning of cargo to save a ship. Âli's so-called political testament is a doubtful source: see appendix C.

[23] Cevdet called them a "unit," or "one being," in his *Maruzat*, quoted in Mardin, *Cevdet*, p. 88, n.99.

ful before the sultan, Fuad sometimes blunt in his advice or flatly opposed to the imperial desires; Âli was autocratic and jealous of rivals, Fuad less given to holding personal grudges and excluding others from power. Some of the difference between the two was put in capsule form in one of Fuad's witticisms, which for the benefit of Sultan Abdülaziz compared Âli, Fuad himself, and Mütercim Mehmed Rüşdi Paşa, who was often associated with the other two. "When we come to the edge of a river and want to cross," said Fuad, "if I have seen a bridge I throw myself on it at once. Âli Paşa begins to investigate whether or not the bridge is sound, and looks for a ford. Rüşdi Paşa won't set foot on the bridge until after a regiment of troops has crossed it."[24] Cevdet Paşa somewhat more acrimoniously described Fuad as "a man who in all matters likes invention and innovation."[25] Fuad was more western in his personal habits than Âli, and more given to westernization. This tendency showed up not only in affairs of state, but in small matters; Fuad, for instance, flouted Muslim custom by having statuary in his garden. It was quite proper that he should be called the *gâvur* pasha more commonly than was Âli.

Much of the difference between Âli and Fuad can be explained only in the imponderable terms of personality. But there were other significant differences in their backgrounds. Âli was the son of an unprosperous tradesman and doorkeeper in one of İstanbul's bazaars. Fuad came from a well-known family, was the son of the famous poet Keçecizade İzzet Molla, and was privileged to have more formal education than Âli, since he did not have to start work so young. It is noteworthy too that while Âli had the advantage of learning French and western ideas in the translation bureau and in European diplomatic posts, Fuad had this and more. He was the product of all three of the important educational processes of the time which led to a knowledge of the West. He had studied at the medical school in İstanbul, where instruction was in French and the scientific slant was now western. He had then shifted from medicine to diplomacy, entered the translation bureau in his early twenties, and rose to be first dragoman of the Sublime Porte. And he also served in diplomatic missions to European powers. He was for three years a secretary in the London embassy, headed a special mission to Spain, negotiated successfully in

---

[24] Abdurrahman Şeref, *Tarih musahabeleri*, p. 102. Cevdet called these three statesmen a trinity: *Tezâkir*, p. 16.
[25] *Ibid.*, p. 67.

St. Petersburg on the question of the 1849 Hungarian refugees, went on a mission to Egypt, and in 1858 represented the Porte at the Paris conference on the Danubian principalities. His first term as foreign minister, a post which he was to occupy five times, was in 1852, when he was thirty-seven years old. That year marked the first time when Âli and Fuad worked together as grand vezir and foreign minister.

This career had given Fuad his westernisms and his French, which language he commanded so fluently that his bons mots became famous in the capital and in diplomatic circles throughout Europe. He could use his French wit to crushing effect. When an Englishwoman badgered him with questions about the number of wives which he as a Muslim had, he replied, "The same as your husband—two, only he conceals one and I don't."[26] This career had inculcated also a certain catholicity of view and lack of prejudice, and had apparently destroyed some of Fuad's roots in the past. Fuad was, like Âli, a Freemason. Islam meant less to Fuad than to Âli. "Islam was for centuries, in its environment, a wonderful instrument of progress," he said to the editor of *La Turquie.* "Today it is a clock which is behind time and must be set."[27] To some, including westerners, such attitudes on Fuad's part seemed the mark of superficiality and dilettantism. Reşid used to complain that Fuad was changeable.[28] But though Fuad might be more superficial and more modernist or even secular in his religion than Âli or most other Ottoman statesmen, he was no less devoted to the service and preservation of the state. "The first and most important task of a Government is to look to its own preservation," he instructed Ottoman diplomats.[29]

This, Fuad believed, had to be accomplished through effective application of the doctrine of Ottoman equality. The grant of liberties to the non-Muslims would, he thought, keep them from thinking nationalistic thoughts.[30] Fuad recognized fully the contagious effect of the western concept of national self-determination now operating in the empire's Balkan provinces. His remedy was to counteract this

[26] Henry Drummond Wolff, *Rambling Recollections* (London, 1908), I, 261-262.
[27] Mismer, *Souvenirs,* p. 110.
[28] Cevdet, *Tezâkir,* part 15, quoted in Mardin, *Cevdet,* p. 172, n.136; cf. Fatma Aliye, *Cevdet,* p. 109.
[29] Austria, Auswärtige Angelegenheiten, *Correspondenzen des Kaiserlichköniglichen Ministerium des Äussern* (Vienna, 1866-1874), I (1867) 98, Fuad's circular of 20 June 1867.
[30] Orhan F. Köprülü, "Fuad Paşa," *Islâm ansiklopedisi,* IV, 679, citing the holographic draft of a memorandum by Fuad.

sort of subversion with equality for all subjects without exception.[31] But Fuad did not intend, really, that Muslim Turks should give up their dominant position. He had earlier remarked that the Ottoman Empire was built on four bases: the Muslim millet, Turkish state, Ottoman sultans, and İstanbul as capital.[32] These indispensable bases would continue along with equal treatment for all subjects. In these views he paralleled Âli. He also was as intent as Âli on trying to keep the council of ministers free from interference by the sultan and the Palace. Fuad went beyond Âli in his apparent inclination toward a national parliament, though whether he regarded its establishment as feasible is not clear.[33] But, at least so far as Balkan peoples were concerned, Fuad qualified the principle of popular sovereignty as "excessive" and "mischievous."[34] His parliament, had he actually established one, would presumably not have had strong control over the ministry or sultan.

Though Fuad's power of resistance to monetary gifts was not above suspicion, especially when gifts were offered by the governor of Egypt, he labored as vigorously as Âli to keep the empire together, and actually lost his second grand vezirate by refusing to let Sultan Abdülaziz marry a daughter of the khedive Ismail—a union which would have given the Egyptian governor greater influence in the palace.[35] In acting to repress the Lebanese revolt of 1860 and to keep foreign intervention at a minimum, Fuad was so severe as to get the local nickname of "father of the cord."[36]

The neatest summary of Fuad's views on Ottoman politics and reform is his "political testament," a letter purportedly written to Abdülaziz by Fuad from his deathbed in Nice in 1869.[37] In part, it deals

---

[31] Cf. his letter of resignation from the grand vezirate in 1863: Mehmed Memduh, *Mirât-ı şuunat* (İzmir, 1328), pp. 127-133, giving the text, though evidently misdated. Cf. also Ali Fuad, *Rical-i mühimme*, pp. 163-164.

[32] Cevdet, *Tezâkir*, p. 85.

[33] E. Z. Karal, *Islahat fermanı devri, 1861-1876* (Ankara, 1956), pp. 143-144; cf. Bernard Lewis, *The Emergence of Modern Turkey* (London, 1961), pp. 371, 374. On parliament: Ali Fuad, *Rical-i mühimme*, pp. 173-174.

[34] Mehmed Memduh, *Mirât-ı şuunat*, p. 130.

[35] Aspersions on Fuad's honesty in Morris to Seward, confidential and private, 12 February 1868, USNA, Turkey 20; Millingen, *La Turquie*, pp. 280-283, 324-326, with a bias against Fuad; Edward Dicey, *The Story of the Khedivate* (London, 1902), p. 58; N. P. Ignatyev, "Zapiski Grapha N. P. Ignatyeva," *Isvestiia Ministerstva Inostrannykh Diel*, 1914, I, 130; Köprülü, "Fuad Paşa," p. 675.

[36] J. F. Scheltema, ed., *The Lebanon in Turmoil* (New Haven, 1920), p. 38.

[37] For texts and discussion of authenticity see R. H. Davison, "The Question of Fuad Paşa's 'Political Testament,' " *Belleten*, 23:89 (January 1959), 119-136.

with the foreign policy which Fuad believed the Porte should follow. It sets forth also Fuad's premise on reform: that the empire is in danger and that its only salvation is progress rapid enough to keep pace with England, France, and Russia. To do this "we must change all our institutions—political and civil." Such change does not contravene religious principles. Islam, as the sum of all truth, is not a closed system, but can accept new truths even if they are developed in Europe. The aim of the Ottoman administration should be the absolute equality and fusion of all races. The state should be placed above religious questions. Separatisms based on religious differences should be stifled. To achieve effective equality it will be necessary to institute a new system of justice, a new system of public instruction, and to build roads and railroads. The leader in this, said the dying Fuad, should be Âli, "whose friend and brother I have always been."[38]

Whether or not Fuad actually wrote the "political testament" attributed to him, it did reflect his views. These were remarkably parallel to the opinions Âli expressed in his memorandum of 1867. The fact that the two men could agree on so much, and could work effectively together, gave the Ottoman government a greater stability than it had enjoyed for some time or was to enjoy after their passing. Both Europe and the peoples of the empire knew with whom they had to deal. The collaboration of Âli and Fuad, and their long tenure of office, meant also that the promises of the Hatt-ı Hümayun might really be fulfilled. Though parts of that document were destined to remain paper promises only, it was usually not for want of effort on the part of Âli and Fuad, nor for want of good laws, but a result of the familiar difficulties: the climate of opinion, the lack of first-rate personnel, haphazard execution of law, and foreign complications. Changes were slow, but they came. Beginnings were made. In 1856, the year of issue of the Hatt-ı Hümayun, attention was first turned to the status of non-Muslims in the empire. It was entirely natural that this should

[38] Fuad, like Âli, lacks a solid biography. Orhan Köprülü, "Fuad Paşa," İslâm ansiklopedisi, IV, 672-681, is exceptionally full and soundly based; Ali Fuad, Rical-i mühimme, pp. 141-171, is a reasonably good sketch; İnal, Son sadrıâzamlar, I-II, 149-195, is less scholarly than Köprülü, but informative; Abdurrahman Şeref, Tarih musahabeleri, pp. 98-104, is a short life with anecdotes. Portraits by contemporaries are in Werner, Türkische Skizzen, II, 166-171; Mordtmann, Stambul, I, 25-26, and II, 143-150; Augsburger Allgemeine Zeitung, 9 May 1855, Beilage; L. Raschdau, "Diplomatenleben," pp. 402-403; Mismer, Souvenirs, pp. 13-16; Millingen, La Turquie, pp. 272-284; Ubicini, Turquie actuelle, pp. 177-184; Levant Herald, 27 November 1861; Morris to Seward, #301, 17 February 1869, USNA, Turkey 20; Challemel-Lacour, "Les hommes d'état," pp. 917-923.

be the first of the reforms to be considered, since the European powers had insisted on Christian rights, and this insistence had provided them with a pretext for interference in Ottoman affairs. Further, if egalitarian Ottomanism were to be achieved, this was the necessary point of departure.

Three months after the Hatt-ı Hümayun was proclaimed, the first Christian delegates were appointed to sit on the Supreme Council of Judicial Ordinances. Thus for the first time in Ottoman history an organ of central government was affected by the representative principle, as the provincial councils had been earlier. Whether the members appointed in May 1856 were actually representative in any sense except that they were members of important non-Muslim millets is open to serious doubt. They were not elected by their communities, but named by governmental fiat. They were, further, chosen from among prominent families of İstanbul whose interests attached them closely to the Ottoman Porte. The Gregorian Armenian member was Ohannes Dadian, of the family which provided directors for the imperial powder works; Ohannes had the farm of the İzmir and Beirut customs. The Armenian Catholic member was Mihran Düzian, director of the imperial mint. The Jewish representative was Halim the younger, a wealthy banker. Stephen Vogorides (İstefanaki Bey), also an officeholder and strong supporter of the Ottoman government, sat for the Greek millet. These non-Muslims were, further, to sit and vote only when matters of general concern to all Ottoman subjects were debated—a regulation which justified Fuad Paşa's explanation to Muslims of the significance of this promise in the Hatt-ı Hümayun.[39] How much influence such a small group of non-Muslims would have is problematical. Yet at the beginning no more could be expected. By 1867 the non-Muslim members of the council held their seats just like their Muslim colleagues, on a permanent rather than a provisional basis.[40] When the Supreme Council was transformed in 1868 into the Council of State, the non-Muslim membership was expanded, and the

[39] Thomas X. Bianchi, *Khaththy Humaïoun ou charte impériale* (Paris, 1856), pp. 21-22 n.; Prokesch to Buol, #39A-E, 16 May 1856, HHS, XII/56; Edouard Engelhardt, *La Turquie et le Tanzimat* (Paris, 1882-1884), I, 145; Thouvenel, *Trois années*, p. 355; Cevdet, *Tezâkir*, pp. 166, 177; Y. G. Çark, *Türk devlete hizmetinde Ermeniler* (İstanbul, 1953), pp. 62-65, 78-79.
[40] Fuad's memorandum of 1867 in Abdolonyme Ubicini and Pavet de Courteille, *Etat présent de l'Empire ottoman* (Paris, 1876), p. 253.

now-established principle that all millets be represented in the central lawmaking body received further confirmation in the first parliament elected under the 1876 constitution.

Equality of all Ottomans in military service had also been promised in the *hat*, and was confirmed by government action within the year. The question was still as touchy as it had been after the Hatt-ı Şerif of Gülhane or during the Crimean War, when the attempt to introduce equal military service remained abortive. Muslims wanted their non-Muslim brethren to share in the burdens of defending the empire, but naturally did not want to serve under native Christian officers or to arm Christians who might revolt. Although the Ottoman Christians may have wanted equality in theory, they preferred in practice to pay a tax and so gain exemption from five years of service and possible death, and to devote their time to trade or agriculture. When the question was debated in the government councils,[41] it was decided to proceed to a census of all non-Muslims eligible for military service, who on the basis of available figures were believed to number about two million. Officials and priests cooperated in drawing up the lists. It was further decided that, because of opposition to the measure and because of the practical difficulties involved if suddenly a full quota of untrained non-Muslims were to be introduced into a battle-hardened Muslim army, the entrance of non-Muslims into the army would be staggered. Of a presumed first contingent of sixteen thousand eligible non-Muslim recruits, only four thousand would be taken the first year. In fact, not even this was done. The Hatt-ı Hümayun had admitted the principle of buying off from military service, and this was reintroduced with a new tax, the *bedel-i askerî*, a contribution for exemption which was essentially the old *cizye*.[42] Theoretical equality was maintained in principle, because Muslims too were allowed to buy exemption. Equality was, however, denied in fact, since Muslims had to pay a much greater sum.[43]

[41] Bianchi, *Khaththy-Humaïoun*, n. 2, says it was in the Supreme Council with its new non-Muslim members; Sıddık Sami Onar, "Bedel-i askerî," *Islâm ansiklopedisi*, II, 439, says it was in the Tanzimat Council.

[42] At first called the *iane-i askeriye*. The *bedel* continued to be regarded by non-Muslims as nothing but the old capitation tax, still referred to in some quarters as *haraç*: G. Muir MacKenzie and A. P. Irby, *Travels in the Slavonic Provinces of Turkey-in-Europe* (London, 1866), p. 20 and n. Cf. above, chapter I, n. 80, and chapter II, n.6.

[43] Cf. A. Heidborn, *Manuel de droit public et administratif de l'Empire Ottoman* (Vienna, 1908-1912), II, 155-157, for explanation of the amount of the tax; also Young, *Corps de droit*, V, 275-276.

REFORM AND CONSPIRACY, 1856-1861

Eventually the whole matter of non-Muslim military service was buried, to the general satisfaction of both Christians and Muslims, by a special commission appointed to sit on the question. The non-Muslims continued to pay the *bedel-i askerî*, collected at first by government officials, then by the millet hierarchies. It is probable, though not certain, that this theoretical equality and practical discrimination was the best solution obtainable at the time.[44] But with this sort of temporization a chance to increase effective Ottomanism was lost. Some, including the commander in chief Ömer Paşa, believed that equal service in mixed, rather than separate, units was quite possible.[45] Muslims continued to complain that for a small payment the non-Muslims escaped sharing in the blood tax that should fall equally on all Ottoman subjects.[46] Although there is some suspicion that the Phanariote aristocracy of İstanbul tried to preserve its own dwindling influence by discouraging any enthusiasm for military service among the Greek Orthodox of the empire, there was no discernible desire among non-Muslims generally to assume the burden. Instead, many of them profited by the absence of their Turkish compatriots on military service to get control of lands and trade.[47] When the question again arose in the parliaments of 1877 and 1878, only a few Christian voices were raised in favor of equal military service. Most of the Christian deputies balked at the prospect, and Turkish deputies showed more enthusiasm for equality than they.[48]

[44] A very revealing report by Âli, revised by Reşid, on a special session on this question, gives arguments for and against Christian military service: Mehmed Selâheddin, *Bir türk diplomatının evrak-ı siyasiyesi* (İstanbul, 1306), pp. 144-49. Undated, probably 1856 or 1857.

[45] Dr. K. (Josef Koetschet), *Erinnerungen aus dem Leben des Serdar Ekrem Omer Pascha* (Sarajevo, 1885), p. 252, who blames the Palace, and battle-shy Armenians, for the failure to realize it. Cf. Antonio Gallenga, *Two Years of the Eastern Question* (London, 1877), I, 184-197.

[46] Mithat Cemal Kuntay, *Namık Kemal* (İstanbul, 1944-1956), I, 185; Felix Kanitz, *Donau-Bulgarien und der Balkan* (Leipzig, 1875-1879), III, 151; G. G. B. St. Clair and C. A. Brophy, *Twelve Years' Study of the Eastern Question* (London, 1877), pp. 125-134, a Turcophil discussion.

[47] Great Britain, *Parliamentary Papers*, 1861, vol. 67, *Accounts and Papers*, vol. 34, "Reports . . . Condition of Christians in Turkey," #8, encl. 2.

[48] Hakkı Tarık Us, *Meclis-i meb'usan 1293:1877 zabıt ceridesi* (İstanbul, 1940-1954), I, 323-324, and II, 64, cited in Robert Devereux, *A Study of the First Ottoman Parliament, 1877-1878* (George Washington University, unpublished M.A. thesis, 1956), pp. 111-113. On the question of non-Muslim military service see, in addition to the sources cited in preceding notes, Koetschet, *Erinnerungen*, p. 47 (Ömer was a member of the special commission on the question); Engelhardt, *La Turquie*, I, 141-142, 145-146; Andreas D. Mordtmann, *Anatolien, Skizzen und Reisebriefe* (Hannover, 1925), pp. 254-256; Paul Fesch, *Constantinople aux derniers jours*

In other ways the years after 1856 gave evidence of a slow but continued trend toward Ottoman equality, until the Muslim reaction of the 1870's, and of more effective protection extended by government to Ottomans of all creeds. The Porte continued to give assurances and to issue orders on equal treatment for all.[49] More important, local officials began to echo these principles, and sometimes to act on them. The secretary of the governor of Erzurum in 1858 announced, in dealing with a sectarian dispute, that the government "looks upon all the nations of the Empire in the same light."[50] A classic pronouncement was delivered by the governor of Ankara in 1865, who caused a herald to cry publicly, "It is commanded by the ruling authorities that all subjects cease to deride one another as Moslems and Rayahs, as Armenians and Protestants, since all are equally the dependent subjects of the royal government, and it is further commanded that mutually respecting and honoring one another, all shall dwell together in brotherly love."[51] In its way this pithy proclamation was a masterly summary of the official policy of equality among adherents of all religions, of the concept of Ottoman citizenship, and of the antidefamation clause of the Hatt-ı Hümayun, revealing that the governor understood perfectly what the Porte had announced. That the civil authority should command all men to live together in brotherly love

---

d'Abdul Hamid (Paris, 1907), pp. 247-266; Karal, Islahat fermanı devri, pp. 181-183; Prokesch to Buol, #39A-E, 16 May 1856, HHS, XII/56, who makes a connection between the appointment of the first Christians to the Supreme Council and the need of the Porte to supplement its Muslim military strength from the Christian millets. Some Christians, graduates of the military medical school, had apparently served in the army with officer rank, beginning in 1841: Osman Ergin, Türkiye maarif tarihi (İstanbul, 1939-1943), II, 626. Discussions in government commissions in 1856 and again in 1861 envisioned the admission of thirty-odd Christian officer-candidates in various military schools: ibid., pp. 606-607; Mehmed Selâheddin, Bir türk diplomatının evrak-ı siyasiyesi, pp. 144-149. In 1864 thirty-five Christian students were admitted to the officers' training school: Morris to Seward, #81, 3 March 1864, USNA, Turkey 18. Whether they were ever commissioned, or served, the author does not know. Fuad Paşa in his 1867 review of the Hatt-ı Hümayun's execution reported it had been necessary to limit the number of Christian officers until more Christian soldiers should be enrolled, but gave no figures and did not indicate whether any native Christian officers were actually serving. He pointed out that, despite the lack of equality in military service (for which he blamed the non-Muslims "almost exclusively"), there were Christians serving in two mixed Cossack regiments in the Ottoman army: text of his memorandum in Ubicini and Pavet de Courteille, Etat présent, pp. 249-250, 251-252.

[49] As in a circular of 1858 to provincial governors: Halil İnalcık, "Tanzimat nedir?" Tarih araştırmaları, I (1940-1941), 257.

[50] ABCFM, Trowbridge's Diary, p. 51.

[51] Ibid., vol. 284, #331, 21 September 1865.

was undoubtedly as commendable as it was unenforceable. But in this instance the dispute was between Gregorian and Protestant Armenians; local officials surely enforced equality with greater conviction and delight in such cases than when Muslims were involved. But even where Muslims were involved, there was a change in official attitudes. In one of the rare instances of apostasy of a Turkish Muslim family to Christianity the Porte investigated, found no compulsion, and gave protection to the converts, saying that "the Musselman is now as free to become a Christian as the Christian is free to become a Musselman. The government will know no difference in the two cases."[52] But public opinion was aroused, so that the converted family fled for safety despite the Porte's protection.[53] In matters apart from the delicate question of apostasy there was uneven progress. Christian testimony was accepted in mixed courts and occasionally in Muslim courts.[54] More non-Muslims were given official posts of some importance, although it was apparently only in 1868 that the first non-Muslim, Krikor Agaton, achieved full ministerial rank as minister of public works.[55] In this sporadic progress toward a more genuine equality there was a triple dichotomy: the Porte was ahead of Muslim opinion; the capital was ahead of the provinces; and while some non-Muslim Ottomans improved their status and advanced in official positions, many of their brethren went the opposite way toward separatist nationalism.[56]

The Hatt-ı Hümayun had also promised that penal and commercial law, and procedural law for mixed tribunals, would be codified as soon as possible. This was actually done within a few years. The reform here was twofold: codification, which was badly needed, and also a considerable borrowing from western secular law, which gave greater impetus to the extension of the principle of Ottoman equality. Although various European codes were consulted, it was

[52] *Ibid.*, Armenian Mission v, #276, 5 September 1857.
[53] *Ibid.*, Armenian Mission v, #277, 21 September 1857.
[54] Cf. George Hill, *A History of Cyprus* (Cambridge, 1940-1952), IV, 209-210, 213.
[55] Esat Uras, *Tarihte Ermeniler ve ermeni meselesi* (Ankara, 1950), p. 186; Çark, *Ermeniler*, pp. 199-201. Cf. Cyrus Hamlin, *Among the Turks* (New York, 1878), pp. 371-375, listing Christian officials.
[56] There is continuing evidence of the lack of absolute equality, but also of the advance of Porte-appointed officials over local Muslim sentiment. See, for example, Mackenzie and Irby, *Travels*, passim; and on the question of nonadmission of Christian testimony against Muslims, *ibid.*, pp. 178, 263, 396.

French law which provided the basic model. This was true of the penal code which was promulgated in 1858; it represented, after the commercial code of 1850, the second code that borrowed extensively from the West.[57] The chairman of the drafting commission, significantly, and the man principally responsible for the code, was Ahmed Cevdet Efendi. Cevdet was the member of the ulema furnished by the *şeyhülislâm* when Reşid Paşa had asked for a man well versed in Muslim law, but conscious also of the necessities of modern life. The code which he worked out superseded the previous penal code of 1840 and its successor of 1851, which were not western-inspired. The product of 1858 endured, with some alterations, until the Kemalist regime. Though it was crude and somewhat inelastic, it was "based on principles of common sense, common morality, and common justice," and as such represented "a very 'workable' piece of legislation."[58] It not only carried out the promises of 1856 by providing penalties for graft among officials, for molesting the worship of any sect, and so forth; it also reflected the new age of westernization in its provisions about tampering with telegraph lines or setting up an unauthorized press. Although an outstanding member of the ulema had prepared the code, and although it contained recognition of the şeriat and the religious courts, there was a rather vague opposition to its application—an opposition which seems, however, to have been born of ignorance and resentment against innovation rather than of fanatic religious defense of the holy law. Fuad Paşa admitted in 1867 that application of the new code was imperfect, owing to the ignorance and inexperience of judges trained in an older law.[59] Yet by 1878 it was estimated that, as far in the interior as Kayseri, nine tenths of the cases were tried under the new code.[60] Codes of procedure for mixed commercial courts

[57] Texts of the code in *Düstur*, I (İstanbul, 1289), 537-596; George Young, *Corps de droit ottoman* (Oxford, 1905-1906), VII, 1-54; Grégoire Aristarchi, *Législation ottomane* (Constantinople, 1873-1888), II, 212-268; Charles G. Walpole, *The Ottoman Penal Code 28 Zilhidje 1274* (London, 1888); Erich Nord, *Das türkische Strafgesetzbuch vom 28. Zilhidje 1274* (Berlin, 1912), with the 1911 additions.

[58] Walpole, *Penal Code*, p.v. Walpole was an English judge in Cyprus who actually administered the provisions of the code in his court.

[59] Fuad's memorandum of 1867, Ubicini, *Etat présent*, p. 247.

[60] Hamlin, *Among the Turks*, p. 367. On the penal code see, further, Ebül'ulâ Mardin, "Development of the Shari'a Under the Ottoman Empire," in Majid Khadduri and Herbert J. Liebesny, eds., *Law in the Middle East*, I (Washington, 1956), 285-289; Tahir Taner, "Tanzimat devrinde ceza hukuku," in *Tanzimat*, I (İstanbul, 1940), 230-232.

and of maritime commerce followed in 1861 and 1863 respectively; in each case French law was the basic source.[61]

This was not true of the code of land law, promulgated also in 1858. The same commission worked on this code as on the penal law, but its effort here was not to introduce western principles. Instead, the object was a classification and regularization of the customary forms of tenure of land (principally state land) which had grown out of the practices of the Ottoman sultans from earliest times, the collection and codification of provisions of scattered *kanun*'s, and the bringing up to date of rules and terminology outmoded since the demise of the fief system. A further aim was the registration of titles in the names of individuals whom the state could then hold directly responsible for the pertinent taxes.[62] The further illegal conversion of state-owned land (*mîrî*) into freehold property (*mülk*), and then into *vakıf*, could also be prevented by proper registration. The land code represented also an effort to increase the power of the central government by decreasing the influence of large landowners in the provinces—those tribal *şeyh*'s, *âyan*'s, and others who had acquired extensive properties and commensurate local political and economic domination. It was especially provided that one individual could not hold the lands of an entire village.[63] But, in actual fact, the code, both because of its provisions and the haphazard method of its application, failed to achieve the desired ends. The code did not deal with all aspects of land law, but referred to the classical religious lawbooks on some matters. Nor, in practice, did it succeed in establishing clear individual title and so creating a greater equality among individual Ottoman subjects. The code took no account of the collective ownership and share tenancy forms of land tenure which were common in many parts of the empire; the individuals involved in these systems, long-established by custom, thus failed to gain legal recognition or protection of their rights. Further, when registration of titles was carried out, many a peasant registered his lands in the name of someone else, often a local *şeyh* or large landowner, because he feared that the land census was

[61] Texts in *Düstur*, I, 780-810 and 466-536; also Young, *Corps de droit*, VII, 155-170 and 103-154; Aristarchi, *Législation*, II, 374-400, and I, 344-419.

[62] The question of land registration and taxation had already been discussed by a general assembly during the Crimean War. It had been decided to use the districts of İzmir and Salonika as pilot projects: Cevdet, *Tezâkir*, p. 50.

[63] Texts of land law in *Düstur*, I, 165-199; Young, *Corps de droit*, VI, 45-83; Aristarchi, *Législation*, I, 57-170.

only preliminary to the familiar state demands for more taxes and military recruits. Thus the man with the legal title-deed (*sened tapu*) was often someone quite other than the actual cultivator who had customary rights of tenure, which the cultivator could not now defend at law. And the state, although it established tax responsibility, failed to reduce the power of large landholders, many of whom now had proper legal tenure of state (*mirî*) land, including the former fief lands, which they were able to treat effectively as outright freehold property (*mülk*).[64]

As the drive to import European ideas and to extend effective Ottoman equality gathered momentum during Âli Paşa's grand vezirate, which extended from January 1858 to October 1859, an important although somewhat inchoate opposition began to develop. Based on a rather widespread dissatisfaction with the government, the opposition finally took shape in the conspiracy of 1859, known to Turks as the Kuleli incident.[65] The conspiracy has frequently been hailed as the first rising in Ottoman history aimed at securing constitutional government.[66] Although some of the conspirators may have been infected by western ideas, the bulk of them undoubtedly were not.[67] In fact,

[64] Ömer Lutfi Barkan, in *Tanzimat*, I, 369-421; Hıfzı Veldet in *Tanzimat*, I, 180-187; Mardin, "Development of the Shari'a," pp. 285-288; Doreen Warriner, *Land and Poverty in the Middle East* (London, 1948), pp. 15-18; Halil İnalcık, "Land Problems in Turkish History," *Muslim World*, 45 (July 1955), 226; R. C. Tute, *The Ottoman Land Laws* (n.p., n.d.—Jerusalem, 1927?), passim; W. Padel and L. Steeg, *De la législation foncière ottomane* (Paris, 1904), passim. The last two works provide references to supplementary regulations on registration and other land regulations to 1876 and beyond: Padel, pp. 6-7; Tute, pp. 129ff.

[65] From the fact that the conspirators, when apprehended, were confined and interrogated in the Kuleli barracks on the Asiatic shore of the Bosporus.

[66] For example, by Nicholas Jorga, *Geschichte des osmanischen Reiches* (Gotha, 1908-1913), V, 517; by Thouvenel, *Trois années*, p. 354, n., seeing here a precedent for the New Ottomans; by Engelhardt, *La Turquie*, I, 158; by Millingen, *La Turquie*, p. 159; by Ahmed Rasim, *İstibdaddan hakimiyeti milliyeye* (İstanbul, 1342), II, 56; by Ahmed Bedevi Kuran, *İnkılâp tarihimiz ve Jön Türkler* (İstanbul, 1945), pp. 7-8, cited in Recai G. Okandan, *Umumî âmme hukukumuzun ana hatları* (İstanbul, 1948), pp. 75-76 and n.24; by Wanda, *Souvenirs anecdotiques de la Turquie* (Paris, 1884), pp. 69-76.

[67] Some of the army officers in the plot probably imbibed political ideas from Polish or Hungarian colleagues. This is most likely to be true of General Hüseyin Dâim Paşa, a Circassian who had European friends: Millingen, *La Turquie*, p. 159; Wanda, *Souvenirs*, pp. 69-76; Hermann Vambéry, *His Life and Adventures* (New York, 1883), pp. 22-24; Walter Thornbury, *Turkish Life and Character* (London, 1860), I, 62; Thouvenel to Walewski, #68, 28 September 1859, AAE, Turquie 341. Possibly it is true also of Cafer Dem Paşa, an Albanian officer, who had English friends.

the basic motif of the conspirators was opposition to westernization. Their general dissatisfaction with the government may have arisen from many sources—from the excessive spending of Sultan Abdül-mecid, from the fact that army pay was in arrears, from a generally difficult economic and financial situation—but it crystallized as a defense of the şeriat, a resentment against the government's edicts according equality and various specific privileges to non-Muslims, and anger at the European pressures behind these edicts. Overzealous foreign humanitarians had, in fact, printed and circulated copies of the Hatt-ı Hümayun, leading the native Christians to expect more than was really possible.[68] The moving spirit in the conspiracy was one Şeyh Ahmed, a teacher in the medrese attached to the Sultan Beyazid mosque, who had been voicing such sentiments. He indicated that he regarded the great reform decrees of 1839 and 1856 as contraventions of Muslim law because they accorded Christians equal rights with Muslims. A good many ulema, including theological students, were involved in the conspiracy, as well as army officers and others. These men took an oath to support Şeyh Ahmed and to sacrifice themselves. Beyond these generalizations, in the present state of knowledge, it is impossible to be more precise on the ideology of the conspiracy, and the fuzziness of some of the conspirators' concepts leads to the suspicion that there may have been no precise formulation. Their immediate object was to get rid of Abdülmecid and, presumably, his current ministers, and to raise Abdülaziz to the throne. The latter, however, was not privy to the plot.

The conspiracy was betrayed to the government by an army officer who had been asked to join, and in mid-September of 1859 some forty-odd ringleaders were arrested. In İstanbul the news of the arrests provoked the usual rumors that a massacre of Christians was, or was not, in prospect; that from five thousand to fourteen thousand soldiers were involved; that the conspirators wanted, or did not want, increased westernization in the empire. It seems certain that many more persons than those arrested were prepared to support a revolt, had it actually occurred; various şeyh's promised the aid of several thousand disciples, and presumably soldiers could have been rallied too. A good deal of opinion in the capital seems to have supported the conspirators. Arrests were hindered, and theological students who had not been

[68] Great Britain, *Parliamentary Papers*, 1861, vol. 67, *Accounts and Papers*, vol. 36, "Reforms in Turkey," #9, Bulwer to Russell, 26 July 1859.

REFORM AND CONSPIRACY, 1856-1861

arrested put up posters appealing to the Muslim public to save their brethren at Kuleli in the name of religion and patriotism. Âli Paşa's administration evidently tried to play down the whole affair and to pass it off as the action of a few discontented Circassians and Kurds, but it took measures to limit the number of theological students in the capital, packing a good many off to the provinces; it also imposed a tax on the property of mosques and dervish tekkes, to curb somewhat the influence of the professional men of religion. The Porte also took the precaution of distributing to the garrison in the capital three months' back pay. With the arrests, the conspiracy fell to pieces. The leaders were interrogated by a government commission of the highest officials under Âli's chairmanship, and the future grand vezir Midhat Paşa, then second secretary of the Supreme Council, took part in the investigation. The conspirators were sentenced to varying punishments, principally imprisonment or exile in provincial spots. The few death sentences were commuted. Thus the abortive conspiracy left behind it only a tradition and an example for the future. This was not an example of revolt for parliamentary or constitutional government, but it was an example of a plot to overturn the government, and one which counted on a rather widespread public support. As such, it served as a precedent for the abortive New Ottoman plans of 1867, and for the successful coup of 1876. There is no directly traceable connection between the conspiracy of 1859 and either of the later incidents, though in all three cases some of the antigovernment feeling was fairly conservative and Islamic in nature.[69]

[69] The best study of the conspiracy of 1859 is Uluğ İğdemir, *Kuleli Vak'ası hakkında bir araştırma* (Ankara, 1937). Foreign embassies were generally well informed, though they received conflicting reports: cf. Thouvenel to Walewski, #65 and encl. and #68, of 21 and 28 September 1859, AAE, Turquie 341; Bulwer to Russell, #164 and encl., and #179, of 20 and 27 September 1859, FO 78/1435; Collett to Manderström, #12 and #14, of 20 and 30 September 1859, SRA, Depescher från Svenska Beskickningen i Konstantinopel; Williams to Cass, #53 and #54 with encl. of İstanbul press of 20 and 28 September 1859, USNA, Turkey 16; also Schauffler to Anderson, #92, 12 December 1859, ABCFM, Armenian Mission VIII. İU. A. Petrosian, *"Novye Osmany" i bor'ba za konstitutsiiu* (Moscow, 1958), p. 25, though he has used Russian archives, cites none on this incident. In addition to the accounts cited in notes 66 and 67 see Abdurrahman Şeref, *Tarih musahabeleri*, p. 172; Ahmed Midhat, *Üss-i inkılâb*, I, 75 n.; *idem, Kâinat*, IV (İstanbul, 1298), 548-549; Halûk Y. Şehsuvaroğlu, *Sultan Aziz* (İstanbul, 1949), pp. 9-15; Tarik Z. Tunaya, *Türkiyede siyasî partiler* (İstanbul, 1952), pp. 89-90; Ahmed Rasim, *İstibdaddan hakimiyeti milliyeye*, II, 56-60; Kuntay, *Namık Kemal*, I, 89, n.12, and 597, n.3, and II, part 1, 513 and n.5; Thornbury, *Turkish Life*, I, 37-40, 54-68, which reproduces (Anon.), "The Late Insurrection in Turkey," *Chamber's Journal*, 12:326 (31 March 1860), 193-197; Millingen, *Turquie*, pp. 235-236; *idem, Les imams et les derviches*

Although the conspirators had been unable to depose Abdülmecid, a part of their objective was attained a month after the Kuleli affair broke, when Âli Paşa was replaced as grand vezir by the more conservative Kıbrıslı Mehmed Emin Paşa. Mehmed, a native of Cyprus as his nickname indicated, was actually a product of the old education and the new. He had been one of the last students of the old palace school, in the time of Mahmud II. Thereafter he had entered the new army which Mahmud created after the destruction of the Janissaries, and rose to the rank of general. His early military training was completed by several years' study in Paris and in Metz, and service with the French dragoons. Since he knew French, as well as Greek and Turkish, Kıbrıslı Mehmed not only filled a half dozen provincial governorships before the Crimean War, but was also for a brief period ambassador to the Court of St. James and went on a mission to St. Petersburg at the time of Alexander II's accession. On his second tour of duty in Paris Kıbrıslı Mehmed had met and married the widow of Dr. Millingen, Byron's physician. Melek Hanım was half French, one quarter Greek, and one quarter Armenian, and a curious person by her own account, not above using her position for shady financial gain. Kıbrıslı Mehmed managed to survive the wave of scandal caused by his domestic life, his divorce from Melek, her reversion to Catholicism, and the conversion of his daughter to the same faith. He first became grand vezir for six months in 1854, and at the end of the Crimean War was acting grand vezir while Âli was at the Paris peace congress; thus he had presided at the ceremony of proclamation of the Hatt-ı Hümayun in 1856.

Despite his considerable knowledge of Europe, his early association with Reşid, and his later cooperation with Âli and Fuad, Kıbrıslı Mehmed never developed into a convinced westernizer. Indeed, it was exactly because he was not known as a westernizer that he, instead of Fuad, was chosen as acting grand vezir when the Hatt-ı Hümayun was proclaimed, so that he might act as a shield against Muslim curses.[70] He became, along with Âli and Fuad, a political rival of Reşid, but then broke with the other two as well. His estranged wife later wrote that his western education was "a thin surface of knowledge veneered over a thick mass of ignorance" and that he had "preserved

---

(Paris, 1881), pp. 204-205; Adolphe d'Avril, *Négociations relatives au Traité de Berlin* (Paris, 1886), pp. 55-59.

[70] Cevdet, *Tezâkir*, p. 66.

below the varnish of civilization the stamp of the old Turk."[71] Her judgment was harsh and biased, but it was true that Kıbrıslı Mehmed leaned more to the old than did Âli or Fuad. He was, however, an honest and energetic public servant, dedicated to improvement and the rooting out of abuses. Fuad is supposed to have remarked that, while Âli was all head, Kıbrıslı Mehmed was all legs. Certainly Mehmed was less thoughtful and less hesitant than Âli, more straightforward and more inclined to act. "An impatient man," Cevdet called him, "not given to long thinking."[72] His most significant action as grand vezir came in the field of provincial administration, which was now crying for attention.[73]

Although the Hatt-ı Hümayun had promised a reform of the provincial councils, as well as measures to improve communications, agriculture, and the system of tax collection, nothing along these lines had been effected by 1859. Instead, it became obvious that discontent and disorder in various provinces of the empire were in no way diminished. The preceding year had witnessed a rebellion in Crete occasioned by the tax system, a rising of Christian peasants in Bosnia against oppression by Muslim landlords, a renewal of Bulgarian agitation for bishops of their own people to replace the domineering Greek hierarchy, and a Montenegrin attack on the borders of Herzegovina. In some places Christians complained of Muslims; in other places Muslims complained of Christians. A fanatic mob in Jidda murdered the French and English consuls. Arab, Kurd, and Yezidi tribes ravaged the Mosul district in 1859. These provincial disturbances had several important consequences. To these problems the Porte had to devote money, men, and attention which might better have been spent in

[71] Melek Hanum, *Thirty Years in the Harem* (London, 1872), pp. 277-278.

[72] *Tezâkir*, p. 88.

[73] Kıbrıslı Mehmed Paşa, like other Ottoman statesmen, lacks a biographer. The best portrait is in Werner, *Türkische Skizzen*, II, 172-182. İnal, *Son sadrıâzamlar*, I, 83-100, is more informative on some points but a hodgepodge of quotations, largely from Cevdet. Melek Hanum, *Thirty Years*, is quite informative though biased; her *Six Years in Europe* (London, 1873) has less information about her ex-husband. Melek's son, Frederick Millingen (Osman-Bey) defends her throughout his *Les Anglais en Orient* (Paris, 1877). See also Ubicini, *Turquie actuelle*, pp. 173-177; Barnette Miller, *The Palace School of Muhammad the Conqueror* (Cambridge, Mass., 1941), p. 7; Drummond Wolff, *Rambling Recollections*, II, 4-5; *Tezâkir-i Cevdet*, #5, quoted in Mardin, *Cevdet*, p. 51, n.81; *La Turquie*, 9 September 1871. HHS XII/58 (Varia), p. 75, contains an anonymous letter of 25 October 1856 to Cevdet, a sample of the slander to which Mehmed was subject. His honesty may be suspect from Melek Hanum's accounts, but is generally defended by other contemporaries. İnal, *Son sadrıâzamlar*, I, 37, recounts that he rejected a large gift offered by the khedive, whereas Âli accepted.

working out basic reforms. Further, the authority of the Porte over the empire was more shaken by such disturbances than it would have been before the increased centralization of governmental authority under Mahmud II. Also, provincial unrest provided the European powers with an excuse for intervention, which the Porte always feared would result only in a process of separation from its control such as was now in full swing in the Danubian principalities. The ambassadors of the powers at İstanbul did, in fact, present the Porte on October 5, 1859, a memorandum urging immediate fulfillment of the promises of the Hatt-ı Hümayun. Russia pressed especially for an international inquest on conditions in the Balkans.[74] It is probable that the fall of Âli from the grand vezirate was in part occasioned by the powers' representations, as well as by the Kuleli incident of three weeks before and by Âli's disputes with Abdülmecid over the latter's spendthrift habits. Kıbrıslı Mehmed was thus faced with the provincial problem as soon as he took office. Although he was out again in two months, he was back as grand vezir in May of 1860, and this time remained in the post until August 1861. Provincial administration continued to occupy his attention.

Kıbrıslı Mehmed attempted no immediate reorganization of provincial government. Instead, he fell quite naturally into the time-honored method of sending out commissioners on inspection.[75] In the late spring of 1860 he himself left İstanbul on an inspection tour as head of a commission composed of some of the best men of the empire: three Turks in addition to himself—Cevdet Efendi, Afif Bey, and Besim Bey; two Armenians—Artin Dadian and Kabriel Efendi; and two Greeks—Musurus and Photiades.[76] The commission spent four months in and around the cities of Ruschuk (Rusçuk, Ruse), Shumla (Şumla, Shumen, Kolarovgrad), Vidin, Nish (Niş, Niš), Prishtina (Prİştine, Priština), Scopia (Üsküb, Skopje), Monastir (Manastır, Bitola), and Salonika (Selânik, Thessalonike). Its methods were characteristic of Kıbrıslı Mehmed, who received countless petitions in person and dispensed justice on the spot himself, or through ad hoc

---

[74] Engelhardt, *La Turquie*, I, 161-163. Another Russian note of 23 April 1860 stressed the problem: *Archives diplomatiques*, I (1861), 113-115.

[75] See above, pp. 27, 47-48.

[76] The Russians claimed that they provoked the tour: Ignatyev, "Zapiski Grapha N. P. Ignatyeva," *Izvestiia Ministerstva Inostrannykh Diel*, 1914, I, 103; the French claimed that their ambassador suggested the trip: d'Avril, *Négociations*, p. 63. British backing helped the Porte evade the Russian demand for an international commission.

mixed courts. The number of individual petitions received was extraordinary—some four thousand in the province of Nish alone. Most of them dealt with disputes between individuals, which reflected laxity or corruption in the administration of justice, and the exclusion of Christian testimony in the courts. Some of the petitions were spurious, prepared by agitators who had their own ends in view. Some Christians were obviously afraid to enter complaints, but many were not. In October 1860 the inspection tour was cut short by the Druze-Maronite feud in the Lebanon, which made imperative Kıbrıslı Mehmed's return to the capital. But the four months in the field were sufficient to expose the conditions of local government, to re-establish the formula of checking on provincial administration by inspection tours, and to lay the basis for the vilayet experiment of 1864.[77]

Despite Russian claims that the commission did not admit the true extent of misgovernment and oppression, the revelations of its report seem to be fairly accurate.[78] Six conclusions were reached, and some of these were acted upon on the spot. The first was that there was no systematic oppression of Christians by Muslims, officially or unofficially, but that Christians could justly complain that their testimony was often refused in court. The second was that the Greek hierarchy was frequently tyrannical and unjust—the archbishop of Şarköy, for instance, was convicted of extortion and of the violation of a Bulgarian girl. Thirdly, the commission found malfeasance in office among a number of Turkish officials. The governor of Nish and some underlings were convicted of accepting bribes, removed from office, and

[77] Great Britain, *Parliamentary Papers*, 1861, vol. 67, *Accounts and Papers*, vol. 34, "Reports . . . Condition of Christians in Turkey, 1860," includes considerable information from British consuls who watched the commission in action. #6, Mayers to Green, Ruschuk, 18 July 1860, encl. 2, gives a French translation of Kıbrıslı Mehmed's temporary instructions to provincial governors; *ibid.*, "Papers . . . Administrative and Financial Reforms in Turkey, 1858-1861," #40, Âli to Musurus, 21 November 1860, gives a French translation of Kıbrıslı Mehmed's report to the sultan. Ahmed Rasim, *İstibdaddan hakimiyeti milliyeye*, II, 52-54, discusses tour and report. See also *Journal de Constantinople*, 14 June and 15 October 1860; Kanitz, *Donau-Bulgarien*, I, 102-112; Moustapha Djelaleddin, *Les Turcs anciens et modernes* (Paris, 1870), p. 177.

[78] The Russian government issued a memorandum of 4 January 1861 belittling the results of the tour and containing some just criticisms: *Archives diplomatiques*, II (1861), 220-233. The Porte refuted this in an undated memoir of February 1861: *ibid.*, pp. 107-114. The truth lay between the two statements, but the Russian seems more overdrawn. The British reports cited above generally parallel the Turkish, and are often somewhat Turcophil in this period.

imprisoned; it does not appear that they were simply sacrificed as scapegoats to appease local and foreign opinion. Some of the local meclises also were dissolved and reconstituted. The commission was, fourthly, dissatisfied with the tax-farming system; some of the *iltizamcı*'s were imprisoned for bribery and extortion, and the accountant-general (*muhasebeci*) of Nish was imprisoned for accepting a bribe from a Jewish tax farmer. Kıbrıslı Mehmed tried to curb extortion by ordering that a committee of local notables control the assessments made by the *iltizamcı* on the produce of each individual. The commission decided, fifthly, that the local roads needed improvement, and, finally, that the police system had to be strengthened.

From 1860 until 1864 the Porte regularly used the system of imperial inspectors to supplement the normal eyalet government. The *müfettiş* (inspector) became a familiar figure in the Balkans and Anatolia, though he was not a regular visitor to the Arab provinces. Among the men sent out on inspection were some of the most able and intelligent of the empire. Ahmed Vefik Efendi covered western Anatolia; Bursalı Ali Rıza Efendi was in northeastern Anatolia; Abdüllâtif Subhi Bey, known as a numismatist and a man learned in western science, went to Bulgaria; and Ziya Bey, the writer and palace secretary and later New Ottoman leader, went to Bosnia. Cevdet was appointed head of a special office in the Sublime Porte to coordinate the reports sent in by the inspectors and to see that they were acted upon. The system of provincial inspection was admittedly a palliative, not a solution, for the problems of provincial government. Fuad Paşa remarked that each of the four inspectors interpreted his instructions differently and acted as an individual.[79] Ziya turned out to be poor at his job, and had to be replaced by Cevdet himself. Ahmed Vefik acted in so highhanded and arbitrary a manner that the complaints of the citizens of Bursa led to his recall. Yet, on the whole, the system seems to have provided an effective and recurring check on provincial officials, on tax farmers, and on local councils in the eyalets, and to have rendered the administration of justice more equitable. The inspectors did not hesitate to fire corrupt officials. It is reported that Subhi Bey "lacked neither energy to punish nor shrewdness to detect" and that only one mayor (*müdür*) in his area could boast of having passed the inspection with spotless hands.[80] Provincial governors were

---

[79] İnal, *Son sadrıâzamlar*, II, 188.
[80] Mackenzie and Irby, *Travels*, pp. 78-80.

inspired to clean house by the impending arrival of inspectors, and at least one of them emulated the grand vezir, on a smaller scale, by touring his own province with a commission of Muslims and Christians.[81]

The Porte also, in some instances, followed the time-honored practice of sending out commissioners with extraordinary powers, often both civil and military, as trouble shooters to provinces affected by active discontent or genuine revolt. In this period, for example, Fuad Paşa went to Syria with extraordinary powers to deal with the Druze massacre of Maronites, and Cevdet was sent to Scutari (İşkodra, Shköder) to suppress a rebellion. The Syrian outbreak in particular showed how sensitive to provincial disturbances the Porte was: its concern was not only to get rid of the French military expedition to pacify Syria, which Fuad succeeded in doing, but also to fend off any resultant disorders in İstanbul which might shake the government. In August 1860 there was real fear in the capital, and the Porte forbade inhabitants to speak of Syria on the streets.[82] The long-run result of such special missions was to encourage the further sending of regular inspectors. This system in its turn produced an increased central control over the provinces and a check on the wider powers accorded provincial governors by the ferman of 1852. It also gave the Porte greater familiarity with provincial conditions, provided the basis for sending out the capable Midhat Paşa to be governor of Nish in 1861, and laid the groundwork for the reform of provincial administration by the vilayet law of 1864. The Syrian disorders led to a special constitution for the Lebanon which also influenced the later vilayet law.[83]

[81] Hüseyin Hüsni Paşa in Salonika: *Journal de Constantinople*, 14 January 1861. On the inspection system in this period see: Mordtmann, *Stambul*, I, 170, and II, 10-11; Kanitz, *Donau-Bulgarien*, II, 111-112; *Journal de Constantinople*, 13 August 1864, giving the grand vezir's official report for 1863-1864; Karl Ritter von Sax, *Geschichte des Machtverfalls der Türkei*, 2nd ed. (Vienna, 1913), pp. 372-373; Abdurrahman Şeref, *Tarih musahabeleri*, pp. 223-224; Mardin, *Cevdet*, pp. 53-55 and n.85-87; Ali Ölmezoğlu, "Cevdet Paşa," *İslâm ansiklopedisi*, III, 116; A. H. Tanpınar, "Ahmed Vefik Paşa," *ibid.*, I, 208; Hill, *Cyprus*, IV, 229, where he reports a travesty on the inspection system; *Smyrna Mail*, 1 September and 1 October 1863.

[82] Williams to Cass, #89, 7 August 1860, USNA, Turkey 16; Schauffler to Anderson, #9, 21 August 1860, ABCFM, Western Turkey Mission IV.

[83] See below, chapter V. Despite the vilayet law, both the special commissioner and the regular inspector were used again. See instructions for a new wave of inspectors in 1871, in *La Turquie*, 30 October and 27 December 1871. The investigation commission was also used at times as a delaying move to ward off foreign intervention or separatism: see Âli's proposals on such a commission in the Principalities in 1861: Riker, *Roumania*, p. 312.

In the midst of this chaotic period Sultan Abdülmecid died, on June 25, 1861. His passing seemed to be an unmixed blessing for the empire. His youthful enthusiasm for reform, exemplified by the backing he had given to Reşid's projects, had waned. Palace expenditures had mounted steeply in his later years; Abdülmecid had spent lavishly for new palaces and other construction, and this contributed to his growing unpopularity with the public. But Abdülmecid had been a mild and humane sultan, who usually did not dominate his government. The significance of the change in monarchs would become apparent only when the character of Abdülaziz should become known. At the time of his accession, after an abortive move to bypass him for his nephew Murad, Abdülaziz was quite an unknown quantity. Both conservatives and reformers counted on him to strengthen their hands; if anything, the conservatives hoped for more from him, as it was generally rumored that he was an "Old Turk." Abdülaziz had passed his thirty-one years apart from the public gaze, although he had enjoyed more freedom in his confinement than any prince in two and a half centuries, having been allowed to marry and have a son even before his accession. His brother Abdülmecid had, however, been suspicious of him in the last few years, thought once of sending him away to Tripoli in Africa, and required him to live with his mother Pertevniyal. As sultan-mother, Pertevniyal was to have a strong influence on Abdülaziz; what this might portend was unknown. It was known only that Abdülaziz had had a simple Muslim education, was strong, handsome, and healthy in contrast to his brother, and loved wrestling and the chase.[84]

[84] On the change in monarchs and on Abdülaziz in 1861 see Şehsuvaroğlu, *Sultan Aziz*, pp. 15-24; *Augsburger Allgemeine Zeitung*, 7 July 1861, Beilage; Melek Hanum, *Thirty Years*, pp. 265-268; Millingen, *La Turquie*, pp. 251-253, 262-263; Ubicini, *Turquie actuelle*, p. 136; A. D. Alderson, *The Structure of the Ottoman Dynasty* (Oxford, 1956), pp. 21, 35; A. H. Ongunsu, "Abdülaziz," *İslâm ansiklopedisi*, I, 57-58; Count Greppi, "Souvenirs d'un diplomate italien à Constantinople," *Revue d'histoire diplomatique*, 24 (July 1910), 372, 379-383. The move to put Murad on the throne was apparently a bit of personal politics on the part of Rıza Paşa, enemy of Abdülaziz's brother-in-law Damad Mehmed Ali Paşa, but was generally thought to have French backing also: Mehmed Memduh, *Mirât-ı şuunat*, p. 29; Anton Graf Prokesch-Osten, "Erinnerungen aus Konstantinopel," *Deutsche Revue*, IV (1880), 70-72; L. Raschdau, ed., "Diplomatenleben am Bosporus," *Deutsche Rundschau*, 138 (1909), 386; Bamberg, *Geschichte*, p. 458; Brown to Seward, #8, 26 June 1861, USNA, Turkey 17. But the French ambassador of two years before, at the time of the Kuleli incident, had said that Abdülaziz should make a better sultan than the dissipated Murad: Thouvenel to Walewski, #65, 21 September 1859, AAE, Turkey 341. The author does not know what influence the reported Bektashi affiliations of Pertevniyal may have had: J. K. Birge, *The Bektashi Order of Dervishes* (London, 1937), p. 81.

Abdülaziz's accession *hat* shed no particular light on his future course. It confirmed the reform decrees of 1839 and 1856, and stressed the equality of all Ottoman subjects, but seemed also to lay unusual emphasis on conformity with the holy law of Islam.[85] As it turned out, the new sultan was unable to make his full influence felt in the affairs of government for ten years after his accession, and his personal proclivities became decisively important only in 1871. This was so because at the very beginning of his reign Âli and Fuad secured their dominant position and maintained it for a decade. Although the conservative Kıbrıslı Mehmed had been confirmed in office as grand vezir by Abdülaziz on his accession, six weeks later Âli Paşa had the job. From August 6, 1861, until Âli died on September 6, 1871, either he or Fuad was grand vezir, with only two brief interludes which totalled thirteen months. During the same time span one or the other was foreign minister, with no interruptions at all. Though the duumvirate aroused bitter opposition among rival statesmen and in some segments of public opinion, it ruled. Abdülaziz ruled only when both were dead.[86]

Abdülaziz had succeeded to the throne at a time when two crises threatened the empire. One was a rising of Christian peasants in the Herzegovina, which attracted the armed support of Montenegro in 1862. A successful military campaign under Ömer Paşa put a temporary end to these outbreaks, though it brought no solution to the fundamental problems involved. Even more serious than the Christian risings was the financial crisis of the Porte, which in 1861 became acute. The Ottoman ministers were gratified that Abdülaziz at once pledged economy in the palace, broke up Abdülmecid's large and expensive harem, and declared that he would be satisfied with one wife only. Yet these measures were insufficient. On December 11 there seemed

[85] Texts in *Das Staatsarchiv*, I (1861), 97-99; *Archives diplomatiques*, III (1861), 318-320; *Düstur*, I, 14-15; Ahmed Midhat, *Üss-i inkılâb*, I, 294-296.

[86] Grand vezirates in this period: Âli, 6 August-2 November 1861; Fuad, 22 November 1861-2 January 1863; Yusuf Kâmil, 5 January 1863-1 June 1863; Fuad, 1 June 1863-5 June 1866; Mütercim Mehmed Rüşdi, 5 June 1866-11 February 1867; Âli, 11 February 1867-6 September 1871. Foreign ministries: Fuad, 6 August 1861-22 November 1861; Âli, 22 November 1861-11 February 1867; Fuad, 11 February 1867-12 February 1869 (died); Âli (who now took the foreign ministry while keeping the grand vezirate), 12 February 1869-6 September 1871 (died). Âli was continuously in one of these two offices, without breaks. Fuad was more likely to fall out of the sultan's good graces and to vault back in; in addition to these two offices, he was for brief periods in early 1863 president of the Supreme Council and minister of war, and was out of office for eight months in 1866-1867.

to be danger of revolution in the capital. On that day the only circulatory medium in İstanbul, paper money known as the *kaime*, which was already heavily discounted in terms of gold, sank one hundred per cent in value on the Galata exchange. Merchants refused to accept it, business stood still, mobs formed, bakeries were sacked. Quick action by Fuad's government to support the *kaime* brought temporary relief. Revolt might otherwise have spread to the provinces, where the soldiers' pay was in arrears just as it had been at the time of the 1859 conspiracy.[87]

The immediate origin of the crisis was clear: it stemmed from the unbalanced condition of the treasury, a want of confidence in the government's ability to repay heavy short-term advances by local Galata bankers, and a complete distrust of the paper money. This situation, in turn, was the product of the hopeless muddle of state finances coupled with general economic underdevelopment and an unfavorable balance of trade. The Crimean War had imposed a heavy burden on the treasury, which was increased thereafter by the expense of other military expeditions to rebellious provinces. Abdülmecid's heavy spending was added to the deficit. Treasury receipts, on the other hand, were decimated by the graft of officials and tax farmers. That there was not more taxable land and produce was due in part to the generally backward condition of agriculture, of industry, and of means of communication and transport. It was due in part also to the fact that perhaps three fourths of the arable land of the empire had been transformed, legally or illegally, into *vakıf* property, which was partially tax-exempt and which often was not kept up or cultivated as adequately as it should have been. The state *evkaf* ministry, created by Mahmud II to supervise and administer the properties of the charitable endowments, was a drain on the treasury because the expenses of administration and upkeep usually ran ahead of receipts.[88] Customs revenues were low largely because trade treaties with the European nations imposed a uniform ad valorem import duty of five per cent, which the Porte could not unilaterally raise. To get revenue, then, it imposed on domestic products an export duty of twelve per cent. There was also an internal tariff on the transportation of goods

[87] Morris to Seward, unnumbered, 18 December 1861, USNA, Turkey 17.
[88] Fuad Köprülü, defending the institution of *vakıf*, points out that Fuad dipped into *evkaf* funds to rectify treasury deficits, and so helped further to undermine the institution and depreciate the properties: "L'institution du Vakouf," *Vakıflar dergisi*, II (1948), 32-33.

from place to place within the empire. Native industry was naturally discouraged by such practices. Bursa, under such conditions, was full of Bursa towels made in Manchester.[89]

To offset the lack of sufficient revenue the Porte had resorted to three expedients. The first was the issue of the *kaime*, unnumbered so that the public could not know in what quantities, and of other sorts of interest-bearing paper which covered annual deficits. The second was short-term borrowing from local bankers. The third was borrowing in Europe—a method which the Crimean War had made possible and which by 1860 had resulted in four large loans.[90] All three methods proved ruinous. The paper money was issued in large quantities and was easy to counterfeit. The local rates in Galata were steep. When interest and amortization on the European loans were added, the annual service of the Ottoman public debt was such as to leave insufficient funds for the business of government. Therefore, further deficits were incurred. The European loan of 1860, moreover, had failed of complete subscription; this initiated the crisis that came to a head in 1861.

In the face of these difficulties, the grand vezir Fuad took over personal supervision of treasury affairs and submitted to Abdülaziz plans for retiring the *kaime*, cutting expenses, and increasing revenue. A permanent finance council which included an Austrian, a Frenchman, and an Englishman was established by the Porte. This council with great difficulty drew up a first budget for 1863-1864 and proposed changes in the tax system; the European members complained, however, of a lack of power. With aid from Britain and France the Porte finally succeeded in converting the Galata loans that fell due and in creating the Imperial Ottoman Bank, which was backed by some of the largest European financial houses. The founders of the bank negotiated for the Porte in 1862 a loan which was subscribed four times over and was used to retire the paper money, although holders received only forty per cent in specie and the remainder in government obligations. Public joy was reflected in a chronogram, the last line of which, with the numerical value of 1279 (A.D. 1862 corre-

[89] Hamlin, *Among the Turks*, p. 59. Ömer Celel Sarç surveys the weakness of Ottoman industry in *Tanzimat*, I, 424-440.

[90] European loans had been considered just before the Crimean War, but vetoed by Abdülmecid. Damad Fethi Paşa predicted: "If this state borrows five piasters it will sink. For if once a loan is taken, there will be no end to it. It [the state] will sink overwhelmed in debt." Cevdet, *Tezâkir*, p. 22, and Fatma Aliye, *Cevdet*, p. 87.

sponded to A. H. 1279), said "the name *kaime* has been banished from the world." New commercial treaties which were negotiated in 1861 raised the import duty to eight per cent and provided for the gradual reduction of the export duty to one per cent.[91]

For the moment the credit of the empire was saved, and public confidence was restored. The fundamental difficulties, however, were not solved. Mustafa Fazıl Paşa,[92] minister of finance in 1863-1864, found many obstacles in his path as he tried to work out a rational financial system. In the ensuing decade more internal and external debts were contracted, Abdülaziz's good intentions on economy vanished as his harem and his love of ironclad warships increased, corruption continued, and budgets were disregarded. Despite the fundamental weakness of the financial structure, to which Âli and Fuad contributed in so far as they satisfied various of the sultan's wishes in order to stay in office, no new acute crisis intervened until 1875. The Tanzimat ministers were thus able to give more attention to fundamental administrative reorganization, which had been in abeyance since 1856. Two projects, the reorganization of the non-Muslim millets and of the provincial administration, were already under consideration.

[91] One gets the impression from many authors, both Turkish and western, that Ottoman history from 1856 to 1876 was nothing but one long crisis of provincial rebellion and financial catastrophe. Almost all Turkish memoirs of the period, and later accounts, include substantial sections, frequently in very general terms, on palace expenditures, corruption, and the European loans. For this period of financial crisis the most useful is A. Du Velay, *Essai sur l'histoire financière de la Turquie* (Paris, 1903), pp. 130-196 and 260-264. This work has recently been translated into Turkish as "Türkiye malî tarihi," *Maliye mecmuası,* #12 (1939) and following issues. Charles Morawitz, *Die Türkei im Spiegel ihrer Finanzen,* trans. by Georg Schweitzer (Berlin, 1903), pp. 20-44, and Grégoire Poulgy, *Les emprunts de l'état ottoman* (Paris, 1915), pp. 41-54, are sketchier and add little. Ahmed Rasim, *Istibdaddan hakimiyeti milliyeye,* II, 63-73, and Refii Şükrü Suvla in *Tanzimat,* I, 270-275, analyze the loans. Abdolonyme Ubicini, *Letters on Turkey,* trans. by Lady Easthope (London, 1856), I, 254-358, gives background on general economy. Cevdet, *Tezâkir,* pp. 20-23, and Fatma Aliye, *Cevdet,* pp. 84-87, are useful on this subject though relating to 1851-1852. Ali Fuad, *Rical-i mühimme,* pp. 72-74, deals with financial troubles in 1858-1859. On the *kaime* see Şükrü Baban in *Tanzimat,* I, 246-257, and J. H. Mordtmann in *İslâm ansiklopedisi,* VI, 106-107. Documents on the 1860-1861 crisis from English, Turkish, and French sources are in *Das Staatsarchiv,* I (1861), 317-341. English reports are in Great Britain, *Parliamentary Papers,* 1861, vol. 67, *Accounts and Papers,* vol. 34, "Papers Relating to Administrative and Financial Reforms in Turkey, 1858-1861"; *ibid.,* 1862, vol. 64, *Accounts and Papers,* vol. 36, the report of the English commissioners; and *ibid.,* 1875, vol. 83, *Accounts and Papers,* vol. 42, "Turkey No. 1, 2, 3, 6," on the 1862 loan. Du Velay contains the essence of these. Chronogram in *Zeitschrift der Deutschen Morgenländischen Gesellschaft,* 17:3/4 (1863), 712.
[92] On him see below, chapter VI.

113

CHAPTER IV

REORGANIZATION OF THE NON-MUSLIM
MILLETS, 1860-1865

New constitutions for the principal non-Muslim millets of the empire were the first fruit of the Porte's efforts for basic administrative reform. In 1862 and 1863 the Greek Orthodox and Armenian Gregorian communities were placed under organic laws which diminished the power of the clergy and increased lay influence correspondingly. Ottoman Jews received a similar charter in 1865. The impetus for these changes came both from within the millets themselves and from the Turkish government. An inner upheaval in each religious community manifested itself in mid-century, and the Porte urged on each the elaboration of new constitutions. Probably Kıbrıslı Mehmed's findings of Greek Orthodox corruption in Bulgaria in 1860 helped to speed the action. But the Hatt-ı Hümayun had already promised reform of the millets, while confirming the ancient privileges and freedom of worship accorded them. Lord Stratford and the French and Austrian ambassadors, in the discussions leading up to the proclamation of the *hat*, had warmly supported millet reorganization, particularly in the direction of extending lay control, limiting clerical authority, and fixing clerical salaries.[1] Each community was required by this edict to set up a commission to reform its own administration and to submit the results for the Porte's approval, in order to bring millet organization into conformity "with the progress and enlightenment of the times." This phraseology, an echo of the nineteenth-century cult of progress, obscured the real reasons which led the Porte to insist on millet reorganization.

Several considerations seem to have urged the sultan's government toward this course. The most immediate was the hope that European intervention in favor of the minorities, especially Russian pressure favoring the Greek Orthodox, would be curbed if the power of an obscurantist clerical hierarchy, which tried to keep its flock in subjection, were decreased.[2] It is likely also that the Tanzimat statesmen

---

[1] Great Britain, *Parliamentary Papers*, 1856, vol. 61, *Accounts and Papers*, vol. 24, "Correspondence Respecting Christian Privileges in Turkey," pp. 38, 42, 47, 61; Prokesch to Buol, 24 January 1856, HHS, XII/56.
[2] *Ibid.*

had in mind the furtherance of Ottoman brotherhood and egalitarian citizenship, which was implicit in the whole tone of the Hatt-ı Hümayun. The more that religious dogma and clerical control could be pushed into the background, the greater would be the chances for consolidating the empire on the basis of Ottomanism. Such millet reform would help to increase the separation of state and religion, as the gradual adoption of secular law was already doing. It is dubious, however, that either Âli or Fuad intended the millet constitutions to be a trial run for a form of representative government that might later be extended to the whole empire, despite an assertion to this effect by an informed Ottoman statesman.[3] It would also be to the Porte's advantage if, by diminishing clerical influence in the millets, some of the sectarian warfare among the Christians could be avoided. These squabbles caused the Porte considerable trouble simply in the maintenance of domestic order, and in addition offered further opportunity for intervention by great powers who were partisans of one sect or another. It is possible, further, that aside from political motives there was among Porte officials some desire simply to alleviate the legal and financial tyranny exercised by the Greek and Armenian hierarchies over their flocks. An added practical consideration for the Tanzimat statesmen was to diminish Christian antagonism aroused against the Porte by provincial metropolitans who told their flocks that what they collected for their own pockets was an exaction by the state.[4]

The misfortunes of the ordinary non-Muslims of the empire were not, of course, due solely to the dominion of the ecclesiastical hierarchies. It has been noted before, but is worth repeating, that the non-Muslims were still considered by the Turks to be second-class subjects, and were very conscious of their inferiority. Though by 1860 the condition of the Christians, who were the vast majority among the non-Muslim subjects, had improved considerably over what it had been only a few years before, they could still complain legitimately about unequal treatment. They still protested the general prohibition

---

[3] İsmail Kemal Bey later claimed that the Armenian constitution "was intended as an experiment in constitutions and was to form a model for later use." Sommerville Story, ed., *The Memoirs of Ismail Kemal Bey* (London, 1920), p. 254. It is true that there was some Armenian influence on the Ottoman constitution of 1876, as will be seen below in chapter x, but İsmail Kemal is probably reading back into the earlier act an intention which did not then exist.

[4] Mehmed Selâheddin, *Bir türk diplomatının evrak-ı siyasiyesi* (İstanbul, 1306), pp. 184-185. Reşid Paşa in this undated document calls the Greek metropolitans "unfit" and "corrupt."

of bells on their churches, the frequent rejection of their testimony in Turkish courts, occasional rapes of Christian girls or forced conversions, and other sorts of personal mistreatment. The Armenians of eastern Anatolia had strong complaints about the marauding habits of armed Kurdish bands. There were occasional fanatical outbursts against Christians by local Muslim groups. There was still no equality in opportunity to hold public office. It was these undeniable injustices which usually attracted the attention of European writers of the time, and which often produced biased accounts and special pleading.[5] It might, in fact, have been argued that the Turks were less oppressive of their subject peoples than were the Russians of the Poles, the English of the Irish, or the Americans of the Negroes. But this was generally forgotten in Europe. Some writers were prepared to admit that Ottoman officials were much fairer in their treatment of minorities than local Muslim notables whom the officials were powerless to control or afraid to thwart. But few Europeans knew or admitted that in many respects the Muslims and Christians suffered equally—from brigandage, from corrupt tax collection, or from general misgovernment—and that in some instances Christian notables and tax farmers were themselves the oppressors of Muslims.[6] In some ways the Christians were better off than the Turks, since they were exempt from military service and sometimes had foreign consuls to lean on. It was reported from İzmir that "the Turkish villager is, without doubt, more frequently subject to oppression than the Christian."[7] There is evidence to show that in this period there was emigration from independent Greece into the Ottoman Empire, since some Greeks found the Ottoman government a more indulgent master.[8] The sum of the picture is that in many respects all the Ottoman peoples were on the same level, and that the Christian minorities, although of status in-

[5] Such as the pamphlet of the Rev. William Denton in just this period: *The Christians in Turkey* (London, 1863). He culled from the travel accounts of MacFarlane and Senior, and the Blue Books on the condition of Christians in 1860, the outstanding examples of Turkish oppression, while suppressing contradictory evidence from the same sources.

[6] There were probably a fair number of instances like that of 1858 reported in ABCFM, *Trowbridge's Diary*, pp. 38-40, where a Greek müdür who had purchased his office was supported by the Turkish governor in his mistreatment of a Turkish woman.

[7] Great Britain, *Parliamentary Papers*, 1861, vol. 67, *Accounts and Papers*, vol. 34, "Reports . . . Christians," #8, encl. 2, Blunt to Bulwer, 28 July 1860.

[8] Nassau W. Senior, *A Journal Kept in Turkey and Greece* (London, 1859), pp. 82, 190, 272-294; Albert Dumont, *Le Balkan et l'Adriatique* (Paris, 1874), pp. 85-89, 383-390.

ferior to the Turks, did not suffer continuously and exclusively from Turkish oppression.

But the Christian minorities were subject, in addition, to an oppression of their own from their ecclesiastical hierarchies. Simony was usual, particularly in the Greek church. The patriarch purchased his office from the Ottoman government, and in consequence sold bishoprics to make good his expenses. The ultimate sufferer was the ordinary village Greek, who was subject to overtaxation and extortion by his own clergy and by the *kocabaşı*'s, or elected lay headmen of his village, who were a part of the system. "Here, as everywhere else in Turkey," reported a British consul from a Greek town, "every sort of injustice, malversation of funds, bribery and corruption is openly attributed by the Christians to their clergy."[9] The position of Bulgars within the Greek church provided a particular sore spot. European observers likened the Greek clergy there to clerical tax farmers, bent on recouping presents made to their superiors for investiture. It was not unknown for Greek priests to lend money at sixty per cent interest to Bulgar peasants. Villagers tried to avoid the luxury of a resident priest because of the expense entailed. Meanwhile the services were in Greek, higher ecclesiastical offices were kept out of Bulgar hands, and the Greek clergy failed to establish Bulgar schools.[10] The whole

[9] Cathcart (Preveza) to Bulwer, 20 July 1860, encl. 2 in #10, Great Britain, *Parliamentary Papers*, 1861, vol. 67, *Accounts and Papers*, vol. 34, "Reports . . . Christians." Abdolonyme Ubicini, *Letters on Turkey*, trans. by Lady Easthope (London, 1856), II, 132, 136, 157-168, gives a picture of the simony, oppression, shibboleths, and the ignorant lower clergy of the Greek Orthodox church of this period. Cyrus Hamlin, in ABCFM, Armenian Mission V, #269, 1867, draws an even more devastating indictment, though allowance must be made for his vigorous Protestantism and iconoclasm; he accuses the Greek church of having corrupted the native honesty of the Turk. For an earlier picture of Greek church corruption, but an opposing view that the Turks were responsible for it, see Theodore H. Papadopoullos, *Studies and Documents relating to the History of the Greek Church and People under Turkish Domination* (Brussels, 1952), pp. 131-147. Cf. examples in C. T. Newton, *Travels and Discoveries in the Levant* (London, 1865), I, 218-222; *Accounts and Papers*, 1861, vol. 34, "Reports . . . Christians," #4, encl. 2; #8, encl. 2.

[10] Dumont, *Le Balkan*, pp. 85, 149-152, 371; G. G. B. St. Clair and C. A. Brophy, *Twelve Years' Study of the Eastern Question in Bulgaria* (London, 1877), pp. 71-75, 81-83; Halil İnalcık, *Tanzimat ve Bulgar meselesi* (Ankara, 1943), pp. 78-79, on *kocabaşı*'s. On the Bulgar struggle for freedom, see Alois Hajek, *Bulgarien unter der Türkenherrschaft* (Stuttgart, 1925), pp. 186-220. The Porte finally in 1870 recognized an independent Bulgarian exarchate, which, of course, was as much a political as a religious move: ferman in George Young, *Corps de droit ottoman* (Oxford, 1905-1906), II, 61-64. In 1872 the İstanbul Orthodox synod created a new heresy of nationalism and declared the Bulgars schismatics: Heinrich Gelzer, *Geistliches und Weltliches aus dem türkisch-griechischen Orient* (Leipzig, 1900), p. 129.

clerical oppression was supported by certain influential lay elements in the capital whose power and wealth was served by the alliance.

In the Gregorian Armenian millet the situation was as bad, although not complicated by a problem like that of the Bulgars. The Armenian *sarraf*'s, or bankers and moneylenders, were in league with members of the Ottoman bureaucracy to cheat the government and squeeze their people. The later Armenian revolutionaries condemned the bankers who "never ceased to exploit their compatriots, sometimes doing them more wrong than perhaps the Turks themselves."[11] In the provinces also Armenian notables and Turkish officials often worked together to exploit the villager. Although Armenians in a town near Adana were oppressed by the Turkish governor, "they were oppressed still more by their own head men. These collect the taxes for the governor; and while they collect one piastre for him, they collect three for themselves."[12] At Bandırma the leading Armenians (*çorbacı*'s) formed "an unholy league with the Turkish governors, judges, and authorities of the neighbouring places, and the Armenian bishop, whoever he might be. . . . All in office, ecclesiastical and civil, of all religions, unite in one object and in one only, to oppress and fleece the people and cheat the government."[13]

The Greek and Armenian millets, then, had become corrupt machines of business and politics, manipulated for the advantage of the hierarchies. Each millet, of course, had been political since its earliest recognition by the Ottoman sultans, because of the attribution to the patriarchs of considerable civil authority in matters of personal status, justice, and taxation.[14] Thereafter it was to the interest of each hierarchy to maintain its power by keeping the mass of its flock in relative ignorance, by making sure of the cooperation of the Ottoman authorities, and by fighting any sort of religious or political heresy which might subtract tax-paying members from its communion. Thus both hierarchies fought Protestant and Catholic inroads on their membership, and the Orthodox fought the Bulgar demands for a national church in particular. The Greek hierarchy struggled to maintain its position as the first among the non-Muslim millets, while the Ar-

[11] Varandian, quoted by Frédéric Macler, *Autour de l'Arménie* (Paris, 1917), p. 253.

[12] ABCFM, Central Turkey Mission I, #238, end of 1860.

[13] *Ibid.*, Armenian Mission V, #298, 24 September 1859.

[14] H. A. R. Gibb and Harold Bowen, *Islamic Society and the West*, I, part 2 (London, 1957), survey the general status of millets up to the nineteenth century in chapter 14.

menian was worried about any possible increase of Greek influence in the empire. Both enjoyed looking down on the Jewish millet as the least of the big three. What actual persecution the Jews suffered was due less to the Muslims than to the Christians of the empire.[15] How far the millet organization could be used for private political purposes is shown by a number of instances in the years immediately following the Hatt-ı Hümayun, when various individuals sought to shift from one millet to another for completely worldly reasons. Sometimes the motive was to escape clerical taxation, sometimes to conserve personal political influence, sometimes to gain the support given to members of a particular millet by a foreign power. When, for instance, four Gregorian Armenian *çorbacı*'s who had been exploiting the populace ran up against a reforming bishop, they claimed to turn Protestant. A Gregorian Armenian bishop who was in danger of being disciplined or despoiled by a superior turned Catholic and remained under French consular protection until the danger was past.[16]

Since the non-Muslim millets were in fact so political in character, the Porte could reform them without prejudice to religious freedom or to the purely ecclesiastical prerogatives of the patriarchs. The hope was that, by diluting the clerical control, some of the tyranny and corruption could be rooted out and some of the intersectarian warfare eliminated. The Greek and Armenian millets were the chief objects of the Porte's concern; they were by far the largest, and most in need of reform.[17] The Jewish millet was less so, partly because the grand

[15] Especially at Easter, because of an old superstition that at this time of year the Jews immolated a living Christian child. *Neue Freie Presse*, 3 April 1867; Boker to Fish, #43, 20 August 1872, USNA, Turkey 24; and a refutation of this superstition in M. Franco, *Essai sur l'histoire des Israélites de l'Empire ottoman* (Paris, 1897), pp. 220-233.

[16] These instances in ABCFM, Armenian Mission V, #298, 24 September 1859, and Central Turkey Mission, I, #238, end of 1860. Cf. other instances in *ibid.*, Armenian Mission VIII, #392, Tocat [Tokat] 1857 Report, and *Trowbridge's Diary*, p. 136; Henry J. Van Lennep, *Travels in Little-Known Parts of Asia Minor* (London, 1870), II, 176-177; Henry Harris Jessup, *Fifty-Three Years in Syria* (New York, 1910), I, 53, 242-245.

[17] The Greek Orthodox numbered about 6,600,000 at mid-century and the Gregorian Armenians some 2,400,000. The Jews, third in importance, were far behind, with perhaps 150,000. These figures follow Ubicini, *Letters*, I, 18-26, and II, 174 and 299. Other religious communities had been recognized by the Porte before 1860, although they were small and did not possess such extensive powers: Armenian Catholics, Latin Catholics, and Protestants. To these Ubicini and Pavet de Courteille, *Etat présent de l'Empire ottoman* (Paris, 1876), pp. 187-189, add Greek uniates (Melkites) (1847) and Bulgar uniates (1861). These smaller communities were newly organized and not in serious need of reform, except for the Armenian Catholics,

rabbi, although his civil powers were commensurate with those of the Greek and Orthodox patriarchs, was not at the head of an ecclesiastical hierarchy as they were. But in all three of the major millets there arose by mid-century strong protests against the existing order. The protests were voiced by bourgeois laymen, usually by artisans who were members of the various *esnaf*'s, or trade gilds, and by some of the more enlightened professional men. The Porte, while trying to appease all interests within the millets, favored the agitation for reform. It was in the Armenian millet that the reform movement first spread extensively, and here also that the most significant changes were achieved with the elaboration of a written constitution.

Until the last years of Mahmud II's reign, management of the affairs of the Gregorian Armenian millet was nominally in the hands of the patriarch of İstanbul and of the highest clergy. The patriarch, while subordinate in spiritual matters to the Catholicos of Echmiadzin and Catholicos of Sis, was the independent head of the civil administration for members of his church in the Ottoman empire. But in actuality the patriarchate of İstanbul had come to be dominated by some two hundred members of the wealthy urban aristocracy, known as the *amira*. A split in this group occurred over the question of an Armenian college established in İstanbul in 1838, and this opened the way for greater influence of the artisans in community affairs. On one side of the split were the *sarraf*'s, or moneylenders, bankers, and great merchants; on the other side were those Armenian notables who held such official Ottoman posts as imperial architect, director of the mint, and superintendent of the imperial powder works. The artisans allied themselves with the latter group, in support of the college. When the bankers withdrew their support from the college, a financial board of twenty-four artisans was established by the patriarch to manage millet finances. They had insufficient financial strength. Despite intervention by the Porte, which resulted in an imperial edict of 1841 confirming an elected council of tradesmen in control of civil affairs, the artisans still could not manage without the financial sup-

---

who were badly split after 1869 over the question of control from Rome raised by the bull Reversurus and the dogma of papal infallibility. This so-called Hassunist controversy caused the Porte endless trouble for a few years thereafter.

port of the bankers, and had to surrender their administrative rights in the following year.[18]

The turmoil induced by this schism on civil administration of the community was alleviated when a new patriarch, Matteos, succeeded in 1844 in forming a combined council of tradesmen and bankers. But the continued domineering attitude of the *sarraf*'s, especially their pretensions to influence in the election of provincial bishops, forced Matteos to champion the rights of the artisans. In 1847 he created two councils, one civil and one ecclesiastical, to manage millet affairs. This the Porte sanctioned by ferman. Bankers and artisans were about equally balanced on the civil council. The patriarch presided over both councils, and a lay logothete was appointed to carry on business with the Porte. This system endured for some ten years.[19]

Meanwhile the Armenian community was beginning to be affected by a cultural renaissance. There had already been in the eighteenth century a revival of classical Armenian learning, centered in the Mekhitarist monastery at Venice. As the nineteenth century wore on, the written language began to approach the vernacular. The vernacular Armenian Bible of the American missionary Elias Riggs was one of the harbingers of the movement. A more popular literature arose following the work of Kachadur Abovian (d. 1848). The Mekhitarist fathers took to nonreligious subjects. In the 1840's the Armenian press began to expand and to turn from the classical church language to the vernacular. *Massis,* the most important Armenian journal of İstanbul, was founded in the next decade by Garabed Utujian. The secular and vernacular literature, together with the concomitant growth of national consciousness, was the first of three influences which were to strengthen the position of the lay reformers of the millet.[20]

Utujian was representative of a new element which introduced modern French ideas to the Ottoman Armenians. He and other Armenian intellectual leaders of the rising generation had lived and studied in Paris in the 1840's, and some had been there in the exciting times of

[18] Leon Arpee, *The Armenian Awakening: A History of the Armenian Church, 1820-1860* (Chicago, 1909), pp. 173-181.

[19] Arpee, *Armenian Awakening,* pp. 182-183; Malachia Ormanian, *L'Eglise arménienne* (Paris, 1910), p. 72; Young, *Corps de droit,* II, 77; Esat Uras, *Tarihte Ermeniler ve ermeni meselesi* (Ankara, 1950), pp. 159-160.

[20] A. O. Sarkissian, *History of the Armenian Question to 1885* (Urbana, Ill., 1938), pp. 118-120, 133-134; H. J. Sarkiss, "The Armenian Renaissance, 1500-1863," *Journal of Modern History,* IX (December 1937), 437-438; Prince M. Dadian, *La société arménienne contemporaine* (Paris, 1867), pp. 31ff.

the 1848 revolution and the second republic. Paris became the center for the progressive intellectuals, who on their return home were known as the Loussavorial, the enlightened ones, as opposed to the Khavarial, or obscurantists. Among the Loussavorial were Nigoghos Balian, of the family of architects; Nahabed Rusinian, author of a textbook on philosophy; Garabed Utujian; Krikor Agaton; and others whose names became household words in the history of Armenian reform. It was said that in Paris Balian and Rusinian sketched the preliminary lines of the coming Armenian constitution.[21]

From the Protestant missions came a third influence which affected Armenian reform. At about the time when the artisan element was beginning to bestir itself, American and English missionaries started to work among the Armenians of the capital and in Anatolian centers. The number of converts was probably not over five thousand.[22] But the influence of the missions was far greater than the mere number of conversions would indicate. As has been seen, some Gregorian Armenians looked to Protestantism for political reasons. When in 1850 the Protestants, with strong backing from the British ambassador, secured a separate millet status by imperial ferman, the manner in which they proceeded to organize the community furnished an example to the Gregorian church.[23] The Protestant millet was from the start based on the representative principle and on lay control. In 1851 a popular assembly at İstanbul provided for the election of thirteen representatives to manage community affairs, to choose an executive committee, and to select the *vekil* ("agent") authorized by the Porte as the civil head of the millet. Shortly after the Hatt-ı Hümayun a tentative Protestant constitution was drawn up and submitted to a popular assembly. The constitution dealt only with civil affairs: it provided for a representative assembly which should control the budget, appoint an executive committee from its own membership, and elect

---

[21] Macler, *Autour de l'Arménie*, pp. 230-231, condensing from Mikael Varandian, *Haygagan Sharjuman Nakhapalmouthiun* (The Origins of the Armenian Movement) (Geneva, 1912), I; Sarkissian, *Armenian Question*, pp. 120-121; K. J. Basmadjian, *Histoire moderne des arméniens* (Paris, 1917), pp. 78-80; Uras, *Tarihte Ermeniler*, pp. 153-154, quoting from Saruhan, *The Armenian National Assembly* (in Armenian) (Tiflis, 1912), pp. 5-12 (?).

[22] Ubicini, *Etat présent*, p. 226. Some estimates are rather higher: Noel Verney and George Dambmann, *Les puissances étrangères dans le Levant en Syrie et Palestine* (Paris, 1900), p. 25; Young, *Corps de droit*, II, 107.

[23] Ferman in *ibid.*, pp. 108-109. An earlier Protestant charter, vezirial rather than imperial, of 1847 in William Goodell, *Forty Years in the Turkish Empire*, ed. by E. D. G. Prime, 5th ed. (New York, 1878), p. 483. Cf. Uras, *Tarihte Ermeniler*, p. 156.

the *vekil,* who had to be a layman. The Protestant rules for the conduct of millet business were printed up and distributed in Turkish and Armeno-Turkish, and apparently exercised some influence on the reform movement in the Gregorian millet. There was also a negative influence which came from the Protestant organization—the Gregorian patriarchs realized that increased lay participation in the direction of their millet affairs would be necessary to forestall further defections to Protestantism.[24]

Strengthened by the literary renaissance, the influx of French political ideas, and the Protestant example, the leading bourgeois of the Gregorian millet began to work seriously for a constitution. The principal leadership came from some of the French-trained intellectuals who were members of an educational committee formed in 1853. Before the constitution took its final form, ten years later, it went through four or five committees and three drafts, meeting at each stage opposition from the moneylending magnates. A draft of 1857, accepted by a millet assembly, had a life of two months. A new draft, prepared by a committee on which Krikor Odian, Rusinian, Servichen (Serovpe Vichenian), and others of the new intellectuals were prominent, was adopted on June 5, 1860, by another general assembly and actually was put into operation for sixteen months. Further strife within the millet between the Loussavorial and the Khavarial caused the Porte to suspend operation of the constitution in October 1861. Then the Ottoman government itself appointed a committee of Armenians, which included clergy, officials, and some intellectuals, to revise the 1860 draft. In February of 1862 Âli Paşa, the minister of foreign affairs, sent a formal communication to the acting patriarch Stepan, requiring that the civil and ecclesiastical councils of the millet elect a seven-man committee to review the amended draft with the Porte-appointed committee.[25] This was done, and a joint report was drawn up for the Ottoman government.[26] Final approval of the revised constitution was not immediately forthcoming from the Porte, and in the interval impatient Armenians, presumably tradesmen,

---

[24] Arpee, *Armenian Awakening,* pp. 190-191, n.; ABCFM, Western Turkey Mission II, #260, 28 February 1860; H. G. O. Dwight, *Christianity Revived in the East* (New York, 1850), pp. 37, 53-56, 146-149.

[25] Text in Uras, *Tarihte Ermeniler,* pp. 161-162, and in Arshag Alboyajian, "Azkayin Sahmanaterouthiun," *Entertzag Oratzoytz sourp Perkechian Hivantonotzy Hayotz* (1910), p. 400.

[26] Text in H. F. B. Lynch, *Armenia: Travels and Studies* (London, 1901), II, 446-448.

stormed the patriarchate and broke the furniture. Turkish troops were sent to keep order. Finally, the official approval was accorded on March 29, 1863, the assembly of 1860 was reconvened to accept the constitution, and it appointed a committee to supervise the execution of the provisions. Thus was the Armenian millet launched on its constitutional life.[27]

The constitution maintained the patriarchate and the civil and ecclesiastical councils, but subordinated them to a general assembly, which was the kernel of the new organization.[28] This assembly elected the patriarch and the two councils. The patriarch was still the medium of communication between the millet and the Porte, but had to account to the assembly for his actions and was paid a fixed stipend. Through the councils the assembly controlled all Armenian affairs. The religious council was concerned with dogma, religious education, and ordination of clergy. The civil council operated chiefly through a number of standing committees appointed to look after education, hospitals, millet property, finance, justice, and the like. Final control of all these committees was, of course, vested in the general assembly.

In this organizational scheme the composition of the assembly was fundamental. Of its hundred and forty members, only twenty were clergymen; here was a real victory for the lay element. The İstanbul bourgeoisie also secured a dominant position, with a disproportionately large representation in the assembly.[29] Eighty of the lay deputies and all the ecclesiastical deputies were elected from the capital; the prov-

[27] On drafting and acceptance of the constitution: Alboyajian, "Azkayin Sahmanaterouthiun," pp. 389, 396-404; Uras, *Tarihte Ermeniler*, pp. 161-165; Arpee, *Armenian Awakening*, pp. 184-185; Basmadjian, *Histoire moderne*, pp. 77-81; Macler, *Autour de l'Arménie*, pp. 115-119; Dadian, *Société arménienne*, pp. 21-23; Sarkissian, *Armenian Question*, pp. 120, 127; Ormanian, *Eglise arménienne*, pp. 72-73.

[28] Text of the constitution (*Sahmanaterouthiun*, and entitled in the Turkish version *Ermeni Patrikliği Nizamatı*, "Regulations of the Armenian Patriarchate") in Lynch, *Armenia*, II, 448-467. Young, *Corps de droit*, II, pp. 79-92, gives a defective version, with omissions, and an error on p. 88 indicating that all members of the general assembly were clergymen. *Düstur*, II, 938-961, gives the text but omits the preamble. Summaries in Uras, *Tarihte Ermeniler*, pp. 167-174; Dadian, *Société arménienne*, pp. 23-27; Télémaque Tutundjian, *Du pacte politique entre l'Etat ottoman et les nations non musulmanes de la Turquie. Avec un exposé de la Constitution arménienne de 1863* (Lausanne, 1904), pp. 61-104.

[29] Of 2,400,000 Armenians in the empire, the capital had about 180,000: Ubicini, *Etat présent*, p. 202, n.3. The estimates vary, as usual. Lorenz Rigler, *Die Türkei und deren Bewohner* (Vienna, 1852), I, 141, gives 250,000, citing an 1846 census; Sarkis Atamian, *The Armenian Community* (New York, 1955), p. 44, approves 135,000.

inces, therefore, had only two sevenths of the total representation for more than nine tenths of the Armenian population. Perhaps this was justified by the lack of advanced political consciousness among the provincial Armenians. The electorate was restricted to those who paid a basic millet tax; males were not mentioned, but presumably female suffrage was not even considered. In İstanbul election was direct, but based upon a list of candidates prepared by an electoral council in each quarter, which amounted almost to election at two degrees. In the provinces election was really at three degrees, for the delegates to the national assembly were chosen by provincial assemblies which had already been elected on the basis of lists prepared by local councils.

The provincial governments were constituted like the central, with a metropolitan elected by the provincial assembly at the head of each. The lay element was dominant in these assemblies also. The various provincial committees were responsible to their counterparts in İstanbul. Taxation was based on the ability to pay, and the proceeds were devoted in part to local, in part to the central administration. All in all, the Armenian millet constitution, despite lack of clarity on some points and lack of detail on the provincial organization, was a fairly sophisticated document setting up reasonably complex but workable machinery. As its preamble emphasized, the representative principle was fundamental.

Difficulties arose in the early years of parliamentary government in the Armenian millet. The constitution had been a heavy blow to the magnates of İstanbul and destroyed the clerical control of the millet which the magnates had operated to their advantage. But public interest in voting, even in the capital, was hard to arouse; the first elections in İstanbul brought out only a small number of eligible voters. The Porte had to see that the constitution was carried out, and suspended it for three years following 1866 when the civil and ecclesiastical councils fell into disagreement. But from 1869 until 1892, when tension between the Ottoman government and the Armenians mounted, the constitution functioned and the general assembly met regularly. In this period the voice of the provincial Armenians was more clearly heard in the assembly, despite their underrepresentation. A committee of the assembly collected and examined complaints from the provinces and the peasantry, and submitted to the Porte recommendations on tax reforms, on curbing Kurdish depredations, and on stricter control by the Ottoman government over the acts of provincial officials.[30]

In the Greek millet reform was slower in making its appearance than in the Armenian community.[31] This was in part due to the fact of less agitation among the Greek laymen. Probably the majority of politically conscious Greeks in the empire were more interested in the old dream of the *megale idea*—the grand concept of reviving the Byzantine Empire—than in millet reform as such.[32] Further, the Bulgarian communicants were interested in an autocephalous national church rather than in mere reform under the İstanbul patriarch. The patriarchate, in turn, was probably more concerned to keep its grip on the Bulgars and not to lose this portion of the ecclesiastical income, especially since Orthodox church properties in the Roumanian principalities, which also produced a considerable revenue, were about to slip from the patriarch's control. But the Greek patriarch of İstanbul was still the most powerful figure among all the non-Muslims of the empire, and his reluctance to weaken this position was also among the causes for the slowness of Greek reform.

Although the Greek church within the empire was not organized into a single ecclesiastical hierarchy, the patriarch of İstanbul was vastly more influential than the spiritual chiefs of the other autocephalous Greek churches. The patriarchs of Alexandria, Antioch, and Jerusalem headed territories which were less extensive and less wealthy, and the autocephalous church of Cyprus was confined to that island alone. The most important distinction was, of course, that the Ottoman sultans had conferred on the İstanbul patriarch alone the

---

[30] Arpee, *Armenian Awakening*, pp. 190-192; Macler, *Autour de l'Arménie*, p. 129; Sarkissian, *Armenian Question*, pp. 35-39; Uras, *Tarihte Ermeniler*, pp. 178-182; Atamian, *Armenian Community*, pp. 32-41.

[31] Although in the Greek church of Cyprus there seems to have been an early and partly effective reform movement in the 1830's that included some degree of representative government. Cf. George Hill, *A History of Cyprus* (Cambridge, 1940-1952), IV, 153-155, 204-205, 367-368.

[32] This sentiment seems to have taken an upsurge in connection with the revolution of 1862 in Greece: Morris to Seward, #33, 6 November 1862, USNA, Turkey 17; Henry G. Elliot, *Some Revolutions and other Diplomatic Experiences* (London, 1922), pp. 117, 121, 128. Cf. Nassau W. Senior, *A Journal Kept in Turkey and Greece* (London, 1859), pp. 205-206. In 1862 the Porte imposed a censorship on books and periodicals imported from abroad, because of anti-Ottoman propaganda sent in by Russians and by Greeks living abroad: Morris to Seward, #35, 11 November 1862, and #36, 27 November 1862, the latter enclosing Âli's note, USNA, Turkey 17.

supreme civil authority over all Greek Orthodox peoples in the empire, even though canonically he was only *primus inter pares*. In the exercise of these, as well as his spiritual, powers the patriarch was assisted by a synod of archbishops. With the synod he had powers of jurisdiction in all cases between members of the millet except in criminal actions; he had also powers of taxing for church support, and of appointment and destitution of bishops under his control. Each bishop, in turn, had powers similar to those of the patriarch, and a council to assist him. At the base of the hierarchy was the village or parish organization. Here the adult males gathered annually on St. George's Day to elect several elders and a *kocabaşı* to manage local community affairs. The last-named individual administered the finances of church and school, collected ecclesiastical revenues, exercised minor judicial functions, and also after Mahmud II's time collected the tax in lieu of military service, the proceeds of which he forwarded to the Porte through bishop and patriarch. The patriarch was elected by the synod and a vaguely defined assembly of Greek notables and members of the trade gilds. But actually, since the mid-eighteenth century, the effective power not only of selecting the patriarch but of administering millet affairs was in the hands of five metropolitans, the *gerontes*, who were members of the synod. These, like the Armenian magnates, had a vested interest in forestalling any increase in democratic lay influence within the millet administration.[33] The Porte had already failed in 1847 in an effort to add three lay members to the all-powerful synod.[34]

Since the reform movement was not nearly so self-generating within the Greek millet as in the Armenian, the Porte had to apply continued pressure after the proclamation of the Hatt-ı Hümayun of 1856. The synod was opposed to application of the reform promises in the *hat*. The patriarch ostensibly professed himself in 1856 favorable to a separation of temporal and spiritual matters and to stated salaries for the hierarchy, but was afraid of the intrusion of the lay

[33] F. Eichmann, *Die Reformen des osmanischen Reiches* (Berlin, 1858), pp. 19-39, and Ubicini, *Letters*, II, 118-142, 175-193, describe the mid-century organization. See Papadopoullos, *Studies and Documents*, pp. 48-60, for evolution of the synod, and Jacques Visvisis, "L'administration communale des Grecs pendant la domination turque," (*L'Hellénisme Contemporain*), *1453-1953: Le cinq-centième anniversaire de la prise de Constantinople* (Athens, 1953), pp. 221-235, on the basic village organization.

[34] Karl Beth, *Die orientalische Christenheit der Mittelmeerländer* (Berlin, 1902), p. 16.

element into the management of millet affairs.[35] The next year the Porte found itself obliged to send a note to the patriarch prescribing the rules for selecting a provisional committee to work out a constitution and mentioning also the most important features which the constitution should possess.[36] The deliberations of this committee were interrupted by the stubborn opposition of the five *gerontes*, and the Porte was eventually forced to order their return to their respective dioceses.[37] With this obstacle removed, the committee produced a series of laws between 1860 and 1862 which, taken cumulatively, were the equivalent of the more formal constitution elaborated by the Armenians.[38]

Clerical control remained much stronger in the new Greek organization than in the Armenian. There was no permanent general assembly, but only a body convened especially for patriarchal elections. In this assembly the lay element was a large majority, and had specifically to include one banker, five merchants, ten artisans, four professional men, eight public officials, the members of the new mixed council, and twenty-eight representatives of the provincial bishoprics. Three names of candidates for the patriarchate were selected by this assembly from a list prepared by the bishops, to which additions might then be made. Ultimate selection of the patriarch was by the clerical members of the assembly alone, from among the three final candidates. The Porte reserved the right to strike from the original list any candidate of whom it disapproved. The patriarch, once he was selected and confirmed by the Porte, carried on millet administration with a synod and a mixed council. There was no purely civil council such as the Armenians set up, and in questions to be decided by the two councils sitting together the clergy were in a majority. The synod per se was concerned with dogma and ecclesiastical discipline. Its

[35] Prokesch to Buol, #22F, 13 March 1856, HHS, XII/56; Edouard Engelhardt, *La Turquie et le Tanzimat* (Paris, 1882-1884), I, 147-148.
[36] Text in L. Petit, "Règlements généraux de l'église orthodoxe en Turquie," *Revue de l'Orient chrétien*, III (1898), 397-401; also I. de Testa, *Recueil des traités de la Porte ottomane avec les puissances étrangères* (Paris, 1864-1911), V, 170.
[37] Beth, *Orientalische Christenheit*, pp. 12-13; Petit, "Règlements généraux," pp. 403-404.
[38] Text of the Greek organic laws (*Kanonismoi*, and entitled in the Turkish version *Rum Patrikliği Nizamatı*, "Regulations of the Greek Patriarchate," which is more accurate than the similar title for the Armenian constitution) in *ibid.*, pp. 405-424, and *ibid.*, IV (1899) pp. 228-246; also *Düstur*, II, 902-937. Young, *Corps de droit*, II, 21-34, is less complete. Summaries in Beth, *Orientalische Christenheit*, pp. 13-38; Ubicini, *Etat présent*, pp. 191-196; and F. van den Steen de Jehay, *De la situation légale des sujets ottomans non-musulmans* (Brussels, 1906), pp. 96-107.

membership of twelve was rotated among the seventy-odd bishops, so that none might obtain overmuch power; the system was automatic rather than electoral. The mixed council supervised finances, schools, hospitals, and functioned as a court of appeal. It was composed of four bishops from the synod and eight laymen. In the election of the latter, only the Greeks of Istanbul and its suburbs had a voice, and they alone were eligible for council membership. The election was at two degrees: Istanbul residents voted for members of an electoral college, which chose the lay councillors. Provincial government also was far less developed than in the Armenian system. All bishops were appointees of the central synod, which could proceed without regard to the public opinion of the diocese affected. There were no provincial assemblies; most of the power remained in the bishop's hands. All salaries were regulated by law, excepting that the lowest clergy were continued on the vicious system of living on fees.

Perhaps the small degree of popular participation allowed by the Greek organic laws was more in keeping with the mentality of the period than the more extensive lay participation and suffrage of the Armenian constitution. The Greek reorganization did break the power of the *gerontes*, did provide that the synod should not have a vested interest in corruption, and did lay down specific financial rules. These were not always observed, since bishops still paid considerable sums to the patriarch on investiture and the patriarch still did the same to the Porte for his investiture.[39] But corruption seemed to be on the wane, and the sinecures in the Istanbul patriarchate, long a sore on the millet organization, existed no longer. What remained chiefly to correct was the ignorant and penniless condition of the lower clergy.[40]

The Jewish millet also acquired a new constitution in this period. Like the Armenian community a few years before, in the early 1860's the Jews of the capital were torn by bitter argument over the subjects to be taught in a Jewish school. A progressive lay element, led by the richest of the Istanbul notables, was opposed by a conservative rabbinical group. Their dispute came to a head in 1862 and 1863.[41]

[39] Dumont, *Le Balkan*, p. 371; Elliot to Derby, #324, confidential, 30 March 1876, FO 78/2456; C. D. Cobham, *The Patriarchs of Constantinople* (Cambridge, 1911), p. 36.

[40] Beth, *Orientalische Christenheit*, pp. 29-33, 35-38.

[41] Franco, *Essai*, pp. 162-166; Abraham Galanté, *Histoire des Juifs d'Istanbul*

The grand vezir Fuad Paşa had to intervene not only to restore order, but to order compliance with the millet reform stipulated in the Hatt-ı Hümayun. Upon the election of Yakir Gueron as locum tenens of the grand rabbinate, he was told by the Porte to convene a commission of lay and spiritual leaders to elaborate a constitution for the Jewish community.[42] This was done, and the constitution was approved by the Porte in 1865.[43]

As did the Armenian constitution, so also the Jewish represented a victory for the laymen. The *hahambaşı*, or grand rabbi, remained civil head of the millet under the new instrument, as well as spiritual head of the region of İstanbul. But he was powerless to act without the consent of the two councils, spiritual and civil, created by the constitution, and he received a fixed salary. Both councils were elected by a general assembly of eighty, composed of twenty rabbis and sixty laymen elected by the Jews of İstanbul and its suburbs. The general assembly also elected the grand rabbi, from a list of candidates controlled by the rabbis; for this election forty delegates from the provinces were added to the assembly. The whole constitution bore a strong resemblance to the Armenian instrument approved two years before, except that the latter was more complete. The Jewish millet was unlike the Armenian and Greek in that it had no clerical hierarchy. Since each local community organized itself and selected its rabbi, the grand rabbi of İstanbul exercised no absolute spiritual authority except over the Jews of the capital. The constitution, therefore, provided no provincial organization, and only İstanbul was represented in the normal general assembly. But the Porte recognized the grand rabbi as civil chief of the millet throughout the empire, and he was the channel of communication between provincial communities and the Ottoman government—hence the addition of provincial delegates to the electoral assembly.

For a few years immediately following the elaboration of the constitution, the affairs of the Jewish millet ran smoothly. But then a revival of rabbinical influence threatened the domination of the pro-

---

(İstanbul, 1941), I, 31, 76, 130-131, largely following Franco; Young, *Corps de droit*, II, 144-145.

[42] Text of the Porte's notes in Franco, *Essai*, p. 167, and Young, *Corps de droit*, II, 145-146. Cf. Galanté, *Histoire*, I, 131-133, 230-232.

[43] Text of the constitution in Young, *Corps de droit*, II, 148-155; *Düstur*, II, 962-975, entitled *Hahamhane Nizamatı*, "Rabbi Office Regulations." Summaries in Ubicini, *Etat présent*, pp. 206-208, and Steen de Jehay, *Situation légale*, pp. 349-355.

gressives, and the leader of the reformers, Abraham Camondo, left
İstanbul for Paris. Further, no grand rabbi was elected according to
the constitutional provisions, and a locum tenens continued in office.
Financial distress was caused both by extravagance on his part and by
the small return from the various millet capitation and excise taxes.
Some of the congregations in the provincial cities also had their own
difficulties with corruption in the rabbinate. Up to the time of Abdülhamid's accession the Jewish millet had not solved its administrative
problems under the new order.[44]

The effect of these changes in the organization of the major non-
Muslim millets is hard to assess. None of the three constitutions operated smoothly, but difficulties were to be expected with any such
innovation. Corruption within the millets was no more wiped out
than it had been in the empire as a whole by the reform efforts up to
this point. There was perhaps less of it, and the stipulation in each
constitution of fixed salaries for the higher clergy might have been
expected to produce some improvement. The intersectarian warfare
was not perceptibly abated. As for the Porte's hope that separatist
tendencies on the part of the minority peoples might be checked and
foreign interference in their behalf diminished, it simply went un-
fulfilled. This was so despite the fact that the Porte could rebuff such
interference on individual occasions, as in 1868 when the Catholicos of
Echmiadzin attempted on Russian inspiration to send a legate to
İstanbul in imitation of the Pope's legate. The Porte refused him,
with the statement that only the patriarch of İstanbul had authority
over Ottoman Armenians.[45] So far as the Greek millet was concerned,
it was ironic that just as the reorganization of this religious community
was completed, the emphasis in propaganda emanating from Russia
began to swing away from the old line of "Orthodox brethren" to
the new line of Panslavism, thus providing a new basis of appeal to
the Ottoman peoples of the Orthodox communion. These peoples
were receptive to such appeals simply because, like other minority
peoples within the empire, their national consciousness was fast developing. This national consciousness, ending up in a full-blown mod-

---

[44] Franco, *Essai*, pp. 180-190; Young, *Corps de droit*, II, 146; David S. Sassoon,
A History of the Jews in Baghdad (Letchworth, 1949), pp. 157-162.
[45] The Catholicos' letter and Porte's reply in FO 195/893, #426 and #427.
Cf. Engelhardt, *La Turquie*, II, 66-69.

ern nationalism, was obviously the greatest single impediment to the achievement of an Ottoman brotherhood which would wipe out separatist ambitions. The reorganization of the millets was powerless to halt the new feeling.

In fact, millet reorganization was involved in a double paradox. The first was this: that although the reorganization was intended to eradicate abuses, extend the principle of popular government, and increase the loyalty of minorities to the Ottoman state, the mere fact that the reorganization was along millet lines helped to reemphasize the lack of homogeneity among Ottoman peoples. The separate nature of the millet, simply because it was reformed as a millet, was confirmed. Even though the power of the clergy was lessened and some degree of secularization introduced, the lines of religious distinction between Ottoman peoples were retraced, not obliterated. Osmanlılık was not yet the universal creed, even on paper.[46] The second paradox followed from the millet reorganization itself: the increased lay participation in millet administration, and particularly the growing emphasis in all the non-Muslim communities on secular education, gave a new élan to nationalist feeling. The secular education tended naturally in this direction, as was true all over nineteenth-century Europe. This process would undoubtedly have taken place without any reorganization of the millets whatsoever, but the nature of the reorganization, as well as the impetus which came to it from the lay upheaval within the millets, seems to have speeded up the process. Press and schools among the Greeks, Armenians, and Jews of the empire expanded rapidly in the second half of the nineteenth century.[47] Greeks and Armenians, many of whom had completely lost their national languages and knew only Turkish, began to relearn them.[48] The Greeks already had the independent state of Greece, and the *megale idea*, to look to. From Greece came financial and diplomatic support in the later 1860's for new Greek-language schools and textbooks within the

[46] It is interesting that the millet reorganization made no change in the channel of relationships of the millet chiefs with the Ottoman government, which was principally through the minister of foreign affairs, although there were, on occasion, relations with other ministries also. It appeared as if the millets were considered to be foreign states. Only in 1878 was the practice changed to put relationships tacitly in the hands of the minister of justice: Sesostris Sidarouss, *Des patriarcats* (Paris, 1906), p. 282.

[47] Cf. Osman Ergin, *Türkiye maarif tarihi* (İstanbul, 1939-1943), II, 611-637, 651-666, on schools, foundations, and learned societies among these minorities.

[48] This was noted in the mid-sixties, just as the millet reorganizations were completed, by Van Lennep, *Travels*, I, 297, 299.

Ottoman Empire.[49] A new generation of Armenian revolutionaries began also to arise, rivalling the older group of Armenians on whom the Porte had relied a good deal in the years since the Greek revolt of 1821.[50] The Bulgars, of course, went their own way, not content with the Greek millet reform, and in 1870 obtained their own ex- archate as a way stage to national independence. The Turks were quite aware of the educational progress among the minority peoples, and some of them were also aware of its ultimate implications.[51] Their remedy was not to stop it, but to deflect it by establishing mixed schools for all Ottoman subjects and to help Turks themselves catch up in the educational world.

But the millet reorganization did not contribute to this. It pointed away from Osmanlılık in so far as secular education was permitted to increase within each millet. In fact, it might be argued that the old clerical obscurantism, which kept the mass of the non-Muslims in ignorance, was a better ally of continued Ottoman dominion, although not, of course, of Osmanlılık, than the new order in the millets. The joint committee on the Armenian constitution said in 1862 that the millet administration had an obligation to the imperial government "to preserve the nation in perfectly loyal subjection."[52] But such was not the result. Among the major non-Muslim communities, only the Jews were, in the long run, content to continue a dual allegiance to the Ottoman state and their own millet. They were simply in no posi- tion to entertain separatist ambitions. Ardent reformers among the Turks were profoundly annoyed at this continued attention of non- Muslims to millet interests instead of Ottoman interests. They looked to their own religious and nationalist aims, and were all wrapped up in "Greekism, Armenianism, Bulgarianism, . . . Orthodoxy, Hassun- ism, anti-Hassunism, Protestantism . . . ," complained Süleyman Paşa in 1876.[53]

When this lack of effectiveness of the millet reorganizations is con-

[49] Dumont, *Le Balkan*, pp. 368-369.
[50] On the rise of Armenian nationalism to 1876 see Sarkissian, *Armenian Question*, pp. 119-135; Macler, *Autour de l'Arménie*, pp. 235-236, 240-245, 272-273; Bas- madjian, *Histoire moderne*, pp. 124-129 and ff.; *Augsburger Allgemeine Zeitung*, 17 September 1876; *Aspirations et agissements révolutionnaires des comités arméniens* (Constantinople, 1917), pp. 35-36.
[51] There are a good many comments by Âli, Fuad, and the New Ottomans on this. Cf. also Ahmed Midhat, *Üss-i inkılâb* (İstanbul, 1294-1295), I, 119.
[52] Lynch, *Armenia*, II, p. 448.
[53] *Süleyman Paşa muhakemesi* (İstanbul, 1328), p. 76.

ceded, it still remains to assess the impact of this movement on the reform of the empire as a whole. This was probably greater than has usually been recognized. The reorganization potentially affected nearly nine million non-Muslims, almost a third of the empire's population if the tributary self-governing territories be excluded. Undoubtedly the new constitutions helped to prepare these peoples for more intelligent participation in the Ottoman elections and parliament as set up in the laws and constitution of 1876. Further, the millet reorganization must have influenced the thinking of some Ottoman statesmen. A number of high officials, including Âli and Fuad, were occupied with this problem for several years. Their insistent encouragement of millet reform, one suspects, may have focussed more of their attention on the two dominant trends observable in the reform—secularization of government and popular participation in government on some sort of representative principle. Âli and Fuad were, of course, already committed to a gradual divorce of religion from government; but one might surmise that their experience with millet reform confirmed this tendency, which found strong expression in Âli's memorandum of 1867 and Fuad's political testament of 1869.[54]

The written constitutions elaborated for each millet, and the general national assembly which each instrument created, contributed also to the adoption of a constitution for the whole empire in 1876. A good many Ottoman statesmen must have gained from this experience some familiarity with the concepts of written constitution, national parliament, and popular representation. It is dubious, as noted above, that Âli and Fuad deliberately set out to create the Armenian constitution as the prototype for a form of government later to be extended to the whole empire. But it can be shown that Midhat Paşa, the principal author of the 1876 constitution, was directly influenced by the Armenians. Krikor Odian Efendi, one of the authors of the Armenian constitution, was for years an adviser to Midhat, and himself participated in the discussions on the later Ottoman constitution.[55] Odian, Servichen, and others plied Midhat with constitutional arguments.[56] Namık Kemal, the most influential of the New Ottomans, and also himself a member of the drafting commis-

[54] See references to these in chapter III, above. Bertrand Bareilles, *Le rapport secret sur le Congrès de Berlin* . . . (Paris, 1919), p. 25, says that Dr. Servichen was the "éminence grise" of Fuad Paşa, but offers no evidence.

[55] See below, chapter X.

[56] Mikael Kazmarian, ed., *Krikor Odian* (Constantinople, 1910), I, xiv.

sion for the Ottoman constitution of 1876, referred as early as 1867 to the assemblies of the Christian millets which, he said, could serve as models for a chamber of deputies.[57] More such influence may have come through Krikor Agaton Efendi, another of the drafters of the Armenian constitution, who was the first non-Muslim appointed to a full ministerial post in the Ottoman government. The electoral provisions of 1876 reflected in some ways the millet constitutions, particularly in the system of indirect voting and in the special status accorded citizens of İstanbul.

The most immediate influence of the millet reorganization was on the reform of provincial administration which began one year after the Armenian constitution was put into effect. It may have been mere chance that the complicated electoral systems and councils of the millet and vilayet statutes were suggestive of each other. But there may again have been direct influence, since Fuad Paşa and Midhat Paşa were the principal authors of the new law for the provinces. Further, the extension of the representative principle in the make-up of provincial councils and general assemblies was likely to be more successful because the millet constitutions, particularly the Armenian, had lessened the tyrannical influence of the clergy who played so large a part in public life. Some of the clergy, who under the new provincial law were automatically to take seats in various local councils, were now elected by their people instead of appointed by the hierarchy. But the new provincial organization, of course, had a wider sweep because it affected all Ottoman subjects, not simply the non-Muslims. The problem had actively occupied the Ottoman ministers since Kıbrıslı Mehmed Paşa's inspection trip of 1860. In 1864 they turned their full attention to it.

---

[57] Namık Kemal's "Answer to the *Gazette du Levant*," text in Mithat Cemal Kuntay, *Namık Kemal* (İstanbul, 1944-1956), I, 185.

~~@ CHAPTER V @~~

PROVINCIAL GOVERNMENT: MIDHAT PAŞA AND
THE VILAYET SYSTEM OF 1864 AND 1867

A successful system of administering the provinces and their subdivisions was an absolute necessity if the Tanzimat were really to set the
empire on a new path. Millet administration was important, but it
concerned non-Muslims only. Central government was, of course,
supremely important, but most of the sultan's subjects had contact
with it only through its provincial proliferations. Ottoman statesmen
had been occupied with the problem of reorganizing provincial government ever since the breakdown of the Ruling Institution and the
system of fiefs, and had done a good deal of experimenting. Their
constant dilemma in the Tanzimat period was how to maintain centralized control over the far-flung empire while allowing sufficient
latitude and authority to local officials so that administration might
be efficient and expeditious. They sought also to represent in the
same organization the desires and needs of the heterogeneous elements of the population, contributing to the development of Osmanlılık and of representative institutions. The answer to these problems
in the period after the Hatt-ı Hümayun was a set of regulations, first
elaborated in 1864 and further developed in later years, known as
the vilayet law, from the new name given to the provinces. This grew
out of the experience and experiment of the years since Mahmud II.[1]

After Mahmud II's destruction of the *derebeyi*'s, the number of
eyalets had undergone some revisions and the status of some was, in
fact, different from that of others—Egypt and Tunis most promi-
nently. But there were always some thirty-odd of these provinces, each
centered on an important city.[2] Each was headed by a governor (vali)
whose authority increased or decreased according as the Porte tried to
give him latitude for the efficient conduct of business, or held a short
rein to assure his remaining under central control. In the 1840's the

---

[1] There seems to be no adequate study in any language of Ottoman provincial
administration and its actual workings in the nineteenth century. A systematic collection of the evidence would be useful.

[2] For lists of eyalets roughly about mid-century see Abdolonyme Ubicini, *Letters
on Turkey*, trans. by Lady Easthope (London, 1856), I, 14-18; Ahmed Rasim,
Istibdaddan hakimiyeti milliyeye (İstanbul, 1924), II, 101-106.

vali was subject to a double check of subordinate officials directly responsible to the Porte instead of to him and of the council (meclis) introduced by Reşid Paşa. This arrangement often succeeded only in impeding efficient administration, and it became fashionable for governors to say that "their hands were tied by the Tanzimat."[3] By 1852 the Porte realized that the governor needed greater authority, both to make his responsibility real and to avoid tedious reference of problems to İstanbul. A ferman of that year gave the vali more power over his subordinate officials and over the political subdivisions of the eyalet. Yet Fuad Paşa found in 1855 that the powers of the governor were still insufficient. When he was acting as commissioner at Janina (Yanya, Ioánnina) with extraordinary civil and military powers, he refused the request of a deputation of local Christian and Muslim notables that he stay on as vali. Later he explained his refusal on the ground that to accomplish anything the extraordinary powers were necessary; otherwise, were he an ordinary vali, his important memoranda would simply go into the brief case of the provincial accountant-general and rot there.[4] The trend toward decentralization of administrative authority was continued in regulations of 1858 which gave the vali further responsibility for the hierarchy of provincial officials below him and made him the local representative of all competent offices of the central government. This, of course, piled up work now centralized in the provincial capitals and slowed it down in the subdivisions.[5]

These changes in regulations seemed to have little effect in the provinces, where the problems that had heretofore existed continued to exist. Ömer Lûtfi Paşa's administration of the Baghdad eyalet just after the Crimean War furnishes instructive illustrations. Ömer was well-intentioned and fairly able. Yet he had trouble with corrupt subordinates, including wastrel efendis who were sons of a personal friend of his. He had trouble with local officials who speculated in commodities and sent bread and meat up to six and seven times their worth. He had trouble with Arab revolts against oppressive taxation caused by competitive bidding for the farm of taxes, with the resultant squeeze on the population. Ömer was driven to arbitrary actions, among them the exemplary execution of seven rebellious tribes-

[3] George P. Badger, *The Nestorians* (London, 1852), I, 362.
[4] Ali Fuad, *Rical-i mühimme-i siyasiye* (İstanbul, 1928), p. 152.
[5] Edouard Engelhardt, *La Turquie et le Tanzimat* (Paris, 1882-1884), I, 107; Sıddık Sami Onar, *İdare hukukunun umumî esasları* (İstanbul, 1952), pp. 551-552.

men without trial and without order from the capital—an act which he tried to justify with a covering *mazbata*, or minute, from his meclis. This act constituted the basis for his recall. Actually, political wire-pulling by rivals in the capital, a common phenomenon of the times, was instrumental in his destitution; Ömer's presents of fine Arab steeds to various high officials were in this instance unavailing. The vicious effect of these rivalries was often enhanced by the *kapıkâhyası*, the personal agent whom each vali maintained at the capital and through whom he communicated to the Porte. The *kapıkâhyası* often played a double game, condemning his own employer to enrich himself.[6] The governors themselves apparently made no direct annual reports to the Porte, since these were proposed as an innovation in the grand vezir's review of the provincial inspection tours of 1863.[7]

Much of the inefficiency and corruption in provincial administration was, of course, due to the manner in which governors were appointed and shifted about. Appointment was frequently the result of intrigue, influence, and bribery rather than of merit; sometimes it was simply a means to remove a politically influential man to a post of honorable exile far from the Porte. The governor was sent to a province about which he often knew nothing, where he would stay only briefly, and where he set about not only to recover his financial outlay but to support a mass of personal servants and hangers-on who were given official positions, though in reality they were members of the governor's own household. Since the positions were often unsalaried, fees and exactions levied on the people resulted. Provincial officials "lived off the air," dependent on income from fees and fines. Some subordinate officials, including those appointed directly from the capital, were salaried, but at a rate which made honesty and a reasonable standard of living incompatible. A certain amount of bribery and corruption was probably not inconsistent with reasonably good provincial government providing the officials were men who commanded respect and were not too often shifted, but by the mid-nineteenth century this was seldom the case. Even able governors were usually not long in one place,

[6] Dr. K. (Josef Koetschet), *Erinnerungen aus dem Leben des Serdar Ekrem Omer Pascha* (Sarajevo, 1885), pp. 47-120, recounts Ömer's governorship in Baghdad. Koetschet in Osman Pascha, *Der letzte grosse Wesier Bosniens* (Sarajevo, 1909), pp. 2-27, gives an account of Osman as vali in Bosnia in the 1860's. Cf. Hans Wachenhusen, *Ein Besuch im Türkischen Lager* (Leipzig, 1855), pp. 104-113, for a good account of the externals of the life and daily round of a vali in this period in Vidin.

[7] *Journal de Constantinople*, 13 August 1864.

and in addition to their salaries required "revenue under the door." The system affected provincial judges of the religious courts also, who were unsalaried and lived on fees.[8]

Under these conditions there appeared a popular longing for the old *derebeyi*, who had often been a fairly good governor in his district, better able to keep order than a transitory vali, and less interested in bleeding the people on whose continued prosperity his own future depended. In some regions of Anatolia there seems to have been a marked decline in prosperity after Mahmud II crushed the power of the local *derebeyi*; in other regions towns once ruled by *derebeyi*'s seemed still to be better off than those which had never known such an overlord. This seemed particularly to be so when members of the old *derebeyi* family were ensconced in official positions in the eyalet hierarchy, and continued to act somewhat independently of the Porte, their provincial seats "really not included in the charmed circle of the Tanzimat."[9] The only advantage of the vali over the *derebeyi* from the viewpoint of the local population was probably that the former, if he proved exceptionally bad, might be recalled by appeal to the sultan.[10]

[8] Ahmed Midhat, *Üss-i inkılâb* (İstanbul, 1294-1295), I, 97-102, a review of pre-1864 provincial administration, which admits improvement since 1800 or so; Ahmed Saib, *Vaka-i Sultan Abdülaziz* (Cairo, 1320), pp. 47-48; cf. the pre-nineteenth-century picture in H. A. R. Gibb and Harold Bowen, *Islamic Society and the West*, I, part 1 (London, 1950), 197-198, 205-207. Damad Mehmed Ali, navy minister and Abdülaziz's brother-in-law, was said to have accumulated great wealth from bribes soliciting his aid on provincial appointments: Morris to Seward, #27, 11 August 1862, and #35, 11 November 1862, USNA, Turkey 17. On salaries: Great Britain, *Parliamentary Papers*, 1861, vol. 67, *Accounts and Papers*, vol. 34, "Reports . . . condition of Christians in Turkey," #3, encl. 1; #4, encl. 1; #16, encl. 2. A special administrative problem existed in those areas where tribal groups resisted control. In the Kurdish area the Porte experimented rather unsuccessfully in these years with appointing tribal leaders or bandit chiefs to government office: Henry J. Van Lennep, *Travels in Little-Known Parts of Asia Minor* (London, 1870), I, 136, and II, 21-29; Frederick Millingen, *La Turquie sous le règne d'Abdul Aziz* (Paris, 1868), p. 21; idem, *Wild Life Among the Koords* (London, 1870), pp. 183-187; O. Blau, "Nachrichten über kurdische Stämme," *Zeitschrift der Deutschen Morgenländischen Gesellschaft*, 16 (1862), 625-626. But at least near Harput in 1872 the experiment seems to have brought order among the Kurds: Allen to Clark, 13 December 1872, ABCFM, Eastern Turkey Mission I, #121.

[9] Andreas D. Mordtmann, *Anatolien; Skizzen und Reisebriefe (1850-59)*, (Hannover, 1925), pp. 106, 109. Other information *ibid.*, pp. 34, 113-114, 482; Felix Kanitz, *Donau-Bulgarien und der Balkan* (Leipzig, 1875), I, 90; Pierre de Tchihatcheff, *Asie Mineure* (Paris, 1850), p. 44; Christine Belgiojoso, *Asie Mineure et Syrie* (Paris, 1858), pp. 3-11; E. Sperling, "Ein Ausflug in die isaurischen Berge," *Zeitschrift für Allgemeine Erdkunde*, Neue Folge 16 (1864), 55-57.

[10] Cf. Nassau W. Senior, *A Journal Kept in Turkey and Greece* (London, 1859), p. 22.

Though they were caught in a corrupt system, it is doubtful that the intellectual and moral character of individual provincial officials was lower at mid-century and after than it had been at any time in the recent past. One meets accounts of good, bad, and indifferent officials. But the great edicts of the Tanzimat in 1839 and 1856 and the various supplementary regulations and admonitions issued by the Porte carried the implication that now the machinery of government would be operated by an efficient and honest sort of civil service on the European model. Naturally this did not happen. Men brought up in old relationships determined by status, influence, and bribery did not suddenly become new-style civil servants. Some of the Stambuli efendis employed in provincial posts were, of course, half-westernized in costume, habits, and even habits of thought, but this did not necessarily mean an improvement in administration.[11] The Porte did try to train provincial officials below the rank of governor in a school set up for that purpose in 1859, along lines laid down by the Tanzimat Council. Here the students were exposed to a smattering of international and domestic law, economics, statistics, and other liberal disciplines in a course which, originally two years in duration, seems soon to have been extended to three or four years. The students' preparation for such study was meagre, and those who received the diploma were not always sent out to provincial posts. By 1864 at least fifteen graduates of this Mekteb-i Mülkiye were absorbed into the system of local government, and a number of other provincial officials were reappointed after completing a refresher course in the school.[12] But it is impossible to discover what impression, if any, such men made on provincial administration. Osman Paşa as governor of Bosnia set up two schools in his province—a secondary school and a "law school"—which produced most of his capable local officials.[13]

A large part of the difficulty in provincial administration arose from the way in which the meclis instituted by Reşid had worked out in prac-

---

[11] Cf. above, chapter I, pp. 32-35; G. Muir Mackenzie and A. P. Irby, *Travels in the Slavonic Provinces of Turkey-in-Europe* (London, 1866), pp. 55, 341-352.

[12] Osman Ergin, *Türkiye maarif tarihi* (İstanbul, 1939-1943), II, 495-502; Andreas D. Mordtmann, *Stambul und das moderne Türkenthum* (Leipzig, 1877-1878), I, 137; *Tanzimat*, I (İstanbul, 1940), 448; *Journal de Constantinople*, 13 August 1864. Some of the school's graduates evidently entered offices in the capital or in diplomatic missions abroad. Some of the graduates of a more general training course for government officials set up in 1862, the Mekteb-i Mahrec-i Eklâm, may also have gone into provincial service; cf. Ergin, *Maarif tarihi*, II, 397-400; Morris to Seward, 26 March 1862, USNA, Turkey 17.

[13] Koetschet, *Osman Pascha*, p. 4.

tice. This council, attached to each vali and to each governor of the subdivisions of the eyalet, was intended to represent the views of the governed and to apply a brake to the arbitrary acts of governors. It also sat as a court of justice. The council's sealed *mazbata* was required to sanction the governor's acts. Though experience with the meclis varied in different parts of the empire, the result was rarely satisfactory, and the abuses apparent in Reşid's time[14] continued unabated. Sometimes the council controlled the governor, having influence enough locally and in the capital to thwart the best-intentioned of administrators sent from İstanbul. Sometimes the governor could dominate the council, which became a rubber stamp for his actions. It sometimes happened that council members would sign any *mazbata* without reading it. Occasionally the governor even kept the seals of all the members. There were, to be sure, instances of able governors who could gain the co-operation of a meclis, or dominate it; but more usually it seems that the meclis served as a check on a good governor, and as an accomplice of a bad one. In Tokat there existed what was probably a common situation—an oligarchy of local notables controlled the administration of affairs, and to each of these notables a section of the populace contributed goods or services for protection. Against their influence İstanbul and its delegates were usually ineffectual.[15] This was representation of a sort, which undoubtedly in many instances helped to protect the interests of those who contributed to the notables, but it was not representation of a sort which would help to improve the processes of government and the progress of reforms. Because a position in the meclis carried no remuneration, men of no means could not sit on one except as paid creatures of some influential notable. The members of the meclis themselves sometimes became tax farmers through dummy representatives. Christians and Jews on the councils were no better than the Muslims. In most districts these minorities were underrepresented, and their delegates on the council sided with the Muslim majority either through parallel interest or through fear. But in some regions, as, for example, in some of the villages around İzmir, Christians were in majority control of the local councils and acted exactly as did their Muslim counterparts elsewhere. The Porte had never regulated election of the non-Muslim members of the meclis, and the power nat-

[14] See above, chapter I, pp. 48-49.
[15] Van Lennep, *Travels*, I, 159-60; cf. *Accounts and Papers*, 1861, vol. 34, #7, encl.

urally fell into the hands of the more powerful notables among them and of the clergy. For this reason the millet reorganization, in weakening the power of a corrupt clergy, was a useful preliminary to the reform of provincial administration. In sum, the meclis up to 1864 was not truly representative, and not a true instrument of progress. Muslim or Christian, it was invariably more retrograde than the officials sent out from İstanbul.[16]

The vilayet law of 1864 was aimed at correcting this situation in the provinces—at combining central control with local authority, at expediting the conduct of public business in the provincial capital, and at improving the representative quality of the meclis. The Hatt-ı Hümayun of 1856 had already promised that "steps will be taken for a reform in the composition of the provincial and communal councils to guarantee the sincerity of delegates of the Muslim, Christian and other communities and to guarantee freedom of voting in the councils." But until 1864 nothing was done along this line.

A number of influences which converged in the early 1860's help to explain the climate in which the new law was born, and probably the reasons for its elaboration at that point. One such influence was the series of provincial tours of inspection by Kıbrıslı Mehmed and by groups of imperial commissioners from 1860 on.[17] Four inspectors had gone out in 1863 with instructions to check on local officials, effect economies, inspect police and prisons and *vakıf* administration, advise on measures to improve communications and agriculture, and reform the conduct of the local councils and village notables. Though this was a large order, the inspection did accomplish something and produced suggestions on the reform of elections to the meclis which were studied in the Supreme Council of Judicial Ordinances at the

---

[16] Best descriptions of the meclis in this period are in *Accounts and Papers*, 1861, vol. 34, #3, encls. 1 and 2; #4, encl. 2; #5, encl. 7; #8, encl. 2; #9, encl.; #10, encl. 1; #13, encl.; #14, encl. 1; #15, encl. 1; #16, encl. 2; #20, encl. 2; #23, encls. 1 and 2, all of which are reports of British consuls dated in 1860. See also George Hill, *A History of Cyprus* (Cambridge, 1940-1952), IV, 206-209; Millingen, *La Turquie*, pp. 214-216; Mackenzie and Irby, *Travels*, pp. 257-258, 409; Sperling, "Ausflug," pp. 46-48; F. Eichmann, *Die Reformen des Osmanischen Reiches* (Berlin, 1858), p. 32; C. T. Newton, *Travels and Discoveries in the Levant* (London, 1865), I, 73-76; Ziya Bey in Hürriyet, #41 (21 zilhicce 1285), quoted in *Tanzimat*, I, 821.

[17] See above, chapter III, pp. 105-108.

capital, one section of which had already been concerned with the selection of competent local officials.[18]

It is likely also that the revision of the statute of the Lebanon by the Porte and the powers in conference in 1864 influenced both the form and the time of issuance of the vilayet law. Under a provisional law of 1861, established after the massacres of 1860, the Lebanon had been successfully administered by Garabed Artin Dâvud Paşa, a Roman Armenian, who was given wide powers as governor. Under the 1864 revision of the Lebanon's organic statute his powers were enlarged further, his meclis was made more representative of the various sects in the Lebanon, and the influence of the clergy in the government was held to a minimum. The revised statute was issued on September 6, 1864, just two months before the vilayet law was promulgated.[19] It is quite possible that the vilayet law was influenced not only by some of the terms of the Lebanon statute, but also by a desire on the part of the Porte to regulate the administration of its other provinces without the intervention of the European powers, to which it was obliged to agree in setting up the Lebanese administration.

The views of Fuad Paşa also exerted a major influence on the vilayet law. His general concern for holding the empire together had been reinforced by a number of experiences with wayward provinces in the decade before the law came into being. As special commissioner in Janina during the Crimean War he had to deal with separatist influences flowing from Greece; after the Crimean War he was negotiator on the matter of the Danubian principalities, which were rapidly slipping from the Ottoman grasp; in 1861 he had dealt, again as special commissioner, with the Lebanon in revolt. The governor of Egypt, Ismail, was also trying to make his province as independent of the sultan as possible, and Fuad in 1863 had direct experience of this as he, now briefly minister of war, accompanied Abdülaziz on a visit there. Fuad on this occasion distinguished himself by efforts to treat Ismail, despite Egypt's special status, as if he were just another

[18] The Tanzimat Council had been reintegrated with the Supreme Council in 1861, and the latter had been subdivided into sections: see below, chapter VII, p. 239. On the 1863 inspection: *Journal de Constantinople*, 13 August 1864; Morris to Seward, #59, 13 July 1863, USNA, Turkey 17.

[19] Text in George Young, *Corps de droit ottoman* (Oxford, 1905-1906), I, 140-149, and Grégoire Aristarchi, *Législation ottomane* (Constantinople, 1873-1888), II, 204-210.

vali; somewhat mischievously Fuad refused the horse assigned him but walked by Abdülaziz's stirrup, forcing the angry Ismail to forego his own mount and follow the example.[20] Fuad's ideas on the dangers of provincial separatism were set down in the letter of resignation as grand vezir which he handed to Abdülaziz in January 1863. Here he dwelt particularly on Serb, Greek, Bulgar, and Roumanian sedition, and the encouragement of this nationalist separatism by European powers.[21] Obviously stronger and more equitable provincial government seemed the remedy. And on the necessary measures for this sort of reform Fuad, who in June of 1863 was again grand vezir as the result of the imperial favor he regained while on the trip to Egypt,[22] was without doubt influenced by the activity of the governor of the eyalet of Nish, who was at that moment the most efficient and forward-looking of all Ottoman provincial governors, and much concerned also with combatting Balkan separatisms. It is reasonable to suppose that the grand vezir read carefully the reports sent from this turbulent province to İstanbul by the energetic governor.

This man was Ahmed Şefik Midhat Paşa, destined to achieve far greater stature than his administrative experience had so far given him. He had been born in 1822 in İstanbul, the son of a judge who had filled several posts in the Balkans. Midhat's education was, at the beginning, old-fashioned. At ten he was a *hafız*, one who knew the Koran by heart. In his teens he began as a clerk in government offices, studying Arabic and Persian at the same time. In the 1840's he served as secretary to a number of officials in the Asian provinces, including a stint with the inspection commissions. After 1850 he became specialized as a trouble shooter on provincial mission, first in Damascus and Aleppo to investigate the conduct of Kıbrıslı Mehmed Paşa there, then during the Crimean War in Edirne and surrounding Balkan areas to wipe out brigandage, then in Bursa on earthquake relief, then on an

---

[20] Ali Fuad, *Rical-i mühimme-i siyasiye*, pp. 165-166. Egypt's special status dated from 1841. Among other privileges was the right of the family of Mehmed Ali, to which Ismail belonged, to hereditary governorship of Egypt in the male line. Text of the ferman of 1 June 1841 in J. C. Hurewitz, *Diplomacy in the Near and Middle East* (Princeton, 1956), I, 121-123.

[21] Summary of the document in Ali Fuad, *Rical-i mühimme-i siyasiye*, pp. 163-164. Cevdet said that Fuad also wanted to give extensive powers to able governors in order to free the central administration from routine provincial business. See the quotation from his "Maruzat" in E. Z. Karal, *Islahat fermanı devri, 1861-1876* (Ankara, 1956), p. 153.

[22] Mehmed Memduh, *Mirât-ı şuunat* (İzmir, 1328), p. 32.

inspection commission in Vidin and Silistria. His provincial work was more and more concentrated in the Balkan area, interspersed with periods in the Porte. After the Crimean War, when he was about thirty-five, Midhat began the study of French. Most of those officials who knew French had studied it at a younger age, and Midhat was always at a disadvantage here; he never was completely at home in the language. In 1858 he took six months' leave and went to Europe for his own education, visiting Vienna, Paris, Brussels, and London.

It was in 1861 that Midhat was made vali of the eyalet of Nish, which was now clearly recognized as one of the potential trouble spots of the empire. The appointment came as the result of Kıbrıslı Mehmed's tour of the Balkan provinces in 1860, and Midhat was by experience and ability the logical man for the job, though it might be suspected also that the grand vezir, whom Midhat had investigated and ousted in Syria a decade earlier, was happy to put Midhat in a difficult position. In Nish Midhat was remarkably successful, particularly in keeping public order, suppressing brigandage, and building roads. He was always wary of Bulgarian nationalist sentiment, which was now beginning to grow and which found encouragement from groups across the frontiers of the autonomous Serb and Roumanian provinces. It was characteristic of Midhat that, while suppressing separatism, he customarily followed a practice in each locality of calling together notables, Muslim and Christian, to get their complaints and views on various matters, as well as agreement on a program of action. As a person Midhat already had developed a reputation for energy, brusque speech and decisive action, inclination toward westernization, Ottoman patriotism and suppression of separatism, but just treatment of minorities within the Ottoman framework, and for absolute honesty.[23] He was not a devout Muslim in the orthodox sense and was suspected of Bektashi leanings. Even clearer was his tendency toward secularism, much like that of liberal nineteenth-century Europe. "In forty or fifty years people will not build churches or mosques any more," he remarked a few years later, "but only schools and humanitarian institutions."[24]

[23] His honesty was fifteen years later impugned by Cevdet Paşa, who was, however, a personal antagonist, in the matter of using inside information to profit from the sale of Ottoman bonds: Ebül 'ulâ Mardin, *Medenî hukuk cephesinden Ahmed Cevdet Paşa* (İstanbul, 1946), pp. 131-132, n.113; the charge is not proven, and Midhat is defended on this question by Mithat Cemal Kuntay, *Namık Kemal* (İstanbul, 1944-1956), II, part 1, 347, n.23.

[24] In 1867, to the Ritter von Sax: *Geschichte des Machtverfalls der Türkei* (Vien-

Out of this atmosphere came the new law of 1864, worked out in consultation between the grand vezir Fuad and the provincial governor Midhat. Fuad telegraphed Midhat to return to İstanbul, where a special commission had already been formed to reconsider the methods of provincial administration. Working at night together on the project, and obviously with the French departmental regulations or a summary of them as reference, the two statesmen drafted a new law which was then approved by the whole council of ministers and promulgated by imperial irade as of November 8, 1864.[25]

By this law a revised hierarchy of provinces and subdivisions was established.[26] The name of the reorganized province was changed from eyalet to vilayet, an older term for "region" or "native country" that had sometimes been applied to provinces. Each vilayet was subdivided into a number of sancaks (sometimes also called "liva," a subdivision of the old eyalet), each sancak into kazas, and each kaza into *kariye*'s (either communes, or town quarters with at least fifty houses), and *nahiye*'s (groups of rural hamlets). Although the law was somewhat vague on the exact relationship of the *kariye* and *nahiye* to the higher

---

na, 1913), p. 376 n. On Midhat's early career and character: Ali Haydar Midhat, *Midhat Paşa: Hayat-ı siyâsiyesi*, vol. 1: *Tabsıra-i ibret* (İstanbul, 1325), pp. 3-23; idem, *The Life of Midhat Pasha* (London, 1903), pp. 32-38; İbnülemin Mahmud Kemal İnal, *Osmanlı devrinde son sadrıâzamlar* (İstanbul, 1940-1953), II, 315-318; Le duc Louis Antoine Léouzon, *Midhat Pacha* (Paris, 1877), pp. 6-33; Franz Babinger, "Midhat Pasha," *Encyclopaedia of Islam*, III, 481-482; M. T. Gökbilgin, "Midhat Paşa," *İslâm ansiklopedisi*, Cüz 82, pp. 270-271; Cyril E. Black, *The Establishment of Constitutional Government in Bulgaria* (Princeton, 1943), pp. 11-12; Mehmed Selaheddin, *Bir Türk diplomatının evrak-ı siyasiyesi* (İstanbul, 1306), pp. 167-170; Berissav Arsitch, *La vie économique de la Serbie du sud au dix-neuvième siècle* (Paris, 1936), pp. 31-32.

[25] A. H. Midhat, *Tabsıra-i ibret*, pp. 23-24, gives the best though brief account; also Ahmed Midhat, *Üss-i inkılâb*, I, 102-103. The author has nowhere found an authoritative statement that Fuad and Midhat actually had the French law in front of them as they worked. Napoleon III had recently enlarged the powers of prefects in the departments—a decentralizing move. In 1864 Alexander II inaugurated measures involving district assemblies that elected provincial councils (*zemstvo*'s), but there is probably no connection between Russian and Ottoman developments. Midhat claims to have worked out plans for provincial reorganization as early as the Crimean War period: A. H. Midhat, *Tabsıra-i ibret*, p. 7; idem, *Life*, pp. 34-35.

[26] Text of the law for the Tuna (Danube) vilayet of 7 Cemaziyelâhir 1281 (7 November 1864) in *Düstur* (İstanbul, 1282), pp. 517-536, and in I. de Testa, *Recueil des traités de la Porte ottomane* (Paris, 1864-1911), VII, 469-484, though evidently misdated in the latter. The law was slightly revised when it was made general in 1867; text in *Düstur*, I (İstanbul, 1289), 608-624; Testa, *Recueil*, VII, 484-493; Aristarchi, *Législation*, II, 273-295; Young, *Corps de droit*, I, 36-45 (defective). The revisions were largely concerned with the titles of provincial officials and elimination of special criminal courts. Because the changes were slight, and the 1867 titles of officials became general, the following discussion is based on the latter version of the law.

divisions, it represented, as a whole, a more integrated hierarchy than had hitherto existed, stretching from the sultan down to the rural community. Governors of the highest three divisions—vali, mutas-arrıf, and kaymakam respectively—were appointed by the sultan; only the headmen (*muhtar's*) of the communes were elected by the people, with two headmen for each "class of people," which presumably meant religious community or millet. Likewise other vilayet officials were named from the capital—those in charge of finance, correspondence, public works, and agriculture—but they had a curious double responsibility, both to the appropriate ministry in İstanbul and to the vali. Somewhat surprisingly, each vilayet had a functionary to see to the "foreign affairs" of the province, which meant treaty execution and liaison with consuls; he was nominated by the foreign minister in İstanbul. This hierarchy of officialdom represented a mixture of centralization and decentralization. There was popular selection of only the lowest officials, and all the other channels of authority led directly to the Sublime Porte. But in this chain of command the vali had wide powers, specified in the law, over police, political affairs, financial affairs, the carrying out of judicial decisions, and the execution of imperial laws. Viewed from İstanbul, this represented a decentralization of authority wherever the vali could act on his own initiative. Viewed from the provinces, this represented considerable centralization in the vilayet.

Alongside the hierarchy of appointive officials, the 1864 law set up also a hierarchy of councils attached to these officials, expanding the scope of the provincial meclis that Reşid had created and building on Midhat's experience in Nish. Now there was to be an administrative council (*meclis-i idare*) in each of the three top tiers, attached to the governor of each vilayet, sancak, and kaza. The law did not spell out the powers of the administrative council, but obviously it was a deliberative and advisory body which dealt with political, financial, and economic matters. Among the members of each council were local officials who took their seats ex officio—a fact which assured a majority of Muslims. But the representative principle was extended to all three levels of council, though in a peculiar fashion. In the councils of the sancak and kaza the local spiritual heads of the non-Muslim millets automatically had seats. This was an extension to lower levels of the principle that Reşid had inaugurated, while at the same time the former practice of seating such clerical chiefs on the vilayet council was discontinued. But in addition, and more significantly, the administrative council on each of the three levels was now to contain also some elected members: two Muslims and two non-Muslims on the vilayet and sancak councils; and three members, religion unspecified, for the kaza councils. This represented the first general extension of the elective and representative principles down into the lower divisions.

The electoral system itself, which the 1864 law also provided, was, however, a far cry from any true democratic concept. It was indirect and complex, reminiscent in some respects of the electoral system set up in the constitution of the Armenian millet the year before. The basis of the electoral system was the council of elders (*ihtiyar meclisi*) of each religious community in each commune. This council was no innovation in 1864, but had existed traditionally among both Muslims and Christians. Now it was directly incorporated into the administrative hierarchy of the empire as a whole. The councils of elders, by the law of 1864, automatically included the spiritual chiefs—imams and non-Muslim clergy—but a majority of the elders (the councils ran from three to twelve members) were elected annually by all Ottoman subjects of the locality over eighteen years of age who paid fifty piasters a year in direct taxes. Each council of elders served now as an electoral body to choose the elective members of the administrative council of the kaza. But they "elected" from a list prepared by the administrative officers of the kaza, which contained three times the requisite number of names, simply by eliminating one third of these. The list of twice the necessary number of names was then given to the mutasarrıf of the sancak, on the level above the kaza, who eliminated half the remaining names to make the final selection of the "elected" members of the kaza administrative council. The real choice thus rested with the administrative officers at all times. For election of members to the administrative councils of the sancak and the vilayet the same process was repeated, with each element—the nominating officials, the "electoral" councillors, and the determining voice of the governor—one step higher in the hierarchy. Under this system it was in the Porte itself that the final choice of elective members for the vilayet administrative council was made. To be eligible for membership in this, the most important *idare meclisi*, a candidate had to pay a yearly direct tax of at least five hundred piasters, which was in those days a considerable sum, but probably not out of line with property qualifications for voting in western European states of the day.

In this travesty on popular election there was only a shadow of democratic participation. The system was an improvement over that of Reşid's day, since the influence of non-Muslim clergy in the administrative councils was less and in the vilayet council was practically eliminated. This improvement had also been made in the Lebanon organic statute. But the combination of Turkish officials in each meclis, plus the determining voice of officials in choosing the "elected" members, meant that a Muslim majority was assured from vilayet down through kaza even in those Balkan regions where the Christian population was a great majority. For these reasons the law of 1864 has been severely criticized.[27] There were reasons, however, for this sort of system, even apart from the ever-present consideration of regard for sensitive Muslim opinion. A part of the cause for the indirect elective system lay simply in the lack of experience of the common people, the "foot-dust," in representative government. An equally important justification for the new system was the desire to avoid the corrupt meclis that had heretofore existed, by giving a preponderant voice to the Istanbul-appointed officials, whom experience had shown to be more forward-looking than the notables who had sat as "representative" members on the provincial meclis since the 1840's. The recent reform of the Armenian millet gave hope that provincial ecclesiastics of that church who sat ex officio on the lower councils would be more representative of their people than heretofore; the same was less likely for Greek bishops, who under the new millet constitution were still appointed by the patriarch.

Two other institutions inaugurated in the vilayet law were more nearly representative than the administrative councils, although elections to each were also controlled by the Porte's officials. One was the civil and criminal court created for each vilayet, sancak and kaza.[28] Each court was presided over by the nominee of the *şeyhülislâm;* the judge so appointed had also the additional function of taking charge of the şeriat courts. But the other members of the civil court were, at each level, three Muslims and three non-Muslims, chosen by the same process as the elective members of the administrative councils. In Muslim districts this allocation gave Christians an undue representation, while the reverse was true for Christian districts; yet

[27] See, for example, Benoît Brunswik, *Etudes pratiques sur la question d'Orient* (Paris, 1869), pp. 33-39.

[28] In the kaza there was a civil court only. Vilayet and sancak were also given a commercial court, to be governed by the westernized commercial code.

the system was reasonably equitable, as the court would take account principally of mixed cases involving litigants of more than one faith. By the creation of these courts, justice and administration were more clearly separated in the provinces than had been the case before.

The other representative institution was the general assembly (*meclis-i umumî*) created for each vilayet. It was composed of four elected representatives from each sancak, two Muslims and two non-Muslims, chosen by the elected council members of the kazas in each sancak. The assembly thus formed was competent to discuss public works, taxes, police, agriculture, and commerce, but it was essentially advisory since no measures could be carried out without imperial sanction. The vali, as presiding officer, had considerable power in the assembly and could decide which petitions submitted by members on behalf of their constituents would be considered; he also was responsible for sending *procès-verbaux* of the sessions to İstanbul. The assembly was to meet annually for a maximum of forty days. For the empire as a whole a provincial assembly, adapted from the French model, was an innovation. It existed already only in the Armenian millet and in some of the autonomous or privileged provinces.[29]

The intention of the law was obviously not only to improve the efficiency of government in the provinces, but to eliminate local complaints and foreign complaints in favor of minorities by extending the representative principle. It is an interesting question whether the latter aspect was in 1864 intentionally conceived as a step toward constitutional government. Midhat Paşa, in brief memoirs written nearly twenty years later, asserts that the new vilayet system was intended by Âli and Fuad "as a preface to a chamber of deputies (*meclis-i meb'usan*)," and that it "had for some time been taking shape in their minds."[30] Later writers, searching for hopeful signs of constitutional development in the empire, have seized on this law and Midhat's statement as forecasting genuine parliamentary government.[31] It is quite unlikely that Âli would have favored a chamber of deputies. Possibly Fuad was favorable to such a step in the indeterminate future, and Midhat himself may possibly have entertained at this early date

[29] See, for instance, the assembly in the island of Samos, which had some legislative power: text of law of 1852 in Young, *Corps de droit*, I, 116-119.

[30] A. H. Midhat, *Tabsıra-i ibret*, p. 23.

[31] Ahmed Rasim, *İstibdaddan hakimiyeti milliyeye*, II, 73-74; Ali Fuad, *Rical-i mühimme-i siyasiye*, p. 173. Neither cites a page reference to Midhat, but obviously the above passage is indicated. The latter implies that Fuad alone favored a parliament.

ideas about the parliamentary system which he was to inaugurate in 1876. But, as in the case of similar interpretations of the Gülhane decree of 1839 and the Armenian millet constitution, it is dangerous to impute specific motives of this sort. Fuad and Midhat may already have had general inclinations in this direction, but Midhat may in his memoirs be seeking, consciously or not, to justify the course of action he later pursued as grand vezir. The principal aim of the law was sound provincial administration.

To test the new system, one vilayet was set up in 1864 and christened the Tuna, or Danube, vilayet. It was formed of the eyalets of Silistria, Vidin, and Nish, and thus was rather sizable, as well as geographically somewhat unwieldy, since it included the region of Sofia, which was cut off from the rest by the Balkan range. The Tuna vilayet represented a key area in which to try out a system designed to hold the empire together. It was close to İstanbul, for which it was the connecting link to Ottoman provinces as far off as Bosnia. It was a sensitive area also, in view of the developing Bulgarian national consciousness. Of the surrounding Balkan regions, Serbia and Roumania were rapidly increasing their degree of independence of the Porte. From across their frontiers came encouragement to Bulgar separatism, which was further incited from Russian sources. Any governor here, laboring under the eye of İstanbul, and with the wide responsibilities given him under the new law, would have his hands full. There was an additional problem of considerable magnitude at this period—the flood of Tatar and Circassian refugees from Russia who were relocated in this area. Between the Crimean War (1855) and the inauguration of the vilayet law thousands of Tatars and Circassians entered the Ottoman Empire.[32] The influx continued for at least two years more. The Ottoman government, faced with the problem of resettling the refugees, sent many of them to the area of the Tuna vilayet, with the idea that they would help to serve as a border defense against Serbia and along the Danube, and perhaps also as a countermeasure to separatist activity among Bulgars. The local authorities were then faced with the question of supplying land, houses, animals, and temporary

---

[32] According to Ottoman statistics, which seem rather high, 600,000 from 1855 to 1864, and 400,000 more in the next two years: Salaheddin Bey, *La Turquie à l'exposition universelle de 1867* (Paris, 1867), p. 213; *Journal de Constantinople*, 13 August 1864.

provisions for the Circassians, and also with the problem of local resentment against the refugees. There were sometimes local crises of great proportions, as when the population of Varna (Stalin) was increased overnight by fifty per cent owing to such an influx.[33] Such problems, in addition to the usual burdens of local administration, would test any governor as well as the new regulations.

Midhat Paşa was, logically, chosen to carry out the experiment as governor of the Tuna vilayet. Contemporaries generally acclaimed him successful, although grudgingly in many cases and not without admixture of criticism. What impressed travellers and residents in Bulgaria first was the program of public works, vigorously pushed and much of it completed, an achievement unheard of in other parts of the empire. Paved roads, bridges (fourteen hundred by Midhat's count!), street lights, public buildings, schools, steamer service on the Danube, model farms with agricultural machinery imported from Europe, all served to bring both the appearance and the fact of prosperity to the province. Of greater importance for the prosperity of the ordinary farmer were the agricultural credit cooperatives established by Midhat. In each village, peasants cultivated half an acre for the cooperative fund; the council of elders sold the produce to provide the capital from which loans up to two thousand piasters might be made to such peasants as needed them, at a low rate of interest. Both Christians and Muslims participated in the administration of the scheme. Thus the grip of the moneylender, with his high interest rate, was avoided by many peasants. Midhat is still acclaimed in Turkey as the father of the agricultural bank, and in Bulgaria today as the founder of the best-developed credit cooperatives in the Balkans.[34] There seems to have been no important industrial development,

[33] Reiser (Varna) to Stenerzin, 17 January 1865, Svenska Riksarkivet, Beskickningen i Konstantinopels. See on the refugees generally Kanitz, Donau-Bulgarien, I, 295-298, 309-310, 314-319; G. G. B. St. Clair and C. A. Brophy, Twelve Years' Study of the Eastern Question in Bulgaria (London, 1877), pp. 166-182; Sax, Geschichte des Machtverfalls, p. 371; A. H. Midhat, Tabsıra-i ibret, pp. 34-36; Ludwik Widerszal, Sprawy Kaukaskie w polityce europejskiej w latach 1831-1864 (Warsaw, 1934), p. 174.

[34] On the cooperatives: A. H. Midhat, Tabsıra-i ibret, pp. 29-30; Ahmed Midhat, Üss-i inkılâb, I, 105; Sıddık S. Onar, "The Analysis . . . of the Public Corporations in Turkey . . . ," Revue internationale des sciences administratives, I (1954), 17; Robert L. Wolff, The Balkans in Our Time (Cambridge, Mass., 1956), p. 172; Clician Vassif, Son Altesse Midhat Pacha (Paris, 1909), p. 12. Arsitch, La vie économique de la Serbie, pp. 31-32, dates the banks from Midhat's previous period in Nish, with a different system of peasant contributions; St. Clair and Brophy, Twelve Years'

but craftsmanship was promoted by Midhat's establishment of training schools in Nish, Ruschuk, and Sofia where poor and orphaned children could learn a trade. One of these was so novel as to be a girls' trade school, attached to a factory in Ruschuk which made clothing for the military.[35] Prosperity was increased also by vigorous use of regular troops and gendarmes to suppress brigandage.

The administrative machinery through which all this was achieved was that laid down in the 1864 law. The Danube vilayet was divided into seven sancaks and forty-eight kazas, in which Midhat's subordinates organized the appropriate administrative councils down to the town and village level. Even the elective members of some of the councils—probably the higher ones—seem to have been paid a salary. The general assembly met annually, though published records give no indication as to the nature of its deliberations. The application of the system was infused with a conciliatory spirit aimed at dealing equally with Muslims and Christians; this gave Muslims cause to condemn Midhat as the *gâvur* pasha, but as his administration continued they referred to him more often as *gözlüklü*, "the bespectacled." The first official provincial newspaper in the empire, the *Tuna*, was published at the capital, Ruschuk, in Turkish and Bulgarian. Midhat surrounded himself with officials of considerable ability; he seems to have been able to influence the selection even of those appointed directly from İstanbul. The salaries paid them were adequate, and certainly bribery and embezzlement were decreased if not eliminated. Abdurrahman Paşa at Varna seems to have been an exemplary mutasarrıf. Odian Efendi, one of the authors of the Armenian constitution, was an able "minister" of foreign affairs, and occasionally represented Midhat in İstanbul as well as in the vilayet. Leskofçalı Mustafa Galib Bey, a fairly well-known poet of the old school, was chief secretary of Midhat's administrative council and editor of his newspaper. Midhat took into his service a brilliant young man (brother of yet another of his provincial officials) who served in various secretarial positions and then became editor of the *Tuna*. This was Ahmed

---

Study, pp. 293-294, criticize the system and claim that Christian clerks corrupted it. A. A. Popova, "Politika Turtsii i natsionalno-osvoboditelnaia bor'ba bolgarskovo naroda v 60-x gg. xix veka," *Voprosy istorii*, x (1953), 58, claims that only the *çorbacı*'s, "agricultural and trading-usurping bourgeoisie," profited from the cooperatives: cited in İU. A. Petrosian, *"Novye Osmany" i bor'ba za konstitutsiiu* (Moscow, 1958), p. 79, n.23. Cf. A. Du Velay, *Essai sur l'histoire financière de la Turquie* (Paris, 1903), pp. 205-210, on the extension of the system to all vilayets.
[35] Ergin, *Maarif tarihi*, II, 572.

Midhat, to whom Midhat Paşa gave his own name and who later achieved an independent literary fame. Midhat's own secretary was Kiliçyan Vasıf Efendi, a Croat. İsmail Kemal, the famous Albanian, was in Midhat's service, and he too worked on the newspaper *Tuna.* One of İsmail's uncles was also an official. Wherever he found talent, Midhat used it. He had as subordinates a good many non-Muslims, both Ottoman subjects and foreigners, in addition to Vasıf and Odian. Among the foreigners were a sizable number of Polish refugees working as civil and military engineers, telegraph employees, teachers, and cartographers. Midhat Paşa praised the integrity and ability of his officials and their cooperation: "all the vilayet officials, big and small, were united like the members of a family."[36] This was overenthusiastic, and certainly there were other officials like Bursalı Senih Efendi who opposed Midhat's policies of innovation and quit his service.[37] Apparently there were no Bulgars in any other than minor posts in the vilayet. Midhat's team of officials, nevertheless, served to keep the new administrative machinery in running order.[38]

Bulgar nationalism, which from the Ottoman viewpoint was, of course, seditious and revolutionary, was undoubtedly the reason for the lack of higher Bulgar officials in the vilayet, though the low educational level may have been a contributing factor. Throughout his three-year period as governor Midhat tried to combat the nationalism in three ways. The first was simply to win over the ordinary inhabitants of the province by good government and equitable treatment, and in this Midhat must have been reasonably successful, to judge by the comments of impartial observers and also by the protests of Bulgar nationalists against some of his measures. The second was by providing good education in mixed schools to be attended by both Muslims and Christians. Midhat was, in any case, a strong proponent of modern education and undertook a reform of elementary schools in the vilayet which became the model for a general reform in the

[36] A. H. Midhat, *Tabsıra-i ibret*, p. 41.
[37] Kuntay, *Namık Kemal*, I, 24, n.10; A. H. Midhat, *Tabsıra-i ibret*, p. 25.
[38] On officials: Ahmed Midhat, *Üss-i inkılâb*, I, 105; Sommerville Story, ed., *The Memoirs of Ismail Kemal Bey* (London, 1920), pp. 27-28, 30; Reiser (Varna) to Swedish Foreign Ministry, 8 April 1856, Svenska Riksarkivet, Beskickningen i Konstantinopels; Moustapha Djelaleddin, *Les Turcs anciens et modernes* (Paris, 1870), pp. 104, 179-181; Cevdet Perin, "Ahmed Midhat Efendi . . . ," *Garp filolojileri dergisi* (İstanbul, 1947), pp. 137-139; Abdurrahman Şeref, "Ahmed Midhat Efendi," *Tarih-i osmani encümeni mecmuası* III:18 (1328), 1114; Alaettin Gövsa, *Türk meşhurları* (İstanbul, n.d.), p. 147; Adam Lewak, *Dzieje emigracji polskiej w Turcji (1831-1878)* (Warsaw, 1935), p. 201.

empire some years later.[39] But he was vitally interested in establishing a complete school system which should provide opportunities for the Bulgars and keep them from going to schools in Kishenev, Odessa, and elsewhere in Russia.[40] Presumably it was for this system that Namık Kemal consulted works on the organization of provincial schools in France and sent information to the secretary of Midhat's administrative council.[41] The plan was, however, not carried out, and nationalists among the Bulgars resisted this attempt to amalgamate them into an Ottoman brotherhood.[42]

When agitation or rebellion appeared openly, Midhat did not shrink from ruthless suppression. Some of the "brigandage" he stamped out was actually infiltration of agitators from across the frontiers. The Porte regarded this as Russian-inspired, and certainly it was the policy of Ambassador Ignatyev at İstanbul to bring about the breakup of the Ottoman Empire into national autonomies.[43] Midhat supported a proposal by a refugee Polish leader of the 1863 revolt against Russia to create a Polish military unit in Bulgaria, and also to organize Bulgars and Pomaks under Polish officers.[44] This plan was frustrated, but regular Turkish troops and Circassians were sufficient to quell a premature rising by a section of the Bulgarian revolutionary organization which was sponsored and financed by Russia. Midhat conducted an inquisition, and probably hanged innocent and guilty alike.[45] In the same year Midhat dealt somewhat cavalierly with international law in arresting on an Austrian boat in the Danube two Slavic agitators with foreign passports.[46]

A group of moderate Bulgar nationalists proposed early in 1867 a plan to create a dual monarchy which would give self-government to

[39] Ergin, *Maarif tarihi*, II, 388-390.
[40] A. H. Midhat, *Tabsıra-i ibret*, pp. 42-43; idem, *Life*, pp. 40-41; Halil İnalcık, *Tanzimat ve Bulgar meselesi* (Ankara, 1943), p. 24, n.1, quoting a memorandum of 1868 by Midhat.
[41] Kuntay, *Namık Kemal*, I, 24.
[42] (Anon.), *Les Turcs et la Bulgarie* (Paris, 1869), p. 19.
[43] Lyons to Stanley, #210, 24 May 1867, enclosing Mayers (Ruschuk)-Lyons, 17 May 1867, FO 78/1960; Lyons to Stanley, #303, confidential, 9 July 1867, FO 78/1962; B. H. Sumner, "Ignatyev at Constantinople," *Slavonic Review*, 11 (1933), 346.
[44] Lewak, *Emigracji polskiej*, p. 212.
[45] Alois Hajek, *Bulgarien unter der Türkenherrschaft* (Stuttgart, 1925), pp. 235-236; B. H. Sumner, *Russia and the Balkans* (Oxford, 1937), p. 110; A. H. Midhat, *Life*, pp. 42-45.
[46] Morris to Seward, #224, August 1867, USNA, Turkey 20; A. H. Midhat, *Life*, pp. 45-46; Story, *Ismail Kemal*, p. 32.

Bulgaria. Inspired by the Austro-Hungarian Ausgleich of that year, the proposal envisioned Abdülaziz as sultan of the empire and tsar of Bulgaria, to be represented in the latter kingdom by a Bulgarian viceroy elected by a national assembly. The plan was submitted to the sultan, along with protestations of loyalty to him and assertions of opposition to the Greek *megale idea* of recreating the Byzantine Empire. The petition asked also for an autocephalous Bulgar Ortho-dox church, free of the control of the Greek patriarch of İstanbul.[47] The Porte paid no attention to the scheme, and soon the moderate Bulgars were eclipsed by a more revolutionary type of leadership. Midhat was probably quite opposed to the proposal, as he was an-tagonistic not only to Bulgarian autonomy but also, evidently, to the autocephalous church which Âli Paşa was inclined to favor. Any such plan ran counter to Midhat's efforts to create Osmanlılık.[48]

After three years as vali, Midhat was recalled by the Porte for reasons which are not clear. A number of European observers thought he was sacrificed to avoid further complications over the affair of the Austrian steamer. It is possible also that he was recalled to avoid Russian pressure on Turkey after his severe repression of Slavic sep-aratism. It may be also that he was called specifically to assume the presidency of the reorganized Council of State in İstanbul. It is also possible that friction between Âli and Midhat had something to do with it—friction not only on vilayet matters and the Bulgar exarchate, but also stemming from Âli's jealousy of Midhat's growing reputa-tion. Âli had become grand vezir the year before Midhat's recall.

What is clear is that Midhat's administration of the Tuna vilayet was, given the times and the situation, a resounding success. His suc-cess, rather than any failure, may have contributed to his recall. Legitimate criticism may be made of Midhat's sometimes overhasty action, of his beginning too many things without being able to carry them to completion, of a certain superficiality in his knowledge of the bases of western civilization. He was not always popular in the

[47] Petition text in *Le Nord* (Brussels), 26 and 27 March 1867; and Morris to Seward, #199, 2 April 1867, USNA, Turkey 19. Cf. Hajek, *Bulgarien*, pp. 209, 231-233.

[48] It is possible that this proposal may have influenced Midhat's plans for a federal-ized empire, which he broached when grand vezir in 1872; see below, pp. 290-291, on this. But the model in 1872 was the federal German empire proclaimed in 1871 rather than the Ausgleich. In 1878 Midhat did declare for an autonomous Bulgaria: Midhat Paşa, "The Past, Present, and Future of Turkey," *Nineteenth Century*, III (June 1878), 990-991, 999. But this was under pressure of later events and in al-tered circumstances, after the Treaty of San Stefano.

vilayet, especially when problems of Circassian resettlement caused him to draft the local peasantry into forced labor to assist in the projects. The terms of the vilayet law and the size of his vilayet undoubtedly produced a degree of inefficiency; a number of observers were sure that smaller units would have been better governed. But Midhat made the system work reasonably well, in the opinion both of Turcophils and Bulgarophils. After his recall he was remembered in the vilayet with favor and sometimes with affection, both for his own attitude and deeds and by contrast with his successors.[49] One indication of Midhat's success may be that Ottoman officials, in the period immediately after Midhat left the Tuna vilayet, were said to consider Ruschuk to be the highest provincial post.[50]

In a memorandum of May 15, 1867, addressed to the European powers, Fuad Paşa hailed the vilayet experiment as emerging triumphant from its first test. The empire had found, said the foreign minister, "a form of administration corresponding altogether to the needs of the country, to the customs of the populations, and to the demands of the concept of civilization which presses upon the empire from all directions."[51] He described the electoral system as "appropriate to the condition of the mores in the provinces of the Empire." He promised, finally, an extension of the new system within a few weeks to all the provinces. The vilayet law was soon formally communicated to the great powers.[52] Fuad was writing his memorandum for foreign consumption, and in reply to French and Russian notes reminding the Porte to fulfill its promises of reform. But there is no

[49] Useful general accounts and estimates of Midhat as Tuna vali: A. H. Midhat, *Tabsıra-i ibret*, pp. 26-61; idem, *Life*, pp. 38-47; Ahmed Midhat, *Üss-i inkılâb*, I, 105-106; Story, *Ismail Kemal*, pp. 27-32; Clician Vassif, *Midhat Pacha*, pp. 10-14; Mordtmann, *Stambul*, II, 82-84, 167-169; St. Clair and Brophy, *Twelve Years' Study*, pp. 281-294; Djelaleddin, *Les Turcs*, pp. 179-185; Kanitz, *Donau-Bulgarien*, I, 112-114, 150, and II, 46, and III, 175 (some of which refers to Midhat's period in Nish); Paul Fesch, *Constantinople aux derniers jours d'Abdul-Hamid* (Paris, 1907), pp. 18-24, largely based on Kanitz; Gökbilgin, "Midhat Paşa," pp. 272-273; Léouzon, *Midhat*, pp. 40-43; Amand von Schweiger-Lerchenfeld, *Serail und Hohe Pforte* (Vienna, 1879), pp. 238-243; (Anon.), *Les Turcs et la Bulgarie*, pp. 12-30; Ahmed Saib, *Vaka-i Sultan Abdülaziz*, pp. 48-49.

[50] Koetschet, *Osman Pascha*, p. 26.

[51] Text in Testa, *Recueil des traités*, VII, 459.

[52] Fuad's note to the powers in Young, *Corps de droit*, I, 36-37, n.1. The vilayet law which he enclosed with this communication was the 1867 revision of the 1864 law which his memorandum, above referred to, had said was in process.

reason to doubt that Âli and Fuad were pleased with the way the law had worked out in the Tuna vilayet. As Midhat had applied it, it helped to curb separatism at a crucial time when Crete was in revolt and agitators there sought *enosis* with Greece, when the governor of Egypt was pressing to extend his independent authority, and when Charles of Hohenzollern was just launched on his rule as prince in the vassal state of Roumania. Though he may have disliked Midhat, the grand vezir Âli disliked separatism even more. He had once, just after the American Civil War started, offered his sympathy to the American chargé d'affaires with the statement that he "warmly deprecated the principle of 'secession' as vicious to all governments."[53] The vilayet administration in Bulgaria had shown also that the way of Osmanlılık and westernization could advantageously be pursued under the new law. Sultan Abdülaziz, returning by way of the Danube vilayet from his trip to Paris in the summer of 1867, was impressed by Midhat's work of modernization.[54] The Porte was already planning to extend the vilayet system. In March Fuad had so stated, and Midhat had been called from Ruschuk to sit on a commission charged with improving the regulations.[55]

Some parts of the empire were apparently reconstituted as vilayets even before Fuad's memorandum promised to extend the system. After the Tuna vilayet, Erzurum, Edirne, Bosnia, Aleppo, Syria, and Tripoli in Africa were the first to be so organized.[56] Egypt was also regarded as a vilayet. Within a year the whole empire was so organized, at least on paper, except for Baghdad and the Yemen.[57] Crete became a vilayet in 1867 after the insurrection was put down. Its

---

[53] Brown to Seward, #10, 17 July 1861, USNA, Turkey 17. In his negotiations over recognizing Prince Charles in 1866, Âli attached the statement that the Principalities were "an integral part of the Ottoman Empire"; even in the face of contrary fact he clung to the principle: T. W. Riker, *The Making of Roumania* (London, 1931), pp. 563-564. Similarly, during Fuad's first grand vezirate, regulations of 1862 on administration of salt monopoly revenues stated, "Since Egypt and Moldavia-Wallachia form integral parts of the empire . . . ," but then proceeded to make special rules for them: Young, *Corps de droit*, v, 130.

[54] Ebüzziya Tevfik, "Yeni Osmanlılar tarihi," *Yeni Tasviriefkâr*, installment 80, cited in Kuntay, *Namık Kemal*, I, 125; Charles Mismer, *Souvenirs du monde musulman* (Paris, 1892), pp. 18-19.

[55] Pisani to Lyons, #67, 19 March 1867, FO 195/887.

[56] Salaheddin, *La Turquie*, pp. 176-177, 192-193, 206, quoting from the *Salname* (official yearbook) of 1283/1866-1867.

[57] Ubicini and Pavet de Courteille, *État présent de l'Empire ottoman* (Paris, 1876), p. 90, n.3. Further exceptions to this were the vassal or privileged states of Serbia, Roumania, Tunis, and, in fact, Egypt, Montenegro, Samos, and the Lebanon; İstanbul also had a special organization.

organic statute was modified from the vilayet standard to give Christians greater representation in the various councils, the courts, and the general assembly.[58] The Sporades also, Greek-inhabited islands which had been allowed effective self-government with a tributary status, were in the years 1869 to 1873 assimilated into the vilayet system.[59] In all, twenty-seven vilayets were created in the period down to 1876, in the place of the old eyalets, which had ranged in number from thirty-two to nearly forty. Most of the vilayets were consequently bigger than the former administrative units.[60]

Though the vilayet law was revised in some minor aspects in 1867, it was not until 1871 that a more thorough revision was made by a committee of the new Council of State established in 1868.[61] The chief virtue of the new law was to eliminate some of the blurred areas of the regulations of 1867 by making more explicit the powers of the various officials and meclises. The vali was given even more extensive powers than before over officials in the vilayet and its subdivisions, as well as over troops stationed there. The double responsibility of various provincial officials to the vali and to İstanbul was not specifically denied, but the vali's authority was increased. To a long list of specific duties and powers of the vali was added a prescription that he go on inspection tour in his province once or twice a year. The whole impression of this portion of the new law is that it catalogued the things Midhat had done in the Tuna vilayet and was now doing as vali in Baghdad.[62] The powers of the general assembly of the vilayet were somewhat extended, and it was apparently given in a backhanded way the right to interpellate vilayet officials. The 1871 law created some new provincial offices, including that of vilayet director of public instruction. It added a new division to the administrative hierarchy by redefining the *nahiye*, a collection of villages or farms, as an intermediate step between the kaza and the village

---

[58] Text of law in Aristarchi, *Législation*, II, 169-203, including three supplementary sets of regulations; summary in Ubicini and Pavet de Courteille, *Etat présent*, pp. 107-112.

[59] Young, *Corps de droit*, I, 156-157; Antonio Gallenga, *Two Years of the Eastern Question* (London, 1877), II, 227-228 n.

[60] The *Salname* for 1286/1869-1870, pp. 124-129, lists twenty-three vilayets; for 1289/1872-1873, pp. 144-150, twenty-five vilayets; for 1291/1874-1875, pp. 138-167, twenty-five vilayets. Ubicini and Pavet de Courteille, *Etat présent*, pp. 91-96, list the vilayets and subdivisions as of 1876, based on the *Salname* for 1293.

[61] Text in Aristarchi, *Législation*, III, 7-39; *Düstur*, I, 625-651; Young, *Corps de droit*, I, 47-69 (defective).

[62] On which see below.

(*kariye*). The *nahiye* was in charge of a *müdür*, and had its own administrative council composed of representatives from the village councils of elders within its circumscription. Finally, the revised statute of 1871 created the municipality as an administrative entity, with a president and a council to see to local sanitation, public works, and the like. This was an innovation for the empire as a whole. If it had been vigorously carried out, considerable local improvement might have resulted. But, in fact, this part of the law remained largely unapplied, and the growth of municipal administration in the provinces began only after 1877.[63]

It was not long before Baghdad too was brought under the vilayet system. This was one of the most difficult of Ottoman provinces to govern, owing not only to its vast extent from Mosul to Basra, but to the independent-minded Kurd and Arab tribes. The area had been brought back under the direct control of the Porte only in the latter days of Mahmud II, and although there had been some reasonably good governors thereafter, the typical Ottoman bureaucrat there had been the partly westernized Stambuli efendi who was contemptuous of the Arabs and little concerned with improving their lot. A policy of tribe-smashing failed to achieve its ends, or to produce any desirable results.[64] Midhat Paşa was the obvious man for the governorship, and was sent out in 1869 to tackle the job. He had been for the past year the first president of the reorganized Council of State, and might have continued in this post except for the death of Fuad Paşa in February 1869. Midhat and Fuad got along famously, and Âli, out of regard for Fuad, held his dislike of Midhat in check. But, with Fuad gone, Âli was in complete control of the Porte; he himself assumed Fuad's foreign ministry portfolio, while keeping the grand

[63] The sixth district, or "cercle," of the capital, including Pera and Galata, had been set up as a pilot project in 1858 and functioned effectively, largely under foreign and non-Muslim impulsion. Even before the 1871 law some municipal administration existed in places—in the Tuna vilayet, in Cyprus (and in the almost autonomous Tunis and Egypt)—and Midhat between 1869 and 1872 made a start at municipal organization in the Baghdad vilayet. But the lack of municipal organization remained general. Cf. Bernard Lewis, "Baladiyya—(1) Turkey," *Encyclopaedia of Islam*, new ed., I, 972-974, and his *Emergence of Modern Turkey* (London, 1961), pp. 389-392.

[64] Stephen H. Longrigg, *Four Centuries of Modern Iraq* (Oxford, 1925), pp. 280-292, on the period 1839 to 1869. Midhat took advantage of Wahhabi internal quarrels to extend by conquest a tenuous Ottoman control over the Hasa and Kuwait: *ibid.*, pp. 301-304.

vezirate, and at the same time removed his most prominent rival from the capital by sending him to Baghdad.[65]

Midhat went out to Baghdad with a team of hand-picked subordinates, including his young protégé Ahmed Midhat and at least one of his Polish engineers from the Tuna vilayet.[66] As in Bulgaria, his energy made itself felt in all corners of public life. Some of his activity, especially in material improvements, duplicated what he had done in the Tuna vilayet. In the city of Baghdad he began to westernize the outer aspect with pavements and street lights, created a public park, started a water supply system, built the only bridge the city was to know until the twentieth century, and tore down part of the old wall to give the city room for rational expansion. He built a tram line, out to a suburb, which was successful as the first joint-stock company in Baghdad and which operated, beginning with horsecars in Midhat's time, for sixty years. For public enlightenment he established several schools, including a secondary school and an academy for military cadets; Christians and Jews were admitted, though not many applied, along with Muslims. Ahmed Midhat in Baghdad began to produce modern school texts. The first newspaper in Iraq, the *Zaura*, was begun as a semiweekly in Arabic and Turkish. Midhat Paşa was active also in the field of social welfare, organizing charitable and relief projects and subscriptions for a civil hospital which provided free treatment. He inaugurated quarantine measures. He founded a technical school where orphans could get training in a craft along with an elementary education. Also in the economic sphere he established a savings bank, wool and cotton mills, a factory to produce military clothing. He promoted shipping in the Persian Gulf, established a ship repair yard at Basra, began dredging operations on the river, promoted regular steamship service on the Euphrates; his interest in the latter stemmed partly from the opening of the Suez Canal under a French company in 1869, which momentarily revived British concern for a Euphrates route to India. Some of these activities were opposed as *bid'at*, or heretical innovation, by the local population. A good many were regarded suspiciously. Some worked well; some did not. Some remained beginnings only, abandoned by Mid-

---

[65] *Journal des Débats*, 15 February 1869; Mardin, *Cevdet*, pp. 60, 88, n.99; Clician Vassif, *Midhat Pacha*, p. 17.

[66] Ten officials are named in Fahmi al-Mudarris, *Maqālāt siyāsiyya*, I (Baghdad, 1931), 55-56; Lewak, *Emigracji polskiej*, p. 191. Midhat employed also a Viennese physician as sanitation director: Bernhard Stern, *Jungtürken und Verschwörer* (Leipzig, 1901), pp. 128, 138.

hat's successors. The dredges worked poorly. The river steamer service was unsatisfactory. Years later the Baghdad wall was still only partly demolished, and heaps of ruins remained. Midhat's actions were sometimes overhasty, his projects sometimes poorly thought out.[67] But the sum of material achievement was impressive.

On more fundamental questions of land development, irrigation, tribal settlement, taxation, Midhat also made progress in varying degrees. His Polish engineer started a model farm with a well-irrigated garden, but the total work of irrigation seems to have been slim, aside from a little dam construction and cleaning out of canals. The culture of date palms on the lower Euphrates and the Shatt-el-Arab, however, increased greatly in Midhat's time, with pacification and settlement of the tribes and a fair system of tax assessment. The key to many problems—public order, regular conscription of army recruits, collection of tax income, improved agriculture—lay with the nomadic tribes. Midhat had a double authority in dealing with them. He was at the same time vali and commander of the Sixth Army corps, an unusual position for a governor under the new dispensation, and he did not hesitate to suppress revolts against conscription or against innovations generally. He may have been unnecessarily severe in dealing with some tribal leaders; he executed Şeyh Abdülkerim, who had written to other tribal şeyh's that Midhat desired to destroy the Arab tents and force them into the degrading and dishonorable occupation of farming, in settled villages.[68] Settlement of the tribes was, in fact, Midhat's program, though he recognized the difficulties involved. He wanted, among other things, to get land titles registered and under state control, instead of under tribal control, and to put land in the hands of cultivators; to stop Bedouin marauding and get them also under state control; and to increase public order as well as tax income by these means. The Bedouin were, of course, suspicious, and success was partial. But a good many nomads were settled, land on secure tenure at low payments was sold to the cultivators, land titles were registered, and an increase in prosperity and security did

[67] There is an incredible story that Midhat thought he could run a railless railroad across the desert; the desert triumphed, and the locomotive rusted, stuck in the sand. Stern, *Jungtürken*, p. 140, based on information from Midhat's physician in Baghdad.

[68] Col. Herbert (Baghdad) to Elliot, 30 August 1871, encl. in Elliot to Granville, #346, 26 Sept. 1871, FO 78/2177; Habib K. Chiha, *La province de Bagdad* (Cairo, 1908), pp. 71-72.

result. Apparently *şeyh*'s were consulted,[69] tribal customs respected as far as possible in this process, and taxes arranged suitable to local conditions rather than on the city or village model.

Administratively, Midhat organized the councils and the courts according to the vilayet law.[70] He also inaugurated municipal councils in Baghdad and other cities, though their chief development came after his time. Contrary to his practice in Bulgaria, he appointed a good many natives of the vilayet to jobs in government offices; he was "an education for the Iraqis."[71]

Among the people of the Baghdad vilayet Midhat had aroused considerable resentment by his measures, but he had also won considerable approval for the justice and the progress of his administration. When he left the post, after a three-year tenure, his own circumstances were so straitened that he had to send an agent out to sell a gold box he had received from Sultan Abdülaziz; the purchaser, however, recognized it and again made a present of it to Midhat.[72] Well into the twentieth century Midhat was remembered in Iraq with respect as an enlightened administrator. A man like this is not produced by the wombs of mothers, says one of his Iraqi biographers.[73] In 1910 the Basra municipality voted to erect a statue of Midhat in memory of his services.[74] But in the Sublime Porte, Midhat was by 1872 not so highly regarded. Âli Paşa had died in the previous autumn, and his successor in the grand vezirate was Mahmud Nedim Paşa, an even more determined opponent of Midhat. Mahmud Nedim tried to

[69] Şiddīq al-Damlūji, *Midḥat Bāshā* (Baghdad, 1952-1953), p. 49.

[70] The author has found no mention of the general assembly here.

[71] Mudarris, *Maqālāt siyāsiyya*, I, 60. Accounts and estimates of Midhat's work in Baghdad generally: *ibid.*, pp. 52-60; Damlūji, *Midḥat Bāshā*, pp. 33-51; A. H. Midhat, *Tabsıra-i ibret*, pp. 66-95; *idem*, *Life*, pp. 47-52; Stern, *Jungtürken*, pp. 128-143; Longrigg, *Four Centuries*, pp. 298-318; Chiha, *Province de Bagdad*, pp. 65-72; Léouzon, *Midhat*, pp. 81-84; Schweiger-Lerchenfeld, *Serail und Hohe Pforte*, pp. 243-245; Grattan Geary, *Through Asiatic Turkey* (London, 1878), I, 92-93, 115, 134, 138, 209; Albertine Jwaideh, *Municipal Government in Baghdad and Basra from 1869 to 1914* (unpublished B.Litt. thesis, Oxford, 1953), pp. vi, 5, 136, 178-179, 181-182; Schweiger-Lerchenfeld, "Ingenieur Josef Cernik's technische Studien-Expedition . . . ," *Petermann's Mittheilungen*, Ergänzungsheft #44, 27-31; Richard Coke, *The Heart of the Middle East* (New York, 1926), pp. 111, 119-125; *idem*, *Baghdad, the City of Peace* (London, 1927), pp. 274-275; D. G. Hogarth, *The Nearer East* (New York, 1915), pp. 200-201; Ernest Dowson, *An Inquiry into Land Tenure* (Letchworth, 1931), pp. 18, 50; Max von Oppenheim, *Die Beduinen*, III, part 2 (Wiesbaden, 1952), 200; Gökbilgin, "Midhat Paşa," pp. 273-274.

[72] Mudarris, *Maqālāt siyāsiyya*, I, 54; Damlūji, *Midḥat Bāshā*, p. 51; Geary, *Through Asiatic Turkey*, I, 250-251, who calls it a "watch."

[73] Mudarris, *Maqālāt siyāsiyya*, I, 52.

[74] A. H. Midhat, *Hâtıralarım* (İstanbul, 1946), pp. 229-230.

siphon off from the Baghdad vilayet a good deal of the increased revenue Midhat's policies had achieved, while Midhat wanted to keep it for local use. Midhat published in the *Zaura* a defense of his achievements as vali, which earned for the İstanbul newspapers that reprinted it a warning from Mahmud Nedim.[75] The argument led to Midhat's resignation, and he started back to İstanbul to take up the political fight at close quarters.

The vilayet system thus inaugurated by law and tested successfully under Midhat Paşa in two of the most difficult of the empire's provinces remained thereafter the basis of local administration in the Ottoman Empire. There was periodic amendment or addition to the law, and considerable tinkering with the boundaries of vilayets and with their subdivisions.[76] The heterogeneity of the empire made it difficult in practice to put all its provinces into the hierarchical strait-jacket that Midhat and Fuad had devised. Cyprus, for instance, formerly separately governed under an independent mutasarrıf, was in 1868 assimilated into the vilayet of the Dardanelles with a capital so distant (at Çanak) as to make good administration impossible, and other arrangements had to be found.[77] Even in theory the system was not perfect. The jurist Cevdet Paşa criticized the tergiversations of reforming statesmen who had not decided whether the empire was really to be governed on centralizing or decentralizing principles and had fallen somewhere between the two.[78] But Cevdet's criticism on this point seems to be based on an impossible counsel of perfection, for any large state must somehow combine local and central authority in a flexible system where lines are sometimes blurred. The real test of the system was in its working.

Opinions varied on how well the system actually worked in its first few years of operation. Namık Kemal was critical of the new system, in part because he thought it was instituted to please Europe and the Christian minorities, and in part because he viewed Midhat Paşa as

[75] Mordtmann, *Stambul*, II, 84-85.
[76] In 1876 the electoral law was simplified: Young, *Corps de droit*, I, 45-47; and also an elaborate set of instructions was sent to valis: Sublime Porte, Ministère des Affaires Etrangères, *Instructions relatives à l'administration générale des vilayets* (Constantinople, 1876); Young, *Corps de droit*, I, 88-95; Aristarchi, *Législation*, V, 50-59.
[77] Hill, *Cyprus*, IV, 239-241, 250-251.
[78] His memorandum of 1289 (1872-1873) in Mardin, *Cevdet*, p. 348.

the only effective governor, and even his work did not keep the Bulgars firmly in check. Of the valis of the newly formed vilayets in Anatolia, "some are in their dotage, some corrupt, and some incompetent," he said.[79] His colleague Ziya Bey a few months later maintained that improvements made in such provinces as the Tuna vilayet were soon annulled when the governor was replaced.[80] Ahmed Midhat, looking back from the end of the 1870's, saw great advantages: an end to the evils generated from the previous system when so many local officials were personal servants in the vali's household; a rational and ordered system of appointed officials and partly elected councils; better justice and a cleaner separation of judicial and administrative functions.[81] But he also recognized that the new regulations were not always applied, that former abuses continued, and that not all vilayets measured up to the standard set in Bulgaria by Midhat.[82] After the constitution of 1876 the debate still went on, centered for a short time in the chamber of deputies, where the delegates in considering a new revision of the 1867 law tried to limit the power of Porte-appointed officials in favor of increased popular rights and where demands that various provincial officials be tried for malfeasance were raised.[83] Complaints about the system were always numerous, but may be seen in better perspective when it is remembered that after three years Austrian administration in Bosnia was just as unpopular as Ottoman rule had been.[84] Any government that actually collected taxes was objectionable to many people.

Whether the vilayet system worked well or poorly depended in the end, as some of the foregoing comments recognize, on the quality of the administrators, especially of the valis. They now had extensive powers and a large territory. Fuad had said in 1867 that it was deemed prudent to give extensive powers to the valis, now that the tradition of the independent *derebeyi* was quite destroyed.[85] He was right in

[79] *Hürriyet*, #14 (29 eylûl 1868) and #22 (23 teşrin-i sani 1868), quoted in Kuntay, *Namık Kemal*, I, 134, n.2 and n.3.

[80] *Hürriyet*, #40 (29 mart 1869), quoted in *Tanzimat*, I (İstanbul, 1940), 821.

[81] *Üss-i inkılâb*, I, 103-105, 107-108; also Ahmed Midhat, *Kâinat* (İstanbul, 1288-1299), IV, 552-553.

[82] *Üss-i inkılâb*, I, 106. Here Ahmed Midhat tries to exculpate officials by blaming lapses not on the system, not on the men applying it, but on the perplexity of officials on how to apply the regulations.

[83] Robert Devereux, *A Study of the First Ottoman Parliament, 1877-1878* (George Washington University, unpublished M.A. thesis, 1956), pp. 135, 152-153.

[84] Charles Jelavich, "The Revolt in Bosnia-Hercegovina, 1881-1882," *Slavonic and East European Review*, 31:77 (June 1953), 421-423.

[85] Vetsera to Beust, 4 October 1867, in Testa, *Recueil des traités*, VII, 501.

so far as it was now unlikely that governors—those of Egypt excepted—would be able to establish hereditary positions in their provinces, independent of İstanbul. But the question of good administration remained a question of officials. If Midhat, a man of energy but imperfect vision, could operate the vilayet system in difficult areas, there was great hope. But the experience of the vilayet system varied from province to province and from year to year. Only a few provincial administrators could approach the standard Midhat set.[86] Some officials, at least at the start, actively tried to undermine the system.[87] But in most cases the difficulty was simply that a new system could not be staffed immediately with new administrators, nor infused at once with a new spirit. The evidence is overwhelming that the Stambuli efendi sent out to the provinces was ineffectual, although sometimes well-meaning, and that in many other instances he was interested only in his own pocket or in getting back to a job in the capital. An occasional administrator was in league with local brigands: one European traveller, set upon and robbed, received from the bandits for the amount taken a money order which the local kaymakam cashed.[88] Worse than actual corruption was the apathy of many officials in the face of local difficulties, which in times of crisis amounted almost to criminal negligence. During the great Anatolian famine of 1874 Turks who contributed funds for relief were not willing that the regular provincial administrators, most of whom had done nothing to alleviate conditions, should administer the aid, but employed special agents or foreigners.[89]

The administrative councils functioned indifferently. In some localities the wealthy Christian *çorbacı*'s dominated both the meclis and the Turkish officials. In other places a Muslim aristocracy thwarted the efforts of administrators sent out from the Porte. In still other places administrators dominated the meclis; Christians in Edirne referred to the council as *peki*, "yes-men." Some councils continued

---

[86] As Mehmed Raşid Paşa and Abdüllâtif Subhi Paşa in Syria: Mordtmann, *Stambul*, II, 50-53; Mehmed Said Paşa in Cyprus: Hill, *Cyprus*, IV, 248; the general experience in Salonika: P. Risal, *La ville convoitée—Salonique* (Paris, 1914), pp. 241, 246-247; and some of the governors in Bosnia: Koetschet, *Osman Pascha*, pp. 54, 63, 74-76.

[87] A. H. Midhat, *Tabsıra-i ibret*, p. 25, where Midhat Paşa accuses some officials of trying to arouse religious opposition to the vilayet system on the orders of the şeyhülislâm Sadeddin Efendi.

[88] Schweiger-Lerchenfeld, *Serail*, pp. 279-280.

[89] Mordtmann, *Stambul*, II, 63-82.

for several years with the same membership, as no elections were held. The *mazbata* process was misused as before to cover up misdeeds, or to confirm on paper what was not so in fact.[90] The new courts sometimes functioned reasonably well, where there was no interference from other officials, but there were always complaints about the administration of justice. The general assemblies of the vilayets met only at the beginning of the system, evidently into the early 1870's, and then were discontinued.[91] Because of the Porte's constant financial troubles, a disproportionate amount of the revenue of the provinces went to the capital and left the vilayets without the needed funds for improvement.

Mahmud Nedim Paşa, who became grand vezir in September 1871, surveyed the vilayet system at that point in a curiously unctuous circular to all valis. It could only have been designed to please the sultan and ward off critics.[92] The vilayet system is not working too well, observed the grand vezir; this is not the fault of Abdülaziz, who put so much personal effort into it, nor of the central administration, which issued all needed directives, nor yet of the people, so remarkable for their intelligence and aptitude and so heedful of the call of progress and civilization. It is the fault of the provincial authorities, who are not sufficiently imbued with the generous intentions that motivated this work of regeneration. Mahmud Nedim went on to warn these authorities to pay more attention to justice and education and less to newspapers, yearbooks, and roads built only to wash away. It was true that the valis, following Midhat's example, had begun to establish provincial newspapers, and yearbooks as well.[93] True also that some of their roads and other public works were shoddy. But Mahmud Nedim's circular sounded not only like an attempt to ingratiate himself with the sovereign, but also like a political attack on Âli's era, with its emphasis on vilayet reorganization. The

[90] Useful general accounts of provincial situations after the vilayet law are in Albert Dumont, *Le Balkan et l'Adriatique* (Paris, 1874), pp. 61-101, on Edirne; Midhat's report on Syria in 1878 in Clician Vassif, *Midhat*, pp. 161-168; Koetschet, *Osman Pascha*, pp. 6-10, 37-76, on Bosnia; Mordtmann, *Stambul*, II, 25-50, more general.

[91] Young, *Corps de droit*, I, 60, n.8; cf. *ibid.*, 40, n.13. The author does not know at what date they were discontinued. Koetschet, *Osman Pascha*, p. 7, speaks as if the Bosnian *meclis-i umumî* met annually in Sarajevo at least to 1874.

[92] Elliot to Granville, #382, 24 October 1871, FO 78/2177, encl.

[93] Belin, "Bibliographie ottomane," *Journal asiatique*, Series VI: 4 (August-September 1871), 152-154, analyzes one yearbook and names the nine vilayets that had so far produced them.

circular was followed by a series of articles in the semiofficial newspaper *La Turquie* harshly criticizing the whole vilayet law as setting up "little absolute states" in which the valis had the powers of proconsuls, quasi-independent vassal princes, *derebeyi*'s revived.[94] It may be that Mahmud Nedim was warring not only against the system[95] but against the possibility of any vali's becoming powerful or popular and, in particular, against Midhat, whose success in Baghdad quite possibly made Mahmud Nedim jealous.

Mahmud Nedim himself only helped to intensify the deficiencies of the vilayet system by speeding up the shifting of officials that had been one of the curses of provincial government through the previous forty years. Such shifting had occurred in Âli Paşa's time too: one German-born local official wrote that Ramazan was the month of changing officials and that "they change governors here as we change shirts at home."[96] But now Mahmud Nedim, evidently in an effort to isolate Abdülaziz from the influence of any potential rival, capriciously shifted officials, competent or not, from one post to another, and the chaos he inaugurated continued throughout the confused period up to 1876.[97] Ahmed Esad Paşa, a prominent statesman of European education, held twelve of the most important posts in the empire between 1867 and 1875, including five different governorships.[98] Mehmed Rauf Paşa was appointed vali of Salonika; arrived there, he was sent as vali to Bosnia; after two days in this post he was named commander of troops in Herzegovina; ten days later he was made vali of Monastir.[99] The London *Times* correspondent said of the situation about 1875 that provincial pashas lived only in the saddle, and that the İstanbul press had given up as sheer mockery the formula of congratulating each vilayet on "its good fortune in being entrusted to the care of a Pasha so universally known for his wisdom, justice, and humanity."[100] While the sultan and competing

---

[94] *La Turquie*, 23 November through 11 December 1871. The articles appear to be written by a European, are dated "1868" at the end, were reprinted from the *Impartial de Smyrne*, but it is noted that they could be published only after the grand vezir's circular. All phases of the law, including election process and courts and Christian-Muslim equality, were criticized, sometimes quite soundly.

[95] Evidently he "suspended" the vilayet system for a time, and Midhat restored it in August 1872 on becoming grand vezir: Ubicini, *Etat présent*, p. 90, n.3.

[96] Georg Schweitzer, *Emin Pascha* (Berlin, 1898), pp. 57, 70.

[97] On Mahmud Nedim's administration generally, see below, chapter VIII.

[98] *Levant Herald*, 30 November 1875.

[99] F. Bianconi, *La question d'Orient dévoilée* (Paris, 1876), p. 58.

[100] Gallenga, *Two Years*, I, 127.

statesmen played politics with provincial posts, the effect in the provinces was, of course, to deprive the minority of energetic and honest
administrators of both opportunity and incentive to undertake any
serious improvements. "I have been at Egin six months," said a kaymakam early in 1877. "I may be dismissed at any moment. What inducement is there for a man to try and improve the condition of the
people, when all his work may be upset by his successor?"[101]

Quite naturally, under these circumstances, voices were again raised
asking for the return of the good old days in provincial administration. To some this meant the *derebeyi* who was rooted in the soil he
governed, and not susceptible to reassignment by the Porte.[102] Others
called for the reinstitution of the system of provincial inspectors. Âli
Paşa's "political testament," supposedly written in 1871, called for
this. Mahmud Nedim actually did this in 1871, sending out *jurnalcı*'s,
or informers, from the Council of State to get information from the
people rather than from officials and to check up on one another at
intervals as well.[103] In 1876 there were again calls for inspectors—
as an Arabic journal of Istanbul expressed it, for a system of honest
commissioners like Ahmed Vefik Paşa.[104] Throughout these complaints
the emphasis was as much on the character of the officials as on the
system itself.

For it was true that the vilayet system, while imperfect and not
equally suited to all parts of the empire, could be made to work by
capable and honest men. This was clear to leading statesmen. The
qualifications which should be sought in officials had long been known
to Ottoman rulers and ministers. During the Crimean War, Sultan
Abdülmecid had insisted to a gathering of ministers and notables that

[101] Frederick Burnaby, *On Horseback Through Asia Minor* (London, 1877), II, 36.
[102] Hermann Vambéry, *Der Islam im neunzehnten Jahrhundert* (Leipzig, 1875), p. 127; Friedrich von Hellwald, *Der Islam* (Augsburg, 1877), pp. 36, 38; W. G. Palgrave, *Essays on Eastern Questions* (London, 1872), pp. 37-41, 158; J. L. Haddan, "Turkish Resources," *Journal of the Society of Fine Arts* (21 February 1879), p. 287; Wassa Effendi, *The Truth on Albania* (London, 1879), pp. 38-45; Ziya in *Hürriyet*, #41 (5 nisan 1869), quoted in *Tanzimat*, I, 821. Ziya regretted also the absence of the old weapons of confiscation and execution. Moustapha Djellaleddin, *Les Turcs*, pp. 62-63, in 1870 compared provincial officials unfavorably with the old feudal regime.
[103] Elliot to Granville, #392, 31 October 1871, FO 78/2177; *La Turquie*, 30 October 1871 and 27 December 1871. The author does not know how long this revival of inspection continued.
[104] Mordtmann, *Stambul*, II, 60, citing *El Dschewaib* [*al-Djawā'ib*]; *Diplomatic Review*, 24 (July 1876), 165.

industry and integrity were required.[105] Midhat and some others possessed these qualities. Also needed were a sensitivity to situations, and farsightedness, which critics of Midhat said he did not sufficiently possess.[106] The most penetrating analysis of the problems of government personnel in this period was made by Cevdet Paşa in his memorandum of 1872.[107] Sound education is needed for officials, said Cevdet, and the curriculum of the Mekteb-i Mülkiye must meet the needs of the times. Officials also need the ability to sense local situations and to apply policy accordingly, which means that they must have experience. Good officials must be suitably rewarded so that they stay in the civil service, rather than leaving it only to the misfits. The state must also decide on definite civil service rankings and on the duties of officials—in short, a table of organization and job descriptions—instead of the present vaguenesses. Then the effort must be made to find the right man for the job, not to find a job for the man. Cevdet recognized here the interconnection of men and system. Good men were necessary to operate any system. But a good system made it far easier, as the jurist Léon Ostrorog later pointed out, to employ as well as possible men of very medium ability; the regulations would make it as easy as possible for the officials to do their job right and as hard as possible to do it wrong.[108]

This was the direction in which the vilayet law tended, despite all its imperfections. The new system worked indifferently except where men like Midhat, of more than average ability, were in charge. But it served as a training school for better administrators in the future. It provided a small amount of experience with popular representation on administrative councils and provincial assemblies, which could serve as preparation for further democratization later and for a national assembly, should the time for such ever be ripe. A certain amount of public education was fostered by the vilayet system, not only with the councils and schools established in the provinces, but with the spread of local newspapers.[109] Finally, the vilayet law did

---

[105] Cevdet, Tezâkir, p. 51.

[106] Abdurrahman Şeref, Tarih musahabeleri, p. 204: to be nabızgir, sensitive to another's pulse and acting accordingly, and to have durbinlik, the quality of a telescope.

[107] In Mardin, Cevdet, pp. 342-348. The document deals with both judicial and administrative organization.

[108] Léon Ostrorog, Pour la réforme de la justice ottomane (Paris, 1912), p. 4. He speaks here of the administration of justice alone, but the principle is universal.

[109] By 1873 all but three vilayets had their own journals: Levant Herald, 8 April 1873.

provide some degree of local flexibility which hopefully might solve some administrative problems and contribute to the official goal of creating an amalgamated Ottomanism in the empire.

Whether in fact the vilayet system would realize its potential depended on many things, among them the existence of a forward-looking and stable ministry in the capital, the general progress of education among the people, and the development of more officials who were intelligent, hard-working, and patriotic. Critics could easily find that none of these conditions was developing. Among the most important critics of the period were a small group of men who in the later 1860's represented the beginnings of the first modern Turkish public opinion. Their influence, brought to bear on questions of education, administration, and the preservation and general progress of the empire, was first felt in the period of the vilayet law's initiation, in the time of Âli and Fuad. They called themselves the New Ottomans.

CHAPTER VI

POLITICAL AGITATION: THE NEW OTTOMANS

The year 1867 was the most eventful of the years between the Crimean War and the deposition of Sultan Abdülaziz in 1876. Crete still seethed in rebellion. The Cretan question brought strained relations between Greece and the Porte. Revolutionary Bulgars staged a premature uprising. Unrest in Montenegro produced border raids. There was an ephemeral revolt in Syria. Under pressure, the Turks withdrew their last garrison from Serbia. Prince Michael of Serbia was meanwhile occupied with plans for a movement of the united Balkans against Ottoman rule. These events, in particular the Cretan revolt for *enosis* with Greece and the departure of the last Turkish soldiers from Belgrade, roused Muslim feeling within the empire. At the same time France, Russia, and Britain were severally engaged in assessing the fulfillment of the Hatt-ı Hümayun's promises and in pressing the Turkish ministers for more extensive reforms. By the force of internal events and external pressure the Turks were led to take stock of their position.

Sultan Abdülaziz was moved to break precedent and show himself in 1867 in Europe—the first Ottoman ruler to travel outside his domains except at the head of an army. The impression he made on the West probably did the Ottoman Empire no lasting good, though it brought some immediate diplomatic benefit; but the impression that western technological advance made on him was considerable. Fuad wrote in 1867 for foreign consumption his memorandum on the fulfillment of the Hatt-ı Hümayun, in which he emphasized the steps taken toward equality and administrative modernization, with particular praise for the vilayet experiment. In the same year Âli's memorandum, written for the Porte only, laid down his belief in the necessity of a fusion of the empire's peoples, of westernized education, and of admitting Christians to the highest offices. These were the voices of the central government.

For the first time, in 1867 also, other voices which criticized the government made themselves distinctly heard. Some of them belonged to men prominent in the public life of the empire—Mustafa Fazıl Paşa, Halil Şerif Paşa, Hayreddin Paşa—who wrote reform proposals which circulated more or less publicly. Other voices belonged to a small group of young men who were quite discontented with both the international and the domestic situation of the Ottoman Empire. Although they all held government jobs at various times, their importance arises from the fact that they symbolized the growing intellectual ferment of the time and that they constituted, in effect, the beginning of modern political agitation in the empire. They engaged in conspiracy, like the men of 1859, but their real medium was the press, and a good deal of their inspiration came from their knowledge of French and their firsthand observation of western Europe. Loosely grouped together under several different labels, these young men in a hurry came to call themselves the "New Ottomans."

Frequently the New Ottomans have been called "Young Turks," and some of them on occasion used the French term "Jeune Turquie" to describe their group. But the terms "Young Turk" and "Young Turkey" have introduced endless confusion into Ottoman history, and should be avoided except for reference to the later generation of agitators who from 1889 on worked against Abdülhamid II's regime. Well before the New Ottomans were organized as a group in 1865, these expressions were current in Europe, and continued to be so throughout the Tanzimat period.[1] But they were so loosely used as to defy definition. The commonest early use by Europeans was to indicate young Turks who knew French, who might have been to Europe for education or travel, and who in attitudes and manners often tried to ape the West.[2] Shortly *Jeune Turquie* (sometimes capitalized and sometimes not) began to be used to identify any Turkish statesman or group who wanted some sort of change, whether reactionary or progressive. Thus in 1855 the French writer Ubicini designated Mahmud II's *jeune Turquie* as a group of conservative statesmen on the model of Kıbrıslı Mehmed or Ahmed Vefik who wanted reform by return to the old ways, while Sultan Abdülmecid's *jeune Turquie*

---

[1] The claim of Ebüzziya Tevfik, historian of the New Ottomans, that the term "Young Turk" was first seen by European newspapers in a letter of Mustafa Fazıl published by *Le Nord* on 7 February 1867 cannot be true: Ebüzziya, "Yeni Osmanlıların sebebi zuhuru," *Yeni tasvir-i efkâr*, 1 June 1909, cited in Mithat Cemal Kuntay, *Namık Kemal* (İstanbul, 1944-1956), I, 289, n.12.

[2] So in Edouard Driault, *L'Egypte et l'Europe* (Cairo, 1930-1931), II, #106, letter of 7 May 1840 to İbrahim Paşa's agent from Constantinople; Lady Hornby, *Constantinople During the Crimean War* (London, 1863), p. 64, letter dated Therapia, 26 October 1855; Georges Perrot, *Souvenirs d'un voyage en Asie Mineure* (Paris, 1864), p. xv. Cf. Schauffler to Redhouse, Bebek, 19 June 1856, ABCFM, Armenian Mission VIII.

headed by Reşid, Âli, and Fuad drove willy-nilly toward a superficial westernization.[3] In his diary for May 2, 1864, the American missionary Van Lennep noted that "there is a party, chiefly composed of young men educated in Europe, who may be denominated 'Young Turkey,' whose object and endeavour is to introduce a general and radical reform into all branches of the administration. . . . They claim that the civil code of the Koran is no longer adapted to the wants of mankind; that Religion and the State should no longer be identical; and that the latter should be thoroughly renovated and reconstructed upon an European model. . . ." Many people, he noted, mistakenly identify these Young Turks with the heterodox Kızılbaşı sect.[4] Yet another keen observer of the Turkish scene could call those who wanted to restore the Janissary power "Young Turks."[5] The leaders of the fanatical part of the ulema were also said to call themselves "Young Turks."[6] A later generation of historians contributed to the confusion by applying the name "Young Turk" to Selim III as well as to Mahmud II and Abdülmecid and also to Midhat Paşa, represented as leader of a party of pan-Islamic fanatics dedicated to opposing pan-Slavism.[7] Such undisciplined use of the term has made "Young Turk" nearly meaningless for the Tanzimat period, although, unfortunately, later Turkish writers have on occasion used it as an alternative term for the "New Ottomans."[8] For this period, if "Young Turk" has any meaning at all, it is in the sense in which European journals most frequently used it—to indicate a somewhat westernized view, the opposite of "Old Turk." The influence of Mazzini's Young Italy, and its brother organizations in his Young Europe, on western

[3] Abdolonyme Ubicini, *La Turquie actuelle* (Paris, 1855), pp. 160-165. This categorization is followed, capitalized, by Hippolyte Castille, *Réchid-pacha* (Paris, 1857), p. 35.

[4] Henry J. Van Lennep, *Travels in Little-Known Parts of Asia Minor* (London, 1870), I, 32.

[5] Andreas D. Mordtmann, *Stambul und das moderne Türkenthum* (Leipzig, 1877-1878), I, 66. In other places he calls them "reactionaries" and "Old Turks": *ibid.*, 217-218; *Anatolien: Skizzen und Reisebriefe* (Hannover, 1925), p. 77.

[6] Mordtmann, *Stambul*, II, 170.

[7] Soubhy Noury, *Le régime représentatif en Turquie* (Paris, 1914), p. 61; Bernhard Stern, *Jungtürken und Verschwörer* (Leipzig, 1901), pp. 108-109; Edouard Driault, *La question d'Orient* (Paris, 1921), pp. 203, 450; W. Allison Phillips, *Modern Europe* (London, 1908), pp. 210, 492-493.

[8] Cf. Abdurrahman Şeref, "Ahmed Midhat Efendi," *Tarih-i osmani encümeni mecmuası*, III:18 (1328), 1115; *idem*, *Tarih musahabeleri* (İstanbul, 1339), p. 172. These use "Genç Türkiye" and "Genç Türkler." Cf. also Halide Edib, *Turkey Faces West* (New Haven, 1930), p. 86; Mehmed Zeki Pakalın, *Mahmud Nedim Paşa* (İstanbul, 1940), p. 136.

nomenclature for progressive Turks is evident. But for the young political agitators of the later 1860's the name "New Ottomans" (Yeni Osmanlılar)—their own choice—is far better.

The New Ottomans were never a political party in the modern sense, although they have sometimes been so called. In the empire of that day there were no parties aside from the "ins" and the "outs," subdivided into groups formed about one or another of the rival Turkish statesmen or around one of the embassies in the capital.[9] The period of greatest cohesion of the New Ottomans came in 1867 when, in this fashion, they were gathered around Mustafa Fazıl Paşa, whose transitory, though significant, role will be discussed hereafter. But essentially the New Ottomans were a loose group of individualistic intellectuals who had some common attitudes toward the situation of the empire in the mid-1860's. For one thing, they were opposed to the tight grip which Âli and Fuad maintained on the Ottoman administration. Âli was their especial bugbear. New Ottoman hatred of Âli was reinforced by personal grievances which some of them had against him. Another and even stronger bond among them was the passionate resentment at European interference in the affairs of the empire, and at the diminution of the empire's strength exhibited by the Cretan revolt and the evacuation of Belgrade. Of all the excited Muslim reaction to these events, the New Ottomans' was the greatest and most vocal. Their opposition to Âli stemmed in part from this, for Âli as foreign minister or grand vezir was forced on many occasions to yield to the pressure of the great powers and to deal with rebellion by conciliation as well as by repression. A further bond among the New Ottomans, and in part an explanation of their origin as a group, was their participation in the literary renaissance of the day—the revolt against classicism, the emulation of some western examples, and the rise of independent Turkish journalism in the empire. The New Ottomans did not initiate the renaissance, but sought to hurry it along. In the years after the Crimean War this intellectual and literary revival was already under way. It was one of the major characteristics of the Tanzimat period.

Ottoman literature, the poetry in particular, had long been under the influence of the Persian not only in form, but in subject matter,

---

[9] Cf. Dr. K., *Erinnerungen aus dem Leben des Serdar Ekrem Omer Pascha* (Sarajevo, 1885), pp. 253-255.

imagery, vocabulary, and construction. Since poetic subjects were restricted, variations had to occur in the intricacy and subtlety of expression. The literary result was far removed from the language of
the ordinary Turk. Although in the eighteenth century there had
been a decline in Persian influence, the classical tradition continued
strong well into the nineteenth century. Of course, by that time it had
lost all vigor and originality. Even the *âşık*, the popular poet who
filled the role of wandering minstrel in the market places and coffeehouses of the empire, was considerably influenced by Persian style.
There was a brief Persianist revival, the last gasp of the old order,
as late as the 1860's.[10] Prose also continued to be complex. The peasant
could not understand a Turkish newspaper even when it was read to
him. Even people of some education complained about mid-century to
Alfred Churchill, editor of the semiofficial *Ceride-i havadis* (*Register
of Events*), which was written in "middle Turkish" rather than "eloquent Turkish," that they had difficulty in understanding it. Pure
Turkish words were largely missing from the literary vocabulary,
and when Persian and Arabic words did not fill the needs, European
importations were used.[11] In the government bureaus official style, to
which efendis continued to give great attention, tended to remain
complex and contorted. Some officials were contemptuous of simplicity; even at the end of the Tanzimat period it was possible to write
a thirteen-page document in two sentences.[12] Punctuation was almost
unknown. Further, the Arabic alphabet, really unsuited to the representation of Turkish sounds, complicated the task of easy and accurate reading and writing. To cap it all, there were nine different
calligraphic systems in use in Turkey.[13] The adequacy of the educational system entirely aside, it is small wonder that even by the end

---

[10] E. J. W. Gibb, *A History of Ottoman Poetry* (London, 1900-1909), IV, passim;
also V, 30, on the 1860's. Cf. M. F. Köprülü, s.v. "Turks," *Encyclopaedia of Islam*,
IV, 954. On the *âşık: ibid.*; Edmond Saussey, *Littérature populaire turque* (Paris,
1936), pp. 37-40; Mustafa Nihat [Özön], *Metinlerle muasır türk edebiyatı tarihi*
(İstanbul, 1934), pp. 194-195; Van Lennep, *Travels*, I, 252-254.

[11] Andreas D. Mordtmann, "Ueber das Studium des Türkischen," *Zeitschrift der
Deutschen Morgenländischen Gesellschaft*, III (1849), 351-353.

[12] Summary of an interrogation of Midhat Paşa in İsmail Hakkı Uzunçarşılı,
Midhat ve Rüştü Paşaların tevkiflerine dair vesikalar (Ankara, 1946), pp. 87-100.
Cf. Hermann Vambéry, *Sittenbilder aus dem Morgenlande* (Berlin, 1876), pp. 196-
197.

[13] T. X. Bianchi, "Bibliographie ottomane," *Journal asiatique*, Series V: 16 (October-November 1860), 335-337.

of the Tanzimat period only four to five per cent of the Ottoman population were literate.[14]

Book publication had increased considerably throughout the nineteenth century, but it remained true that the majority of works which appeared in İstanbul or from the great press at Bulak in Egypt from 1856 on to 1877 dealt with traditional subjects in the old-fashioned manner: commentaries on law and religion, essays on mysticism, classical poetry, literary criticism, biographical dictionaries, chronicles of the Ottoman sultans, and the like.[15]

The situation here described, though characteristic, was never static. By the start of the nineteenth century, it has already been noted, new influences began to compete with the old as the knowledge of French increased, as military and technical works were translated and published, as secular educational institutions multiplied. The reaction against the old ways took several forms—efforts to introduce more Turkish words into the literary vocabulary, to simplify style, to clarify spelling. At the same time there was a trend toward a broader range of subject matter for published works, toward increased translation from western languages, toward using western forms, as in journalism and drama. In most of these trends a number of the New Ottomans ultimately participated, and occasionally pioneered. A number of leading Ottoman statesmen were also prime movers in the movement away from tradition and toward intelligibility.

The drive to include more Turkish words in the literary vocabulary found encouragement from a number of sources. The commission on education set up in 1845, of which Âli and Fuad were members, sought to introduce a popular literary language purged of many Arabic and Persian elements.[16] The Encümen-i Daniş which was founded shortly thereafter discussed the compilation of an Osmanli dictionary which should limit the Arabic, Persian, and other foreign words to be accepted for common usage, and appointed a commission

---

[14] J. Østrup, "Den moderne, literaere bevaegelse i Tyrkiet," *Nordisk Tidskrift för Vetenskap, Konst och Industri* (Stockholm, 1900), p. 215.

[15] Valuable lists of new publications appeared quite regularly by Hammer-Purgstall and Schlechta-Wssehrd in the *Sitzungsberichte der K.U.K. Akademie der Wissenschaften zu Wien, Philologisch-Historische Klasse*, and were continued by the latter after 1866 in the *Zeitschrift der Deutschen Morgenländischen Gesellschaft*; also by Bianchi and Belin in the *Journal asiatique*. On historians see also Franz Babinger, *Die Geschichtsschreiber der Osmanen und ihre Werke* (Leipzig, 1927).

[16] Freiherr F. W. von Reden, *Die Türkei und Griechenland in ihrer Entwicklungsfähigkeit* (Frankfurt a.M., 1856), p. 308.

to work on this.[17] The resurgence of Bektashism in this period may also have contributed, since the Bektashi order had through centuries preserved the popular language in the face of the dominant Persian influence.[18] So may the writing of Feth-Ali Ahondof, a Turk of Russian Azerbayjan, who wrote in a clear Turkish.[19] The culmination in this period of the move toward Turkishness in vocabulary was the dictionary compiled by Ahmed Vefik Paşa, and published in 1876, which was based on the living language, emphasizing Turkish words.[20]

Probably more progress was made in simplifying style than in replacing Arabic and Persian words with Turkish. An increasing number of writers became convinced that greater clarity and simplicity were important, among them the historian Cevdet Paşa who, after finishing five volumes of his history, began to modernize his style with the sixth.[21] Most of the new generation of journalists, including the New Ottomans, had like tendencies.[22] The process was abetted by an 1855 statute which made mandatory the simplification that had already begun in administrative ordinances: "In the future, the *nizamat* laws or ordinances will no longer be written in obscure or ambiguous words, they shall be stated and explained in clear, easy and concise terms."[23] The Hatt-ı Hümayun of 1856 was in simpler style than documents theretofore.[24] Also a milestone was the first modern Turkish grammar to appear in the empire, done by Cevdet together with Fuad, published in 1851. The language, however, was still called "Osmanli."[25]

[17] Fatma Aliye, *Ahmed Cevdet Paşa ve zamanı* (İstanbul, 1332), p. 76.

[18] J. Kingsley Birge, *The Bektashi Order of Dervishes* (London, 1937), pp. 16-17.

[19] H. J. Kissling, "Die türkische Sprachreform," *Leipziger Vierteljahrschrift für Südosteuropa*, I (October 1937), 74.

[20] *Lehçe-i osmanî* (İstanbul, 1293). Cf. Babinger, *Geschichtsschreiber*, pp. 373-374; A. C. Barbier de Meynard, "Lehdjè-i-osmani . . . ," *Journal asiatique*, Series VII:8 (August-September 1876), 275-280; idem, *Dictionnaire turc-français* (Paris, 1881-1886), I, ii-v.

[21] Babinger, *Geschichtsschreiber*, p. 378. *Ibid.*, pp. 360-362, credits Hayrullah Efendi (d. 1866) with being the first to write Ottoman history in straightforward rather than bombastic style. Cf. T. X. Bianchi, *Khaththy Humaïoun* (Paris, 1856), pp. vii-viii. The movement toward simplified style and vocabulary is surveyed with many examples in Agâh Sırrı Levend, *Türk dilinde gelişme ve sadeleşme safhaları* (Ankara, 1949), pp. 96-162, and briefly in Bernard Lewis, *The Emergence of Modern Turkey* (London, 1961), pp. 423-424.

[22] Ahmed Midhat, who began his journalistic career with Midhat Paşa in the Tuna vilayet, felt very strongly on this: *Üss-i inkılâb* (İstanbul, 1294-1295), I, 121-122.

[23] Law of 26 November 1855 quoted from *Takvim-i vekayi* in Bianchi, *Khaththy Humaïoun*, p. viii.

[24] *Ibid.*, p. vi.

[25] *Kavaid-i osmaniye* (İstanbul, 1268), trans. by H. Kellgren as *Grammatik der os-*

Hand in hand with the movement toward a simpler style went efforts to clarify the orthography. The practical leaders seem again to have been Fuad and Cevdet. In their grammar they employed two diacritical marks to show accurately some of the vowel sounds. Cevdet did the same in the third volume of his *History*. In the imperial year-book (*salname*) for 1858-1859 Fuad caused diacritical marks indicating vowel pronunciation to be inserted for the first time.[26] Münif Efendi (later Paşa), one of the best-educated Turks of his day, and a product of the translation bureau and the diplomatic service, was much concerned with the need for systematizing the spelling, saying that every word could be read five ways and wanting at least better signs for vowel sounds.[27] He is said to have harbored thoughts of giving up the Arabic alphabet altogether.[28] The Azerbayjani Feth-Ali came to İstanbul in 1863 to propose an alphabet reform to the government, but it was not accepted. He also was willing to adopt the Latin alphabet.[29]

When measured against modern Turkish, the progress toward clarity and simplification seems to have been abysmally slow. But within a decade after the Crimean War the change was unmistakable to those who knew the old. "Taste in matters of style has been singularly modified," wrote one of the foremost orientalists in 1865. "The hereditary predilection of Ottoman writers for periods of an excessive length is disappearing little by little. The artificial combinations of rhymed prose, . . . the puns as well as the frequent quotations from the Arabic and Persian are more and more losing their centuries-old charm, and yielding to the conviction that in matters of wording, clarity, simplicity, and precision are qualities more to be appreciated than the

---

manischen Sprache (Helsingfors, 1855). Cf. Âli Ölmezoğlu, "Cevdet Paşa," *İslâm ansiklopedisi*, III, 115, 122, and the critical comments by Mordtmann and Hammer-Purgstall in *Zeitschrift der Deutschen Morgenländischen Gesellschaft*, VI:3 (1852), 410-411.

[26] Barbier de Meynard in *Journal asiatique*, Series VII:8 (August-September 1876), 279-280; O. Blau, "Nachrichten über kurdische Stämme," *Zeitschrift der Deutschen Morgenländischen Gesellschaft*, 16:4 (1862), 607.

[27] Agâh Sırrı Levend in *Ulus*, 9 August 1953, quoted in William A. Edmonds, "Language Reform in Turkey . . . ," *Muslim World*, 45:1 (January 1955), 57.

[28] Martin Hartmann, *Der islamische Orient* (Berlin, 1899), I, 21-22 n.

[29] Edmonds, "Language Reform in Turkey . . . ," p. 58; A. A. Pallis, "The Language Reform in Turkey," *Royal Central Asian Journal*, 25:3 (June 1938), 439-440; Mirza Bala, "Feth-Ali Ahund-zâde," *İslâm ansiklopedisi*, IV, 579. On these moves to simplify orthography see, further, Fevziye Tansel, "Arap harflerinin islâhı ve değiştirilmesi hakkında ilk teşebbüsler ve neticeleri (1862-1884)," *Belleten*, 17:66 (April 1953), 224-226; Levend, *Türk dilinde gelişme*, pp. 167-171; Lewis, *Emergence*, pp. 421-422.

most harmonious phraseology." This advance he credited to the influence of Reşid, Fuad, Âli, Cevdet, and others, and cited progress made in indicating vowels, in better spelling, and in the start of regular punctuation.[30]

Among the books published at İstanbul there began to appear works written sometimes in the old style, but infused with a new spirit, and indicative of an interest in a broader range of subject matter. This is evident, for instance, in the histories. Where the official historiographer twenty years before had pointed out in vain that events in other countries should be included, by the 1860's Hayrullah Efendi was trying to put Ottoman history in its world context, and Ahmed Hilmi was translating from the English and improving a world history.[31] Cevdet Paşa in his history and Subhi Paşa in his work on numismatics followed careful research methods.

The symbol of this broadening interest, showing clearly the influence of secular western thought and of the trend toward Osmanlılık, was the founding of the Ottoman Scientific Society (Cemiyet-i İlmiye-i Osmaniye) in 1861. This was principally the work of the liberal and enlightened Münif Efendi, just as the earlier Academy of Learning (Encümen-i Daniş) reflected the concerns of the more conservative but equally enlightened Cevdet Paşa. Münif was not only grounded in oriental languages, but knew several European tongues as well, had studied in Berlin while serving as secretary of the embassy there, and had broad contacts, among them the American missionaries in İstanbul. For translating bits from Voltaire, and reportedly helping to put the Bible into Turkish, he was denounced on occasion as an atheist.[32] The Scientific Society's constitution set forth as its object the extension of knowledge of the arts and sciences in the empire through translations, book publication, and teaching, while it was to refrain from discussing political or religious questions of the moment. Membership was open to all, regardless of race or religion, who knew Turkish,

[30] O. Schlechta-Wssehrd in the preface to K.K. Orientalische Akademie in Wien, Osmanische Sprichwörter (Vienna, 1865), pp. vii-x.

[31] J. H. Kramers, Analecta Orientalia, I (Leiden, 1954), 18; Babinger, Geschichtsschreiber, pp. 360-362, 364-365. Hayrullah was a product of the medical school, Ahmed Hilmi of the translation bureau.

[32] On him see Mordtmann, Stambul, I, 173-176; Amand von Schweiger-Lerchenfeld, Serail und Hohe Pforte (Vienna, 1879), pp. 228-229; George Washburn, Fifty Years in Constantinople (Boston, 1909), pp. xvii-xviii, not naming Münif but evidently referring to him; İ. A. Gövsa, Türk meşhurları (İstanbul, n.d.), p. 267; Levant Herald, 13 February 1877, calling him a member of Jeune Turquie, though so far as the author knows he was not one of the Young Ottomans.

Arabic, or Persian plus French, English, German, Italian, or Greek. The society established a library open three days a week and offered public courses in five languages, in arithmetic, and in political economy. Its journal, the *Mecmua-i fünun* (*Journal of Sciences*), carried articles on a wide range of subjects, including history, geography, astronomy, geology, child education, financial problems, and transportation. With its fourth number the *Journal* began to run articles on foreign political questions as well. The language of the *Journal* was, as Münif promised in the first issue, clear and simple "so as to be understood by all."[33] Where earlier salons or groups had tended to cluster around literary men who were poets or philosophers, the new trend was toward combining literary interests with the discussion of science and national economy.[34]

Concurrently with the movements toward a purer vocabulary, a simpler style, better spelling, and a broader range of subjects came a growing stream of translations from western languages, principally from the French. Now to the translations of textbooks and scientific works were added an increasing number of histories, novels, poems, and plays.[35] What a vogue some of the translated works might have is shown by the history of Fénelon's *Télémaque*. This was among the French novels best known to Levantine society in Pera.[36] Yusuf Kâmil Paşa, one of the outstanding statesmen of the empire, translated it into Turkish in 1859—the first novel put into Turkish. After three years of circulating from hand to hand, it was published twice, the second time in 1863 at Şinasi Efendi's *Tasvir-i efkâr* press, during the period when Yusuf Kâmil was grand vezir. This rendition was into Turkish of the old bombastic style.[37] *Télémaque* seems to have had a

[33] T. X. Bianchi, "Bibliographie ottomane," *Journal asiatique*, Series VI: 2 (August-September 1863), 237-261; Series VI: 5 (January-February 1865), 174 n.; "Schreiben des Hrn. Dr. Busch an Prof. Brockhaus," *Zeitschrift der Deutschen Morgenländischen Gesellschaft* 17:3/4 (1863), 711-713; Levend, *Türk dilinde gelişme*, p. 99. Cf. Ragıp Özdem, "Tanzimattan beri yazı dilimiz," *Tanzimat*, I (İstanbul, 1940), 883-884.
[34] Franz von Werner [Murad Efendi], *Türkische Skizzen* (Leipzig, 1877), II, 75; Benoît Brunswik, *Etudes pratiques sur la question d'Orient* (Paris, 1869), pp. 57-58.
[35] Cf. Özön, *Muasır edebiyatı tarihi*, 20-22, 42-44, 331-332; Otto Hachtmann, "Türkische Übersetzungen aus europäischen Literaturen," *Die Welt des Islams*, VI:1 (1918), 1-23; İsmail Habib [Sevük], *Avrupa edebiyatı ve biz: Garpten tercümeler* (İstanbul, 1940-1941), especially vol. 2.
[36] Ubicini, *Turquie actuelle*, pp. 456-457.
[37] Özön, *Muasır edebiyatı tarihi*, pp. 83, 295, 331; *Augsburger Allgemeine Zeitung*, 6 July 1876 Beilage.

considerable popularity in translation. Münif Paşa praised it in an early number of his *Mecmua-i fünun.*[38] Ahmed Vefik Paşa, immensely irritated at Yusuf Kâmil's ornate prose, later put *Télémaque* into a simpler Turkish.[39] Ziya Paşa also translated it.[40] There was more than pure fiction in the work, for it contained a protest against the tyranny and maladministration of Louis XIV, and set forth ideas for a model state. Its political influence on other writers, and perhaps on larger groups, may have been fairly wide. The leader of a small Muslim heterodox sect that exhibited French secular ideas and called itself Protestant as well as truly Muslim and truly Christian claimed to interpret *Télémaque* in spiritual terms.[41]

The reaction against the classical tradition extended also to the introduction of westernized drama. The Turks had long enjoyed their traditional varieties of drama, such as the shadow play.[42] But the new stimulation of the stage came from western contacts. For some years European pieces had been played to the foreign element in İstanbul. Many were typical, in their second-rate quality and bad acting, of the specimens of European culture that found their way to Turkey. Of one play the *Levant Herald* complained that "the dialogue is as heavy as the allusions are indelicate. . . . Of such a piece the less said of the acting the better."[43] Other plays were performed in Turkish translation, but by Armenian actors with execrable Turkish accents, and the women's parts taken by men. Better stimulation came through those Turks who had been to Europe and liked the western stage, especially French drama. Molière in particular had an appeal. Many of his comedies were translated and adapted by Ahmed Vefik Paşa.[44] The drama, whether translated or original, provided a new means for developing Turkish language and thought. Of this, as of other literary media, the New Ottomans made good use.

[38] Bianchi, "Bibliographie ottomane," *Journal asiatique*, Series VI:2 (August-September 1863), 248.

[39] Özön, *Muasır edebiyatı tarihi*, p. 295; İsmail Habib [Sevük], *Avrupa edebiyatı ve biz*, II, 57-59.

[40] Gibb, *Ottoman Poetry*, V, 59.

[41] Schauffler to Clark, 1 February 1868, ABCFM, Western Turkey Mission IV, #26.

[42] Cf. Nicholas Martinovich, *The Turkish Theatre* (New York, 1933); George Jacob, *Geschichte des Schattentheaters* (Berlin, 1907), pp. 82-108.

[43] November 6, 1867.

[44] Özön, *Muasır edebiyatı tarihi*, pp. 202-204; Mordtmann, *Stambul*, I, 163; Bianchi, "Bibliographie ottomane," *Journal asiatique*, Series V:13 (June 1859), 541-542; Sevük, *Avrupa edebiyatı*, II, 44-50.

The man who stands as a symbol of these innovations, who is a link between the new literary currents and the New Ottomans, and who in addition first developed the independent Turkish journalism which was the particular medium of the New Ottomans, was İbrahim Şinasi Efendi. Şinasi, the son of a deceased artillery captain, was in the 1840's working as a clerk in the imperial arsenal, writing some occasional verse in the old style, and beginning to learn French. His application to be sent to Paris for study at government expense was approved by Reşid Paşa's administration. During his stay of approximately five years Şinasi was ostensibly to study economic and scientific subjects, but developed a great interest in literature as well. He met Lamartine and other men of letters. On his return to İstanbul, probably in 1853 when he was about twenty-seven years old, Reşid's patronage secured public office for him. Although Âli and Fuad dismissed him, they were eventually reconciled to him through Yusuf Kâmil Paşa.[45]

İbrahim Şinasi is sometimes said to have taken part in the revolution of 1848 and to have returned from Paris a republican and an atheist.[46] This is problematic. Throughout his later life Şinasi showed himself to be rather nonpolitical, and some, at least, of his poetry has a strong theistic note.[47] What he obviously brought back with him were some general notions on western cultural development, some specific ideas on literary forms and simplicity of style, and probably some concept of western-style patriotism, to all of which his writing after his return bears testimony. In 1859 Şinasi published a booklet of poetical fragments translated from Racine, Lamartine, La Fontaine, and others, in which the French text appeared on the page opposite his Turkish rendition. This was the first western poetry to be put into Turkish, and although its immediate influence was as slim as the volume, the long-run implications of the influence of French imagery and form on Turkish poetry were vast.[48] Another new departure by Şinasi was the

[45] On his early life see Gibb, *Ottoman Poetry*, V, 22-25; Jean Deny, "Shinasi," *Encyclopaedia of Islam*, IV, 371; Özön, *Muasır edebiyatı tarihi*, pp. 27-28, n.1; Ahmed Rasim, *İlk büyük muharrirlerden Şinasi* (İstanbul, 1927), pp. 23-29.

[46] Deny, "Shinasi," who says he can find no evidence (p. 372); Vambéry, *Sittenbilder*, p. 36; Halide Edib [Adıvar], *The Conflict of East and West in Turkey*, 2nd ed. (Lahore, 1935), p. 189; several of her statements about Şinasi are suspect. A. H. Tanpınar, *XIX. asır türk edebiyatı tarihi*, 2nd ed. (İstanbul, 1956), pp. 155, 159, says Şinasi went to Paris only after the 1848 events.

[47] Examples in Gibb, *Ottoman Poetry*, V, 35-36, 40.

[48] Bianchi, "Bibliographie ottomane," *Journal asiatique*, Series V:16 (October-November 1860), 341-343; Gibb, *Ottoman Poetry*, V, 32; Paul Horn, *Geschichte der türkischen Moderne* (Leipzig, 1902), p. 10. Horn names the wrong volume for this

first original play to be written in Turkish in the empire. *Şair evlenmesi* (*A Poet's Marriage*), evidently inspired by the Molière that Şinasi had seen in Paris, was a crude satire on the Muslim custom of making marriage contracts through intermediaries, and turned on the substitution of an ugly bride for a pretty one. As drama, the comedy was less important than it was for the introduction of playwriting to Turkish literature.[49] Şinasi experimented in some of his original poetry with a few verses using Turkish words only, and he published also his own collection of Turkish proverbs.

Of far greater immediate impact than his rather slight achievement in poetry and drama was Şinasi's work in journalism. Here he carried on the reforming trends toward simplifying style and making it suit the subject, toward using more Turkish vernacular expressions, toward introducing punctuation—in short, toward making written Turkish more widely intelligible and more useful for discussions of social, political, and scientific subjects. As important as these questions of style was the fact that his venture into the newspaper world marked the beginning of independent Turkish journalism. Until this time there were in the empire, especially in the capital, a good many newspapers in foreign languages or the languages of the minority peoples, but only two in Turkish, and both were government-connected. The one was the *Takvim-i vekayi*, the official paper established by Mahmud II; the other was the semiofficial *Ceride-i havadis*, edited by Alfred Churchill, son of its founder, William Churchill, which had a government subvention.[50] Then on October 22, 1860, appeared the first

year, confusing the translations of 1859 with a later volume of selected poems. The volume was published at the plant of the *Presse d'Orient*, whose editor Jean Piétri gave support to the New Ottomans.

[49] Özön, *Muasır edebiyatı tarihi*, pp. 202, 206-207, who dates the play as 1860 and says it was first published in the *Tercüman-ı ahval*; the same author in his *Son asır türk edebiyatı tarihi* (İstanbul, 1941), p. 133, dates it 1859; Vambéry, *Sittenbilder*, p. 36, who dates it as about 1858-1859 and erroneously says it was published in the *Ceride-i havadis*; followed by a translation into German, pp. 37-46. Turkish original in Ahmed Rasim, *Şinasi*, pp. 140-150.

[50] There had been also since 1828 a Turkish-Arabic paper in Cairo, the organ of Mehmed Ali's government: M. Hartmann, "Djarīda," *Encyclopaedia of Islam*, I, 1018. A very influential Arabic weekly, *al-Djawā'ib*, began publication in İstanbul in late July 1860, two months before Şinasi's venture, but it acquired a subsidy from the Porte: C. Brockelmann, "Fāris al-Shidyāk," *Encyclopaedia of Islam*, II, 67-68. On the development of the press in the empire from the beginnings to the 1860's see Abdolonyme Ubicini, *Letters on Turkey* (London, 1856), I, 246-253; Ahmed Emin [Yalman], *The Development of Modern Turkey as Measured by its Press* (New York, 1914), pp. 27-38; Server İskit, *Türkiyede matbuat idareleri ve politikaları* (Ankara?, 1943), pp. 3-28; Özön, *Muasır edebiyatı tarihi*, pp. 698-702;

number of the *Tercüman-ı ahval* (*Interpreter of Conditions*). The publisher was Agâh Efendi, a product of the triple westernization of premedical education, employment in the translation bureau, and service as secretary in the Paris embassy.[51] The editor was Şinasi, who had resigned his government positions to take up the new profession. After a few months Şinasi left this journal to start his own, the *Tasvir-i efkâr* (*Representation of Opinions*), which appeared first on June 27, 1862.[52] This biweekly sheet of four pages contained bits of foreign and domestic news, but also supplementary articles on historical, literary, and social matters, intended for the education of the public, and in a style whose shorter sentences, punctuation, and simpler construction were designed to serve the same end.[53]

Shortly Şinasi was joined on his paper by a young man of twenty-three or so, Namık Kemal. Scion of a family distinguished in the Ottoman public service, Namık Kemal had been immersed in studies of Persian and Arabic and the old-school poets, whose style he imitated in verse of his own which he began composing in his early teens. Coming to İstanbul from the provinces at about eighteen, he won entrée to poetic groups. The turning point in his life came about the year 1863, when he secured a position in the translation bureau and thus regularly came in contact with the French language and with European affairs. Then also he met Şinasi, who persuaded him to help with the *Tasvir-i efkâr*. These influences channeled Kemal's energies into translating articles from European newspapers, discussing current questions, and generally raising the level of Ottoman culture—his lifetime purpose. New ideas came more quickly to him than new style, although in helping to create a simpler and more vigorous Turkish he soon went beyond Şinasi.[54] When in 1864 Şinasi suddenly left

---

Özdem, "Tanzimattan beri yazı dilimiz," *Tanzimat*, I, 859-896 (largely extracts); Vedad Günyol, "Matbuat," *İslâm ansiklopedisi*, VII, 367-369; Selim Nüzhet [Gerçek], *Türk gazeteciliği 1831-1931* (İstanbul, 1931), passim to p. 48; Ahmed Rasim, *İstibdaddan hakimiyeti milliyeye* (İstanbul, 1923), II, 41-46; H. W. V. Temperley, *England and the Near East: The Crimea* (London, 1936), pp. 244-245, 403, n.33.

[51] Kuntay, *Namık Kemal*, I, 394-400.

[52] Facsimile of page 1 of the first issue in Ahmed Rasim, *Şinasi*, p. 32. Özön, *Muasır edebiyatı*, p. 702, gives this date; Bianchi, "Bibliographie ottomane," *Journal asiatique*, Series VI:2 (August-September 1863), 233, gives June 15, which is the Julian style used on the masthead.

[53] *Ibid.*, pp. 233-237.

[54] On Kemal's early life: Mehmed Kaplan, *Namık Kemal, hayatı ve eserleri* (İstanbul, 1948), pp. 34-53; Th. Menzel, "Kemal, Mehmed Namık," *Encyclopaedia of Islam*, II, 847-848; Özön, *Muasır edebiyatı tarihi*, pp. 42-43, n.1, and 82; İhsan

İstanbul for Paris, the responsibility of editing *Tasvir-i efkâr* fell completely on young Kemal's shoulders.[55] The challenge helped to develop his talents, and shortly he was embarking on a series of vigorous articles touching questions of internal reform, language and literature, and even foreign policy. Şinasi, meanwhile, led a fairly quiet life in Paris, putting most of his work on a monumental Turkish lexicon which remained incomplete at his death. But his early influence was not lost, since it carried on through Namık Kemal into fields of greater political significance, especially upon Kemal's association with the coterie of the New Ottomans.

It is difficult to gauge the impact of these independent newspapers on the Ottoman public, but at least in the capital it must have been considerable. The two official organs suddenly found they had competition, and to meet it the *Ceride-i havadis* put out a supplementary daily news bulletin. The *Tercüman-ı ahval* boasted of its independence, pointing out that its competitors, official and semiofficial, had the imperial government and an Englishman as proprietors, while it represented the "people of Islam." A further argument on questions of education between Şinasi's paper and Churchill's caused the first official suspension of a Turkish journal; the *Tercüman-ı ahval* was shut down for two weeks. By 1862 the Ottoman government felt obliged to set up a press directorate, and in 1865 to establish a press law. An earlier law of 1857, concerning the licensing of printing presses and prepublication censorship of books and pamphlets, had mentioned newspapers only in connection with foreign subjects, whose presses also had to be licensed.[56] The new law of 1865 obviously followed the none-too-liberal model of Napoleon III. It required the obtaining of an official permit for each new paper or new editor, specified that a signed copy of each issue be delivered to the government for review, and provided all sorts of penalties for infraction of the regulations.

Sungu, *Namık Kemal* (İstanbul, 1941), pp. 3-4; Kuntay, *Namık Kemal*, I, 2-28. The chapter on Kemal by Riza Tevfik for Gibb's *Ottoman Poetry* was written but not published.

[55] The date of Şinasi's departure is sometimes given as 1865. The reasons vary. Gibb, *Ottoman Poetry*, V, 27, says Şinasi left to avoid appointment to an unwanted official post. Deny in *Encyclopaedia of Islam*, IV, 372, says it was to avoid arrest after a revolutionary friend of his Paris days had been arrested. Cf. İsmail Habib [Sevük] *Edebi yeniliğimiz* (İstanbul, 1931), I, 70; Tanpınar, *XIX. asır*, pp. 159-160; Ahmed Rasim, *Şinasi*, p. 31.

[56] Grégoire Aristarchi, *Législation ottomane* (Constantinople, 1873-1888), III, 318-319; *Düstur*, II (1289), 227-228.

These forbade publishing anything detrimental to public morals, religion, or good customs, as well as anything against the sultan or the ministers, and further forbade complicity in any move which might disturb domestic order.[57] Obviously Âli and Fuad were concerned about the possible effect of independent journalism on Ottoman stability and on their own positions. Their concern was justified. For although so far only the two papers started by Şinasi and a few magazines—the *Mecmua-i fünun* the best of them—existed as independents, the number of journals grew remarkably within the next decade and proved to have an explosive force, giving to opponents of the administration a voice heretofore denied them except for rumor and the sort of conspiratorial rising that had been attempted in the Kuleli affair of 1859. There was still no important Turkish middle class to play the role taken by the bourgeoisie in western countries, and most of the intellectuals were attached to the administration through official posts of one sort or another. Yet they could oppose the administration, and maladministration, now that they had found a printed voice. Later writers, looking back on the events of the decade after 1865, could comment with assurance on the increasing importance of public opinion.[58] To develop this public opinion became one of the chief tasks of the New Ottomans.

In such an atmosphere of political and cultural ferment the group of New Ottomans began to take shape. The year was 1865. Fuad Paşa was grand vezir, Âli foreign minister, and there seemed no prospect that their grip on the administration would soon be loosed. One Saturday evening in June half a dozen young intellectuals gathered in the Bosporus villa of one of their number, and on the following day went up the Bosporus to the Belgrad forest for a lunch prepared by a cook and two servants who had been sent on ahead. At this *fête champêtre* it was decided to form a secret society, the object of which was

---

[57] İskit, *Türkiyede matbuat idareleri*, pp. 11-19; text of law in İskit, *Türkiyede matbuat rejimleri* (İstanbul, 1939), pp. 691-695; George Young, *Corps de droit ottoman* (Oxford, 1905-1906), II, 321-326; Aristarchi, *Législation*, III, 320-325; *Düstur*, II, 220-226. İskit dates the law as 1864, but it became effective on January 1, 1865: Morris to Seward, #103, Constantinople, 18 January 1865, USNA, Turkey 18. Cf. A. Djiveleguian, *Le régime de la presse en Turquie* (Paris, 1912), pp. 25-36, on discussion of the law.

[58] Cf. Ahmed Midhat, *Üss-i inkılâb*, I, 122, and his definition of the functions of the press; also Cevdet as quoted in Recai G. Okandan, *Umumî âmme hukukumuzun ana hatları* (İstanbul, 1948), I, 141, n.47.

to bring about change in the Ottoman administration—to get rid of absolutism and to promote constitutionalism. The name which apparently they first gave to themselves was the İttifak-ı Hamiyet, or the Patriotic Alliance. So was born the group which by 1867 became the New Ottoman Society.[59]

But much about the origins of the New Ottomans remains obscure. It is not only the exact date of the first meeting that is lacking, but the program or statutes of the İttifak-ı Hamiyet, a membership list, and certainty as to whether there was a leader of the group and, if so, who he was. Even this traditional account of the Sunday picnic may not represent accurately the occasion of the founding of the secret society.[60] Much remains to be learned about the motivation and political ideas of the early members of the group.[61] But it seems certain that the moving spirits were all young men, only one or two having reached thirty; most had a literary bent, and some were journalists; almost all had some contact with westernizing influences, including knowledge of French; several were employees of the translation bureau.

The one of the traditional six founders who gained greatest prominence later was Namık Kemal, translation bureau employee and *Tas-*

[59] This account follows that of Ebüzziya Tevfik, "Yeni Osmanlılar," *Yeni tasvir-i efkâr*, 20 June 1909, which has been generally followed by Turkish historians, as Ebüzziya was early associated with the original group. The author has not seen the original, but has used the citations of Ebüzziya in Kuntay, *Namık Kemal*, I, 293, n.2, and 415, n.4; Ibnülemin Mahmud Kemal İnal, *Son asır türk şairleri* (İstanbul, 1930-1942), fasc. 5, p. 943. See the summary and evaluation of published accounts, including Ebüzziya's, in Kaplan, *Namık Kemal*, pp. 54-59. A new detailed, scholarly study by Şerif Mardin, *The Genesis of Young Ottoman Thought* (Princeton, 1962), pp. 10-14, 20-23, gives further references. On the name for the society, Kuntay, *Namık Kemal*, I, 18, and 289, n.11; Tarik Z. Tunaya, *Türkiyede siyasî partiler, 1859-1952* (İstanbul, 1952), p. 91.

[60] Cevdet Paşa, for instance, in his *Maruzat*, indicates that the New Ottomans sprang from a group of literati who gathered habitually in Churchill's editorial office of the *Ceride-i havadis*: quoted in İnal, *Türk şairleri*, fasc. 6, p. 1020. This seems unlikely if the rivalry between the *Ceride-i havadis* and the papers of Şinasi and Namık Kemal was still strong.

[61] What connections they may have had, before 1867 in particular, with European writers and editors in İstanbul, with Polish and Hungarian refugees there, with Mustafa Fazıl of the ruling family in Egypt, and with the royal princes Murad and Abdülhamid is not clear. It is still also an open question as to whether the New Ottomans were used, wittingly or unwittingly, by Âli Paşa to frighten Sultan Abdülaziz into continued reliance on him, by Polish exiles as a weapon against Russia, or by Ismail of Egypt to further his own dynastic ends. It is, of course, perfectly clear that the New Ottomans were used by Mustafa Fazıl, as will appear hereafter. Further, what were the relations between the few prominent New Ottoman exiles to Europe in 1867, and the rest of the reputed 245 members who remained in the empire?

vir-i efkâr editor.[62] A second, who has been called the "spirit and chief" of the society, was Mehmed Bey.[63] Mehmed came of an important family whose members had served faith and state. He had had a part of his education in France, and had worked also in the translation bureau.[64] Quite possibly he was the original organizer; the Saturday evening gathering had been in his father's villa. Ayetullah Bey, later to be a newspaper editor, came of a wealthy and well-educated family of statesmen, learned French in his youth, and served also in the translation bureau.[65] It was Ayetullah who is reported to have drawn up the statutes of the organization in 1865. The fourth of the traditional six was Refik Bey, always identified as the owner of the *Mir'at* (*Mirror*), a magazine founded in 1863 after the *Mecmua-i fünun* had pointed the way. Refik also had been in the translation bureau as well as in journalism.[66] Nuri Bey had also learned some French, worked in the translation bureau, and was later for a time a journalist.[67] The sixth was Reşad Bey, whose major distinction was later to volunteer for the French army in the Franco-Prussian War.[68]

Whether or not all of these six young men actually were in the original New Ottoman group, and whether they were the only founders, is not certain. Many other men have been named as early members, some as founders, others as "supporters" although not formal

[62] Gibb, *Ottoman Poetry*, VI, vi, states that Kemal was the "chief founder"; Geoffrey Lewis, *Turkey* (New York, 1955), p. 36, calls him the "prime mover"; other writers, including Kemal's son, refrain from calling him a founder but imply that he soon became the leading spirit: Ali Ekrem [Bolayır], *Namık Kemal* (İstanbul, 1930), p. 46; İsmail H. Danişmend, *İzahlı osmanlı tarihi kronolojisi* (İstanbul, 1947-1955), IV, 212, says the assertion that Kemal was not an original member is a "feeble report." This is typical of the lack of precise information.

[63] Abdurrahman Şeref, "Yeni Osmanlılar ve hürriyet," *Sabah*, 12 April 1334, quoted in Mehmet Zeki Pâkalın, *Tanzimat maliye nazırları* (İstanbul, 1940), II, 32-33.

[64] İnal, *Son asır türk şairleri*, fasc. 5, pp. 943-948; Gövsa, *Türk meşhurları ansiklopedisi*, p. 246; Kuntay, *Namık Kemal*, I, 414-424, on his career.

[65] Gövsa, *Türk meşhurları*, pp. 55, 344 (s.v. Sami Paşa, Abdurrahman), 358 (s.v. Suphi Paşa, Abdüllâtif); İnal, *Türk şairleri*, fasc. 1, pp. 145-151. Fehmi Caner, one of the later Young Turks, in a letter of March 25, 1941, named Ayetullah as one of the three New Ottoman founders, with a "Vezir Sami Paşazade" who may also be the same Ayetullah, since Sami Paşa was Ayetullah's grandfather: Ernest E. Ramsaur Jr., *The Young Turks* (Princeton, 1957), p. 21, n.24. Ayetullah's father was the numismatist Subhi Paşa.

[66] Özön, *Son asır türk edebiyatı tarihi*, p. 8; Emin, *Development of Modern Turkey*, p. 44. Refik died in 1865, and so plays less of a role than his colleagues: Ebüzziya, "Yeni Osmanlılar," *Yeni tasvir-i efkâr*, 20 June 1909, in Kuntay, *Namık Kemal*, I, 293, n.2.

[67] Gövsa, *Türk meşhurları*, p. 288; Kuntay, *Namık Kemal*, I, 389-393.

[68] *Ibid.*, pp. 381-388; Gövsa, *Türk meşhurları*, p. 320.

members.[69] It would seem quite logical that Agâh Efendi, whose background corresponded closely to that of the six, should have been an early member, and perhaps a founder. It stands to reason also that Mustafa Fazıl Paşa, the Ottoman-Egyptian statesman who had serious disagreements with the grand vezir Fuad, should have been in touch with members of the İttifak-ı Hamiyet. Mustafa Fazıl's house by early 1866 had become a center for critics of the Ottoman government.[70] But whether Mustafa Fazıl could have been among the original organizers of the group is quite dubious, given his position and background. It seems clear that the heir-apparent to the Ottoman throne, the prince Murad, son of Abdülmecid and nephew of the reigning sultan Abdülaziz, was somehow associated with the thinking if not the planning of the group, principally through Namık Kemal.[71] Murad was of an age with the young intellectuals of the İttifak-ı Hamiyet, and although their relationship grew tenuous, he was their hope for a constitutional monarch if Abdülaziz should be deposed. This was one of the germs of the 1876 revolution.

Among the early members of the New Ottoman group were two who, with Namık Kemal, gained the greatest prominence for their writing and their impact on the public. They were Ziya Bey (later Paşa) and Ali Suavi Efendi. Ziya may have been one of the founders of the İttifak-ı Hamiyet, and is sometimes spoken of as the New Ottoman leader.[72] Except for the Egyptian prince Mustafa Fazıl Paşa,

[69] For example, Şeyh Naili Efendi, named by Fehmi Caner in Ramsaur, *Young Turks*, p. 21, n.24, as one of the three founders, who may have been confused with the Hungarian refugee Ömer Naili Paşa, mentioned as a member in Kuntay, *Namık Kemal*, I, 359, and Kaplan, *Namık Kemal*, p. 58. Cf. Tunaya, *Siyasî partiler*, pp. 91-92, for additional names, including some of prominent officials and bankers. Kuntay, pp. 357-358, also includes as members Mustafa Fazıl's steward Azmi Bey as accountant or treasurer of the group, and Ahmed Ağa as an ordinary villager representing the upright common man. Melek Hanum, *Six Years in Europe* (London, 1873), pp. 97-98, mentions as members of the group Mustafa Fazıl Paşa, Ziya Bey, and a Pole who was a major in a Turkish regiment.

[70] Marcel Colombe, "Une lettre d'un prince égyptien du XIXè siècle au Sultan ottoman Abd al-Aziz," *Orient*, 5 (First Quarter, 1958), 24.

[71] Kuntay, *Namık Kemal*, I, 79-82, 257-258; Bolayır, *Namık Kemal*, pp. 46-47; Halûk Y. Şehsuvaroğlu, *Sultan Aziz* (İstanbul, 1949), pp. 51-55; Tunaya, *Siyasî partiler*, pp. 91, 94. The latter two accounts rely a good deal on İbnülemin Mahmud Kemal [İnal], "Abdülhamidi Sani'nin notları," *Türk tarih encümeni mecmuası*, 13/90-15/92 (1926), and Abdülhamid may not be a reliable source on such matters, given his opposition to the New Ottomans. The suspicion was mutual, for Kemal feared Abdülhamid, as he later told his son Ali Ekrem: Kuntay, *Namık Kemal*, I, 257. Abdülhamid connected Murad, Mustafa Fazıl, and Namık Kemal, saying that meetings often took place in Mustafa Fazıl's garden.

[72] Vambéry, "Erinnerungen an Midhat Pascha," *Deutsche Revue*, II (May 1878),

Abdülhamid Ziya Bey was the most distinguished of the early New Ottoman group, and also the oldest, having reached forty in the year of the founding of the İttifak-ı Hamiyet. In his earlier life Ziya had pursued a more traditional career in clerical and administrative offices of the government than had his translation-bureau colleagues. He had been thoroughly immersed in the Persianized poetry, which he him-self also composed, and led a bohemian after-hours life with brother poets in the taverns of İstanbul. But, through the influence of the great Reşid Paşa, Ziya had in 1855 been appointed third secretary in the imperial palace. Thereafter he abandoned the dissolute life of the Persianist cafe habitués and began also to study French, which he had mastered sufficiently within a year to translate Viardot's history of Moorish Spain into Turkish. From this time on, Ziya produced a fair number of other translations from the French, as well as original po-ems influenced in their modes of thought, though not yet in language, by French example. The most famous of these, his *Terciibend,* exhibits the influence of western science and agnosticism, a cry of intellectual bewilderment in a world of confusion and injustice. Ziya also became a contributor to Agâh Efendi's *Tercüman-ı ahval.* After the accession of Sultan Abdülaziz in 1861, Ziya lost his palace job, undoubtedly be-cause of Âli Paşa's jealousy of his brilliant mind and his influence in the palace. Ziya had made clear his own ambition, and was evidently trying to warn Abdülaziz against Âli's domination. From 1862 to 1866 Ziya held a variety of administrative posts, most of them de-signed to keep him out of the capital. He made an unsatisfactory pro-vincial inspector, as has been noted previously, but in a six-month pe-riod as governor of Cyprus established an enviable reputation for en-lightenment and energy. Whether he was in İstanbul in 1865 at the founding of the İttifak-ı Hamiyet is not clear, but he was there the next year. His bitterness against Âli, based on personal grievance and reinforced by political considerations, continued and undoubtedly had the effect of drawing Ziya closer to the New Ottomans.[73]

192; Th. Menzel, "Kemal, Mehmed Namık," *Encyclopaedia of Islam,* II, 848, calls Ziya the founder of the group, and associates no one else with him in this capacity.
[73] For Ziya's own account of his early life, taken from *Mecmua-i Ebüzziya,* 14-15 (1 and 15 rebiülâhır 1298), see Gibb, *Ottoman Poetry,* V, 42-51, further information 51-61, 65-67, and a translation of most of the *Terciibend,* 87-95. On his *Endülüs tarihi* translation from Viardot: Vambéry, *La Turquie d'aujourd'hui et d'avant qua-rante ans* (Paris, 1896), p. 9; idem, *Der Islam im neunzehnten Jahrhundert* (Leipzig, 1875), pp. 276-278. Cf. also Kuntay, *Namık Kemal,* I, 394; George Hill, *History of Cyprus* (Cambridge, 1940-1952), IV, 234-235; İnal, *Osmanlı devrinde son sadrı-*

Ali Suavi Efendi was a completely different sort of person, of humble origins, a product both of *rüşdiye* and of the old religious education, who became a teacher in the new *rüşdiye*, or secondary schools, in the provinces—first in Bursa, then in Philippopolis (Filibe, Plovdiv).[74] Wherever he went, he was a stormy petrel, criticizing the government in sermons and lectures which he gave in mosques; his tone was often political, somewhat fanatic, and chauvinist. He later explained that paternal influence, his study of the Prophet's life, and experience of unjust provincial administrators gave him his iconoclastic bent.[75] Ali Suavi, nevertheless, enjoyed, at least for a time, the patronage of some important men, among them Sami Paşa, the grandfather of the New Ottoman member Ayetullah. It was Sami who evidently secured the teaching jobs for Ali Suavi, and through this relationship may have come the latter's connection with the New Ottomans. It is not evident that up to 1865 or 1866, when he returned from Philippopolis to İstanbul, Ali Suavi knew any French or much about the West. Back in İstanbul, he continued his fiery preaching in the mosques and became a newspaper editor. His *Muhbir* (*Intelligencer*) began appearing on January 1, 1867. Probably before that time he had some connection with the İttifak-ı Hamiyet members.[76]

It must have been difficult to hold together an organization containing so many brilliant individual minds and to draw up a program of action on which all could agree. The statutes of the İttifak-ı Hamiyet were reportedly to be drawn up by Ayetullah, who was charged by the others with this task.[77] If it be assumed that they were actually drawn up, no copy of such statutes has been discovered by modern

âzamlar (İstanbul, 1940-1953), I, 19-20; Mehmed Memduh, *Mirât-ı şuûnat* (İzmir, 1328), pp. 30-31.

[74] Ali Suavi's own curriculum vitae seems fanciful, except for the first phrase: "Osmanli-Muslim born in İstanbul, having travelled the whole extent of the Ottoman Empire, in Asia Minor, Iraq, Arabia, Africa, and Europe, I have studied on the spot science, religion, men and things, knowledge which has made me a hoca": Ali Suavi, *A propos de l'Herzégovine* (Paris, 1875), preface. But he seems to have made the pilgrimage to Mecca.

[75] Ali Suavi, "Yeni Osmanlılar tarihi," *Ulûm*, 2:15 (1869?), 892-932, cited in İsmail Hami Danişmend, *Ali Suâvi'nin türkçülüğü* (İstanbul, 1942), pp. 9-11.

[76] On his early life: Kuntay, *Namık Kemal*, I, 466-467; idem, *Sarıklı ihtilâlci Ali Suavi* (İstanbul, 1946), pp. 7-21; Gövsa, *Türk meşhurları*, p. 40; Mordtmann, *Stambul*, I, 224-225; Schweiger-Lerchenfeld, *Serail*, p. 66. The date for *Muhbir* is usually put in 1866, but İhsan Sungu, "Tanzimat ve Yeni Osmanlılar," *Tanzimat*, I, 806, n.49, gives the above date.

[77] Ebüzziya, "Yeni Osmanlılar," *Yeni tasvir-i efkâr*, 20 June 1909, cited by Kuntay, *Namık Kemal*, I, 415, n.4. Ayetullah is said to have had two books, on the Carbonari and on Polish secret societies: Kaplan, *Namık Kemal*, p. 58.

historians. It is usually said that the Carbonari furnished a model for the organization, and that there were secret cells of seven whose members were not supposed to know members of other cells.[78] The purpose of the İttifak-ı Hamiyet has been stated thus—to submit to Sultan Abdülaziz on his visit to the Sublime Porte a petition or proposal for constitutional government, to which the sultan should swear in the Chamber of the Prophet's Mantle.[79] Certainly the members of the group were opposed to absolute government, for personal or public reasons or both, and opposed in particular to Âli and Fuad—though it should be noted that Âli was at this time only foreign minister and that the grand vezir Fuad was never so detested by the New Ottomans as his colleague and in some respects stood rather nearer to their viewpoint. The implication of the constitutional petition was to remove the control of Âli and Fuad, and perhaps also to depose Abdülaziz. Possibly the use of violence was contemplated, and the new secret society has been accused of plotting the assassination of the sultan himself.[80] What emerges from the slim evidence is the obvious fact that the group was united in its opposition to the government of the day and that most of the members wanted some kind of constitutional check on administrative authority. What kind of constitutionalism is not sure; the opinion that there were two hundred and forty-five members and two hundred and forty-five different "constitutionalisms" represented in the group may not be far off the mark.[81] Ali Suavi preached a kind of constitutionalism, though he was reported to include only Muslims in his argument that state affairs should be based on the Koranic doctrine of the public taking of

[78] Although Süleyman Paşa's son says that his father, leader of the thirty-fifth cell, knew the leaders of the other thirty-four: Süleyman Paşa zade Sami, ed., *Süleyman Paşa muhakemesi* (İstanbul, 1328), pp. 18-19. What is known of the organization does not allow a good comparison with the Carbonari's lodges and grades of initiates. Mazzini's "Young Italy," a descendant of the Carbonari, may well also have furnished inspiration.

[79] This is presented as article 1 of the İttifak-ı Hamiyet program in Tunaya, *Siyasî partiler*, p. 93, quoting L. Eroğlu, "Bizde siyasî cemiyet ve partilerin tarihçiği," *Aylık ansiklopedisi*, 52 (1948), 1489. The date for petitioning the sultan is here given as 15 muharrem, which in 1865 fell on June 10, and thus would leave little time after a Sunday meeting (on June 4) to draw up the proposal.

[80] Namık Kemal's son records the talk about deposition and elevating Murad to the throne: cited in Kuntay, *Namık Kemal*, I, 257; so does the prince Abdülhamid, cited in Şehsuvaroğlu, *Sultan Aziz*, p. 53. Abdülhamid also speaks of assassination: *ibid.*, p. 54.

[81] Kuntay, *Namık Kemal*, I, 358, 363. The figure 245 comes from Ebüzziya, "Yeni Osmanlılar tarihi," *Yeni tasvir-i efkâr*, 1 September 1909; cf. Kuntay, p. 358, n.5.

counsel.[82] But probably Namik Kemal is the best exponent, in the years 1865 to 1867, of what the newly constituted group sought.

Kemal was still editing the *Tasvir-i efkâr*, which he did not attempt to make into an outright spokesman for constitutionalism or political reform.[83] He was still concerned with raising the general cultural level of his people. One of his major articles argued vigorously for simpler, clearer writing, closer to the spoken language, with due regard for Turkish grammar and syntax; meaning and natural expression were all-important, so that writing might be understood.[84] Other articles dealt with history, such as his "Devri istilâ" ("The Period of Conquest"), which pointed to the early growth of the Ottomans toward greatness.[85] He also did a good deal to foster the concept of patriotism, not only with his emphasis on Turkish speech, but in his interest and pride in Ottoman history and in his frequent use of the word *vatan* to mean "fatherland." The word did not yet have its full emotional content, nor was it yet narrowly nationalistic, since Kemal could include the Greek Orthodox peoples in his *vatan* on occasion; yet it indicated a strong pride in fatherland, a real patriotism, and the germ of nationalism.[86] These feelings were obviously deepened by the Cretan revolt, on which Kemal began to comment, cautiously at first, but with a patriotic and antirebel tone.[87] Throughout his writing there ran a concern for people in general, which began to show also in his praise for experiments in parliamentary government in Egypt and Roumania, connecting them with the desiderata of free expression of popular opinion, progress, and prosperity.[88]

Others of the New Ottoman group undoubtedly held such opinions, and after their exile in May of 1867 expressed them without restraint in their writings. It is dangerous, however, to read back into 1865 and

---

[82] Mordtmann, *Stambul*, I, 225; Schweiger-Lerchenfeld, *Serail*, p. 66; Kuntay, *Sarıklı ihtilâlci*, pp. 29-32.

[83] Kuntay, *Namık Kemal*, I, 58.

[84] Özön, *Muasır edebiyatı tarihi*, pp. 581-582.

[85] *Ibid.*, p. 452.

[86] Examples of his use of the term in Kuntay, *Namık Kemal*, I, 50-51, 55, 184 (in the 1856 Hatt-ı Hümayun form of *vatandaş*), 186, 291. In his comment on p. 55 Kuntay says that the word *vatan*, after waiting for centuries on the threshold of the Ottoman language, entered it with Kemal's couplet at the head of his "Yangın" (Fire) article of 3 zilkade 1282 (March 20, 1866). This can hardly be so, since the word had been used from about mid-century; see above, chapter II, n.15. Şinasi used it also —for example, in the first editorial statement of purpose in the *Tercüman-ı ahval*: Özön, *Muasır edebiyatı tarihi*, p. 701.

[87] Kuntay, *Namık Kemal*, I, 59-60.

[88] *Ibid.*, pp. 59, 212, n.25; Sungu, *Namık Kemal*, p. 6.

1866 the ideas expressed in 1868 and later years, ideas which probably were affected by the plain fact of exile. If one seeks a reasonably comprehensive statement of what the New Ottomans—still presumably the İttifak-ı Hamiyet—stood for before their exile, an article which Namık Kemal wrote, evidently in February or March of 1867, provides the best indication.[89] Here Kemal identifies himself with pride as a member of a party or society which, however, is not formally organized with a constitution and president. In fact, says Kemal, it has no individual leader. Its members are held together by "a brotherhood of opinion and kinship of the heart." They are the product of a mentality of change. The members are men who have had the advantage of travel and of contact with western-educated relatives, and include at Kemal's guess ninety per cent of the progressive leaders in the army, the maritime services, the press, medicine, and literature, most of whom naturally are government employees. Possibly Kemal was trying to cover up, by this general description, the existence of the secret İttifak-ı Hamiyet. But it is reasonable also to suppose that by early 1867 there was a loose group of progressives such as Kemal described, and that the İttifak-ı Hamiyet may, in fact, have had neither tight organization nor strong leadership, despite the Carbonaro model.

Three general categories of ideas emerge from Kemal's description of what this progressive group believed. First is an emphasis on equality and Osmanlılık, not far in most of its aspects from what the leading Tanzimat statesmen of the day themselves sought. Kemal calls all subjects of the Porte Osmanlis, decries all special privilege to any particular group, and asks for equality of duties as well as rights. All Christians in the empire, except those Greeks who insist on the *megale idea*, are accepted as equals. But Kemal inveighs especially against the privileges that Christians already have—protection by their own patriarchs and by European powers, exemption from military service, and the chance to grow rich while Muslims serve the state. He admits that Christians suffer from certain legal disabilities in matters of court testimony and property disposal, but he considers that their privileges overbalance these. He perceives the fundamental incompatibility of Christians' demanding yet more privileges without giving complete

[89] This appears not to have been published at the time. It is given in Kuntay, *Namık Kemal*, I, 183-187, 290-291. The two sections are actually reversed in order. Kuntay obtained the article in Kemal's holograph from a private collection. It was intended as an answer to an article that appeared in the *Gazette du Levant*, a French weekly in İstanbul, of 19 February, presumably 1867.

devotion to the government that grants them. But he conceives that real equality will be preferred by the Christians to "the emptiness of the honor of the title of sovereign nation." Kemal was not the first to fall into this misunderstanding of the growing strength of nationalism. And his Osmanlılık, obviously, was tinged with a special regard for the position of the Muslim.

This special regard verges into the patriotic views which Kemal expresses—not specifically Turkish, but Ottoman. His patriotism is evident in part from his strictures on Christian exemption from the army, on their desire for top administrative jobs, and on their inability to write correctly in official Ottoman style. It is evident also from his assertion that his party is willing to undergo great trials for the fatherland and looks back to Ottoman heroes of old for inspiration. It is quite clear also from his denunciation of separatism and his opposition to interference in Ottoman affairs by the great powers.

In addition to the ideas of equality and patriotism, Kemal expresses also a general desire for reform. There is no specific defense of constitutionalism, but a hint that chambers of deputies are a good thing. He is emphatic on the need for freedom of thought and expression. Finally, there is praise for members of the party who have started newspapers in Turkish and utilized literary reform as a cardinal means of fostering progress. This, in fact, was what Namık Kemal was now doing with his *Tasvir-i efkâr*, and Ali Suavi with his *Muhbir*, by early 1867. They were trying to create a public opinion favorable to change. The effort had important consequences, but it was still small. It is recounted that one stormy day Namık Kemal was crossing the Bosporus in a caïque, together with Ziya, Reşad, and Nuri. Reşad was afraid and Namık Kemal asked him if he were afraid of dying. "I'm not afraid of dying," answered Reşad. "But if the caïque sinks I'm afraid public opinion will sink too."[90]

Despite the humorous exaggeration, there was considerable truth in what Reşad said. The New Ottomans in İstanbul were nurturing public opinion. Early in 1867 they got unexpected assistance from the Egyptian prince Mustafa Fazıl Paşa, who now was catapulted into the forefront of New Ottoman pamphleteering and political agitation as the result of Egyptian dynastic intrigue.

[90] *Ibid.*, I, 571, quoting Ali Ekrem [Bolayır], "Sahâyif-i hâtırat," *Yeni Gün*, 24 January 1920. The exact date is not given.

Mustafa Fazıl was the brother of the governor of Egypt, Ismail Paşa. An intelligent man, product of a westernized education, speaking French like a Frenchman, he was also an imposing though corpulent figure, his round face framed by reddish hair and a reddish beard. From about 1845 on, he was away most of the time from his estates in Egypt and occupied some of the highest offices in the Ottoman government in İstanbul. In the early 1860's he held briefly the portfolios of education and then of finance.[91] Although he may have looked forward at times to the chance of becoming grand vezir, his dominant wish was to succeed his brother Ismail as ruler of Egypt.

Such succession was a distinct possibility, for, according to the system then followed, Mustafa Fazıl was next in line.[92] Mehmed Ali, founder of the line of Egyptian rulers, had in 1841 secured by ferman from Sultan Abdülmecid the right to pass on the governorship of Egypt as hereditary title to males in his immediate family. Succession was not, however, stipulated as father to son, but oldest male to oldest male, which meant that the title might pass to an uncle, brother, or nephew rather than to a son.[93] When Ismail Paşa, the son of Mehmed Ali's son Ibrahim, succeeded to the governorship of Egypt in 1863, the next in line was his brother Mustafa Fazıl, born only a few months after him in Ibrahim's harem.[94] After Mustafa Fazıl would come Halim, the fourth son of Mehmed Ali and so actually uncle to Ismail and Mustafa Fazıl, but born just after them. It was Ismail's fondest desire, however, to secure the succession to his own son. The desire was natural, and Ismail was not the first to want to change the succession system to one of primogeniture. Both of his immediate predecessors had tried, though in vain, to do so.[95] Should Ismail be successful where his predecessors had failed, both Mustafa Fazıl and Halim would be unceremoniously cut out of the line of succession.

[91] A somewhat disordered sketch of his life is in Pâkalın, *Tanzimat maliye nazırları*, II, 3-65. Cf. also Edwin De Leon, "The Old Ottoman and the Young Turk," *Harper's*, 44 (1872), 612; Horace Rumbold, *Recollections of a Diplomatist* (London, 1902), II, 329-331; Colombe, "Une lettre d'un prince égyptien," p. 23.

[92] In the event Mustafa Fazıl would never have succeeded because Ismail outlived him.

[93] Text of the ferman of 1 June 1841 in Thomas Holland, *The European Concert in the Eastern Question* (London, 1885), pp. 110-114.

[94] Ismail's older brother Ahmed, who would normally have succeeded, was killed in 1858 in a mysterious train wreck. The common suspicion was that Ismail had planned the accident.

[95] G. Douin, *Histoire du règne du Khédive Ismail* (Rome, 1933), I, 205; Alexandre Holinski, *Nubar-Pacha devant l'histoire* (Paris, 1886), pp. 21-22.

Halim is not essential to the story, and may be dismissed with a word here. On reasonably good terms with Ismail until the end of 1865, Halim broke with Ismail over questions of property and, presumably, the succession. Halim was thus thrown together with Mustafa Fazıl, though the two seem never to have been intimate. Halim went to France and to İstanbul, but appears to have been important only as a factor in keeping up the three-cornered tension that developed between Ismail, Mustafa Fazıl, and the Porte. Involved in this tension were alleged plots by Halim, in which Mustafa Fazıl may also have been involved, to kill Ismail and to raise revolt in Syria in order to carve out a separate domain. The principal incident came in 1868 with the so-called O'Reilly affair. One Eugene O'Reilly, an adventurer who had served as Hasan Bey in the Ottoman army, was evidently planning revolt in Syria with some European financial backing and possibly with the connivance of Halim and Mustafa Fazıl.[96]

Mustafa Fazıl was a far more active opponent of Ismail than was Halim, and could exert considerable influence in the Ottoman capital. Probably it was Mustafa's presence in İstanbul that kept Ismail from pushing the succession change in 1863. Ismail also worried about Mustafa's visit to Napoleon III in 1864, and about the chance that Mustafa might become grand vezir.[97] But two situations in İstanbul worked to Ismail's advantage. One was that Sultan Abdülaziz had the same desire to change the succession in favor of his eldest son as had Ismail.[98] The sultan thus would be happy to have his Egyptian vassal serve as guinea pig to test popular reaction. The other situation was the hostility that developed between the grand vezir Fuad Paşa and Mustafa Fazıl. Their mutual coolness is said to have dated from the time when Fuad was charged with dividing Ibrahim's property between Mustafa Fazıl and his two brothers. But it became acute when they quarreled over financial reforms and the Ottoman budget in the years 1862 to 1866, when Fuad was grand vezir and Mustafa Fazıl finance minister,

[96] W. B. Jerrold, *Egypt under Ismail Pasha* (London, 1879), pp. 83-102; Douin, *Khédive Ismail*, I, 209-213, and II, 86-96; Jacob M. Landau, *Parliaments and Parties in Egypt* (Tel Aviv, 1953), pp. 77-80; W. Gifford Palgrave to Lyons, confidential, Constantinople, 18 June 1867, encl. in Lyons to Stanley, very confidential, 19 June 1867, FO 78/1961. O'Reilly was at one time a favorite aide-de-camp of Fuad Paşa: *Levant Herald*, 30 November 1875.

[97] Douin, *Khédive Ismail*, I, 206, 211-212.

[98] The succession to the Ottoman throne had by custom since 1617 gone not necessarily from father to son, but to the eldest male of the immediate family. See below, chapter VIII, on Abdülaziz's further plans for changing the rule of succession.

then abroad in voluntary exile in Paris, then back in İstanbul as head of a special treasury council. By early 1866 the breach became final, with Fuad and Mustafa Fazıl each seeking to denigrate the other in the eyes of Sultan Abdülaziz. The Egyptian became more and more outspoken against the Ottoman ministers, whereupon he was fired from the treasury council in February 1866. His continued criticism of the government led to the suspicion that he was somehow involved with circulating in İstanbul anonymous letters which criticized the government. The upshot was that Mustafa Fazıl was asked to leave the country. On April 4, 1866, he departed for Paris and lived there comfortably with his great wealth, in half-forced exile.[99]

Whether or not Ismail helped to secure the exile of Mustafa Fazıl, the fact remained that now his major opponent was out of the capital. Within a month Ismail was in İstanbul, where he succeeded almost at once in persuading Abdülaziz to consent to his scheme for changing the succession to the Egyptian governorship. It is commonly suspected that Ismail, as was his wont whenever he sought favors, scattered effective monetary gifts among the influential in the capital. But Abdülaziz probably wanted the succession change anyway, to provide a precedent for his own efforts. What is more difficult to understand is Fuad's consent to the change. He may have been open to pecuniary argument; he may have inclined to the change in Ismail's favor as the result of his feud with Mustafa Fazıl. Some have accused him of favoring Ismail's scheme in order to open the way to the succession of Abdülaziz's young son and the establishment of a regency in the empire, which Fuad himself might head.[100] All this is curious in view of Fuad's known desire, shared with Âli, to keep the empire together and treat Ismail like any other provincial governor, and also in view of Fuad's reported opposition to the suc-

[99] Ebüzziya Tevfik, "Yeni Osmanlıların sebebi zuhuru," *Yeni tasvir-i efkâr*, 31 May 1909, quoted in Kuntay, *Namık Kemal*, I, 311, n.1; İnal, *Son sadrıâzamlar*, II, 173-174; Melek Hanum, *Six Years*, pp. 98-99; Frederick Millingen, *La Turquie sous le règne d'Abdul Aziz* (Paris, 1868), pp. 279, 340-343; Vicomte de la Jonquière, *Histoire de l'Empire ottoman* (Paris, 1914), II, 24-25; Colombe, "Une lettre d'un prince égyptien," pp. 23-24; Douin, *Khédive Ismail*, I, 213-214.

[100] Cf. Şehsuvaroğlu, *Sultan Aziz*, p. 45, which is accepted by A. D. Alderson, *The Structure of the Ottoman Dynasty* (Oxford, 1956), p. 52. Millingen, *La Turquie*, pp. 337, 340-343, also accuses Fuad, and reports current at the time in İstanbul confirm this view: Morris to Hunter, #117, 3 July 1865, USNA, Turkey 18; Morris to Seward, #153, 22 May 1866, USNA, Turkey 19; and French dispatches cited in Colombe, "Une lettre d'un prince égyptien," pp. 24-25, n.9.

cession change in 1865.[101] Yet the ferman of May 27, 1866, formally changed the succession in Egypt to the rule of father to eldest son, on the grounds of helping the prosperity and stability of the province by eliminating rivalry among collateral heirs, and also, as Abdülaziz's preamble said to Ismail, "appreciating . . . to their full extent the efforts thou has made with this object. . . ."[102] These efforts must have lightened Ismail's purse considerably, as well as costing Egypt's treasury henceforth a doubled annual tribute to İstanbul. Whatever Fuad's role in the affair had been, he fell within a week from the grand vezirate which he had occupied for three years. Though various other statesmen were working against him, the issue on which he fell was ironically one of Egyptian influence in the palace: Fuad opposed Abdülaziz's desire to take Ismail's daughter, Tevhide, as a wife, on the grounds that Ismail then would have too favorable a backstairs entrée to the sultan.[103] But Ismail's own privileges did not suffer, and indeed were extended the next year to give him the title of khedive, the rank of grand vezir, and extensive rights for internal legislation and the negotiation of nonpolitical treaties.[104]

To Mustafa Fazıl the ferman of 1866 was a real blow, eliminating at one stroke any prospect of his becoming ruler of Egypt. It was undoubtedly the succession question rather than his spat with Fuad which turned Mustafa Fazıl toward vigorous agitation against the Ottoman ministers, and thus toward the camp of the New Ottomans.

[101] Douin, *Khédive Ismail*, I, 6, 206-207. Cf. above, chapter v, on Fuad's trip to Egypt in 1863.

[102] Text of ferman in Holland, *European Concert*, pp. 114-116; Douin, *Khédive Ismail*, I, 218-220.

[103] Ottoman historians usually recount this as the affair of the "little slip of paper." Fuad's objection to the love match was written on a small paper and given to the head chamberlain who, instead of reading it to Abdülaziz, handed it to him. The sultan was insulted, Fuad was fired, but the marriage plans were cancelled. Cf. Mehmed Memduh, *Mirât-ı şuûnat*, pp. 36-37; Ali Fuad, *Ricâl-i mühimme-i siyasiye* (İstanbul, 1928), pp. 166-170; Abdurrahman Şeref, *Tarih musahabeleri*, p. 108; Orhan F. Köprülü, "Fuad Paşa," *İslâm ansiklopedisi*, IV, 677; Alderson, *Ottoman Dynasty*, p. 89; Douin, *Khédive Ismail*, I, 229-231. Differing interpretations of Fuad's dismissal in Millingen, *La Turquie*, pp. 352-354; and Morris to Seward, #157, 8 June 1866, USNA, Turkey 19.

[104] Text of ferman of 8 June 1867 in Holland, *European Concert*, pp. 116-118. On Ismail's campaign for the new concessions in the spring of 1867, when the Porte was embarrassed by Cretan and Serbian affairs and the New Ottoman attacks, see the dispatches of Lyons in İstanbul to Stanley, #77, confidential, 26 February 1867; #95, 13 March 1867; #97, 19 March 1867; #106, 26 March 1867, all in FO 78/1958, and further #242, 13 June 1867; #243, confidential, 13 June 1867; and #269, 19 June 1867, in FO 78/1961.

How close his relations with the New Ottomans had been before he left İstanbul it is hard to say. Nor is it clear what relationship, if any, existed between the Egyptian prince in Paris and the young intellectuals in İstanbul through the summer and fall of 1866 and the winter of 1866-1867. This was the period when the Ottoman government was confronted by the necessity of recognizing Charles I as monarch of an autonomous Roumania, of dealing with the Cretan revolt, whose leaders had proclaimed union with Greece, of finding a solution for the Serbian agitation to get rid of the last Ottoman garrisons, and of shunting aside Ismail's scheming for greater independence. Presumably in this situation the New Ottomans looked with favor on so outstanding an opponent of the slowly weakening Ottoman administration as was Mustafa Fazıl, whose exile certainly increased his fame. Quite possibly Mustafa Fazıl had contact with the New Ottomans through French journalists in Paris and İstanbul, who play a shadowy role on the edges of the burgeoning movement.

In any case, by late January of 1867 Mustafa Fazıl was mentioned in a dispatch from İstanbul as the head of the party of the *jeune Turquie*. The indication was that at least for some weeks he had been believed to be its chief. Further, it was said that Mustafa Fazıl had already sent to the sultan a memorandum on the dangerous situation of the empire, and would in a subsequent memorandum set forth his plan for reorganization.[105] Then on February 5, 1867, Mustafa Fazıl addressed to *Le Nord* in Brussels a letter, published on February 7, proclaiming himself the representative of the *Jeune Turquie*. After defending himself against charges that he was interested in financial gain for himself, he continued: "It matters not whether one is Muslim, Catholic, or Greek Orthodox to be able to put the public weal ahead of private interest. For that it is sufficient to be a man of progress or a good patriot, which is one and the same thing. Such is at least, Sir, the inmost conviction of the great party of the *Jeune Turquie* which I have the honor to represent. This party knows neither the resignation of fatalism nor the abdication of discouragement. That is to say that the insurrection of Crete, and the other greater troubles which are promised us in certain quarters, find it unshakable in its resolution

---

[105] *Journal des débats*, 6 February 1867, correspondence from Constantinople of 25 January 1867. This is a reasonably accurate description of Mustafa Fazıl's letter to Abdülaziz, on which see below. Cf. also *Le Nord* (Brussels), 9 February 1867, for the same dispatch.

to carry out the reform projects which thought, experience and suffering have matured."[106]

It is not clear whether Mustafa Fazıl intended to proclaim himself the representative of the İttifak-ı Hamiyet, about which he may or may not have had information, or simply of the amorphous *Jeune Turquie*, used in its usual loose sense of reformers with liberal tendencies. Nor is it clear whether he made the proclamation on his own initiative, or was persuaded to do so by European intriguers and journalists with whom he may have been in touch in Paris.[107] But in any case the move could serve his own purposes in trying to overthrow the Ottoman administration that had denied him the Egyptian throne: it would appeal to liberal sentiment in Europe, it would embarrass Âli and Fuad, and it might attract to his support the New Ottoman journalists of İstanbul. The same considerations would apply to the much longer and more famous open letter written by Mustafa Fazıl to Sultan Abdülaziz from Paris. Here again there may be question as to whether Mustafa Fazıl took the initiative, or whether he was, in fact, the original or the sole author of the letter.[108] But whatever its origin, it undoubtedly represented Mustafa Fazıl's rather advanced ideas and served his individual purposes as well.

Written originally in French, the *Lettre adressée à Sa Majesté le Sultan* was a fairly lengthy document which set forth in vigorous

[106] *Le Nord*, Thursday, 7 February 1867. Though published in Brussels, the editorial offices were in Paris, in charge of M. Théophile Franceschi. *Le Nord* was commonly known as an organ of the Russian government, and most of its dispatches from the Near East were slanted in an anti-Turk fashion, as was editorial comment. Colombe, "Une lettre d'un prince égyptien," p. 25, cites a defective copy of the letter which makes Mustafa Fazıl say he represents "a large part" of the Jeune Turquie.

[107] This, for instance, is the opinion of Léon Cahun, who had some contact with the New Ottomans in Paris the next year: Ernest Lavisse and Alfred Rambaud, eds., *Histoire générale*, XI (Paris, 1899), 547.

[108] The *Diplomatic Review* (24 July 1876), for instance, in an article on " 'Reform' in Turkey," p. 159, says that intriguers wrote the letter, hoping to make Mustafa Fazıl grand vezir and to get money from him, and then flatly names the Wallachian journalist Gregory Ganesco, then operating in Paris, as the author. The *Diplomatic Review* was an organ devoted to David Urquhart's conservative Turcophil gospel, and its statement may be suspect. On Ganesco see Jules Hansen, *Les coulisses de la diplomatie* (Paris, 1880), p. 319. Another Wallachian journalist also supported Mustafa Fazıl's claims to the Egyptian throne, at least in 1869—Mons. N. Bordeano, editor of *La Turquie*. But since *La Turquie* was a semiofficial paper usually close to the views of the current Ottoman administration, this support may reflect simply a period of official antagonism toward Ismail. Cf. *Levant Times*, 28 September 1869. It is also possible to suspect relations between Jean Piétri, editor of the *Courrier d'Orient* in İstanbul, and Mustafa Fazıl. Their ideas seemed to run on similar lines, and it was through Piétri that Mustafa Fazıl made contact in 1867 with Ziya and Namık Kemal.

language the evils and dangers besetting the Ottoman Empire and proposed reforms of a constitutional and egalitarian nature.[109] The whole was couched in the form of a ringing, emotional appeal to Abdülaziz to take the lead in regenerating his empire—an appeal reminiscent of Mazzini's eloquent letter of 1831 to Charles Albert of Piedmont. It began with a sentence that lingered in the minds of Ottoman reformers, to be quoted on later occasions: "Sire, That which enters the palace of princes with the greatest difficulty is the truth." There followed an outline of present evils—depopulation and a decline in Turkish virility, moral degeneration and loss of morale, intellectual stagnation, the injustices and exactions of subordinate officials who were insufficiently controlled, treasury crises and the general lack of industrial, agricultural, and commercial development. These evils, Mustafa Fazıl made clear, weighed as heavily on Muslims as on Christians of the empire, if not more so, since the former had no great power on the outside to succor them. But the essential division of the empire was not along religious lines; it was along lines of power. "Your subjects of all sects are divided into two classes: those who oppress without restraint, and those who are op-

---

[109] It seems likely that Mustafa Fazıl's letter was actually written in 1866, since its existence and its essence, if not the exact text, were known in İstanbul by January 25, 1867. But the author has found no copy that can be clearly identified as printed in 1866. The earliest copy in the Bibliothèque Nationale, *Lettre adressée à Sa Majesté le Sultan par S. A. le Prince Mustapha-Fazil-Pacha* (Paris, Imp. Ch. Schiller, 16 pp.), has no date of publication, but the date of the "dépôt légal" stamp is 1867. This is quite possibly what the *Journal des débats* of 26 March 1867 refers to as Mustafa Fazıl's letter "just published in French in pamphlet form." Printed copies of another edition in French with the same title were circulating in İstanbul before March 20, 1867. This edition, 11 pp., indicates no publisher, place, or date; it may have been sent in from Paris through the foreign post offices, or it may have been printed in İstanbul itself. The British ambassador Lyons enclosed a copy with his dispatch to the Foreign Office, #101, 20 March 1867, FO 78/1958; there is another copy of the same, still in pristine uncut form, in FO 195/893. Colombe reports in "Une lettre d'un prince égyptien," p. 25, that the letter was also published in France in the *Liberté*, a Paris journal, of 24 March 1867. Colombe curiously does not say which of the many copies of the document he reproduces on pp. 29-38 of his article, but since the *Liberté* publication is the only one he identifies specifically, perhaps he takes the text from that source. He refers obliquely to printed copies sent before March 24 to Napoleon III and to his foreign ministry, but does not cite them exactly. Except for very minor variations a few times in wording, capitalization, and punctuation (aside from typographical errors) all these editions are so close as to give assurance that any one may be used. The Cairo edition of 1897 dates the letter both in the title and at the end of the text as 1866, but advances no proof. On this and later republications, as well as on translation and publication in Turkey in 1867, see the discussion following, and notes thereto. If Ebüzziya's date, quoted in Kuntay, *Namık Kemal*, I, 108, n.29, is correct, the Turkish translation could not have been from the *Liberté* version, since the translating was done on 1 zilkade 1283 (March 7, 1867).

pressed without pity." The origin of all these evils was an antiquated political system, which served well in its time, but now produced only "tyranny, ignorance, misery, and corruption." Islam was not responsible—it was no more fatalist than Christianity. Mustafa Fazıl twice compared the Ottoman situation to pre-1789 France, implying the need for radical change.

The cure, therefore, was a reformed political system. "Sire, save the Empire by transforming it! Save it by giving it a Constitution." Mustafa Fazıl did not stop for details of the constitutional project which, he said, he and his friends had worked out and would send along later.[110] But he suggested freely elected provincial assemblies, delegates from which would form a national assembly. The constitution would also guarantee individual rights, as well as perfect equality of Muslim and Christian. The monarch would be limited only in his power to err or commit excesses. The fruit of a constitution would be liberty and the restoration of individual initiative, which would produce the necessary atmosphere for the development of culture and economy. A constitution would in addition strengthen the empire internationally by removing grounds for foreign intervention. It would bring European public opinion to the Turkish side. Citing the example of Italy, which had quite an appeal for Turks of the mid-nineteenth century, Mustafa Fazıl pointed out that the liberal Piedmontese constitution of 1848, granted by the king, was the first step toward national regeneration. There was also more than a hint of secularism in the letter—religion governs souls and points to the future life, says the Egyptian prince, but it does not regulate the rights of peoples, and must keep to "the sublime domain of eternal truths." Political reform would regenerate loyalty, morals, culture, the economy, military strength. The Turks had before them the examples of European countries—and even of the parliamentary beginnings in Egypt, Tunis, Moldavia, Wallachia, Serbia. But time was pressing, and the Muslims were coming to the end of their patience.

Despite its superficialities and its sometimes inept historical examples, the letter as a whole makes a considerable impact. It became, in fact, one of the great documents of Turkish liberty, referred to and reprinted over a period of more than forty years whenever political

[110] The author does not know whether Mustafa Fazıl ever submitted such a draft. And who were the friends?

agitation was resumed or press freedom was allowed.[111] A part of its appeal undoubtedly lay in its patriotic, even slightly nationalist, tone. The letter exhibited pride in the Ottoman past and in the Turkish character, praised the deed of 1453, and contained some not-too-oblique disparagement of the Byzantines and the moral character of the conquered peoples. In fact, this aspect of the letter, like its emphasis on the equality of all Ottomans and on the need for reforms, parallels the sentiments of Namık Kemal recently cited.[112] But in his pleas for constitution and for liberty Mustafa Fazıl, in the freedom of exile, went much farther than Namık Kemal, still in İstanbul, dared to go.

Mustafa Fazıl's two letters became known in İstanbul at a time propitious for their welcome reception among the New Ottomans and a rather wider group of critics of the government. Part of the atmosphere was the result of the work of Jean Piétri, editor of the *Courrier d'Orient*, who may have been in direct contact with Mustafa Fazıl. The *Courrier* was reported so early as January 1867 to have been echoing the plans and hopes of the *jeune Turquie* party, and to have affirmed that Muslims as well as Christians felt the need for the convocation of a national assembly on the basis of free elections.[113]

[111] Mustafa Fazıl's letter was reprinted in December 1876 or January 1877, in the period when the first Ottoman constitution was proclaimed, by the İstanbul newspaper *İstikbal*. Sultan Abdülhamid evidently feared "the famous letter," as his chief secretary called it, and complained about the publication: Ali Haydar Midhat, *The Life of Midhat Pasha* (London, 1903), p. 125. This was, so far as the writer knows, the first open publication of the letter in the capital. In 1897, when the Young Turk agitation was vigorous, the letter was published in Cairo, which, of course, was under British control though still a part of the empire: *Lettre adressé* [sic] *au feu Sultan Abdul Aziz par le feu Prince Moustapha Fazil Pacha, 1866* (Cairo, A. Costagliola, 1897), italicizing the words *liberté* and *constitution* wherever they appeared. Just after the Young Turk revolution the letter was again reprinted openly in the capital at least four times: as *Bir eser-i siyasî* (İstanbul?, Edep Matbaası, 1326); as *Parisden bir mektub* (İstanbul, Artin Asadoryan Matbaası, 1326); as *Bir Padişaha bir mektub* (Türk Matbaası, 1327), listed in Enver Koray, *Türkiye tarih yayınları bibliyografyası* (Ankara, 1952), #775; and in serial form in Ebüzziya Tevfik's "Yeni Osmanlıların sebebi zuhuru," *Yeni tasvir-i efkâr*, 31 May-7 June 1909, cited in Kuntay, *Namık Kemal*, I, 286, n.7. The author has seen only the first two of these four.

[112] At least one recent scholar reports that it was said Namık Kemal had composed Mustafa Fazıl's letter, though this evidently is based, in part, on the misconception that the letter was originally written in Turkish: Şiddīq al-Damlūjī, *Midḥat Bāshā* (Baghdad, 1952-1953), p. 19, n.1.

[113] *Journal des débats*, 6 February 1867, correspondence from Constantinople of

In early February the *Mecmua-i havadis* (*Review of Events*), an İstanbul journal published in Turkish but with Armenian characters, maintained that Turkey would solve her own problems by emancipating the Christians and by reestablishing Christian-Muslim harmony.[114] This was followed by the circulation of a letter or pamphlet on February 12, arguing the necessity of a constitutional and egalitarian regime in Turkey to save it from foreign intervention and to raise the economic level. The author of this was another Egyptian, Halil Şerif Paşa, related to the Egyptian ruling family, who had already served as Ottoman ambassador to Athens and St. Petersburg. Halil Şerif was almost completely westernized in his education and tastes, virtues and vices; he had a reputation as a great gambler and drinker, as an amateur of Courbet's nudes, and as an intelligent man and a liberal.[115] Presumably Halil Şerif was in touch with Mustafa Fazıl, whose daughter he later married. Just the day before his pamphlet appeared, on February 11, the New Ottomans' pet enemy, Âli Paşa, had been appointed grand vezir. The French and Russians were now bombarding the Porte with advice about reform, while the evacuation of the Serb fortresses was in prospect, and the Cretan revolt had stirred up sympathetic feeling among the Ottoman Greeks and antagonism among the Muslims.[116]

Into this atmosphere came Mustafa Fazıl's letter to *Le Nord*, which began to make the rounds of the İstanbul press. Reprinted ap-

25 January; and 31 January 1867, telegram from Constantinople of 29 January. Cf. *Le Nord*, 9 February 1867. Jean Piétri (also spelled "Giampiétri"), a Frenchman, had edited the *Presse d'Orient* for its French founder, M. Baligot de Beyne. Mardin, *Genesis*, p. 33, finds the original spelling in the *Courrier* to be "Giampietry." Though the *Presse* was suppressed in 1859 for its Francophilism on the issues of the principalities and the Suez Canal, it was resurrected in late 1860 or early 1861 by Jean Piétri under the new name *Courrier d'Orient*: Perrot, *Souvenirs d'un voyage*, pp. 16-20. Perrot praises both the independent spirit and the Frenchness of the *Courrier*, which he claims was read from Trabzon and Bucharest to Alexandria.

[114] *Journal des débats*, 11 February 1867.

[115] On him see Douin, *Khédive Ismail*, II, 313-314; Kuntay, *Namık Kemal*, I, 329-335; Schweiger-Lerchenfeld, *Serail*, pp. 49 and 53-54; Rumbold, *Recollections*, II, 332; Frédéric Loliée, *Les femmes du second empire* (Paris, 1906), pp. 81-86; Elliot to Derby, confidential, #404, 30 July 1875, FO 78/2384. The memoir by Halil Şerif is quoted in Edouard Engelhardt, *La Turquie et le Tanzimat* (Paris, 1882-1884), I, 231. The author has not seen a copy, and Engelhardt says it was unpublished. It is referred to also in Bernhard Stern, *Jungtürken und Verschwörer*, 2nd ed. (Leipzig, 1901), pp. 120-121, and Soubhy Noury, *Le régime représentatif en Turquie* (Paris, 1914), pp. 62-63.

[116] Greeks living in villages on the European shore of the Bosporus had in January demonstrated for their "Byzantine ideas," shouting: "Long live Greece! Down with Turkey!" *Journal des débats*, 6 February 1867.

parently first in the *Courrier d'Orient*, it was translated in Ali Suavi's paper *Muhbir* on February 21, 1867. Two days thereafter Namık Kemal reprinted *Muhbir's* translation in his own *Tasvir-i efkâr*, adding some laudatory comment of his own. The translation of Mustafa Fazıl's French was not very literal, and *Jeune Turquie* was at first clumsily rendered as "the possessors of new thought of the Ottoman nation." Namık Kemal did better, translating *Jeune Turquie* as *Türkistanın erbabı şebabı*, "the youthful ones of Turkey."[117] For a time in the spring of 1867 this term served as a designation for the group of would-be reformers clustered around the members of the İttifak-ı Hamiyet in İstanbul and represented, on his own assertion, by Mustafa Fazıl in Paris.[118] Namık Kemal did not accept Mustafa Fazıl as representative or leader of the group, and, in fact, disclaimed acquaintance with him.[119] Yet he expressed appreciation for Mustafa Fazıl's patriotism and many of his ideas, and pride in the fact that the prince should consider himself "one of us." Similarly, Ali Suavi at first disclaimed any desire for close association with Mustafa Fazıl. Indeed, by Ali Suavi's own account, the prince's letter had been published in *Muhbir* by the owner of the paper without the knowledge of himself, the editor.[120] Yet the prince and the İstanbul journalists were rapidly being drawn together.

At almost the same time as Mustafa Fazıl's letter to *Le Nord* was arousing excitement in İstanbul—perhaps a few days later—his open letter to Sultan Abdülaziz came into the hands of Namık Kemal and his friends. On March 7, 1867, it too was translated into Turkish. The translation was made by Kemal's friend Sadullah Bey, who had also been trained in the translation bureau, in order that Kemal's own

[117] Sungu, "Tanzimat ve Yeni Osmanlılar," *Tanzimat*, I, 777, n.1; Ebüzziya Tevfik, "Yeni Osmanlıların sebebi zuhuru," *Yeni tasvir-i efkâr*, 1 June 1909, quoted in Kuntay, *Namık Kemal*, I, 290, n.12. This is probably what Th. Menzel refers to when he says that the expression "Young Turk" first appeared in the *Tasvir-i efkâr*: "Kemal, Mehmed Namık," *Encyclopaedia of Islam*, II, 848. Otherwise the assertion makes no sense, for the expression had long been used in English and French. The use of "Türkistan," a term with somewhat more nationalist connotations than "Memaliki Osmaniye" or other labels for the Ottoman Empire, was not unusual in this period, especially among the New Ottomans. The text of *Muhbir's* translation, evidently slightly tailored to a Muslim audience, is in Kuntay, *Sarıklı ihtilâlci*, p. 23; of Namık Kemal's comment in Kaplan, *Namık Kemal*, pp. 52-53 (English translation in Mardin, *Genesis*, pp. 37-38).

[118] The term is, for instance, sprinkled through Namık Kemal's answer to the *Gazette du Levant*: Kuntay, *Namık Kemal*, I, 183-187, 290-291.

[119] Kuntay, *Namık Kemal*, I, 290-291, 184-185.

[120] Cited *ibid.*, I, 469.

well-known style might not betray the source. The work was done in one night, Sadullah dictating to Ebüzziya Tevfik, while Kemal was on hand to consult with them. Then arrangements for lithographing were made through Jean Piétri with the French printing firm of Cayol in İstanbul. Reportedly fifty thousand copies of the letter were lithographed and distributed by men who in most cases had some close connection with Namık Kemal and the *Tasvir-i efkâr* press.[121] At least in the capital, and probably in other cities, the letter rapidly became known. No newspaper in İstanbul dared reprint it, though the *Levant Herald* published a short abstract.[122] Thus the letter of Mustafa Fazıl brought increasing sympathy between him and the New Ottoman journalists in İstanbul. Quite probably his public stand helped to embolden the New Ottomans in their next move.

This was to condemn the administration of Âli Paşa more openly than they had hitherto done in their newspapers. The attack came principally on the diplomatic issues of Serbia and Crete. Ali Suavi's *Muhbir* carried articles critical of the Ottoman government on such subjects as foreign loans, and especially on the question of Turkish evacuation of the Belgrade fortress. A further article by Ali Suavi on the desires of Ismail Paşa of Egypt and his agent Nubar Paşa led to the suspension of *Muhbir* by the Porte, by order of March 9, 1867. When the proprietor of *Muhbir*, Filip Efendi, protested the suspension, Namık Kemal printed the protest and commented cautiously but favorably on it in his *Tasvir-i efkâr* of March 10. In the same issue appeared Namık Kemal's famous article on the Eastern Question, criticizing the Porte and the intervention of the powers in the Cretan affair.[123] Âli Paşa, confronted with a difficult diplomatic situation, was understandably annoyed at the increasing vehemence of these journalist gadflies. In disregard of the procedures laid down in

[121] Pâkalın, *Maliye nazırları*, II, 17-18; Tunaya, *Siyasî partiler*, p. 92, and n.8; Kuntay, *Namık Kemal*, I, 108, n.29, 277, 279-281. The Greek Revelaki, formerly Lord Stratford's dragoman, was somehow involved also, but it is not clear whether he helped in the Turkish translation, or published the letter in French in İstanbul: Pâkalın, *loc.cit.*; Kuntay, *Namık Kemal*, I, 245. The figure 50,000 seems high, but is commonly accepted. Henri Cayol had set up in business in İstanbul in the 1830's. On him see Mordtmann's letter of 11 July 1851, *Zeitschrift der Deutschen Morgenländischen Gesellschaft*, VI:3 (1852), 409 and n.1; Belin's note in *Journal asiatique*, Series VI:8 (October-November 1866), 439-440.

[122] Alfred de Caston, *Musulmans et chrétiens* (Constantinople, 1874), II, 354-357: *Neue Freie Presse*, 4 April 1867.

[123] Tanpınar, *XIX asır*, pp. 198-199; Kuntay, *Namık Kemal*, I, 63-64 and n.23.

the 1865 press law, Âli issued an administrative edict under which immediate action could be taken against a portion of the local press described as the inflammatory organ of extremist groups, subversive of public order and of the foundations of the empire itself.[124] The *Tasvir-i efkâr* was cut off after its issue of March 24. The same issue carried official notice that Namık Kemal was to be rusticated to Erzurum in an administrative post.[125] Âli Paşa had obviously decided to rid the capital of his most virulent critics, for Ziya Bey, who had written for *Muhbir* on occasion, was similarly assigned to a post in Cyprus, and Ali Suavi was already simply exiled to Kastamonu near the Black Sea. Tension in the capital mounted, as rumors of a conspiracy of Muslims against the Sublime Porte and Christians alike began to circulate, and as the first Turkish soldiers began to leave Belgrade.[126]

Namık Kemal and Ziya dragged their feet and did not actually go to their posts of exile. Instead, approached by Mustafa Fazıl through the medium of Jean Piétri, they accepted the invitation of the Egyptian prince to join him in Paris.[127] They escaped on May 17 by steamer to Italy, where they were joined by Ali Suavi, who had meanwhile got himself back from Kastamonu, and the three proceeded to Paris, where they found both Mustafa Fazıl and Şinasi. Şinasi appears to have maintained little connection with the newly arrived exiles.[128] But now for a time the New Ottoman journalists were thrown into close contact and collaboration with Mustafa Fazıl.

Meanwhile the other members of the İttifak-ı Hamiyet who were left in İstanbul were, of course, suspect to the Porte. It is possible, as has been charged, that Âli Paşa knew something of the designs of the organization, if not about the organization itself, and allowed it

[124] Text in Aristarchi, *Législation*, III, 325-326, dated 12 March 1867; in Young, *Corps de droit*, II, 326, dated 6 March 1867; in Kuntay, *Namık Kemal*, I, 521-522, dated 14 March 1867 (8 zilkade 1283), which is probably correct; İskit, *Türkiyede matbuat rejimleri*, p. 696, dated 16 March (10 zilkade).

[125] Kuntay, *Namık Kemal*, I, 522.

[126] Lyons to Stanley, #112, confidential, 27 March 1867, FO 78/1958; T. W. Riker, "Michael of Serbia and the Turkish Occupation," *Slavonic and East European Review*, 12 (April 1934), 652-658. Muslim feeling, roused by the Cretan rebellion, was also rising in Beirut and Bursa: ABCFM, Vol. 292, #240, 3 April 1867, and Western Turkey Mission III, #525, 9 March 1867.

[127] Pâkalın, *Tanzimat maliye nazırları*, II, 19-21, based on Ebüzziya's account.

[128] Despite the assertion of Frederick Millingen, *Les Anglais en Orient* (Paris, 1877), pp. 345-346, that he (Millingen) and Şinasi were very close to Mustafa Fazıl in Paris, and that Şinasi begged Millingen to recruit Garibaldi's help for a military expedition against the Ottoman province of Tripoli.

to continue up to this point so that he might gain credit with Sultan Abdülaziz by denouncing the conspirators, and so reinforce his dominance over the fearful sultan.[129] But the combination of the growing diplomatic crisis with Mustafa Fazıl's outspoken letters from Paris and the critical journalism of the New Ottomans in İstanbul now made the agitators left in the capital a force to be reckoned with, since they could well arouse feeling among the populace. Indeed, Mehmed Bey, of the original conspiratorial group, had just been or was even now attempting exactly that among the ulema in the medreses.[130] So late as March 20, 1867, when Mustafa Fazıl's letter to the sultan was first circulating in the capital, the British ambassador had been able to report that the party nicknamed "la jeune Turquie" were neither numerous nor important.[131] By April 10, even before Namık Kemal and Ziya escaped to Paris, his opinion was that the so-called Young Turks could feed on a very great discontent of the Muslim population in the capital, exacerbated by the distress of those government employees whose salaries were in arrears.[132] Sometime in May Âli Paşa evidently decided to break up the conspiratorial group. Further arrests and exiles were ordered.[133]

The exact chronology of the changing aims of the members of the İttifak-ı Hamiyet in İstanbul is not completely clear. Certainly they kept to their original aim of 1865 to alter the composition of the administration and to get Âli, in particular, out.[134] At some point, evidently in the spring of 1867, members of the İttifak-ı Hamiyet had gathered in the mosque of Aya Sofya to discuss future moves and had reached no agreement on a replacement for Âli Paşa. Mehmed

---

[129] Schweiger-Lerchenfeld, *Serail und Hohe Pforte*, pp. 48, 179-183. Cf. *Levant Herald*, 5 July 1876. Denunciations of conspiracies, even of wholly fictitious ones, were a not unusual method of currying the imperial favor. There was another example the next year: Morris to Seward, private and confidential, 29 October 1868, USNA, Turkey 20. Namık Kemal denied any New Ottoman complicity: Kuntay, *Namık Kemal*, I, 303.

[130] Kuntay, *Namık Kemal*, I, 358 and n.4. Cf. *Neue Freie Presse*, 4 April 1867, charging similar activity by Ali Suavi.

[131] Lyons to Foreign Office, #101, 20 March 1867, FO 78/1958.

[132] Lyons to Stanley, 10 April 1867, in Lord Newton, *Lord Lyons: A Record of British Diplomacy* (London, 1913), I, 167.

[133] Tanpınar, *XIX. asır*, p. 199, fixes the first arrests on Monday, May 20, 1867, evidently on Ebüzziya Tevfik's authority. Cf. Morris to Seward, private, 31 May 1867, USNA, Turkey 20.

[134] The reported plot of three young men, two of them connected with the Young Ottomans, to seize Sultan Abdülaziz in 1866 and to enthrone Murad in his place is not clear: Schweiger-Lerchenfeld, *Serail*, pp. 201-206.

Bey wanted his uncle Mahmud Nedim Paşa, then vali of Tripoli in Africa, as grand vezir.[135] Others wanted Ahmed Vefik Paşa.[136] It may be that already some of the group were planning to assassinate Âli and other ministers. This becomes more likely at the time of what appears to be a second meeting of the group, which probably occurred after the flight of Namık Kemal and Ziya, although accounts in Turkish give it no date. Gathering in the Veli Efendi meadow, some forty conspirators planned to raise an *émeute* on the occasion of Sultan Abdülaziz's visit to the Sublime Porte, and presumably to kill Âli and others if necessary. The leader here was Mehmed Bey, although Mustafa Fazıl's steward, Azmi Bey, is also said to have been a promoter of the meeting. It looks as if Mehmed, alarmed by the Porte's measures against the press and New Ottoman journalists, had decided to try more violent action. But the Porte got wind of the plot through Ayetullah, one of the group, who was horrified at the thought of killing. Further arrests were made, whereupon Mehmed, Nuri, and Reşad succeeded in making good their escape to join their colleagues in Paris.[137] The date of their escape is not certain, but it must have been early June of 1867.[138] For information given by Âli and Fuad to European diplomats discloses that about fifty conspirators met in a garden outside the capital (presumably the Veli Efendi meadow) on Monday, June 3, and that the police gained knowledge of it through betrayal by one of the group. By June 10, at least sixteen arrests had been made. Among those arrested were Azmi Bey, Mustafa Fazıl's steward; Hüseyin Daim Paşa, one of the leaders of the 1859 Kuleli conspiracy, who, of course, may this time not have been involved at all; and presumably arrested also was Mustafa Asım Paşa, second in command of the gendarmerie, who is usually considered to have been a member of the İttifak-ı Hamiyet.

[135] By some authors, Mahmud Nedim is accounted a member of the İttifak-ı Hamiyet and a conspirator against Âli—an assertion that goes back to Ali Haydar Midhat, *Midhat Paşa*, II: *Mirât-ı hayret* (İstanbul, 1325), p. 19.

[136] On this supposed meeting in Aya Sofya: Abdurrahman Şeref, *Tarih musahabeleri* (İstanbul, 1339), p. 173. Danişmend, *Kronolojisi*, IV, 212, calls reports of this meeting "weak."

[137] On the Veli Efendi meeting and its results: Şehsuvaroğlu, *Sultan Aziz*, pp. 55-57; İnal, *Son asır türk şairleri*, I, 149-150; idem, *Son sadrıâzamlar*, II, 264-265; Kuntay, *Namık Kemal*, I, 245.

[138] Abdurrahman Şeref, quoted in Pâkalın, *Maliye nazırları*, II, 33, and followed by Danişmend, *Kronolojisi*, IV, 212, puts the escape of these three *before* that of Namık Kemal, Ziya, and Ali Suavi. This seems unlikely; if true, it destroys the above reconstruction of events.

The Turkish ministers were sure that Mustafa Fazıl was somehow implicated, and reported that the plan was to assassinate all ministers but one when they met in council on Wednesday, June 5.[139] Although Âli and Fuad, in disclosing the plot to European diplomats, tried to play down the importance of the opposition to their administration, they tried at the same time to make diplomatic capital by observing that it was popular discontent over Crete and the possibility of losing control of the island that really put the government in danger. The ministers may have been more alarmed than they admitted. Possibly an order of June 13 prohibiting the importation of revolvers was connected with the episode.[140] When reports of the plot and the arrests reached Europe, Ziya Bey wrote a letter to Paris newspapers denying complicity of Mustafa Fazıl or himself and saying that those arrested were not connected with his group.[141]

Âli and Fuad were for the moment secure in the capital. They could go ahead with plans for the sultan's visit to Paris and London and with trying to implement the Tanzimat program. The New Ottomans in the capital had lost their leadership, which now re-formed in Paris with the aid of Mustafa Fazıl.

The exiles who gathered about Mustafa Fazıl Paşa in Paris were few in number. Four of them were from the presumed original six of the İttifak-ı Hamiyet of 1865: Namık Kemal, Mehmed, Reşad, Nuri. Three others had been, in one way or another, their colleagues in journalism in İstanbul—Ziya, Ali Suavi, Agâh—and probably also members of the Patriotic Alliance. They were joined in Paris by one

---

[139] Pisani (dragoman) to Lyons, #145, 5 June 1867, FO 195/887; Lyons to Stanley, #245, 13 June 1867, and #258, confidential, 16 June 1867, both FO 78/1961; Bourée to Moustier, telegram, 5 June 1867, and Bourée to Moustier, #100, 5 June 1867, both AAE, Turquie 371.

[140] Text in Young, *Corps de droit*, II, 302; Aristarchi, *Législation*, III, 104.

[141] See, for example, report in *Le Nord* (Brussels), 25 June 1867, reprinted from the *Augsburger Allgemeine Zeitung*; also Caston, *Musulmans et chrétiens*, II, 364-365. Caston makes Ziya speak of five or six thousand potential demonstrators. Melek Hanum, *Six Years*, who had left İstanbul before the affair broke, speaks of a conspiracy of 30,000 associates, p. 100. Léon Cahun reports that in 1868 some of the exiles in Paris told him the New Ottoman plot was to establish a constitutional monarchy under a new sultan as a prelude to a republic, while Arabs would elect a caliph at Mecca to "give investiture" to the Ottoman republic: Ernest Lavisse and Alfred Rambaud, *Histoire générale*, XI (Paris, 1899), 547. This is fantastic, yet Cahun by his own admission and the word of some Turks had reasonably close contact with the exile group: Abdurrahman Şeref, *Tarih musahabeleri*, p. 186; Kuntay, *Namık Kemal*, I, 530-532.

Kani Paşazade Rifat Bey, who left his job in the Ottoman embassy there, and at some later date by a former general of brigade, Hüseyin Vasfi Paşa.[142] What Mustafa Fazıl wanted of these men was their journalistic talent, to be employed against Âli and Fuad, presumably in hopes that he might regain the right to succeed to the Egyptian governorship, or at least knock the ministers out of office and himself become grand vezir, and thus Ismail's superior. In return, the New Ottomans would get financial support from Mustafa Fazıl's vast wealth; he had already financed their trips into exile. But the Egyptian pretender and the New Ottomans were now also thinking along parallel, if not identical, political lines since the publication of Mustafa Fazıl's letter to Sultan Abdülaziz, and they might, therefore, expect to reach agreement on a plan of organization and of campaign for political reform of the Ottoman Empire. Such agreement was not immediately achieved. It was held up partly by the state visit of Abdülaziz to Paris, which lasted from June 30 to July 10. The government of Napoleon III, through the Ottoman ambassador, obliged the New Ottomans to leave during this period; some went to London, and some to the isle of Jersey.[143] But by August they were gathered again in Paris, and met on the tenth of that month at Mustafa Fazıl's house to decide on a program of action. The eight young revolutionaries, under Mustafa Fazıl's temporary chairmanship, decided that Ali Suavi should publish a newspaper—a new *Muhbir*—and that a capital fund of a quarter of a million francs would be under Ziya's control. The capital came from Mustafa Fazıl, who also provided monthly salaries for the propagandists.[144]

The actual statutes of organization of the exile group seem to have been completed on August 30, 1867.[145] The first article of the statutes, drawn in French and entitled "Organisation de la Chancellerie de la Jeune Turquie," was considerably revised from that of 1865. It now read:

"The party of the Jeune Turquie is constituted. It has as aims:

"a) The carrying out of the reform program of prince Mustafa

[142] *Ibid.*, I, 376, 395, 401; Léon Cahun, *loc.cit.*, p. 548.
[143] Kuntay, *Namık Kemal*, I, 546, 582.
[144] *Ibid.*, p. 482 (mostly from Ebüzziya), where it is reported also that Ziya and Kemal were to publish a paper called *Hürriyet* (*Liberty*). In view of the later history of the exile publications, the decision on *Hürriyet* at this date seems more doubtful.
[145] Engelhardt, *La Turquie et le Tanzimat* (Paris, 1882-1884), II, 3, gives April 30, which seems quite unlikely if the first New Ottomans fled from İstanbul only in May.

Fazıl contained in his letter addressed to the sultan, and consequently the changing of the regime and of the men who presently oppress the Ottoman Empire.

"b) The destruction of the Russian influence and propaganda in the East, which are so dangerous for the very existence of the Ottoman Empire, the diminution of czarism by the emancipation of the Christian populations in Turkey from the Muscovite protectorship and by the reestablishment of the heroic Polish nation in its former independence, as bulwark against the encroachments of the barbarity of Russia."[146]

What is startling in this document is the association of New Ottoman and Polish revolutionary aims, a subject that will require considerably more investigation. How much contact there was between the two groups, and how much actual cooperation—whether in the Ottoman Empire or among exiles in western Europe—is not clear. But it does seem clear that there were connections, which may have been furthered through Mazzini and other Italian exiles.[147] A Turkish army officer of Polish origin was associated with the New Ottoman group in exile.[148] Ziya was also in contact with a leader of the Polish rising of 1863, Marjan Langiewicz, who had been sent to the Ottoman Empire on Mazzinian funds to further the cause of the Balkan Christian separatisms, but who found the Christians to be tools of Russia and who attempted instead (in vain, owing to Âli's opposition) to set up a Bulgar-Pole military unit to support the Turks against Russia.[149] Through Langiewicz, Ziya gained the support of Count Wladyslaw Plater, a Pole of the 1830 exile with great experience in nationalist propaganda and European diplomacy, and of Simon Deutsch, an Austrian socialist politician in exile who was also vigorously anti-Russian. These men, in fact, and Plater in particular, seem to have assisted Ziya in drawing up the statutes of August 30. The signers of the statutes were Mustafa Fazıl, Ziya, Namık Kemal, Plater, and Deutsch.[150] Since Deutsch was a member of the First

[146] Adam Lewak, *Dzieje emigracji polskiej w Turcji (1831-1878)* (Warsaw, 1935), p. 214, n.62.

[147] *Ibid.*, pp. 211, 213.

[148] Melek Hanum, *Six Years*, pp. 97, 100, 106; Cahun in Lavisse and Rambaud, *Histoire générale*, XI, 548.

[149] Lewak, *Emigracji polskiej*, pp. 211, 213.

[150] *Ibid.*, pp. 213-214. Deutsch and Plater are mentioned also by Schweiger-Lerchenfeld, *Serail und Hohe Pforte*, pp. 206-207; Deutsch as an old friend of Namık Kemal

International, and a participant in the Paris Commune, the question of his possible influence on the New Ottoman exiles is an interesting one.[151] Undoubtedly the New Ottomans in exile had some contact with Mazzinians, Polish exiles, socialists, Freemasons, and others on the radical fringe of European society of the 1860's. It is not unreasonable to suppose that the New Ottomans attracted some cooperation and support from other exiles, and probably also from unstable characters and second-rate journalists seeking a livelihood.[152] How much the activities and views of the New Ottomans were influenced by these temporary combinations and marriages of convenience is still an open question.

The constitution of the New Ottoman group provided that the Turks would handle internal and military matters, while Plater and Deutsch would take over external policy and press propaganda (in the European press, presumably). Mustafa Fazıl was to bear the cost of an annual budget of three hundred thousand French francs.[153]

---

is mentioned in a letter of later date by Léon Cahun: Kuntay, *Namık Kemal*, I, 531. Mordtmann mentions a Dr. Simon Deutsch as Mustafa Fazıl's physician: *Augsburger Allgemeine Zeitung*, 28 February 1878, Beilage.

[151] On Deutsch: *La grande encyclopédie*, XIV, 352. The International at its 1866 Congress in Geneva voted to support the reconstitution of Poland, and at its 1867 Lausanne congress voted for democratic suffrage, among other things.

[152] For instance, Frederick Millingen, *Les anglais en Orient*, pp. 361-364, says that Ziya and Ali Suavi depended on him to launch the newspaper *Muhbir* when it began to appear in London; Gregory Ganesco, the Wallachian who is said to have written Mustafa Fazıl's letter to the sultan, is also said to have published the 1867 statutes in his own journal in that year: " 'Reform' in Turkey," *Diplomatic Review*, 24 (July 1876), p. 159.

[153] Lewak, *Emigracji polskiej*, p. 214. He does not give the literal text of the statutes beyond article 1, and unfortunately the original document in the Biblioteka Narodowa in Warsaw was destroyed in World War II. The summary here is incomplete. This seems, however, to be the same document to which Engelhardt refers as of April 30; his summary of article 1 nearly coincides with Lewak's text. It is close also to the summary of the same article cited by Tunaya, *Siyasî partiler*, p. 93, from L. Eroğlu, "Bizde siyasi cemiyet ve partileri tarihçiği," *Aylık ansiklopedisi*, #52 (1948), 1489. " 'Reform' in Turkey," *Diplomatic Review*, 24 (July 1876), 159-160, publishes what it calls article 13 of the statutes, in which Mustafa Fazıl guarantees an annual subvention of 300,000 francs; it says, further, that the complete statutes except for this article were published in Paris in 1867 in the *Tablettes d'un Spectateur*, which I have not yet been able to find. The discrepancy over article 13 may be due to the fact that the budgetary provision, according to Lewak, was in a postscript added by Mustafa Fazıl next to his signature. Lewak's document was signed in Paris. Schweiger-Lerchenfeld, *Serail und Hohe Pforte*, refers evidently to the same document, but places its concoction and signature at Baden-Baden in August 1867 (pp. 52-53, 60-61, 206-207). Actually the Baden-Baden meeting in August seems to have involved only Mustafa Fazıl and Namık Kemal: Kuntay, *Namık Kemal*, I, 325. Schweiger-Lerchenfeld says, further, that Mustafa Fazıl at first refused to sign

The results of these August decisions were two-fold. Within the empire Langiewicz was to set up an agency in İstanbul and nine branches in the Balkans to counteract Russian influence and win the cooperation of Balkan Christians for the New Ottoman movement. He was provided with a small fund by the newly established New Ottoman Society. But, instead, he reverted to his old plan for creation of a Bulgar-Pole military unit. This, coupled with rumors that his military force was to compel Sultan Abdülaziz, under threat of deposition, to make Mustafa Fazıl the grand vezir in Âli's stead, meant that his usefulness was ended, and he got nowhere with his plans.[154] Outside the empire the New Ottomans had more immediate success, as *Muhbir* appeared in its revived form on August 31, 1867. Because of restrictions in France, Ali Suavi published it in London, proclaiming at the head of the first issue that *Muhbir* could again appear since it had found a country where truth-telling was not forbidden. It was issued in the name of, and carried the seal of, the new society which had been formed earlier that month and christened in Turkish the Yeni Osmanlılar Cemiyeti, or the Society of New Ottomans.[155] But from the beginning *Muhbir* under Ali Suavi's direction had more of a Muslim tone, and paid less attention to the avowed aims of the Yeni Osmanlılar, than Namık Kemal and Ziya and others of the group liked.[156] This boded ill for the united front.

So also did the separation of Mustafa Fazıl from the rest of the Yeni Osmanlılar in September, though the bad results were not immediately apparent. The Egyptian prince had not been banished from France when Sultan Abdülaziz visited, but, instead, had talked with him and accompanied him on a part of his European tour. The upshot was some sort of agreement between the two, based, one suspects, on a promise by the sultan that he would move toward constitutional government or that he would appoint Mustafa Fazıl to an important position, or both. Whatever the promise may have been, Mustafa Fazıl was induced to return to İstanbul, which he did about

---

a compromising document, but that Ziya, Deutsch, and Plater got him to sign one copy, which remained in Ziya's possession and which was saved when English police raided Ziya's house later in London. Ziya could then use the document to put pressure on Mustafa Fazıl.

[154] Lewak, *Emigracji polskiej*, pp. 214-215.

[155] İhsan Sungu, "Tanzimat ve Yeni Osmanlılar," *Tanzimat*, I, 777, n.1, illustration facing p. 801, 807, n.49.

[156] Tanpınar, *XIX. asır*, p. 200.

the middle of September 1867. Before his return, he talked with Namık Kemal in Baden-Baden, so that the latter was not only reconciled to the prospect, but thought that Mustafa Fazıl might become a constitutional grand vezir, or at least work in that direction. The Egyptian left funds to keep the New Ottoman publication going.[157] But this was in fact the beginning of a breach that grew wider, and a success for Âli Paşa in that it separated the New Ottomans from their financial backer. No big step toward constitutional government was taken. The Council of State created in the spring of the next year was a far cry from a chamber of deputies.[158] Mustafa Fazıl did, in fact, regain high office as president of the new Council of Justice and then as minister of finance, though only in 1869 and 1870, evidently as a result of new friction between the khedive Ismail of Egypt and the sultan.[159] But his efforts to ingratiate himself with the sultan and Âli, and to gain such office, led to his increasing impatience with the publications of the New Ottoman exiles, since these consistently attacked Âli, and thus widened the breach between Mustafa Fazıl and the exiled journalists. Ultimately this had disastrous results for the New Ottoman finances. Ziya became particularly bitter, and in his satiric Zafername depicted Mustafa Fazıl as the nightly drinking companion of Âli.[160]

Even had Mustafa Fazıl not returned to İstanbul, the New Ottoman coterie could not long have stuck together. The members were too different in temperament, character, grievances, ambitions, and in views about the prerequisites for salvation of the Ottoman Empire. Ali Suavi's Muhbir became more vitriolic and fanatically Muslim in tone. Mustafa Fazıl finally ordered it stopped in the spring of 1868, after Namık Kemal and Ziya had become quite disgusted with Ali Suavi. The two, with Mustafa Fazıl's backing, started a new paper in London, Hürriyet, which first appeared on June 29, 1868, and contained some of their best political writing. Yet not all the other New Ottomans liked Hürriyet, some considering it not radical enough.

---

[157] Kuntay, Namık Kemal, I, 315, 325, 546-552, largely based on unpublished letters of Namık Kemal.

[158] See below, chapter VII, on the Council of State.

[159] Colombe, "Une lettre d'un prince égyptien," p. 28, n.13. Schweiger-Lerchenfeld, Serail und Hohe Pforte, pp. 56-58, connects the friction with Ismail's success in playing host to European royalty at the Suez Canal opening.

[160] Actually in the prose commentary on the Zafername which Ziya maliciously attributed to Hüsni Paşa, the gendarmerie commander: Gibb, Ottoman Poetry, V, 61-62, 98, n.1.

By the middle of 1869 Mustafa Fazıl found *Hürriyet*'s criticism of the Ottoman government and of Âli too much also, in view of his climb back into official favor. Ziya irritated Mustafa Fazıl more than did Namık Kemal, for Ziya evidently had hopes of regaining the sultan's favor through violent criticism of the ministers. Ziya's subsidy was cut off. Finally Namık Kemal broke with Ziya in late summer of 1869. Ziya struggled to continue *Hürriyet* by himself for a while. Namık Kemal remained throughout the most respectable and reasonable of the New Ottomans, and stayed on in London with some financial assistance from Mustafa Fazıl to see to the printing of an edition of the Koran. Some of the others got into scrapes of one sort or another, including extramarital adventures. Ziya was in the hands of the English police briefly for publishing an article by Ali Suavi which encouraged the assassination of Âli Paşa. To avoid trial Ziya skipped to Geneva, and there again revived *Hürriyet* for a time. Meanwhile Ali Suavi had started an encyclopedic journal of his own, *Ulûm (Sciences)* in Paris. Mehmed started his own *İttihad (Union)* in Paris, and then Mehmed and Hüseyin Vasfi set up a more radical sheet, *İnkılâb (Revolution)*, in Geneva. The khedive Ismail tried and failed to buy Namık Kemal, but evidently succeeded in buying Ziya after the subsidy from Mustafa Fazıl had stopped. By the spring of 1870 the group had fallen completely to pieces. And Mustafa Fazıl was now being used by Âli as a weapon against Ismail, just as earlier Mustafa Fazıl himself had used the New Ottomans against Âli.[161]

The New Ottoman Society was never again reconstituted. Mehmed, Nuri, and Reşad fought for France against Prussia. Ziya was still presumably in Ismail's pay. Namık Kemal, assured that he could return safely, went back to İstanbul at the end of 1870. There he did resume his journalistic career, and for a period after Âli Paşa's death in 1871 he was quite effective, especially with his new paper *İbret (Admonition)*. But, though some of his old friends worked with him, the former New Ottoman group was not resurrected in İstanbul. The other exiles drifted back at intervals during the following years, Ali Suavi not until 1876.

The effectiveness of the New Ottomans is not solely to be judged,

[161] Kuntay, *Namık Kemal*, I, 444, n.66, 482-504, 518-519, 533-544, 562-574; Sungu, "Tanzimat ve Yeni Osmanlılar," pp. 779, n.6, 855; Tanpınar, *XIX. asır*, pp. 200-202; Mordtmann, *Stambul*, I, 68-70; Schweiger-Lerchenfeld, *Serail und Hohe Pforte*, pp. 58-72; Danişmend, *Ali Suâvi'nin türkçülüğü*, pp. 9, 12-15; Mardin, *Genesis*, pp. 47-56; Kaplan, *Namık Kemal*, pp. 61-72.

however, by their cohesion or lack of it. They were never a political party, though in İstanbul in 1867 they might have created an effective conspiratorial group. Their main function was journalistic agitation to mold a new public opinion. This effort had some impact, both immediate and on events in 1876 and after. How great the immediate impact was it is hard to judge. In part, the New Ottomans aimed to influence European opinion against the regime of Âli Paşa, and to persuade westerners that there was a salvation for the Ottoman Empire and that Islam was compatible with sound reform. *Muhbir* issued a summary sheet in French, with translations of some of its articles. But neither the thought processes of the New Ottomans, nor their personal conduct, nor their condemnations of European action in the Eastern Question seem to have elicited much approval among westerners, and probably there was as much criticism as there was praise of them in Europe.[162] To Europe, Âli and Fuad were more likely to appear the sound and progressive reformers, going ahead with new measures on the western model in exactly the same years during which the New Ottomans were in exile.[163] The New Ottomans' major aim, however, was to influence opinions and politics within the empire. Here they had rather more success, though again measurement is hard.

One measure is the reaction of Âli's government. Certainly Âli must have felt the personal attacks on him keenly. He was mercilessly castigated as kaiser, despot, tyrant, grafter, inefficient, weak, destroyer of the faith of believers in the might of the Padishah and Caliph. He was derided as *kapıcızade*, "son of a doorkeeper"—an allusion to his humble origin.[164] Fuad was also attacked, but never quite so vigorously; furthermore, his illness and death left Âli supreme by early 1869. The New Ottoman attacks also, of course, hampered the conduct of business by the Ottoman government, and posed a possible threat to its security and a real threat to its prestige. The publications of the

---

[162] Vambéry, *Der Islam im neunzehnten Jahrhundert*, pp. 276-278; *idem*, "Freiheitliche Bestrebungen im moslemischen Asien," *Deutsche Rundschau*, 78 (October 1893), 64-65; *Augsburger Allgemeine Zeitung*, 18 September 1876; Mordtmann, *Stambul*, I, 66-67; Cahun in Lavisse and Rambaud, *Histoire générale*, XI, 545-546, and XII, 485-486.

[163] See below, chapter VII, on these measures.

[164] *Hürriyet*, 14 September 1868, cited in Kuntay, *Namık Kemal*, I, 270; *Le Mukhbir*, 7 November 1867; summary of a *Muhbir* supplement in FO 195/893, #120; Ali Suavi, *Ali Paşa'nın siyaseti* (İstanbul, 1325), pp. 11-12, quoted in Kuntay, *Namık Kemal*, I, 270, n.7.

exiles went into the empire through the foreign post offices, in evasion of article nine of the 1865 press law which forbade the introduction and circulation of periodicals from abroad which, dealing with political or administrative matters, were published with an intent hostile to the Ottoman government. *Ulûm* was, in fact, published in small format so that it could be mailed in an envelope like an ordinary letter.[165] None of the papers was large. At least in İstanbul, and very possibly in some provincial cities, these publications attracted considerable attention. The first two issues of *Hürriyet* were read openly by riders on the Bosporus ferries in the relatively liberal days following the opening of the Council of State in 1868. Then the police began to crack down. But copies continued to get into the empire, and to be distributed by a French bookseller in Pera.[166] A single issue of *Hürriyet* smuggled into İstanbul is said to have commanded a price of one Turkish lira.[167] The Porte asked the British government to forbid its post office in İstanbul to distribute *Muhbir*, and later made the same request with regard to *Hürriyet*.[168] But the journals continued to circulate in the empire.

So also did various brochures which the exiles produced, against the circulation of which the Porte also protested. The best known of these was by Ziya, attacking the rumored plans of Abdülaziz to change the order of succession to the throne by by-passing the heir-apparent, Murad, in favor of his own son, Yusuf İzzeddin.[169] It is impossible to say whether or not this had any impact on the sultan himself; he did not, at least, permanently abandon his dream. It would, in fact, be interesting to know whether Abdülaziz was at all influenced by the New Ottomans—whether by Mustafa Fazıl's letter, or by the memorandum on reforms which Ziya presented to the sultan as he passed through London, or by the personal attacks of the more radical New Ottomans, who depicted him as mad.[170]

The major effect of the New Ottomans in exile on the growing public opinion in the empire was achieved by hammering away at a

[165] Danişmend, *Ali Suâvi'nin türkçülüğü*, p. 9.

[166] Şehsuvaroğlu, *Sultan Aziz*, p. 58; Fazli Necip, *Külhani Edipler* (İstanbul, 1930), p. 39. The French bookseller is variously named as "Kok" or "Vik."

[167] Ahmed Saib, *Vaka-i Sultan Abdülaziz* (Cairo, 1320), pp. 115, 147.

[168] FO 195/893, *note verbale* of the Sublime Porte, 5 October 1867; and Safvet (Foreign Minister) to Elliot, 14 October 1868, in FO 195/893, #368.

[169] Şehsuvaroğlu, *Sultan Aziz*, p. 47.

[170] On the latter two, cf. Sungu, "Tanzimat ve Yeni Osmanlılar," pp. 838-840, 852.

few ideas which, despite the individual variations among the exiles, they generally held in common. Basic to all of their arguments was their conviction that the Ottoman Empire had to be preserved intact, by arresting its lamentable decline and increasing its strength. Ziya in his *Zafername* attacked Lebanese autonomy, the withdrawal of the Turkish garrison from Belgrade, concessions to the Cretan rebels, concessions to the Montenegrins.[171] Concessions were weakness.

> "The Turkish virtues old are all, alack, undone;
> The ancient Turkish zeal abideth in ne'er an one;
> The Turkish glory of yore is past away and gone;
> The Turkish State is come into such a plight that none
> The signs and portents sad of approaching doom can see."[172]

But the word that Ziya used was not "Turkish," but "Osmanli."[173] It was the Ottoman virtues and the Ottoman Empire that the New Ottomans wanted to revive. Mixed in with this Ottoman patriotism and pride in the empire's past was also a pride in Islam and its past.

The love of fatherland, of *vatan*, was most vigorously expressed by Namık Kemal during his exile and after in both prose and poetry. In one forceful passage he gives a series of reasons for patriotism, each explosive sentence beginning, "A man loves his country, because...."[174] This is still Ottoman patriotism rather than Turkish nationalism, though the germs of the latter were contained within it. It was not only the patriotic sentiment that went in this direction, but the concern of the New Ottomans with the common man, and with the Turkish language, their use of the terms "Türk" and "Türkistan" as names for their people and country, and their interest in the Turkish past. The latter is particularly true of Ali Suavi, who developed more of a feeling for Turkish racial qualities than did his colleagues.[175]

Yet even Ali Suavi remained an Ottoman, and never made the transition to Turkish nationalism, which in view of the desire to defend the whole Ottoman Empire would have been almost impossible. "All the populations which today compose the Ottoman Empire constitute

---

[171] Gibb, *Ottoman Poetry*, V, 97-105.
[172] Gibb's translation, *ibid.*, p. 108.
[173] Cf. the Turkish text, *ibid.*, VI, 376.
[174] In *İbret*, 22 March 1873, quoted in Mustafa Nihat Özön, *Namık Kemal ve İbret gazetesi* (İstanbul, 1938), pp. 264-265.
[175] Danişmend, *Ali Suâvi'nin türkçülüğü*, pp. 27-31. He even proposed Turkish as the language for the ritual of worship: *ibid.*, p. 32.

only one nationality: the Osmanli," he wrote in 1875, and then plunged off into some quite untenable racial theories.[176] The New Ottomans generally defended Osmanlılık, but there was an ambivalence in their defense. Sometimes they argued that all peoples of the empire should have equal treatment, that all should equally love and defend the empire, that it was impossible to separate them. But true Osmanlılık suffered whenever they defended Islam as the proper legal base for the state, or let their anger at Christian rebellion or privileges for Christians carry them away, or when they vented their wrath on Âli Paşa for his supposed favoring of Christians.

> "For of Greeks and Armenians doth he make Bey and Mushir;
> The equality of rights to perfection brought hath he."

So wrote Ziya with bitter sarcasm during his exile.[177] This attitude accounts, in part, for the fact that while Reşid Paşa, though criticized on occasion, generally found favor in New Ottoman eyes, Âli and Fuad did not. Reşid had in the Gülhane *hat* of 1839 proclaimed the equality of all and had begun with this decree the strengthening of the state and had called in the aid of European powers to help him in his program. Âli and Fuad, on the other hand, had been led by the European powers when they issued the *hat* of 1856, had permitted their intervention in domestic affairs, had announced special privileges for Christians, and so had weakened the state.[178]

When it came to their views on the necessary reforms in the empire's political machinery, the New Ottomans were also strongly influenced by their reaction to Âli. Their political concepts were a product of the events of the day; no more than Âli's were their ideas developed in a vacuum and by the study of political theory. Âli was, in the New Ottoman view, the symbol and apex of a tyrannical bureaucracy. Namık Kemal wrote with effective irony about the peasant who, visiting İstanbul and seeing many fine houses, thinks there must be many sultans. There are many sultans, the peasant is told, but they

[176] Ali Suavi, *A propos de l'Herzégovine*, pp. 16, 20-21, 23-35.

[177] Gibb, *Ottoman Poetry*, v, 108. Cf. Ziya in *Hürriyet*, #12, 14 September 1868, quoted in Sungu, "Tanzimat ve Yeni Osmanlılar," pp. 794-795: "You [Sublime Porte] made valis, pashas, civil officials of the highest rank out of Christians."

[178] *Hürriyet*, #4, 20 July 1868; #27, 28 December 1868; #34, 15 February 1869; all quoted in *ibid.*, pp. 795-796, 783-784, 780 respectively. Cf. Namık Kemal in *İbret*, #9, 25 June 1872; #28, 10 October 1872; #46, 5 November 1872; all quoted in *ibid.*, pp. 778-779, 781-782.

lack the title. They are ministers.[179] The power of these pseudo sultans of the bureaucracy would have to be subject to some kind of popular check, in the New Ottoman view. Âli would have to go. Some believed also that there must be a change in sultans as well, but Âli was always in the New Ottoman eyes the first among tyrants. Personal animosities were involved in this antagonism, but the New Ottomans had come upon the basic truth that since the reforms of Mahmud II, which broke the Janissary and the *derebeyi* power, there were no further effective checks upon the central executive authority. Sometimes they called for the reestablishment of provincial *âyan*'s and *derebeyi*'s and even hinted that Janissaries had been a good thing.[180] But their real prescription for political reform involved popular sovereignty, representative government, and some form of constitutional monarchy.

In theory, the New Ottomans even went so far as to defend the principle of republicanism. "Who in the world can deny this right [to establish a republic]? Was not Islam a sort of republic when it first arose?" asked Namık Kemal.[181] Ziya expounded at length the virtues of republican government in contrast to personal autocracy.[182] But neither advocated republicanism for the Ottoman Empire, or indeed thought it possible or desirable.[183] Instead, they envisioned some sort of a representative assembly which should have legislative power and act as a brake on the executive authority. For this concept Namık Kemal was the chief and most consistent spokesman. Ziya evidently had less enthusiasm for a parliament, though he had agreed to the program in Mustafa Fazıl's letter to the sultan. Ali Suavi spoke for parliamentary methods, but was later accused by Namık Kemal of having written articles in exactly the opposite sense to regain favor with the sultan's government.[184] Some others apparently abandoned any belief in parliamentary government. "I thank God," said one New Ottoman who visited the French National Assembly at Versailles in

[179] *Hürriyet*, #27, 28 December 1868, quoted in Kuntay, *Namık Kemal*, I, 128.

[180] *Le Mukhbir*, #10, 7 November 1867; *Hürriyet*, #41, 5 April 1869, quoted in Sungu, *loc.cit.*, pp. 821-822; *Hürriyet*, #12, 14 September 1868, quoted in *ibid.*, p. 848.

[181] *Hürriyet*, #12, 14 September 1868, quoted in *ibid.*, p. 853.

[182] *Hürriyet*, #99, 14 May 1870, quoted in *ibid.*, pp. 855-856.

[183] Danişmend, *Ali Suâvi'nin türkçülüğü*, pp. 25-26, advances a dubious argument that Ali Suavi actually wanted an Ottoman republic.

[184] Fevziye A. Tansel, *Namık Kemal ve Abdülhak Hamid* (Ankara, 1949), pp. 50-51, Namık Kemal's letter of 10 March 1877.

1871, "who, among so many evils, has spared my country from that of a chamber of deputies."[185] But Namık Kemal was consistent in his advocacy of a parliament.

His views as expressed while he was in exile, beginning with the first issue of *Hürriyet*, seem to have crystallized in favor of a parliament representing all peoples of the empire, which would have a general supervision over the actions of the administration and which should have the sole legislative authority. Namık Kemal was insistent that legislative and executive powers had to be separate; otherwise absolutism remained. The assembly or parliament would represent popular opinion, and not only was the voting process healthy and educational in itself, but sovereignty belonged to the people, who had to exercise that right. He went so far as to imply that the people might choose the sultan and caliph: "The imamate is the right of the people." And certainly the ministers would be responsible to the parliament for acting justly according to law. Namık Kemal took cognizance of various objections to an Ottoman parliament—that it was undesirable innovation, that the people were too ignorant, that the language differences were too great. But he argued that a parliament was no more *bid'at* than steamships. Should the Ottoman Empire then not buy steamships, and let the Greeks capture Crete with their little lemon boats? Further, an assembly set up by consensus of the community was not *bid'at*. As for ignorance, there was no more of it among Ottomans generally than among Serbs, Montenegrins, and Egyptians who had embryonic popular assemblies. And, of course, there would be an official language for debates. There was no use waiting for a man on horseback to appear as savior. Let the people act.[186]

Exactly how Namık Kemal conceived the structure and functioning of representative government for the Ottoman Empire is unclear. At one point he spoke of the French model of Napoleon III, modified to Ottoman needs, as the best, with a council of state to prepare laws, a popular chamber to vote them and check the budget, and a "senato" of important men as guardian of constitution and general freedom.

[185] Léon Cahun in Lavisse and Rambaud, *Histoire générale*, xii, 483.

[186] These arguments are developed in *Hürriyet*, #1, 29 June 1868; #4, 20 July 1868; #12, 14 September 1868; #13, 21 September 1868; #14, 29 September 1868; #18, 26 October 1868; all quoted extensively in Sungu, "Tanzimat ve Yeni Osmanlılar," pp. 844-851. Also *Hürriyet*, #11, 7 September 1868, quoted in Okandan, *Umumî âmme hukukumuz*, p. 98, n.24.

But elements of the British system also appealed to him. In any case, the lower chamber was, in his view, to represent the empire's peoples as a whole (the *ümmet*, here used not for the religious community but for all peoples under one government), to be freely elected and to contain an opposition party.[187] Of the so-called representative assembly instituted by Ismail in Egypt, Namık Kemal was sarcastically critical: it was created to elicit European approval, its deputies were elected "to the crack of the gendarme's lash," and then when the government explained to the deputies that the opposition sat on the left, they trampled each other in a general rush to the right.[188] The Ottoman parliament was to be different—a genuinely representative body independent of administrative authority.

It is clear also that Namık Kemal, and with him most of the New Ottomans, regarded Islamic law as the fundamental framework within which the parliament as well as other political reform would naturally fit.[189] One of the recurring New Ottoman criticisms of Âli and Fuad was that they exhibited a shallow secularism, abandoning the şeriat. Even Reşid was not immune from New Ottoman criticism on the score of having disregarded the şeriat.[190] So the Tanzimat statesmen not only lost important ties to the past, but did away with one of the important checks on bureaucratic autocracy, and abandoned the essential democracy of Islam. The duality of law introduced into the empire by the Tanzimat was bad; the şeriat properly interpreted and applied could meet all needs. Not only did the şeriat contain the necessary principles of justice but also, in Namık Kemal's view, it laid the political basis for civilization and progress. A constitution could be

---

[187] Kaplan, *Namık Kemal*, pp. 106-109; Tanpınar, *XIX. asır*, p. 203; *Hürriyet*, #13, 21 September 1868, in Sungu, *loc.cit.*, p. 849. Lewis, *Emergence*, pp. 141-142, says Namık Kemal favored the English model; Mardin, *Genesis*, p. 311, that he favored the French, though he later spoke of the Belgian constitution as the "best available."

[188] In *Hürriyet*, #59, 9 August 1869, quoted in Kuntay, *Namık Kemal*, I, 556. This same story is told by Jonquière, *Histoire de l'Empire ottoman* (Paris, 1914), II, 681, of Ahmed Vefik and the Ottoman chamber under the 1876 constitution!

[189] Ali Suavi, despite his religious training and rather fanatic tone in *Muhbir*, was by the time he published *Ulûm* evidently veering away from Islamic law as the basis for the state, and also denied that the sultans were rightful caliphs: Danişmend, *Ali Suâvi'nin türkçülüğü*, pp. 23-25; Sungu, "Tanzimat ve Yeni Osmanlılar," pp. 856-857. Earlier, his *Muhbir* had called the sultan the rightful head of 100,000,000 Muslims as far as China: FO 195/893, #120, "Translation of the Supplement of the Muhbir . . . March 25, 1868."

[190] *Hürriyet*, #41, 5 April 1869, quoted in Sungu, "Tanzimat ve Yeni Osmanlılar," pp. 800-801.

grounded in Islam. Islam taught the principle of *şûra* ("council"), of *usul-u meşveret* ("the method of consultation"). Islam was democratic and, in its beginnings, a kind of republic. Islamic law, Namık Kemal further claimed, had kept legislative and executive authority separate.[191]

This was a somewhat idealized concept of Islam. It was true that Islam taught the equality of all believers, the principle of an elective caliphate, the virtue of consultation among the faithful, and the obedience of the caliph to the law. But in fact Islam had throughout almost all its history produced authoritarian government. What is important, however, is that Namık Kemal and the New Ottomans believed what they said about the essential political democracy and progressiveness of Islam. This gave them a vital point of contact with other Muslims in the empire, conservatives among them, and a base for persuasion. Namık Kemal hewed to the same line after his return from exile. In his new paper *İbret* he wrote that "our only real constitution is the şeriat" and that the method of consultation should be included in a constitution for the Islamic caliphate. "The Ottoman state is based on religious principles," he said further, "and if these principles are violated the political existence of the state will be in danger."[192] Freedom of thought, sovereignty of the people, and the method of consultation made up his prescription for the properly constituted Islamic state. This was to have its effect in the events of 1876.

In addition to their castigation of the Tanzimat statesmen, their inculcation of Ottoman patriotism and of a certain feeling of Turkishness, and their preaching of representative government grounded in Islamic law, the New Ottomans in exile also strongly advocated educational and economic progress to catch up with the achievements of the non-Muslims of the empire and with western Europe generally. Their concern came partly from comparison of the educational and economic position of the Christian minorities of the empire with that of the Turks; partly from their concern over the effects of bad taxing

[191] *Hürriyet*, #12, 14 September 1868; #18, 26 October 1868; #23, 30 November 1868; #30, 18 January 1869; #41, 5 April 1869; #50, 7 June 1869; all quoted in Sungu, *loc.cit.*, pp. 804-807. Also *Hürriyet*, #1, 29 June 1868; #9, 24 August 1868; #11, 7 September 1868; #50, 7 June 1869; all quoted in Okandan, *Umumî âmme hukukumuz*, pp. 98, n.23, and 106-107, n.45.

[192] *İbret*, #46, 5 November 1872, quoted in Sungu, *loc.cit.*, pp. 844-845, and #24, 4 October 1872, quoted in Okandan, *Umumî âmme hukukumuz*, p. 98, n.23.

methods and of the foreign debt piled up through successive loans since the Crimean War; partly from comparing European progress to Ottoman backwardness. Ziya wrote:

"I travelled the land of the infidel, towns and mansions
I saw;
I wandered Islamic countries, all ruins I saw."[193]

The New Ottomans seem to have imbibed also something of the mid-century European cult of material progress. For the Ottoman Empire they advocated better education, a great increase in literacy, the learning of European languages, the improvement of agriculture, establishment of banks and new industry, and in general acquiring the learning and products of western science.[194] There seems to be something also in New Ottoman thought of the belief that autocracy harmed economic progress, while representative government assisted it. Ziya wrote that the autocrat regarded the state as his own farm, working and robbing the millions of people in it.[195] Namık Kemal, writing about the virtues of representative government and the example of Europeans, said that "because their affairs are well regulated, their wealth is greater."[196] His economic arguments were also strongly tinged with patriotic feeling: Why should the Turks, who once had been on a level with Europe, not regain that equality? Why should their commerce and finance be in non-Muslim hands?[197]

Probably the most effective work of the New Ottomans in exile was their criticism of the weaknesses of the Ottoman Empire and of the conduct of its statesmen. It was easy to seize on obvious weaknesses, and the New Ottomans, who had no responsibility for the conduct of affairs, did so in vigorous language. It is not unreasonable to suppose that their criticism of Âli's conduct and of his westernisms helped to bolster the reaction and the Islamic sentiment that developed after his death in 1871.[198] But the New Ottomans left a mark

[193] Ali Canip, *Türk edebiyatı antolojisi* (İstanbul, 1934), p. 18.
[194] *Hürriyet*, #5, 27 July 1868; #7, 10 August 1868; #21, 16 November 1868; #22, 23 November 1868; #41, 5 April 1869; #47, 17 May 1869; #54, 5 July 1869; #56, 19 July 1869; all quoted in Sungu, "Tanzimat ve Yeni Osmanlılar," pp. 840-841, 825-827, 828-830, 830-834, 822, 834-835, 841-842 respectively.
[195] *Hürriyet*, #99, 14 May 1870, quoted in Sungu, *loc.cit.*, p. 856.
[196] *Hürriyet*, #13, 21 September 1868, quoted in *ibid.*, pp. 848-849.
[197] Cf. H. Z. Ülken, "Tanzimattan sonra fikir hareketleri," *Tanzimat*, I, 761; Sungu, *Namık Kemal*, p. 16; *Hürriyet*, #42, 12 April 1869, in Sungu, "Tanzimat ve Yeni Osmanlılar," p. 787.
[198] On this see below, chapter VIII.

also with their propaganda for patriotism and for representative government. Their theories, conceived in the crisis period of 1867, were to bear their first fruit when the next crisis period of 1875-1876 offered an occasion.[199]

In the years 1867 to 1870, while the New Ottomans were publishing in Europe, other proposals for reform of the empire appeared in print also. The ideas advanced paralleled, in many cases, those of the New Ottomans. A "Memoir addressed by several patriotic Mussulmans to the Ministers of the Sublime Porte," circulating in French and Turkish in the spring of 1867 in İstanbul, was said by the *Levant Herald* to read "like a leaf out of the programme of Young Turkey." The anonymous authors of the pamphlet laid down as the conditions of national prosperity "equality of all citizens before the law; liberty of conscience; personal liberty; inviolability of property; inviolability of thought; division of power; independence of the judicial function; inviolability of all rights which flow from these principles; and finally, the necessary guarantees against the exercise of arbitrary power." The Koran, they continued, was no bar to progress, but was in harmony with the requirements of humanity and civilization. But in a regime of equality, they pointed out, lay two dilemmas: not only would Christians, better-educated, take over too many government jobs, but their desires might well push them toward national independence rather than Ottoman unity.[200]

More impressive, because it was written by a leading Muslim statesman, was a lengthy argument advanced on September 9, 1867, by Hayreddin Paşa. Hayreddin was a Circassion by birth, brought as a slave to Tunis, who was given a westernized military education and commanded fluent French. He rose rapidly in the military service of the Bey of Tunis, and then in a political career. Hayreddin went on a number of diplomatic missions, became minister of marine, president of the council, in later years the prime minister in Tunis, and then, in 1878, grand vezir in İstanbul. In these positions Hayreddin made

[199] Lewis, *Emergence*, pp. 138-142, 166-170, 330-335, summarizes Namık Kemal's thought, emphasizing the Islamic as well as western content. Mardin, *Genesis*, pp. 283-384, gives a detailed analysis of the political theory of Namık Kemal, Ziya, and Ali Suavi.
[200] *Levant Herald*, 1 May 1867; cf. Morris to Seward, #205, 3 May 1867, USNA, Turkey 20. The *Herald* speculates that the real author might be a European.

a name for himself as an enlightened administrator.[201] He was strong-ly influenced by his knowledge of European civilization, as well as by his thorough grounding in Islam. His ideas developed also under the pressures of the time, for he was concerned not only theoretically with raising Muslim states to the European level, but practically with resisting the spread of French influence in North Africa. To help stave off the French, the Bey had already sent him in 1864 to İstanbul to reaffirm Tunisian allegiance to the sultan and arrange for the an-nual tribute.[202] His book of 1867 reflected these concerns, particularly the acquisition of European ideas and techniques in order to ward off European control.

Hayreddin's *Akwām al-masālik fī maʿrifat aḥwāl al-mamālik* was an ambitious survey of the history, geography, administration, and econ-omy of many states of the world. It was in the preface that his ideas on reform appeared.[203] Though his arguments were often couched in general terms, Hayreddin was speaking about the Ottoman Empire in particular. He took it as axiomatic that the integrity of the empire had to be preserved and all foreign interference rejected. The capitu-lations too were evil.[204] To preserve the empire, European economic, political, and cultural institutions must be copied. Hayreddin offered elaborate proof, with quotations from caliphs and doctors of the law, that nothing in Islam prohibited borrowing ideas and institutions from other cultures; far from being *bidʾat*, such borrowing was meritorious if it increased the welfare of the faithful. Europe was ahead of the Muslim world in scientific and economic matters because of good gov-ernment and liberal institutions. Material prosperity could come only under such conditions. Unjust government had destroyed the earlier Muslim prosperity.[205]

[201] Th. Menzel, "K̲h̲air al-Din Pas̲h̲a," *Encyclopaedia of Islam*, II, 873; İnal, *Son sadrıâzamlar*, fasc. 6, pp. 895-896; A. Demeerseman, "Un grand témoin des premières idées modernisantes en Tunisie," *IBLA*, 19:76 (1956), 359-363; Heap (Tunis) to Second Secretary, #160, 23 October 1873, and Heap to Hunter, #193, 31 December 1874, USNA, Tunis 11.

[202] Morris to Seward, #100, 7 December 1864, USNA, Turkey 18. Cf. A. Demeerse-man, "Doctrine de Khéréddine en matière de politique extérieure," *IBLA*, 21:1 (1958), 13-29; *idem*, "Indépendance de la Tunisie et politique extérieure de Khéréddine," *IBLA*, 21:3 (1958), 229-277.

[203] Translated into French as "Le Général Khérédine," *Réformes nécessaires aux états musulmans* (Paris, 1868). Translated also into Turkish, though in what year the author is not sure. Its circulation was forbidden: İnal, *Son sadrıâzamlar*, fasc. 6, p. 934.

[204] *Réformes*, pp. 40-42.

[205] *Ibid.*, pp. 7-31.

Hayreddin's prescription for good government was based in fact on the necessity for curbing an arbitrary ruler and in theory on the Koranic injunction that the ruler should take counsel before acting. He reproduced what he claimed was the political code of Süleyman the Lawgiver, prescribing that the ministers and ulema warn the ruler if he contravened the law, and even that, as the ultimate remedy, they go so far as to depose him. Hayreddin then drew a perfect analogy between this check on the authority of a sovereign and the parliaments of nineteenth-century Europe. Without indicating any details, he advocated the delegation of responsibility to ministers, and a popular base for government through representatives who would check a bad ruler and assist a good one. To the common objection that the peoples of the empire were not ready for such institutions Hayreddin replied that of course institutions must be tailored, as they were in Europe, to the readiness of the people, but that good institutions would in themselves be educational.[206]

Hayreddin's book drew favorable comment from Âli Paşa.[207] It would seem at first a matter for surprise that Âli should praise a man whose sentiments seemed to parallel those of the New Ottomans. But in fact Âli would agree with most of what Hayreddin had said: the need for material progress and for borrowing from Europe, the adaptability of Islam to new things, a check on the ruler's power. Nor was there any attack on Âli or the Tanzimat statesmen in Hayreddin's writing; quite the reverse. He praised the *hat* of 1856 as well as that of 1839, and in general endorsed the reforms carried out since the time of Mahmud II. This view set Hayreddin apart from the New Ottomans. Hayreddin was, further, more cautious than they in proposing representative government, and although he agreed with them in principle he warned them that in advocating a parliament they must be quite sure that the non-Muslims would help to preserve the empire.[208] Namık Kemal, indeed, did not like Hayreddin's book, which he later called "ridiculous."[209] In part, his distaste seemed to arise from the fact that Hayreddin was really a non-Turk, an official of what was almost an autonomous Arab country. And though Hayred-

---

[206] *Ibid.*, pp. 32-77.

[207] Mehmed Memduh, *Esvât-ı sudûr* (İzmir, 1338), p. 13, quoted in Kuntay, *Namık Kemal*, I, 202.

[208] *Réformes*, pp. 38-41.

[209] Kuntay, *Namık Kemal*, I, 202. Cf. pp. 203-204.

din's political proposals were more cautious than Namık Kemal's, the major difference was that Hayreddin lacked the burning patriotism that Kemal exhibited. The two reformers agreed on the need for economic growth, educational progress, borrowing from the West, curbing autocracy, setting up some kind of representative assembly, and basing the reform on Islamic teaching. Hayreddin's work, like the New Ottoman writings, may also have had some influence on the momentous reform efforts of 1876, for in that year it was reissued (evidently in French) and circulated in İstanbul, among other places.[210]

A year after Hayreddin's book appeared in Paris another work advocating Ottoman political reform, with much more specific detail, was published in French in İstanbul.[211] It may be significant that the publisher was Jean Piétri's *Courrier d'Orient* press, though since Piétri was hospitable to many reform ideas this does not imply any necessary connection with the New Ottomans. The author was Mustafa Celaleddin, a Turkish army officer who had graduated from the military academy, had risen through ability and personal bravery, and who as general of division was to die in the summer of 1876 fighting the Montenegrins. But Mustafa Celaleddin was by origin a Pole, born Konstanty Polkozic-Borzęcki, who after the disturbances of 1848 had fled to France and then to the Ottoman Empire.[212] To the end of his life he preserved a vigorous Russophobia born of his early experiences. His Turcophilism was equally strong. Much of his writing, including half or more of his *Turcs anciens et modernes*, developed an early kind of Turkish nationalism, based on historical and linguistic argument. Mustafa sought to prove that the Turks were related to European peoples, that there was a "Touro-Aryan" race, and that Turkish was not only akin to Greek, Latin, and other European tongues but might be the father of them all.[213]

[210] Demeerseman, "Indépendance de la Tunisie," p. 277.
[211] Moustapha Djeladeddin, *Les Turcs anciens et modernes* (Constantinople, 1869). It was reissued in Paris in 1870.
[212] On his life see Lewak, *Emigracji polskiej*, p. 87; Aktchoura Oglou Youssouf Bey [Yusuf Akçura], "L'oeuvre historique de Mustafa Djelalettin Pacha . . . ," 7ᵉ Congrès des Sciences Historiques, *Résumés*, II (1933), 233; Dr. K., *Erinnerungen . . . des Serdar Ekrem Omer Pascha*, p. 54; Benoît Brunswik, *La réforme et les garanties* (Paris, 1877), pp. 52-53.
[213] Cf. comments of Aktchoura, *loc.cit.*, pp. 234-236. Moustapha Djelaleddin, *L'Europe et le touro-aryanisme* (n.p., n.d.) seems to be the end of his *Turcs anciens et modernes*. The copy of the former work in the Bibliothèque Nationale carries many corrections and footnotes in a neat hand, possibly Djelaleddin's own, with a signature at the end in the same hand, "Général Moustapha Djelaleddin." The theories here

In his political argument Mustafa Celaleddin defended the Turks as being essentially progressive, and denied that Islam was an obstacle. Christians and Muslims in the empire could get along well so long as Russia did not interfere. The essential need, in his opinion, was a national representative assembly, the basis for which already existed in the various councils of the vilayet organization. Mustafa Celaleddin went beyond Hayreddin and the New Ottomans in proposing an exact apportionment of seats in the elective chamber: 100 Muslims, 25 Armenians, 25 Bulgars, 14 Greeks, 7 Roman Syrians, 7 Jews, 4 Orthodox Albanians, 3 Roman Albanians, 4 Orthodox Bosniaks, 3 Roman Bosniaks, 3 Wallachs, 2 Nestorians, 2 Roman Armenians, and 2 Protestants. The total made 101 non-Muslims to 100 Muslims. Mustafa would retain the vilayet law's electoral system of eliminating candidates from a prepared list until a new law should be established by the assembly. There should also be a small senate of notables. Ministers should have greater responsibility, the grand vezir less than heretofore. The assembly, however, should have legislative power and budgetary control, and its members should be paid. For local governments he advised somewhat smaller provinces and considerable autonomy. All this, said Mustafa Celaleddin, would bind the heterogeneous empire together, and there were enough men of wisdom in the provinces so that representative government would work.[214] Despite the lack of discernible connection between Mustafa Celaleddin and the New Ottomans, the parallels in their thinking are obvious.

There is a danger in overestimating the impact of the New Ottomans and of other reform proposers on the course of events in the Ottoman Empire. Whether the suggestions came from Namık Kemal, Ziya, Ali Suavi, Mustafa Fazıl, Halil Şerif, Hayreddin, or Mustafa Celaleddin, the immediate effect was small. Yet a cumulative effect there undoubtedly was. Some of this was apparent in 1876, some not until the years of agitation preceding the revolution of 1908. All these critics and would-be reformers were part of a process of creating a new public opinion, and part of the new era of journalism and pamphleteering. With much of what they said, Âli and Fuad certainly

advanced may have influenced Ali Suavi, and curiously foreshadow some developed later in Turkey.

[214] *Les turcs anciens et modernes*, pp. 173-193, 209-211.

agreed, though often not with the manner in which it was said. The critics of the 1860's were neither the first nor the last to advocate borrowing from the West the means to oppose to the West a stronger and more united state. Âli and Fuad were also engaged in this process, and during the same years between 1867 and 1870 they continued in their path of piecemeal reform and westernization to strengthen the empire.

CHAPTER VII

THE FINAL ACHIEVEMENTS OF ÂLI AND
FUAD, 1867-1871

While their New Ottoman opponents poured forth abuse and criticism from Paris, London, and Geneva, Âli and Fuad in İstanbul were occupied with the business of government. Their first job was to hold the empire together. Though the Cretan rebellion went on, draining the Porte's treasury[1] and obliging the grand vezir Âli Paşa to make an extended trip there in the fall of 1867, the island was under control in 1868, and the vilayet organization as extended to Crete allowed the Christians a special status in local administration. By 1868 also the possible united drive of Balkan peoples against the Turks was averted by the death of its Serb leader, Michael Obrenovich. The Bulgar nationalist agitation for an autochthonous church organization was actually used to advantage by Âli when in 1870 the ferman creating a separate Bulgar exarchate set Greek against Bulgar in a contest for the cure of Macedonian souls. From 1868 until 1871, when Âli died, the customary irritation of revolts and diplomatic crises was somewhat reduced. And collective European diplomatic intervention in the affairs of the Ottoman Empire was unlikely because of the diametric opposition of French and Russian views on Ottoman reform.

Âli and Fuad used these years to pursue their program of westernization, secularization, and the furtherance of Osmanlılık by small steps. They were firmly in control of the sultan and the administration. Their most vocal critics, at home or abroad, could do little immediate damage. When Fuad died in February of 1869, Âli, instead of getting another foreign minister, combined Fuad's former duties with his own. By the time of Âli's death, in September of 1871, his grand vezirate of over four and a half years was the longest since 1839, and the third longest in a century of Ottoman history. What reform was carried out bore his stamp and Fuad's.

The major measures involved the creation of a new Council of State, a new venture in nonsectarian schooling and a revamped educational system, the codification of part of the civil law, an attack on

---

[1] Reportedly fighting the revolt cost at least three million pounds sterling just to the end of 1867: Elliot to Stanley, #76, 28 December 1867, FO 78/1965.

the capitulations, and a considerable improvement in the military organization. Much of this showed the influence of France, which was strongly asserted in these years; yet the two statesmen had not had a French program forced on them. Their natural inclinations went in that direction. In 1867 both France and Russia had presented fairly detailed plans for Ottoman reform. The French plan led toward amalgamation of the peoples of the empire into an Ottoman nationality through extension of equal rights, mixed education, and minimization of religious influence.[2] The Russian plan suggested dividing the empire into autonomous regions based on nationality.[3] No Ottoman minister could have favored the Russian plan. It would have led, as Fuad epigrammatically told the Russian ambassador Ignatyev, to the establishment of the "Etats Désunis de Turquie."[4] The French plan, however, accorded with the proclivities of Âli and Fuad. They counted, further, on French and British support against Russian designs, and in 1867 Napoleon III was still a distinguished patron despite his setbacks in Mexico and Luxemburg. This trend toward French-influenced reform was measurably strengthened by the trip which Sultan Abdülaziz took to Paris in the summer of 1867.

No Ottoman sovereign had ever before set foot outside the empire except on military campaign. A number of considerations counselled that Abdülaziz should break with precedent. His ostensible reason for travel was to see the Paris exhibition of 1867 at Napoleon III's invitation. The real reason was to reestablish Turkish credit, shaken by the events in Crete, in the capitals of western Europe, and to try to forestall any possible Franco-Russian cooperation in favor of the Cretan rebels. Alexander II had just been to Paris, and the sultan's trip might counteract the tsar's influence. Incidentally, Abdülaziz might counteract also the influence of the khedive Ismail, who visited Europe at the same time, and of his critic Mustafa Fazıl, then in Paris. To do this, the sultan would have to appear as the head of a state that was making

---

[2] I. de Testa, *Recueil des traités de la Porte ottomane* (Paris, 1864-1911), VII, 418-422, French memorandum of 22 February 1867.

[3] "Zapiski Grapha N. P. Ignatyeva," *Izvestiia Ministerstva Inostrannykh Diel*, 1914, II, 77-80, and III, 94-98; Edouard Engelhardt, *La Turquie et le Tanzimat* (Paris, 1882-1884), I, 217-222, and II, 4-6. Testa, *Recueil*, VII, 446-455, gives the Russian memorandum of 18 April 1867. Cf. the Russian memorandum of 24 March, *ibid.*, pp. 433-441.

[4] "Zapiski . . . Ignatyeva," *loc.cit.*, 1914, III, 96. Fuad's report to the British ambassador of this witticism put it as "La Monarchie de la République des Etats non unis de la Turquie." Lyons to Stanley, #200, confidential, 22 May 1867, FO 78/1960.

progress. At the same time, Âli and Fuad intended that the trip have not only diplomatic effect, but domestic repercussions also. Abdülaziz himself should see something of western monarchical government and of western material progress. The two statesmen undoubtedly worked hard to persuade Abdülaziz to go.[5] And they prepared the ground for presenting Abdülaziz and his empire in the most favorable light possible. The process had already been started with Fuad Paşa's memorandum of May 15, 1867, recounting in glowing terms the progress in reform made since the Hatt-ı Hümayun of 1856, while candidly admitting certain shortcomings to be corrected as soon as possible.[6] Fuad also spoke to the western ambassadors of new reforms coming: a Council of State on the French model, the removal of legal restrictions on certain types of property, including *vakif* land, and legislation to allow foreigners to own real estate in the empire.[7] Europe was further assured by Fuad that no woman, slave, eunuch, or other person offensive to western feelings would be in the sultan's party.[8] Fuad went on the trip officially as foreign minister, but also to keep Abdülaziz from embarrassing errors in personal conduct. During the sultan's forty-four-day absence from his dominions Âli Paşa attained the height of his political power as regent, the first and only time an Ottoman subject was so appointed.

Abdülaziz arrived in Paris on June 30, 1867, and after a brilliant visit of eleven days went to London on Queen Victoria's invitation for a visit of equal length. He returned via Brussels, Coblenz, Vienna, and Budapest, meeting Leopold II, Wilhelm I, and Franz Joseph. On August 3 he reached Ottoman territory in the Tuna vilayet, where he showed appreciation for the work of the vali, Midhat Paşa. Three days later he was back in his own capital, greeted by a tumultuous welcome.[9] There were two unfortunate side effects of the trip

[5] On reasons for the trip see: "Zapiski . . . Ignatyeva," *loc.cit.*, 1914, II, 89; Haluk Y. Şehsuvaroğlu, *Sultan Aziz* (İstanbul, 1949), p. 34; Andreas D. Mordtmann, *Stambul und das moderne Türkenthum* (Leipzig, 1877-1878), II, 173; Lyons to Hammond, private, 10 June 1867, FO 78/2010. Cf. Frederick Millingen, *La Turquie sous le règne d'Abdul Aziz* (Paris, 1868), pp. 376-378.
[6] Text in Grégoire Aristarchi, *Législation ottomane* (Constantinople, 1873-1888), II, 24-35, and Testa, *Recueil*, VII, 457-467. The British, and undoubtedly the French, were furnished with an advance draft: "Considérations sur l'exécution du Firman Impériale du 18 Février 1856," endorsed "Rec'd May 2d 1867 from Fuad Pasha," FO 195/893. Compare Fuad's optimistic picture here with Engelhardt's gloomy assessment of reform as of 1867: *La Turquie*, I, 237-252.
[7] Lyons to Stanley, #199, 22 May 1867, FO 78/1960.
[8] Lyons to Stanley, #237, 10 June 1867, FO 78/2010.
[9] On the trip generally see: Şehsuvaroğlu, *Sultan Aziz*, pp. 34-44; İ. H. Daniş-

for the sultan personally. One was the shock to conservative Muslims that the sultan-caliph should visit infidel lands; in their view of etiquette it was the inferior who always visited his superior.[10] The other concerned Abdülaziz's relationships with his nephew Murad, the heir-apparent. Evidently fearing to leave Murad and Murad's brother Abdülhamid in the capital while he was abroad, the sultan took both nephews with him, as well as his own son, Yusuf İzzeddin, a boy not yet ten. Murad made quite a favorable impression in Europe, which evidently aroused Abdülaziz's jealousy for his own son, and various rumors arose regarding Murad which only increased the sultan's suspicion of him. Other rumors, probably with some basis in fact, that Abdülaziz wanted to change the order of succession to put his own son first, also increased, and aroused opposition to the sultan. After the return to İstanbul, therefore, the reigning sultan kept Murad under closer watch than ever, and the gulf between the two deepened.[11]

Yet on the whole the trip was a success. Abdülaziz, certainly in part owing to Fuad's watchfulness, committed no major blunders.[12] Diplomatically, the trip marked a point of decrease in Franco-Russian cooperation over Crete.[13] Of equal importance was the impression made on Abdülaziz by western civilization. The material, especially the military, aspects appealed to him most. He inspected several British dockyards and naval arsenals attentively, and saw naval maneuvers at Portsmouth, after which Victoria gave him the Order of the Garter

---

mend, *İzahlı osmanlı tarihi kronolojisi*, IV (İstanbul, 1955), 216-223; Charles Mismer, *Souvenirs du monde musulman* (Paris, 1892), pp. 18-19; Adam Lewak, *Dzieje emigracji polskiej w Turcji (1831-1878)* (Warsaw, 1935), pp. 192-193.

[10] Fuad recognized that the shock would come: Lyons to Stanley, #199, 22 May 1867, FO 78/1960. Cf. Morris to Seward, unnumbered, 2 July 1867, USNA, Turkey 20; H. J. Van Lennep, *Travels in Little-Known Parts of Asia Minor* (London, 1870), I, 12.

[11] Among the various rumors were: that Victoria wanted Murad to marry one of her daughters; that Napoleon III wanted Murad to study government in France; that Murad was to stay abroad as a threat to the monarch, like Prince Cem; that Murad was to slip back to İstanbul before Abdülaziz and be proclaimed sultan: Şehsuvaroğlu, *Sultan Aziz*, pp. 38, 41-42; Amand von Schweiger-Lerchenfeld, *Serail und Hohe Pforte* (Vienna, 1879), pp. 74-75, 174-175; Mithat Cemal Kuntay, *Namık Kemal* (İstanbul, 1944-1956), I, 549, n.16; A. D. Alderson, *The Structure of the Ottoman Dynasty* (Oxford, 1956), p. 95, n.1. On succession change see: Şehsuvaroğlu, *Sultan Aziz*, pp. 45-47; Osman Nuri, *Abdülhamid-i Sani ve devr-i saltanatı* (İstanbul, 1327), I, 10-11; Ahmed Midhat, *Üss-i inkılâb* (İstanbul, 1294-1295), I, 198.

[12] Fuad is reported to have said to Âli on return, "There! I give back our efendi safe and sound to his *lâla* ["tutor"], but I am done in." Ali Fuad, *Rical-i mühimme-i siyasiye* (İstanbul, 1928), p. 170.

[13] A. J. P. Taylor, *The Struggle for Mastery in Europe, 1848-1918* (Oxford, 1954), p. 184.

with her own hand. He reviewed French and Prussian troops, admiring particularly the weapons and the discipline of the latter.[14] Undoubtedly his renewed enthusiasm for ironclad warships, for new weapons, and for support for the Ottoman military reorganization of 1869 derived from these experiences. Railroads also impressed Abdülaziz. He had already shown great interest in the İzmir-Aydın line in 1863.[15] In the fall of 1867 there were new negotiations between the Ottoman government and various European entrepreneurs, looking toward the building of lines from Belgrade to İstanbul and İstanbul to the Persian Gulf.[16] The craze for railroad-building mounted in the 1870's. In 1873 Ignatyev reported that Abdülaziz was "victim of a veritable railroad fever."[17] Not only the need for railroads, but also the desirability of an enlarged program of public instruction and of building up the material basis for such prosperity as the West exhibited seized Abdülaziz's mind. In a *hat* issued on his return from Europe, and in talking with his council of ministers, he stressed these points.[18]

It is hard to say whether Abdülaziz was much influenced by the samples of constitutional monarchy he had seen in his brief trip. Certainly he did not return a constitutionalist, despite a visit to a session of the House of Commons. But he may have decided that some form of enlarged representative council was compatible with his imperial position. One of the specific pieces of advice sent to London by the British ambassador in İstanbul was that Abdülaziz should be exposed to the splendor of Queen Victoria's position, since the opponents of constitutionalism in the Ottoman Empire were telling the sultan that there was no splendor without absolutism.[19] Undoubtedly Napoleon of the Liberal Empire and the constitutional monarch Victoria did impress him. In an unprecedented exhibition of individual democracy, Abdülaziz on his return to İstanbul shook hands with a visiting ambassador and asked him to sit down.[20] Probably also it was his Euro-

---

[14] Mehmed Memduh, *Mirât-ı şuûnat* (İzmir, 1328), p. 89.

[15] *Smyrna Mail*, 28 April 1863.

[16] Cf. Barron to Stanley, #58, 15 October 1867, and #60, 17 October 1867; also Elliot to Stanley, #39, 19 November 1867—all FO 78/1964; also Elliot to Stanley, #49, 2 December 1867, FO 78/1965.

[17] B. H. Sumner, *Russia and the Balkans, 1870-1880* (Oxford, 1937), p. 103.

[18] Outrey to Moustier, 14 August 1867, Testa, *Recueil*, VII, 494; Şehsuvaroğlu, *Sultan Aziz*, p. 44.

[19] Lyons to Hammond, private, 10 June 1867, FO 78/2010.

[20] Barron to Stanley, #26, confidential, 27 August 1867, FO 78/1963. The ambassador was Ignatyev.

pean experience which led Abdülaziz to sanction the transformation
of the old Supreme Council of Judicial Ordinances into a Council of
State on the French model.

The Supreme Council of Judicial Ordinances (Meclis-i vâlâ-yı
ahkâm-ı adliye) had been set up by Mahmud II in 1838 to discuss
and draft new regulations. After the proclamation of the Hatt-ı Şerif
of Gülhane in 1839 this council was given the special function of working out into law the general principles enunciated in the *hat*, and was
endowed with internal rules resembling those of western parliamentary procedure. In 1854 the legislative function of the Supreme Council had largely passed to the Tanzimat Council (Meclis-i âli-i tanzimat), which was split off from the parent body to elaborate reform
measures. The Supreme Council, which retained certain judicial and
supervisory functions, was given a number of appointed non-Muslim
members in 1856, thus carrying out one of the promises of the Hatt-ı
Hümayun of that year.[21] In 1861 the two bodies were again fused as
the Supreme Council of Judicial Ordinances, which now had three
working divisions: administrative, legislative, and judicial. It is not
apparent that after 1861 this council was effective or influential.[22] That
the non-Muslim members had any voice at all in the Supreme Council's
legislative division (*Daire-i kavanin* or *kanun dairesi*) is unlikely. But
so long as it existed, the Supreme Council represented a potential basis
for the development of a deliberative legislature constructed on the
principle of representation of all elements of the empire.

Possibly Fuad had such a development in mind, though he was not
in favor of a parliament in 1867, and criticized Midhat Paşa in that
year as a man "who saw in the parliamentary regime a remedy for
all evils, without suspecting that politics rebels against panaceas even
more than medicine."[23] Fuad had broached the idea of a Council of
State of both Christians and Muslims in March of 1867.[24] Âli had sent
back from Crete late in 1867 his famous memorandum in which he

---

[21] On these developments see above, chapters I, II, and III.
[22] *Hat* of 1861 combining the two councils in *Archives diplomatiques*, III (1861),
436. See, further, on the fusion Cevdet's account in Ebül'ulâ Mardin, *Medenî hukuk
cephesinden Ahmet Cevdet Paşa* (İstanbul, 1946), p. 53 and n.84. Engelhardt, *La
Turquie*, I, 251, claims the Supreme Council met only once between 1856 and 1867,
which seems impossible.
[23] Mismer, *Souvenirs*, p. 20.
[24] Moustier to Bourée, 15 March 1867, in Testa, *Recueil*, VII, 429-430.

advised that Christians be given full chance to participate in government. He and Fuad seem, further, to have felt that the wide powers given to valis under the new vilayet law required some machinery for strengthening contact between the vilayets and the capital, which a Council of State might provide.[25] In addition to the desires to expand slightly the representative principle and to check overdecentralization, there was evidently a feeling on the part of Ottoman statesmen that, as Europeans urged them, judicial functions should be made independent of the legislative and executive.[26] This had already been done at the provincial level in the vilayet law. Finally, there was the European example. In these years the Council of State, especially in France and Austria, was a device for law-drafting and administrative purposes, which might develop either toward constitutionalism or as a mechanism to support absolutism in the absence of a parliament.[27] Abdülaziz had visited both states, and after his return was willing to endorse the concept of Âli and Fuad. Little was done while Âli was on his special mission to Crete for nearly five months from October 1867 to February 1868. But in this interval Fuad, as acting grand vezir, called Midhat to İstanbul to discuss vilayet matters, and evidently the two discussed a Council of State also. On March 5, 1868, less than a week after Âli's return, the order was issued to replace the old Supreme Council with two new bodies, a Council of State (Şura-yı devlet) and a Judicial Council (Divan-ı ahkâm-ı adliye) which became, in effect, a supreme court of appeal and cassation. Midhat Paşa was appointed to head the Council of State, Cevdet Paşa to head the Judicial Council. Each exercised considerable influence in drawing up their respective statutes.[28]

The *règlement organique* of the Judicial Council was promulgated on April 1, 1868.[29] The council was to take cognizance of cases that

[25] Ahmed Midhat, *Üss-i inkılâb*, I, 106-107; Ahmed Saib, *Vaka-i Sultan Abdülaziz* (Cairo, 1320), p. 49; *Le Stamboul*, 27 December 1875.

[26] Cevdet in his *Maruzat*, quoted by Mardin, *Cevdet Paşa*, pp. 58-60.

[27] Robert C. Binkley, *Realism and Nationalism, 1852-1871* (New York, 1935), pp. 143, 145-146. The author is not sure whether the assembly created by Ismail in Egypt in November 1866 influenced the Ottoman decision. Cf. Jacob M. Landau, *Parliaments and Parties in Egypt* (Tel Aviv, 1953), pp. 8-11.

[28] Mardin, *Cevdet Paşa*, pp. 58-60; Âli Ölmezoğlu, "Cevdet Paşa," *İslâm ansiklopedisi*, III, 116; Ahmed Midhat, *Üss-i inkılâb*, I, 107; A. H. Midhat, *Midhat Paşa: Hayat-ı siyâsiyesi*, vol. I, *Tabsıra-i ibret* (İstanbul, 1325), 61; Louis Antoine Léouzon, *Midhat Pacha* (Paris, 1877), pp. 74-75, giving the wrong date.

[29] Text in Testa, *Recueil*, VII, 514-516; Aristarchi, *Législation*, II, 42-43; *Düstur* (1289 ed.), I, 325-327.

arose under the new westernized law—criminal, and commercial and civil—but not of cases under the şeriat or those which would be handled by the millet courts or by the new mixed commercial tribunals. The members, once appointed, were irremovable except if regularly tried and convicted; the executive authority was specifically forbidden to interfere in the court's functions. Thirteen members were appointed to the council in addition to Cevdet Paşa, its president. Of these, two were Armenian Catholics, one a Gregorian Armenian, one a Greek, and one a Bulgar. Among the Muslim members were several of the ulema.[30] Cevdet was quite pleased with the calibre of the Muslim members and with the way he himself organized the council's functioning.[31]

The *hat* setting up the Council of State was issued just a month later, on May 1.[32] By its terms this council was to discuss and draft all projects of law and regulations, to keep a general watch on administration and report deficiencies, to act as a court to judge cases of administrative conflict or of individual officials, and to give general advice whenever asked by the sultan or the ministers. Decisions of the council were to be by majority vote, which could be secret if so desired. *Procès-verbaux* were to be kept. Some of the council members, further, were to participate in the annual examination of the budget and financial condition of the empire. To carry out these functions, five sections of the council were set up: police, army, and navy; finances and *evkaf*; legislation; public works, commerce, and agriculture; and public instruction. Each of the sections was to have its own president, and five to ten of the council members would serve on each. The whole organization was on the French model. In addition, it was provided that the council should discuss with three or four delegates who would be sent each year from the provincial general assemblies the desires contained in memoranda drawn up by those assemblies. Here, obviously, was the potential check on the powers of the valis, and the link between local and central representative government. The ex-

[30] List of members in FO 195/893, #160.
[31] *Tezâkir-i Cevdet*, 19, quoted in Mardin, *Cevdet Paşa*, pp. 60-61.
[32] Text in Testa, *Recueil*, VII, 518-521; Aristarchi, *Législation*, II, 38-41; Young, *Corps de droit*, I, 3-5; *Düstur*, I, 703-706. The *Düstur* and Young give the date as 1 April 1868 (8 zilhicce 1284), the same day as the Judicial Council's statute was issued. Testa and Aristarchi give 1 May 1868 (8 muharrem 1285), which is also given on the official brochure distributed to embassies: FO 195/893, #159. The author is unable to explain the discrepancy. The internal regulations of the council, as of 1869: Young, *Corps de droit*, I, 7-11 (extracts); *Düstur*, I, 707-718.

perience of a central council to discuss legislation, with its own parliamentary procedure, which had existed since 1839, was here being combined with the experience of the 1845 assembly of representatives from the provinces, but on a regular basis.

The Council of State has been greeted by many writers as a major step toward parliamentary government, and by some as so consciously planned by Âli and Fuad.[33] In several senses the former assertion is true. The separation of judicial functions from legislative and administrative was accepted in principle. A regular sort of parliamentary procedure was set up within the council. The delegations from the elected general assemblies of the vilayets were to participate in discussing the questions they brought before the council. One might justly call the council a parliament in embryo. But Âli certainly was no partisan of parliamentary government. Whether the council would develop in that direction depended on events of the future. Members were not elected, but appointed by the sultan. According to its own statute of 1868, further, the council had no initiative in legislation, but could discuss only matters laid before it by the grand vezir, and all reports went back from the council to him and the ministers. By its internal regulations the president of the council had extensive powers. Even if it did not itself develop into a parliament, however, the council by its provisions for free discussion, majority vote, and keeping of *procès-verbaux* was a "school for the training of statesmen."[34]

The council, further, was part of a conscious effort to extend the principle of representative government to the national level. This was evident not only in the provision for occasional delegates from vilayet general assemblies, but in the official list of members appointed in 1868.[35] Of the thirty-seven men named in addition to Midhat Paşa, who had already been appointed president, eight were provincial notables from important cities of the empire. Eleven, including some of the notables, were non-Muslims, and in the official list were rather naïvely designated by sect, evidently in order to impress Europe. Four of the eleven were Armenian Catholics—a tremendous overrepresen-

[33] Ahmed Rasim, *İstibdaddan hakimiyeti milliyeye* (İstanbul, 1924), II, 77-79; Abdurrahman Şeref, *Tarih musahabeleri* (İstanbul, 1339), p. 96; Halil İnalcık, "Tanzimat nedir?" *Tarih araştırmaları, 1940-1941* (İstanbul, 1941), p. 257; Danişmend, *İzahlı . . . kronolojisi*, IV, 226-227.

[34] Ahmed Midhat, *Üss-i inkılâb*, I, 107.

[35] In FO 195/893, #160. E. Z. Karal, *Islahat fermanı devri, 1861-1876* (Ankara, 1956), pp. 148-149, gives a total of forty-one members a year later, of whom thirteen were non-Muslims, but he mentions no Jews at all.

tation of a tiny minority; three were Greeks, two Jews, and one each Bulgar and Armenian Gregorian. Among both the Muslim and non-Muslim members were men of considerable experience and ability. One was Odian Efendi, the Armenian constitutionalist and Midhat's man. A similar proportion of about thirty per cent non-Muslims was maintained in the staff positions of the council.

On May 10, 1868, Sultan Abdülaziz formally inaugurated the Council of State and the Judicial Council at the Sublime Porte in a red-carpeted chamber done over as an amphitheatre.[36] His speech, by whomever written, evidently still reflected the impressions of his European trip.[37] Condemning arbitrary government, and endorsing individual liberty within the proper limits of society's welfare, the sultan proclaimed the separation of judicial from executive authority and the need for good administration to promote prosperity and catch up with Europe. The old ways were insufficient. He reiterated the concept of Osmanlılık—all subjects of whatever creed are "children of the same fatherland." There was also a hint of secularism in his speech, since he mentioned the separation of executive from judicial, religious, and legislative authority. The speech was greeted with praise in the European journals, with thanks by the moneylenders of Galata, and by a rise in the quotations on Ottoman bonds.[38] And for a year or so there was more press freedom, as if the Council of State were inaugurating a "liberal Empire" on Napoleon III's model.[39] The new institutions did not meet with universal approval, however. From London Namık Kemal indicated that popular supervision of government was still needed, and further separation of legislative from executive authority, while Ziya criticized the appointment of Christians to the Council of State as evidence of the Porte's weakness.[40]

While Midhat Paşa was its president, the Council of State was active in the preparation of new measures. Among its products were the new nationality law, the new organization of public education, and regulations on mining, the metric system, and a lending bank to extend credit to small employers.[41] Midhat was jealous of the preroga-

[36] Şehsuvaroğlu, *Sultan Aziz*, pp. 32-33.
[37] Text in Testa, *Recueil*, VII, 521-523.
[38] Ahmed Rasim, *Istibdaddan hakimiyeti milliyeye*, p. 79.
[39] Şehsuvaroğlu, *Sultan Aziz*, p. 34.
[40] *Hürriyet*, #1, 29 June 1868, quoted in İhsan Sungu, "Tanzimat ve Yeni Osmanlılar," *Tanzimat*, I (İstanbul, 1940), 845-846; *Hürriyet*, #12, 14 September 1868, quoted in *ibid.*, 795.
[41] A. H. Midhat, *Tabsıra-i ibret*, pp. 61-65; *idem*, *The Life of Midhat Pasha*

tives of the Council of State, and got into argument with Âli over the nonapplication of measures it had drawn up and over the nonreferral of other matters Midhat deemed important. This, coupled with the personal friction between the two which was heightened after Fuad's death in February 1869, caused Midhat's transfer out of İstanbul to the governorship of Baghdad.[42] It is not apparent that Midhat was trying to build the council into a parliament, though he may have entertained such thoughts on its eventual functions. After his departure the council was less active and was in almost constant reorganization, though its approval was still required on important matters.[43] This lack of effectiveness was partly due to the overlapping of functions between the sections of the council and the various ministries, and partly because in the period after Âli's death in 1871 Mahmud Nedim and Abdülaziz seem to have used the council as a dumping ground for ministers out of office, often second-rate men.[44] In the period 1871 to 1876 it sometimes acted to obstruct useful measures rather than to expedite them.[45] At best, the council remained in those years another administrative device which might work well or badly. Because it was a small-scale example of national representation, and employed some parliamentary methods, it was also another in the long chain of steps which might lead logically, though not inevitably, to the creation of a parliament sometime in the future.

At the same time as Âli and Fuad undertook the formation of the Council of State, they were contemplating reform of the educational system also. Both had been members of the commission of 1845 which had recommended creation of a state system of secular education, from the lowest school to the university. Under the ministry of education

---

(London, 1903), p. 17; Engelhardt, *La Turquie*, II, 23; Sommerville Story, ed., *The Memoirs of Ismail Kemal Bey* (London, 1920), pp. 41-42. İsmail Kemal was one of the council's staff.

[42] A. H. Midhat, *Tabsıra-i ibret*, p. 66; İ. A. Gökbilgin, "Midhat Paşa," *İslâm ansiklopedisi*, fasc. 82, p. 273; Mardin, *Cevdet Paşa*, pp. 88-89, n.99.

[43] Sıddık Sami Onar, *İdare hukukunun umumî esasları* (İstanbul, 1952), p. 549; Abdolonyme Ubicini and Pavet de Courteille, *Etat présent de l'Empire ottoman* (Paris, 1876), pp. 83-84; *Le Stamboul*, 27 December 1875.

[44] Mordtmann, *Stambul*, I, 30, and II, 171; Elliot to Derby, #340, 13 July 1875, FO 78/2384.

[45] Elliot to Derby, #306, 23 June 1875, FO 78/2383. But see Story, *Ismail Kemal*, pp. 46-47, where İsmail Kemal bypassed the council in 1869 on the plea of "erratic discussion."

which was subsequently established there had been quite an increase in the number of elementary schools.[46] The increase in the number of higher elementary (or secondary, depending on the viewpoint) schools, the *rüşdiye*, had been less. The university had never really functioned at all. Figures furnished by Subhi Bey, minister of education, show that in 1867 the Ottoman government claimed 11,008 primary schools with a student population of 242,017 boys and 126,454 girls. There were also 108 *rüşdiye*'s with 7,830 students, and a pitiful 225 students in four specialized higher civil schools.[47] All these students were Muslims. The non-Muslim millets operated their own schools, which according to Subhi numbered 2,495, almost all primary, with 125,404 students. Medreses, which continued under control of the ulema, were not included in these figures, nor were the higher specialized schools such as the naval and military schools and the medical school. Only in these higher schools was there any mixed education of Christians and Muslims, though the Christians were few. Students from the various non-Muslim millets were sometimes mixed together in schools run by foreigners, as in the American Robert College, founded in 1863, or the İzmir school of the Kaiserwirth deaconesses.

The Hatt-ı Hümayun of 1856 had been strangely silent on the need for educational advance, except for the promise that Christians should have equal opportunity to enter the state civil and military schools, and for a reconfirmation of the right of the millets to operate their own educational institutions. But the Tanzimat statesmen were not unaware of the educational problem, and in the 1860's were constantly reminded of it by their New Ottoman critics. The problem was not only one of establishing more schools to broaden the educational base, but of improving the calibre of instruction to reach the level already attained by some of the non-Muslim millet schools and to come closer to the European level. This involved creating more

---

[46] "Modernized elementary government schools are being opened everywhere all over Turkey," Schauffler to Anderson, 12 December 1859, ABCFM, Armenian Mission VIII.

[47] Subhi Bey to Elliot, rec'd. 18 November 1867, FO 195/893. These figures exclude African provinces. They are considerably lower, and probably more accurate, than comparable figures for 1864 from the same ministry: Ubicini, *Etat présent*, pp. 155-156. Karal, *Islahat fermanı devri*, pp. 194-195, 200-201, gives the same figures as Ubicini. For a sample description of the educational facilities in an important provincial center (Edirne) as of 1868 by an impartial observer, see Albert Dumont, *Le Balkan et l'Adriatique* (Paris, 1874), pp. 102-106.

state schools, outside the control of the ulema, with improved curricula and teaching staff. But the problem was yet more complex, if Osmanlılık were to be promoted. Mixed schools for Muslims and non-Muslims, such as Midhat Paşa had begun to establish in the Tuna vilayet, would be necessary if the lines of demarcation between millets were to be obliterated. This had been considered by a special commission, discussing the reforms of 1856, which agreed that it was better to have non-Muslim children in Ottoman rather than foreign schools, but found that the religious method of instruction still characteristic of the *rüşdiye* made a mixed student body too difficult.[48] The French note of February 1867, placing before the Porte its reflections on the fulfillment of the Hatt-ı Hümayun, laid great stress on the need for more schools, especially for secondary schools, for mixed schools, for a university, and for the training of teachers.[49] Âli Paşa's memorandum sent from Crete at the end of November 1867 made some of the same points just as strongly, especially the need for better education for Muslims and for mixed schools.

The first big breach in millet barriers to mixed education occurred in 1868 with the establishment of the *lycée* of Galatasaray. This, like the Council of State, had been taking shape before Sultan Abdülaziz's trip to Europe. The French pressed hard for a school patterned on their own, and with an expert from Napoleon III's ministry of education Âli and Fuad had already worked out a plan for a *lycée* in the spring of 1867.[50] After the sultan's trip, and after Âli's return from Crete, the latter renewed the proposal of such a school in a memorandum to the sultan.[51] An imperial ferman was issued accordingly.[52]

[48] Mehmed Selaheddin, *Bir türk diplomatının evrak-ı siyasiyesi* (İstanbul, 1306), p. 145.

[49] Text in Testa, *Recueil*, VII, 419-420.

[50] Moustier to Bourée, 15 March and 22 March 1867, and Bourée to Moustier, 22 May 1867, in Testa, *Recueil*, VII, 429, 432-433, 467-468. Cf. İhsan Sungu, "Galatasaray Lisesinin kuruluşu," *Belleten*, VII: 28 (October 1943), 315-347, which uses these dispatches as well as contemporary İstanbul newspapers. The French motive appears not to have been solely altruistic, but to promote French influence and possibly Catholic influence. Jesuit ultramontanism was suspected by Protestants: George Washburn, *Fifty Years in Constantinople* (Boston, 1909), pp. 24-25; Mordtmann, *Stambul*, I, 44.

[51] Text in Sungu, "Galatasaray," pp. 323-324.

[52] Text in Aristarchi, *Législation*, III, 315-317; Young, *Corps de droit*, II, 377-380; *Düstur*, II, 245-248. The latter is the fullest. Young's text is based on the *Düstur*, but omits parts. These two are undated. Aristarchi's text is as communicated to foreign powers on April 29, 1868. Young notes one of the significant differences, p. 377. There are others he does not note—for instance, in the curriculum laid down. It may be that Aristarchi's text was drawn for foreign consumption, but it

The ferman stated explicitly that the new school was for boys of all creeds and was to be a conscientious copy of western schools. The five-year course prescribed was essentially a European curriculum. Religious instruction and services for boys of each millet would be in charge of leaders of their own faith. Bulgars, Greeks, and Armenians might study their own tongues as well as French, Latin, and Turkish. A large number of scholarships for needy students was established by the Ottoman government.

The lycée of Galatasaray was an immediate success, for which the only demonstrable cause was the comparative excellence of the instruction. Despite opposition on the part of Greek Orthodox leaders, Sephardic Jews, and the Pope—all of whom feared that the tolerant atmosphere of the new institution would wean the rising generation away from their control—341 students were enrolled at the opening in September 1868. Of this number 147 were Muslims, 48 Gregorian Armenians, 36 Greek Orthodox, 34 Jews, 34 Bulgars, 23 Roman Catholics, and 19 Armenian Catholics. At the end of the second year there were over 600 students. Complaints arose among the Turkish students about food, bathroom facilities, Latin, and the little emphasis given to the Turkish language. But on the whole differences in religion and customs and language seem not to have destroyed a harmonious functioning. The principal language of instruction was French, as were the teachers and the headmaster, M. de Salve.[53]

Namık Kemal, from abroad, criticized Galatasaray for virtually ignoring Turkish. He also called it an ostentatious display created at the insistence of the French ambassador, though presented as the work of the Council of State, and not enough to make a dent in the tremendous educational problems of the empire.[54] The criticisms all had some foundation, yet he exaggerated. The school continued to be a

---

is just as likely that the *Düstur* text is a later emendation. Not only is it undated, but it omits the provision in Aristarchi's text that half the students must be Muslim; the *Düstur* text, therefore, may be an accommodation to the fact that in 1868 well under half the students enrolled were Muslims. Part of the ferman as given in Sungu, "Galatasaray," p. 325, is taken from the Turkish text as published in the newspaper *İstanbul* on June 16-18, 1868. It resembles the text in Aristarchi, which seems to indicate that the *Düstur* version is not the original.

[53] De Salve, "L'enseignement en Turquie: le lycée impérial de Galata-Séraï," *Revue des deux mondes*, 3rd period, V (15 October 1874), 846-849; Engelhardt, *La Turquie*, II, 12-16. Turkish complaints: Osman Ergin, *Türkiye maarif tarihi* (İstanbul, 1939-1943), II, 404.

[54] *Hürriyet*, #49, 31 May 1869, and #56, 19 July 1869, quoted in Sungu, "Tanzimat ve Yeni Osmanlılar," pp. 841-843.

good one and survived some vicissitudes. Enrollment fell after the French defeats of 1870, as the prestige of the French language suffered. Mahmud Nedim, grand vezir after Âli's death in 1871, hurt the school by his "economies." M. de Salve resigned, to be followed in turn by an Ottoman Armenian, two Ottoman Greeks, and in early 1877 by the stormy petrel Ali Suavi, who was a disaster as the director of the school. The school was bodily moved for a time from the Christian quarter to the Muslim atmosphere of İstanbul. In the long run, however, the diminution of French control was undoubtedly beneficial, and even in 1876 the enrollment was fairly sizable.[55]

One year after the Galatasaray *lycée* opened its doors a comprehensive law of reorganization for the state school system was issued.[56] This was the product of deliberation in the Council of State and of the work of Safvet Paşa, the minister of education. The whole scheme, much more thoroughgoing than that of 1846, was an attempt to rationalize the educational system by integrating what had been a somewhat haphazard growth of parts into an orderly pattern, from the elementary grades to the university level. It was justified not on this ground alone, however, but on the grounds that glaring deficiencies in Ottoman education had to be corrected to meet the demands of nineteenth-century civilization.[57] There was also implicit in the system a strong element of Osmanlılık. Five levels of schooling were set up: two primary (*sıbyan* and *rüşdiye*), two secondary (*idadiye* and *sultaniye*), and the higher special schools and the university at the top. According to the plan, schools of the first three levels were to be provided for each village, town, or quarter of a stipulated population, with *sultaniye*'s in each vilayet capital. Curricula were prescribed, and a complete administrative organization laid out. The utmost fairness in regard to language and religion was shown to non-Muslim minorities. In the two primary school levels Christians and Muslims were to be separated, evidently to avoid practical difficulties. From the sec-

[55] Ergin, *Maarif tarihi*, II, 405; Washburn, *Fifty Years*, p. 25; Mordtmann, *Stambul*, I, 45; Schweiger-Lerchenfeld, *Serail*, pp. 227-228; Antonio Gallenga, *Two Years of the Eastern Question* (London, 1877), I, 180-181; Charles de Moüy, *Lettres du Bosphore* (Paris, 1879), p. 181.
[56] Text in Aristarchi, *Législation*, III, 277-315; Young, *Corps de droit*, II, 355-375 (defective); *Düstur*, II, 184-219.
[57] Cf. the memorandum in Sadrettin Celâl Antel, "Tanzimat maarifi," *Tanzimat*, I, 450-451. Possibly the Egyptian law of 1867 putting *mekteb*'s under state control had some influence: cf. J. Heyworth-Dunne, *An Introduction to the History of Education in Modern Egypt* (London, 1938), pp. 362-375.

ondary schools on, education was to be mixed. The law recognized also the existence of private schools maintained either by individuals or by millets, providing only that their teachers should hold state certificates. Under the new system the *sıbyan* school was to be free and compulsory, the *rüşdiye* free but not compulsory. Boys were obliged to attend school to age eleven, girls to age ten.

In theory the scheme was fine, though it was greeted with some apathy at home and scepticism abroad. The *Times* of London described the plan as the French system with an admixture of English denominationalism, but admitted that if it were applied it would do a lot to amalgamate the Ottoman peoples.[58] Such a vast scheme could, of course, not be carried out quickly. It remained, with some changes, the basis for Ottoman education until the end of the empire, and was a strong indication that the state rather than the millet was now considered responsible for schools. But the state, partly for lack of money and teachers, was able by the end of the Tanzimat period to increase significantly only the number of schools in the two elementary categories. The *rüşdiye*'s in particular were rapidly developed. The *idadiye*'s, however, remained theoretical only, except in İstanbul, and Galatasaray was the only one of the *sultaniye*'s in existence.[59] A few other sorts of schools were opened or enlarged in the years 1869 to 1875—teacher training schools, including one for women; preparatory schools for the military academies; refresher courses for provincial officials; part-time courses for the poor, especially gild apprentices.[60]

While the secondary schools remained wanting, another attempt was made, as it had been in the 1840's, to start educational development at the top also, by a new formal opening of the university at İstanbul. Tahsin Efendi, a liberal member of the ulema who had been in Paris and had had contact with the New Ottomans, was its head. Inaugurated on February 20, 1870, the university soon ran into difficulties, partly from lack of proper teachers, students, and books, but also because lectures by the famous Jemaleddin el-Afghani aroused protest on the part of the *şeyhülislâm* and other members of

[58] October 15, 1869.
[59] Ubicini, *Etat présent*, pp. 156-159, based on the *salname* for A.H. 1293 (A.D. 1876-1877): Bertold Spuler, *Die Minderheitenschulen der europäischen Turkei* (Breslau, 1936), pp. 71-72, 84-85; Karal, *Islahat fermanı devri*, pp. 202-203.
[60] Ergin, *Maarif tarihi*, II, 405-412, 418-423, 557-572; Antel, "Tanzimat maarifi," pp. 449-450; Ubicini, *Etat présent*, pp. 163-166.

the ulema. The university was therefore closed again in 1871, not to reopen until after the end of the Tanzimat period. There remained a faculty of law, which seems, however, actually to have been on the *lycée* level in combination with Galatasaray.[61]

At best, this was spotty educational progress. There were many difficulties. Western institutions were copied, but western-trained teachers were few. Some of the lack was supplied, for the civil schools, by men trained in the military schools.[62] Where teachers were foreign, instruction was often in French, as in Galatasaray or in the military medical school. This aroused protest on the part of patriotic Turkish students, and in 1869 the medical school actually switched to Turkish.[63] The elementary schools did not increase rapidly enough, and the teaching in them was modernized very slowly. In 1873 *Basiret (Foresight)*, a conservative newspaper, was again voicing the familiar complaint that Greek and Armenian schools were ahead of the Turkish, and better supported by their communities.[64] Education in the provinces lagged well behind that in the capital. Some of the higher specialized schools, like the university, were on no better than a *lycée* level.[65] Yet it is unfair to compare actuality, even by the end of the Tanzimat period, with the master blueprint of 1869. The deficiencies and the disappointments were real, but so was the progress made. Turkish education was more widespread, and somewhat different in tone and in quality, from what it had been in 1856. The state had assumed responsibility, a program of modernization had been adopted officially, some schools were improving. Together with the westernized military schools, the new developments in literature and the press, and the increased contact of individuals with Europe, the civil schools were contributing to the creation of a new educated class formed outside the old patterns of the medrese.

[61] Ergin, *Maarif tarihi*, II, 462-468, 581; Antel, "Tanzimat maarifi," pp. 448-449; Ubicini, *Etat présent*, p. 162; Young, *Corps de droit*, II, 382-383; A. Heidborn, *Manuel de droit public et administratif de l'Empire Ottoman* (Vienna, 1908-1912), I, 280-281, n.218; Ölmezoğlu, "Cevdet Paşa," p. 117. On Jemaleddin see below, chapter VIII.

[62] Ergin, *Maarif tarihi*, II, 361.

[63] *Université de Stamboul: historique . . .* (İstanbul, 1925), pp. 21-22. A new civil medical school founded in 1866 used Turkish from the start: Ergin, *Maarif tarihi*, II, 545.

[64] Cited by Mordtmann, *Stambul*, I, 148-150. See the general review of Turkish education as of about 1875 in Hermann Vambéry, *Der Islam im neunzehnten Jahrhundert* (Leipzig, 1875), pp. 171-185.

[65] Ergin, *Maarif tarihi*, II, 355.

At the same time as the educational system in the empire was being redrawn, the legal system was also being reexamined. Like the Ottoman schools, Ottoman laws had been modernized and rearranged piecemeal since 1840. Before 1860, western-inspired codes of commercial law, penal law, and some procedural law had come into being, and the traditional land law had been somewhat better systematized. But the bulk of the civil law, which concerned matters of personal status (marriage, divorce, alimony, inheritance, wardship, and the like) and matters of contract and obligation, so far remained untouched. Courts in these areas followed the prescriptions of the şeriat. But these prescriptions were not always plain. The last codification had been centuries before. Judges had to have recourse to many commentators, but often in practice did not know where to look for legal guidance, and did not know enough law and enough Arabic to use the guides and precedents. "Sacred jurisprudence resembles a boundless ocean," said, in 1869, the commission appointed to redraft a part of the civil law, "and as difficult as it is to draw up pearls from the ocean, so great ability and learning are required for a man to find always in the law the necessary rules for the solution of each question." And in the nineteenth century, continued the commission, such men of learning were becoming rarer, both in the new "regular" or westernized civil courts and in the şeriat courts.[66] Some systematization for ready reference was needed.

The problem had first been tackled at the end of 1855 by a commission of jurists created within the Tanzimat Council. One of the members was Cevdet, Reşid Paşa's protégé, who had not only a thorough knowledge of the religious law, but was an exceptional member of the ulema in having learned French and enjoyed close contact with the reforming statesmen of the Tanzimat.[67] This committee was occupied, as Cevdet described its task, with putting into one book in Turkish the religious law on transactions, so that every-

[66] From the preface of the *Mecelle*: W. E. Grigsby, *The Medjelle or Ottoman Civil Law* (London, 1895), pp. iii-iv. Cf. Sıddık Sami Onar, "Les transformations de la structure administrative et juridique de la Turquie . . . ," *Revue internationale des sciences administratives*, IV (1955), 773.

[67] There is some argument on how well Cevdet knew French. Evidently his reading knowledge was fairly good, but he could not speak it freely: Fatma Aliye, *Ahmed Cevdet Paşa ve zamanı* (İstanbul, 1332), p. 34; Mardin, *Cevdet*, pp. 30-33, n.56. His knowledge of western law was also not great at the start, though it increased: *ibid.*, pp. 9-10. On Cevdet in general see, in addition to the above two works, Harold Bowen, "Aḥmad Djewdet Pasha," *Encyclopaedia of Islam*, new ed., I, 284-286, and Ölmezoğlu, "Cevdet Paşa," pp. 114-123.

one could understand it. The work remained incomplete, however.[68] A part of the motivation came from the increased commercial contacts with Europe and the question of whether to accept French law.[69] This was always a delicate matter, given religious sensitivity among Muslims, though the law of obligations and contracts was less affected by this sensitivity than the law of personal status.

By 1867, however, Âli Paşa as grand vezir was willing, at least, to consider the adoption of large parts of western civil law, and so proposed in his memorandum of that year. He knew something of the French civil code. This had already been translated into Arabic under Egyptian government sponsorship. Âli, evidently with the thought that equality and Osmanlılık would best be promoted by the adoption of one secular law for men of all creeds within the empire, asked that the Arabic version be translated into Turkish.[70] But it is a question as to how far Âli wanted to go in applying the French civil law to the Ottoman Empire. To take over the whole Code Napoléon of 1804 would have been, for the time, a far more radical measure than was, under the republic, the creation of a new civil code based on the Swiss in 1926. Âli's proposal in his memorandum of 1867 was restricted: that the French civil code be used for the mixed courts in cases involving Muslims and non-Muslims.[71] Âli was a cautious man by nature. Quite possibly he intended that only those portions of the French civil code bearing on commercial transactions should be adopted, as a supplement to the already French-based commercial code. For the French memorandum of February 22, 1867, had pointed out specifically that the Ottoman commercial code lacked those general principles needed which were to be found in the French civil code, and that these provisions should be added.[72] The French ambassador evidently thought that some such process was going on when he reported that progress was being made by the commission charged with extracting from the *code civile* some fifteen hundred or sixteen hundred articles that could advantageously be borrowed.[73] Cevdet Paşa, he said, was regarded by Âli and Fuad as a liberal spirit who could

[68] Cevdet Paşa, *Tezâkir 1-12*, ed. by Cavid Baysun (Ankara, 1953), pp. 62-63.
[69] *Ibid.*
[70] Said Paşa, *Hatıratı* (İstanbul, 1328), I, 6. Cf. Mardin, *Cevdet*, pp. 173-174, n.138; Ergin, *Maarif tarihi*, I, 230.
[71] Hıfzı Veldet, "Kanunlaştırma hareketleri ve Tanzimat," *Tanzimat*, I, 200-201.
[72] Testa, *Recueil*, VII, 420.
[73] Bourée to Moustier, 10 March 1868, *ibid.*, p. 511.

guide the fusion of European and Turkish law. The question of the French code and its possible adoption was argued in the council of ministers, evidently on a broad base, and defeated. Fuad is said to have supported Cevdet and others who opposed such a move. The şeriat won out.[74]

The upshot was the establishment in 1868 of a new commission of Muslim jurists under the chairmanship of Cevdet Paşa to take up again the abortive work of 1855 on the law of obligations and contracts. Two years before, Cevdet had made the transition from the ranks of the ulema to the civil service hierarchy. He was involved in other jobs also, and was shuffled about in various posts in the capital and as provincial governor during the eight years that the commission worked. For a time he was removed from the commission, and complained that the work in that period was badly done. The vagaries of Ottoman politics after Âli's death affected the commission's work.[75] But the commission, after a preliminary report in 1869, finished between 1870 and 1876 sixteen books of the law of transactions, known as the *Mecelle-i ahkâm-ı adliye*.[76]

The *Mecelle* was not a complete civil code, and in fact was not so intended. The delicate matters of personal status were left out of consideration entirely by the committee. It is considered by some legal experts not to be a code at all, but simply a guide to the law for the use of those Turkish judges and jurists who otherwise were at sea in the older lawbooks and collections of *fetvas*'s. Nevertheless, the *Mecelle* was meant to render reference to the older books unnecessary wherever possible. Its 1,851 articles gave a clear and orderly exposition of the law of transactions derived from the şeriat. Part of the *Mecelle* was also concerned with civil procedure. The basis for most of the work was the Hanefite law, which was the prevailing rite in the Ottoman Empire. As Cevdet said, the *Mecelle* resolved controversial points in the Hanefite law.[77] He was quite pleased with the result, quoting a comparison of his own work and Justinian's code to the benefit of himself.[78]

---

[74] Ölmezoğlu, "Cevdet Paşa," p. 116; Ebül'ulâ Mardin, "Mecelle," *İslâm ansiklopedisi*, fasc. 74, p. 434.

[75] Cf. Mardin, *Cevdet*, p. 103; Veldet, "Kanunlaştırma hareketleri," p. 189; Mardin, "Mecelle," pp. 434-435.

[76] Text in Aristarchi, *Législation*, VI and VII; Young, *Corps de droit*, VI, 169-446; and sprinkled through *Düstur*, I, II, and IV. English translation by C. R. Tyser, *The Mejelle* (Nicosia, 1901), following the Turkish rather literally.

[77] *Tezâkir*, pp. 62-63. [78] *Ibid.*, p. 64.

Later jurists have criticized Cevdet's work as having taken too narrow a base, and having missed both the opportunity to profit from western law and the chance to incorporate useful points from the other Islamic schools of law.[79] Western influence on the *Mecelle* was, in fact, limited to its organization into numbered articles. The coincidences between various of its provisions and the French civil code seem to be fortuitous, or the result of some far older influence of Roman on Islamic law.[80] Some jurists have said also that the *Mecelle* was simply insufficient to meet the needs of rapidly changing times. But it is not clear that a commission of jurists in the then condition of the Ottoman Empire could have gone much farther. Cevdet was the most enlightened of the commission, but he had his doubts about innovation and could certainly not have been given sole responsibility for the work.

Though most legal specialists have offered the criticisms mentioned above, they are not agreed on what weight to give these criticisms when balanced against the advantages of the *Mecelle*. The greatest advantage was order and clarity, which was a big step forward. Another was that the sanction of the Ottoman government was behind the *Mecelle*, making it an authoritative work and opening the way for further secularization.[81] The sultan's authority was mentioned in the *Mecelle* itself, though undoubtedly the pertinent provision could not be enforced: "When by order of the sovereign, the opinion of one doctor of the law having been found in conformity with public interest and the needs of the times, it has been ordered to judge according to this opinion, judges cannot validly base their decisions on a contrary opinion."[82] Further, it has been argued that the *Mecelle* had not so narrow a base as first appears. The drafting commission stated in its preface that it had selected, among varying Hanefite opinions, those which best met the demands of modern times and cases. The *Mecelle*, in consequence, was "based not exclusively on the dominant Hanafi opinion regarding every point, but rather on an eclectic selection of

---

[79] Cf. Veldet, "Kanunlaştırma hareketleri," pp. 191-194; Sıddık Sami Onar, "The Majalla," in Majid Khadduri and Herbert Liebesny, eds., *Law in the Middle East*, I (Washington, 1955), 298, 307; Mardin, *Cevdet*, pp. 171-175.

[80] Leon Ostrorog, *The Angora Reform* (London, 1927), pp. 77-78; Veldet, "Kanunlaştırma hareketleri," p. 195, criticizing Young's citation of French law parallels, as well as the translation.

[81] *Ibid.*, pp. 194-195; Gotthard Jäschke, "Der Islam in der neuen Türkei," *Die Welt des Islams*, N.S., I:1/2 (1951), 12-13.

[82] Article 1801.

provisions that had received recognition of some sort in the Hanafi school (even though some of them had in fact originated elsewhere). This was an innovation of outstanding importance. . . ."[83]

The *Mecelle* was to be applied both in the şeriat and in the *nizamiye* courts.[84] The former, under supervision of the *şeyhülislâm*, judged civil cases among Muslims only, according to the religious law.[85] The latter, under the ministry of justice, were the westernized "regular" courts, a product of the Tanzimat period, established to take cognizance of all criminal cases and of cases involving Muslims and non-Muslims or non-Muslims of different sects. These courts applied the new westernized laws of the empire, such as the penal code, as well as religious law where that was the sole applicable standard. Westernized courts had grown in haphazard fashion, starting with the mixed commercial courts and İstanbul police courts of the 1840's.[86] There had been periodic revisions and additions to the number of westernized courts—in particular, commercial courts that operated under the commercial code of 1850 and appendices thereto, new police courts that operated under the penal code of 1858,[87] and the *nizamiye* courts composed of Muslims and non-Muslims set up under the vilayet law in every vilayet, sancak, and kaza. When the *Divan-ı ahkâm-ı adliye* was established in 1868, it was to act as a court of appeal for cases that came up from the various *nizamiye* courts. But the whole judicial apparatus required better systematization.

So in 1869, when Cevdet Paşa was minister of justice—a position into which his presidency of the Judicial Council had been transformed—a new set of regulations was prepared in an effort to clarify the situation.[88] The courts were thereby organized into a hierarchy. At the lowest level the council of elders in the *nahiye* served as a court of conciliation, and could settle cases only when both parties accepted the solution. Courts in the capitals of kazas, sancaks, and vilayets had

[83] J. N. D. Anderson, *Islamic Law in the Modern World* (New York, 1959), p. 24. Cf. Heidborn, *Manuel de droit public*, II, 286, n.230.

[84] Cevdet, *Tezâkir*, p. 63.

[85] Tribunals with analogous functions, though, of course, not so extensive, existed within the non-Muslim millets also for their own members.

[86] For a review of the courts before 1854 see Abdolonyme Ubicini, *Letters on Turkey* (London, 1856), I, 47-49, 168-185.

[87] Veldet, "Kanunlaştırma hareketleri," pp. 196-197, 203.

[88] Text in Testa, *Recueil*, VII, 535-540, dated 21 zilhicce 1285 (4 April 1869); Aristarchi, *Législation*, II, 289-295, dated 4 muharrem 1286 (16 April 1869).

the usual judicial powers, but their competence was carefully defined
for both civil and criminal cases, those in the larger divisions taking
the more important cases. Appeal procedures were specified. Presiding judges in the *nizamiye* courts continued, however, to be appointees
of the *şeyhülislâm*, as laid down in the vilayet law. And confusion in
jurisdiction between religious and secular courts was not yet entirely
removed.[89] Nor, despite the acceptance in principle of the separation
of powers, were the courts completely independent of the administrative authorities. Some confusion persisted in the *nizamiye* courts, as
well as the confusion inherent in the characteristic dualism of the
Tanzimat period as two sets of institutions, in this case religious and
secular courts, stood alongside each other. New regulations were,
therefore, periodically issued, and the *nizamiye* courts were to get
their final organization only after the constitution of 1876 was promulgated.[90] Entirely aside from the matter of court organization, however, the administration of justice suffered from the traditional defects: the ignorance or venality of judges, and the practice of sub-
orning witnesses. Complaints on these counts, too numerous to catalogue, continued to the end of the Tanzimat period. Muslims and
non-Muslims alike felt these shortcomings.

Fuad Paşa had said in the spring of 1867 that some reform measures concerning land tenure were coming soon. Before Sultan Abdülaziz left on his trip to Europe, three decrees had actually been
issued. Each had relatively small effect on the total pattern of landholding in the Ottoman Empire. Yet, taken together, since each
freed some type of land from some legal restrictions, the measures
represented an increase in the transferability of land and a step toward a more secular, western concept of landholding. Further involved in the measures were small but significant attacks on the system of *vakıf* and on the system of capitulations.

In the past the practice of dedicating land or other immovable
property to the support of religious and charitable objects—whether
of mosques, medreses, hospitals, or poor relief—had been of immense
benefit to Islamic civilization. Such endowments could even be created

[89] Veldet, "Kanunlaştırma hareketleri," pp. 203-204; Young, *Corps de droit*, I,
291-293.
[90] See, on court development in general, Heidborn, *Manuel de droit public*, I,
216-228; Ubicini, *Etat présent*, pp. 147-151.

for what, by the nineteenth century, were coming to be recognized as public works that ought to be state-supported, such as roads and bridges. In the course of time many abuses had arisen—the turning of state land illegally into *vakıf*; the establishment of "camouflage" *vakıf*'s, the income from which went essentially to the creator of the trust and his heirs rather than to charitable objects; graft on the part of administrators of the endowments; and so forth.

While these abuses were important in themselves for hurting the whole *vakıf* system, their significance here is in the economic effect on the state and the individual in the nineteenth century. So far as the state went, it suffered whenever any of its land was transformed illegally into *vakıf*, since *vakıf* was exempt from most kinds of taxes. The state suffered, in fact, simply because so much property was *vakıf*, legal or not. It was variously estimated in the nineteenth century that between half and three quarters of all arable and built-on property in the Ottoman Empire had become *vakıf*.[91] Almost the entire city of İstanbul had become *vakıf* by the start of the nineteenth century. The whole village of Bebek, up the Bosporus from İstanbul, was the property of one mosque.[92] The state suffered further because *vakıf* property, as experience showed, tended to degenerate, among the reasons for which was the simple fact that he who leased or worked the property was not the owner and often had little interest in long-term repair or improvement. Consequently the general economy suffered again from low productivity. The *vakıf*'s also supported many unproductive idlers. Mahmud II attempted to counteract some of these bad effects by creating a ministry to supervise *vakıf*'s. In fact, the effect was small, since the state usually paid out more to maintain the endowments than it received in income from them, and the deficit was enhanced by the expense of paying the bureaucrats involved, by inflation that ate into the real income from *vakıf* leases, and by illegal diversions of funds to other state purposes.[93]

[91] Ubicini, *Letters*, I, 261; Prokesch to Beust, 15 March 1867, in Testa, *Recueil*, VII, 738; Heffening, "Wakf," *Encyclopaedia of Islam*, IV, 1100; Young, *Corps de droit*, VI, 113.

[92] Fuad Köprülü, "L'institution du vakouf: sa nature juridique et son évolution historique," *Vakıflar dergisi*, II (1942), 32; Schauffler to Anderson, 12 December 1859, ABCFM, Armenian Mission VIII, #92.

[93] On the institution of *vakıf* in general, and abuses, see H. A. R. Gibb and Harold Bowen, *Islamic Society and the West*, I, part 2 (Oxford, 1957), 165-178; Köprülü, "L'institution du vakouf," pp. 3-48; *La Turquie*, 1/2 August 1875; Onar, "Les transformations," pp. 759-764; Halim Baki Kunter, "Türk vakıfları ve vakfiyeleri üzerine mücmel bir etüd," *Vakıflar dergisi*, I (1938), 103-129.

Of just as great concern to the state, and of greater concern to the individual in the nineteenth century, was the fact that *vakıf* property was taken out of the channels of normal commercial transaction and inheritance. The act of dedication made the property God's, in perpetuity, and fixed the purposes for which the revenues might be used. The property could be leased, but not bought or sold like freehold property; it was not subject to suit and seizure for nonpayment of debt, so could not be used in the ordinary way as security for borrowing. In the Ottoman Empire a system of what amounted to almost perpetual lease had been worked out by statute, thus circumventing the general rule of Islamic law that leases of *vakıf* property should be for one year.[94] The direct heirs of the holder could inherit the right to use the property, but in default of direct heirs the religious or charitable institution took over, other members of the family being excluded. Such leases still did not amount to freehold property. "The principle is pushed so far," as Fuad explained, "that the grandchild cannot succeed, if his parent dies in the life time of the grand parent; only the son or daughter of the last holder can inherit."[95] There were many other obstacles to freedom of transaction as far as *vakıf* property went, and some complex situations, such as that one party could hold the right to land as *vakıf*, while another could own outright trees and buildings thereon.

As European ways and commercial connections grew in the nineteenth-century empire, and as the abuses in the whole *vakıf* system became more and more apparent, there was a tendency on the part of the top westernized bureaucrats to try to do away with these legal restrictions on so much of the real estate in the empire, even to abolish the *vakıf* system itself.[96] This would open up possibilities for further economic development. European powers urged such reform on the Porte periodically in the Tanzimat period, in part with the desire to help the empire, in part to ease the way for their own nationals to invest there. Any secularization of *vakıf*'s, or steps in that direction, would also be a further blow at the influence of the ulema, whose stipends and support depended so much on the endowments and whose influence as administrators of *vakıf*'s was often considerable.

In the years after the Hatt-ı Hümayun of 1856 there were recur-

---

[94] This was lease by *icareteyn*, or "double rent." Cf. Henry Cattan, "The Law of Waqf," in Khadduri, *Law in the Middle East*, p. 209.
[95] Lyons to Stanley, #199, 22 May 1867, FO 78/1960.
[96] Köprülü, "L'institution du vakouf," p. 34.

rent reports that some such step toward secularization was about to be taken. So early as December of 1859 the measure that was ultimately adopted in 1867 was rumored to be forthcoming—an extension of the right of heritability to more distant relatives of *vakıf* leaseholders, so that, in effect, the property would be closer to *mülk*, or property held in fee simple. In return for the extension of the right of inheritance, the government would collect an extra five per cent of the income from the property.[97] By this means, the property technically would remain *vakıf*, and so would avoid the odium of secularization. Probably because of opposition from the ulema, the project was dropped, and similar proposals in 1863 and 1865 failed also.[98] By 1867 the urging of France, plus the difficult position of the treasury in meeting costs of suppressing the rebellion in Crete, plus undoubtedly a desire on the part of Âli and Fuad to create a liberal nimbus for Abdülaziz before he went to Europe, brought the project to the fore again.[99] Possibly complete secularization of *vakıf*'s was contemplated for a moment.[100] But this was likely to arouse too much opposition among the ulema.

What resulted, then, was that the idea of 1859 was revived in two edicts of May 21 and June 18, 1867.[101] The first allowed the extension of the right of inheritance from relatives of the first to the seventh degree for *vakıf* and state (*miri*) properties which were held of the state by *tapu*, or official title-deed of possession.[102] In return, the state collected, in addition to the usual tithe on the produce of the land, a fifteen per cent tax on the income for the next year, though the collection of the increase was spread over five years. The second decree allowed a similar extension of the right of inheritance, in return for an additional payment, of rural (*müstağallat*) and urban (*müsakkafat*) *vakıf*'s held by double rent (*icareteyn*).[103] Conversion to extended heritability was optional with the holder. "The principle

[97] Schauffler to Anderson, 12 December 1859, ABCFM, Armenian Mission VIII, #92.
[98] Morris to Seward, #70, 4 December 1863, USNA, Turkey 17; Morris to Seward, #129, 18 October 1865, and #133, 22 November 1865, USNA, Turkey 19. The government evidently did take over some property of the Mevlevi dervishes about 1864: Van Lennep, *Travels*, II, 235.
[99] Engelhardt, *La Turquie*, I, 209; Morris to Seward, #195, 27 February 1867, USNA, Turkey 19; Prokesch to Beust, 15 March 1867, in Testa, *Recueil*, VII, 737-738.
[100] Young, *Corps de droit*, VI, 113.
[101] Texts in Testa, *Recueil*, VII, 740-745; Young, *Corps de droit*, I, 316-318 (defective); Aristarchi, *Législation*, I, 254-263; *Düstur*, I, 223-226.
[102] These are not the same degrees of relationship as in western civil or canon law.
[103] Cf. Omer Hilmi, *A Treatise on the Laws of Evkaf* (Nicosia, 1899), pp. 45-49.

of the new laws is to assimilate the vacoufs and 'terres seigneuriales' to freehold property," Fuad explained to the British ambassador.[104] This was only partially true. Many sorts of *vakıf* were not touched by the laws, but only those founded by members of the imperial family or those administered by the state after the founder's family had died out.[105] Further, not many *vakıf*'s appear to have been converted in accord with the new law. So far as the state lands were concerned, the benefit accrued not necessarily to the cultivators of the land, but to those who held the official title of possession, the *tapu*. Europeans were disappointed. Property was not much more mobile than before.[106] Yet a cautious step in the direction of secularization had been taken, opening the way for further such steps and for consideration of more radical measures.[107]

The third of the land laws of 1867, also announced on June 18, granted permission to foreigners to own real estate in the Ottoman Empire. This was not only a liberalization of legal restrictions on transactions in land, but a weapon used by Âli and Fuad to attack the capitulations. Behind the edict lay a history of considerable controversy. Under Ottoman law foreigners were not allowed to own Ottoman real estate. In fact they sometimes did, but only through a dummy representative, subject of the Porte, who was the nominal owner.[108] But this involved legal troubles and the risk that the dummy would cheat the owner. Of course, the foreigner had an advantage in that, if bankrupt, property not held in his name could not be seized. But the whole situation curbed foreign ownership and investment. The powers pressed for free ownership of land by foreigners, which the Hatt-ı Hümayun of 1856 had promised. But the Porte would concede this only if the powers should give up capitulatory privileges

[104] Lyons to Stanley, #199, 22 May 1867, FO 78/1960.

[105] *La Turquie* of 1/2 August 1875 put all these in the category of "customary *vakıf*'s," as opposed to those whose revenues went entirely to religious or charitable objects.

[106] Mordtmann, *Stambul*, II, 206; *La Turquie*, 27 and 30 November and 2 December 1871, and 1/2 August 1875; Halil İnalcık, "Land Problems in Turkish History," *Muslim World*, 45:3 (July 1955), 227.

[107] As in 1873 and 1875: Engelhardt, *La Turquie*, II, 125-128; Maynard to Fish, #67, 20 May 1876, USNA, Turkey 29; *La Turquie* 1/2 August 1875. Evidently on each occasion a more drastic *vakıf* secularization law remained ineffective.

[108] Nasim Sousa, *The Capitulatory Regime of Turkey* (Baltimore, 1933), p. 82 and n.37. İzmir was an exception, where foreigners could hold property in their own names.

in respect of the property.[109] The Ottoman position was maintained until 1867, and reiterated in Fuad's memorandum of that year on the Hatt-ı Hümayun. Finally, France and Austria seemed to recognize that extensive extraterritorial privileges were no longer justified. The new edict permitted foreigners to hold real property in the empire, except in the Hijaz.[110] But they could hold it only on the same basis as any Ottoman subject—on condition of conforming to local police regulations, submitting to Turkish civil courts, and paying the usual taxes. The next year a protocol accepting the new dispensation was signed by France, and soon thereafter by other powers.[111] The protocol accorded certain privileges of consular protection to the persons, movable goods, and court appearances of foreign property owners.

Ziya Bey, from exile in London, bitterly attacked the granting of permission to foreigners to own property. He conjured up a picture of Turks, already suffering from western predominance in trade and industry, selling out in İstanbul to foreigners and migrating, homeless, with barefoot children, to Anatolia. What would it profit the Turks if İstanbul, bought by the blood of their forebears, were rebuilt like Paris, but foreigners owned the property?[112] Ziya did not recognize that the measure was also an attack on the capitulations. But westerners did, and some of them criticized the new measure just as bitterly as Ziya, for opposite reasons. They called it a snare, depriving foreigners of all capitulatory protections.[113] Ignatyev, Russian ambassador to the Porte, thought that Âli and Fuad were counting on a great influx of English and French colonists whose tax payments would aid Turkish finances and whose political weight would support Turkish sovereignty against particularist Christian nationalisms.[114]

[109] Testa, *Recueil*, VII, 733-740, especially Âli's note of 3 October 1862; Morris to Seward, #36, 27 November 1862, USNA, Turkey 17; Young, *Corps de droit*, I, 334-335.

[110] Text in Testa, *Recueil*, VII, 745-747; Aristarchi, *Législation*, I, 19-21; Young, *Corps de droit*, I, 337-341; *Düstur*, I, 230-231.

[111] Text in Testa, *Recueil*, VII, 730-733; Aristarchi, *Législation*, I, 22-25; Young, *Corps de droit*, I, 341-345. Cf. Engelhardt, *La Turquie*, I, 213-214. The United States resisted signing longer than any power: Elliot to Granville, #91, 26 March 1873, FO 78/2226; Boker to Fish, #116, encl., 4 June 1873, USNA, Turkey 24.

[112] *Hürriyet*, #21, 16 November 1868, quoted in Sungu, "Tanzimat ve Yeni Osmanlılar," pp. 835-836.

[113] Benoît Brunswik, *Etudes pratiques sur la question d'Orient* (Paris, 1869), pp. 65-87; Morris to Seward, #265, 25 July 1868, USNA, Turkey 20; *Levant Herald*, 29 July 1868.

[114] "Zapiski . . . Ignatyeva," 1914, III, 97. Cf. Morris to Seward, #13, 19 March 1862, USNA, Turkey 17.

Possibly they indulged in this hope, though it seems farfetched. The essential in Âli's mind seems, however, to have been that a breach should be made in the capitulations. The last paragraph of the protocol recognized that the Porte reserved to itself the right of coming to an agreement with the powers as to revision of the old treaties of capitulation.

For the Tanzimat statesmen, notwithstanding that they often welcomed the support and followed the advice of the western powers in their reform measures, were at the same time waging a battle against foreign intervention of all sorts. They objected strenuously to such intervention in times of crisis, like the Cretan rebellion. They also objected continuously to the capitulations, and nibbled away at the privileges of foreigners in the empire whenever it was possible. Âli had begun this at the negotiations in Paris following the Crimean War, trying to get rid of the capitulations, which he called "an insuperable obstacle to all improvements."[115] The powers, of course, resisted any weakening of their privileges, and with reason, given the state of Turkish courts and of the tax collection system. But the Tanzimat statesmen persisted.[116] They tried to assimilate foreigners to the legal status of Ottoman subjects wherever they could. The press law of 1865 had already provided that foreigners might publish periodicals in the empire only if they accepted the jurisdiction of Ottoman officials and courts.[117] The law on the ownership of property by foreigners was another step in the same direction. Then in 1869 came an even more significant attack on the capitulations, in the form of a law on nationality.

Europe was surprised by the issue of the law on nationality and naturalization on January 19, 1869.[118] The powers at first claimed that such a measure, affecting all nations, should have been the product of international discussion. The Porte maintained that it was a domestic question. As it became apparent that the law would not be applied retroactively, and would not be used to punish Greeks in the empire after the tension over the Cretan affair, protests were allowed

[115] Great Britain, *Parliamentary Papers*, 1856, vol. 61, *Accounts and Papers*, vol. 24, "Protocols of Conferences held at Paris . . . ," p. 54.

[116] They got some aid from the Roumanian position on the same question: T. W. Riker, *The Making of Roumania* (London, 1931), pp. 230-235.

[117] Article 3.

[118] Text in Testa, *Recueil*, VII, 526-527; Aristarchi, *Législation*, I, 7-8; Young, *Corps de droit*, II, 226-229; Düstur, I, 16-18.

to drop.[119] Superficially the new law seemed only to be a step in the direction of secularization and Osmanlılık. It substituted modern political definitions of nationality and naturalization for the old criterion of conversion to Islam. So the empire moved toward Europe's secular standards. But the law also stated that all persons domiciled in Ottoman territory were to be considered Ottoman subjects unless they could prove the contrary and, further, that no Ottoman subject might become a citizen of another state without the preliminary consent of the Porte. This provision was aimed at the woeful state of affairs wherein all manner of Ottoman Christians and Levantine rabble obtained the protection of great powers by a nominal transfer of citizenship.[120] Although aimed at an abuse of capitulatory rights, this measure might also be construed as part of an attack on the system itself. The nationality law was supplemented in the summer of 1869 by three others. One established a commission to inquire into the status of presumed Ottoman subjects who claimed foreign nationality or protection. The other two set up a more stringent passport control for both Ottoman and foreign subjects.[121]

Âli's purpose in all this, as Ignatyev readily saw, was to sabotage the capitulatory privileges one by one, instead of launching a frontal attack.[122] Âli evidently contemplated a more general offensive in the spring of 1869. He inspired the semiofficial *La Turquie* to denounce the capitulations.[123] A memorandum from the Porte to the powers carried on the offensive.[124] This dealt only with abuses under the capitulations, but Âli's bitterness against the system was evident throughout. He ended his memorandum with the statement that "we have pointed out many times how the very existence of the capitulations hinders the regular functioning of the institutions, and the progressive advance of civilization, in the Empire." European opposition,

---

[119] Testa, *Recueil*, VII, pp. 529-534, 540-545, 554-560; Aristarchi, *Législation*, I, 9-11; Young, *Corps de droit*, II, 224-225.

[120] See above, chapter II. The Porte had made previous efforts to curb this abuse: Sousa, *Capitulatory Regime*, pp. 100-104. In 1860 the Porte had required that Ottoman subjects naturalized as foreign subjects leave the empire within three months after selling their goods: Safvet's note of 11 September 1860, in Williams to Cass, #98, 17 September 1860, USNA, Turkey 16. It is not apparent that this was effective.

[121] Texts in Testa, *Recueil*, VII, 561-563; Aristarchi, *Législation*, III, 99-102; Young, *Corps de droit*, II, 238-240, 272-273.

[122] "Zapiski . . . Ignatyeva," 1914, VI, 154-155. Cf. Brunswik, *Etudes pratiques*, pp. 167-267.

[123] Mordtmann, *Stambul*, I, 68.

[124] Text in Testa, *Recueil*, VII, 548-554; Young, *Corps de droit*, I, 268-274. Cf. Sousa, *Capitulatory Regime*, p. 104.

nevertheless, was too strong to permit any wholesale change in the capitulations. Instead, the policy of tangential attack was pursued. Some of the majesty of the position of the foreign consuls was removed by a regulation of 1870, signed by Âli Paşa as foreign minister, that they should no longer be greeted by salvos.[125] After Âli's death there were other efforts.[126] But the capitulations remained a galling sign to the Turks that, though admitted to the European family of nations, they were still considered inferior. Europe's attitude continued to be a psychological block to more general Turkish acceptance of western-oriented reform.

The one area in which western-oriented reform was most acceptable was the military. Since the later eighteenth century, and more rapidly since Mahmud II's destruction of the Janissaries, the army had undergone progressive changes in this direction. During the Tanzimat period the army was considerably improved, although it never reached the desired standard. The common soldier was no problem; it was generally admitted that the Turk soldier was among the best in the world.[127] What was needed was better organization, a better officer corps, better equipment, better training, better supply, better sanitation, and a general economic and educational development such as would undergird a modern army. Progress of some sort came in all these ways in the Tanzimat period, but principally in organization and equipment. This was due, in large measure, to the interest of Sultan Abdülaziz in military affairs, particularly in the visible aspects of equipment, and to the work of Hüseyin Avni Paşa, who became Âli's minister of war in 1869.[128]

Hüseyin Avni had started life as a theological student, but had switched to the military school and had capped his twenty-year army

[125] Text in Young, *Corps de droit*, III, 42, n.1; Aristarchi, *Législation*, IV, 24.

[126] Cf. Young, *Corps de droit*, I, 258-259, on an attempt to deny foreign dragomans the right to appear in the new civil and criminal courts, 1875; and IV, 342, on an Ottoman protest against the foreign post offices as an anachronism and violation of sovereignty, 1874.

[127] "Your privates proved that they are without equal," Francis Joseph was reported to have said to Âli, of the Crimean period: Cevdet, *Tezâkir*, p. 44.

[128] For varying estimates of the Ottoman army between 1856 and 1869 see Engelhardt, *La Turquie*, I, 115-121; Millingen (an officer), *La Turquie*, pp. 38-61, 439-444; Mordtmann, *Stambul*, I, 16-18; F. W. von Reden, *Die Türkei und Griechenland in ihrer Entwicklungsfähigkeit* (Frankfurt a.M., 1856), pp. 317-329.

career as a successful general in Crete, fighting rebellion.[129] When he came to be minister of war, the Ottoman army was still organized on the plan adopted in 1842. Infantry, cavalry, and engineer corps were on the French model, artillery on the Prussian. The six army corps, plus reserves, and a dubious 120,000 men owed by the tributary states, gave a maximum of 500,000 possible effectives. Soldiers were required to do five years' active service and to spend a further seven in the reserves.[130] Since that time, a good many modern weapons had been acquired, and the training of officers improved, but no basic changes had been made. Hüseyin Avni calculated that such an army was insufficient for the defense of the empire, and submitted to Abdülaziz in 1869 a memorandum which outlined a reorganization that would produce a dependable army of over 700,000, if needed.[131] The law issued later that year on the basis of his recommendations placed the reserves for the first time on an effective and rational basis.[132] The Prussian organization of 1860 served as the model. The period of active service was reduced from five to four years, and a new active reserve status of two years was created, along with two further reserve categories of six and eight years respectively. There were not in fact enough trained officers to command the reserves, so that the actual strength was estimated at something over 300,000 by some.[133] Yet a seventh army corps was created, based on the Yemen, and in the Russo-Turkish War of 1877-1878 there were 750,000 under arms.[134]

Although all kinds of imperfections remained—notably still an officer corps of most uneven quality, lack of good communication and supply and even of maps—the army by the end of the Tanzimat period seems to have been in reasonably good shape. It was equipped with Henry-Martini and Snider rifles, with heavy Krupp guns, and outfitted in comfortable Zouave costume. Though the Turkish army was defeated in 1878 by the Russians, the first two categories of reserves were shown to be as good as the regulars.[135] The Russian ambassador

---

[129] Ahmed Saib, *Vak'a-i Sultan Abdülaziz*, pp. 80-81; J. H. Mordtmann, "Ḥusain 'Awnī Pasha," *Encyclopaedia of Islam*, II, 342.

[130] H. Zboinski, *Armée ottomane* (Paris, 1877), pp. 12-13.

[131] Text in *ibid.*, pp. 13-21.

[132] Text in Aristarchi, *Législation*, III, 514-519.

[133] Ubicini, *Etat présent*, pp. 178-179.

[134] Necati Tacan, "Tanzimat ve Ordu," *Tanzimat*, I, 135.

[135] W. E. D. Allen and Paul Muratoff, *Caucasian Battlefields* (Cambridge, 1953), pp. 111-114, 217; Zboinski, *Armée ottomane*, pp. viii, 75-77, 85. Zboinski was a Belgian, professor at the İstanbul military school. For a more cynical picture by a

Ignatyev, who would have the best reason of any to follow Ottoman military progress closely, thought the reorganized army quite effective and generally underestimated.[136] Cevdet Paşa somewhat complacently observed in 1872 that the military service had been brought up to the required level.[137] An Austrian officer who had served in the Ottoman army during the Crimean War observed a great improvement by 1874 in the officer corps and in general *esprit*. He noted also that, whereas formerly most officers had risen from the ranks, now the products of the westernized military education were increasing, creating a class distinction among the military.[138] This was to have its effect later on Ottoman political life as well as on the army. And Hüseyin Avni, the reorganizer of the army, could count on the support of a good many officers and cadets when he combined with Midhat to overthrow Abdülaziz in 1876.

The Ottoman navy was Abdülaziz's favorite plaything. Through his efforts it was, by 1876, the third most powerful in Europe with regard to the number and armament of its ships. More than twenty ironclads had been acquired since 1864.[139] But in personnel and spirit it could not match the army, and there was no organizer like Hüseyin Avni to make it effective. Hobart Paşa, the English sailor and adventurer who took charge of the Halki naval school about 1867, did not fill the bill. It is likely, however, that the increase in naval as well as land strength gave the Turks an increased confidence and contributed to their increasingly pugnacious attitude toward Europe and European intervention in the 1870's. The armed forces were a bulwark for the empire that the Tanzimat statesmen were trying to resuscitate. But the forces did not support the sultan who had shown such interest in them. The navy also took a hand in the deposition of Abdülaziz in 1876.

The years 1870 and 1871 marked the end of an era in the Ottoman Empire as much as in western Europe. Âli Paşa died in September

---

French engineer working in the Balkans, see F. Bianconi, *La question d'Orient dévoilée* (Paris, 1876), pp. 137-148.

[136] "Zapiski . . . Ignatyeva," 1915, IV, 228-230.

[137] Mardin, *Cevdet*, p. 345.

[138] Murad Effendi [Franz von Werner], *Türkische Skizzen* (Leipzig, 1877), II, 118-132.

[139] Zboinski, *Armée ottomane*, pp. ix, 121-128. Cf. Ubicini, *Etat présent*, p. 183, who seems to list some wooden ships as armored.

1871. Thereafter the lack of a strong hand in guiding the empire toward gradual westernization was sorely felt. But, even before Âli's death, his policy had suffered when the Second Empire met defeat at the hands of Prussia. The collapse of France affected the Ottoman Empire's domestic situation, as well as its relationships with the powers, since the French support and example had been the strongest in the preceding decade.

Little indications of the French defeat were at once noticeable in İstanbul. The editor of *La Turquie* said that, sitting in a public garden in the capital, he could see French prestige fall as the war bulletins came in.[140] The study of French declined. An Armenian father asked that Robert College teach his son "Prussian" instead of French.[141] Âli, who favored France though he remained diplomatically reticent during the war, was hurt by the French defeat. He was also worried by Russia's seizure of the chance to declare null the Black Sea clause of the Paris treaty of 1856, which forbade Russian armament on the Black Sea. He tried to put the best face possible on both matters, accepting the Russian action since there was no great power support to combat it, declaring that French influence in the Ottoman Empire had not always been good, and hoping that Prussia would help to maintain the empire.[142] But the new German Empire was not yet ready to fill the gap, and for a time the defeat of France meant that Russian influence in İstanbul, in the person of Ambassador Ignatyev, was in the ascendant. The French defeat was not unpleasing to some—conservative opponents of Âli, palace intriguers, even Abdülaziz himself. The sultan may have harbored a dislike of Napoleon III, and he certainly had admired Prussian arms since his trip in 1867.[143] Possibly Abdülaziz also felt that the French defeat would help to loosen the control of Âli, under which he chafed.

Âli, in fact, survived the Second Empire only by a year. In June of 1871 he fell ill and kept to his house in Bebek. Since at this time Âli

---

[140] Mismer, *Souvenirs*, p. 174.

[141] Wood to Clark, 10 October 1871, ABCFM, vol. 286, #404. Cf. De Salve, "L'enseignement en Turquie," p. 849.

[142] Mordtmann, *Stambul*, I, 26; Mehmed Memduh, *Mirât-ı şuûnat*, p. 42; Ahmed Saib, *Vaka-i Sultan Abdülaziz*, p. 46; Ludwig Raschdau, "Aus dem politischen Nachlass des Unterstaatssekretärs Dr. Busch," *Deutsche Rundschau*, 137 (December 1908), 386-388; Anton Graf Prokesch-Osten, "Erinnerungen aus den Jahren 1870 und 1871," *Deutsche Revue*, IV (1880), 19; "Zapiski . . . Ignatyeva," 1914, IV, 90-93.

[143] Raschdau, "Nachlass . . . Dr. Busch," pp. 387-388; Georges Douin, *Histoire du règne du Khédive Ismail* (Rome, 1933-1934), II, 581.

was acting as grand vezir, foreign minister, and minister of the interior, it was difficult to conduct the business of government. Characteristically, Âli clung to power and to life as long as possible, while the various public men who aspired to the grand vezirate pulled all possible wires to assure themselves the succession. Little cliques formed, each with its palace contact, to struggle for the mantle. The khedive Ismail, who had never been able to buy Âli, now used his money and his influence against Mustafa Fazıl and Halil Şerif, and to bribe in his favor Mahmud Nedim, Safvet Paşa, and other worthies. Nor did he fail to satisfy Abdülaziz's craving for rare birds and animals of all sorts for his collection.[144]

At once it became apparent that Âli had no obvious successor. For ten years he and Fuad had conducted the business of the government with almost no interruptions. After Fuad's death in February 1869 Âli's grip on the administration had tightened. He dug a wide moat around his tenure of office and trained up no political heirs. This was his greatest disservice to the state. Neither in the conduct of foreign relations, at which he had excelled, nor in the domestic program of gradual reform, had Âli reared any outstanding disciple. His failure in this regard may have been due to his innate jealousy of office or to his memory of how he and Fuad, Reşid Paşa's disciples, had quarreled with the master at the end of his life. Potential rivals had been kept either in specialized positions—men like Safvet or Edhem Paşas —or, for the most part, in provincial governorships—like Midhat Paşa.[145] The sultan also had been kept relatively isolated from affairs and from other statesmen by Âli and Fuad. In part, this accorded with the sultan's wish, since he abhorred interviews with foreign ambassadors. In part, it was a necessity for the welfare of the state, since Abdülaziz was growing more peculiar, exhibiting signs of possible mental unbalance.[146] But Abdülaziz was tired of his tutelage to the elder statesman. The agent of the khedive Ismail reported on July 26 that Abdülaziz was pleased at the prospect of Âli's death.[147]

At the end of August Âli retired into his harem, never to emerge.

[144] Douin, *Khédive Ismail*, II, 599-607; Pierre Crabitès, *Ismail the Maligned Khedive* (London, 1933), pp. 179-192.
[145] Cf. Raschdau, "Nachlass . . . Dr. Busch," p. 388; "Zapiski . . . Ignatyeva," 1914, IV, 90.
[146] Raschdau, "Nachlass . . . Dr. Busch," pp. 384-387; *idem*, "Diplomatenleben am Bosporus," *Deutsche Rundschau*, 138 (1909), 400-402.
[147] Crabitès, *Ismail*, p. 179.

On September 6, 1871, he died. The next day *La Turquie* appeared with black borders. It was generally recognized that a great man was gone. Some, among European observers particularly, used language tinged with a sense of tragedy like that used in 1890 when Bismarck was dropped from office by the young kaiser; the great stabilizing influence was gone.[148] But Âli was criticized also in the obituaries that appeared.[149] And within the empire interest centered on the question of who would succeed Âli. Mahmud Nedim, at the moment minister of the navy and once the candidate of some of the New Ottomans, was the one whom Sultan Abdülaziz appointed. But Abdülaziz himself seemed desirous of exercising a greater influence within the administration. In reality there was a sort of political vacuum, now that Âli was gone and French influence had declined. No single individual could fill Âli's shoes. And his policy of gradual secularization, of pursuit of Osmanlılık, of general modernization, received a setback. In its place came a renascent Islamic sentiment and a rising anti-Europeanism which colored the events of the next few years.

[148] Cf. Elliott to Granville, #318, 7 September 1871, FO 78/2177.
[149] Cf. *Levant Herald*, 7 September 1871.

CHAPTER VIII

THE PERIOD OF CHAOS, 1871-1875

For four years after Âli Paşa's death the Ottoman domestic situation became progressively more confused. Mahmud Nedim's grand vezirate of almost a year produced only administrative instability. Within the next three years there followed six grand vezirates. These changes at the top intensified a process of office-shifting in lower ranks that became chaotic at times. Meanwhile Sultan Abdülaziz, whose personal vagaries grew with the years, exercised more influence within the administration than before, and added to the instability by resurrecting his plan to alter the succession to the throne. Economically, the empire suffered also, both from an agricultural crisis in 1873 and 1874 and from a treasury crisis which came to a head in 1875. A long-drawn-out war against tribesmen in the Yemen added to the financial difficulties. Ismail of Egypt pursued his course of cajolery and bribery to attain yet greater independence of the Porte. By the summer of 1875 the revolt in Herzegovina, which in other circumstances might not have had such serious results, was almost the last straw. It brought renewed European pressures on the empire and increased financial problems. The half decade proved to be a prelude to revolution in 1876, for within these years various sorts of personal, economic, and political discontent arose which finally merged to facilitate the overthrow of Abdülaziz himself.

The currents of discontent were not well defined. Some men simply complained of capricious government or of economic want. Others complained of autocracy and looked to constitutional government as the remedy. Still others sought to reject the Tanzimat, to return to conservative Islam, and to express this politically by emphasizing the sultan's role as caliph of all Muslims. If there were in the years 1871 to 1875 any common denominator, it was the familiar broad desire to strengthen the empire against European pressures and domestic separatism. This was most often expressed in the 1870's by a renascent antiwesternism which had within it some elements of Ottoman patriotism, rather more of Islamic conservatism, and even a bit of pan-Islamic sentiment.

In part, the new wave of religious sentiment seems to have been simply a reaction against the secularizing policies of Âli and the pressures of Europeans. It probably drew strength, however, from new sources also. One of these was Jemaleddin el Afghani, who appeared in İstanbul in 1870 after a somewhat stormy early career in Afghan politics. Jemaleddin had already acquired quite a reputation for learning, and seems to have been greeted with acclaim in the capital, welcomed by Âli, and given a position on the council of education. Shortly he was invited to lecture in the mosques of Ayasofya and Sultan Ahmed, and also to give an address under the auspices of the ephemeral university then being recreated after the education reform of 1869. Before an audience of statesmen and journalists he spoke of prophecy and philosophy as the soul of the body politic. Hasan Fehmi, *şeyhülislâm* at the moment, was apparently jealous of Jemaleddin's popularity, and accused him of unorthodoxy in insinuating that prophecy was a craft and the Prophet a craftsman. The ensuing controversy aroused such furor that the Porte asked Jemaleddin to leave. He departed for Cairo in March of 1871, there to be given a stipend by Ismail's government, with freedom to teach.[1]

How much influence Jemaleddin had on Turkish opinion during his short stay it is hard to say. His later influence in Egypt, in Iran, and again in the Ottoman Empire in the 1890's was certainly greater. But it is a legitimate surmise that his preaching of a revived Islam, of borrowing from the West to combat the West, and of the need for Muslim peoples to work together contributed something to the intensified Islamic and anti-European sentiment of the 1870's in the empire. In some of these views Jemaleddin paralleled opinions of the New Ottomans.[2]

Another of the sources for revived Islamic sentiment was the in-

---

[1] Edward G. Browne, *The Persian Revolution of 1905-1908* (Cambridge, 1910), pp. 2-30; Ignaz Goldziher, "Djamāl al-Dīn al-Afg̲h̲ānī," *Encyclopaedia of Islam*, I, 1008-1011; Charles C. Adams, *Islam and Modernism in Egypt* (London, 1933), pp. 6, 13-14; Auriant, "Un émir afghan, adversaire de l'Angleterre en Orient; Djemmal ed Dine, ténébreux agitateur," *Mercure de France*, 288 (1 December 1938), 316-330; Ettore Rossi, "Il centenario della nascita di Gemal ud-Din el-Afghani celebrate a Kabul," *Oriente Moderno*, 20:5 (May 1940), 262-265.

[2] Auriant, "Emir afghan," pp. 320-321, claims that Jemaleddin got along well with the "Young Turkey" party. But during Jemaleddin's stay in İstanbul the leading New Ottomans were still in Europe, except that Mustafa Fazıl had returned and Namık Kemal came back at the end of 1870. Auriant says also that Jemaleddin was initiated into a Freemasonic lodge in İstanbul, which may have been the same that Mustafa Fazıl and Namık Kemal had joined.

terest of Ottoman Turks and of their government in their Muslim Turkish brethren of Central Asia. Because the nineteenth-century Ottoman Empire was so inextricably bound to the West by its reform programs, its Balkan problems, and the actions of European powers, the continuing contacts with the Muslim world of the East are often forgotten. They existed, nevertheless, represented by occasional outstanding individuals like Jemaleddin, by a greater number of nameless travellers or of pilgrims to Mecca, who sometimes came on to İstanbul, and by dervishes from Central Asia who lived in tekkes maintained for them in İstanbul by pious Muslims.[3] In the 1860's and 1870's the Ottoman Turks' awareness of other Muslim and Turkish peoples was increased by upheavals in inner Asia. The Panthais, Chinese Muslims in Yunnan province, revolted and set up a state of their own. Yakub Beg successfully wrested Turkestan from Chinese control and governed it as a Muslim state, centered on Kashgar. Meanwhile the sporadic Russian advance against the independent Turkish khanates east of the Caspian had been seriously resumed in the 1860's. By 1870 Tashkent, Bokhara, and Samarkand were under Russian dominion, while Khiva and Khokand were threatened.[4] The awareness was not only religious and cultural, but political, since the Turkish peoples of Central Asia were caught in the great Anglo-Russian contest that had begun in the 1830's, and they appealed to the Ottoman Empire, as well as to Britain, for help. Between the Crimean War period and 1871 missions to İstanbul had come from Khiva, Khokand, Bokhara, and Kashgar, and even from the Afghans and the Panthais. The Porte had evidently sent a military instructor to Bokhara, but the longing of the Central Asian Muslims for support from İstanbul met with no real satisfaction. Obviously the Ottomans were in no position to wage war beyond the Caspian—much less so than in the Caucasus, where the Circassians and Shamil had gone down before Russian might despite Ottoman sympathy for them. The only tie was a vague recognition by the Turkestanis of Abdülaziz as caliph and his acceptance of this empty honor, symbolized by the ceremonial reception of Central Asian embassies.[5]

[3] Cf. "Zapiski Grapha N. P. Ignatyeva (1864-1874)," *Izvestiia Ministerstva Inostrannykh Diel*, 1915, IV, 227; Arminius Vambéry, *History of Bokhara* (London, 1873), p. 419 and n.; *idem*, "Jugendwanderungen," *Globus*, 25 (1874), 171; D. C. Boulger, *The Life of Yakoob Beg* (London, 1878), p. 170.

[4] B. H. Sumner, *Russia and the Balkans, 1870-1880* (Oxford, 1937), pp. 36-37, 45-46, 51-52.

[5] On political and sentimental connections 1854-1871: Cevdet Paşa, *Tezâkir 1-12*,

While Âli Paşa lived, Ottoman connections with Central Asia remained ceremonial only, though Âli is said to have expressed interest in the desire of Turkomans to become subjects of the sultan and so gain protection against Russia.[6] But after 1871 the Porte was willing to go a little farther. Bokharan appeals to the sultan and to Britain for aid evidently met with no results in İstanbul.[7] Yakub Beg, however, whose state was a going concern in the 1870's, got more positive results. His envoy Seyyid Mahmud Yakub, who since the early 1860's had been shuttling between Central Asia and İstanbul as representative first of Khokand and then of Kashgar, appeared again in İstanbul in 1873. The mission, facilitated by Britain, travelled via India. It returned to Kashgar with a group of Ottoman Turks, among them four army officers to act as military instructors, and with a few light weapons. Seyyid Mahmud Yakub also brought back from İstanbul the title of *âmir* for Yakub Beg and some kind of promise of protection, however unreal, from Abdülaziz as "suzerain." Yakub proceeded to strike coins in the sultan's name which bore the inscription "Protected Kashgar," and Abdülaziz's name was mentioned in the prayers.[8] Again in 1875 the same envoy came to İstanbul, was well re-

ed. Cavid Baysun (Ankara, 1953), pp. 46-47; Fatma Aliye, *Ahmed Cevdet Paşa ve zamanı* (İstanbul, 1332), p. 89; Boulger, *Yakoob Beg*, pp. 169-170; Eugene Schuyler, *Turkistan* (New York, 1876), I, 355, n.1, and II, 303, 308; Vambéry, *History of Bokhara*, p. 390; idem, *Travels in Central Asia* (New York, 1865), pp. 71, 157-158, 162, 175, 221, 484-485; Robert Shaw, *Visits to High Tartary, Yarkand, and Kashghar* (London, 1871), pp. 208-209; Ethel Forsyth, ed., *Autobiography and Reminiscences of Sir Douglas Forsyth* (London, 1887), p. 60; Jean Deny, *Sommaire des archives turques du Caire* (Cairo, 1930), plates LI and LII; Morris to Hunter, #117, 3 July 1865, USNA, Turkey 18; Sublime Porte to British Embassy, 3 October 1868, FO 195/893, #353; Elliot to Stanley, #55, encl., 4 December 1867, FO 78/1965; "Zapiski . . . Ignatyeva," 1915, IV, 227.
[6] Vambéry, *His Life and Adventures* (New York, 1883?), p. 321. Fuad's political testament also shows awareness of the ring of Sunni Muslims around Iran: James L. Farley, *Turks and Christians* (London, 1876), p. 241.
[7] Stanton (Cairo) to Granville, #2, 10 January 1872, FO 78/2229; Elliot to Granville, #76, 1 July 1872, and #85, 6 July 1872, FO 78/2218.
[8] Elliot to Granville, #147, 14 May 1873, #155, confidential, 20 May 1873, and #172, 30 May 1873, FO 78/2267; Forsyth, *Autobiography*, pp. 134-135, 158; H. W. Bellew, *Kashmir and Kashghar* (London, 1875), pp. 188, 213, 304; Boulger, *Yakoob Beg*, p. 196. There is some question as to whether Yakub sought, himself took, or was granted by Abdülaziz the designation of *âmir ul müminin*, "commander of the faithful," a title used by the caliphs and sometimes by Ottoman sultans: Bellew, *Kashmir and Kashghar*, p. 304; Owen Lattimore, *Pivot of Asia* (Boston, 1950), p. 35; Julius Debelak, "Die central-asiatische Frage," *Streffleur's Oesterreichische Militärische Zeitschrift*, 16 (1875), 129; Louis E. Frechtling, "Anglo-Russian Rivalry in Eastern Turkistan, 1863-1881," *Royal Central Asian Journal*, 26:3 (July 1939), 479. This seems unlikely.

ceived by Abdülaziz, and returned with two thousand Snider breech-loading rifles and six fieldpieces—a fact which he tried to conceal from Ignatyev, whom he called "Satan personified."[9] But the cordial reception accorded the embassy, the decorations given its members, and the fact that Turkish officers were on loan to Yakub Beg were well publicized in İstanbul.[10] So also, the next year, was the position of Yakub Beg as "vassal" to the sultan.[11]

Inevitably there was greater interest among Ottomans in the Turks of Central Asia, especially as the Russian advance continued in the 1870's, first against Khiva and then Khokand. Ali Suavi, still in Paris, tried to stimulate the interest with a little book on Khiva which emphasized the support given it by Ottoman sultans up to Mahmud II.[12] Various accounts of travel in Turkestan were translated into Turkish.[13] Turkish merchants and villagers, even in the Balkans, were reported eager for news of Central Asia and growing more anti-Russian in their sentiment.[14] The khan of Khiva hoped for another Crimean alliance to beat back the Russians. The Porte knew this to be impossible; yet some Ottoman Turks, as the tensions with Russia grew, would have liked to act to free Central Asia.[15] There may have been some nascent feeling of Turkishness or of pan-Turkism in these expressions of interest in Central Asia; if so, it was extremely slight.[16] The main components of public feeling in the 1870's were a political Russophobia and an emphasis on Islam which more and more verged on pan-Islamic sentiment.

Pan-Islamism was, in part, manufactured in the Muslim world outside of the Ottoman Empire. Some Muslim Turks, threatened by Russia and looking to the sultan for aid, hoped he would declare a jihad.[17]

[9] Elliot to Derby, #247, 18 May 1875, FO 78/2383; #331, 5 July 1875, FO 78/2384; #464, 22 August 1875, FO 78/2385. Cf. Schuyler, *Turkistan*, II, 324-325.
[10] *La Turquie*, 31 July and 4 August 1875.
[11] *Levant Herald*, 19 August and 14 September 1876.
[12] *Hive* (Paris, 1290), republished as *Hive fi muharrem 1290* (İstanbul, 1326). Cf. İ. H. Danişmend, *Ali Suâvi'nin türkçülüğü* (İstanbul, 1942), pp. 27-28, 35-36.
[13] MacGahan (? "Mageman")'s, as *Hive seyahatnamesi ve tarihi* (İstanbul, 1292); Schuyler's, as *Musavver Türkistan tarihi ve seyahatnamesi* (İstanbul, 1294).
[14] W. G. Palgrave, *Essays on Eastern Questions* (London, 1872), p. 61; "Opinions of the Turkish People on Central Asia," *Diplomatic Review*, 21:2 (April 1873), 134-136. Both sources are Russophobe.
[15] *Ibid.*; Fred Burnaby, *A Ride to Khiva* (New York, 1877), pp. 258-259; *idem*, *On Horseback Through Asia Minor* (London, 1877), II, 51.
[16] Ali Suavi had some such feeling, which Danişmend, in *Ali Suâvi'nin türkçülüğü*, tends to exaggerate.
[17] Vambéry, *Travels*, p. 221.

Some Indian Muslims, wistfully longing for their vanished glory, also wanted a jihad, but directed against Britain. Among them were a group of exiles living in Istanbul, on stipends granted by the Ottoman government, who had fairly wide Muslim connections.[18] Englishmen also contributed to building pan-Islam, both in order to combat Russia and also to keep the affection of Indian Muslims by demonstrating support for the Ottoman Muslims and the sultan-caliph.[19] Probably Russians contributed unwittingly to the rise of pan-Islamism; there are grounds for suspecting that pan-Slavism, which came of age in the late 1860's, helped to produce a pan-Islamic reaction. In part, pan-Islamism was manufactured by Tunisian Arabs within the empire who sought the sultan's support against great power threats just as did the Muslims of Central Asia. Hayreddin Paşa, arriving in Istanbul in 1871 to secure the desired ferman, declared that the sultan had a great hold over the popular Muslim mind in Tunis.[20] Then again, a sort of Arab-Turk pan-Islamism was used by the Ottomans as a weapon against separatist Egyptian tendencies. The newspaper *Basiret* in 1871 carried an article promoting the concept of the unity of Islam and suggesting that Turkish troops occupy Egyptian ports while Egyptian troops should be used elsewhere in the empire. The semiofficial *La Turquie* followed the same tack in proclaiming that the Ottoman task was to link the scattered Muslim elements of the empire, Egypt and Tunis included. "Islam is not only a religion, it is a nationality," declared *La Turquie*. "The Arabs like the Turks recognize the sultan of Constantinople as legitimate sovereign and caliph."[21] Ottoman arms were soon engaged in the reconquest of the Yemen in an attempt to keep yet another Arab area from going the way of tribal independence or succumbing to Ismail's intrigues.[22] In 1871 also the official

[18] Elliot to Derby, #339, confidential, 12 July 1875, and encl., FO 78/2384.

[19] D. E. Lee, "The Origins of Pan-Islamism," *American Historical Review*, 47:2 (January 1942), 284-286; H. A. M. Butler-Johnstone, *The Eastern Question* (London, 1875), p. 3.

[20] Elliot to Granville, #348, confidential, 27 September 1871, FO 78/2177. The Bey wanted not only protection against France, Italy, and Egypt, but wanted to make his position hereditary in his own family: cf. Elliot to Granville, #323, confidential, 8 September 1871, and #347, confidential, 23 September 1871; İ. H. Uzunçarşılı, "Tunus'un 1881'de Fransa tarafından işgaline kadar burada valilik eden Hüseynî âilesi," *Belleten*, 18:72 (October 1954), 556-557, 568-569.

[21] Georges Douin, *Histoire du règne du Khédive Ismail* (Rome, 1933-1934), II, 586-587; M. Sabry, *L'empire égyptien sous Ismail* (Paris, 1933), p. 126.

[22] (Anonymous), "A Glimpse of the Yemen Insurrection," *Chambers's Journal*, 14 October 1871, pp. 641-644, and 21 October 1871, pp. 659-662; Douin, *Khédive Ismail*, II, 591.

journal of the Baghdad vilayet, where Midhat was still governor, boldly asserted that the Algerian Arabs in revolt against France were
legitimate subjects of the Porte.[23]

In response to these various events and pressures the tendency toward pan-Islamic sentiment grew in İstanbul. The irrepressible *Basiret*
made itself the spokesman for the Muslim world. It was the *Basiret*
press which published the translated accounts of travel in Turkestan.
The newspaper looked beyond the Arab and Turk worlds, calling in
1873 for a campaign against China to aid the Panthais and for a Muslim crusade against Europe to help the Algerians and the Muslims of
India.[24] *Basiret*'s most extravagant pan-Islamic excursion concerned
the Dutch East Indies. The sultan of Atchin, fighting the Dutch in
Sumatra, appealed to Abdülaziz as his suzerain for aid. The Porte
was embarrassed by the impossible request, but the Ottoman sultan as
head of the Muslim religion, said the foreign minister, could not refuse to receive the emissary from Sumatra. *Basiret* then declared with
joy in July 1873 that the Porte would send eight warships against the
Netherlands. Upon this, *Basiret* was suspended for a time, and the
matter settled by negotiation between the Dutch and the Turks,
probably at the insistence of European diplomats and especially of
Ignatyev, who feared the precedent of armed aid to non-Ottoman
Muslims.[25] *Basiret* represented a fairly large segment of Turkish opinion. It was reputed the most widely read İstanbul paper.[26] Its tendencies accorded with the drive against the capitulations which Âli had
initiated, with the emphasis on the cultural bonds of Islam characteristic of the New Ottomans, and with the natural inclination of Turks
to think of their sultan as the ruler of the world, superior to other
rulers, even non-Muslim. And Abdülaziz seems to have indulged in
some dreams of restoring the glory of the caliphate.[27] A pamphlet
entitled *The Union of Islam*, written by a functionary of the mixed

[23] Edouard Engelhardt, *La Turquie et le Tanzimat* (Paris, 1882-1884), II, 117
and n.1.

[24] A. D. Mordtmann, *Stambul und das moderne Türkenthum* (Leipzig, 1877-
1878), I, 241-242.

[25] Elliot to Granville, #145, 8 May 1873, and #160, 23 May 1873, FO 78/2267;
Mordtmann, *Stambul*, I, 240-241; "Zapiski . . . Ignatyeva," 1915, IV, 226.

[26] Mordtmann, *Stambul*, I, 242.

[27] "Zapiski . . . Ignatyeva," 1915, I, 170, and IV, 225, 227; Mordtmann, *Stambul*, I, 240; Karl Braun-Wiesbaden, *Eine türkische Reise* (Stuttgart, 1876), II, 44-
45; Murad Efendi [Franz von Werner], *Türkische Skizzen* (Leipzig, 1877), I, 95.

maritime commercial court in İstanbul, enjoyed a considerable success and was translated into Arabic. Esad Efendi, its author, called on pilgrims to come to Mecca to unite and spread Islam everywhere.[28]

Pan-Islamism, of course, amounted to nothing as a political movement. The Muslims of the world did not unite against Russia, Britain, France, China, and the Netherlands. The Ottoman Empire did not aid Muslims outside its borders, nor did they, in turn, aid the Ottoman Turks. This phase of pan-Islamism was a futile search for military aid and a sentimental attachment to the concept of the caliphate. But within the Ottoman Empire the pan-Islamic movement did have some concrete results. It helped to produce a sort of Islamic patriotism, an antiwestern rigidity, which was revealed in the crisis of 1876-1877. When the newspaper *Sabah* during that crisis warned Europe of attack by 300,000,000 Muslims, this was an empty threat; but Ottoman diplomacy at the same time was more unyielding than it had previously been, supported as it was by this kind of sentiment.[29] The more immediate practical effect of the pan-Islamic movement was to reinforce after Âli's death the slowdown of the secularizing, westernizing reform program. *Basiret* was also the organ for expressing this kind of anti-Europeanism.[30]

The anti-Europeanism of the 1870's became almost tangible. "Hostility to foreigners, and jealousy of their presence and operations of every description, commercial, educational, and religious, are on the evident increase," wrote in early 1874 an American who had lived in Syria since the Hatt-ı Hümayun.[31] The hostility was observable in many little ways—in the progressive Turkification of Galatasaray, in the battle of students in the military medical school against Pera Levantines over whether a French chanteuse should sing a song about the "joli Turque" instead of the "Marseillaise," in the actions of a mob that wrecked a modernized school that gave "*gâvur*" lessons.[32]

---

[28] Mordtmann, *Stambul*, II, 129-130. Esad was also an editor of *Basiret*. Cf. chapter x below, n.40.

[29] On *Sabah*: *ibid.*, I, 258. Cf. George Campbell, *A Handy Book on the Eastern Question* (London, 1876), p. 41.

[30] V. Hoskiær, *Et Besøg i Grækenland, Ægypten og Tyrkiet* (Copenhagen, 1879), p. 174.

[31] Henry Harris Jessup to Rev. F. F. Ellinwood, 12 February 1874, quoted in Jessup, *Fifty-Three Years in Syria* (New York, 1910), II, 438.

[32] *Levant Herald*, 18 January 1873; Osman Şevki Uludağ, "Tanzimat ve hekimlik," *Tanzimat*, I (İstanbul, 1940), 975 and n.2; Osman Ergin, *Türkiye maarif tarihi* (İstanbul, 1939-1943), II, 395-397.

The government sponsored in 1873 a picture book of costumes of the Turkish people wherein were found sentiments not current before 1870 in official Tanzimat circles. The "Europeanizer," the "progressive," was derided, while the "bourgeois Muslim of the old school" was praised, who had "remained in spite of, in opposition to, and against all, faithful to the old usages and national customs."[33] In Anatolia the precepts of Islam seemed to be more rigorously observed than heretofore.[34] Foreign missionaries felt the change in atmosphere. Whereas in 1864 a temporary closing of the American mission bookstore was revealed to be a political maneuver by Âli to keep the respect of conservatives, a prohibition in 1874 of the sale of Christian scriptures in Turkish, if printed in Arabic characters, was motivated by a deeper antiforeign feeling. The government also placed new obstacles in the way of converting Muslims to Christianity.[35] By 1876 *Basiret*, as might be expected, was attacking mission schools run by Americans, British, and Germans as founts of the foreign poison of Protestant proselytism, while *Hakikat* (*Truth*), the journal of the ministry of war in İstanbul, generally blamed European poison for the bad conditions in the empire.[36]

In view of this climate of feeling in the 1870's, it was a disaster for the progress of Ottoman reform that there was no statesman of the calibre of Âli to take charge. The ensuing administrative chaos was, in part, caused simply by the lack of an heir to Âli. In part, it was calculated policy by Mehmud Nedim. In part, it came from Abdülaziz, who now embarked on a period of personal rule such as the empire had not seen since the death of Mahmud II. The Janissary and *derebeyi* counterweights existed no more. The Porte's bureaucracy was partially paralyzed by the constant shifting of officials. In this the sultan seems to have played a large part. His character, his interests, and his idiosyncracies further added to the chaos.

[33] Hamdy Bey, *Les costumes populaires de la Turquie en 1873* (Constantinople, 1873), plates I and II, and pp. 13-14.

[34] Palgrave, *Essays*, pp. 111-120, 160.

[35] Brown to Seward, #8, 23 July 1864, and Morris to Seward, private, 8 September 1864, USNA, Turkey 18; Greene to Clark, 11 August 1874, ABCFM, vol. 354, #21, and "Memorandum in regard to Religious Toleration in Turkey," 14 November 1874, ABCFM, vol. 352, #73; Leland J. Gordon, *American Relations with Turkey* (Philadelphia, 1932), p. 228; Charles T. Riggs, "The Turkish Translations of the Bible," *Moslem World*, 30:3 (July 1940), 245.

[36] Mordtmann, *Stambul*, I, 154, and II, 60-62.

When Âli died, Sultan Abdülaziz is reported to have said that he was at last a free man.[37] This was in large measure true. Abdülaziz had, of course, still to depend on ministers and bureaucrats, but they could no longer control him without an Âli. Instead, they truckled to him in their competition for high office. The center of gravity had shifted from the Porte to the Palace. To Halil Şerif, Abdülaziz expressed admiration for the absolutism of the tsar, and said he had learned from this that there should be no first minister, but that each minister should be responsible to the sultan and work with him.[38] The sultan himself seems to have been responsible for a good deal of office-shifting, and to have fired without severance pay "many men whose beards had grown gray from thirty-five to forty years service to the state."[39] It is unclear whether this was pure caprice, or a means of preventing any officials from becoming entrenched in influential positions, or a search for those who would satisfy his whims most fully, or a search for able men. It is likely, however, that the sultan's actions were, in part, simply reaction to Âli's long period of control, and partly a result of his increasing idiosyncracies, which seemed to border on megalomania.

The least of his idiosyncracies was a craze for spending money on warships, on his palaces and harem and household employees, on his collections of small horses and other animals, on music boxes, and on crystal windows for his yacht.[40] This, of course, opened up the way for favor-seeking officials to deplete the treasury to satisfy Abdülaziz, and for outsiders like the khedive Ismail to curry favor with gifts. Another *idée fixe* was to change the succession in favor of his son Yusuf İzzeddin, who when Âli died was an ill-educated boy of almost fourteen.[41] Rumors that such a change was imminent had been current

---

[37] Henry Elliot, "The Death of Abdul Aziz and of Turkish Reform," *Nineteenth Century*, 23 (1888), 277; İbnülemin Mahmud Kemal İnal, *Osmanlı devrinde son sadrıâzamlar* (İstanbul, 1940-1953), p. 28; "Zapiski . . . Ignatyeva," 1915, I, 146.

[38] Douin, *Khédive Ismail*, II, 707. Cf. Horace Rumbold, *Recollections of a Diplomatist* (London, 1902), II, 326; *Levant Herald*, 26 February 1873.

[39] Ahmed Midhat, *Üss-i inkılâb* (İstanbul, 1294-1295), I, 202; Hoskiær, *Besøg*, p. 150.

[40] Ali Haydar Midhat, *Midhat-Pacha. Sa vie, son oeuvre* (Paris, 1908), pp. 28-30, n.1; Ahmed Midhat, *Üss-i inkılâb*, II, 254-255; Mithat Cemal Kuntay, *Namık Kemal* (İstanbul, 1944-1956), I, 102 and n.6,7; Hajo Holborn, ed., *Aufzeichnungen und Erinnerungen aus dem Leben des Botschafters Joseph Maria von Radowitz* (Berlin, 1925), I, 239.

[41] A. D. Alderson, *The Structure of the Ottoman Dynasty* (Oxford, 1956), pp. 12-13; Hoskiær, *Besøg*, p. 149.

in the years 1865 to 1868. In the latter year the heir-apparent, Abdülaziz's nephew Murad, was so alarmed that he consulted Ignatyev on what he should do, and considered flight.[42] The question then lay dormant, but Abdülaziz did not abandon his idea, which was brought up again after Âli's death.[43]

Other idiosyncrasies were such as to cast doubt on Abdülaziz's mental balance and emotional stability. He became more domineering in his personal conduct, demanding that ministers prostrate themselves to him and kiss his son's feet. He wanted no one but himself to be called Aziz; consequently officials who bore that name had to be given some other in documents laid before the sultan. He never forgave Midhat for wearing spectacles in his presence without his permission. It was generally believed, and was quite possibly true, that Abdülaziz had bestowed a high decoration on a victorious fighting cock and had exiled a losing cock for one month. This was hardly the same man who had ascended the throne in 1861. He still neither smoked nor indulged in intoxicants, but both his physical and mental health seemed to be deteriorating. Rumors to this effect had been current since 1862. Probably the early ones can be discounted, but by the 1870's Abdülaziz had such eccentricities that the rumors increased, and the conduct of state affairs suffered.[44]

With the sultan in such condition, it was doubly unfortunate that he chose Mahmud Nedim Paşa to be Âli's successor as grand vezir. Though during the next five years, until his deposition, Abdülaziz often switched the tenants of the post, Mahmud Nedim seems to have been his favorite, and held the office twice for a longer period than any of his rivals: for eleven months after September 8, 1871, and for more than eight months in 1875-1876. The choice of Mahmud Nedim

---

[42] "Zapiski . . . Ignatyeva," 1914, III, 98-99.

[43] See below, p. 283.

[44] Hoskiær, Besøg, p. 150; Amand von Schweiger-Lerchenfeld, Serail und Hohe Pforte (Vienna, 1879), pp. 111-126; Harold Temperley, "British Policy Towards Parliamentary Rule and Constitutionalism in Turkey," Cambridge Historical Journal, IV (1933), 167-169; Sommerville Story, ed., Memoirs of Ismail Kemal Bey (London, 1920), pp. 94-95; Ahmed Midhat, Üss-i inkılâb, I, 200, n.; Josef Koetschet, Osman Pascha, der letzte grosse Wesier Bosniens (Sarajevo, 1909), pp. 61-62; Raschdau, "Aus dem politischen Nachlass des Unterstaatssekretärs Dr. Busch," Deutsche Rundschau, 137 (1908), 383-385; Kuntay, Namık Kemal, I, 98-102; Morris to Seward, #33, 6 November 1862, USNA, Turkey 17; Raschdau, ed., "Diplomatenleben am Bosporus," Deutsche Rundschau, 138 (1909), 213-214; Mehmed Memduh, Mirât-ı şuûnat (İzmir, 1328), p. 86. Cf. aspersions on the sultan's sanity in İnkılâb, April 1870, quoted in Tanzimat, I, 852.

seems to have been the sultan's own, and may be due to the fact that as navy minister at the end of Âli's regime Mahmud Nedim had pleased the sultan by catering to his interest in warships. Mahmud Nedim had had a reasonably distinguished public career, partly in posts as high as undersecretary or acting minister of foreign affairs, or deputy grand vezir. Most of his recent experience, however, had been as provincial governor. He had been the candidate of some of the New Ottomans to replace Âli, but when he actually got the job they became disgusted with him. Almost none of his contemporaries in high office thought well of him. One suspects that there must be more good to say of him than has been said. He had started in political life as Reşid's disciple. He did have some ability, and was at times simply the victim of circumstances. Yet, aside from a general distrust of Âli's secularizing policies, it is hard to say that Mahmud Nedim had political principles other than self-advancement. Even before the Crimean War he had been characterized as clever, hypocrite, sycophant, flatterer, untrustworthy.[45] He was undoubtedly venal. His appeal to Abdülaziz, aside from his ability, must have been based on flattery, on playing up the sultan's role in public affairs, and on gratifying the sultan's financial and other whims. Abdülaziz, in fact, remarked that Mahmud Nedim was the first minister he had had who did what he, the sultan, wanted.[46] One way to Abdülaziz's favor in this period was to criticize Âli, and this Mahmud Nedim was quite willing to do. That Mahmud Nedim had never been outside the empire and knew no European language evidently did not bother the sultan.[47]

Mahmud Nedim's grand vezirate was characterized from its start by an indiscriminate firing and shifting of officials. Whether he initiated the policy, or whether he fell in with Abdülaziz's desires on this score, is unimportant, for it seemed to serve the interests of both. Mahmud Nedim declared that the motives were economy and the removal from office of grafters who had abused Âli's confidence. The grand vezir did, in fact, go so far as to try to divide the official year into nine months of forty days each, and so cut three months' pay

[45] Cevdet, *Tezâkir*, pp. 16-17, 26.
[46] Douin, *Khédive Ismail*, II, 631.
[47] On Mahmud Nedim generally: İnal, *Son sadrıâzamlar*, pp. 259-273; *La Turquie*, 9 September 1871; *Levant Times and Shipping Gazette*, 9 September 1871; Elliot to Granville, #320, 7 September 1871, and #329, 11 September 1871, FO 78/2177; Hoskiær, *Besøg*, p. 155; Raschdau, "Nachlass . . . Dr. Busch," pp. 388-389; Werner, *Türkische Skizzen*, II, 138-140.

from the salary of each official. But the real motives seemed to be to remove from office supporters of Âli's policies, and potential rivals, and to keep any single official thereafter from becoming prominent. In the fall of 1871 Mahmud Nedim exiled the former war minister, Hüseyin Avni, the former justice minister, Şirvanizade Mehmed Rüşdi, the former police minister, Hüsni, and others, all quite summarily. He thereby made for himself some important enemies. Of more immediate concern, the administration suffered badly. Whatever economies were effected only released funds for Abdülaziz's palace expenditures and new ironclads. Public order decreased as dismissed gendarmes took to brigandage themselves. Meanwhile government business bogged down. İstanbul was like a madhouse, said one official, as ministers and valis flew about like rubber balls.[48] "Your officials have gone on promenade," said Franz Joseph to a recalled ambassador. "They are in ceaseless rotation."[49] It was a senseless administrative chaos. Presumably the influence of the Palace, especially of the harem and the *valide sultan* Pertevniyal, increased the chaos and the chances for gaining office through bribery.[50]

The positive results of Mahmud Nedim's grand vezirate, if such they can be called, were a few steps taken ostensibly to improve government, but which, in fact, undid some of the reform of the previous decade. On the day after his accession to power the semiofficial *La Turquie* carried a rather cynical caricature of the Âli-Fuad period: "Heretofore there was talk of reform, improvement, and progress only when the state had a loan in view, only to forget all these beautiful intentions immediately the loan was assured."[51] The six sections of the Council of State were reduced to three. Special agents (*jurnalcı's*) were appointed to check on government officials. But the grand vezir's speech, in which he reported these achievements of nine

[48] Koetschet, *Osman Pascha,* pp. 59-60.

[49] Mehmed Memduh, *Mirât-ı şuûnat,* p. 45.

[50] Brown to Fish, #26, 21 October 1871, USNA, Turkey 23; Elliot to Granville, #361, 6 October 1871, and #381, 24 October 1871, FO 78/2177; Hoskiær, *Besøg,* pp. 155-156; Mahmud Celaleddin, *Mirât-ı hakikat* (İstanbul, 1326-1327), I, 35-36; Abdurrahman Şeref, *Tarih musahabeleri* (İstanbul, 1339), pp. 187-188; İnal, *Son sadrıâzamlar,* pp. 274-275; Ahmed Rasim, *Istibdaddan hakimiyeti milliyeye* (İstanbul, 1924), II, 148-150; "Zapiski . . . Ignatyeva," 1915, I, 147; Mordtmann, *Stambul,* I, 91-96, 105; Elliot to Granville, #169, 5 September 1872, FO 78/2219; Elliot, "Death of Abdul Aziz," pp. 277-278; Schweiger-Lerchenfeld, *Serail,* pp. 183-184.

[51] *La Turquie,* 8 September 1871, quoted in Mordtmann, *Stambul,* I, 92.

months in office, was largely devoted to praise of the sultan.[52] The vilayet system was virtually abandoned by Mahmud Nedim, who began to organize smaller provinces and restricted the communication of resolutions by the vilayet general assemblies to the Porte.[53] Probably he intended to hold a tighter rein on valis, as his argument of 1872 with Midhat, then Baghdad governor, indicates. Mahmud Nedim also fell in with Abdülaziz's desire to change the succession to the throne. In the spring of 1872 young Yusuf İzzeddin, now almost fifteen, was appointed commander of the first army corps, stationed at İstanbul. It was generally believed that this was to pave the way for announcing the succession change in June. Probably because of lack of popular enthusiasm, and because of protests by the British, the announcement was never made.[54]

Mahmud Nedim also reversed the trend of the previous decade in another way. Whereas Âli and Fuad had sought advice and support principally from the British and French ambassadors, Mahmud Nedim was closer to Ignatyev than to any other diplomat. The grand vezir came to be called "Nedimoff" by the populace, and the Russian ambassador was sometimes referred to as "Sultan Ignatyev." Whether money passed between them was unimportant, for the two could cooperate anyway on the basis of their opposition to Âli's policies. Nothing in Ignatyev's published memoirs indicates that Mahmud Nedim was his dupe, but obviously the latter looked to Ignatyev for support. It is significant that Ignatyev's picture of Mahmud Nedim is much more favorable than the usual: a man of intelligence, finesse, and hard work, esteemed by conservatives. But Ignatyev was, of course, opposed to the previous policies of Âli not only for their western orientation, but because they strengthened the Ottoman Empire. After 1871 he was pleased to see the policies of Abdülaziz and Mahmud Nedim weaken the empire and to have his own influence rise. He was suspected of encouraging the talk of changing the order of succession. He later boasted of his good relations with the sultan in

---

[52] Text in *Levant Times and Shipping Gazette*, 17 May 1872.

[53] Elliot to Granville, #138, 13 August 1872, FO 78/2218; George Young, *Corps de droit ottoman* (Oxford, 1905-1906), I, 40, n.13; İnal, *Son sadrıâzamlar*, p. 274.

[54] Mordtmann, *Stambul*, I, 111-113; *Augsburger Allgemeine Zeitung*, 7 May 1872; Rumbold, *Recollections*, II, 324-326; Benoît Brunswik, *La succession au trône de la Turquie* (Paris, 1872); Ahmed Saib, *Vaka-i Sultan Abdülaziz* (Cairo, 1320), pp. 97-102; Elliot to Granville, #94, confidential, 18 July 1872, and #97, confidential, 19 July 1872, FO 78/2218.

this period, while at the same time he was preparing Balkan Christians, Kurds, and Armenians as instruments of tsarist policy, to revolt when it suited Russia.[55]

In addition to Ignatyev, Ismail Paşa of Egypt also obtained greater influence in İstanbul during Mahmud Nedim's grand vezirate. Ismail was constantly on guard lest his aspirations to greater independence be thwarted and his past gains taken away by the Porte. He wanted also to make sure that neither Mustafa Fazıl nor Halim regained the right of succession to the Egyptian throne. While evidently he had been able to buy off Halim, he was much troubled that Mustafa Fazıl from the summer of 1869 on had been included in the Ottoman administration—first as minister without portfolio, then as finance minister—and was still in the fall of 1871, after Âli's death, minister of justice. Ismail was also afraid of the influence of Halil Şerif at the Porte. In addition, Ismail wanted to set up a system of courts divorced from those of the empire, to maintain a strong armament, and to get a new ferman granting him power to appoint a regency for the contingency of his death while his son was yet a minor. To pursue these ends, Ismail maintained in İstanbul, in addition to his regular *kapı kâhyası*, or representative, a special agent, one Abraham Bey. Abraham was an astute Armenian, brother-in-law of the Armenian Nubar Paşa, Ismail's leading statesman. A former Porte official who knew how to move circumspectly among the influential in the capital, Abraham had arguments that were reinforced by khedivial largesse as unfailing as the widow's cruse of oil. In the judgment of Ismail Kemal, Midhat's devoted supporter, Abraham was "the most influential man at the palace."[56] From 1871 to 1873 his gifts to Abdülaziz were fantastic: geese and pheasants in fine cages, the "resplendent lophophore, the crowned goura, the barnacle goose," one hundred dogs, sixty American white mignon ducks, rams and white Tuscan cows, four hundred sheep, three hundred thousand Ottoman bonds, and one million Ottoman bonds, among other things.[57]

[55] "Zapiski . . . Ignatyeva," 1915, I, 145-148, and IV, 229-230; Raschdau, "Nachlass . . . Dr. Busch," pp. 389ff.; Alexander Onou, "The Memoirs of Count N. Ignatyev," *Slavonic Review*, X (1931-1932), 389; Emmerich von Huszar, "Die Memoiren des Grafen N. P. Ignatew," *Oesterreichische Rundschau*, 41 (1914), 174; Kuntay, *Namık Kemal*, II, part 1, 764.

[56] Story, *Ismail Kemal*, p. 94.

[57] Alfred de Caston, *Musulmans et chrétiens: la Turquie en 1873* (Constantinople, 1874), II, 652-654; Pierre Crabitès, *Ismail the Maligned Khedive* (London, 1933), pp. 155-206; Douin, *Khédive Ismail*, II, 309ff., 548, 603, 625, 628, 630-635, 723.

Ismail also maintained a good relationship with Mahmud Nedim, well salted with bribes. While Mahmud Nedim was still navy minister, he had been persuaded to send away from İstanbul an enemy of Ismail's, Hurşid Paşa, formerly Ismail's secret police chief, who had defected to the Porte. When Mahmud Nedim became grand vezir, he was paid liberally by Ismail to make sure that Halil Şerif, then ambassador at Vienna, was not appointed foreign minister, as seemed likely at the time. Mustafa Fazıl was, however, retained as minister of justice until January 1872, perhaps simply to attract larger sums from Ismail. To grease the ways for Ismail's new mixed court system, a modification of the capitulations in Egypt, Abraham Bey offered Mahmud Nedim sixty thousand pounds, and Abdülaziz one hundred and fifty thousand. Even Ignatyev accepted twenty thousand pounds from Abraham in return for a letter favorable to Egyptian judiciary reform. The khedive was painfully surprised when the American minister, George Boker, who voluntarily supported his scheme, refused a large sum of money and diamonds for his wife. Other high Ottoman officials were touched by Ismail's generosity. This sort of corruption seems to have been much more widespread under Mahmud Nedim than it had been under Âli, who had better kept Ismail in his place.[58]

By August of 1872, when his grand vezirate was suddenly ended, Mahmud Nedim had done nothing to strengthen the empire. Nor, in fact, had he done anything to strengthen himself except in the regard of Abdülaziz, Ignatyev, and Ismail. Mahmud Nedim, in his self-seeking, developed an extraordinary faculty for making enemies. The New Ottomans, some of whom had once favored him, were amnestied and began to return from exile during his vezirate. They were soon disillusioned by what they found. Namık Kemal in his new paper *İbret* criticized Mahmud Nedim's rapid shifting of officials, and began to think better of Âli.[59] Ziya Bey, in a dramatic gesture,

[58] Douin, *Khédive Ismail*, II, 325-328, 552-557, 610, 618, 631; Crabitès, *Ismail*, 194, 199-207, 220-223; Edward S. Bradley, *George Henry Boker, Poet and Patriot* (Philadelphia, 1927), 288-289. Boker did accept a trip up the Nile. Cf. Kuntay, *Namık Kemal*, II, part 1, 111-112.

[59] Elliot to Granville, #392, 31 October 1871, FO 78/2177; *İbret*, #20, 30 September 1872, and #97, 20 January 1873, in Kuntay, *Namık Kemal*, I, 231, 152; *İbret*, #46, 5 November 1872, in İhsan Sungu, "Tanzimat ve Yeni Osmanlılar," *Tanzimat*, I, 784-785.

went to Âli's grave to ask forgiveness.[60] Not only the New Ottomans, but all sorts of others became Mahmud Nedim's opponents as the result of his eleven months in office. There were those whom he had summarily dismissed or whose pay he had reduced, including many minor officials and some influential leaders like Hüseyin Avni. There were those who resented his closeness to Ignatyev, especially now that Muslim sentiment was rising in a Russophobe tide. There were others who resented his ties to Ismail, for the fact of bribery if not the amount involved was known. And there were many who disapproved of Mahmud Nedim's catering to the whims and expenditures of Abdülaziz. Those who believed the rumors current about the sultan's mental health could say, in addition, that Mahmud Nedim was giving in to the whims of a madman, instead of opposing them. All this was to have its effect, particularly when Mahmud Nedim next held the grand vezirate in 1875-1876.

The grand vezir had also done a good deal to damage the reputation of the sultan himself, by making a great parade of attributing all authority to Abdülaziz. Thus, whereas the populace heretofore had generally been disposed to blame ministers for bad conditions, leaving the sultan above direct reproach, now the sultan's name had been brought down to the level of market place criticism. "The shake thus given to the system . . . will be far more difficult effectually to remedy . . . than all the other evils" caused by Mahmud Nedim, the British ambassador astutely reported.[61] This also would have its repercussions in 1876, when a new crisis arose. Further, the talk of succession change which Mahmud Nedim encouraged fostered the identification of Abdülaziz and his son Yusuf İzzeddin with Mahmud Nedim's chaotic administration. The logical result was that the hopes of would-be reformers were pinned on Murad more strongly than ever.

Mahmud Nedim's opponents were by no means all of one cast. They included disparate elements among officialdom, the military, the journalists, and the general populace. It was possible that they might in the future coalesce, and Mahmud Nedim by his actions had helped to create a public opinion which could conceivably bring this about. But before this could come to pass, the initiative was seized by Midhat Paşa, governor of the Baghdad vilayet.

[60] İnal, *Son sadrıâzamlar*, p. 41.
[61] Elliot to Granville, #269, 25 November 1872, FO 78/2220.

Midhat Paşa had resigned his governorship in consequence of disputes with Mahmud Nedim, and in May 1872 started back by way of Syria to İstanbul. His reputation as an able administrator was well established, and many in the capital pinned their hopes on him to get rid of the grand vezir. Once arrived, Midhat was visited by various sacked officials, who recounted the horrors of Mahmud Nedim's administration. The latter was obviously worried over Midhat's presence in the capital. On July 29 Midhat's appointment as governor of the Edirne vilayet was announced, evidently a move by Mahmud Nedim without consultation with Abdülaziz to get rid of Midhat. But Midhat obtained an audience with Abdülaziz, and seems to have spoken so forcefully that the sultan in the late evening of July 30 summoned Mahmud Nedim to relinquish the seals of office and appointed Midhat in his stead.[62] The news of the change was greeted by unprecedented public demonstrations of joy on July 31 before the Porte and the palace. Midhat's entry at the Porte was a triumphal procession, while hostile officials gathered in front of Mahmud Nedim's house to hoot him.[63] Shortly, even Abdülaziz seems to have become disillusioned with Mahmud Nedim, referring to him as jealous, duplicit, and corrupt.[64]

The high hopes placed in Midhat were soon deceived, for Midhat was no wizard and had to start simply by trying to remedy some of the mistakes of Mahmud Nedim. His own experience and character, moreover, did not fit him in the best possible manner for the job of grand vezir. During the previous decade and more Midhat had been a provincial governor, except for one year as president of the Council of State in İstanbul. With his energy and efficiency there went a

---

[62] A. H. Midhat, Midhat Paşa, hayat-ı siyâsiyesi, vol. 1, Tabsıra-i ibret (İstanbul, 1325), 133-134; İnal, Son sadrıâzamlar, pp. 276-277, 324-328; Mehmed Memduh, Mirât-ı şuûnat, pp. 45-46; Levant Times and Shipping Gazette, 29 and 31 July 1872; Elliot to Granville, #118, 31 July 1872, FO 78/2218. The unexpectedly sudden change in grand vezirs gave rise to many stories, some probably in part true: that Hüseyin Avni caused the change by means of a harem girl pleasing to the sultan; that Mahmud Nedim crossed some important palace officials; that he proposed making Ismail governor of the Yemen too; that he doused the sultan with water from a toy fire engine! Cf. Douin, Khédive Ismail, II, 647-650; Mehmed Memduh, Mirât-ı şuûnat, pp. 45-46; Elliot to Granville, #154, confidential, 21 August 1872, FO 78/2218; Antonio Gallenga, Two Years of the Eastern Question (London, 1877), I, 160-161.

[63] Levant Times and Shipping Gazette, 1 August 1872; Koetschet, Osman Pascha, pp. 60-61; Aus dem Leben König Karls von Rumänien (Stuttgart, 1894-1900), II, 276; Mordtmann, Stambul, I, 118; Farley, Turks and Christians, p. 30.

[64] Elliot to Granville, #246, confidential, 3 November 1872, FO 78/2220.

brusqueness, even a tactlessness, which served him ill in his relations with Abdülaziz and with others in the capital.[65] Sometimes he was more of a theorist, well ahead of his times, than a practical statesman.[66] He also had powerful opponents. The Russian ambassador Ignatyev had tried in vain to prevent Midhat from ever reaching the capital, by urging Mahmud Nedim to appoint him vali of Aleppo.[67] Thereafter Ignatyev worked constantly for Midhat's fall, and gave himself most of the credit for thwarting the reformer, who was notably hostile to Russia. The khedive Ismail also, finding that Midhat was unamenable to his intrigues and opposed his direct dealings with the sultan, encouraged Abdülaziz with a gift of one hundred and twenty-five thousand pounds to dismiss Midhat.[68] As a result, Midhat's grand vezirate was destined to last only eighty days.

Despite the difficulties inherent in his position, Midhat started out boldly. He recalled from exile those whom Mahmud Nedim had sent away. He succeeded in getting Halil Şerif as his foreign minister when Cemil Paşa, son of the great Reşid, died after only one month in office. He opposed the granting of new concessions to the khedive. He initiated measures to extend education in the provinces, to regularize the collection of the tithe, to advance railroad construction, to get a telegraph line built to the Hijaz, to systematize interdepartmental correspondence and filing methods in the government, to enforce conversion of weights and measures to the metric system. He raised the salaries of lower officials and cut those of the higher, including his own. He restored the cuts made by Mahmud Nedim in the *gendarmerie*, so that brigandage was lessened. Midhat also investigated the finances of Mahmud Nedim's period, and accused him of graft, inaugurating a campaign against him which went too far for the stomach of many other officials and implicated the Palace as well. This was certainly part of the reason for Midhat's undoing. In short, Midhat acted at the Porte as he had as vali—with many vigorous starts, a campaign against corruption, and a disregard for the politics of office-holding.[69]

[65] Cf. Abdurrahman Şeref, *Tarih musahabeleri*, p. 204; Mehmed Memduh, *Mirât-ı şuûnat*, p. 56.

[66] Holborn, *Radowitz*, p. 240.

[67] Elliot to Granville, #162, confidential, 30 August 1872, FO 78/2218.

[68] "Zapiski . . . Ignatyeva," 1915, I, 148-150; Douin, *Khédive Ismail*, II, 657-658, 667-672; Angelo Sammarco, *Histoire de l'Egypte moderne*, III (Cairo, 1937), 217-219.

[69] A. H. Midhat, *Tabsıra-i ibret*, pp. 134-147; idem, *The Life of Midhat Pasha*

Two projects of more far-reaching significance began to occupy Midhat during his grand vezirate—a constitutional plan and a plan for federal organization of the empire. Neither came to a head during his short tenure of office, but each had the support of Halil Şerif, who was continued in the foreign ministry by the sultan for five months after Midhat fell. Halil Şerif probably contributed considerably to each project, for he knew Europe far better than Midhat, had just come from the ambassadorship at Vienna, and had, at least since his memorandum of 1867, had in mind the project of a constitution. Just after becoming minister for foreign affairs, Halil Şerif married Mustafa Fazıl's beautiful and quite Europeanized daughter Nazlı. The marriage seemed to strengthen the cooperation among Halil Şerif, Mustafa Fazıl, and Midhat, all of whom entertained constitutional ideas. Because the western Europeans thought highly of Halil Şerif, and because Abdülaziz knew he would help to attract new loans, the efforts of Ignatyev and Ismail to get rid of him were not at once successful.[70] Probably, therefore, the views that Halil Şerif expressed up to March 11, 1873, when he was dropped, can be taken as representing Midhat's also.

The plan for a constitution seems to have remained in the stage of informal discussion of the general concept, and is known chiefly through the revelations, probably exaggerated, of those who opposed it and who sought to convince Abdülaziz that Midhat was dangerous. Exactly what Midhat's ideas on constitution were in 1872 it is impossible to say. He had contact with Odian and Dr. Servichen and other Armenians who are said to have plied him with constitutional argu-

(London, 1903), pp. 64-66; Hoskiær, Besøg, p. 160; Mahmud Celaleddin, Mirât-ı hakikat, I, 37-38; Douin, Khédive Ismail, II, 672; "Zapiski . . . Ignatyeva," 1915, I, 148-150; Elliot to Granville, #169, 5 September 1872, FO 78/2219; İnal, Son sadrıâzamlar, pp. 278-281; Ali Ölmezoğlu, "Midhat Paşa," İslâm ansiklopedisi, fasc. 82, pp. 274-275; Levant Times and Shipping Gazette, 1 August to 19 October 1872.

[70] Elliot to Granville, #201, confidential, 25 September 1872, FO 78/2219, and #282, confidential, 9 December 1872, FO 78/2220; Hoskiær, Besøg, pp. 178-180; Holborn, Radowitz, I, 240; İnal, Son sadrıâzamlar, p. 137; Douin, Khédive Ismail, II, 667-709. On Ignatyev's opposition to Halil Şerif and Midhat see further G. Giacometti, Russia's Work in Turkey: a Revelation, trans. by E. Whitaker (London, 1877), letters 1-10. These documents, published by the Turks at İstanbul in French and Turkish in 1877, purport to be authentic Russian correspondence, the first ten being by Ignatyev. Their authenticity is questionable, but the verisimilitude is remarkable. All deal with 1871-1873. On authenticity see W. L. Langer, European Alliances and Alignments (New York, 1931), p. 68 and n.2; Sumner, Russia and the Balkans, pp. 130, n.4, 244, 681.

ments during weekly dinners at Odian's house.[71] The khedive Ismail, a month and more after Midhat was out of office, wrote that Midhat, Halil Şerif, and Mustafa Fazıl were in league to take the government out of Abdülaziz's hands, that they were seeking a constitution, and advised the sultan to grant one himself if he wanted it, but not to submit to such pressures.[72] Ignatyev, similarly but more specifically, accused the same three men of seeking power with a plan for an independent and so-called constitutional ministry and a simulation of national representation. He gave himself considerable credit for killing this plan and for warning Abdülaziz that Midhat was nothing but a disguised revolutionary who meant to limit the sovereign rights.[73] Whatever form the constitutional idea had assumed in Midhat's mind by 1872, the dream of constitutional government haunted him thereafter, and he came back to it with other colleagues the next year.

The plan for a federalized empire reached a more advanced stage before it disappeared from the scene. Its essence was to tie the Roumanian principalities and Serbia to the Ottoman Empire in the same way as Bavaria and Württemberg were tied to the newly created German Empire. Evidently conceived during Midhat's grand vezirate, the plan was broached by Halil Şerif only after Mütercim Mehmed Rüşdi had replaced Midhat. As Halil Şerif explained it, the scheme intended "that these Dependencies should be raised nearly to the position of those German states which enjoy their independence subject to the condition of their military resources being at the disposal of the Emperor."[74] The scheme enjoyed British and Austrian support, but naturally was resisted by Ignatyev, who used all his influence against it. According to his own report he succeeded in convincing Mehmed Rüşdi that it was dangerous; the grand vezir then said Midhat was the author of the project. The Germans also disapproved it. To the Serbs and Roumanians the plan, of course, meant lowering rather than raising their status. Plans of federal organization, which were fairly widespread at the time, they would consider only if the plans were anti-Turkish. Halil Şerif's plan meant to them political as well as military subjection, and it is questionable whether the foreign minister really thought he could persuade the Serbs and

[71] Mikael Kazmararian, ed., *Krikor Odian* (Constantinople, 1910), I, xiv.
[72] Douin, *Khédive Ismail*, II, 675-677, 693-694.
[73] "Zapiski . . . Ignatyeva," 1915, I, 149-153.
[74] Elliot to Granville, #259, confidential, 13 November 1872, FO 78/2220.

Roumanians to accept it, even though he offered them autonomy in matters of coinage and decorations and freedom from the capitulations. After December of 1872 no more was heard of it.[75]

Midhat Paşa had by then been out of office for two months. He had not really given himself a good chance to survive as grand vezir. From the outset he had opposed the influence of the palace functionaries, had said that the sultan alone was master, and had also opposed the sultan himself on certain issues as well as implicating him in financial scandal. This was all in decided contrast to the complaisance of Mahmud Nedim. Further, by his blunt manner Midhat had tried to emphasize the supremacy of the Porte, going so far as to ride on horseback into the palace grounds—something that was never done. Âli Paşa would have agreed with the motive, but never with the methods. In addition, Midhat was opposed by Mahmud Nedim, whose influence continued through palace partisans, as well as by Ignatyev and Ismail. The major cause of his dismissal seems to have been argument with the Palace over new privileges granted Ismail in return for bribes—in particular, the right for Egypt to contract foreign loans. The final *hat* on this point was issued behind Midhat's back; he is said to have seen a copy only after his fall from office. Midhat's opposition to Ismail was obstinate. By his son's account, Midhat angrily returned fifty thousand gold pounds which had been delivered by Ismail's agents to his house when he was absent. On October 18, 1872, the sultan called in Mütercim Mehmed Rüşdi Paşa to replace Midhat. Ignatyev congratulated Abdülaziz on getting rid of Midhat. The tributary Balkan states rejoiced that Midhat, "of the unsettled and restless school" of Halil Şerif, was gone.[76]

With the fall of Midhat the Ottoman Empire entered anew on a period of confusion in which the caprice of the sultan, the intrigue of Ismail, the pan-Slavism of Ignatyev, and the deterioration of the

---

[75] Temperley, "British Policy Towards . . . Turkey," p. 179; "Zapiski . . . Ignatyeva," 1915, I, 170-172; Nicholas Iorga, ed., *Correspondance diplomatique roumaine sous le roi Charles Ier (1866-1880)* (Paris, 1923), pp. 95-99.

[76] Elliot to Granville, #180, confidential, 16 September 1872; #205, confidential, 1 October 1872; #214, 14 October 1872; #215, confidential, 14 October 1872; #217, 14 October 1872; #229, 20 October 1872; #233, confidential, 24 October 1872—all FO 78/2219; also #249, most confidential, 6 November 1872, FO 78/2220; A. H. Midhat, *Tabsıra-i ibret*, pp. 147-149; Story, *Ismail Kemal*, pp. 88-89; Mehmed

economic situation set the stage for rising discontent. Office-shifting continued almost as fast as it had under Mahmud Nedim. "The utmost confusion prevails in every department of the State," observed the British ambassador, "the transaction of even the most ordinary routine business having become almost impossible."[77] His judgment was confirmed on all sides. Leading political figures, each ambitious for self, formed parties of one or ad hoc combinations to oust whoever was in office. "Every new Grand Vizier pulls down so far as possible all that his predecessor had built up," said Cyrus Hamlin, who had seen thirty years of Ottoman politics. "These changes have all been from sheer caprice. It disorganizes the administration of government in all its departments. It makes the provincial governors and judges perfectly rapacious. Knowing they will soon be changed they make hay while the sun shines."[78]

At the top of the administrative heap, six grand vezirs were appointed within three years, beginning with Mütercim Mehmed Rüşdi. After him came Esad Paşa, then Şirvanizade Mehmed Rüşdi, then Hüseyin Avni, again Esad, and on August 26, 1875, Mahmud Nedim for the second time.[79] Their rise and fall were due to many different incidental causes, but in the last analysis to the pressures on, and to the whims of, Abdülaziz. Ignatyev, in congratulating the sultan on Midhat's removal, had recommended as best that form of government where the sovereign was master, as in Russia and Turkey, and expressed the hope that Abdülaziz would continue to act independently of his ministers.[80] Abdülaziz, after Âli's death, needed no such

Memduh, *Mirât-ı şuûnat*, p. 47; İnal, *Son sadrıâzamlar*, pp. 328-330; Sammarco, *Egypte moderne*, III, 217-219; A. H. Midhat, *Hâtıralarım, 1872-1946* (İstanbul, 1946), pp. 39-40; Iorga, *Correspondance diplomatique roumaine*, #231, 21 November 1872.

[77] Elliot to Granville, #273, 28 November 1872, FO 78/2220.

[78] Hamlin to Trent, 4 November 1872, ABCFM, vol. 354, #67. Cf. the frustrations of Cevdet Paşa, an able man who never achieved the grand vezirate he desired: Ebül'ulâ Mardin, *Medenî hukuk cephesinden Ahmet Cevdet Paşa* (İstanbul, 1946), pp. 125, n.108, and 128.

[79] Grand vezirates: Mütercim Mehmed Rüşdi, 19 October 1872 to 15 February 1873; Sakızlı Ahmed Esad, 15 February 1873 to 14 April 1873; Şirvanizade Mehmed Rüşdi, 14 April 1873 to 13 February 1874; Hüseyin Avni, 13 February 1874 to 25 April 1875; Esad, 26 April 1875 to 25 August 1875; Mahmud Nedim, 25 August 1875 to 11 May 1876. There is question about some of the dates. These are based on İ. H. Danişmend, *İzahlı osmanlı tarihi kronolojisi* (İstanbul, 1947-1955), IV, 507-509, corrected in three instances from diplomatic dispatches or İstanbul newspapers.

[80] Elliot to Granville, #249, most confidential, 6 November 1872, FO 78/2220.

encouragement. Mehmed Rüşdi the Mütercim blamed his predecessor Mahmud Nedim for confirming Abdülaziz in the belief that now he need not take advice and that his desires would be satisfied anyway.[81] The sultan proceeded to make and unmake ministers without consulting his grand vezirs. Mehmed Rüşdi, a conscientious and honorable man, stood up to the sultan on this issue once, but this was unusual.[82] When Esad replaced Mehmed Rüşdi, the sultan said that he himself would give orders to ministers and that the grand vezir would be more of a figurehead.[83] None of the grand vezirs was without ability. They ranged in character from the young westernized general Esad to Şirvanizade Mehmed Rüşdi, a moderately liberal member of the ulema who had made the transition to the civil service hierarchy; from the intelligent, conscientious, and cautious Mütercim Mehmed Rüşdi to the self-seeking, amoral, and more energetic Hüseyin Avni. Yet none accomplished any great work during his grand vezirate, and it is unprofitable to follow the ins and outs of personal politics which took so much of their attention. The political infighting was vicious at times. Ismail's intrigue, supplemented by his copious purse, was always present as a complicating factor, even after the khedive obtained in 1873 a ferman consolidating all previously granted privileges so that he appeared almost an independent monarch.[84]

During this chaotic period little beginnings adumbrated the course of future events. Both constitution and deposition were discussed by a few high officials. Constitutional plans had, of course, been initiated by Midhat and Halil Şerif in 1872, and the sultan was aware that such ideas were current, for he reproached Halil Şerif with being a partisan of constitutional government.[85] In 1873, during the grand vezirate of Şirvanizade Mehmed Rüşdi, the constitutional idea was evidently mulled over by a somewhat wider group. Şirvanizade himself was a product of medrese training, but no fanatic, rather intelligent, and considered at least by the Russian ambassador to be under British influence.[86] He had also been a member of the New Ottoman

[81] Elliot to Granville, #232, confidential, 24 October 1872, FO 78/2219.
[82] Elliot to Granville, #256, 12 November 1872, FO 78/2220; Douin, *Khédive Ismail*, II, 683.
[83] *Ibid.*, p. 707; Elliot to Granville, #71, confidential, 2 March 1873, FO 78/2226.
[84] Boker to Fish, #123, 2 July 1873, USNA, Turkey 25. Text in J. C. Hurewitz, *Diplomacy in the Near and Middle East* (Princeton, 1956), I, 174-177.
[85] Douin, *Khédive Ismail*, II, 707.
[86] "Zapiski . . . Ignatyeva," 1915, I, 155-156.

group.[87] An opponent of Mahmud Nedim because of his exile in 1871, Şirvanizade was thrown together with Hüseyin Avni and Midhat, who also were bitter rivals of Mahmud Nedim. These three all happened to be ministers during Esad's short grand vezirate early in 1873—Hüseyin Avni for war, Midhat for justice, and Şirvanizade for finance.[88] After they used their joint influence to get Esad out, Şirvanizade was appointed grand vezir.

It is possible that the three had discussed constitutional government during Esad's regime. It is certain that at least Midhat and Şirvanizade did so during the latter's grand vezirate, meeting at the grand vezir's house in the evenings with some other ministers. Hüseyin Avni was no real partisan of constitution, but knew what was going on. According to Midhat's account, the ministers, alarmed by the general situation and especially the financial condition of the empire, agreed that the remedy was a chamber of deputies, but that since such a phrase would alarm the sultan, a reform proposal of more moderate aspect was to be drawn up. Midhat was delegated to do this. His memorandum, much of it in general terms, talked of the rule of law equally over all subjects, but also more specifically recommended recasting the administrative councils and the courts, establishing financial controls to be effected by the Porte, and other measures. Şirvanizade Mehmed Rüşdi one day unintentionally mentioned the forthcoming memorandum to Abdülaziz, who thereupon packed Midhat off to Salonika as vali and shortly fired the grand vezir himself.[89] The memorandum has been described as "a sort of draft of a defective constitution."[90] This is exaggeration. How far the constitutional planning went is not certain. The assertion of Midhat's friend İsmail Kemal that Midhat drew up at this time "a project of organic statutes" including a responsible ministry and popular control of finances seems also to be exaggerated.[91] But certainly Midhat's thinking went in this direction.

Midhat probably had in mind also the possibility of deposition of

---

[87] On Ebüzziya's authority: A. H. Tanpınar, *XIX. asır türk edebiyatı tarihi*, 2nd ed., I (İstanbul, 1956), 196; M. Z. Pâkalın, *Tanzimat maliye nazırları* (İstanbul, n.d.), II, 137-138.

[88] Midhat came into the ministry about a month after the other two: *Levant Herald*, 13 March 1873. This was on the same day that Halil Şerif was finally ousted as foreign minister.

[89] Midhat, *Tabsıra-i ibret*, pp. 150-151, and text of memorandum, pp. 323-326. Cf. Cevdet, quoted in Pâkalın, *Maliye nazırları*, II, 130.

[90] Ahmed Rasim, *Istibdaddan hakimiyeti milliyeye* (İstanbul, 1924), II, 153.

[91] Story, *Ismail Kemal*, p. 103.

Abdülaziz. He, Şirvanizade, and Hüseyin Avni have been accused by others of projecting a change in sultans as early as the first months of 1873.[92] After Şirvanizade Mehmed Rüşdi became grand vezir in April of 1873 the project was entertained by a number of the ministers. Hüseyin Avni seems to have been led by his ambition to reveal such thoughts of his colleagues—undoubtedly with added inventions —to the sultan, and so to get himself appointed grand vezir in Şirvanizade's place, in February 1874. But Hüseyin Avni did not give up the idea of deposition—apparently in his case a product of a personal antagonism to the sultan as much as of desire to benefit the state. He is said to have contemplated it during his grand vezirate in 1874 and 1875 and to have continued to work toward it after he was out of office.[93] Abdülaziz's suspicions were somehow aroused, as Hüseyin Avni was thereafter posted to governorships progressively farther from the capital—first İzmir, then Konya, then the Yemen. The latter assignment was, however, never undertaken, as the events of the Balkan revolt of 1875 brought Hüseyin Avni back to the capital so that his military ability might be used.[94] In the crisis period that started in 1875, the plans for constitution and for deposition would again come to the surface.

So also would a more intense and more emotional patriotic feeling which was developing during these same years. Such feeling was, in part, a natural accompaniment of the renewed emphasis on Islam during the 1870's. It was also, in part, the product of deliberate cultivation by a small group of writers, chief among whom was Namık Kemal. Namık Kemal had not reconstituted in İstanbul the New Ottoman group of Paris. This would have been impossible, because of personal antagonisms and because some, like Ali Suavi, stayed abroad. Ziya Bey, further, on his return to İstanbul seemed to have abandoned his former comrades and ideals; he was being paid considerable sums by Ismail, and accepted employment as second secre-

[92] Cevdet, quoted in Pâkalın, *Maliye nazırları*, II, 129; Danişmend, *Kronolojisi*, IV, 244.

[93] *Ibid.*, pp. 244-246; Story, *Ismail Kemal*, pp. 102-103; Ali Ölmezoğlu, "Cevdet Paşa," *İslâm ansiklopedisi*, III, 117; Charles Mismer, *Souvenirs du monde musulman* (Paris, 1892), pp. 271-275. Mahmud Celaleddin, *Mirât-ı hakikat*, I, 103, alleges that Hüseyin Avni on his trip to Europe in the spring of 1875 secretly saw English ministers who said that Abdülaziz's deposition and Murad's accession would be well received.

[94] Elliot to Derby, #210, confidential, 27 April 1875, FO 78/2382; #392, 27 July 1875, FO 78/2384; #412, 3 August 1875, and #426, confidential, 5 August 1875, FO 78/2385.

tary of Sultan Abdülaziz while still the recipient of Ismail's bounty.[95]
Two of Namık Kemal's comrades in exile, however, Nuri and Reşad,
worked with him, as did also the brilliant young writer Ebüzziya
Tevfik, now in his early twenties. Namık Kemal contributed to several
periodicals, such as *Diyojen* (*Diogenes*), a comic semiweekly quite
popular among the lesser officials in İstanbul for its lampoons on the
administration, which was suppressed by Palace order early in 1873
for insulting Ismail.[96] He contributed also to *Hadika* (*Garden*), edited
by Ebüzziya, until its suspension for two months because of an article
on a strike at the imperial arsenal.[97] But in this world of precarious journalism—in which papers were suspended, and reappeared; were suppressed, and popped up under new names; in which writers were exiled, and their work continued by others—Namık Kemal's chief efforts went into his paper *İbret*.[98]

İbret (*Admonition*) was a Turkish newspaper of İstanbul owned
by a Christian, of which Namık Kemal took over the editorship after
it had been suspended for two months.[99] Its first issue under Namık
Kemal appeared on June 13, 1872, in the grand vezirate of Mahmud
Nedim.[100] Here Namık Kemal pursued the course he had previously
established in *Hürriyet*. He criticized the administration, criticized
Ismail, advocated copying western economic achievement, cultivated
love of fatherland, preached the unity of Islam, praised the şeriat, and
advocated government by consultation. The paper was quite popular
and exercised considerable influence among the young theological students of the capital.[101] Mahmud Nedim was obviously unhappy with
the paper, but its first suspension seems to have come as the result
of pecuniary pressure on the Palace by Ismail, whose efforts to buy
the editor had failed.[102] Late in July *İbret* was suspended, and Namık
Kemal and his three chief collaborators were ordered to provincial
posts. Namık Kemal managed not to take up his appointment until
after Mahmud Nedim fell from office. Midhat, however, on becom-

[95] Crabitès, *Ismail*, pp. 178-179; Douin, *Khédive Ismail*, II, 654-656, 663.
[96] *Levant Herald*, 13 and 17 January 1873; Douin, *Khédive Ismail*, II, 696-697.
[97] *Levant Herald*, 30 January 1873.
[98] Ahmed Midhat, *Üss-i inkılâb*, II, 162-163.
[99] *Levant Times*, 14 June 1872.
[100] Mehmed Kaplan, *Namık Kemal* (İstanbul, 1948), pp. 80-83.
[101] Mustafa Nihat Özön, *Namık Kemal ve İbret gazetesi* (İstanbul, 1938), reproduces a selection of Namık Kemal's articles. Cf. Sungu, "Tanzimat ve Yeni Osmanlılar," pp. 778-779, 781-782, 804, 844; Kuntay, *Namık Kemal*, II, part 1, 104-107;
Şehsuvaroğlu, *Sultan Aziz*, pp. 65-66.
[102] Kuntay, *Namık Kemal*, II, part 1, 110-114.

ing grand vezir insisted that he go to Gelibolu as mutasarrıf, whereupon he went. But *İbret*'s suspension was lifted after about two and
a half months, and Namık Kemal contributed articles to it from his
post of exile. Soon he managed to get himself back to the capital and
resumed the editorship openly in January 1873. A new suspension
of a month was ordered, in the grand vezirate of Esad Paşa, because
of articles critical of censorship of books. Then *İbret* resumed publication, only to be suppressed very soon after events connected with a yet
more audacious piece of writing than Namık Kemal had so far attempted in his newspapers.[103]

The audacity resulted from the combination of one of Namık
Kemal's favorite themes, the passionate love of fatherland, with a
new medium, the stage drama in western style. Aside from translations of western plays, the first modern drama written in Turkish had
been Şinasi's *A Poet's Marriage*, and it is not clear that this was ever
performed. Namık Kemal, on his return from exile, collaborated with
Ebüzziya Tevfik in writing a play, *Ecel-i kaza (Accidental Death)*.[104]
This was actually produced in January 1873 under the sponsorship
of Halil Şerif Paşa on a double bill with a comedy by Ali Bey, the
chief secretary of the quarantine bureau. All the ministers except the
grand vezir, plus Mustafa Fazıl and Midhat, who were out of office,
were present.[105] These plays, and others translated or adapted from
western languages such as Ahmed Vefik's versions of Molière comedies, were staged at the Gedik Paşa theatre in İstanbul. The actors
were Armenians, with indifferent accents. The audience seems to have
enjoyed the action, but not always to have understood all the spoken
parts.[106] The theatre was enjoying an upsurge, its red bills posted
on street corners and mosques. The house was often packed.[107] A
number of figures of the literary renaissance had formed a committee
in January 1873 to promote and improve the new medium. On it were
the above-named dramatist Ali Bey; Namık Kemal; Raşid Paşa, who
had had a Paris education, had served in the translation bureau, and

[103] *Ibid.*, pp. 116-119; *Levant Herald*, 8 April 1873; Sungu, *Namık Kemal* (İs-
tanbul, 1941), pp. 12-13.
[104] E. J. W. Gibb, *A History of Ottoman Poetry* (London, 1900-1909), V, 15. Gibb
mistakenly calls this "the first original Turkish drama."
[105] *Levant Herald*, 25 and 30 January 1873.
[106] Belin, "Bibliographie ottomane," *Journal asiatique*, series VI: 18 (August-September 1871), 126; Werner, *Türkische Skizzen*, I, 100-107, describing a performance
of Schiller's *Die Räuber* in translation.
[107] *Ibid.*, p. 92.

was destined to become foreign minister later that year; Halet Bey, an experienced journalist; and Agop Efendi Vartovian (known as Güllü Agop or Agop Güllian), an Armenian, the director of the acting company.[108] The committee was to improve the acting and diction, and to encourage the translation and composition of dramatic pieces.

Namık Kemal then produced a new play for the Gedik Paşa theatre. In early March it was known that he was writing a piece about the siege of Silistria, where in 1854 the beleaguered Turks had thrown back the Russians.[109] The finished work, entitled *Vatan yahut Silistre* (*Fatherland or Silistria*), was played on Tuesday night, April 1, to a crowded house, which responded enthusiastically. Namık Kemal had packed a tremendous emotional content into the play with his emphasis on patriotism, expressed by the actors in both word and deed, prose dialogue and song. Though the term *vatan* had meant "fatherland" from mid-century on, and had been increasingly so used by the New Ottomans in particular, its association with Namık Kemal's play of 1873 gave *vatan* its full meaning and impact for the future.[110] As drama, *Vatan* left much to be desired. The plot was crude, and its message unmistakable. Kemal also introduced a love story. He began the play with an amorous scene, from which the hero departs for the front to defend his fatherland, upon which he makes a great speech to his beloved. She then dons male disguise and goes to the front to rejoin her man. The succeeding action unrolls at the front, involving a daring raid to fire the enemy's ammunition dump. The whole was tricked out with copious supplies of blood, shouting, cannon, redoubts, and the fanfare of trumpets. The play contained a few unmistakable criticisms of the Ottoman administration. But both these and the love story were secondary to the main theme of Ottoman patriotism, best expressed by Namık Kemal in two songs sung by the volunteers.[111] Typical of the sentiment is this song:

[108] *Levant Herald*, 25 January 1873; Sungu, *Namık Kemal*, p. 18; Cevdet Perin, "Ahmed Midhat Efendi et l'influence française . . . ," *Garp filolojileri dergisi* (İstanbul, 1937), p. 136 and n.2; Kuntay, *Namık Kemal*, II, part 1, 151. Kuntay says also the Young Ottoman Nuri was both member and organizer of the committee. Cf. Y. G. Çark, *Türk devleti hizmetinde Ermeniler* (İstanbul, 1953), pp. 278-279, on origins of the acting company.

[109] *Levant Herald*, 6 March 1873.

[110] On earlier uses, see above chapter II and n.15, and chapter VI and n.86. Cf. the emotional description in 1949 of the emotional experience in 1873 by Kuntay in *Namık Kemal*, II, part 1, 152.

[111] The play has many editions in Turkish. It is also translated into German by Leopold Pekotsch, *Heimat oder Silistria* (Vienna, 1887).

> Blood and sword on our flag are flying,
> On our hills and plains roams no fear of dying,
> A lion in each part of our land is lying,
> We rejoice in the fray martyrs' lives to lay down,
> We are Ottomans, giving up life for renown.[112]

And at the final curtain, upon victory, the cast all joins in:

> Before us the enemy, ready with arms,
> March, heroes, to the aid of the fatherland!
> March onward, march, salvation is ours;
> March, heroes, to the aid of the fatherland![113]

After the performance Namık Kemal was cheered when he came to the stage, and cheered in the streets by crowds shouting, "Long live Kemal!" They shouted also: "What is your wish?" "Here is our wish!" "May God grant our wish!" Since the word for "wish" was *murad*, and since Murad was the heir-apparent, the political implications of the pun were not far to seek.[114] There were demonstrations also after a second performance of *Vatan* two or three nights later. The upshot was that Namık Kemal was arrested and exiled to Famagusta (Magosa) in Cyprus. His journalist friends Nuri and Ebüzziya Tevfik were also arrested and exiled to Acre and Rhodes respectively. Ahmed Midhat, who collaborated with them, and was a well-known liberal journalist who had begun his career with Midhat Paşa's provincial newspapers, was also exiled to Rhodes. *İbret* was suppressed, as was also a lesser liberal paper, *Siraj* (*Lamp*). Two Armenians were also arrested—Sarafian, the managing director of *İbret*, and Güllü Agop, the director of the theatre—but each was shortly released. The Gedik Paşa theatre, however, was placed under censorship, all plays requiring advance police approval.[115]

Various reasons have been advanced for the exiling. Officially, the journalists were sent away because of their journalism, which the

---

[112] Quoted, in new Turkish, in Sungu, *Namık Kemal*, p. 18.

[113] Quoted in *ibid.*, p. 19.

[114] Abdurrahman Şeref, *Tarih musahabeleri*, p. 182; Kuntay, *Namık Kemal*, II, part 1, 155, 163.

[115] *La Turquie*, 8 and 12 April 1873; *Levant Herald*, 8 (Bulletin du Soir), 10 and 12 April 1873; Pekotsch, *Heimat oder Silistria*, pp. iv-v; Elliot to Granville, #112, 19 April 1873, FO 78/2267; Douin, *Khédive Ismail*, II, 712-713; Sungu, *Namık Kemal*, pp. 18-19; Kuntay, *Namık Kemal*, II, part 1, 164-166. Accounts differ as to whether the arrests were made during the second performance or sometime later.

Porte claimed exceeded the bounds of propriety in its criticism. This was certainly a factor. But the play was what moved the government to action. The official censor, Arifi Bey, a well-educated and westernized diplomat by training, explained that *Vatan* was too inciting, with its talk of blood and war. He criticized the westernized theatre in general as dangerous to Turkish culture because sprung from alien soil.[116] But more than this, the play had shown that people could be aroused to demonstrations which were not only patriotic, but might turn against the sultan himself.[117] For Abdülaziz this was serious, since Namık Kemal had renewed his connections with the heir-apparent Murad after his return from European exile. These evidently were facilitated by the British ambassador, Sir Henry Elliot, and kept up through other intermediaries as well. Murad for a time sent a monthly stipend to Namık Kemal's family while the playwright was in exile at Famagusta.[118] Whether or not actual conspiratorial plans were already afoot, as has been alleged, Murad was still the hope of Namık Kemal and others who thought as he did. The Porte may well have feared another conspiracy like that of 1867.

The exiles had to remain in their places of forced residence until after Abdülaziz had been deposed in 1876. Namık Kemal continued active, writing plays, stories, and works on literature and history. During his exile occurred his famous literary quarrel with Ziya Bey over Ziya's anthology, *Harabat (Tavern)*. Some of Namık Kemal's works were published at the time, either anonymously or under others' names. One play, *Gülnihal (Rose-twig)*, a satire on the strife of Abdülaziz and Murad over the succession, was subtle enough to escape the censor in 1875. Another, *Akif*, was laden with emotion on freedom and fatherland.[119] But it was *Vatan*, inferior in literary merit to much of his later work, which became one of the major documents of Ottoman history because of its historic role in first giving dramatic expression to love of fatherland. It fitted in well also with the rising Islamic sentiment of the 1870's, and with the spirit to be expressed in the crisis

[116] Werner, *Türkische Skizzen*, I, 94-96.
[117] *La Turquie*, 12 April 1873, hints at this.
[118] Kuntay, *Namık Kemal*, II, part 1, 120, 159-160, 263, 717, 738; Şehsuvaroğlu, *Sultan Aziz*, pp. 52-55, 60. Cf. the undocumented account in Alma Wittlin, *Abdul Hamid, the Shadow of God* (London, 1940), pp. 75-78.
[119] Mordtmann, *Stambul*, I, 233; Sungu, *Namık Kemal*, p. 22; Gibb, *Ottoman Poetry*, V, 77-85.

years of 1875 to 1878. When the 1908 revolution was successful, *Vatan* was again ritually performed in both Salonika and İstanbul.[120]

In the years 1873, 1874, and 1875 general discontent with the government of Abdülaziz took a new upward surge because of economic distress among large sections of the population. An agricultural crisis was followed by a crisis in the imperial treasury. Would-be reformers like Midhat were to profit from this situation, for it threw temporarily into their hands a large following among which were numbered many ordinarily conservative Turks. The economic misery began with a famine which affected considerable areas of Anatolia in 1873, and even reached to the capital as well. The financial collapse of the Ottoman treasury, which was always in a precarious state, was helped along by the international panic of 1873 and brought to a head by the treasury's inability to meet the payment of bond coupons on the foreign debt in the fall of 1875. The two phases of the economic crisis were related, as tax receipts fell during the famine period.

Bad crop years and various types of natural disaster were quite usual in one or another of the Ottoman vilayets. But from 1873 to 1875 there was a greater concentration of troubles than at any time in recent years. In 1872 central Anatolia had been afflicted with a drought which sent the price of seed up at the same time as the government pressed for new taxes. The Roumanian principalities suffered similarly that year. Cyprus was by then in its third season of drought, with locust plagues in addition. Conditions rapidly grew worse, especially in Anatolia, but the Balkan provinces were also affected. The Porte saw itself obliged, because of bad harvests and threatened famine in the spring of 1873, to forbid the export of grain from the districts of Ruschuk and Vidin. That fall a similar measure had to be applied to the vilayet of Adana in southeast Anatolia. Naturally the capital and other usual markets for this grain suffered from growing scarcity

---

[120] C. R. Buxton, *Turkey in Revolution* (New York, 1909), p. 71; Bertrand Bareilles, *Les Turcs, ce que fût leur empire* (Paris, 1917), p. 238; Kuntay, *Namık Kemal*, II, part 1, 157, 160. Kuntay, in *ibid.*, p. 158, says that *Vatan* was performed five hundred times in Abdülaziz's reign, which seems hardly credible, since the play was suppressed after its second performance. It may have been revived later, but Abdülaziz reigned for only three years more after the first performance. The play continued, however, to be published and sold in bookstores in Abdülhamid II's reign at least to 1889, when the seventh edition appeared. Cf. Pekotsch, *Heimat oder Silistria*, p.v.

and rising prices. The bad harvests of 1873 were followed by a winter unprecedented for seventy years in its severity. Anatolia lay under a mantle of snow deeper than the oldest inhabitant could remember. Communications were brought to a standstill. Wolves devoured men even near the suburbs of Istanbul. Districts around Harput suffered from earthquake also, which rendered many homeless in temperatures far below freezing. Even so far south as Syria rain, hail, and snow washed out roads, swept away travellers, and killed sheep by the hundreds.[121]

The hard winter, coupled with floods when the deep snow melted, raised the famine to a distressing pitch in 1874. Grain was scarce because of the previous poor harvest and because hungry peasants had eaten their seed supplies during the winter. Worse, nine-tenths of the livestock in some regions had perished from natural causes or slaughtering for food. Men starved in the streets and died without burial. In the Kayseri district a camel forty days dead was torn apart by the hungry; when the vali ordered it buried, the people dug it up and ate the rotting flesh, some dying in consequence. Some merchants cornered food supplies and made large profits. Many villagers began to migrate. Some villages were virtually deserted, larger districts sometimes depopulated by a third or more. In this terrible situation the Ottoman government moved very slowly to relieve distress, hampered by distorted reports from officials in the vilayet system, by corruption, by lack of roads. In some districts in some years the tithe on agricultural produce was totally or partially remitted, but it had been recently raised to twelve and a half per cent, and often was only reduced to the original ten per cent; even this was not uniformly done; and in some regions fifteen to eighteen per cent was collected. Some Turkish officials were absolutely incompetent, and some stole from the relief supplies that were sent by the government. The vali of Ankara, one of the hard-hit regions, had to be removed in favor of Abdurrahman Paşa, formerly one of Midhat's best men in the Tuna vilayet, who then carried out some constructive relief measures. It was

[121] *Levant Times*, 7 October 1872; Maynard to Fish, #34, 4 November 1875, USNA, Turkey 28; Boker to Fish, #93, 14 April 1873, USNA, Turkey 24, and #148, 25 September 1873, USNA, Turkey 25; ABCFM, Western Turkey Mission III, #270, 14 February 1874; ABCFM, Eastern Turkey Mission I, #129, 20 January 1874; #131, 14 March 1874; #132, 8 May 1874; #352, 21 May 1874; George Hill, *A History of Cyprus* (Cambridge, 1940-1952), IV, 248-249 and n.4, 257-258; George Washburn, *Fifty Years in Constantinople* (Boston, 1909), pp. 86-87; Jessup, *Fifty-Three Years*, II, 435.

a commentary on the inefficiency of the Ottoman administration that the most effective, though still insufficient, relief was brought by American and English missionaries and Scottish merchants, aided by a relief committee formed in Istanbul under the direction of the British ambassador and the American minister. The regions of Ankara, Kayseri, Talas, and Harput were among the hardest hit; Sivas escaped the worst. Food in the capital became sufficiently dear so that the poorer there also suffered.[122]

By 1875 the famine itself was over, and the harvest of that year was good; yet the results of the ordeal lingered on. Depopulated villages regained only a portion of their former numbers. One kaza in the Ankara vilayet, for instance, retained in 1875 only twenty-five thousand of a population calculated at fifty-two thousand two years before; twenty thousand were dead and seven thousand had emigrated. Sheep there were still only four per cent of the 1873 figure, oxen twenty per cent. Typhus spread. The government, in straitened financial circumstances, now tried to collect heavier taxes from the impoverished peasantry, but many tax farmers were unwilling to try. Even into the spring and summer of 1876 central Anatolia was filled with homeless, with paupers who had been producers, while new droughts in Bosnia and near Sivas caused the government to prohibit cereal exports from those regions.[123] The political effect of the famine was to predispose a large number of ordinarily conservative peasants toward change. The famine had been centered in Turkish-populated areas; by 1875 the Anatolian Turkish peasant was worse off than the Balkan Christian peasant. Economic misery was then capped by the government's calling out Anatolian peasants to fill the army ranks against Balkan rebellion in 1875 and 1876. The peasantry would not initiate a move to overturn the administration, but by 1875 were quite likely to approve such a move. The famine had also affected many

---

[122] ABCFM, Western Turkey Mission II, #41, 15 September 1874; #42, 13 October 1874; #43, 2 March 1875; #437, 26 November 1874; ABCFM, Western Turkey Mission IV, #432, 27 April 1874; ABCFM, Western Turkey Mission III, #706, 1 January 1875; Stamatiades to Hunter, 25 November 1874, USNA, Constantinople Consulate 11; Maynard to Fish, #34, 4 November 1875, USNA, Turkey 28; Hill, *Cyprus*, IV, 248-249 and n.4, 257-258; *Levant Herald*, 10 October 1874 and 21 May 1875; Elliot to Derby, #138, 12 March 1875, FO 78/2381.

[123] ABCFM, Western Turkey Mission II, #732, 15 August 1875; #100, 16 March 1876; and #742, 28 November 1876; Maynard to Fish, #7, 30 June 1875, USNA, Turkey 28; James L. Farley, *Turks and Christians* (London, 1876), pp. 85-87; Fred Burnaby, *On Horseback Through Asia Minor* (London, 1877), I, 133; Elliot to Derby, #138, 12 March 1875, FO 78/2381; *Levant Herald*, 21 May 1875.

cities, including the nerve center of the empire, İstanbul. But probably the financial crisis of the treasury in 1875 affected opinion in the cities even more than did the famine.

The collapse of the imperial treasury had been preparing for many more years than the famine, and had been staved off by palliatives. The 1861 financial crisis had narrowly missed proving fatal to the credit of the empire.[124] Since that time the Porte had walked the edge of the abyss without plunging in, but only at the cost of increased loans from Europe, the interest and amortization charges on which grew with each year. Had the revenues of the Porte increased substantially during this period, the situation would not have proved so serious. But for many reasons the treasury's income, though increased, did not attain nearly the total that might have been possible.

The basic cause was the underdeveloped state of industry and agriculture within the empire. Mineral resources and industrial possibilities remained largely untouched from lethargy, lack of capital, lack of knowledge, lack of administrative facilitation, and from well-founded suspicion of foreign concessionaires. Native trades and crafts had in many cases been killed off in the nineteenth century by European competition; this was partly the simple result of Europe's industrial advance and partly the result of the capitulation treaties which, even after the revisions of the early 1860's, limited import duties to a maximum of eight per cent ad valorem, and so curbed the Ottoman power to protect native crafts. Internal tariffs on transport of domestic goods were an additional handicap. Since industry produced so little tax revenue, and since import duties were so low, the chief source of revenue had to be the various taxes on land and farming.[125]

Agriculture had made little progress since 1856, still hampered by backward methods, by lack of roads to transport produce, by the discouragement of individual initiative on the part of peasants who worked land that belonged to a landlord or was *vakıf*. This was entirely aside from plagues of locusts, drought, and other natural impediments. Especially important was a noticeable depopulation of the Turkish agricultural districts which was well under way by mid-century, and which found its origins in the heavy burden of military service, in

[124] See above, chapter III.

[125] The American minister, noting with sympathy the Ottoman desire to raise import duties to twenty per cent, observed that the United States government in 1875 got two thirds of all its revenue from that source: Maynard to Fish, #32, 2 November 1875, USNA, Turkey 28.

cholera and other plagues, in abortions and other limitations on the size of families, and in a general tendency toward migration to the cities. Unlike a similar tendency in western Europe and the United States, the increase in number of workers in the cities did not mean a higher birth rate, since the workers were largely bachelors. Nor was it compensated for by more productive and mechanized farming methods. The idleness of a bare city subsistence attracted a good many.[126] The whole economic situation of the empire was further aggravated by sporadic brigandage, by the slow development of road and rail transport, by rapacious and frequently shifted officials, and by the tax system. Some taxes, such as that on Christians in lieu of military service, were not onerous and were collected with a minimum of difficulty. But others, as on silk cocoons, were collected in such a way as to increase spoilage and harm the silk industry. This was often true of the major agricultural tax, the tithe on produce; much of the peasant's crop was often spoiled before the assessor arrived to claim his share. The tithe was still farmed to agents who tried to collect as much as they could, certainly far more than the government ever received from them except in disaster years which deceived their preliminary estimates.[127]

On the basis of such an economy the imperial treasury could not hope for a much larger regular income. True, the budget for the financial year 1874-1875 reckoned on rather startling increases in receipts, but these were of a purely temporary nature in many cases and in others were overvalued.[128] There was no indication that the empire

---

[126] Nassau W. Senior, *A Journal Kept in Turkey and Greece* (London, 1859), pp. 164, 183-184, 190-191, 214; Farley, *Turks and Christians*, pp. 103-121; Mordtmann, *Stambul*, I, 185-195; *idem, Anatolien, Skizzen und Reisebriefe* (Hannover, 1925), pp. 12-13, 97-98, 102-103, 290-291, 425; Friedrich Hellwald, *Der Islam* (Augsburg, 1877), pp. 55-56, n., quoting an article in *Basiret* of April 1875. Provincial inspectors in 1863-1864 had been instructed to seek ways of increasing the population: *Journal de Constantinople*, 13 August 1864.

[127] A good history of economic conditions is needed. The literature is widely scattered. For this period see Engelhardt, *La Turquie*, II, 305-312; Mordtmann, *Stambul*, I, 32-36, and II, 117-118, 181-309; Farley, *Turks and Christians*, pp. 48-71; Albert Dumont, *Le Balkan et l'Adriatique*, pp. 11-23, 337-340; James Baker, *Turkey* (New York, 1877), pp. 337-388, 394-412; G. G. B. St. Clair and C. A. Brophy, *Twelve Years' Study of the Eastern Question in Bulgaria* (London, 1877), pp. 114-116, 135-138; Burnaby, *On Horseback*, I, 192; F. Bianconi, *La question d'Orient dévoilée* (Paris, 1876), pp. 65-67; E. Z. Karal, *Islahat fermanı devri, 1861-1876* (Ankara, 1956), pp. 240-273. Cf. also references in chapter III above, n.91.

[128] Sublime Porte, Ministère des Finances, *Budget des recettes et dépenses de l'exercice 1290 (1874-75)* (Constantinople, 1874), and criticism of it in A. DuVelay, *Essai sur l'histoire financière de la Turquie* (Paris, 1903), pp. 317-323.

could escape from borrowing again in Europe to make up for annual operating deficits. The sultan still spent wildly—one fourteenth of the budget was for his civil list, but he managed to spend more than twice that.[129] Between his expenditures, corruption, and charges for interest and amortization, the treasury was left with less than the funds necessary for the ordinary business of government. Short-term loans locally contracted carried high interest rates, and were particularly castigated by a commission of experts, many of them Europeans, called in to examine the 1874-1875 budget.[130] The local obligations should have been consolidated into long-term debt, but money for the empire was growing tighter. The international panic of 1873 affected İstanbul as Viennese banks there failed, dragging down with them a host of wildcat houses sprung up in Turkey since 1870. Vienna was unable to lend, and London was now more interested in Egypt, Suez, and the United States for investment. Only French capital supported the empire in a loan of 1873, which was not at all favorable to the Ottoman government. Despite a momentary enthusiasm for Ottoman securities on the London market in 1874, the situation did not improve. Some still believed that Ottoman credit could be saved, but predictions of disaster mounted constantly.[131]

By the summer of 1875 financial disaster appeared close at hand. The grand vezir, Esad Paşa, admitting that the situation was serious, cut his own and other top officials' salaries and circularized valis on measures of economy. The salary cuts were meant also, he said, to influence Abdülaziz into giving over part of his income to railroad-building. The sultan was actually induced to issue a *hat* on August 1 saying that he would build the Baghdad railway at his own expense —an announcement greeted by *La Turquie* with effusive praise, but discounted by public opinion.[132] The full effects of the famine of 1873-

---

[129] Goodenow to Fish, #17, 23 April 1874, USNA, Turkey 26.

[130] *Ibid.*, enclosing the commission's report of 17 February 1874.

[131] DuVelay, *Histoire financière*, pp. 205, 304-316; L. H. Jenks, *The Migration of British Capital to 1875* (New York, 1938), pp. 310-311; Charles Morawitz, *Die Türkei im Spiegel ihrer Finanzen* (Berlin, 1903), pp. 20-57. A favorable view of Ottoman finances in Bailleux de Marisy, "Moeurs financières de la France, IV: les valeurs orientales, les finances de la Turquie et de l'Egypte," *Revue des deux mondes*, 3rd period, v (1 October 1874), 650-678; unfavorable views in Benoît Brunswik, *La crise financière de la Turquie* (Paris, 1874), and "Zapiski . . . Igna-tyeva," 1915, VI, 109-120.

[132] Elliot to Derby, #288, confidential, 14 June 1875, FO 78/2383; #341, 13 July 1875; #365, 21 July 1875; #377, confidential, 22 July 1875, FO 78/2384; *Courrier d'Orient*, 28 July 1875; *La Turquie*, 22 July, 3 and 4 August 1875; Braun-Wiesbaden, *Türkische Reise*, II, 332.

1874 were now being felt by the treasury. To this was added the strain of revolt which, simmering since the spring, broke into violent uprising in Herzegovina in July. Grounded in an agrarian dispute between the Muslim landlords and the Orthodox peasantry, the revolt was brought to a head by tax collection methods more vicious than usual, as the Porte attempted to get sorely needed revenues. Hampered by lack of rail transport and lack of funds, with military pay in arrears, the Porte moved too slowly to quell the revolt, which, as it spread, put an added burden on the treasury.[133] Abdülaziz was thus faced in the summer of 1875 with a repetition of the same two crises that existed in 1861 at the time of his accession—financial collapse, and Herzegovinian revolt that was likely to attract support from other Balkan Slavs.

At this juncture the ministry was strengthened by the addition of three former grand vezirs. On August 21, 1875, Midhat was named minister of justice, Hüseyin Avni minister of war, and Mahmud Nedim president of the Council of State.[134] This ministry of all the talents was a curious combination. Midhat could cooperate with Hüseyin Avni, and the two had similar views on the need to act vigorously against the Balkan rebels. But both had previously opposed the grand vezir Esad, and both were undoubtedly suspect to the sultan; Midhat had been unemployed for about eighteen months after a brief tour as vali of Salonika, and Hüseyin Avni had been sent to increasingly distant provincial posts.[135] Mahmud Nedim, further, was the enemy of both, as well as of most other leading statesmen. He had been allowed to return to İstanbul from the governorship of Adana because of ill health and his palace connections.[136] It was evidently the sultan's intention to ease Mahmud Nedim back into the grand vezirate. This took place on August 25, four days after Mahmud Nedim had been made president of the Council of State, and Esad was moved down to the ministry of public works.[137]

From the start, Mahmud Nedim's elevation to the grand vezirate meant trouble. Hüseyin Avni evidently opposed him vigorously, and

[133] Ibid., pp. 105-109; Sumner, Russia and the Balkans, pp. 134-142; Langer, European Alliances, pp. 62-72; Elliot to Derby, #446, 17 August 1875, FO 78/2835.
[134] Hat in La Turquie, 22 August 1875.
[135] A. H. Midhat, Tabsıra-i ibret, pp. 151-152; n.94 above.
[136] Elliot to Derby, #148, 19 March 1875, FO 78/2381.
[137] Elliot to Derby, #471, 25 August 1875, and #493, 29 August 1875, FO 78/2385.

was forced out of the ministry by October 2. Midhat Paşa resigned in November. Meanwhile Russian influence was immensely strengthened. Ignatyev made no secret of his glee at the turn of events, and it may be that his influence with the sultan was partly responsible for Mahmud Nedim's appointment.[138] Mahmud was so friendly to Russia that Nelidov, the counsellor of embassy, could write: "Ignatyev was master of the situation in Constantinople, where a grand vezir devoted to Russia and a Sultan hostile to the West were more disposed to follow his suggestions than to listen to the advice of our adversaries."[139] Naturally Ignatyev wanted to maintain this favorable situation, and to keep the initiative in the developing crisis over Herzegovina from passing into Austrian hands. Therefore, though Ignatyev did not believe in the vitality of the empire and scorned the westernized reforms of Âli and Fuad, he advocated, for the moment, a policy of new reform measures and of soft answers to the Balkan insurgents. His influence on the various reforms announced by Mahmud Nedim during the last five months of 1875, and on the lenient policy in dealing with the rebels, was considerable. Mahmud Nedim "gave his beard into the hand of the Russian ambassador Ignatyev," said Cevdet.[140] At the same time Ignatyev kept up his relations with minorities in the empire and supported the mission of the pan-Slav general Fadeyev to reconstruct the khedive's army. Of course Ignatyev's forces were all deployed against Midhat and Hüseyin Avni, the two members of the ministry who wanted to put down the insurrection by force and parley afterward.[141]

While the Balkan revolt increased in scope and intensity, Mahmud Nedim was confronted with the problem of imminent bankruptcy. The immediate question was to find funds to pay the Ottoman bond coupons that fell due in October. Service on the public debt now consumed over forty per cent of the annual budget; but by late September the financial year, though only half gone, showed a deficit of eight and a half million pounds sterling. Evidently a three-month

[138] Sumner, *Russia and the Balkans*, p. 145, baldly credits Ignatyev with bringing about the change. Ignatyev had certainly tried. Cf. Elliot to Derby, #310, confidential, 25 June 1875, FO 78/2383.

[139] Nelidow, "Souvenirs d'avant et d'après la guerre de 1877-1878," *Revue des deux mondes*, 6th period, 27 (1915), 308.

[140] Mardin, *Cevdet Paşa*, p. 131, n.113.

[141] Sumner, *Russia and the Balkans*, pp. 70, 73-76, 143, 145-146; Gallenga, *Two Years*, I, 96-104, 112-113; Elliot to Derby, #553, 15 September 1875, FO 78/2386; Raschdau, "Nachlass . . . Dr. Busch," pp. 392-393.

loan from the Ottoman Bank at eighteen per cent was insufficient. By late September some diplomats, at least, knew that repudiation or reduction of payments was contemplated, and the public also got wind of this.[142] Nevertheless, the actual announcement of default came as a surprise. The irade of October 6, 1875, published in the newspapers the next day, told the Porte's creditors that for five years they would get only one half of the interest due them, the other half to be replaced by new obligations carrying five per cent interest.[143] On the surface this partial default seemed the only sane method of attacking the problem. In its official releases the Porte promised such financial reorganization and economic development that in five years the interest and amortization charges could easily be met.[144] Nevertheless, a storm of protest arose at once. Ignatyev was generally accused of having instigated the default, with a malicious intent to aid the downfall of the Ottoman Empire. For a man who wanted to maintain Mahmud Nedim in office, this was a foolish move. Nevertheless, it is known that Ignatyev gloated over the financial weakness of the empire and, further, that he resented the influence of British and French bondholders. It may thus have been that Ignatyev thought he could defy the western powers at the same time as he guided the destinies of the empire through "Nedimoff." If this actually was his reasoning, it was a miscalculation.[145]

For the default was one of the penultimate steps toward the downfall not only of Mahmud Nedim, for the second time, and thus of Ignatyev's influence, but also of Abdülaziz himself. Already the famine and the Islamic feeling which called for strong measures

---

[142] Sublime Porte, Ministère des Finances, *Budget des recettes et des dépenses de l'exercice 1291 (1875-76)* (Constantinople, 1875); Elliott to Derby, #524, confidential, 7 September 1875; #525, 7 September 1875; FO 78/2386; Elliot to Derby, #581, 24 September 1875; #591, 26 September 1875; #617, confidential, 30 September 1875, and encl., FO 78/2387; *Levant Herald*, 24 September and 7 October (weekly edition) 1875.

[143] DuVelay, *Histoire financière*, pp. 326-334, with the official pronouncements; Mordtmann, *Stambul*, I, 123-124.

[144] *Le Stamboul*, 7 October 1875. Cf. Jenks, *British Capital*, p. 320: "a very sensible moratorium."

[145] Mehmed Memduh, *Mirât-ı şuûnat*, pp. 54-55; Raschdau, "Nachlass . . . Dr. Busch," p. 393; Sumner, *Russia and the Balkans*, p. 103; D. C. Blaisdell, *European Financial Control in the Ottoman Empire* (New York, 1929), pp. 78-80. Cherbuliez, "L'Angleterre et la Russie en Orient," *Revue d'histoire diplomatique*, X (1896), 65-66, absolves Ignatyev of all advance knowledge and implicates Elliot. Jenks, *British Capital*, p. 320, calls Ignatyev's advice "disinterested." Ignatyev's motives and actions are still obscure. Mahmud Celaleddin, *Mirât-ı hakikat*, I, 65, says that the British and French embassies reportedly were consulted and offered no objection.

against the Balkan rebels had aroused many Turks against the government and the sultan. Naturally the default irritated European bondholders, who would be less likely to support a defaulting government. More important for the immediate political situation, the default affected adversely a good many Ottomans who had invested in their government's bonds—not only Greeks and Armenians, but Turks as well, among the wealthier and influential official class. This was true both in the capital and in provincial cities.[146] Just after the announcement of default some passengers on a Bosporus ferry with rather bitter irony offered half the ticket price in cash and five-year bonds for the remainder.[147] Such men would be unlikely to give continued support to the government of Mahmud Nedim, and perhaps would turn against Abdülaziz. They were thus, by the events of 1875, thrown together temporarily with common conservative Turks and with disciples of the New Ottomans, all of whom, for one reason or another, were discontented with the government. Leadership for the discontented would soon be supplied by Midhat and Hüseyin Avni, both of whom were by late fall out of the government.

[146] Mardin, *Cevdet*, pp. 131-132, n.113; Burnaby, *On Horseback*, II, 34-35; Baker, *Turkey*, p. 392; Raschdau, "Nachlass . . . Dr. Busch," p. 397, n.1; Edwin Pears, *Forty Years in Constantinople* (New York, 1916), p. 52. Cevdet Paşa, in Mardin, *Cevdet*, charges that Midhat, Mahmud Nedim, and Ignatyev made use of advance knowledge of the default to sell off bonds and profit greatly. The charge is unproven, at least as regards Midhat. Cf. Kuntay, *Namık Kemal*, II, part 1, 347, n.23; İnal, *Son sadrıâzamlar*, pp. 396-397.
[147] *Levant Herald*, 9 October 1875.

CHAPTER IX

1876—THE YEAR OF THE THREE SULTANS

As the autumn of 1875 wore on into winter, it became increasingly clear that both men and events were conspiring to effect some sort of political upheaval within the Ottoman Empire. Any government would have experienced great difficulty in solving all the problems that confronted the Porte. Mahmud Nedim's government proved quite unable to deal effectively with the problems of insurrection and finance and unable, above all, to allay the popular discontent sprung from Christian revolt, European diplomatic intervention, pan-Slav pressure, famine, economic distress, and the rising tide of Muslim feeling. By the spring of 1876 this general discontent, focussed on the Ottoman government, found leadership in strategically placed groups of civil officials, military leaders, and theological students whose temporary coalescence made possible the coup d'état of May 30.

Had the Turks acted vigorously at the very inception of the revolt to put it down, or had the consuls of the European powers found a solution in the fall of 1875, the whole course of events that ensued might have been altered. But such was not the case. The revolt spread into Bosnia, increased in ferocity, found succor from across the frontiers of Montenegro, Serbia, and Austria-Hungary, and received backing among pan-Slavs. European opinion generally sided with the rebels, and although none of the great powers wanted to precipitate a dissolution of the Ottoman Empire, all became involved in discussions about the situation, while elements within the Austro-Hungarian and Russian governments sought a disposition of Bosnia-Herzegovina that would be favorable to one or the other of them.[1] The Muslim feeling which had been growing among Turks since the early 1870's began to express itself not only against the rebels, but against other Christians of the empire and against the European powers. Occasional outrages were committed against Christians, an undercurrent of opposition to Christians existed in various cities, including İstanbul itself,

[1] The diplomatic complications among the European powers may best be followed in William L. Langer, *European Alliances and Alignments*, 2nd ed. (New York, 1950); David Harris, *A Diplomatic History of the Balkan Crisis of 1875-1878: The First Year* (Stanford, 1936); B. H. Sumner, *Russia and the Balkans, 1870-1880* (New York, 1937); R. W. Seton-Watson, *Disraeli, Gladstone and the Eastern Question: A Study in Diplomacy and Party Politics* (London, 1935).

and some papers in the capital began to accuse Europe of religious fanaticism.[2] Matters were not improved by an abortive rising of Bulgar revolutionaries in September, which led the Porte to enroll Muslim irregulars in Balkan towns to be prepared for any such future risings.[3]

A possible diplomatic solution to the crisis over Bosnia-Herzegovina appeared on December 30, 1875, in the form of the Andrassy Note, worked out by the Austro-Hungarian foreign minister and approved by the other five great powers.[4] The Porte protested vigorously against receiving this reform program for the two provinces in the form of an identic or collective note, and was generally unhappy about foreign interference, saying to the British government with remarkably accurate foreboding that acceptance of such a note "would be fatal to [Sultan Abdülaziz's] influence over his subjects: and the discontent which would be produced by such a step would endanger his throne."[5] Nevertheless, in an effort to avoid further foreign interference, the Porte accepted the proposed plan with slight reservations.[6] Had it been applied by the Porte with the backing of the six powers, further immediate trouble in the empire might have been forestalled. But the insurgents themselves rejected the Andrassy Note as affording insufficient guarantees for enforcement. They used such language as "Our blood cries for revenge!" and "Now or never."[7] Mahmud Nedim's government was thus, in the eyes of its public, saddled with a double failure: it had given in to outside Christian interference, and no beneficial results in Bosnia-Herzegovina had come from this weakness. The Porte was worried about public reaction, did not release the text of the Note to the press, and imposed prepublication censorship on all news stories concerning it.[8]

Such governmental action pointed up the new importance of public opinion in the Ottoman Empire, especially in the capital. There had always been in Ottoman history public opinion of a sort, which had

---

[2] Antonio Gallenga, *Two Years of the Eastern Question* (London, 1877), I, 203-219, 272-312; *Stamboul*, 2 and 5 October 1875; ABCFM, Western Turkey Mission II, #455, 23 December 1875; ABCFM, Eastern Turkey Mission I, #462, 27 January 1876.

[3] ABCFM, Western Turkey Mission II, #551, 27 October 1875.

[4] Text in *Staatsarchiv*, 30 (1877), #5580.

[5] Harris, *Diplomatic History*, pp. 210-211, quoting Raşid to Musurus, 3 January 1876, FO 78/2527, and Derby to Elliot, 14 January 1876, FO 78/2448.

[6] *Staatsarchiv*, 30 (1877), #5587.

[7] *Ibid.*, #5588-#5591.

[8] ABCFM, Western Turkey Mission II, #568 and #569, 9 and 16 February 1876.

operated in political terms even to the point of sanctioning the deposition of some dozen sultans.[9] But by 1875 the growth of the press in İstanbul, the propaganda activities of the New Ottomans, and the growing familiarity of members of the elite groups with the European press and public opinion had given this force an added significance. Accounts of events in these years by contemporaries are full of references to *efkâr-ı umumiye*, public opinion. More than in 1859 at the time of the Kuleli incident, more than in 1867 when some of the New Ottomans planned a coup, the coup of May 1876 represented fairly a public opinion among Turks of the empire which was more and more turned against the government. As in both of the earlier years, opinions voiced were partly conservative, complaining about concessions to Christians and governmental weakness under pressure, and partly liberal, complaining of governmental autocracy. But they were invariably antigovernment. Such sentiments reached out into the provinces, bolstered by the economic distress. "I repeatedly heard with my own ears," wrote the *Times* correspondent in early 1876, "old Mussulmans in remote and peaceful villages of Asia Minor . . . say that 'the Herzegovinians were their best friends, as they were at war against the government, and Inshallah! it might be hoped they would hold out till they had altogether overthrown it.' "[10]

Mahmud Nedim was at first the prime target of the rising discontent. The Austrian ambassador thought him the only progressive Ottoman official who had energy and prestige, but this was obviously untrue.[11] The grand vezir was popularly criticized for his ineffectiveness, his connections with the Russian embassy, and for his attempted reforms.[12] At least by January of 1876 there were rumors of plots afoot to overthrow his government.[13] The criticism did not stop there, however, but went on to include Abdülaziz himself. This had been encouraged by the fact that Mahmud Nedim, as he had during his first grand vezirate, made a great parade of attributing to the sultan

[9] Cf. A. D. Alderson, *The Structure of the Ottoman Dynasty* (Oxford, 1956), pp. 59-60; H. A. R. Gibb and Harold Bowen, *Islamic Society and the West*, I, part 1 (London, 1950), 38.

[10] Gallenga, *Two Years*, I, 295.

[11] Zichy to Andrassy, 14 December 1875, HHS, Varia Turquie I, #96AG, quoted in Harris, *Diplomatic History*, p. 160, n.85.

[12] Ahmed Saib, *Vaka-i Sultan Abdülaziz* (Cairo, 1320), pp. 190-191; Gallenga, *Two Years*, I, 149.

[13] ABCFM, Western Turkey Mission II, #563, 12 January 1876, and III, #29, 18 January 1876. Cf. Elliot to Derby, #181, 10 February 1876, FO 78/2455.

the responsibility for governmental actions. The majority of people, says Cevdet, began to find courage to mutter slanders against the sultan himself.[14] Rumors about possible deposition of the sultan began to be current in the fall of 1875, though these were perhaps not so widely believed as other rumors that Abdülaziz's health was deteriorating.[15] The public regard for the sultan, in any case, declined noticeably through the winter of 1875-1876. Suspicions that Abdülaziz continued to spend large sums while the empire was in financial straits, and that he demanded payment of his Ottoman debt coupons in full when other bondholders received only half, added to his unpopularity. The whole financial situation was, in fact, becoming worse, not better. Salaries of government employees, including military men, were months in arrears, while the Porte accumulated enough funds to meet the half payment on the debt coupons due in January. The payment was met, but at the cost of mounting dissatisfaction especially in İstanbul, where government was the biggest industry. English workmen employed at the imperial dockyard actually went on strike to get their pay; Turks did not go that far, but grumbled. Meanwhile, despite the imposition of new taxes, the financial situation of the government declined to the point where the April coupon payment was defaulted in its entirety. Business generally was in a slump; many individuals were economically distressed.[16]

Mahmud Nedim's government was not behindhand in issuing the various sorts of reform edicts usual to such a period of tension. Fermans went out to provincial valis urging them zealously and impartially to administer justice and to see that all vilayet meclises were freely elected and that members were equally treated and were given freedom of expression.[17] An irade of October 2, 1875, remitted the

[14] Ebül'ulâ Mardin, *Medenî hukuk cephesinden Ahmet Cevdet Paşa* (İstanbul, 1946), p. 133, n.114. Cf. ABCFM, Western Turkey Mission II, #455, 23 December 1875.

[15] *Ibid.*, #550, 20 October 1875; Mardin, *Cevdet*, p. 133, n.114; Gallenga, *Two Years*, I, 236-238; *Levant Herald*, 18 February 1876.

[16] Raschdau, "Aus dem politischen Nachlass des Unterstaatssekretärs Dr. Busch," *Deutsche Rundschau*, 137 (1908), 397, n.1; ABCFM, Western Turkey Mission III, #29, 18 January 1876, and II, #565, 26 January 1876, #575, 5 April 1876, and Western Turkey Mission I, #462, 6 April 1876; *Levant Herald*, 11 January 1876; Elliot to Derby, #11, 4 January 1876, and #78, secret, 20 January 1876, FO 78/2454; #110, confidential, 26 January 1876, FO 78/2455; #226, 22 February 1876, and #240, 28 February 1876, FO 78/2456; Maynard to Fish, #36, 15 November 1875, USNA, Turkey 28.

[17] Texts in Benoît Brunswik, *La Turquie, ses créanciers, et la diplomatie* (Paris, 1875), pp. 101-103, 109-111.

extra two and a half per cent which had been added to the tithe on agricultural produce, as well as certain arrears in taxes; it repeated that vilayet councils were to have elected members truly representative of the local communities; and it promised that delegates from vilayet assemblies should come to İstanbul to make known their wishes on future reforms. The delegates were, however, not to assemble like a national chamber, but to come to İstanbul in separate groups.[18] A yet more sweeping ferman of December 12 promised tax reform, judicial reform, equality of all citizens of the empire in elegibility to public office, and full religious liberty.[19] Further lengthy and detailed instructions to provincial valis issued on February 21, 1876, again emphasized free elections to the provincial councils, recommended to the valis tours of provincial inspection and new regulations on prisons and police, and told them to apply the recent reforms. A sop to the minorities was offered by the provision that court decisions would, where necessary, be rendered into Greek, Armenian, "Bosnian," Bulgarian, and Arabic.[20]

These were all fundamentally restatements of reforms attempted in the Tanzimat period, incorporating the principle of Osmanlılık. The *Levant Herald* thought that, since the ferman of December 12 simply strengthened promises already made, it was not too ambitious for fulfillment.[21] Yet it is hard to take these reform edicts seriously, in view of the past record of Mahmud Nedim and of the fact that at this juncture he was simply trying to keep the great powers off his neck with regard to Bosnia-Herzegovina by promising reforms for the empire as a whole. What is more, although these reforms were issued under the pressure of diplomatic events and with the encouragement of the British ambassador, Sir Henry Elliot, they owed even more to Mahmud Nedim's friend Ignatyev. Ignatyev's interest was simply to quiet the Ottoman Christians for the moment, since Russia was not ready to partition the Ottoman Empire; to keep his influence with Abdülaziz and Mahmud Nedim; to keep the initiative with regard to the Eastern Question in his own hands and out of Andrassy's; and to urge Turkish reforms "favorable to the future centrifugal develop-

---

[18] Text in *ibid.*, pp. 106-108; *Staatsarchiv*, 29 (1876), #5567.

[19] Text in *Staatsarchiv*, 30 (1877), #5575. Original French text as distributed in Elliot to Derby, #833, 14 December 1875, FO 28/2391.

[20] Text in Grégoire Aristarchi, *Législation ottomane* (Constantinople, 1873-1888), v, 50-59; George Young, *Corps de droit ottoman* (Oxford, 1905-1906), I, 88-95.

[21] *Levant Herald*, 18 December 1875.

ment of the Slavs."²² Since the public knew of Mahmud Nedim's closeness to the Russian ambassador, they tended to be sceptical of the grand vezir's moves.²³ His whole performance gives the impression of frenzied activity to stay in office, to ward off the powers, to appease the general domestic discontent, and to offer a little something to the Balkan rebels.

Mahmud Nedim did set up machinery for carrying out reforms which, if it had worked, might have improved the situation. An eight-man executive council, four Muslims and four Christians, was created to supervise the execution of the announced measures, and to it was added a control commission which would revive again the principle of travelling commissioners of inspection to check on provincial administration and hear complaints.²⁴ There is no evidence that the council or the control commission actually functioned. A yet more promising move was made in January 1876, when Raşid Paşa, the foreign minister, called an unprecedented interdenominational conference in which were represented Greeks, Armenians, Jews, Roman Catholics, and Protestants, to discuss ways and means of reform. These non-Muslims were so outspoken in their demands for complete equality, for genuine Osmanlılık, that the government was embarrassed, and no more was heard of such conferences.²⁵ Odian Efendi, already committed to Midhat's cause, was one of the most forthright, in his quality as representative of the Gregorian Armenians. Curiously, two Armenians did sit briefly as members of the council of ministers during Mahmud Nedim's vezirate.²⁶ This looked like a real step toward Osmanlılık, but the appearance was deceiving. Artin Dadian Efendi was only acting foreign minister briefly in November 1875, while the new appointee Raşid was coming back from his ambassadorship in Vienna.²⁷ This was chance. Abraham Paşa was made minister without

²² Alexander Onou, "The Memoirs of Count N. Ignatyev," *Slavonic Review*, X (December 1931), 401-404; Sumner, *Russia and the Balkans*, pp. 146-150; Harris, *Diplomatic History*, pp. 139, 163-165.

²³ Mithat Cemal Kuntay, *Namık Kemal* (İstanbul, 1944-1956), I, 127-128, n.4.

²⁴ *Levant Herald*, 20, 21, and 23 December 1875; Elliot to Derby, #854, 23 December 1875, and #871, 30 December 1875, with encl., FO 78/2391; text in Aristarchi, *Législation*, V, 34-35.

²⁵ ABCFM, Western Turkey Mission III, #30, 22 January 1876, and II, #457, 28 January 1876.

²⁶ Only one Christian had ever been elevated to that eminence before, and that was Krikor Agaton in 1868 as minister of public works.

²⁷ Ibnülemin Mahmud Kemal İnal, *Osmanlı devrinde son sadrıâzamlar* (İstanbul, 1940-1953), I, 47, n.1; Elliot to Derby, #745, 12 November 1875, FO 78/2390.

YEAR OF THE THREE SULTANS

portfolio in the last month of Mahmud Nedim's grand vezirate. But Abraham was the ex-agent of the khedive Ismail, was close to Abdülaziz, and was suspect to almost everybody. He hardly represented his millet.[28]

The total impact of Mahmud Nedim's second grand vezirate, stretching from August 25, 1875, to May 11, 1876, was thus to create more rather than less dissatisfaction with the Ottoman government. Almost all groups of Ottoman society, for one reason or another, seemed to oppose him and his policies. The men most likely to provide leadership for this opposition were the two who had left Mahmud Nedim's cabinet in the fall of 1875. One of these was Hüseyin Avni Paşa, who had presumably been a personal enemy of Mahmud Nedim ever since his exile from the capital by Mahmud Nedim during the latter's first grand vezirate in 1871. Though he had himself been grand vezir for fourteen months in 1874-1875, Hüseyin Avni was still ambitious of power, and even contemplated the deposition of Sultan Abdülaziz. During a trip he took in 1875 to Vichy for the cure he is said to have spoken of a plot already afoot, in collaboration with Midhat, to overturn the government.[29] As minister of war in Mahmud Nedim's government Hüseyin Avni did not last long, forced out on October 2, 1875, evidently because of the personal antagonism between the two men and because Hüseyin Avni wanted much more vigorous measures taken against the Balkan rebels.[30] Thereafter Hüseyin Avni seems to have bent all his efforts to toppling Mahmud Nedim from power. He was named vali of Salonika to get him out of the capital, managed to get that appointment changed to Bursa, which was nearer the capital, and delayed his departure as long as he could.[31] When Hüseyin Avni's house in İstanbul burned in mid-December, rumors sped around the capital that the fire revealed a great store of arms laid up in his house and that these were destined for an

[28] *Stamboul*, 19 April 1876; Elliot to Derby, #396, confidential, 19 April 1876, FO 78/2457.

[29] Charles Mismer, *Souvenirs du monde musulman* (Paris, 1892), pp. 271-275. Several details of the story are garbled, but Mismer could not have made the story up out of whole cloth.

[30] Elliot to Derby, #618 and #619, both 2 October 1875, FO 78/2388; *Levant Herald*, 4 October 1875.

[31] *Stamboul* for December, passim; Elliot to Derby, #784, 25 November 1875, FO 78/2390, and #836, confidential, 19 December 1875, FO 78/2391.

317

insurrection.[32] Whatever the truth about his clandestine activities over the winter of 1875-1876, Hüseyin Avni's motives seem to have been, aside from particular enmities, a personal drive for power and a patriotic determination to crush the Balkan rebellion and thwart the increasing Russian influence. He was no constitutionalist, despite his association with discussions of constitutional government in 1873, and a Tanzimat man only in so far as army reform went. But his ability, his patriotism, and his political eminence might bring him a considerable following, especially among military men, should he attempt to lead a coup against the government.[33]

The other and politically more effective opponent of Mahmud Nedim was Midhat Paşa. Minister of justice since August, Midhat felt that Mahmud Nedim's conduct toward the rebels was too weak, offered them too many concessions, and that his proposed reforms would provide no cure for the financial and political weakness of the Ottoman Empire in the fall of 1875. Evidently a real argument took place in the council of ministers toward the end of November, whereupon an announcement in the press that Midhat was confined to his house by a slight indisposition was followed by another that he had resigned.[34] Resignation was unusual enough in the Ottoman system to cause public comment, but it was almost unprecedented for Midhat to write out his reasons for resignation in a memorandum to the Palace. This move was bound to have an impact on the public because of Midhat's relative popularity. Furthermore, the memorandum circulated in manuscript in İstanbul.[35] Midhat, in fact, wrote two letters of resignation, the first of which modestly asked Abdülaziz to release him from his burdensome office and give him one in internal administration more suited to his training as a provincial governor.[36] But when asked by the Palace for further explanation, or possibly to reconsider, Midhat painted a dark picture of the international and internal situation of the empire, implying his dissatisfaction with meas-

[32] ABCFM, Western Turkey Mission II, #560, 22 December 1875; Gallenga, *Two Years*, I, 128-132.

[33] Süleyman Paşa, *Hiss-i inkılâb* (İstanbul, 1326), pp. 9-10, 17; Ahmed Saib, *Vaka-i Sultan Abdülaziz*, pp. 167-168; *Levant Herald*, 5 July 1876; "Zapiski Grapha N. P. Ignatyeva (1864-1874)," *Izvestiia Ministerstva Inostrannykh Děl*, 1915, I, 156-158; E. de Kératry, *Mourad V* (Paris, 1878), pp. 103-105.

[34] *Stamboul*, 29 and 30 November, 1875.

[35] Gallenga, *Two Years*, I, 107.

[36] Text, dated 28 November 1875 (29 şevval 1292), in Mehmed Memduh, *Mirât-ı şuûnat* (İzmir, 1328), pp. 134-135; also encl. in Elliot to Derby, #831, 14 December 1875, FO 78/2391.

ures taken to deal with the powers, the rebels, the Christian subjects generally, and the financial crisis.[37] Quite possibly Midhat had gone farther than this in expressing his views in the council of ministers, for reports then current said he had compared the empire to a ship without captain or rudder, and had proposed a partly elective council to control budget and finances, as well as complete equality of all subjects before the law and a further decentralization and democratization of provincial rule.[38] Midhat, in fact, repeated privately to Elliot such views, and told the British ambassador that he wanted to go beyond first steps, to institute a senate which, nominated by the government at first, would become elective and exercise a constitutional control over the sultan. He shared, said Midhat, the general opinion now current that in view of Abdülaziz's character real improvement would be nearly hopeless without such control.[39]

Presumably from this period dates Midhat's intensive drive to secure a constitution for the Ottoman Empire. The statesman who earlier had spoken most clearly for constitutional government, Mustafa Fazıl Paşa, had died just at the beginning of December 1875.[40] Midhat was now the most prominent of the few politicians who held such ideas.[41] It would be interesting to have a day-by-day account of Midhat's activities during the next five months, but unfortunately no such is available. Undoubtedly he employed his leisure, as he may have done during his previous eighteen months' unemployment before he became minister of justice, to win support for his ideas. He certainly was fairly close to the British ambassador, and this, in turn, may have given him added prestige among those who were concerned to combat Ignatyev's influence. It may also have given him hopes of British

---

[37] Text, also dated 28 November 1875, in A. H. Midhat, *Midhat Paşa, hayat-ı siyâsiyesi*, vol. 1, *Tabsıra-i ibret* (İstanbul, 1325), 157, n.1; A. H. Midhat, *Life of Midhat Pasha* (London, 1903), pp. 67-68 (here misdated 1874); encl. in Elliot to Derby, #321, confidential, 30 March 1876, FO 78/2456, probably as supplied by Midhat himself to Elliot.

[38] Gallenga, *Two Years*, I, 158-159; Sandison to Elliot, #120, confidential, 5 December 1875, encl. in Elliot to Derby, #819, confidential, 6 December 1875, FO 78/2391; Elliot to Derby, #820, 10 December 1875, FO 78/2391.

[39] Elliot to Derby, #831 and #832, confidential, both 14 December 1875, FO 78/2391. Cf. Henry Elliot, "The Death of Abdul Aziz and of Turkish Reform," *Nineteenth Century*, 23 (February 1888), 279-280, which exaggerates Midhat's views slightly.

[40] Elliot to Derby, #812, 5 December 1875, FO 78/2391.

[41] Halil Şerif had similar views. It has been said, though the author cannot ascertain the facts, that Midhat, Halil Şerif, and Elliot worked up a constitutional draft in the winter of 1875-1876: (Cherbuliez), "L'Angleterre et la Russie en Orient," *Revue d'histoire diplomatique*, X (1896), 68.

support.[42] Midhat did have something of a personal following already, based on a reputation for honesty and good provincial administration, and demonstrated by the popular acclaim that had greeted his appointment as grand vezir in 1872. He would attract those affected by New Ottoman sentiments, those affected by salary arrears and economic distress, and those opposed to Mahmud Nedim and his catering to Abdülaziz's whims. Midhat also seems to have spent considerable effort to win support among the ulema for his views on the need for a constitutional check on the sultan, arguing that the constitutional method (*usul-u meşveret*, "the method of consultation") did not contravene religious law, but rather was in accord with it.[43]

What Midhat and those associated with him were contemplating was better known after the issuance on March 9, 1876, of an anonymous manifesto signed by "the Muslim patriots." Probably Midhat was the principal author of the document, though it may have been written by someone close to him.[44] It is likely that Odian Efendi, long an advocate of some form of constitutional government, was involved in the drafting; possibly Hüseyin Avni and Kayserili Ahmed Paşa, minister of marine, were informed about it.[45] Midhat was the only individual mentioned by name in the document, as an able administrator in the Danube vilayet and as the "enlightened and courageous head of the energetic and moderate party." The manifesto was sent to such European statesmen as Disraeli, Derby, Granville, MacMahon, Thiers, Gambetta, Bismarck, and Visconti Venosta in an effort to show them that further European intervention in Ottoman affairs would only exacerbate the internal situation. It was not, and could not

---

[42] *Stamboul*, 21 and 22 December 1875; George Washburn, *Fifty Years in Constantinople* (Boston, 1909), p. xx.

[43] Ahmed Saib, *Vaka-i Sultan Abdülaziz*, pp. 145-146; Clician Vassif, *Son Altesse Midhat-Pacha* (Paris, 1909), p. 36. Cf. Ignatyev's reports of April 1876 on the discontent and Midhat's use of it: IÜ. A. Petrosian, *"Novye Osmany" i bor'ba za konstitutsiiu* (Moscow, 1958), pp. 84-85.

[44] Clician Vassif, *Midhat-Pacha*, p. 44, says Midhat drafted a reform memorandum, quite possibly this one or its basis; Ahmed Saib, *Tarih-i Sultan Murad-ı Hamis* (Cairo, n.d.), pp. 173-174, attributes it to a group of liberals assembled around Midhat; *Stamboul*, 2 June 1876, attributes it to "the men at the head of the great liberal movement inaugurated by the softas"; Frédéric Macler, *Autour de l'Arménie* (Paris, 1917), p. 269, following an Armenian source, says it is attributed to Midhat and Odian; Andreas D. Mordtmann, *Stambul und das moderne Türkenthum* (Leipzig, 1877-1878), II, 90-91, says that Odian, then undersecretary of public works, translated it into French; *Diplomatic Review*, 24 (July 1876), 161, says the document reportedly was drawn up by a Pole, but gives no name. This journal opposed a parliament such as the manifesto advocated.

[45] Mordtmann, *Stambul*, II, 90-91.

be, printed in the Ottoman Empire until there was a change in sultans, and appeared in public print only on June 2 after Abdülaziz had been deposed.[46] But the manifesto was sufficiently broadcast so that it must have become known not only to the government of Mahmud Nedim, but to wider circles in the capital also.

Many of the points made in the manifesto bore a close resemblance to those Midhat had been making already.[47] It began by pointing out that the reforms proposed by Europe would antagonize the Muslims by seeming to grant special privileges to Christians and to rebels, and that the promise of reforms would further antagonize the Christians because the wretched government of Abdülaziz and Mahmud Nedim would not carry them out. The manifesto then cited evidence of corruption and bad government and of the critical financial situation, laying the blame for all faults at the door of the autocratic system wherein the sultan had ultimately uncontrolled freedom. Muslims suffered from this as much as Christians. The remedy proposed was a consultative assembly, representative of all races and creeds in the empire, which should serve as a counterweight to the sultan. The assembly, it was recognized, could not function perfectly from its inception, and might begin with limited powers over internal affairs only. The eventual model would be the English form of government. Abdülaziz was called a "miserable madman," and his deposition considered a possible, though not an inevitable, necessity. Great stress was laid on the supposed religious prescriptions that the sultan, to be legitimately possessed of his power and place, must be accepted by the nation and take counsel of the nation. The whole tone of the document continued the emphasis of the Tanzimat period on Ottoman brotherhood. It seemed further to echo the constitutional demands of Mustafa Fazıl's letter of 1867. But Mustafa Fazıl's letter had implored the sultan himself to bring about such a change. Now, in 1876, the "Muslim patriots" despaired of the sultan and seemed to look more to their own efforts.

Raşid Paşa, foreign minister in Mahmud Nedim's government, was well aware of the opposition after the appearance of this manifesto, if he had not been before. When asked in March why further con-

[46] *Stamboul*, 2 June 1876, used its whole front page for the text of the manifesto; *Vakit* and *Basiret* also printed it in full, probably a day or two later: *Stamboul*, 6 June 1876.
[47] Text, in addition to *Stamboul* of June 2, is in *Staatsarchiv*, 30 (1877), #5642, and in Mordtmann, *Stambul*, II, 94-106.

cessions could not be made to Montenegro and the Bosnians, he replied that "if we made propositions to the Sultan tomorrow in this
sense, in the evening we shall already be deprived of our positions
and Midhat, Hussein and Derwisch Pascha, who are on the watch,
come in here."[48] Hüseyin Avni was in Bursa as governor, but he may
still have been in touch with Midhat, and may even have come closer
to backing Midhat's liberal plans simply because of anger over his
provincial exile. Just how the planning to overthrow Mahmud Nedim's government developed it is impossible to say. Midhat's memoirs,
as edited by his son, are silent on this point.[49] "Counsel was being taken
in Midhat's Konak," says his son in another place, "among a few patriots who did not yet despair of their country, as to the best mode of
saving the empire."[50] Midhat's secretary may be more accurate in reporting that Midhat, during his period out of office in 1875-1876,
often saw Hüseyin Avni, Mütercim Mehmed Rüşdi, and Hayrullah
Efendi, a prominent member of the ulema; was in touch with the
erstwhile New Ottoman, Ziya Bey; and was also in touch with the
heir apparent, Murad, who is said to have approved the reform memorandum drawn up by Midhat.[51] Midhat evidently proposed to Mütercim Mehmed Rüşdi, who was a generally respected elder statesman
now also out of office, that the two go together to the palace in an
attempt to make Abdülaziz aware of the serious dangers confronting
the state and to get him to change the personnel of the ministry. But
Mehmed Rüşdi, always a cautious as well as a moderate man, thought
the maneuver too risky.[52] Midhat may also have been in touch with
various Greeks of the capital.[53] Whether he received from Sir Henry
Elliot anything more than general moral support in this period must
remain open to conjecture; Elliot's dispatches indicate a general knowledge of Midhat's political views, but no intimate connection.[54]

[48] Dr. K., *Erinnerungen aus dem Leben des Serdar Ekrem Omer Pascha* (Sarajevo,
1885), pp. 269-270. Almost the same account in *idem, Aus Bosniens letzter Türkenzeit* (Vienna, 1905), p. 46. Derviş Paşa was a general.
[49] A. H. Midhat, *Tabsıra-i ibret*, pp. 162-63.
[50] *Idem, Life*, p. 77.
[51] Clician Vassif, *Midhat-Pacha*, pp. 36-44. Cf. Mahmud Celaleddin Paşa, *Mirât-ı
hakikat* (İstanbul, 1326), I, 104.
[52] Clician Vassif, *Midhat-Pacha*, pp. 37-39; İ. H. Uzunçarşılı, *Midhat ve Rüştü
Paşaların tevkiflerine dair vesikalar* (Ankara, 1946), p. 53, giving Midhat's own
later account.
[53] Kératry, *Mourad V*, pp. 80-82.
[54] Elliot has been pictured by some as an active participant in plans for the overthrow of Mahmud Nedim, which would, of course, decrease Russian influence in

Whatever plans were being developed for the overthrow of Mahmud Nedim must have received added impetus from events in the Balkans, news of which raised the pitch of Muslim, anti-Russian, and anti-government sentiment in the capital. Montenegro, late in April, was practically in an open state of war against the Porte, as support flowed across its border to the rebels; yet Mahmud Nedim's government still took insufficient measures to combat this aggression.[55] At about the same time news came to İstanbul that Turkish, Austrian, and Russian diplomatic documents published in Europe showed that Russia as early as 1870 had been arousing Montenegro and the Slav provinces.[56] Also in early May came the rising of Bulgar revolutionaries, pledged to terrorist methods. They had earlier planned to burn İstanbul and other major cities; in May they began to massacre Turks in the Bulgar area.[57] It is important to note that, despite the European sentiment about "Bulgarian massacres" which arose from the indubitably bloody repression of the revolt by Turkish irregulars, Turkish sentiment regarded the revolt as a massacre of helpless Turks by Bulgar rebels incited by Russia.[58] A measure of the Muslim excitement was the assassination on May 6 in Salonika of the French and German consuls—the unfortunate by-product of action by an excited

---

İstanbul. Cf. Kératry, *Mourad V*, pp. 82, 86-88; Mordtmann, *Stambul*, II, 134; Cherbuliez, "L'Angleterre et la Russie," pp. 67-69. The latter also charges H. A. Munro Butler-Johnstone, a conservative M.P. for Canterbury, with furnishing funds to arm the theological students in İstanbul: *ibid.*, pp. 70-71. Butler-Johnstone was one of those curious English Turcophils of the Urquhart school who backed the Turks against Russia. He was a friend of such mavericks as Ali Suavi and Ahmed Vefik, and wrote in 1875 and 1876 articles advocating moderate Turkish reform based on the Koran, some of which were translated into Turkish. Cf. H. A. Munro Butler-Johnstone, *The Eastern Question* (Oxford, 1875), and *The Turks* (London, 1876); also *Diplomatic Review*, 24 (July 1876), 160-161. See, further, on Butler-Johnstone, Seton-Watson, *Disraeli*, pp. 129-130; Sumner, *Russia and the Balkans*, p. 237.

[55] Gallenga, *Two Years*, I, 287-299; Elliot to Derby, #439, 28 April 1876, FO 78/2457.

[56] *Levant Herald*, 29 April 1876. The Russians said the documents were fabricated or altered; Elliot said he ascertained that at least some of them were "beyond all question generally, although not in all cases literally, authentic." Elliot to Derby, #433, 27 April 1876, FO 78/2457.

[57] Alois Hajek, *Bulgarien unter der Türkenherrschaft* (Stuttgart, 1925), pp. 249-293; V. K. Sugareff, "The Constitution of the Bulgarian Revolutionary Committee," *Journal of Modern History*, IV (December 1932), 572-580.

[58] Süleyman Paşa, *Hiss-i inkılâb*, p. 5; *Augsburger Allgemeine Zeitung*, 12 August 1876, quoting *Basiret*. The reports that reached Europe of Bulgar casualties resulting from Turkish countermeasures were also exaggerated and Russian-inspired, as one of Ignatyev's chief assistants admitted: Nelidow, "Souvenirs d'avant et d'après la guerre de 1877-1878," *Revue des deux mondes*, 6th period, 27 (1915), 331-332.

Muslim mob seeking to rescue from some Greeks a Greek Orthodox Bulgarian girl who had announced her intention of adopting Islam.[59] It was a crime, said Süleyman Paşa, director of the military academy, but also a sign that the Islamic millet was losing patience over constant humiliation of religion and the Muslim community, and showed that a religious and national zeal still existed among Muslims.[60]

The tension in İstanbul was almost visible in early May. It was feared that Muslim sentiment might erupt into outrages against the Christian inhabitants. Mahmud Nedim and Abdülaziz were more than ever unpopular. A rising might be directed against them. Gun merchants in the bazaar did a brisk trade, mostly with Muslims, but also with Christians.[61] Ignatyev contributed to the tension by hiring several hundred Croats or Montenegrins to serve as armed guards for his embassy. It was also rumored in the capital that Sultan Abdülaziz, fearing for his own safety, was about to request that thirty thousand Russian soldiers be sent to protect him.[62] The popular reaction was to accuse Mahmud Nedim of complicity, presumably in cahoots with Ignatyev. The Russian ambassador also was reported to have tried to fan religious feeling into open Muslim-Christian warfare in İstanbul itself, by hiring a few Bulgars to dress like softas, or Muslim theological students, and go about in Christian quarters threatening massacre.[63] Whether the rumors were true or false, the effect was the same. The government, fearing outbreaks and inflammatory moves, had already suspended all private telegraphic communication with the outside world. On May 8 it forbade news vendors to call out the headlines, and the next day announced preliminary censorship of all papers—a move which the conservative *Basiret* met with a sardonic issue of three blank pages and a fourth page of advertisements.[64] In fact, no outbreaks against Christians occurred in İstanbul, and sentiment there was directed principally against the government. Possibly Abdülaziz realized this, as possibly also did his mother, the Valide

[59] Documents on the affair in *Staatsarchiv*, 30 (1877), #5733-#5758.

[60] *Hiss-i inkılâb*, p. 5.

[61] Elliot to Derby, #467, 7 May 1876, #474 and #475, both 9 May 1876, #478, 10 May 1876, all FO 78/2457.

[62] A. H. Midhat, *Tabsıra-i ibret*, pp. 163-164; Ahmed Midhat, *Üss-i inkılâb* (İstanbul, 1294-1295), I, 209.

[63] *Ibid.*, I, 207-209; H. Y. Şehsuvaroğlu, *Sultan Aziz* (İstanbul, 1949), p. 66; Kératry, *Mourad V*, p. 93.

[64] *Stamboul*, 5, 9, and 10 May 1876; *Levant Herald*, 9 May 1876; Ahmed Rasim, *İstibdaddan hakimiyeti milliyeye* (İstanbul, 1924), II, 126, n.1.

Sultan. She sent an intermediary to see Midhat at his farm, asking his remedy for current problems. Midhat hinted, not too cautiously, at a constitution in his reply that the need was for administration based on law and the equality of Christians and Muslims; mere military measures would not suffice. But Midhat's prescription was too drastic for the Valide Sultan to suggest to "her lion."[65] Mahmud Nedim undoubtedly realized the threat to the government. He may have tried to get Midhat out of the capital.

Midhat was dangerous because of his reputation and influence among various segments of the population, and now especially among the theological students of the capital. The softas, whose numbers in İstanbul were variously estimated at five thousand to sixty thousand, were publicly and pointedly restless toward the end of the first week in May, buying weapons and threatening mass action.[66] They made themselves the spokesmen of Muslim discontent with a government unable to crush the rebels and fend off the great powers. They represented, in fact, the largest organizable group in the capital, since most soldiers were on campaign in the Balkans. In a way the softas represented public opinion as the Janissaries had at various times in the past. "The unity of the hocas deserved the thanks of the public," wrote a friend in İstanbul, just after the softa action, to Namık Kemal in exile on Cyprus.[67] It is possible that Mahmud Nedim himself attempted to work through the softas, or to assuage them by a bargain concerning the replacement of the current şeyhülislâm, Hasan Fehmi Efendi, whom the students disliked, with a candidate whom they favored.[68] But it seems unlikely that the theological students could have sided with Mahmud Nedim more than provisionally, given his past record and his complaisance toward Ignatyev. Midhat was

[65] Uzunçarşılı, Midhat ve Rüştü Paşalar, pp. 53-54.

[66] Both the higher and the lower figures are Elliot's: to Derby, #475, 9 May 1876, FO 78/2457. ABCFM, Western Turkey Mission III, #33, 16 May 1876, gives 10,000 to 40,000 in İstanbul; Clician Vassif, Midhat-Pacha, p. 44, says "more than 10,000"; Gallenga, Two Years, II, 53, says "conservatively" 20,000; Kératry, Mourad V, p. 88, gives 30,000 to 40,000. Abdolonyme Ubicini, La Turquie actuelle (Paris, 1855), p. 238, had given 22,000 to 25,000 for the Crimean War period.

[67] Kuntay, Namık Kemal, II, part 1, 616.

[68] Elliot to Derby, #543, confidential, 27 May 1876, enclosing Sandison to Elliot #41, confidential, 26 May 1876; Mehmed Memduh, Mirât-ı şuûnat, p. 64. Derviş Paşa, ambitious of power, may also have been involved in attempted maneuvers with softas; Elliot, loc.cit.; K. G. Bolander, Förspelet till Balkankrisen på 1870-talet (Göteborg, 1925), pp. 119-120. Hasan Fehmi, in a prior term as şeyhülislâm, had been responsible for causing Jemaleddin el Afghani's departure from İstanbul. Could Jemaleddin's influence have been felt among the softas in 1876?

much more their man. Midhat was certainly in close touch with a number of the leading ulema and possibly with some students also. He has been accused by his opponents of setting off the softa demonstrations against Mahmud Nedim by distribution of money in the medreses through the medium of Christaki Efendi, the banker of Prince Murad.[69] Midhat's secretary credits him at least with organizing the softa demonstrations, and Mahmud Nedim also attributed the disorders to Midhat.[70] But it is also possible that the demonstrations were partly spontaneous, as such softa demonstrations had also been in 1853 in another period of Russo-Turkish crisis.[71]

About May 8 or 9 the theological students began to go on strike. The stoppage of study spread from one medrese to another. Some of their professors helped to lead the agitation. In addition to buying arms, the softas organized large meetings at the mosques and heard inflammatory speeches about the weakness of the government in the face of rebellion and Russian influence. A committee was put together. After a mass meeting at the Fatih Mehmed mosque on Wednesday evening, May 10, a petition was drawn up asking Abdülaziz for stronger measures to save the empire and for the dismissal of Mahmud Nedim and the *şeyhülislâm*, Hasan Fehmi. On Thursday morning another mass meeting in the Süleymaniye mosque reiterated the students' demands. Both the Palace and the council of ministers were in an agony of indecision, but that morning the dismissal of the two was announced. Meanwhile the streets and squares of İstanbul, especially in front of the Sublime Porte, were filled with five or six thousand softas. Christian merchants, fearing massacre, began to flee their shops, but they were reassured by the softas, and no violence ensued. The rumor spread that Midhat Paşa had been appointed grand vezir, and Halil Şerif foreign minister.[72] Midhat was the man the softas wanted, but the rumor proved false. In fact, while the Palace tried to make up its mind, the government was for a little over twenty-four hours without a grand vezir, and subject to possible mob rule. Again on Friday, May 12, softa bands packed the streets, until it was

[69] Mahmud Celaleddin Paşa, *Mirât-ı hakikat*, I, 104; Mardin, *Cevdet*, p. 133, n.114.

[70] Clician Vassif, *Midhat-Pacha*, p. 44; Mahmud Celaleddin, *Mirât-ı hakikat*, I, 93.

[71] Ubicini, *Turquie actuelle*, pp. 238-239; Mahmud Celaleddin, *Mirât-ı hakikat*, I, 91.

[72] Hüseyin Nazım Bey to Namık Kemal, undated [mid-May 1876] in Kuntay, *Namık Kemal*, II, part 1, 616.

announced that Mütercim Mehmed Rüşdi was appointed grand vezir and Hayrullah Efendi appointed *şeyhülislâm.* Though these appointments did not fully satisfy the softas, they accepted them at least for the moment, and tension in the capital began to ease. "The past week was one of more excitement and fear than I have witnessed during a long residence in Turkey," wrote an American on the spot.[73] "That violent agitation of the public [i.e., the students] has saved the Islamic nation from a dangerous collapse," wrote at about the same time a man who was a friend of Namık Kemal and the son of a liberal member of the ulema.[74]

The new ministry was strengthened by the addition of Hüseyin Avni, at once brought back from Bursa to be minister of war. This was apparently Abdülaziz's own idea; Mahmud Nedim before his fall had tried in vain to warn the sultan that the throne had more to fear from the ambitious Hüseyin Avni than from anyone else.[75] But what the new ministry might accomplish was problematical, since Abdülaziz and palace officials regarded Mütercim Mehmed Rüşdi as overcautious, a chronic complainer and a do-nothing, and a chameleon-like politician who passed his time courting public favor. Hayrullah Efendi they thought of as an intriguer and an ignorant man in the robes of an educated man. Abdülaziz believed that by the ministerial shifts he was appeasing public opinion, and said to Mehmed Rüşdi, "I appointed you because the people wanted you," in a way such as to indicate not that the sultan had regard for the public, but that the grand vezir was only temporarily in office to still the clamor.[76] Abdülaziz evidently wanted to reappoint Mahmud Nedim as soon as possible.

[73] ABCFM, Western Turkey Mission III, #33, 16 May 1876.

[74] Hüseyin Nazım Bey to Namık Kemal, in Kuntay, *Namık Kemal,* II, part 1, 616. Accounts of the events of these days in *ibid.,* pp. 615-617; Mahmud Celaleddin, *Mirât-ı hakikat,* I, 91-94; Mehmet Memduh, *Mirât-i şuûnat,* pp. 64-66; Ahmed Midhat, *Üss-i inkılâb,* I, 209-212; Osman Nuri, *Abdülhamid-i Sani ve devr-i saltanatı* (İstanbul, 1327), I, 14-17; *Levant Herald,* 12 May 1876; Nelidow, "Souvenirs," pp. 313-318.

[75] Mahmud Celaleddin, *Mirât-ı hakikat,* I, 93. A plan to recall Hüseyin Avni to the ministry, and to get Midhat out of the capital by sending him in Hüseyin's place to Bursa, is, however, attributed to Mahmud Nedim himself two days before his fall by Mehmed Memduh, *Mirât-i şuûnat,* pp. 65-66, and by Elliot, on indirect information from Abraham Paşa: Elliot to Derby, #543, confidential, 27 May 1876, enclosing Sandison to Elliot, #41, confidential, 26 May 1876.

[76] Mahmud Celaleddin, *Mirât-ı hakikat,* I, 94-96; Mehmed Memduh, *Mirât-ı şuûnat,* p. 65; Uzunçarşılı, *Midhat ve Rüştü Paşalar,* p. 102.

In view of public opinion, this would have been a most foolish move, and Mahmud Nedim himself refused to consider another grand vezirate unless Mehmed Rüşdi and Hüseyin Avni and Midhat were banished from the capital. But this the sultan would not dare do now in view of the public temper and the influence of the three men.[77] Mahmud Nedim was really unpopular; nearly three years later deputies in the second session of the Ottoman parliament carried a resolution to try him for crimes and incompetence.[78] Instead, Midhat was added to the ministry after a week, though without portfolio. So was Halil Şerif shortly thereafter. But these constitutionalists were counterbalanced by the simultaneous addition of Derviş Paşa and Namık Paşa, who held opposite views.[79] Even with such changes it was doubtful that the ministers might accomplish much. The Palace still had no confidence in them. Abdülaziz was something of an unknown quantity at this point, and much of the communication with him either went through, or was stopped by, his mother. Mehmed Rüşdi was overhesitant of any action, and did not have much confidence in the outspoken activist Midhat. Midhat probably thought that he should himself be grand vezir. Hayrullah had more intelligence than his enemies gave him credit for and was reasonably liberal, but Hüseyin Avni was no liberal and was a self-seeker.[80] All the ministers were probably annoyed at Midhat's popularity, demonstrated when, just after Mahmud Nedim's fall, a group of softas acclaimed Midhat when they met him at Hayrullah's house. Midhat thereupon made a little speech to the students about the liberal and democratic bases of Islam.[81]

In general, the effects of the demonstrations and of the overthrow of Mahmud Nedim seem to have been two. The first was to increase and consolidate patriotic sentiment—or, put negatively, to increase anti-European, especially anti-Russian, sentiment. The *Levant Herald* printed on May 13 an article accusing Ignatyev of acting out a lie, for European consumption, by importing Croat guards for his em-

---

[77] Mahmud Celaleddin, *Mirât-ı hakikat*, I, 96; İnal, *Son sadrıâzamlar*, p. 298.

[78] Robert Devereux, *The First Ottoman Constitutional Period* (unpublished thesis, School of Advanced International Studies of the Johns Hopkins University, 1961), p. 303.

[79] *Levant Herald*, 5 July 1876; Harris, *Diplomatic History*, p. 330.

[80] Uzunçarşılı, *Midhat ve Rüştü Paşalar*, p. 102; Abdurrahman Şeref, *Tarih musahabeleri* (İstanbul, 1339), pp. 202-203; İnal, *Son sadrıâzamlar*, pp. 336-337; Süleyman, *Hiss-i inkılâb*, pp. 14-17; J. T. von Eckhardt, "Islamitische Reformbestrebungen der letzten 100 Jahre," *Deutsche Rundschau*, 104 (1900), 58-59.

[81] Clician Vassif, *Midhat-Pacha*, pp. 47-48.

bassy to make it appear as if Christians in İstanbul were in danger. Though the government felt it had to suspend the paper, the editor was thereupon flooded with congratulations by Muslims and Christians, and the issue became a rarity, selling at premium prices.[82] A plan to allow a European group to control certain Ottoman revenues —customs, salt tax, tobacco tax, part of the tithe—in an effort to consolidate and regularize the Ottoman debt, might have been signed by Mahmud Nedim's ministry, but was now thrown in the wastebasket.[83] The Berlin Memorandum, a new project of Andrassy and the Three Emperors' League to settle the Bosnian question, was rather baldly condemned by the new Turkish ministry on May 21.[84] The Turks were, of course, stiffened in their attitude by the knowledge that Britain had not accepted the memorandum, but they looked on it not only as a danger to the Ottoman state, but as evidence of antihumanitarianism and of a new crusading mentality in Europe.[85] The other effect was to increase the drive for further controls over Abdülaziz, particularly his spending, and to bring closer to possible realization, therefore, either a constitutional regime or the deposition of the sultan, or both. In İstanbul in the last two weeks of May there was considerable speculation about a further political coup and about "constitution," which for most people had no particular meaning except that it was some sort of curb on the caprice of the sultan. The softas spoke for this idea. Their agitation was carefully not directed against the local Christians, with whom they were sometimes seen amicably walking, but against European intervention and their own ruler. Koranic texts were circulating to demonstrate that absolutism was a violation of Muslim law.[86] Certain leaders among the ulema prepared a draft

---

[82] *Levant Herald*, 13 May 1876; Elliot to Derby, #295, 15 May 1876, FO 78/2458; Gertrude Elliot, "Turkey in 1876: A Retrospect," *Nineteenth Century*, 64 (October 1908), 556-558. Though the English were, not too secretly, pleased at the article, the French ambassador was indignant at the attack on a diplomat: Bourgoing to Décazes, #66, AAE, Turquie 404.

[83] Charles Morawitz, *Die Türkei im Spiegel ihrer Finanzen* (Berlin, 1903), p. 57; Elliot to Derby, #352, 7 April 1876, and #374, 13 April 1876, FO 78/2457; ABCFM, Western Turkey Mission II, #580, 19 April 1876, and #587, 25 May 1876.

[84] Text in *Staatsarchiv*, 30 (1877), #5690.

[85] Süleyman, *Hiss-i inkılâb*, p. 6.

[86] Elliot to Derby, #512, confidential, 18 May 1876; #528, confidential, 24 May 1876; #543, confidential, 25 May 1876; #536, most confidential, 25 May 1876—all in FO 78/2458; ABCFM, Western Turkey Mission II, #466, 18 May 1876, and #467, 25 May 1876.

of a *fetva* of deposition. "There was no doubt but what this request was general," said Midhat later.[87]

How general was any desire for the deposition of Abdülaziz must forever remain a matter of speculation. Though Ottoman sultans had been made and deposed in the past by military men, sometimes acting as agents of a wider popular feeling, deposition of a sultan was still a serious matter. There had been none in the empire for nearly seventy years, since Selim III was dethroned in 1807 by Janissaries rebelling against his innovations, and Mustafa IV deposed by other army units the next year. Yet Abdülaziz had of late certainly been subject to increasing popular criticism, especially in İstanbul. Midhat Paşa was concerned to represent any action taken to change the government as the popular will at work. What the situation in May of 1876 provided was a better opportunity to realize a change, with a large measure of popular support, than had heretofore existed. But the actual planning for the overthrow of the sultan was the secret work of a small group of men, not even with the general approval of the ministers and ulema, as Midhat later claimed.[88] Cevdet Paşa, for instance, who had become minister of education on May 8, had according to his own account no inkling of the deposition before it happened and disapproved of the deed.[89] Some of the small group who did plan the deposition had thought about it at least off and on since the time of Şirvanizade Mehmed Rüşdi's grand vezirate in 1873.[90] When their intentions hardened it is impossible to say, but the likelihood is that it was not until May of 1876, except possibly in the case of Hüseyin Avni. It is also most probable that various individuals arrived independently at the idea that deposition was either necessary or desirable, and that before the last two weeks of May there was little concerted planning.[91] The principal men involved were Midhat, minister without porfolio; Hüseyin Avni, minister of war; and Süleyman, director of the military academy. Also involved were Mütercim Mehmed Rüşdi, the grand vezir; Hayrullah, the *şeyhülislâm*; Kayserili Ahmed Paşa, minister of marine; several other high-ranking army officers; Odian Efendi, adviser to Midhat and undersecretary of public works;

---

[87] Uzunçarşılı, *Midhat ve Rüştü Paşalar*, p. 54.

[88] *Ibid.*, p. 54.

[89] Ali Ölmezoğlu, "Cevdet Paşa," *İslâm ansiklopedisi*, III, 117; Cevdet Paşa, *Tezâkir 1-12*, ed. by Cavid Baysun (Ankara, 1953), pp. xxii-xxv; Mardin, *Cevdet*, p. 257.

[90] See above, chapter VIII, pp. 294-295.

[91] This is the general impression given by Süleyman's *Hiss-i inkılâb*, which is probably the most circumstantial account by an insider.

Ziya Bey, the erstwhile New Ottoman and momentarily unemployed; Dr. Capoléone, physician to the heir apparent, Murad; and probably a few other individuals.[92] When the planning began, further, there seem to have been two divergent methods of approach.

One method was Midhat's. In his subsequent references to events Midhat tried to play down his own part in the deposition of Abdülaziz, ascribing to Hüseyin Avni the chief role.[93] But there seems no doubt that Midhat was one of the leaders and played an active part.[94] His method, however, seems to have been one of planning a deposition by some sort of popular action while keeping open alternatives to government reform that might produce a constitution or some sort of effective curb on Abdülaziz. Even before the overthrow of Mahmud Nedim, Midhat had warned the Valide Sultan's emissary that government under law, and equality of all Ottomans, were the only alternatives to more drastic measures. Within the last two weeks of May, after Midhat had become a minister, he repeated some such advice and warning in a memorandum written to the Valide Sultan at her request. In it he posited the necessity for freedom, equality, and ministerial responsibility.[95] At about the same time Midhat seems to have had an audience with the sultan in which Abdülaziz agreed to the necessity of reforms and blamed all evils on Mahmud Nedim. Thereupon Midhat wrote to Mehmed Rüşdi that if the Valide Sultan agreed and guaranteed such reforms, the plans already made might be modified. Please keep all this secret from Hüseyin Avni, added Midhat.[96] But nothing came of these overtures by Midhat to Abdülaziz and his mother. Midhat, therefore, continued to work for a change in sultans. He may have met with Hayrullah and a group of the ulema to plan this just before he became minister without portfolio, and

---

[92] Possibly including a Pole, Karol Brzozowski, said to be very close to Midhat and supposedly involved in the deposition: Adam Lewak, *Dzieje emigracji polskiej w Turcji (1831-1878)* (Warsaw, 1935), p. 245.

[93] This is the general impression in A. H. Midhat, *Life*, and *idem, Tabsıra-i ibret*, as well as the specific statement in Midhat's interrogation of May 8, 1881, when, of course, he was fighting Abdülhamid's charges against him: Uzunçarşılı, *Midhat ve Rüştü Paşalar*, pp. 53-55.

[94] Sometimes, later, Midhat used to drop remarks intended to show that he was the leader, says Cevdet, an unfriendly witness: Mardin, *Cevdet,* p. 259.

[95] Uzunçarşılı, *Midhat ve Rüştü Paşalar*, pp. 53-54; A. H. Midhat, *Tabsıra-i ibret*, p. 164; *idem, Mirât-ı hayret* (İstanbul, 1325), p. 51.

[96] Text in A. H. Midhat, *Tabsıra-i ibret*, pp. 164-165, n.1; A. H. Midhat, *Midhat Pacha. Sa vie—son oeuvre* (Paris, 1908), p. 47, n.1. Cf. İnal, *Son sadrıâzamlar*, III, 337-338. The French edition gives an obviously erroneous date.

Mehmed Rüşdi may also have been approached.[97] Midhat was not inclined to a military coup d'état, but rather to basing a change in regime on the mass demands of softas and the İstanbul populace, meeting presumably in the Nuri Osmaniye mosque. Military action should only set the seal on the popular demand.[98] The ultimate object of all this was, in Midhat's mind, the establishment of constitutional government. He seems to have harbored no personal rancor against Sultan Abdülaziz. His reason for a change in sultans would be simply to secure better government, and evidently he was assured that the heir apparent, Murad, would be favorable to a constitutional regime. "It has been known for some time that the Prince would be ready to proclaim a constitution on the day of his accession," reported the British ambassador on May 25, "and he has certainly been in communication with some of its most influential advocates."[99] Midhat was not without some personal ambition, as even his partisan Elliot realized, and there was some irony in the fact that he who in 1859 had been, as second secretary of the Supreme Council, one of the inquisitors of the Kuleli incident conspirators should now himself be a conspirator.[100] But Midhat's motives here seem essentially pure.

It was otherwise with Hüseyin Avni Paşa, who represented the alternative method of approach to the deposition. In his view a military coup was the sine qua non. He had, of course, a considerable following in the army, whereas Midhat was more popular among civilians. Possibly this fact had its effect on Hüseyin Avni's thinking, since he wanted to be known as the leader of a successful coup and had strong political ambitions. After the coup he tried to make sure that history recorded him the sole leader.[101] In 1876 personal motives probably ranked equally with his patriotic aim of saving the empire from the rebels and from Europe; he seems to have been gnawed by a desire to get even not only with Mahmud Nedim but with Ab-

[97] Osman Nuri, *Abdülhamid-i Sani*, I, 17-19, speaks quite circumstantially of this but cites no sources, and his date is garbled. Ismail Kemal says that about May 16 he had a letter from Odian Efendi concerning Midhat's plans to depose Abdülaziz: Sommerville Story, ed., *The Memoirs of Ismail Kemal Bey* (London, 1920), p. 108.

[98] Clician Vassif, *Midhat-Pacha*, pp. 53-54, 61-62; A. H. Midhat, *Life*, p. 83; Kératry, *Mourad V*, p. 110; Uzunçarşılı, *Midhat ve Rüştü Paşalar*, p. 54; Şehsuvaroğlu, *Sultan Aziz*, p. 75.

[99] Elliot to Derby, #535, confidential, 25 May 1876, FO 78/2458.

[100] Elliot to Derby, #559, 31 May 1876, FO 78/2458; İ. H. Danişmend, *İzahlı Osmanlı tarihi kronolojisi*, IV (İstanbul, 1955), 190.

[101] Mardin, *Cevdet*, p. 259.

dülaziz for his exile to a provincial governorship in 1871 and for subsequent slights of the same sort.[102] Probably the chance that Mahmud Nedim might again be brought to the grand vezirate, and that he might again be exiled from the capital as Mahmud Nedim was known to have demanded, excited Hüseyin Avni soon after May 12 to immediate planning for a deposition.[103] Hüseyin Avni then began sounding out a few officers.[104] He evidently did not speak so much of reforms as did Midhat. Hüseyin Avni was no wholesale westernizer, and even opposed the changes Süleyman had brought about to make the military academy more like St. Cyr, saying, "We aren't like Europeans, and don't need to copy them."[105] In the same vein, Hüseyin Avni was no partisan of constitution, but apparently went along with the concept for the sake of the success of the plot. Four days before the deposition Süleyman wrung from him a rather grudging promise that a "konstitusyon" or something like that would be adopted.[106]

Süleyman Paşa, director of the military academy, was also a partisan of a military coup, and had on his own initiative, evidently before any approach by Hüseyin Avni, begun to speak to various officers about a deposition.[107] But he was also, in addition to being a vigorous patriot, a strong supporter of a constitutional regime, and thus something of a bridge between the views of Midhat and Hüseyin Avni. Süleyman's own career had been purely military.[108] But his interests were not narrow, and, in addition to being an intense patriot and incipient nationalist, he had become a convinced reformer and something of a westernizer. For a period he had taught literature and history at the military academy. In 1876, at the age of thirty-eight, he had already been for a year or more director of the academy and a strong champion of westernized education, which took him so far as to urge on Hayrullah changes in the medrese curriculum, saying that the ulema needed more training in the mathematical and natural sciences. The progress of the Islamic millet depended on education, thought Süleyman.[109] He believed also in political reform, and was said to

---

[102] Ibid., pp. 259-260, n.176; İnal, Son sadrıâzamlar, pp. 337-338.
[103] Mahmud Celaleddin, Mirât-ı hakikat, p. 96; Şehsuvaroğlu, Sultan Aziz, p. 73.
[104] Süleyman, Hiss-i inkılâb, pp. 6-7; A. H. Midhat, Tabsıra-i ibret, p. 166.
[105] Süleyman, Hiss-i inkılâb, pp. 10-11.
[106] Ibid., p. 13.   [107] Ibid., p. 8.
[108] Cf. Süleyman Paşa zade Sami, ed., Süleyman Paşa muhakemesi (İstanbul, 1328), pp. 3-10; Amédée Le Faure, Procès de Suleiman pacha (Paris, 1880), pp. 20-21; İ. A. Gövsa, Türk meşhurları ansiklopedisi (İstanbul, n.d.), p. 360.
[109] Süleyman, Hiss-i inkılâb, pp. 14-16.

have been the leader of a New Ottoman cell.[110] By 1876, thoroughly aroused by Ottoman misgovernment, Balkan rebellion, and great power pressure, he had also become a convinced partisan of constitutional government as the salvation for faith, state, and fatherland. Four days before Abdülaziz was deposed, Süleyman, in conversation with Hüseyin Avni, said tersely that the event would lose all meaning if the next sultan were also despotic, that he would get the oath of loyalty only if he accepted "the method of consultation." To Midhat three days thereafter he indicated his desire that Murad should announce for constitutional government even before his accession.[111] Süleyman, like Midhat, was not motivated by personal enmity for Abdülaziz.[112] Süleyman was convinced that he himself represented national sentiment and, further, that the soldiers would patriotically support a change in regime and would not be held back by ties to the Palace. Of this he seems to have convinced Hüseyin Avni also.[113]

By Friday, May 26, the tentative plans made by these several individuals began to jell. That night Süleyman and General Redif Paşa, head of the military council, met with Hüseyin Avni at the latter's shore house to begin coordination of military measures. Midhat and Kayserili Ahmed Paşa, the minister of marine, were informed. The next day Süleyman and Hüseyin Avni continued their planning, while Hayrullah and Mehmed Rüşdi were brought up to date on the arrangements. It was decided to carry through the deposition on Wednesday, May 31. The meetings and planning continued over the next two days. Some of it must have aroused suspicion, for all the comings and goings could not be concealed. The daily *Stamboul* reported on Monday that Mehmed Rüşdi and Hüseyin Avni had spent a long time in conference at Midhat's town house.[114] There is some question as to whether Ignatyev, undoubtedly aware of an impending coup if not accurately informed in detail, warned Abdülaziz to take strong measures.[115] There is also a question as to whether Midhat or anyone

---

[110] Sami, *Süleyman Paşa muhakemesi*, pp. 18-19.
[111] Süleyman, *Hiss-i inkılâb*, pp. 3-6, 13, 23-24.
[112] *Ibid.*, p. 23; Sami, *Süleyman Paşa muhakemesi*, p. 45.
[113] Süleyman, *Hiss-i inkılâb*, pp. 6, 12-13, 48.
[114] *Stamboul*, 29 May 1876.
[115] Sumner, *Russia and the Balkans*, p. 168; N. Jorga, ed., *Correspondance diplomatique roumaine* (Paris, 1923), #270, 24 May 1876. More improbably it has been asserted that Ignatyev planned to occupy İstanbul with Russian troops and rescue Abdülaziz with a Russian ship; perhaps there was a rumor to that effect: Amand von Schweiger-Lerchenfeld, *Serail und Hohe Pforte* (Vienna, 1879), p. 246; Felix Bamberg, *Geschichte der orientalischen Angelegenheiten* (Berlin, 1892), p. 460.

associated with him had already asked of, or secured from, Ambas
sador Elliot a promise that the English squadron which had just been
sent to Besika Bay would be ready to come up to Istanbul in case
of need.[116] At some point during these days Midhat must have abandoned his objections to a military coup, though he may still have
hoped for popular demonstrations to accompany it. Midhat was at the
same time asked to get in touch with Murad, which he did through
Ziya, who saw Dr. Capoléone, who saw Murad. Murad was reported
to be, quite naturally, fearful of the attempt if something went wrong.
Something might have, for the suspicions of the Palace were aroused.
On Monday, May 29, the time for the coup was, therefore, advanced
by twenty-four hours and reset for the early morning of May 30.
This change meant that, if Midhat still had plans to provoke a demonstration of the popular will, he had to abandon them now. There
was time to prepare nothing but a military coup. Murad himself
seems not to have been told of the change.[117]

May 29 was a stormy day. Rain fell without cease, streets were
covered with water, trees were uprooted. The plotters, nevertheless,
met at Hüseyin Avni's house that night to make their final arrangements. Midhat was challenged by a sentry for having no lantern, but
was allowed to pass; the boatman he hired to take him there recognized him, but said that whatever he was doing out on such a miserable night must be for the welfare of the millet.[118] Then the plotters
scattered. At about three in the morning of Tuesday, May 30, the
palace of Dolmabahçe, where Abdülaziz was staying, was surrounded
by two battalions under Süleyman's orders on the land side, while
ships of the navy guarded the Bosporus side. Another naval vessel was
stationed off the Russian summer embassy farther up the Bosporus, to
prevent any move by Ignatyev. Süleyman then persuaded the fearful
Murad to leave the apartments where he had been confined and to go
with Hüseyin Avni to the ministry of war. All this took place a little

---

[116] Osman Nuri, *Abdülhamid-i Sani*, I, 21; Washburn, *Fifty Years*, p. 104; Dwight
E. Lee, *Great Britain and the Cyprus Convention Policy of 1878* (Cambridge, Mass.,
1934), p. 25, n.59.

[117] Aspects of the planning are recorded, with differences and some conflicts, in
Süleyman, *Hiss-i inkılâb*, pp. 6-9, 14, 20-23; Mehmed Memduh, *Mirât-ı şuûnat*,
pp. 69-70; Uzunçarşılı, *Midhat ve Rüştü Paşalar*, p. 54; A. H. Midhat, *Hâtıralarım,
1872-1946* (İstanbul, 1946), p. 12; *idem, Tabsıra-i ibret*, p. 166; Clician Vassif,
Midhat-Pacha, pp. 53-64; Kératry, *Mourad V*, pp. 110-123; Sumner, *Russia and
the Balkans*, p. 168. Şehsuvaroğlu, *Sultan Aziz*, pp. 73-80, offers a fairly good reconstruction.

[118] A. H. Midhat, *Hâtıralarım*, p. 13.

before dawn. Meanwhile Midhat and others convened at the war ministry. There Hayrullah read the *fetva* of deposition which had already been prepared, justifying the act on the grounds of Abdülaziz's mental derangement, ignorance of political affairs, diversion of public revenues to private expenditure, and conduct generally injurious to state and community.[119] The ministers present, including Mehmed Rüşdi, the grand vezir, took the oath of loyalty (*biat*) to Murad V. As dawn broke one hundred and one cannon from Kayserili Ahmed's ships in the Bosporus announced to the capital the change in sultans. Abdülaziz was sent to confinement in the Topkapı palace. Murad then went to the Dolmabahçe palace, where a larger gathering took the oath of loyalty.[120] The bloodless revolution was completed. There had been no violence, not even an increase of tension between Christians and Muslims, although the significance of the cannonade was at first not clear. Until late morning many residents of the capital thought Abdülaziz had died or had been killed. Some thought the firing meant that Russian naval units had come into the Bosporus.[121] Neither surmise was true.

Doubt was succeeded by great public jubilation, set off by the soldiers surrounding Dolmabahçe palace, who for two hours shouted long life to the new sultan and, significantly, long life to the millet (which to them probably still meant the Islamic millet, but also now with overtones of "nation"). Quotations on Ottoman bonds rose overnight by fifty per cent on the local market. Christians celebrated with Muslims; softas and Christian clergy went together to see Murad at Dolmabahçe. Turkish newspapers referred to the "Osmanlı nation" rather than to the Islamic millet alone. Osmanlılık was again in the air. Public demonstrations of joy continued at least through Friday, June 2, when Murad V's first visit to the mosque of Ayasofya provided a new occasion. Christians and Muslims cheered, while Murad bowed and acknowledged the acclaim like a western monarch. Softas climbed onto his carriage.[122] Aside from a general supposition that now things would

[119] Text in Ahmed Midhat, *Üss-i inkılâb*, I, 396-397; *Levant Herald*, 5 July 1876.

[120] *Stamboul*, 30 May 1876; *Levant Herald*, 5 July 1876; Süleyman, *Hiss-i inkılâb*, pp. 42-43, 48-49; Cevdet, *Tezâkir*, pp. xxii-xxv; A. H. Midhat, *Life*, pp. 83-86; Nelidow, "Souvenirs," pp. 324-325; *Basiret*, 30 May, trans. in Elliot to Derby, #566, 1 June 1876, FO 78/2459.

[121] Cevdet, *Tezâkir*, pp. 22-23; Gallenga, *Two Years*, II, 81-83; ABCFM, Western Turkey Mission II, #110, and III, #35, both 30 May 1876.

[122] Osman Nuri, *Abdülhamid-i Sani*, I, 31; Süleyman, *Hiss-i inkılâb*, pp. 58-59; Gallenga, *Two Years*, II, 88-91; *Augsburger Allgemeine Zeitung*, 7 June 1876; Neli-

be better, the public joy seems to have had two bases. One was the expectation that the change in monarchs would produce a more vig-orous opposition to rebellion, to European intervention, and to Rus-sia. This was symbolized by the friendship shown to Britain: "God Save the King" was played along with the Turkish imperial march when Murad visited Ayasofya, and Lady Elliot was cheered. The French ambassador wryly reported that Elliot did not hide his satisfaction at the turn of events; further, that the Turks, encouraged by Britain's rejection of the Berlin Memorandum and the increase in her naval forces in the Mediterranean, had begun to speculate on a revival of the old Crimean coalition. In fact, the Berlin Memorandum, which the five ambassadors had decided on May 29 to present to the Porte at noon the following day, was never presented because of the deposi-tion. Ignatyev recognized that the deposition was a blow to his influ-ence, and a gain for Elliot's, and complained that Murad was "a prisoner in the hands of an oligarchy of pashas."[123] The other basis for joy was the general expectation that a constitution would be pro-claimed—meaning to most people a curb on the sultan's expenditures and on capricious administration. *Stamboul* baldly announced on May 30 that the ministers were expected to meet that evening under Mu-rad's chairmanship and to proclaim a constitution. Two days later softas paraded to Midhat's house and cheered him, Murad, and a national assembly (*şura-yı ümmet*).[124] The deposition of Abdülaziz and Murad's accession seemed in fact to be, as Süleyman Paşa more than once called it—using a term the Turks had often applied to Mahmud II's destruction of the Janissaries in 1826—an "auspicious event" (*vaka-i hayriye*).

This judgment appeared to be confirmed by the official acts and documents that followed immediately on Murad's accession. Among Abdülaziz's effects in the palace were found millions of dollars' worth of Ottoman bonds, jewelry, and gold coin, which Murad turned over to the treasury, excepting for the customary distribution of considera-

---

dow, "Souvenirs," pp. 325-327; ABCFM, Western Turkey Mission III, #36, 1 June 1876; *Levant Herald*, 5 July 1876.

[123] *Levant Herald*, 5 July 1876; Bourgoing to Foreign Ministry, 30 May 1876, and Bourgoing to Décazes, #84, 7 June 1876, both AAE, Turquie 404; Harris, *Diplo-matic History*, p. 324; Sumner, *Russia and the Balkans*, pp. 169-170.

[124] *Stamboul*, 30 May and 1 June 1876; cf. ABCFM, Western Turkey Mission II, #35, 30 May 1876.

ble sums to civil and military officials as accession presents.[125] Abdülaziz's fantastic animal collections were opened to the public, and his
palace entertainers were fired.[126] More important, Murad was por-
trayed as a kind of citizen king. The official announcement by the
foreign minister said that he had become sultan "by the grace of God
and the will of the people."[127] Murad's own accession *hat* of June 1,
addressed to his grand vezir Mehmed Rüşdi, struck the same note:
he ascended the throne "by the favor of the Almighty and the will
of my subjects."[128] In his proclamation Murad ordered reorganization
of the Council of State and the ministries of finance, justice, and public instruction. He gave up sixty thousand purses from his civil list.[129]
He confirmed all the ministers in their positions. The şeriat was to
be respected, but all subjects without distinction were to enjoy complete
liberty. All this was to be for the benefit and defense of the fatherland,
the state, and the nation (*vatan, devlet, millet*). These were the sentiments of Osmanlılık, of the Tanzimat period. All Ottoman subjects
were grouped together, without singling out the Islamic millet, and
all were part of the fatherland. The İstanbul newspaper *Sabah* [*Morning*] praised these words, saying that all patriots, even all humanity,
would weep for joy because Murad put *vatan* before *devlet*.[130]

The accession *hat*, however, contained no word about a constitution.
It emphasized, to be sure, the will of the people, and so sounded more
like Midhat than like Hüseyin Avni; it said nothing about the military
or the coup d'état. Yet a constitution seemed to be expected among
many elements of the population, and Turkish newspapers in İstanbul
kept up the demand for constitutional government with a parliament
elected by the people.[131] It was also reasonable to expect that Murad
was favorable to a constitution. He was thought to be a friend of constitutional government, and had so expressed himself to various visi-
tors, including some foreigners. Murad had, as a matter of fact, en-

[125] Uzunçarşılı, *Midhat ve Rüştü Paşalar*, p. 124; Ahmed Midhat, *Üss-i inkılâb*,
I, 228; Elliot to Derby, #597, 8 June 1876, FO 78/2459; *Levant Herald*, 5 July
1876.
[126] *Stamboul*, 3 June 1876.
[127] Text in *Staatsarchiv*, 30 (1877), #5700.
[128] Text in Ahmed Midhat, *Üss-i inkılâb*, I, 401-403; official French version enclosed in Maynard to Fish, #69, 5 June 1876, USNA, Turkey 29.
[129] i.e., 300,000 Turkish pounds, one third of the total.
[130] *Sabah*, 2 June 1876, cited in Kuntay, *Namık Kemal*, II, part 1, 744.
[131] ABCFM, Western Turkey Mission II, #469, 12 June 1876; Lazzaro (Salonika)
to Maynard, 21 June 1876, encl. in Maynard to Fish, #86, 20 July 1876, USNA,
Turkey 29.

joyed a little more freedom than any previous heir apparent since the introduction of the *kafes* system in 1603. He had learned some French, liked western music, had been to Europe in 1867, was allowed by his uncle Abdülaziz to have his own house outside the palace, had occasionally been able to leave his house to see Europeans, corresponded with some, and had become a Freemason. He had had contact with Namık Kemal and possibly others of the New Ottomans. His inclinations seem to have been generally liberal, and specifically in favor of improved secular education for all Ottoman subjects equally.[132] These inclinations and connections were known to his younger brother Abdülhamid and to Sultan Abdülaziz; the latter had restricted Murad's freedom over the past five years or so, which led Murad to overindulgence in alcohol.[133] Hüseyin Avni also disliked Murad's emphasis on equality of Muslims and Christians, accusing him of harboring Masonic ideas.[134] It is possible also that Murad had specific constitutional ideas. He is said to have had a French citizen, a lawyer living in the European quarter of İstanbul, draw up for him the draft of a constitution along lines which he had sketched.[135]

That a constitution should be promulgated immediately upon Murad's accession was, of course, beyond the realm of possibility, even though some seemed to expect this. The elaboration of such a document would certainly take several months. But it would have been quite possible to insert in the accession *hat* a declaration of intentions about a constitution. That this was not done was possibly owing to the shock and fatigue Murad had experienced in suddenly being taken at night by armed men from his apartments and declared sultan. Cevdet Paşa claimed to have seen signs of mental weakness as well as bodily fatigue on the Tuesday of the accession.[136] Midhat and Hüseyin Avni also noticed that Murad was upset, so they stayed in the palace for two nights after the accession, along with Mehmed Rüşdi and Hayrullah.[137] But the more probable reason was that the coali-

---

[132] Alderson, *Ottoman Dynasty*, p. 35; Schweiger-Lerchenfeld, *Serail*, pp. 177-178; Kératry, *Mourad V*, pp. 40-45, 62-72; Demetrius Georgiades, *La Turquie actuelle* (Paris, 1892), pp. 58-59; Osman Nuri, *Abdülhamid-i Sani*, I, 7-8; Edmund Hornby, *Autobiography* (London, 1928), p. 153; Kuntay, *Namık Kemal*, II, part 1, 742-743, 751-752. See also chapter VI above, n.71.

[133] Alderson, *Ottoman Dynasty*, p. 35.

[134] Kératry, *Mourad V*, pp. 139-140; Clician Vassif, *Midhat-Pacha*, pp. 67-68.

[135] Osman Nuri, *Abdülhamid-i Sani*, I, 11.

[136] Cevdet, *Tezâkir*, pp. xxiv-xxv. Cf. Mehmed Memduh, *Hal'ler-iclaslar*, p. 132, cited in Kuntay, *Namık Kemal*, II, part 1, 740, 744-745, n.1.

[137] A. H. Midhat, *Tabsıra-i ibret*, pp. 168-169; *idem*, *Life*, p. 88.

tion of conspirators, united only on the deposition, had begun to split apart. On Tuesday, May 30, after the ceremony of the oath of loyalty was finished, Midhat had produced the draft of an accession *hat* which stipulated constitutional government and ministerial responsibility. He showed it to Süleyman, who was pleased. But Mehmed Rüşdi and Hüseyin Avni were unwilling to go that far. Both opposed the draft. They joined Sadullah Bey,[138] former minister of commerce who had just been appointed palace secretary, in saying: "Our Sultan does not wish to form a national assembly. The knowledge and the training of our nation are not suitable for such a step. However, in order to eliminate the insecurity which prevails, he must bind the administration by strong laws, and must, for instance, reform financial matters. This is the desire of our Sultan." Thereafter Midhat's draft of the *hat* was altered, again presumably by Mehmed Rüşdi, as grand vezir, to eliminate any reference to constitution. Süleyman accuses the grand vezir of autocratic tendencies, Hüseyin Avni of hypocrisy, and Midhat of weakness in this confrontation.[139]

Yet a constitution was now seriously under discussion at the top level of Ottoman administration. During the nights of May 30 and 31, which Midhat, Hüseyin Avni, and Mehmed Rüşdi spent in the palace, Midhat argued with the other two. He had already prepared—when he had done so is not clear—at least a partial draft of a constitution, said to have been composed of only nineteen articles. In addition to desiring a mention of constitution in the accession *hat*, he wanted to make public his draft, so that the hopes of the populace would be kept up. Mehmed Rüşdi and Hüseyin Avni opposed him on both counts, and argued against some of the basic articles of his draft.[140] But on June 2 the manifesto of the "Muslim patriots" was published in İstanbul, and this undoubtedly served Midhat's aim of publicity to some extent.[141] Midhat and Halil Şerif were said to be considering as a model the Belgian constitution of 1831, which had been influential in many European states.[142] Süleyman Paşa was also impatient, and said to Hüseyin Avni that if no progress were made on reform, there

---

[138] Sadullah was the friend of Namık Kemal who in 1867 had assisted in the translation of Mustafa Fazıl's letter to Abdülaziz, which proposed a national assembly.

[139] Süleyman, *Hiss-i inkılâb*, pp. 60-61; Sami, *Süleyman Paşa muhakemesi*, pp. 45-46; Mahmud Celaleddin, *Mirât-ı hakikat*, I, 117-118, 126.

[140] A. H. Midhat, *Tabsıra-i ibret*, pp. 170-172; Mahmud Celaleddin, *Mirât-ı hakikat*, I, 126.

[141] See above, n.46.

[142] Bourgoing to Décazes, #84, 7 June 1876, AAE, Turquie 404.

was no point to the deposition.[143] Evidently a meeting of the council of ministers, at which Murad himself is said to have presided, was held in the palace a few days later, about June 3. Midhat again produced his draft and pleaded in eloquent language for a constitution. Mehmed Rüşdi spoke only of necessary administrative measures. Hüseyin Avni took a Bismarckian line, saying that violent and vigorous measures, not assemblies and discussion, were needed to save the Ottoman state. The ministers reached no conclusion.[144]

Before constitutional discussions could proceed, there occurred an event which cast a shadow on further reform attempts in Murad's reign. This was the suicide of the ex-sultan. Abdülaziz had been miserable in the old palace of Topkapı, and, on his rather piteous request to Murad, was transferred with family and servants to quarters at the Çırağan palace, a little up the Bosporus from Dolmabahçe.[145] There on the morning of Sunday, June 4, Abdülaziz was found with the veins in his arms slashed and one artery severed. He died, by one account in his mother's arms, before medical help arrived. According to the generally accepted reconstruction of events, he had committed suicide with a pair of small scissors which he had asked for to trim his beard. His reason for doing so could only have been his already unstable mental condition, worsened by the shock and ensuing depression caused by his sudden deposition five days before.[146] After his body had been removed to the guardhouse nearby, nineteen of the most prominent physicians in the capital, including several attached to embassies of the great powers, examined the corpse and the room where Abdülaziz had been. Their unanimous conclusion, based on the nature and direction of the wounds and a view of the scene and the scissors, was that he had killed himself.[147] This apparently was also

---

[143] Abdurrahman Şeref, *Tarih musahabeleri*, p. 198.

[144] Şehsuvaroğlu, *Sultan Aziz*, pp. 111-112; Osman Nuri, *Abdülhamid-i Sani*, pp. 37-39; Kératry, *Mourad V*, pp. 142-143; Ahmed Saib, *Tarih-i Murad-ı Hamis*, p. 100, who seems to discuss both this and the June 8 meeting, with a wrong date. Could there have been only one meeting? Kératry seems the source for this one.

[145] Cevdet, *Tezâkir*, pp. xxiv-xxv; Ahmed Midhat, *Üss-i inkılâb*, I, 397-398, giving Abdülaziz's two notes to Murad abridged as one.

[146] Contemporary statements on the circumstances of Abdülaziz's death are Cevdet's, in Mardin, *Cevdet*, pp. 257-258; Mehmed Rüşdi's, in 1881, in Uzunçarşılı, *Midhat ve Rüştü Paşalar*, pp. 125-127; Mehmed Memduh's in *Mirât-ı şuûnat*, pp. 80-81; Şehsuvaroğlu, *Sultan Aziz*, pp. 125-129, based on Yusuf İzzeddin's and evidently other statements; *Le Stamboul*, 5 and 9 June 1876; *Levant Herald*, 5 July 1876. A. H. Midhat, *Hâtıralarım*, pp. 227-229, adds later statements by contemporaries.

[147] Text of the doctors' signed report in French (presumably the original language) in *La Turquie*, 4 June 1876 Supplement; in Turkish in Ahmed Midhat,

the public view at first.[148] But soon people began to believe that Abdülaziz had been assassinated, probably by order of some of the ministers.[149] Ignatyev evidently helped to spread the rumor of murder, and his counsellor of embassy, Nelidov, was convinced that was the fact.[150] The investigation had, of course, been grossly mishandled. There was no coordination between Palace and Porte, the body had been moved before the physicians saw it, and Mehmed Rüşdi and others appear to have been delinquent in not taking charge of a more thorough investigation. There was, of course, no autopsy. If it was murder, those like Midhat and Hüseyin Avni who had led the coup against Abdülaziz, and who would have most to lose if the ex-sultan should again return to the throne, would be suspect. Midhat insisted, and there seems no reason to doubt him, that he was the last of the ministers to learn of Abdülaziz's death.[151] But suspicions persisted. In the phrase of a witty journalist, "Abdülaziz was suicided."[152]

Actually, the cause of reform was seriously set back by the death of Abdülaziz. Midhat had nothing to gain from such an unfortunate event, particularly as any suspicion of murder would, in turn, throw

---

Üss-i inkılâb, I, 398-400, misspelling some doctors' names; in English in A. H. Midhat, Life, pp. 90-91. Further medical statements by Dr. E. D. Dickson, British embassy physician and one of the signers of the above report, in Elliot to Derby, #580, 5 June 1876, FO 78/2459; letter in Stamboul, 8 June 1876; letter to the Lancet, dated 23 June 1876, reprinted in Levant Herald, 5 July 1876; article in British Medical Journal (July 1876), cited in Seton-Watson, Disraeli, p. 36, n.1; cf. Elliot, "The Death of Abdul Aziz," pp. 285-287, citing Dr. Millingen, another of the signers, as well as Dr. Dickson. Another report dated more than twenty-four hours later and signed by five doctors, generally confirming the first report, is referred to by Şehsuvaroğlu, Sultan Aziz, p. 134, n.1. Report of Dr. A. Marroin, French embassy physician, enclosed in Bourgoing to Décazes, #83, 7 June 1876, AAE, Turquie 404. The only doctor's statement the author knows of which affirms murder instead of suicide is one twelve years later by Dr. Mavroyeni, who was not one of the examining physicians in 1876. Mavroyeni was, significantly, physician to Abdülhamid II: Desjardin (Paul de Régla), Au pays de l'espionnage (Paris, 1902), pp. 42-44. "The Death of the ex-Sultan," The Lancet (10 June 1876), 872-873, says that the suicide conclusion of the nineteen doctors is medically unconvincing.

[148] Cevdet, Tezâkir, p. xxv.

[149] Washburn, Fifty Years, pp. 105-106; Fred Burnaby, On Horseback Through Asia Minor (London, 1877), I, 15-17.

[150] Elliot to Derby, #591 and #592, both 7 June 1876, FO 78/2459.

[151] A. H. Midhat, Tabsıra-i ibret, p. 172; idem, Mirât-ı hayret, pp. 57-60; Uzunçarşılı, Midhat ve Rüştü Paşalar, p. 88; Şehsuvaroğlu, Sultan Aziz, pp. 132-133.

[152] Charikles, Türkische Skizzen in Briefe an eine Freundin (Berlin, 1877), p. 16. The suspicions were revived in 1881 under Abdülhamid II by charges that Abdülaziz had been murdered, and that Midhat, Mehmed Rüşdi, Hüseyin Avni, and Hayrullah had been involved. Probably the charges were baseless. See appendix D.

suspicion on the motives of the reformers.[153] But the impact of his uncle's death on Murad V was the gravest blow. Already shaken by the manner of his leaving confinement for the throne, he was now troubled anew by Abdülaziz's suicide. When the news reached him, he was at table; palace officials said he rose and vomited. Both Midhat and Mehmed Rüşdi, who saw him shortly thereafter, found him grief-stricken.[154] All dates assigned to the start of Murad's mental illness are the result of guesswork, but it may well be that this was the event which unsettled his mind the most.[155] The ceremonial girding of the sultan with the sword of Osman, which usually took place between five and fifteen days after accession, should have been scheduled within the week or ten days following Abdülaziz's death.[156] It was put off, evidently owing to Murad's mental condition. Though there was talk of it through the rest of June, the girding of Murad, the hope of the constitutionalists, never took place. Nor does he seem to have taken any effective part in government business.

The next discussion of a constitution was at a special and enlarged meeting of the council of ministers on Thursday, June 8, but Murad did not attend. In addition to the ministers, there came to the Bab-ı fetva (the *şeyhülislâm*'s office) Redif Paşa and Süleyman Paşa, two key military men in the deposition, plus two prominent members of the ulema, Kazasker Seyfeddin Efendi and the Fetva emini (commissioner of *fetva*'s) Halil Efendi. Mehmed Rüşdi pursued a conservative line, saying that the people of the empire were not yet capable of constitutional government; it would be better to content them by a show of empty privileges which would arouse their gratitude toward the government. Süleyman, who had been ordered by Hüseyin Avni not to speak unless military matters were under discussion, could not contain himself, but jumped up from his corner and said: "Your Excellency, the deposition did not take place in order to maintain the present absolutism. Every one undertook this sacrifice in order to assure the future of the nation. Those who did this had no personal animosity toward the deposed sultan and no special relationship to the

---

[153] Midhat later referred specifically to the bad public impression: Uzunçarşılı, *Midhat ve Rüştü Paşalar*, p. 95.

[154] Şehsuvaroğlu, *Sultan Aziz*, p. 133; Uzunçarşılı, *Midhat ve Rüştü Paşalar*, pp. 126-127; Cevdet, *Tezâkir*, p. xxvi.

[155] A. H. Midhat, *Mirât-ı hayret*, p. 60. Cf. Kuntay, *Namık Kemal*, II, part I, 744-745, n.1.

[156] Alderson, *Ottoman Dynasty*, pp. 41-42.

present one. Please continue the discussion with this point in mind."
But Mehmed Rüşdi was unmoved. When Namık Paşa, minister without portfolio, proposed a parliament like Britain's but composed of Muslims only, the grand vezir turned on him, saying, "Then you have become a Red."[157] He derided Midhat's and Halil Şerif's constitutional ideas as well. Further, said Mehmed Rüşdi, give the people something, and they ask for more. Look at the demands of the Cretans since they were given privileges.[158] Midhat advocated a national assembly, but did not criticize Mehmed Rüşdi vigorously at this meeting, evidently seeking to bring about some kind of unity. But this was a vain hope. Although both Server and Raşid Paşas spoke mildly for constitutionalism, the majority of those present remained silent, while several, including Cevdet and Seyfeddin, tried to reconcile differences. But at least three strongly backed the grand vezir, while Halil Efendi spoke out for government by the traditional elite. "Will you ask opinions and courses of action of a collection of ignorant leftovers from Anatolia and Rumelia?" When Midhat said that Süleyman had translated the French constitution, and proposed that he should read it, Halil rejoined that no national assembly, but simply a body of ulema, was needed as an advisory group.[159]

The meeting adjourned without reaching a conclusion. It revealed how the lines of conflict were drawn. Midhat and Süleyman, though unlike and even critical of each other in many ways, were united in favor of speedy action for a constitution.[160] Süleyman Paşa indeed, in the month of June, and perhaps before the meeting at the Bab-ı fetva, had hurriedly drafted a constitution of forty-five articles. Despite its

---

[157] Namık had been known in his youth as a liberal, fluent in French, and one of Reşid Paşa's men; later he was known as a conservative or reactionary Muslim, but he had indicated even before the deposition that he would support some kind of parliamentary control over the sultan, though probably a parliament of Muslims only. Cf. A. Henry Layard, *Autobiography and Letters* (London, 1903), II, 28-29; Elliot to Derby, #628, 3 October 1875, FO 78/2388, and #532, confidential, 24 May 1876, FO 78/2458.

[158] In 1867. See above, chapter V, pp. 158-159. The Christians in the Cretan assembly were asking new concessions in the summer of 1876: cf. *Augsburger Allgemeine Zeitung*, 24 August.

[159] The fullest account of this meeting, though written from his viewpoint, is in Süleyman, *Hiss-i inkılâb*, pp. 61-64, and most of it is repeated in Sami, *Süleyman Paşa muhakemesi*, pp. 46-48. Mahmud Celaleddin, who was also there, reports the meeting in *Mirât-i hakikat*, I, 126. Süleyman says that no record was kept. Cf. İnal, *Son sadrıâzamlar*, I, 142-143; Gad Franco, *Développements constitutionnels en Turquie* (Paris, 1925), pp. 23-24.

[160] Kuntay, *Namık Kemal*, II, part 1, 712-713. Süleyman, like many others, found that Midhat had autocratic tendencies.

disorganization, it is of great interest in its combination of Muslim representation on a geographical basis with non-Muslim representation on a millet basis, in a proportion of two to one. Egypt, Tunis, Serbia, Roumania, and Montenegro would also have deputies. There is no evidence, however, that Süleyman's draft was either made public or discussed by the ministers.[161] Raşid and Server, each with European diplomatic experience, supported Midhat and Süleyman. Mehmed Rüşdi was backed by several speakers and by the inarticulate majority in his contention that a constitution was too radical a departure. Interestingly, most of the argument was on secular lines; only Kara Halil and Namık seem to have introduced religious considerations, while two members of the ulema (Cevdet and Seyfeddin) were moderates, as well as Safvet, who had also had European diplomatic experience. The meeting was erroneously reported the next day to have reached a unanimous decision to create a national assembly and a ministry responsible to it, and to have appointed Midhat to work out the details.[162] But the public went on discussing a constitution and a parliament, and probably expecting such reforms, which Turkish papers in the capital continued to advocate.[163]

Immediate elaboration of a constitution was unlikely, however, until the serious divergences within the council of ministers could be resolved. One of the antagonisms had remained unvoiced at the meeting, but was real enough. This was the opposition of Hüseyin Avni not only to a constitution, but to an increase in the influence of Midhat or of anyone but himself. Hüseyin Avni had since May 30 been the dominant figure in the ministry, posing as the strong man of the deposition and hoping to control both ministry and Palace. Some suspected him of wanting to be dictator.[164] He was a stronger personality than Mehmed Rüşdi, the grand vezir, and as minister of war had military power to back him. He had a more important position than Midhat, who had been without portfolio until early June, when he was given

---

[161] Text in Sami, *Süleyman Paşa muhakemesi*, pp. 62-66, n.1.

[162] *Stamboul*, 9 June 1876. This may have been a story planted by Midhat partisans. *Démenti* in issue of 15 June 1876.

[163] Cf. the letter of Halil Ganem, a Syrian Christian and later deputy to the Ottoman parliament, in *Stamboul*, 8 June 1876; ABCFM, Western Turkey Mission II, #591, 14 June 1876; Edouard Engelhardt, *La Turquie et le Tanzimat* (Paris, 1882-1884), II, 158.

[164] Elliot to Derby, #601, 8 June 1876, FO 78/2459; Gallenga, *Two Years*, II, 133; *Stamboul*, 17 June 1876; Kératry, *Mourad V*, pp. 169-170. It may have been of Hüseyin Avni that Raşid Paşa was speaking when he said to a Bulgar that the government was living in terror: Hajek, *Bulgarien*, pp. 294-295.

the presidency of the Council of State. Then, just a week after the ministers' meeting at the Bab-ı fetva, Hüseyin Avni was violently removed from the scene. A Circassian army officer, Hasan, broke in upon a meeting of the ministers held at Midhat's house on Thursday, June 15, and killed both Hüseyin Avni and Raşid Paşa, the foreign minister. Several others were wounded. Hüseyin Avni was Hasan's target, for the assassination was an act both of personal and political vengeance. Hasan's sister was the second of Abdülaziz's "wives," and Hasan evidently wanted to avenge his sister and the fallen sultan. He may also have believed that Hüseyin Avni had murdered Abdülaziz. In addition, Hasan had been aide-de-camp to Abdülaziz's son, Yusuf İzzeddin, whose hopes of succeeding directly to the sultanate had now been dashed with his father's deposition. Hüseyin Avni had ordered the Circassian out of İstanbul to duty in Baghdad; instead of going, Çerkez Hasan had slain the war minister.[165] But it appeared to some that Midhat might have planned the murder to rid himself of a dangerous rival, since the attack had occurred at his house and he himself was unhurt.[166] This suspicion appears to be unfounded. Yet the fact was that, after Hüseyin Avni's death, Midhat was the strongest personality in the ministry, and might now dominate the more vacillating Mehmed Rüşdi. Sultan Murad was so sick and bewildered at this point that he was not even told of the event.[167] News of a second violent death within two weeks could only unsettle the sultan's mind further. The murder was unsettling enough for the ministers.

Other developments, with one exception, boded ill for further serious work on a constitution. The exception was the recall from exile of Namık Kemal and other New Ottoman associates. Ziya Bey, who had been back in İstanbul since 1872, was on May 30 appointed Sultan Murad's first secretary. He made it his first business to persuade

---

[165] Accounts written by, or based on information from, those present: Mehmed Memduh, *Mirât-ı şuûnat*, pp. 96-99; A. H. Midhat, *Tabsıra-i ibret*, pp. 183-186; Elliot to Derby, #634, 17 June 1876, FO 78/2459 (from Mehmed Rüşdi); Nelidow, "Souvenirs," pp. 328-330 (from Mehmed Rüşdi and Kayserili Ahmed); Schweiger-Lerchenfeld, *Serail*, pp. 145-160 (assertedly from Midhat). Detailed accounts also in Kératry, *Mourad V*, pp. 172-193; Gallenga, *Two Years*, II, 105-113; *Levant Herald*, 5 July 1876; Şehsuvaroğlu, *Sultan Aziz*, pp. 153-158, including Hasan's statement. Hasan's sister had died three days before, apparently from an attempted abortion: Alderson, *Ottoman Dynasty*, table 48 and n.3; Elliot to Derby, #631, 16 June 1876, FO 78/2459.

[166] Washburn, *Fifty Years*, p. 106; ABCFM, Western Turkey Mission II, #471, 16 June 1876.

[167] Mehmed Memduh, *Mirât-ı şuûnat*, p. 100.

Murad to release Namık Kemal and the others from their *résidence forcée*. Because of this exhibition of his influence, and probably because of Mehmed Rüşdi's fear that he might dominate Murad, Ziya was after one day shifted to be deputy minister of public instruction. But the exiles returned, Namık Kemal bringing with him his desire for a parliamentary regime and his burning love of fatherland. In the ensuing summer his *Vatan yahut Silistre* was often played.[168] Otherwise, things looked worse. Muslim fanaticism seemed to be on the increase. The government went back to the process of curbing the press, suspending five İstanbul papers in June.[169] By the end of June, Serbia and Montenegro were openly at war against their sovereign, Murad V, even though Prince Milan of Serbia protested that he believed in the integrity of the Ottoman Empire.[170] So the Turks were thrust into a situation in which Slavic principalities supported Slavic rebels in the Balkans and the Serb army was commanded by the pan-Slav Russian general Chernyaev, who had previously fought the Muslim khanates in Central Asia. The Turks, therefore, began to rouse themselves for a real struggle, which began to look like a religious as well as a national war. There were some Armenian and Greek volunteers for the campaign against Serbia.[171] But it was more characteristic that the Muslim theological students should volunteer, and also be out arousing the countryside. They were now on vacation, and their public agitation seemed less and less directed toward constitutional reform, more and more toward propagating the doctrine of holy war.[172] A vezirial proclamation in Arabic, posted in Antep (Aintab), called for a "warring of the whole family of Islam" against the "seekers of evil" who sought to ruin "the foundation of the state and of the faith of our government." The reserves were being called up in the name of Islam.[173] This was hardly the atmosphere for calm deliberation on a constitution.

[168] Kuntay, *Namık Kemal*, II, part 1, 728; *Stamboul*, 5 and 14 June 1876; *Augsburger Allgemeine Zeitung*, 6 July 1876 (Ausserordentliche Beilage); Mehmed Kaplan, *Namık Kemal* (İstanbul, 1948), p. 97.
[169] ABCFM, Western Turkey Mission II, #470, 15 June 1876, and #592, 21 June 1876; *Stamboul*, 9 June and 3 July 1876; Elliot to Derby, #649, 20 June 1876, FO 78/2459.
[170] Langer, *European Alliances*, pp. 89-90.
[171] *Levant Herald*, 15 July 1876; *Augsburger Allgemeine Zeitung*, 19, 29 July and 3 August 1876; Gallenga, *Two Years*, II, 193-196.
[172] ABCFM, Western Turkey Mission II, #593, 28 June 1876; *Augsburger Allgemeine Zeitung* 9, 13, 14 (Beilage), 19 (Beilage), 20 (Beilage), 21 July 1876.
[173] Text in translation in Maynard to Fish, #86, 20 July 1876, USNA, Turkey 29.

Midhat was, nevertheless, going forward with his plans, with some encouragement from the British ambassador.[174] Midhat had on June 22 a meeting at his house of some of the most influential of the fanatical ulema, and said they had agreed to the necessity of a representative council, partly nominated and partly elected, to control finances. They agreed also that Christians could not be excluded from it. He was not aiming at the impossible, Midhat told Elliot, and would compromise if needed to carry the ministry along. His main problem he foresaw as the administration of equal justice without abolishing the religious courts.[175] Midhat evidently continued to work on a revision of his draft of a constitution.[176] An opportunity to present it came when a grand council of notables (*meclis-i umumî*) was convened at the Sublime Porte on Saturday, July 15, to consider the difficulties caused by Austria's closing the harbor of Klek.[177] Including the ministers, a number of ulema, about seven Christians, and other notables, this gathering of seventy-six heard Mehmed Rüşdi outline the precarious position of the empire in its struggle for life. Persuaded either by Midhat or by the worsening situation, or both, the grand vezir spoke of the need for reorganization of the government. Midhat presented his revised constitutional draft, the basic principles of which the council is reported to have approved, though it remanded to a commission of the Council of State under Midhat's presidency the task of making further emendations. If the reports were true, the grand council's decision marked a radical departure from the past. Among the basic principles were complete equality of Christians and Muslims, eligibility of Christians for all offices including that of grand

---

[174] Ignatyev regarded Elliot as the instigator of Midhat's plans: Ignatyev to Kartsov, 29 June 1876, quoted in Sumner, *Russia and the Balkans*, pp. 169-170. Early in 1876 Elliot had said to Abdülaziz that there ought to be some constitutional control over the government: Elliot to Derby, #492, 12 May 1876, FO 78/2458.

[175] Elliot to Derby, #664, confidential, 24 June 1876, FO 78/2460. Namık Paşa meanwhile expected his parliamentary program, excluding Christians until they had proved their loyalty, to be adopted: Elliot to Derby, #679, confidential, 28 June 1876, FO 78/2460.

[176] *Augsburger Allgemeine Zeitung*, 2 and 4 July 1876. The latter issue reports a meeting of ulema at the Bab-ı fetva which approved Midhat's plans.

[177] Klek was the only Adriatic port through which the Turks could supply their forces in Herzegovina by sea. Gorchakov and Andrassy in their secret meeting at Reichstadt on July 8 agreed that it would be closed. Cf. Sumner, *Russia and the Balkans*, pp. 140, n.2, and 170. I am here assuming that the *meclis-i umunî* described in A. H. Midhat, *Tabsıra-i ibret*, p. 182, is that of July 15, and that it was not in late August as reported by Franco, *Développements constitutionnels*, p. 24, who repeats Midhat's account.

vezir, a chamber of elected deputies—sixteen from İstanbul and four from each vilayet, a ministry responsible to the chamber, the admission of Christian testimony against Muslims in the courts, and security of tenure of judges and civil officials. A copy of Midhat's draft was to be furnished to each of the royal princes and to other persons. Another grand council was to be called later to consider the further revisions.[178]

It does not appear that a second grand council was convened. Instead, the rise of passions and the exigencies of the war against Serbia and Montenegro led the ministers to publish on August 3 an order forbidding public discussion of a constitution. Under the pressure of events, said the order in explanation, even the government could not find time for proper consideration of the constitutional question.[179] Shortly thereafter Midhat received from a group of softas a letter attacking the concepts of constitution and parliament and upbraiding Ziya for trying to justify those concepts with Koranic quotations. So long as England, France, and Russia did not give a proper share in government to the numerous Muslims of their empires, the softas were indisposed to let Christians—whom their ancestors had conquered—participate in Ottoman government.[180] Midhat was said to have received at the same time a letter threatening him with the fate of Hüseyin Avni should he persist in his constitutional plans. Something of a stopgap measure was the reorganization about August 15 of the Council of State under the presidency of Midhat. Whereas Mahmud Nedim had curtailed its functions, Midhat expanded them again under four sections: administrative, judicial, public works, and reform.

[178] *Levant Herald*, 17 July 1876; *Augsburger Allgemeine Zeitung*, 18, 19, 23, 24, 28, and 29 July 1876; A. H. Midhat, *Tabsıra-i ibret*, p. 182, which reports a second meeting at the Bab-ı fetva with no further details. Additional details on the July 15 meeting from the Russian archives and press are in Petrosian, "Novye Osmany," pp. 103-104. *Augsburger Allgemeine Zeitung*, 5 August 1876, gives additional principles for the constitution, said to have been cut by Midhat from 140 to 70 articles, and adds that supposedly it will be in force in two weeks. The whole dispatch seems exaggerated. About four weeks later it was reported that a committee of five Muslims and three Christians, chaired by Server Paşa, minister of public works, had been appointed to examine the constitutional draft: *Augsburger Allgemeine Zeitung*, 18 and 24 August 1876. I do not know what, if anything, the committee accomplished.

[179] Text in *Staatsarchiv*, 30 (1877), #5775. Cf. *Augsburger Allgemeine Zeitung*, 9 and 11 August 1876; Gallenga, *Two Years*, II, 280-281.

[180] Text in *Augsburger Allgemeine Zeitung*, 16 August 1876, and Maynard to Fish, #89, 10 August 1876, USNA, Turkey 29.

Christians were quite liberally represented in the membership of the sections.[181]

Conditions continued to grow worse for any calm discussion of reforms. As volunteers thronged the recruiting offices in İstanbul, as reserves were called up in the interior, as Egyptian contingents arrived by ship, as Tatar and Kurd and Tunisian leaders enrolled and supported volunteers, the atmosphere was at once that of a national and a religious war. The ministry tried its best to play down the religious, and play up the Ottoman, aspect, and would not let the newspapers speak of a jihad. Public subscription lists for aid to the wounded were opened, one of them headed by Midhat's wife—a new departure in public action for women of the empire. Many Turks—and even Armenians, excited by exaggerated reports of risings of their brethren in the Caucasus—began to think of the war effort as directed essentially against Russia rather than against Serbia and Montenegro.[182] The undoubted religious overtones weakened any sense of Osmanlılık and heightened tensions within the empire, although overt incidents, aside from some plundering by Zeybek and Circassian irregulars, were few.

Mehmed Rüşdi's government also encountered in the summer and fall of 1876 financial difficulties inherited from the time of Mahmud Nedim, but now aggravated by the burden of war costs. Interest payments on the Ottoman debt were again postponed in July.[183] The government's appeal to its subjects for contributions and loans assumed in some vilayets the aspect of a forced loan.[184] These measures did not suffice, and by early August the government had come back to the old and dangerous method of financing its needs by the issue of paper money. *Kaime*'s, supposedly backed by the civil list and by income from coal mines, were printed in Paris; in August two million Turkish pounds' worth were issued, and another million in November. The paper currency began at once to depreciate, reaching by December a discount of twenty-four per cent and going much lower thereafter.[185] Meanwhile unusual heat followed by unusual rains de-

---

[181] *Levant Herald*, 15 August 1876, listing names; *Augsburger Allgemeine Zeitung*, 22 and 23 August 1876.

[182] *Augsburger Allgemeine Zeitung*, 23, 26, 28, 29 July and 1, 2, 3, 6, 7, 17 August 1876; ABCFM, Western Turkey Mission II, #474, 1 August 1876, and Eastern Turkey Mission I, #212, 26 July, and #213, 13 September 1876.

[183] *Levant Herald*, 13 July 1876.

[184] *Augsburger Allgemeine Zeitung*, 13 and 14 (Beilage) July 1876.

[185] A. Du Velay, *Essai sur l'histoire financière de la Turquie* (Paris, 1903), pp.

stroyed much of the grain harvest in western Anatolia, while in other parts the drafting of men and beasts for military service left fields untended and crops unharvested.[186] The agricultural situation was not so bad as it had been in 1874, but the economic and military difficulties that plagued the government tended to postpone constitutional discussion.

✛

One problem that the ministry faced was, however, greater than any of the foregoing. This was the incapacity of Sultan Murad V. The Ottoman system demanded a sultan at its head, even to consider and promulgate a constitution which might limit the powers of that sultan. Murad had been the hope of the reformers. But from the earliest days of his reign he had evidently been able to take little part in public business. His girding had been deferred, and he seemed never to have recovered sufficiently from the shock of events to go through with the ceremony. Rumors that he was in poor health had circulated since the start of his reign, although until mid-August these rumors were just as consistently denied. Dr. Capoléone, Murad's personal physician, said that by July 11 he was convalescing satisfactorily from the shock of Abdülaziz's death, complicated by a carbuncle, boils, ague, and fever.[187] But by mid-July there were rumors that his abdication or deposition would be forthcoming soon, and such reports continued throughout the next month.[188] One rumor added that Abdülhamid, Murad's younger brother, would assume a regency. These reports too were consistently denied. Nevertheless, Dr. Max Leidesdorf, a Viennese specialist whom Queen Victoria had consulted, was called to İstanbul to see Murad. He arrived on August 10, and after thorough examination reported on the 13th that Murad was in a bad mental and nervous state, but in fairly good physical condition. His prognosis was that, with proper measures, a cure might be effected in about three months.[189] Although Ottoman statesmen

---

354-356; Maynard to Fish, #111, 18 December 1876, USNA, Turkey 30; *Augsburger Allgemeine Zeitung*, 2 (Beilage) and 22 August 1876.
[186] *Augsburger Allgemeine Zeitung*, 4, 6, 23 July 1876; Gallenga, *Two Years*, II, 176.
[187] Elliot to Derby, #730, confidential, 11 July 1876, FO 78/2460.
[188] *Augsburger Allgemeine Zeitung*, 22, 30, 31 July, and 3, 5, 9 August 1876.
[189] His report is in İsmail Hakkı Uzunçarşılı, "Beşinci Sultan Murad'ın tedâvisine ve ölümüne ait rapor ve mektuplar, 1876-1905," *Belleten*, x:38 (April 1946), plate 33, and Turkish translation, pp. 326-328. A portion was published in *Levant Herald*,

sometimes later referred to his "madness," the probable truth seems to be that Murad had really suffered a nervous breakdown, induced by his confinement under Abdülaziz, his excessive drinking, the shock of being taken by soldiers to his sudden accession, and the further shocks of Abdülaziz's suicide and the Çerkez Hasan murders. Though in time he might recover, he could not for the immediate future be an active head of state.[190]

Since the sovereign could not receive ambassadors, take part in public functions, lead the war effort, or act as arbiter in discussions of the constitution, the ministers were faced with the critical decision as to whether they should await Murad's convalescence or seek another sultan. It is not clear how early in Murad's reign the ministers, or some of them, began seriously to consider deposing Murad. Evidently there were some palace officials and military men, with whom Cevdet, the minister of justice, may have been associated, who sought an increase in their personal influence by replacing Murad with Abdülhamid.[191] But a second deposition would be an extremely serious matter. Midhat and Mehmed Rüşdi evidently came reluctantly to the conclusion that it was a necessity, because of the stagnation in government, and the grand vezir even went to the extreme of consulting Elliot on August 25 at his summer embassy on the wisdom of the change.[192] Possibly before this interview, possibly even before Dr. Leidesdorf's visit, the ministers are said to have sent Midhat to Abdülhamid to see if the latter would consent to act as regent until Murad should be cured.[193] There was, however, no Ottoman prece-

---

21 August 1876. Uzunçarşılı also gives earlier physicians' reports on Murad, pp. 323-325. Cf. also *Levant Herald*, 11, 14, 19 August; *Augsburger Allgemeine Zeitung*, 17 August 1876. There is some question as to whether Dr. Leidesdorf in a second report, or privately, said Murad was incurable: Clician Vassif, *Midhat-Pacha*, pp. 71-72; Gallenga, *Two Years*, II, 116.

[190] Alderson, *Ottoman Dynasty*, pp. 69-70; *Augsburger Allgemeine Zeitung*, 14 September 1876.

[191] See the charges in A. H. Midhat, *Life*, pp. 94-96; *Augsburger Allgemeine Zeitung*, 3 September 1876.

[192] A. H. Midhat, *Tabsıra-i ibret*, p. 183; Mehmed Memduh, *Mirât-ı şuûnat*, p. 102; Ahmed Saib, *Tarih-i Murad-ı Hamis*, pp. 252-304; Elliot, "The Death of Abdul Aziz," pp. 291-292.

[193] Osman Nuri, *Abdülhamid-i Sani*, I, 93-94; Ahmed Saib, *Tarih-i Murad-ı Hamis*, p. 302; Alderson, *Ottoman Dynasty*, p. 48; Georges Dorys, *Abdul Hamid intime* (Paris, 1901), p. 31. Cf. Albert Fua, *Abdul Hamid II et Mourad V* (Paris, 1909), p. 32, on Midhat's supposed plan to have Abdülhamid tell his brothers at a banquet that he was regent only, during Murad's illness, and Abdülhamid's portrayal of the banquet as a plot to murder him: Uzunçarşılı, *Midhat ve Rüştü Paşalar*, pp. 2, n.1, 98, 154-157.

dent for a regency except that confided briefly to Âli Paşa in 1867, and a provisional sultan raised the question of who was the supreme imam in Islam. Abdülhamid would have none of it, and wanted medical certification that Murad was incapable of ruling. He was anxious for the throne, but not on a conditional basis. Circumspectly, Abdülhamid sought to advance his chances through contacts with influential men. He even sent an Englishman he knew to tell Elliot that he was determined on economy, would stop abuses, and, moreover, had studied the British blue books and parliamentary debates on Turkey and agreed with much that was said there.[194]

Abdülhamid was, in fact, willing to make extensive promises to get the throne. Midhat went again to see Abdülhamid at his residence in Musluoğlu, and returned to the council of ministers with Abdülhamid's word to abide by three conditions—that he would promulgate the constitution without delay, that he would act in governmental matters only with the advice of responsible advisers, and that he would reappoint as palace secretaries Sadullah, Ziya, and Namık Kemal Beys.[195] In this manner the ministers hoped to protect themselves from such a resurgence of Palace influence as had taken place in the last five years of Abdülaziz's reign. There were for years rumors current that Abdülhamid had made one further promise, and indeed had made it in written form—to abdicate should Murad completely recover his health. This seems quite unlikely, in view of Abdülhamid's attitude about the regency. In any case, no documentary proof has ever come to light.[196]

The result of Midhat's interview with Abdülhamid was satisfactory enough to him and to the grand vezir so that they went ahead to work out the details of deposing Murad. Meetings of the ministers were held on August 28 and 30. Between them, Mehmed Rüşdi and

<hr/>

[194] Elliot to Derby, #915, very confidential, 27 August 1876, FO 78/2462; Alderson, *Ottoman Dynasty*, pp. 52-53, 70; Osman Nuri, *Abdülhamid-i Sani*, I, 96. The stories in Fua, *Abdul Hamid* II, pp. 29-31, seem exaggerated.

[195] A. H. Midhat, *Life*, pp. 97-98; Ahmed Saib, *Tarih-i Murad-ı Hamis*, p. 303; Osman Nuri, *Abdülhamid-i Sani*, I, 95-98. Petrosian, "Novye Osmany," p. 105, citing Mehmed Ziya, *Yenikapı Mevlevihanesi* (İstanbul, 1329), pp. 184-185, says the meeting was arranged by the Mevlevi şeyh Osman Efendi. Midhat had evidently been in touch with Osman for some time: Mahmud Celaleddin, *Mirât-ı hakikat*, I, 104. A. H. Midhat, *Midhat Pacha*, p. 64, says that the ministers decided that if Abdülhamid refused the conditions they would offer the throne to his younger brother Mehmed Reşad, and that Midhat's wife was to probe the latter's attitude on reforms! Story, *Ismail Kemal*, p. 117, says that Midhat on August 27 actually read to Abdülhamid a draft of, or the bases of, the constitution.

[196] See appendix E.

Midhat conferred with Hayrullah, the *şeyhülislâm*. Two *fetva*'s were drawn up to justify the deposition, of which the more strongly worded was chosen, apparently at Abdülhamid's wish. It spoke of Murad's confirmed insanity.[197] As a medical basis for the *fetva*, Mehmed Rüşdi is said to have obtained from six İstanbul physicians, four of them attached to embassies, a certificate that they had reported on Murad's health and concluded that his complete recovery was not to be expected.[198] An extraordinary meeting of the ministers was convened at the Porte on Wednesday, August 30, at which Mehmed Rüşdi and Midhat spoke strongly for deposition. Their views were upheld, despite some opposition from Rıza Paşa, general in command of the arsenal, who said that Murad might recover. Abdülhamid was sent a message that the ministers had decided on the change in sultans—but, as Mehmed Rüşdi cautiously said, it was not done by the ministers' decision, but by consensus of the community and authority of the şeriat. Invitations to a grand council to be held the following morning were sent to all civil, religious, and military notables. In order to minimize the chance of open opposition, the council was to meet not at the Porte, but in the old Dome Chamber of the divan, at the Topkapı palace, where soldiers and stacked weapons would be on hand.[199]

There on Thursday, August 31, Mehmed Rüşdi spoke to the assembled notables of the discouraging medical reports on Murad's health and of the ministers' discussion the day before. His voice trembled, and he wiped his eyes with a handkerchief. Midhat, more vigorously, said that the government could not operate without a sultan, the final resort in all matters, and called for the reading of the *fetva*. Hayrullah handed it to Kara Halil, the commissioner of *fetva*'s, who read it. The council rather passively accepted the whole proceeding, and then Abdülhamid received the oath of loyalty.[200] The change in sultans was accomplished with no disorder whatsoever, but neither was there any rejoicing beyond the officially ordered fireworks, il-

---

[197] *Le Stamboul*, 29 August 1876; *Augsburger Allgemeine Zeitung*, 31 August and 2 September 1876; Mehmed Memduh, *Mirât-ı şuûnat*, p. 105.

[198] Osman Nuri, *Abdülhamid-i Sani*, I, 98. Text of the supposed report in A. H. Midhat, *Life*, p. 98, with the dubious date of August 31. Possibly this is a predated version of a later version dated September 20, printed in Ahmed Midhat, *Üss-i inkılâb*, I, 437-438, or even of an October 20 report. Cf. manuscript texts of the latter two in Uzunçarşılı, "Beşinci Sultan Murad'ın tedâvisine . . . ait rapor . . . ," plates 35 and 36, and pp. 332-333.

[199] Mehmed Memduh, *Mirât-ı şuûnat*, pp. 102-103.

[200] *Ibid.*, pp. 104-105; *Levant Herald*, 31 August 1876. Official notification to powers in *Staatsarchiv*, 31 (1877), #5792.

lumination, and twenty-one gun salutes five times a day for three days.[201] The same atmosphere carried over to the girding of Abdülhamid, which took place just a week later. It looked as if Abdülhamid were anxious to avoid the postponements Murad had encountered and to tighten his grip on the throne. The pageantry on September 7 was colorful, as Abdülhamid II on his white charger moved in procession up from the Golden Horn to the mosque of Eyüb between files of guards and of Count Szechenyi's model fire brigade. But the crowds were orderly and self-contained. The contrast to the jubilation at Murad's accession was marked. Portents of disaster were noted at the time: the Galata bridge sank four feet and almost collapsed; the cable in the tunnel of the Galata-Pera funicular tramway snapped.[202]

The fact was that Abdülhamid was quite an unknown quantity at his accession. He was almost thirty-four years old, but had lived a life of confinement and retirement. His face had an Armenian cast to it, and it was sometimes rumored that he was the son of an intruder into Abdülmecid's harem. As much good as bad was said of him. He was thought to be economical, orderly, healthy, more pious and more sober than Murad, hard-working. Some considered him to be fanatical and reactionary. Those whom he received in audience in the first year of his reign generally, however, carried away an impression of an intelligent, well-intentioned, fairly liberal sovereign.[203] What his rule might be like was anyone's guess. An American long resident in Istanbul recorded a shrewd estimate the day before the girding. Abdülhamid "is said to have explained his policy thus: Now, my policy is to obey the ministry. After I have learned what is needed, I shall change my policy and make the ministry obey me."[204]

It was some time before Abdülhamid's inaugural *hat* appeared,

[201] *Levant Herald*, 1 September 1876; *Augsburger Allgemeine Zeitung*, 8 September 1876.

[202] *Levant Herald*, 8 September 1876; Gallenga, *Two Years*, II, 121-130; Nelidow, "Souvenirs," p. 339; *Augsburger Allgemeine Zeitung*, 13 and 14 September 1876.

[203] Elliot to Derby, #962, September (n.d.) 1876, FO 78/2463, and #1321, confidential, 29 November 1876, FO 78/2467; *Augsburger Allgemeine Zeitung*, 5, 6, 14 September 1876; Gallenga, *Two Years*, II, 326-327; Hermann Vambéry, *Ueber die Reformfähigkeit der Türkei* (Budapest, 1877), pp. 50-51; Ahmed Midhat, *Üss-i inkılâb*, II, 165-167; Charles de Moüy, *Lettres du Bosphore* (Paris, 1879), pp. 250-251; Léouzon le Duc, *Midhat Pacha* (Paris, 1877), p. 112; Paul Fesch, *Constantinople aux derniers jours d'Abdul Hamid* (Paris, 1907), p. 190, n.; Seton-Watson, *Disraeli*, pp. 207, 406.

[204] ABCFM, Western Turkey Mission II, #603, 6 September 1876.

which was quite in contrast to the publication of Murad's two days after his accession. Meanwhile the new sultan demonstrated some independence of mind by appointing to palace positions men of his own choice, who were not favorable to Midhat. To some of these appointments the ministers entered no objections. But Abdülhamid broke one of his three promises by naming Küçük ("Little") Said Bey and Lebib Efendi as his secretaries instead of Sadullah, Ziya, and Namık Kemal. The grand vezir protested and stayed home for some days on pretense of illness; he is said even to have tendered his resignation, which the sultan refused to accept.[205] The sultan's *hat*, which had been held up not only by differences among the ministers, but by emendations which Abdülhamid wanted to make, finally was read on September 10.[206] It laid greater stress than had been usual for some years on the necessity of strict observance of the religious law. It promised in general terms improvements in the administrative bureaucracy, in education, in provincial government, and energetic measures against the Balkan rebels. It confirmed all ministers in their offices. It also promised in vague terms a grand council or general assembly (*meclis-i umumî*), which might mean anything or nothing. This was a far cry from what Midhat wanted. He had himself drawn up the first draft of the imperial *hat*, in which the sultan was made to promise the adoption of constitutional government, that the grand vezir would bear the title of prime minister, that schools would be established to which all Ottoman subjects would be admitted, that palace expenditures would be sharply reduced, and that the slave trade would be prohibited in the empire and all palace slaves freed.[207] Abdülhamid had safeguarded his own privileges, had reduced much of Midhat's specific language to generalities, and had, in particular, cast doubt on his own preaccession pledge of the speedy introduction of constitutional government.[208] The lines for a struggle over the constitution were being drawn.

[205] Osman Nuri, *Abdülhamid-i Sani*, I, pp. 104-106; Elliot to Derby, #977, 8 September, and #980, confidential, 9 September 1876, both FO 78/2463; Story, *Ismail Kemal*, p. 122; Kératry, *Mourad V*, p. 209; A. H. Midhat, *Life*, pp. 103-105.

[206] Text in Ahmed Midhat, *Üss-i inkılâb*, II, 281-285; *Levant Herald*, 12 September 1876; *Staatsarchiv*, 31 (1877), #5800.

[207] Text of Midhat's draft in Ahmed Midhat, *Üss-i inkılâb*, II, 285-291; A. H. Midhat, *Life*, pp. 106-109, showing Abdülaziz's excisions, as does Osman Nuri, *Abdülhamid-i Sani*, I, 115-119. Some of Midhat's points had been rumored to be in the final draft: *Augsburger Allgemeine Zeitung*, 12 September 1876, which here attributes them wrongly to Damad Mahmud Celaleddin Paşa, grand marshal of the palace.

[208] Cf. the rather sycophantic justification of the sultan's changes in Ahmed Midhat,

It is impossible to know what might have been the situation in the Ottoman Empire if Murad's health had not weakened. But it is quite conceivable that a vigorous sultan, committed to working out a constitution as Murad was, would have seen such a project to completion by the early fall of 1876. A parliament might have met regularly thereafter; it might have helped both to educate and to transform the empire. In view of the man who succeeded him, it is not too much to say that Murad's deposition after a short three months was a tragedy for his people as much as for himself—much as was the death of the liberal Friedrich III of Germany after a three-month reign in 1888, and his succession by the very different Wilhelm II. Abdülhamid II was a capable and strong-willed sultan, but his ideals were different from Murad's. He could not, in the difficult international situation arising from the Balkan rebellions, at once replace all his ministers or flatly go back on all his promises. But his accession *hat* and his palace appointments showed, at least, that he was reluctant to go ahead speedily with a constitutional regime which had already been a matter of public discussion for six months, and of official deliberation for three. When finally Abdülhamid was to consent to it, his action was more a maneuver in international politics than a result of conviction. Meanwhile Midhat, still influential within the ministry, bent every effort throughout the fall of 1876 to deliver the constitution whose birth pains added to the troubles of an already harassed government.

Üss-i inkılâb, II, 169-178, and the quite opposite viewpoint in A. H. Midhat, *Life*, pp. 109-112.

CHAPTER X

THE CONSTITUTION OF 1876

One auspicious event ushered in the reign of Abdülhamid II—a resounding Turkish victory over Chernyaev and the Serbs on September 1. This led to an armistice of ten days, followed by renewed fighting which culminated in the virtual disintegration of the Serb army after another Turkish victory at the end of October. Though the Ottoman armies were now in a position to advance on Belgrade itself, the fruits of victory were denied them by great-power action. The Russians, patrons of the Serbs, had already been probing for an armistice and an international conference. Now, on October 31, they suddenly confronted the Porte with a forty-eight-hour ultimatum to accept a six- to eight-week armistice or suffer a break in diplomatic relations. The Porte, unable to count on Britain's backing because of sentiment there over the Bulgarian massacres, yielded on November 1. The British government had, in any case, been trying to arrange a conference on the Balkan question, which it formally proposed on November 4. Confronted with an unusually violent speech by the tsar, by his order on November 13 for the mobilization of six army corps, and by the agreement of the six powers to Britain's proposal, the Porte also bowed on November 18 to the demand for a conference. This was to meet late in December in İstanbul and to be preceded by a preliminary conference among the powers, but without the Turks, to concert on a reform program.[1]

Naturally the great-power pressures, especially the Russian truculence, heightened the Ottoman patriotic sentiment and the religious sentiment that had been developing over the past year. The tsar wrote that "there is no longer any effective government in Turkey. The men in power are overwhelmed by the fanatical masses used to murder and pillage."[2] The tsar must have known that he was not telling the truth about the Porte. Yet he was partly right about the masses. During the fall of 1876 patriotic and anti-Russian feeling among Turks continued to mount. Victories over the Serbs served only to

[1] On the diplomatic aspects see B. H. Sumner, *Russia and the Balkans* (Oxford, 1937), pp. 196-243; William L. Langer, *European Alliances and Alignments*, 2nd ed. (New York, 1950), pp. 95-109.

[2] To Francis Joseph, 23 September 1876, quoted in Sumner, *Russia and the Balkans*, p. 208.

intensify the Turkish war fever, which affected the capital and all parts of Anatolia, especially those near the Russian frontier, where the Turks were building their military strength.[3] The Turkish press in Istanbul began to breathe war, and to defend the Bulgarian massacres, even as a new investigating commission under Sadullah Bey was sent out to the Bulgar area. *Ittihad* [*Union*] praised Islam as the religion of the sword. *Basiret* went too far in arousing Muslim fanaticism and preaching military preparedness, so that the Porte suspended it briefly.[4] A little of the fanaticism spilled over to create incidents between Christians and Muslims within the empire, as when police at the Sublime Porte beat some Armenian editors whose newspapers had carried stories of Turkish cruelty against Armenian notables in Trabzon. But the Porte tried hard to avoid and to repress all such incidents, in the interest of maintaining Ottoman unity.[5] Its task was easier than might be supposed, since many Armenians of the empire were in 1876 anti-Russian, owing to tsarist rule over their brethren, while many Greeks were also anti-Russian because of Russian support for Serb and Bulgar territorial and separatist political ambitions.[6] Yet the anti-Russian spirit helped also to create a nascent pan-Turkism and to invigorate pan-Islamic feeling. These currents were strengthened by interest in the reported exploits of Yakub Beg—even by hopes that he would help the Ottomans; by the presence of Circassian and Turkoman refugees from Russia in the Ottoman Empire; and by addresses of support from Indian Muslims. The anti-Russian war spirit also carried overtones of Anglophilism and hopes of help from the British.[7]

[3] Fred Burnaby, *On Horseback Through Asia Minor* (London, 1877), I, passim; *Augsburger Allgemeine Zeitung*, 1 and 10 September 1876.

[4] ABCFM, Western Turkey Mission II, #606, 4 October 1876; *Levant Herald*, 17 October 1876; *Augsburger Allgemeine Zeitung*, 24 and 26 September 1876.

[5] Antonio Gallenga, *Two Years of the Eastern Question* (London, 1877), II, 340-342; A. D. Mordtmann, *Stambul und das moderne Türkenthum* (Leipzig, 1877-1878), II, 43-46. The Porte, besides suspending the papers, obliged the editors to go with an investigating commission to Trabzon, the source of their supposedly false news: *Levant Herald*, 27 October 1876. Cf. the similar punishment meted out by Mustafa Kemal to editors: Ahmed Emin Yalman, *Turkey in My Time* (Norman, Okla., 1956), pp. 152-157.

[6] L. Raschdau, ed., "Die Botschafterkonferenz in Konstantinopel und der russisch-türkische Krieg," *Deutsche Rundschau*, 141 (1909), 22; Burnaby, *On Horseback*, I, 246, and II, 12-14; ABCFM, Western Turkey Mission II, #383, 10 November 1876.

[7] Burnaby, *On Horseback*, I, 169-170, 178-180, 235, 244-245, 248-252, and II, 20-22, 173-174; Gallenga, *Two Years*, II, 205-241; *Augsburger Allgemeine Zeitung*, 19 and 27 September 1876; *Levant Herald*, 17 October 1876.

It was in this situation of diplomatic pressures and exaggerated feelings that Midhat had to try to bring the constitution to birth. The diplomatic distractions were a hindrance. The heightened feelings hurt calm debate. The European diplomatic intervention generally worked against the issuance of a constitution; Sir Henry Elliot alone among the diplomats took it seriously. But there were also advantages in the situation. Midhat could portray himself and the constitutionalists to all Ottoman subjects as spokesmen for an Ottoman pride that rejected foreign interference and that insisted on a home-grown constitution as an act of national independence.[8] He had some of the same advantages which Reşid Paşa had in the crisis of 1839 when Reşid secured the agreement of a new sultan and hesitant conservatives to the Hatt-ı Şerif of Gülhane. The crisis situation of 1876 likewise gave Midhat arguments for action and speed, as well as for a display of national unity in progressive reform.

Midhat's desire for a constitution was not, however, simply a matter of the moment. He has often been attacked, especially by those who accept Salisbury's judgment of him in 1876, as shifty, dishonest, vain, and a bigger liar than Ignatyev.[9] Another English diplomat described him at the same time as "one of the most cruel and unscrupulous men in the Turkish Empire."[10] The implication of all this is that Midhat's constitutionalism was fraudulent. These charges may be dismissed as themselves fraudulent, except for the charge of vanity. What is true about Midhat is that he was no man of destiny, no genius in statecraft; that he was best at provincial administration where he was in complete control of a restricted area; that his actions were sometimes hasty or arbitrary; that he began more tasks than he could successfully complete; that he was so blunt and outspoken as to lack a much-needed diplomatic finesse. His contemporaries recognized these traits.[11] At the same time they recognized his ability, energy, sincerity, and clarity of expression. Namık Kemal, who did not always agree with Midhat and who acknowledged Midhat's limitations

---

[8] Cf. Charles de Moüy, "Souvenirs d'un diplomate," *Revue des deux mondes*, 4th period, 157 (1900), 621.

[9] R. W. Seton-Watson, *Disraeli, Gladstone, and the Eastern Question* (London, 1935), pp. 122-123; *Die Grosse Politik der Europäischen Kabinette* (Berlin, 1922-1926), II, #271.

[10] Seton-Watson, *Disraeli*, p. 122, quoting White to MacColl.

[11] İbnülemin Mahmud Kemal İnal, *Osmanlı devrinde son sadrıâzamlar* (İstanbul, 1940-1953), pp. 398ff.; Süleyman Paşa zade Sami, ed., *Süleyman Paşa muhakemesi* (İstanbul, 1328), p. 102.

in political learning, praised his sincerity and greatness of heart, his power of giving good advice, and his inclination to and experience in consultation with others. He was no genius, but who else might save the empire?[12]

What specific ideas Midhat may have had about constitutionalism in the years when he was vali in the Tuna province are not certain, though he is said to have begun thinking about a constitution in the middle 1860's.[13] By 1872, when he was briefly grand vezir, he seems to have envisioned a responsible ministry and some kind of national representation in an assembly. In 1873, with Şirvanizade Mehmed Rüşdi, he had discussed a chamber of deputies and the equality of all Ottoman subjects under the law.[14] From the fall of 1875 on, Midhat had been constantly occupied with constitutional schemes. The available evidence indicates that he went ahead cautiously, either from a recognition of the difficulties inherent in bringing a parliament to the heterogeneous and illiterate empire, or from a need to persuade more conservative and reluctant colleagues. To Elliot in December he spoke of a senate, first to be nominated and later elected, which would have control over the sultan. The manifesto of March 9, 1876, advocated a consultative assembly of all races and creeds having at first power over domestic affairs only. With the accession of Murad he had managed to make the constitutional issue a matter of official discussion, and shortly thereafter had persuaded a group of influential ulema to accept an assembly of all creeds, partly nominated and partly elected. The *meclis-i umumî* of July 15 had accepted in principle Midhat's constitutional proposals, this time including a chamber that was entirely elective. Abdülhamid II had come to the throne only after promising Midhat that a constitution, presumably the one already under consideration, would be speedily promulgated. It cannot, therefore, be charged that Midhat came to the idea of a constitution only in the fall of 1876 as a dodge to avoid more serious reform proposals by the six great powers. This remains true even though he, as well as Abdülhamid, was willing to use the proclamation of the constitution as a diplomatic weapon.

[12] Namık Kemal to Abdülhak Hâmid, 10 March 1877, in F. A. Tansel, *Namık Kemal ve Abdülhak Hâmid* (Ankara, 1949), p. 51. Namık Kemal is replying to Abdülhak Hamid's strictures on Midhat as average in political knowledge, and untrustworthy.
[13] A. H. Midhat, *Midhat Paşa, hayat-ı siyâsiyesi*, I: *Tabsıra-i ibret* (İstanbul, 1325), p. 170.
[14] See above, chapter VIII, p. 294.

Midhat's philosophy of constitutionalism is nowhere synthesized in one place, and probably was not very profound. His primary aim was certainly to preserve by a constitutional regime the independence and integrity of the empire, by revitalizing its government and creating a true equality among its subjects. He seems, like Âli and Fuad before him, to have thought that this would curb separatist nationalisms. A more practical and immediately necessary objective was to limit the power of the sultan, especially with regard to capricious spending. Midhat wanted to restore the control of Porte over Palace —to regain the situation of Âli's time.[15] But he wanted to go beyond Âli with the establishment of a national chamber, which would be a check on the Porte as well as on the Palace. He seems to have had a certain confidence, probably based on his experience as vali, in the good sense of men from the provinces.[16] The best exposition of his views is contained in an article published by Midhat in 1878 in two European journals.[17] This may be suspect, since he was then, as an exile in the West, justifying his drive for a constitution in 1876. But there is no reason why, with the exception of certain propositions concerning Russian actions and Bulgaria, it should not represent the opinions which Midhat actually held in 1876. The whole document exhibits a certain naïveté, especially as regards minority nationalisms and the causes therefor. It attributes the separatist movements principally to Russian influence, but, apart from that, to bad government which, however, weighs as heavily on Muslims as on Christians. The remedy is true Osmanlılık, a "fusion" of the peoples of the empire, and a constitutional regime to insure that the needed reforms and progress of all peoples of the empire are achieved. In some places Midhat's article sounds much like Âli's memorandum of 1867, especially when it deals with equality and "fusion." Midhat further jus-

[15] Cf. Mahmud Celaleddin, *Mirât-ı hakikat* (İstanbul, 1326), I, 126; Midhat to Derby, 17 December 1876, in A. H. Midhat, "English and Russian Politics in the East," *Nineteenth Century*, 53 (1903), 71.

[16] Cf. memorandum of 5 June 1877 in Tenterden Private Papers, FO 363/5/769, cited in Harold Temperley, "British Policy towards Parliamentary Rule and Constitutionalism in Turkey (1830-1914)," *Cambridge Historical Journal*, IV (1933), 182.

[17] Midhat Pasha, "The Past, Present, and Future of Turkey," *Nineteenth Century*, III (1878), 981-993; idem, "La Turquie, son passé, son avenir," *Revue scientifique de la France*, 2nd series, VII (1878), 1149-1154. It was published also in Turkish in 1879 as *Midhat Paşa Hazretlerinin "Memalik-i Osmaniyenin mazi ve hal ve istikbali" unvanıyla neşir buyurdukları makaledir ki gazetelerden naklolunmuştur* (İstanbul, 1295).

tifies the feasibility of his constitutional proposal by attempting to show that Islamic governmental theory rests on essentially democratic bases, having always recognized the principle of "national sovereignty," and, further, that Islam and the Turks have traditionally been tolerant of other religions.[18] Midhat also seems to have thought of a parliamentary regime, as have others in the Near East both then and later, as the mysterious secret of the political success and economic prosperity of western nations.[19]

Midhat has on occasion been charged with aiming in fact at republicanism. Enemies of his said that three days after Murad's accession Midhat had spoken, in a discussion with other officials, of creating a republic.[20] Such accusations were repeated from time to time, even long after Midhat's death.[21] Midhat denied the accusation, which was brought up again in his interrogation and trial in 1881.[22] It is quite likely, however, that he had toyed intellectually with the idea of republicanism, just as had Namık Kemal. Midhat may have spoken about republicanism without much caution on some occasions, for he tried out a wide range of ideas on all sorts and conditions of men. Mütercim Mehmed Rüşdi said that he had heard secondhand reports to this effect from lower-class people.[23] Midhat had at some point a correspondence with Gambetta in which they discussed republican government.[24] But it is just as unlikely that Midhat actually thought that the Ottoman Empire could be transformed into a republic in 1876, or at any early date. Despite his tendency to theorize, he was also a practical man in trying to get things done and in searching for agreement on a constitution. As he said in the *meclis-i umumî* that decided on Murad's deposition, "This state cannot be governed without

[18] Cf. Midhat Pacha, *Question d'Orient. Adresse des positivistes à Midhat-Pacha* .... (Paris, 1877), pp. 16-19, reprinted also in Clician Vassif, *Son Altesse Midhat-Pacha* (Paris, 1909), pp. 103-106, which puts forth some of the same concepts on Islam and on Osmanlılık.

[19] A. H. Midhat, *Tabsıra-i ibret*, p. 170.

[20] İ. H. Uzunçarşılı, *Midhat ve Rüştü Paşaların tevkiflerine dair vesikalar* (Ankara, 1946), pp. 98, 152-154.

[21] Abdurrahman Şeref, *Tarih musahabeleri* (İstanbul, 1339), pp. 208-209; Şiddiq al-Damlûji, *Midhat Bâshâ* (Baghdad, 1952-1953), pp. 93-94; Ernest Dawn, "Ideological Influences in the Arab Revolt," in *The World of Islam: Studies in Honour of Philip K. Hitti* (London, 1959), p. 237, quoting the memoirs of Abdallah.

[22] Uzunçarşılı, *Midhat ve Rüştü Paşalar*, p. 98; A. H. Midhat, *Tabsıra-i-ibret*, p. 243.

[23] Uzunçarşılı, *Midhat ve Rüştü Paşalar*, pp. 152-154.

[24] A. H. Midhat, *Hâtıralarım, 1872-1946* (İstanbul, 1946), p. 135. His wife burned these letters on Midhat's death.

a Padishah.”[25] His aim in 1876 was an elected parliament, a responsible ministry under a prime minister, a sovereign with powers somewhat limited, and equality of all Ottoman subjects. All these things a constitution would prescribe.

Midhat's views fell into a climate of opinion which was half-ready to receive them. This was not only because of the exigencies of the domestic and international situations. It was also owing to Islamic tradition as it was then construed by some, to precedents in representative government already tried in the empire, and to a public discussion of constitutionalism and parliamentary government in the fall of 1876, promoted by Midhat and his supporters. The arguments from Islamic doctrine and tradition in support of parliamentarism, whether historically true or false, were again advanced as they had been nearly a decade earlier by Namık Kemal and Hayreddin. Midhat himself used these arguments. Islamic society was fundamentally democratic, Islamic doctrine defended liberty, the caliphate was essentially elective. The Koran advised that the ruler act upon consultation, and said that God would reward those whose affairs were directed by consultation among themselves.[26] Hayrullah Efendi published a letter in which he emphasized the need of interpreting the Koran and the traditions in the light of reason.[27]

So far as Ottoman precedent was concerned, there was, of course, an older tradition of a sort of representation in the process of legislation. Reşid Paşa in 1856 had described it as a combination of public opinion, sanction of the şeriat, and imperial fiat, coupled with the calling of a general assembly (meclis-i umumî) if necessary.[28] This assembly was representative in a way, but only of the elite, and only

---

[25] Mehmed Memduh, *Mirât-ı şuûnat* (İzmir, 1328), p. 104. Cf. the statement of 1850 in Abdolonyme Ubicini, *Letters on Turkey*, trans. by Lady Easthope (London, 1856), I, 57: "The word 'Republic' alarms them [the Turks] because they believe it to be synonymous with disorder and anarchy—not the idea itself, which is the foundation of the Mussulman's social system." Isolated examples may be found of interest in a "rimpublic," as a local Anatolian official named it in 1880: Valentine Chirol, *Fifty Years in a Changing World* (London, 1927), pp. 104-105. On the word *cumhuriyet* ("republicanism" or "republic") see Bernard Lewis, "The Concept of an Islamic Republic," *Die Welt des Islams*, New Series, IV:1 (1955), 3.

[26] Sura 3:153 and 42:36.

[27] In *Hakikat*, 14 December 1876: ABCFM, Western Turkey Mission II, #487, 28 December 1876; E. de Kératry, *Mourad V* (Paris, 1878), pp. 296-307. Cf. a *fetva* by the chief müfti of Tunis in 1877 on the virtues of intersectarian consultation by rulers, described in Heap (Tunis) to Hunter, #237, 1 May 1877, USNA, Tunis 11.

[28] Cevdet Paşa, *Tezâkir 1-12*, ed. by Cavid Baysun (Ankara, 1953), p. 80.

of the elite in the capital at any given time.[29] Conservatives in 1876, opposed to the Tanzimat decrees, seem to have wanted the *meclis-i umumî* to be called often as a check on the bureaucracy of the Porte.[30] But since 1839 the representative principle had been increasingly apparent in the new Tanzimat institutions usually cutting across sectarian lines, paying at least lip service to the doctrine of Osmanlılık. Reşid had organized provincial councils in the 1840's which were partially representative. Just after the Crimean War a number of non-Muslims had been included in the Supreme Council to represent their millets. The millet reorganizations of the 1860's had introduced a fairly democratic electoral and representative principle among the Armenians, and a modified version of this among the Greek Orthodox. The vilayet law of 1867 had reconstituted the local and provincial meclises on a more representative and partially elective basis, and had established provincial assemblies. The Council of State became in 1868 more representative than its predecessor had been. There was thus a foundation of experimentation with representative and elective institutions on local and provincial levels, plus a small start toward representation on a national level. None of the Tanzimat institutions were yet truly representative, and all worked indifferently, yet many Ottoman citizens had had some experience of them. None of the councils, except in the millets, were truly legislative (rather than advisory), and none effectively limited the sultan's powers. Parliamentary procedure had, however, already made its appearance in the internal regulations of the Council of State and of its ancestor, the Supreme Council of Judicial Ordinances.[31]

In addition, four tributary provinces of the empire—two Muslim and two non-Muslim—had had advisory or legislative assemblies since the 1860's. The Tunisian constitution of 1861 had been suspended three years later, but Egypt, Serbia, and Roumania still had their national assemblies. It is not clear what effect the existence of these assemblies had on Turkish thinking in 1876, but there may have been some. So early as 1867 both Mustafa Fazıl and Namık Kemal had referred to these parliamentary precedents in arguing for an Ottoman

[29] Cf. the list of categories to be invited to the *meclis-i umumî* on Murad's deposition in 1876: Mehmed Memduh, *Mirât-ı şuûnat*, p. 103.
[30] Cf. text of such a petition from Edirne in *Diplomatic Review*, 24 (July 1876), 172, said on p. 160 to be representative of many such petitions.
[31] On these developments see above, chapters I, III, IV, V, VII.

parliament.[32] Particularly the Egyptian assembly, indirectly elected, which had met from 1866 on, may have been influential, though Namık Kemal was sarcastic about the pusillanimity of its deputies.[33] The first open criticism of the khedive's government by a deputy came only in 1876.[34]

Public discussion of constitutional government was not new in 1876. Men like Namık Kemal, Ziya, Ali Suavi, Mustafa Fazıl, Halil Şerif, Hayreddin, and Mustafa Celaleddin had inaugurated such discussion in the preceding decade. In 1876 Hayreddin's book on needed reforms, advocating a parliament, was circulating (evidently reissued) in İstanbul, and Hayreddin expressed the hope that it would serve to clarify the thinking of Muslims "who are not abreast of the needs of the time."[35] Ziya was now more concerned with official discussion of the constitution than with journalism, and Ali Suavi, returned from exile only on November 3, was not much in sympathy with Midhat's aims. Mustafa Fazıl had died in 1875, Mustafa Celaleddin had been killed fighting the Montenegrins in 1876, and Halil Şerif seems to have published nothing at this point. Namık Kemal, however, though he was appointed to the Council of State on September 18, found time to write a series of articles in October for *İttihad*, vigorously defending constitutionalism and the conformity of parliamentary government with religious law.[36]

Public discussion was taken up by others, and the İstanbul press was active in reporting what news it had of the official deliberations on the constitution that took place in the fall of 1876, and in examining all aspects of parliamentary government. There were proponents and opponents of constitution both on religious grounds and on the grounds of political expediency.[37] Süleyman Paşa lamented that of

[32] Mustapha-Fazil Pacha, *Lettre adressée à Sa Majesté le Sultan* (Paris, n.d.); Mithat Cemal Kuntay, *Namık Kemal* (İstanbul, 1944-1956), I, 212, n.25; *Hürriyet*, #4 (29 September 1868), in İhsan Sungu, "Tanzimat ve Yeni Osmanlılar," *Tanzimat*, I (İstanbul, 1940), 847.

[33] See above, chapter VI and n.188.

[34] On the Egyptian assembly see Jacob Landau, *Parliaments and Parties in Egypt* (Tel Aviv, 1953), pp. 8-20; Georges Douin, *Histoire du règne du Khédive Ismail* (Rome, 1933), I, 294-313; Angelo Sammarco, *Histoire de l'Egypte moderne* (Cairo, 1937), III, 135-141, 413-416.

[35] Hayreddin (Tunis) to Selim Faris (İstanbul), 2 August 1876, quoted in A. Demeerseman, "Indépendance de la Tunisie et politique extérieure de Khéréddine," *IBLA*, 21:83 (3rd quarter 1958), 277.

[36] Kuntay, *Namık Kemal*, II, part 2, 17 and 633 on the appointment, 109-129 reproducing the articles.

[37] Ahmed Midhat, *Üss-i inkılâb* (İstanbul, 1294-1295), II, 178-179.

İstanbul's population of about six hundred thousand there were only some five or six thousand politically conscious Muslims who might support Midhat's views—the other elements being either foreigners, members of minority millets, or Muslims who were illiterate, conservative, or uninterested. Of the politically conscious, some were so unrealistic as to think the Turks could ape the French revolution of 1789, and that problems would be solved by singing the "Marseillaise," by condemnation of autocracy in the coffeehouses, and by shouting long life to Midhat.[38] Yet there was serious discussion, often in simple language aimed at the common man.

Vakit on October 27 carried an effective dialogue of questions and answers to explain the nature of a parliament, that it was compatible with the şeriat and tradition, and that Christians as well as Muslims should be members.[39] At about the same time Esad Efendi, a member of the ulema who was selected by Süleyman Paşa to be a teacher in the military school at Kuleli and who was also secretary of the maritime commercial tribunal in İstanbul, published a pamphlet entitled *Constitutional Government*, likewise in dialogue form.[40] Esad set out to prove that Muslim government was constitutional because it was based on religious and civil law, but that when it turned by error to autocracy the people required a watchdog assembly to check on the administration. Christians should be admitted to the parliament, and also to military service, as a matter of practical necessity. "In this we separate religion (*din*) and nation (*millet*)." Further, parliamentary government is the basis of order and wealth, as English experience has shown. Esad's whole approach was to prove that constitution and parliament were within the Islamic and Ottoman tradition, and that an elective assembly was the best insurance against arbitrary government. He gave little attention to the legislative function of a parliament. This pamphlet, says Süleyman, is a sample of the discussion carried on in these days by public speakers and in printed form.[41]

[38] Sami, *Süleyman Paşa muhakemesi*, pp. 75-77.
[39] Given in Azimzade Hakkı, *Turkiyede meclis-i meb'usan* (Cairo, 1907), pp. 99-110; extracts in Paul Fesch, *Constantinople aux derniers jours d'Abdul Hamid* (Paris, 1907), pp. 282-285.
[40] Esad Efendi, *Hükûmet-i meşrute* (İstanbul, 17 şevval 1293). This is reprinted in Sami, *Süleyman Paşa muhakemesi*, pp. 79-88. On Esad's career see Kuntay, *Namık Kemal*, II, part 2, 59, n.14. Cf. chapter VIII, above, n.28.
[41] Kuntay, *Namık Kemal*, II, part 2, 78. Esad's pamphlet, though authorized by the ministry of public instruction, was shortly seized by the police: *Levant Herald*, 10 November 1876. One suspects the hand of Abdülhamid in the seizure. Fesch, *Constantinople*, p. 274, notes another discussion of a parliament in *Hakikat*. Quite

In this atmosphere of diplomatic tension, war fever, and expectancy Midhat worked to get a constitutional draft accepted and promulgated. For nearly four weeks after the accession of Abdülhamid nothing was done. The influential Damad Mahmud Paşa, commander of the arsenal, and a number of ministers and palace officials, were opponents of the whole concept.[42] But the diplomatic situation led to the calling of several grand councils to discuss reform proposals by the great powers and terms for Serbia. One met on September 12, another just two weeks later, another on October 2.[43] These meetings of the *meclis-i umumî* gave Midhat a chance to propose again his constitutional plan, as a means of avoiding outside intervention in matters of reform. At the meeting of September 26, about seventy notables agreed that a constitution establishing an intersectarian parliament should be drafted. It was variously reported that there would be an assembly of seven hundred and twenty members, which resembled a proposal by Küçük Said Bey, or of one hundred and twenty members of whom three fourths would be elected, which sounded like Midhat's project.[44] Though this suggests that at least two of the constitutional drafts were publicly known in rough outline, the recommendation of the grand council to Abdülhamid probably did not go so far as to advocate one specific plan. The sultan's reply, in an irade of September 30, ordered the establishment of a commission of ulema and civil officials to draft a constitution to be submitted to the ministers and the sultan. The irade laid considerable emphasis on reconciling representative institutions with the şeriat and with Ottoman customs.[45]

The *meclis-i umumî* of October 2, about one hundred and twenty strong and including leading Christians, confirmed the decision on

---

by coincidence a constitution for the Protestant millet was under discussion at the same time, and the Porte commission which reviewed it reported it was unable to understand its democratic form, with no chief priest: ABCFM, Western Turkey Mission II, #614, 29 November 1876.

[42] Bekir Sıtkı Baykal, "93 meşrutiyeti," *Belleten*, VI:21/22 (January-April 1942), 53.

[43] *Augsburger Allgemeine Zeitung*, 20, 28, 30 September; *Levant Herald*, 28, 30 September and 3 October; Ahmed Midhat, *Üss-i inkılâb*, II, 195-196; Robert Devereux, *The First Ottoman Constitutional Period* (Washington, unpublished thesis for the School of Advanced International Studies of the Johns Hopkins University, 1961), pp. 25-27; Mahmud Celaleddin, *Mirât-ı hakikat*, I, 188-190; Elliot to Derby, 27 September 1876, in *Staatsarchiv*, 31 (1877), #5831.

[44] *Levant Herald*, 28 and 30 September 1876.

[45] Ahmed Midhat, *Üss-i inkılâb*, II, 196. Devereux, *First Ottoman Constitutional Period*, p. 27, gives October 7, as does Baykal, "93 meşrutiyeti," pp. 55-56. It is hard to fit this date into the sequence of events.

a constitution, and reportedly advocated both a lower chamber and a senate.[46] Thus the diplomatic crisis pushed the constitutional question off dead center. The reply of the Ottoman Empire to the powers' proposals for special regimes in Bosnia and Herzegovina was to be a reform of the imperial government as a whole. By October 12 work on the constitutional project was far enough along so that Safvet Paşa, the foreign minister, could officially inform all Ottoman representatives abroad that an elective assembly and an appointive senate had been adopted in principle, and that plans were being elaborated by a commission under Midhat Paşa's chairmanship. Now the Porte and the sultan were publicly committed to the adoption of parliamentary government, which Safvet's circular telegram said clearly that Abdülhamid had granted.[47]

The commission had held its first session on October 6.[48] It was composed of twenty-four men, to which number four more were added on November 2.[49] Sixteen were civil officials, ten were members of the ulema, and two were generals of the army. The membership included some of the most intelligent partisans of constitutional government. Midhat Paşa was the chairman.[50] Ziya, undersecretary for education, and Namık Kemal, one of the later appointees, were both influential. Two other members—Server Paşa, now minister of public works, and Seyfeddin Efendi, one of the ulema—had spoken for constitution in earlier grand council discussions. Odian Efendi, for years a close adviser to Midhat and one of the authors of the Armenian millet constitution, was certainly among the more influential on the commission. In addition to Odian there were five other Christians, of whom Alexander Karatheodori was undersecretary for for-

---

[46] *Levant Herald*, 3 and 5 October 1876.

[47] Text in *Staatsarchiv*, 31 (1877), #5862. The circular also promised improvement in the vilayet law and its administration.

[48] The date is not certain. Most accounts furnish none. Baykal, "93 meşrutiyeti," p. 56, and Recai G. Okandan, *Umumî âmme hukukumuzun ana hatları* (İstanbul, 1948), I, 138, both give September 24, which is before the commission was ordered to be appointed. Assuming that this is Old Style, the date then becomes October 6. Kuntay, *Namık Kemal*, II, part 2, 106, n.2, gives Oct. 7.

[49] Lists of members in Kuntay, *Namık Kemal*, II, part 2, 56, 75-80, and variant by İhsan Sungu, *ibid.*, II, part 2, 106, n.2. See the careful corrections to the lists in Devereux, *First Ottoman Constitutional Period*, pp. 44-45. Cf. partial lists in *Levant Herald*, 20 November 1876, and in Léouzon le Duc, *Midhat Pacha* (Paris, 1877), p. 136.

[50] Many accounts name Server Paşa as chairman, but this is clearly an error, which arises probably from the fact that Server was chairman of the previous commission to review the constitutional draft, in Murad's reign. See above, chapter IX, n.178.

eign affairs and Vahan undersecretary for justice. Most prominent among those who might create difficulties were Cevdet, who was quite out of sympathy with Midhat, and Namık, who had earlier expressed himself as favorable to a parliament of Muslims only. So far as one can tell, it was a collection of able men. In addition, others seem to have participated in some of the later sessions, including two strong backers of Midhat, İsmail Kemal Bey and Süleyman Paşa, the latter just returned from the campaign against the Serbs.[51]

Much of the commission's work was done in committees, of which the chief was an editing or drafting committee presided over by Ziya Bey. Its members included Namık Kemal, Savas Paşa, a Greek who was director of the Galatasaray *lycée*, Chamich Ohannes Efendi, an Armenian who was on the Council of State, Abidin Bey, commissioner of the bourse, and Ramiz Efendi, one of the ulema. Their daily sessions resulted in lithographed proposals which, along with those of other committees, were circulated to members of the full commission. The latter met four times a week at the Sublime Porte, or sometimes at the houses of Midhat and Server, and made its decisions by majority vote.[52]

When the commission began its work there were already a number of constitutional drafts and projects available for its use. Abdülhamid later said that some twenty projects had been submitted to him.[53] Süleyman Paşa's draft constitution, although very disordered, may have been one of those considered. So also may the draft which Said Bey, chief palace secretary, had made after a French model. It provided for a 750-man assembly, a senate, and a council of state; Said later described it as a "perfect" or "complete" constitution.[54] And, of course, there was Midhat's draft. Said's was certainly much better

---

[51] Sommerville Story, ed., *The Memoirs of Ismail Kemal Bey* (London, 1920), pp. 137-138; Sami, *Süleyman Paşa muhakemesi*, p. 56 and n.2.

[52] *Levant Herald*, 20 November 1876; Abdurrahman Şeref, *Tarih musahabeleri*, pp. 199-200. Minutes of the commission and its committees would be, if extant, extremely interesting. For some further details see Devereux, *First Ottoman Constitutional Period*, p. 29. See Kuntay, *Namık Kemal*, II, part 2, 57, for a similar committee structure as of January 1877.

[53] "Sultan Hamid'in hatıratı," *Yeni Sabah*, 9 December 1949, quoted in İ. H. Danişmend, *İzahlı Osmanlı tarihi kronolojisi*, IV (İstanbul, 1955), 293.

[54] Text in Ahmed Midhat, *Üss-i inkılâb*, II, 333-355. Which French constitution Said used is not indicated. His draft provided for a monarch, but is often said to have been based on the constitution of the French Republic [First? Second? Third?]. Mehmed Said Paşa, *Hatıratı* (İstanbul, 1328), I, 14. Bernard Lewis, *The Emergence of Modern Turkey* (London, 1951), p. 130, n.9, points out that the French *charte* of 1830 had been published in Turkish as early as 1839.

organized than Süleyman's, and more complete than Midhat's. Other contrasts are also instructive. Said, for example, uses article one to assert that sovereignty resides in the monarch. Süleyman is concerned to state in his first article that the Ottoman state is constitutional and independent. Midhat's article one proclaims the integrity of the empire and the inalterability of its boundaries, as well as that its government is based on the şeriat. Namık Kemal later said that the commission used no one of these drafts as its basis, but proceeded *ab initio*; further, that Said's draft did not even come to the commission. Since Namık Kemal was appointed to the commission only after it had done four weeks' work, he may not be accurate here. It is plain, however, that the commission confined itself to no single source of inspiration, and that certainly some of its members cast about widely for suggestions. Namık Kemal reported that the commission considered a wide range of existing constitutions, many commentaries on them, and consulted at least a thousand volumes.[55]

It seems likely that Midhat's draft had, nevertheless, considerable influence, both because Midhat had been the chief proponent of a constitution and because he was commission chairman.[56] By the fall of 1876 Midhat's draft, which at the time of Murad's accession was quite sketchy, had undergone considerable enlargement and change, undoubtedly affected by discussions in the preceding summer. A little before Murad's deposition the Midhat draft consisted of sixty-three articles divided into seven chapters; Namık Kemal, at Midhat's request, had read it to the London *Times* correspondent in İstanbul.[57] This is very close to Midhat's draft of about sixty (unnumbered) articles and eight chapters that Ahmed Midhat reproduces. In late October, just before he became a member of the commission, Namık

[55] Kuntay, *Namık Kemal*, II, part 2, 90-92. Ahmed Midhat, *Üss-i inkılâb*, II, 197, says that Midhat's draft was the basis, an assertion that called forth Namık Kemal's refutation. It is natural to think that the Belgian constitution of 1831 served as a model for drafting the Ottoman. This is asserted in Gotthard Jäschke, "Die Entwicklung des Osmanischen Verfassungsstaates . . . ," *Die Welt des Islams*, V:1/2 (1917), 38; Friedrich von Kraelitz-Greifenhorst, *Die Verfassungsgesetze des Osmanischen Reiches* (Vienna, 1919), p. 2; Erich Pritsch, "Geschichtliche und systematische Übersicht nebst Anmerkungen zur Verfassung," *Mitteilungen des Seminars für Orientalische Sprachen*, 26/27:2 (1924), 165; Lewis, *Emergence*, p. 356. This may be true in part, but the only contemporary statement to this effect that the author has noticed is a French embassy report of June 7, 1876, that Midhat and Halil Şerif went so far as to talk of the Belgian constitution. See above, chapter IX, n.142.

[56] Text of his draft in *Üss-i inkılâb*, II, 321-333.

[57] Gallenga, *Two Years*, II, 282. The date is not specific, but the context indicates August of 1876.

Kemal gave to the public, through his articles in *İttihad*, a verbatim transcription of many articles of Midhat's draft, and strongly defended it. His numbering of the articles indicates that the draft had undergone yet further modifications.[58]

There are a considerable number of similarities between the final product and Midhat's draft. The latter still had gaps in it—as Ahmed Midhat bitingly observed, it provided for no senate, nor did it elaborate the judicial, financial, or provincial organization.[59] But Midhat may well have considered that provincial organization was taken care of by the 1867 law and later amendments. It is interesting to speculate whether the absence of a senate (a Council of State was provided for) was an effort by Midhat to throw all power into a unicameral legislature without a senatorial check. The 120-man chamber of deputies which his draft provided for was to be two thirds elected in the vilayets and one third appointed by the government, which was in line with Midhat's thinking since December of 1875, but not quite so radical as the entirely elected chamber of July 15. Midhat's draft, although it stated in terms very like those of the final constitution that the sultan's person was sacred and he could not be held to responsibility, was far less insistent on the prerogatives of the sultan than was the final product. By contrast, Midhat would give more power to the council of ministers, which in his draft became the competent authority to deal with all important internal and external affairs, its decisions to be sanctioned by imperial irade. Presiding over the council would be a prime minister (*baş vekil*) in the European style. The office of grand vezir was specifically declared abolished. The prime minister, to be named by the sultan, would, in turn, select the ministers, who would then be appointed by the sultan. The provision for a prime minister was a key element in Midhat's proposal and was soon to cause him trouble, especially as some suspected him—probably rightly—of wanting to hold that office himself. Midhat's draft also provided that all subjects without distinction were to be called Osmanli, though Turkish was to be the official language. (Here called "Türki," not "Osmanli.")

Some of the major decisions in the commission must have come before October 12, when Safvet sent his circular to ambassadors

---

[58] Kuntay, *Namık Kemal*, II, part 2, 119-124, reprinting his articles. Namık Kemal omitted all references to Midhat's provision for a prime minister, probably so as to avoid further criticism.

[59] *Üss-i inkılâb*, II, 199.

abroad announcing an elective chamber and an appointive senate. Midhat's chamber, with one third of its members appointed, had already been abandoned. Some of the ulema evidently raised anew the proposition that Muslims only should sit in the chamber, but Midhat's contrary view prevailed on this point.[60] The details of discussion in the commission and its committees are not clear.[61] Ahmed Midhat, an unfriendly witness, makes fun of the commission's work, saying they did not really understand what they were about.[62] This cannot be true, though the members had to grope for the organization best suited to the empire, and opposing views had to be compromised. Sultan Abdülhamid seems not to have been an obstructionist at this stage, but to have wanted some kind of constitution to emerge.[63] Cevdet Paşa and Midhat did get into some bitter arguments over particular points as the proposed articles came from the drafting committee, section by section. There is no reason to think that Cevdet at this stage opposed a constitution altogether, but on certain articles, possibly those concerned with the sultan's prerogatives, he disagreed strongly with Midhat, and seems to have lost in the commission.[64] Midhat was certainly far less of a traditionalist than Cevdet. The diplomatic situation gave Midhat some advantage, since he was known to have found favor with Elliot, and the Turks did not want to antagonize a great power that might furnish help against Russia. This became particularly important after the Russian ultimatum of October 31 and the subsequent Russian mobilization. Ignatyev was persuaded that the sudden ultimatum, leading the Turks to think that Russia had decided on war, allowed Midhat and the radicals to gain the upper hand.[65]

Meanwhile important opposition to a constitution which would allow Christians to sit in the parliament, and which would curtail the sultan's powers, had developed outside of the commission in mid-October. This was accompanied by rumors that Murad had recovered his health and was entitled to the throne. But the heart of the con-

[60] Devereux, *First Ottoman Constitutional Period*, pp. 30-31.

[61] No minutes have been published. The author does not know whether they exist. Nor have any consecutive accounts by participants been published.

[62] *Üss-i inkılâb*, II, 197-198.

[63] Mahmud Celaleddin, *Mirât-ı hakikat*, I, 220.

[64] Cevdet's account from his *Tezâkir*, #18, quoted in Ebül'ulâ Mardin, *Medenî hukuk cephesinden Ahmet Cevdet Paşa* (İstanbul, 1946), pp. 141-143, n.121, including Mardin's comments.

[65] Alexander Onou, "The Memoirs of Count N. Ignatyev," *Slavonic Review*, x (1931), 405.

spiracy, if such it was, was a group of high-ranking ulema, among them Gürcü Şerif Efendi, who on May 10 had hoped to become *şeyhülislâm*, and Muhyiddin Efendi, once the teacher of Yusuf İzzeddin. The government acted with considerable courage, arresting and exiling a dozen or so either to Aegean islands or to their native towns. The movement thus never got out of hand. It may have had ramifications in the Bulgar area, and some Christians were apprehensive of a massacre. The constitutionalists had saved themselves, but by arbitrary action without judicial proceedings. Although exile of officials without trial had not been unusual in Abdülaziz's reign, a contemporary official pointed out that such had not been the case with the Kuleli affair conspirators in 1859 and that a bad example was being set by a presumably reformist ministry.[66]

A few days after the suppression of these recalcitrant ulema the Porte issued, with Abdülhamid's sanction, a provisional electoral law. This law of October 28 had been worked out by the commission on the constitution even before the draft of the constitution itself was completed; for Midhat urgently wanted to start elections, even to have the chamber meet, before the constitution was promulgated, in order to confront the powers with a fait accompli.[67] There was neither time nor machinery to prepare for direct popular elections. Therefore, the provisional law was built squarely on the vilayet law, using the administrative meclis members in each kaza, sancak, and vilayet as an electoral college to vote directly for deputies to the parliament from each vilayet.[68] The law itself noted that these meclises were already "the results of popular suffrage," and a member of the constitutional commission said that the electoral law was very liberal.[69] But the various meclis members were, of course, themselves the result of indirect election in which Porte-appointed provincial officials played a part. Kaza meclis members were elected at two degrees, sancak meclis members at three, and vilayet meclis members at four,

[66] Mahmud Celaleddin, *Mirât-ı hakikat*, I, 193. Accounts of the movement in *Levant Herald*, 23, 26 and 28 October 1876; ABCFM, Western Turkey Mission II, #609, 25 October 1876, and #483, undated; A. H. Midhat, *Tabsıra-i ibret*, pp. 184-185; Devereux, *First Ottoman Constitutional Period*, pp. 33-35; documents in Ahmed Midhat, *Üss-i inkılâb*, II, 291-297.

[67] Mahmud Celaleddin, *Mirât-ı hakikat*, I, 193-194; Baykal, "93 meşrutiyeti," pp. 63-65.

[68] Text of law in Grégoire Aristarchi, *Législation ottomane* (Constantinople, 1873-1888), V, 306-309.

[69] Benoît Brunswik, *La réforme et les garanties*, 2nd ed. (Paris, 1877), p. 85.

the meclis at each level serving as an electoral college to choose twice the needed number for the next higher level, from which officials selected half.[70] Only at the very bottom of the hierarchy did the people vote directly for electors who chose the kaza meclis. This complex system was a far cry from popular election, but it was workable. For İstanbul, the October 28 law provided a popular vote of all property owners for an electoral college, in which there was no participation of officials.[71] This method, which resembled also the Armenian millet electoral system for the capital, was the closest to direct popular election of any of the 1876 arrangements. Midhat's hopes for enough speed to gather the chamber together before the constitution was promulgated were deceived; the electoral law itself set March 13 as the opening date. But in at least one vilayet elections were under way by early December.[72]

Toward the end of November the commission had completed a constitutional draft of one hundred and forty articles, which included Midhat's desideratum of a prime ministry instead of a grand vezirate. The draft was submitted unofficially to Abdülhamid by Midhat.[73] It was expected that the constitution would be proclaimed within a few days.[74] Arrangements were pushed for the meeting of the parliament, as Midhat and other ministers inspected the İstanbul University building which, unused for its original purpose, was to be converted for the parliament's occupancy.[75] It looked as if the Porte, which on November 18 had yielded to the demand for a great-power conference on the Balkans, would have its constitution, though not a parliament in session, well before the conference should meet. Instead, a new struggle began to take shape as men opposed either to the whole concept of a constitution, or to the draft as it then stood, made themselves heard. Some represented palace officials, a clique afraid of losing influence under the new dispensation. Some were ministers, especially Cevdet and Mehmed Rüşdi. And Abdülhamid now embarked on a course of hesitation and obstruction which revealed

---

[70] This revision of the original electoral process, which is described in chapter v above, had been made by a law of 30 December 1875: text in Aristarchi, *Législation*, v, 85-87.

[71] Cf. *Levant Herald*, 30 January 1877.

[72] In Edirne: *Levant Herald*, 7 December 1876.

[73] Mahmud Celaleddin, *Mirât-ı hakikat*, I, 221; A. H. Midhat, *Tabsıra-i ibret*, p. 183; Osman Nuri, *Abdülhamid-i Sani ve devri-i saltanatı* (İstanbul, 1327), I, 165.

[74] Elliot to Derby, #1299, 22 November 1876, FO 78/2467.

[75] *Levant Herald*, 20 November 1876.

him fearful of losing imperial prerogatives, reluctant at the same time to antagonize any influential group of statesmen, and yet again desirous of using the constitution to thwart the diplomats. He may also still genuinely have wanted some sort of constitution in order to appear in the eyes of his own people to be a reformer. The struggle went on in the palace, in the commission, and in the council of ministers.

Abdülhamid followed a process of asking various ministers and officials for their views on the draft, probably to play one against another. Namık Paşa expressed stubborn opposition to the draft. Mehmed Rüşdi, who had not been a member of the constitutional commission, now reverted to his original hesitations about the whole matter. To the sultan he said that the articles enumerating the sovereign's powers should be struck out, since by such enumeration those powers were limited. He objected to the creation of an office of prime minister, advising, instead, retention of the old grand vezirate, and direct appointment of all ministers by the sultan. In fact, Mehmed Rüşdi declared that only the critical international situation disposed him to a constitution of any sort. Palace officials, seeking to preserve their own influence, backed up the grand vezir's arguments, and insinuated that Midhat, greedy for power, wanted to be to himself a prime minister-dictator.[76] At about the same time Süleyman Paşa, still an ardent constitutionalist, returned from the Serb war and was granted an audience with the sultan on November 22. Süleyman argued vigorously for the promulgation. Abdülhamid, very possibly wary of the general who had played an important role in deposing Abdülaziz, paraded his good intentions to Süleyman, declared himself pleased with the audience, and put Süleyman on the constitutional commission which was then working on the internal regulations for the two houses of parliament.[77]

Midhat was as impatient as Süleyman, urging the dangers of delay, but Mehmed Rüşdi considered Midhat imprudent, saying, "The law he has written in haste will devour his head first."[78] According to Namık Kemal, the grand vezir now favored, instead of a constitution, a statement of general principles like the Hatt-ı Şerif of Gülhane. The sultan, said Namık Kemal further, was insincere in his whole attitude toward the constitutionalists, desiring only a strength-

---

[76] Mahmud Celaleddin, *Mirât-ı hakikat*, I, 221.
[77] Sami, *Süleyman Paşa muhakemesi*, pp. 55-56.
[78] Abdurrahman Şeref, *Tarih musahabeleri*, p. 200.

ening of the imperial prerogatives.[79] Quite possibly Abdülhamid was trying to use the grand vezir to thwart Midhat. The sultan never went so far as to refuse the constitution. But his answer to Midhat's unofficial communication of the draft was a letter to Midhat of November 26 indicating that he wanted the council of ministers to revise the draft in order to safeguard the sovereign rights and to make it accord with the customs and needs of the people. Midhat's reply two days later was to admit that a majority of the articles required modification, but to urge speed in promulgating the constitution so the demands of the coming great-power conference would not have to be accepted. We can put into execution our own reforms in three or four days, said Midhat.[80] Midhat had already the evening before been at the palace with Süleyman and the war minister Redif—a visit that may have been worrisome to the sultan since these three, now that Hüseyin Avni was dead, were the most important surviving members of the group that had overthrown Abdülaziz. But what they discussed is not known.[81] At some point in this process the draft constitution was altered to eliminate the prime ministry and restore the grand vezirate, with power of appointing the ministers remaining in the sultan's hands.

At the very end of November, or the start of December, the draft then went to the council of ministers, as Abdülhamid had ordered. Here the sessions were often stormy. Mehmed Rüşdi, although evidently reluctant to attack Midhat directly because of Midhat's favor with the British ambassador, pushed others to the attack. Among them was Cevdet Paşa, who in Midhat's view was swinging the grand vezir to oppose the constitution. "I cannot find two or three persons to help me in the council," complained Midhat. His arguments with Cevdet descended to personalities, Midhat deriding Cevdet's knowledge of European law, and Cevdet retorting that Midhat's French was not so good as that of an ordinary shoemaker.[82] A good many changes were made in the draft by the ministers, including reduction

---

[79] Sami, *Süleyman Paşa muhakemesi*, p. 57. Cf. Ahmed Midhat, *Üss-i inkılâb*, II, 198-202, impugning Namık Kemal's sincerity and defending that of the sultan.

[80] Texts in A. H. Midhat, *Tabsıra-i ibret*, pp. 328-330; idem, *The Life of Midhat Pasha* (London, 1903), pp. 113-114; idem, *Midhat Pacha. Sa vie—son oeuvre* (Paris, 1908), pp. 79-80, all with divergent dates.

[81] *Basiret*, 29 November 1876, quoted in Sami, *Süleyman Paşa muhakemesi*, p. 56, n.2.

[82] İnal, *Son sadrâzamlar*, p. 345, quoting an account by Vefik Bey, Midhat's son-in-law; Mardin, *Cevdet*, pp. 10, n.7, 142-144, n.121.

of the total number of articles, largely through rearrangement and consolidation.[83] Evidently the council of ministers accepted Mehmed Rüşdi's argument that the enumeration of the sultan's powers would be an unconscionable limitation on his authority, for the council excised these articles at the beginning of the draft and substituted a preface stating general principles like those of the 1839 *hat*. Namık Kemal objected strenuously to this, arguing that this was the work of anticonstitution men, and that the Ottoman dynasty and state would suffer if the ruler's prerogatives were not firmly fixed in the constitution itself, as was the case in other constitutional states. This was paralleled by his desire to see that the ministers should not be in a position to dominate the government entirely, as had been the case in Âli's time; therefore, the sultan's prerogatives must be clearly set forth to counterbalance the Porte's authority. On both of these subjects he wrote memoranda to the palace.[84] It may have been on these matters that a subcommittee of the constitutional commission—chaired by Süleyman, with Namık Kemal, Ziya, and Abidin as members—met two or three times after the ministers had made their revisions in the draft.[85] The council of ministers, however, had already approved their revised constitutional draft at a special meeting on December 6. The next day the document was submitted, this time officially, to Abdülhamid. Its promulgation was expected before the week was out.[86]

Yet more delays supervened. There was further discussion in the palace, perhaps occasioned by Namık Kemal's memoranda, on the royal prerogatives laid down in the constitution. Particular argument also went on over the right of the sultan to exile those who endangered the security of the state. It may be that such a clause had been proposed earlier, and it is not clear whether the ministers in the first week of December had discussed it, or what their decision was. But this was evidently the principal matter over which Abdülhamid now delayed further, even as time pressed—for the great powers' diplomats were about to gather in conference in İstanbul on December 11, Lord Salisbury had already arrived on the 5th full of anti-Turkish prejudice, and Ignatyev had already prepared his maximum

---

[83] For some details on changes see Devereux, *First Ottoman Constitutional Period*, pp. 39-40.

[84] İnal, *Son sadrıâzamlar*, pp. 343-344, n.3; Kuntay, *Namık Kemal*, II, part 2, 88, 90-91, 98.

[85] Sami, *Süleyman Paşa muhakemesi*, pp. 6, 57, n.2.

[86] *Ibid.*, pp. 57-58; *Levant Herald*, 7 December 1876.

and minimum plans for rearranging the Balkans.[87] For about ten days no news came from the palace. Someone in the palace—Küçük Said, chief palace secretary, has most often been accused—had proposed an additional clause to article 113 (which dealt with a state of siege) which would allow the sultan to exile supposedly dangerous persons.[88] Damad Mahmud Paşa insisted on its insertion. The sultan debated this for three nights with him and the two Saids, swinging this way and that, for İngiliz Said, the sultan's chief aide-de-camp, vigorously opposed the clause. Abdülhamid's final decision was to demand the power of exile.[89] He would not take the constitution without the additional clause, said the sultan.

After ten days or so Midhat went to the palace to make inquiry, on the insistence of Ziya and Namık Kemal. He returned with the news that the constitution was accepted, but that the dreaded clause had been added to article 113. Ziya and Namık Kemal exploded at this. They had had experience of exile before. They said that this clause vitiated the whole constitution and, further, would destroy its value in the eyes of Europe.[90] Others, by no means radical, like the Porte's chief secretary for palace correspondence, Mahmud Celaleddin, agreed with them: the men of the palace had sold Abdülhamid a bill of goods, said Mahmud.[91] To the demands of Ziya and Namık Kemal that the clause be rejected, Midhat answered that they were behaving childishly; if he acted thus, the constitution would be further delayed and perhaps would never come to be. Possibly the chamber of deputies could later right the wrong. Midhat and his two supporters were estranged over this issue, Ziya even suspecting Midhat of wanting to exercise the power of exile himself.[92] Theoretically the two erstwhile New Ottomans were right, but in the circumstances Midhat's decision was politically the only thing to do, unless the sultan himself could be persuaded to abandon the clause.

It may have been in an attempt to persuade Abdülhamid to do

---

[87] Sumner, *Russia and the Balkans*, pp. 234-237.

[88] Mahmud Celaleddin, *Mirât-ı hakikat*, I, 222; İnal, *Son sadrıâzamlar*, p. 345. Said himself denied the charge: Said, *Hatıratı*, II, part 2, 243-244, n.1.

[89] Mahmud Celaleddin, *Mirât-ı hakikat*, I, 222; unpublished memoirs of Eğinli (İngiliz) Said Paşa, quoted in H. Y. Şehsuvaroğlu, *Sultan Aziz* (İstanbul, 1949), pp. 182-184.

[90] İnal, *Son sadrıâzamlar*, pp. 344-345; Tansel, *Namık Kemal*, p. 29.

[91] *Mirât-ı hakikat*, I, 222.

[92] Sami, *Süleyman Paşa muhakemesi*, p. 58, n.3; Tansel, *Namık Kemal*, p. 29; İnal, *Son sadrıâzamlar*, pp. 345-346.

this that Süleyman Paşa, after conferring with Namık Kemal, again boldly requested an audience of the sultan. But it is more likely that, as his own account states, Süleyman was concerned simply with terminating the endless delay. In any case, probably on the 16th or 17th of December, Süleyman had a lengthy talk with Abdülhamid, during which he argued heatedly for the immediate promulgation of the whole constitution, including those articles which enumerated the sultan's powers. Abdülhamid protested that he did not oppose the constitution—that he was, in fact, himself a constitutionalist—but that the draft presented by Midhat did not sufficiently harmonize the rights of the sultanate and those of the subjects. He asked Süleyman, Küçük Said, and İngiliz Said to go over the draft again and prepare him a memorandum. This they did that same night, in the palace. Their report approved the constitution, but in the form which it had before the changes made by the council of ministers.[93] Certainly not all the ministerial changes were undone, but the sultan's powers, enumerated, must have been restored at this point; they appeared in the definitive text of the constitution, especially in article 7. That night or the next morning Sultan Abdülhamid consented to the proclamation of the constitution, and so informed the office of the grand vezir. By December 18 the news was published in İstanbul that the sultan had approved the constitution, although the date for its promulgation was not yet known.[94] The constitutionalists appeared to have won. Whether it would be an enduring victory was still to be seen.

On December 19, 1876, Midhat Paşa was appointed grand vezir.[95] Mehmed Rüşdi had resigned because of old age and sickness, said the official announcement. But he had probably never been fully trusted by Abdülhamid, because of his role in the deposition of Abdülaziz; and the presence of a contingent of Egyptian troops which Mehmed Rüşdi had told the khedive could winter in İstanbul made the sultan fear their possible use in his own overthrow. It is quite possible also that Abdülhamid, now that he had made up his mind

---

[93] Sami, *Süleyman Paşa muhakemesi*, pp. 12-14, n.2, and 58-62; Şehsuvaroğlu, *Sultan Aziz*, p. 182. Possibly this report was made a few days earlier.

[94] *Levant Herald*, 18 December 1876.

[95] *Hat* of appointment in *Stamboul*, 20 December 1876, and *Levant Herald*, 21 December 1876, which gives the date as 18 December.

to the constitution, wanted Midhat at the helm as a symbol of reform, and to use Midhat's international reputation as a weapon against the coming diplomatic conference. The appointment was a blow at Ignatyev, who had called Midhat a brigand, a filibuster, and a madman.[96] Abdülhamid was undoubtedly wary of Midhat too, but he could hardly overlook him in the circumstances, and might use him. "Let us make him grand vezir once, and then let him fall from fortune," the sultan is reported to have said.[97]

Midhat was eager to proclaim the constitution as soon as he was in office, hopefully with the objectionable clause of article 113 removed. In the latter aim he was unsuccessful.[98] In the former he succeeded almost at once, after two minor obstacles were overcome. The first was that the official translation of the constitution into French had to be checked and confirmed.[99] The other was a final meeting—perhaps ordered by Abdülhamid because of a new attack of cold feet—to consider the whole document again. This took place on December 21 or 22.[100] Possibly some last-minute alterations were made in the draft. Cevdet Paşa provided the fireworks. Since a wise sultan had ascended the throne, he declared, there remained no need to promulgate a constitution. Midhat's vigorous reply was that since the deposition of Abdülaziz had been motivated by the sacred purpose of proclaiming a constitution to prevent autocratic rule, he would at once resign from the grand vezirate if the other ministers shared Cevdet's view and hesitated to confirm the proclamation of the constitution.[101] Midhat thereby successfully beat down Cevdet's move.

On Saturday, December 23, at about one o'clock in the afternoon, the constitution was formally promulgated. The ceremony, for which hasty preparations had been made, took place in the open square to the seaward side of the Sublime Porte. Despite fairly heavy rain, a

[96] Elliot to Derby, #1373, 19 December 1876, FO 78/2468.
[97] Mahmud Celaleddin, *Mirât-ı hakikat*, I, 222-223; İnal, *Son sadrıâzamlar*, p. 117; Sami, *Süleyman Paşa muhakemesi*, p. 62, who gives Süleyman's audience with Abdülhamid much credit for causing the change.
[98] Mahmud Celaleddin, *Mirât-ı hakikat*, I, 223.
[99] *Levant Herald*, 18 December 1876.
[100] It is not clear what sort of a meeting this was. A. H. Midhat, *Tabsıra-i ibret*, p. 188, explicitly calls it a *meclis-i umumî*, though the remarks quoted indicate it might have been the council of ministers only. *Levant Herald*, 22 December 1876, calls it a meeting of the constitutional commission. A. H. Midhat, *Life*, p. 117, calls it explicitly a council of ministers, and says it met at Damad Mahmud Paşa's house.
[101] A. H. Midhat, *Tabsıra-i ibret*, p. 188, n.1. See comments in Mardin, *Cevdet*, p. 143, n.121; Mardin doubts that Cevdet could have opposed the constitution entire.

large crowd gathered, the people pushing and jostling one another with umbrellas. Said Bey, first secretary of the palace, arrived with a velvet pouch containing Abdülhamid's official decree of promulgation and the text of the constitution. He handed this to the grand vezir Midhat Paşa, who, in turn, reverently handed it to the chief secretary of the Porte in charge of communications to the palace, Mahmud Celaleddin, who read the *hat* aloud. The sultan did not grace the ceremony with his presence, and he was said to be slightly indisposed. Perhaps the words which he had been obliged to sanction hurt him. His *hat*, however, was unequivocal. It described the constitution as compatible with the sacred law, and a natural continuation of the reforms begun by his father, Abdülmecid. It said that the aims of the constitution were the welfare of all Ottoman peoples, who should without distinction enjoy the blessings of liberty, justice, and equality, and the safeguarding of the government from arbitrary domination by one or more individuals. The *hat* outlined briefly the process by which the constitution had been elaborated and the main headings of that document, and finally ordered the grand vezir to see that the constitution was made effective in all parts of the empire and that the laws needed to implement it were worked out at once.[102] Midhat then spoke briefly in thanks to the sultan for the important act of promulgation. This will inaugurate, said Midhat, a new era of enduring prosperity.[103] Writing some forty or more years later, the last official historian of the Ottoman Empire, Abdurrahman Şeref, said that the vibration of Midhat's voice still rang in his ears. After the former müfti of Edirne prayed for long life for Abdülhamid, a salute of one hundred and one guns announced the promulgation to the populace.[104]

The booming of the guns sounded also in the hall where the Constantinople Conference (often called by Turks the Tersane or Admiralty Conference, after its place of meeting) was holding its first plenary session. Safvet Paşa, the foreign minister and first Ottoman delegate to the conference, arose to explain the significance of the

[102] Text in *Staatsarchiv*, 32 (1877), #5984; Ahmed Midhat, *Üss-i inkılâb*, II, 209-212; *Levant Herald*, 26 December 1876. Ahmed Midhat, II, 383-385, gives also the text of an initial draft of the *hat* by Midhat which was not quite so flowery and laid less stress on the role of the sultan and the dynasty.

[103] Text in *Levant Herald*, 26 December 1876.

[104] Descriptions of the ceremony in *Levant Herald*, 23 and 26 December 1876; Abdurrahman Şeref, *Tarih musahabeleri*, pp. 200-201; Mahmud Celaleddin, *Mirât-ı hakikat*, I, 224; Ahmed Midhat, *Üss-i inkılâb*, II, 206-207; *Stamboul*, 26 December 1876; Devereux, *First Ottoman Constitutional Period*, pp. 71-74.

salute. He spoke eloquently of the new reform measure, which meant that the empire needed no foreign suggestions.[105] This theatrical coup failed to arrest the deliberations of the powers. That Midhat should have thought it would stop the conference is inconceivable, for he knew that all, even the British, were committed to the deliberations. Were the six powers, furthermore, to toss aside the reform proposals for the Balkan provinces which they had worked out in nine preliminary meetings without the Turkish delegates, and were now about to present to them? Of course this did not happen. The initial diplomatic significance of the constitutional promulgation is that it gave the Turkish delegates strong ground on which to stand in refusing the powers' proposals as they were advanced—a position which caused the powers to whittle down the proposals.

In İstanbul outside the conference hall, the constitutional proclamation provoked a greater enthusiasm. Of course there were the formal visits of congratulation to the sultan in his palace by the ministers and other officials, and that night houses and shops were illuminated.[106] A more significant visit was that paid the next day by Midhat to the Greek and Armenian patriarchs, as a gesture to help bind all the peoples of the empire in a common bond of Osmanlılık and to show that under the new constitutional regime men of all creeds would be treated equally. Such a visit by a grand vezir was unprecedented in Ottoman history, and probably all the more appreciated by the millet heads, since traditionally it was they who visited Ottoman officials. "We consider you the resuscitator of the Ottoman Empire," said the Greek patriarch in reply to Midhat's words of friendship.[107] Meanwhile on the evening of December 23 groups of young liberals among the Turks had paraded the streets, some going to Midhat's house and to the palace to shout long life to the grand vezir and the sultan. They were joined by groups of softas, some just back from the war against Serbia, and by some of the military academy students. A parade of brokers and money-changers from Galata also indulged in similar demonstrations.[108]

[105] Protocol of 23 December 1876 session in *Staatsarchiv*, 31 (1877), #5949.

[106] Mahmud Celaleddin, *Mirât-ı hakikat*, I, 224.

[107] Midhat's speech to the Greek Orthodox, and patriarch's reply, in A. H. Midhat, *Midhat Pacha*, pp. 97-98. Cf. Ahmed Midhat, *Üss-i inkılâb*, II, 213-214; A. H. Midhat, *Life*, p. 131, which says he also visited the grand rabbi; Théodore Blancard, *Les Mavroyéni* (Paris, 1909), II, 70 and n.1.

[108] *Levant Herald*, 26 December 1876; Ahmed Midhat, *Üss-i inkılâb*, II, 208;

Part of this enthusiasm was for constitutional government; part was simply an expression of patriotic opposition to all foreign interference. But of enthusiasm among much of the literate elite of the capital, both Turkish and non-Turkish, there can be little doubt. The next day *Vakit* summed up the sentiment in an article which began, "Yesterday was for all Osmanlis the beginning of happiness."[109]

Throughout the empire as a whole the reaction to the news that a constitution had been proclaimed was, in general, one of scepticism, indifference, or lack of comprehension. In each provincial capital the vali had the imperial *hat* read publicly. Sometimes the notables in the vilayet capital then returned an address of thanks to the sultan. Only in Edirne does real enthusiasm seem to have been engendered, and this was more for defiance of the powers than for parliamentary rule.[110] In some quarters there was fear that the constitution simply represented new concessions to Christian pressure. Ottoman officialdom seems to have understood the import of the constitution and the difficulties which would arise in applying it. The people as a whole, ignorant and tradition-minded, understood little. Three instances may serve as illustrations. In Ankara a telegram arrived on December 25 with news that the constitution was proclaimed and that official rejoicing should begin. The vali, greatly sceptical that political liberty could be achieved without time for more education and the development of greater tolerance, complied with the orders. He read the telegram to the public, an imam pronounced "Amen," and the one cannon in Ankara was fired one hundred and one times despite fears that it might burst. The vali's son opined that roads and railroads were more important than fifty constitutions. As yet the text of the constitution was unknown in Ankara. Two months later the Ankara vilayet newspaper carried a long article in praise of the constitution as a check to administrative chaos, a block to Russian intervention, and a guarantee of free expression and participation in government which would produce good men to help save the empire.[111] In Tripoli in Africa the promulgation, on January 6, produced a salute of guns, some feeble illumination by oil lamps, and a vast indifference except

---

Stamboul, 26 December 1876; Moüy, "Souvenirs d'un diplomate," p. 627; Mahmud Celaleddin, *Mirât-ı hakikat*, I, 224.

[109] Quoted in Azimzade Hakkı, *Türkiyede meclis-i meb'usan*, p. 125.

[110] Fesch, *Constantinople*, p. 235.

[111] Burnaby, *On Horseback*, I, 120-127, an eyewitness account; *Stamboul*, 27 February 1877, reprinting the Ankara article.

among the Marabouts, who feared that a constitution which diminished the power of the sultan might also lessen their own influence among the people.[112] In Beirut the vali read the imperial *hat* in Turkish and Arabic to representatives of all sects, and asked an old *şeyh* to close with prayer. The latter, using a stereotyped formula, prayed for Abdülhamid's victory, that Allah might "destroy the infidels, tear them in tatters, grind them in powder, rend them in fragments, because they are the enemies of the Mohammedans." Then the müfti pulled at the *şeyh*'s collar and whispered, whereupon the *şeyh* concluded, "O Allah, destroy the infidels because they are the enemies of the Moslems, the Christians, and the Jews."[113]

Of the minority peoples, the Jews could but rejoice in the constitution, for they had no nationalist ambitions, and the Armenians in general seem to have greeted it with pleasure because they conceived that it might mean more liberty for them, and they had been unable to get the powers to consider their lot. Their beloved former patriarch, Mgrdich Khrimian Hairig, wrote rhapsodic praise of the constitution as ushering in an era of justice, and an Armenian poet praised Midhat's deeds and ideals.[114] Greeks, particularly in İstanbul and Edirne, seem to have welcomed the constitution partly for its own sake, and partly because they hoped it would thwart the Bulgarian separatism which the great powers tended to favor.[115] Other Balkan peoples, however, exhibited no jubilation. The Slavs who had taken up arms against the sultan could hardly look forward with pleasure to reintegration into the empire, even a constitutional empire. The Bulgars did not want equality and fusion, but separation.[116]

---

[112] Jones (Tripoli) to Hunter, #8, 12 January 1877, USNA, Tripoli IX.

[113] Henry H. Jessup, *Fifty-Three Years in Syria* (New York, 1910), II, 449. Other examples in Burnaby, *On Horseback*, I, 194; *Levant Herald*, 9 January 1877; Ahmed Midhat, *Üss-i inkılâb*, II, 214-217; Devereux, *First Ottoman Constitutional Period*, pp. 74-78; IU. A. Petrosian, *"Novye Osmany" i bor'ba za konstitutsiiu* (Moscow, 1958), pp. 115-116, citing Russian consular reports.

[114] Fesch, *Constantinople*, pp. 235-237; A. O. Sarkissian, *History of the Armenian Question to 1885* (Urbana, 1938), pp. 51-56; *Aspirations et agissements révolutionnaires des comités arméniens* (Constantinople, 1917), p. 13. Some Armenians in the interior were more sceptical: Burnaby, *On Horseback*, I, 194. This was partly because on December 13 a great fire had destroyed shops in Van, whereupon looting and attacks on Christians followed; Turkish soldiers were suspected of arson: ABCFM, Eastern Turkey Mission I, #464, 22 December 1876; Burnaby, *On Horseback*, II, 238-239.

[115] Sumner, *Russia and the Balkans*, p. 244.

[116] ABCFM, Western Turkey Mission II, #618, 27 December 1876; Nicolas Iorga, ed., *Correspondance diplomatique roumaine* (Paris, 1923), #508, 28 December 1876. İsmail Kemal thought otherwise: Story, *Ismail Kemal*, p. 133.

In Roumania, when Prince Charles got a copy of the constitution on December 28, there was an explosion of protest at the implication in articles 1 and 7 that Roumania was no more than a privileged province which could not for any cause be detached from the Ottoman Empire.[117]

Article 1 of the constitution was, in fact, legitimately frightening to Prince Charles, for it reaffirmed emphatically one of the reasons for which Midhat and others had worked so hard for the promulgation. This was simply the preservation of the independence and the territorial integrity of the Ottoman Empire. Article 1 stated that the empire was composed of its present territories, including the privileged provinces, making a unit "which can at no time and for no cause whatever be divided." Here was an answer for the Balkan nationalists and the great powers. For this indivisible empire the constitution went on to provide the powers of the sultanate, a bill of rights for the people, a council of ministers, each of whom was responsible for his ministry, an appointed senate, an elected chamber of deputies, an independent judiciary, parliamentary control of the budget, considerable provincial decentralization, and obligatory primary education for all Muslims.[118] Many of the provisions would have to be elaborated by further legislation before they would become effective. Even so, the constitution did not pretend to place the Ottoman government under full popular control. It was a product of compromise and of the times. It did set up a framework under which steps in that direction might be taken, yet the framework itself had easily identifiable flaws and loopholes.

In the first place, the sultan retained great powers. Some of them were specifically listed, but none was specifically denied him. He appointed the ministers, appointed the members of the senate, convoked and prorogued the parliament. His legislative authority rested not only on this power of appointment, but on the fact that his irade was required before any bills became law, and no time limit was set for

---

[117] *Aus dem Leben König Karls von Rumänien* (Stuttgart, 1894-1900), III, 85-86; *Levant Herald*, 9 January 1877, quoting *Correspondance de Roumanie* of 6 January.

[118] Texts of the constitution are widely available: Turkish in Ahmed Midhat, *Üss-i inkılâb*, II, 355-383; also in the new characters in A. Ş. Gözübüyük and S. Kili, *Türk anayasa metinleri* (Ankara, 1957), pp. 25-38; French in the official translation in *Constitution Ottomane* (Constantinople, 1876) and *Staatsarchiv*, 31 (1877), #5948; English in *American Journal of International Law* (1908), Supplement, II, 367-387.

the veto power implied by this provision. He sanctioned the acts of ministers. He had the exclusive authority to expel individuals considered dangerous to the state. The sultan was also declared to be caliph, non-responsible for his acts, and his person to be sacred. Sovereignty, in short, still resided in the sultan, and not in the nation. Other flaws in the constitution, from the standpoint of democratic processes, were not far to seek. The ministers were responsible for their acts, but not directly to the chamber, though they could be interpellated. Only the ministry could introduce legislation; suggestions originating in the chamber had to pass through the grand vezir to the sultan and the Council of State before they could be presented as bills. Though the budget was voted by the parliament, the ministry had extraordinary spending powers if the chamber were not in session or if a completed budget had not been voted. Normally the parliament was to be in session only each winter, from November 13 to March 13. So far as the central administration and the legislative process were concerned, therefore, the constitution of 1876 created what might be described, in unorthodox terms, as a limited autocracy.

Other aspects of the constitution afford less room for criticism. Much of the judicial regulation remained to be worked out, but the constitution provided clearly for security of judicial tenure, public trial, and no administrative interference with the courts. It maintained the dichotomy of religious and civil courts, which could hardly have been abolished by one stroke in 1876. The individual rights and civil liberties of Ottoman subjects were generally well stated—individual liberty and freedom from arbitrary punishment, freedom of religion and of privileges accorded the millets, freedom of the press "within the limits of the law," freedom of commercial (but not of political or other) association, the right of petition, security of property and domicile, taxation according to law and the individual's means. Many of these principles had been stated before in the Tanzimat pronouncements from 1839 on, but never all together nor so explicitly.

Probably the most beneficial aspect of the constitution was its emphasis on the equality of all Ottoman subjects—again an extension of the Osmanlılık doctrine characteristic of the Tanzimat period. The enumeration of civil liberties was subject to no qualifications as to race or creed. To be sure, Islam was designated the state religion, and the sultan of all Ottomans was also named caliph of all Muslims and defender of the faith. To this extent the constitution exhibited a split personality. But millet distinctions were as far as then possible conscientiously eliminated. All subjects of the state were without exception to be called "Osmanli," and the expression "Ottoman subjects," which had begun its official career in 1839, recurred throughout the text of the constitution, sometimes with the additional phrase "of whatever religion or sect." All Ottoman subjects were stated to be equal before the law, to have the same rights and duties, and to be equally admissible to public office according to merit. Each member of the chamber of deputies, further, was to consider himself the representative not only of the district that elected him, but of all Ottomans. Only in the lower provincial echelon of the kaza was the millet distinction retained—for electoral councils to supervise charitable funds and the resources of widows and orphans of each religious community. One qualification curtailed somewhat this Ottoman equality—the provision that those admitted to public office, as well as those elected to the chamber of deputies, had to know Turkish, the official language. This would work a hardship on some of the Balkan peoples, and probably just as much of a hardship on the Arab subjects of the empire. An interesting commentary on the literacy level as well as on the linguistic heterogeneity of the empire was the further provision that at the end of four years deputies would have to be able to read Turkish, and to write it as far as possible.

It is obvious that almost the entire constitution was western in inspiration. This was a big step—perhaps too big—in the direction in which Mahmud II had started Ottoman political development. There are many parallels to be found between the 1876 constitution and the Belgian constitution of 1831. But the former did not go nearly so far as the Belgian, which stated flatly that "all powers derive from the nation," which had an elected upper house, which allowed the two chambers initiative in legislation along with the king, and which limited the king to the powers enumerated. In several ways the 1876 constitution was closer to the Prussian of 1850, which gave the monarch greater powers and which had an appointed upper chamber. Still, the inspiration was western.

The Ottoman constitution of 1876 has been subject to merciless criticism, both at the time of its creation and since. Some of the criticism has been unfair and grotesque. That the constitution was not simply a diplomatic maneuver contrived to get rid of the Constantinople Conference will already have been abundantly clear. It was the product of a long process of deliberation, and of interest among Turks extending back at least to 1867, as well as of the Tanzimat developments from 1839 on. Treitschke wrote sarcastically, but with partial truth, that the Turks had finally drunk of the constitutional poison which affected such peoples as whisky affected redskins.[119] Freeman thundered in Olympian rage that all Turkish reform documents were varieties of waste paper; the Midhat constitution was "simply a mockery, a delusion, and a snare, a net spread in the sight of birds who ought to be too wise to be caught by it."[120] MacColl wrote that "in reality, Midhat's Constitution is a crafty contrivance for concentrating the government of the Turkish Empire in the hands of the Pashas which means, taking them all in all, of about two hundred of the most unmitigated scoundrels on the face of the earth."[121] Such criticisms as the latter two may be dismissed out of hand. But others are serious, and point generally to the sultan's extensive powers and to the lack of effective control over legislation by the elective chamber.

The critics, either western Europeans or modern Turks, tend to compare the 1876 constitution to a theoretical ideal, or to British parliamentary government after the second Reform Bill, or to the Third French Republic. In theory, they are right. Recai Okandan, for instance, after a devastating review of the individual provisions of the constitution, concludes that "the system which we have termed constitutionalism was in reality a confirmation and reaffirmation of the principles of absolutism."[122] But these comparisons may be misguided. Comparison should perhaps be made not to the more advanced political regimes of western Europe, but to the Russian Empire, which had neither constitution nor parliament, or to Prussia before 1850, to Austria-Hungary, or to Napoleon III's regime before the "Liberal

---

[119] Heinrich von Treitschke, "Die Türkei und die Grossmächte," *Preussische Jahrbücher*, 37 (1876), 688.

[120] Edward A. Freeman, *The Ottoman Power in Europe* (London, 1877), pp. 268-269.

[121] Malcolm MacColl, "Midhat Pasha on Turkish History and Reform," *Gentleman's Magazine*, 243 (1878), 49.

[122] Okandan, *Umumî âmme hukukumuzun ana hatları*, I, 144-174, quotation on p. 168. For other representative analyses and criticisms see Franck Rouvière, *Essai sur l'évolution des idées constitutionnelles en Turquie* (Montpellier, 1910), pp. 91ff.; Gallenga, *Two Years*, II, 288-293; Eugene Schuyler's comments in Maynard to Fish, #126, 30 January 1877, USNA, Turkey 31. The latest and best-balanced analysis is in Devereux, *First Ottoman Constitutional Period*, pp. 46-70.

Empire." By such standards the constitution of 1876 appears reasonably good.

Certainly the constitution was imperfect. Yet, even as regards the legislative process, it created a system that offered much hope. Despite the sultan's great powers, the constitution prescribed a meeting of parliament once a year; if it were dissolved, it would have to meet again in six months. The deputies of the chamber, each of whom represented fifty thousand males, had four-year terms, were paid a salary and travel expenses, enjoyed freedom of speech in the debates and other parliamentary immunities. The whole import of these provisions was a recognition of the right of the nation to be heard, through its representatives. They might not be heeded by the sultan and the Porte, but they would be heard. Some of the theoretically objectionable provisions of the constitution were defensible on the grounds that they prevented that violent break with the past which Âli and Fuad had always feared would mean the death both of reform and of the empire itself. It can indeed be argued that the constitution, far from being too absolutist, expected too much from the deputies, given the Ottoman tradition and lack of parliamentary experience. But there was a background of experience in various meclises to build on; and the constitution, even though it had been worked out by a top-level commission instead of by a prosperous and well-educated bourgeoisie demanding political voice, as had been the case in the West, met the popular feeling that there ought to be a shift away from the sort of arbitrary government Abdülaziz had exercised. Safvet Paşa's circular explaining the constitution maintained, with an overenthusiasm dubiously designed for diplomatic consumption, that it introduced "the reign of liberty, justice, and equality, that is to say, the triumph of civilization."[123] This was too much. But now at least the constitution was there, the sultan formally committed to it. This was, all elements of the situation considered, a remarkable achievement. A means for further political development had been provided. The test, as with the vilayet law earlier, would be how men used the opportunity.

While preparations for elections and for the first meeting of the parliament were progressing, Midhat used the constitution as a diplomatic weapon against any program which the conference of

[123] Text in *Staatsarchiv*, 31 (1877), #5952, 26 December 1876.

powers, still sitting at the admiralty offices in İstanbul, might try to impose. The conference was now proposing a division of Bulgaria into two provinces, East and West, whose governors should be approved by the powers. There would also be a European commission to supervise reforms. Such arrangements Midhat, despite his known partiality for provincial decentralization, was unable to accept; he saw in them a derogation of Ottoman sovereignty and the beginning of dissolution.[124] Instead, he demanded that the Porte be given a year's grace to inaugurate its new system; after that he would allow the powers to inquire into the effectiveness of reforms. Midhat's general opposition to the conference proposals was backed up by Ottoman opinion which, in part his own creation, in fact would endanger any form of acceptance.[125] It has been said that Abdülhamid II would have yielded to the proposals of the conference had he not feared deposition by his ministers.[126] Probably this was just a means of trying to gain favor with the powers. There is no reason to suppose that the sultan really wanted European intervention any more than did Midhat.

Midhat's counterproposal included a device which at first seems inconsistent with his inflexible opposition to foreign intervention. It was, simply, that the great powers through the conference then assembled should take formal cognizance of the Ottoman constitution and so guarantee it. The application of the constitution by the Porte would, in turn, be sufficient guarantee of reforms for the Balkan Christians, in place of the conference proposals. Midhat had been toying with such an idea even before he became grand vezir, at least in the form of getting British support for the constitution.[127] Said Bey claimed to have had the same idea independently, and to have suggested it to Midhat.[128] It may have been the concept of Odian Efendi, for he served in many instances as Midhat's idea-man. In any case, Odian, who was also one of the constitution's authors, was sent to Paris and London during the Constantinople Conference. Abdülhamid and the ministers approved his secret mission, which was ostensibly

---

[124] Elliot to Derby, 30 December 1876, *Staatsarchiv*, 31 (1877), #5956.

[125] Chaudordy to Décazes, 10 January 1877, *Staatsarchiv*, 32 (1877), #5987.

[126] Story, *Ismail Kemal*, p. 136; Salisbury to Derby, 18 January 1877, *Staatsarchiv*, 32 (1877), #5969; Sumner, *Russia and the Balkans*, p. 246, n.1.

[127] Midhat to Derby, 17 December 1876, in A. H. Midhat, "English and Russian Politics in the East," pp. 71-73; idem, *Souvenir de mon exil volontaire* (Geneva, 1905), pp. 83-86.

[128] Said to Midhat, 11 January 1877, in A. H. Midhat, *Tabsıra-i ibret*, pp. 335-336; idem, *Midhat Pacha*, p. 109.

to talk about European loans and the 1875 moratorium, but in reality to convince the Porte's old allies of the Crimean War that the Ottoman Empire could not accept the servitudes demanded by the conference.[129] Following Midhat's lead, Odian proposed that the powers acknowledge the constitution as guarantee enough of good administration in the Balkans, if the Porte guaranteed to the conference that it would be applied. But when Odian advanced this as a "personal suggestion" to Disraeli, the British prime minister, on January 8, and to Derby, the foreign secretary, two days later, he met a stone wall. Derby refused even to discuss a recognition of the constitution by the powers, and referred Odian to the conference as the proper forum.[130] The conference delegates likewise turned down the proposition. Nothing came of the idea, though both Sir Henry Elliot and his successor Sir Henry Layard thought that Europe should have supported the constitution.[131] Midhat still held the same view in 1878— that the powers could legitimately exercise a collective surveillance over the carrying out of the constitution's provisions, thus checking independent Russian action.[132] Evidently he had in mind not the state of affairs of 1856, wherein the powers forced Âli and Fuad to adopt a reform program, but something more analogous to Reşid Paşa's action in 1839 of getting European backing for a home-grown reform program and the integrity of the empire in which it was to be applied. It is interesting to speculate whether Midhat in 1876 considered the proposed guarantee simply a means to secure diplomatic support against foreign, especially Russian, intervention, or whether he had already developed such suspicion of Abdülhamid that he wanted the powers' guarantee to run against any unconstitutional acts of the sultan. The latter is less likely, but the truth is unknown.

Since the constitution had failed to arrest the proposals of the Constantinople Conference, Midhat had to turn to other methods. The final proposal of the six powers involved special regimes and administrative reforms for Bosnia, Herzegovina, and the two Bul-

---

[129] A. H. Midhat, *Tabsıra-i ibret*, pp. 191-193; *Levant Herald*, 18 January 1877.
[130] Derby to Salisbury, 10 January 1876, *Staatsarchiv*, 32 (1877), #5965.
[131] Henry Elliot, "The Death of Abdul Aziz and of Turkish Reform," *Nineteenth Century*, 23 (1888), 294; Temperley, "British Policy," pp. 175-176, 182-183. On the whole mission of Odian see Bekir Sıtkı Baykal, "Midhat Paşa'nın gizli bir siyasî teşebbüsü," in Türk Tarih Kurumu, *III Türk Tarih Kongresi, . . . 1943* (Ankara, 1948), pp. 470-477.
[132] Midhat Pacha, "La Turquie, son passé, son avenir," *Revue Scientifique* (1878), pp. 1153-1154.

garias. Some of this was acceptable to the Ottoman ministry, but they would not agree to the demand that governors for these provinces be approved by the powers, and that international control commissions supervise the application of reforms.[133] Abdülhamid had earlier rejected an idea advanced by Midhat that the best answer to the powers would be for the Porte itself to name some Christian valis.[134] The only remaining answer to the powers, since they would negotiate with the Turks no further, seemed to be outright rejection of their plan. Midhat took this course, hoping at least for English support. Elliot's attitude, and his "long intimacy" (Elliot's phrase) with Midhat, and the presence in İstanbul of the rabidly Turcophile M.P., Butler-Johnstone, who pretended to be Prime Minister Disraeli's confidential agent, gave him some basis.[135] Midhat did not think that he would find Britain allied with the Ottoman Empire if it came to war against Russia.[136] He did hope for diplomatic support. One result had come from Odian's mission to London—Odian's conviction, based on conversation with Derby, that if the Porte torpedoed the Constantinople Conference, the British would take no action. This Odian telegraphed to İstanbul about January 17, which was one day before a *meclis-i umumî* was convened there to consider the plan of the great power conference.[137]

Obviously Midhat wanted an expression of popular or national opinion to back his rejection of the powers' plan. It would be impossible to convene the parliament, as provided for under the constitution, soon enough. Therefore, an exceptionally large *meclis-i umumî* of some 237 or more notables, including representatives of the non-Muslim millets, was convoked on January 18. To this grand council Midhat outlined the powers' proposals, his objections, and the dangers of war

[133] Sumner, *Russia and the Balkans*, p. 246.
[134] Said Bey to Midhat, 23 December 1876, in A. H. Midhat, *Midhat Pacha*, pp. 87-88.
[135] Elliot to Derby, #1396, 28 December 1876, FO 78/2468; Seton-Watson, *Disraeli*, pp. 124, 135-136; Sumner, *Russia and the Balkans*, pp. 236-237; Dwight E. Lee, *Great Britain and the Cyprus Convention Policy of 1878* (Cambridge, Mass., 1934), p. 49, n.10. On Butler-Johnstone see above, chapter IX, n.54; also *Diplomatic Review*, 24 (1876), 44-50, 160-161; Mordtmann, *Stambul*, I, 181-182; *Stamboul*, 18 December 1876. He was raising money at this point for Turkish soldiers in the field. Butler-Johnstone was, in İstanbul, the guest of Ali Suavi, himself newly arrived there; Ali Suavi was, curiously, no friend of Midhat: Clician Vassif, *Midhat-Pacha*, pp. 131-133.
[136] Midhat to Musurus, 10 January 1877, in A. H. Midhat, "English and Russian Politics," p. 76.
[137] Hohenlohe (Paris) to Bismarck, 4 February 1877, *Grosse Politik*, II, #275.

which might pit the weakened Ottoman Empire against Russia if the conference plan were rejected. In a remarkable demonstration of patriotic unity, the notables spoke almost with one voice for rejection. The Greek and Armenian patriarchs and the Bulgar exarch had stayed away, pleading illness, which was the only diplomatic position they could assume. But the vicars of the first two came and voted for rejection. Only the head of the Protestant Armenian millet, along with Prince Halim of Egypt and a few others, advised caution and acceptance.[138] Sultan Abdülhamid approved the decision of the grand council to reject the powers' demands and to retain independence of action for domestic reform.[139] Safvet Paşa, at the next conference session, informed the powers of this decision. He assured them that most of the points of their program were acceptable, but that the initiative must come from the sovereign Ottoman Empire, which could not be subjected to external compulsion.[140] On January 20 the conference broke up, never to reassemble, and the plenipotentiaries left İstanbul as soon as possible, to show their displeasure.

There could be no doubt that such public opinion as existed in the Ottoman Empire, apart from the Slavic provinces, backed the stand of the grand council and the ministry. Opposition to foreign, especially to Russian, intervention was strong, and was encouraged by the Porte when it published during the Constantinople Conference a collection of alleged Russian diplomatic documents proving pan-Slav intrigues in the Balkans.[141] The martial spirit which had been developing since the summer of 1876 had by now reached considerable proportions. A good many Turks expected war with Russia. False reports that Russian armies had crossed the Pruth were published in İstanbul even during the Constantinople Conference. As the conference closed, a

---

[138] Story, *Ismail Kemal*, pp. 139-142; *Levant Herald*, 19 January 1877, giving the figure of 260 notables; Danişmend, *Kronolojisi*, IV, 295-296, giving reported figures of 240 or 300, including 60 non-Muslims; A. H. Midhat, *Midhat Pacha*, pp. 103-106; idem, *Tabsıra-i ibret*, pp. 189-190; Sumner, *Russia and the Balkans*, p. 246, n.1; Fesch, *Constantinople*, pp. 253-254; Mordtmann, *Stambul*, I, 180; Gallenga, *Two Years*, II, 295-301; Salisbury to Derby, 18 January 1877, and Derby to Salisbury, 19 January 1877, *Staatsarchiv*, 32 (1877), #5969-#5970.

[139] Said to Midhat, 21 January 1877, in A. H. Midhat, "English and Russian Politics," p. 74.

[140] Safvet's summary of the situation, dated 25 January 1877, in *Staatsarchiv*, 32 (1877), #5990.

[141] G. Giacometti, *Les Responsabilités de la guerre* (Constantinople, 1877). Cf. Sumner, *Russia and the Balkans*, pp. 244, 681. The Porte was shortly reported also to be preparing a diplomatic Red Book of its own: *Stamboul*, 19 February 1877.

delegation of Hungarian students arrived in Istanbul to honor the Turks as conquerors of the Serbs. The Porte gave them an official reception. For their entertainment Namık Kemal's play *Vatan*, with all its patriotic sentiment and anti-Russian overtones, was staged again.[142] This was a dangerous spirit, which Midhat was probably foolish to have encouraged, though possibly he believed he could control it.[143] His main task, of course, was not to pick a fight with Russia, but to get the constitution into operation. A booklet issued anonymously in Istanbul on January 29, 1877, summed up the situation accurately. It reflected Midhat's attitude, and may have been inspired by him. The revolts of 1875, it declared, should have been suppressed at once. European intervention was inadmissible, and contrary to the Treaty of Paris of 1856. The grand council, truly national, was, in a sense, the first application of the constitution. The Constantinople Conference should have helped the empire to establish its constitution instead of proposing international intervention in the Balkans. The constitution was a start in the right direction, but it would not automatically ensure either reforms or progress, which would depend not only on the maintenance of peace, but on capable officials and a tremendous activity.[144] Perhaps this was too great a demand, but such was Midhat's task. If any Ottoman statesman of the day could do it, Midhat, with all his personal deficiencies, was that man.

Yet Midhat was not vouchsafed the time to do this. His tenure of the grand vezirate lasted only forty-nine days, a period shorter than his term of office in 1872. The cause for Midhat's dismissal was the friction that had been built up between him and the sultan, which made it practically impossible for them to work together. There seems to have been no sympathy at all between them even before Midhat's appointment on December 19. After that date, in addition to Abdülhamid's final hesitations over the constitution, particular points of argument separated the two even farther, though the final split did not come until after the European plenipotentiaries had been safely packed off to their homelands. One source of friction concerned Midhat's relations with Namık Kemal and Ziya—relations

---

[142] Elliot to Derby, #1398, 29 December 1876, FO 78/2468; *Levant Herald*, 30 December 1876 and 23 January 1877; Sumner, *Russia and the Balkans*, p. 244.

[143] Cf. the strictures of İzzet Paşa, based on "certain papers that I have recently had in my hands": *Denkwürdigkeiten des Marschalls Izzet Pascha* (Leipzig, 1927), pp. 79-81.

[144] *La Turquie après la Conférence* (Constantinople, 1877).

which were far too close to suit the sultan. Midhat was accused of talking freely to them about government business, and probably he did so. They were often at his house. Furthermore, these two and others had been active in promoting a committee to send clothing, tobacco, and other gifts to soldiers stationed on the Serb-Montenegrin front during the winter; Midhat had presided at meetings. Now the offices of this relief committee, as the war spirit grew, became a recruiting center for the Asâkir-i milliye, a sort of volunteer national guard, the members of which were given to shouting long life to Midhat and Namık Kemal and to singing the latter's patriotic songs from *Vatan*. Obviously to Abdülhamid this looked as if Midhat were not only gaining popularity among soldiers, but might enjoy the support of a kind of private army. Redif Paşa, the war minister, was ordered to abolish this volunteer militia and absorb it into the regular army, but it resisted the move. The sultan thereupon wanted to get Namık Kemal and Ziya out of İstanbul, and even Midhat's friend İsmail Kemal gave him similar advice.[145]

Abdülhamid further objected to Midhat that the İstanbul press was allowed a freedom which it abused. Again Ziya was involved, for he was suspected of inspiring articles in the *İstikbal* (*Future*)—edited by the liberal Theodore Cassape (Kasap), who had once been a protégé of Alexandre Dumas—to throw doubt on the sultan's sincerity in issuing the constitution and to imply that he, Ziya, was one of the principal originators of that document. *İstikbal* had moreover, said the sultan, quite unnecessarily published Mustafa Fazıl's notorious letter of 1867 to Abdülaziz. Having already in vain ordered Midhat to appoint Ziya ambassador to Berlin, Abdülhamid was now incensed to learn from the newspapers that Ziya was a popular candidate for election to the chamber from İstanbul. His candidacy was unacceptable, said the sultan, who thereupon ordered Midhat to rusticate Ziya as vali of Syria. Ziya gave in, and left for his post. But Namık Kemal resisted appointment to a post of exile, and Midhat refused to force him to take one. Meanwhile the sultan ordered Midhat to elaborate a press law which would curb the liberty to which the press pretended

[145] Mahmud Celaleddin, *Mirât-ı hakikat*, I, 266-267; Sami, *Süleyman Paşa muhakemesi*, pp. 63-73, 78; Kuntay, *Namık Kemal*, I, 295-296; Story, *Ismail Kemal*, pp. 136-137; Y. A., *Midhat-Pacha, la constitution ottomane et l'Europe* (Paris, 1903), p. 11; Chaudordy to Décazes, 10 January 1877, *Staatsarchiv*, 32 (1877), #5987.

under the new constitution, and to have it done in four days.[146] Beyond question, some of the İstanbul papers were highly irritating to the sultan.

There were other sources of friction between the sultan and the grand vezir. One was over official appointments, particularly over replacing the finance minister, Galib Paşa, whom Midhat accused of incompetence.[147] Another was over the question of admission of non-Muslims to military schools.[148] But all this friction was only symptomatic of a basic incompatibility which was compounded of two interrelated elements. One element was Abdülhamid's very natural fear of a grand vezir who had a considerable popular following, and who had already been a principal figure in deposing two sultans and in creating two. Abdülhamid certainly feared for the security of his own throne. He was more antagonistic to Midhat than might otherwise have been the case because he knew that in the depositions Midhat had acted purely for the good of the state, and not because of personal rancor against the reigning sultans. Such a man could not be suborned, and he might so act again, as the self-appointed interpreter of the common weal—this time against Abdülhamid. Of course, Abdülhamid owed his throne to Midhat as much as to anyone, but this would not make him grateful; quite to the contrary, he would not wish to be beholden to Midhat as kingmaker, and would inevitably want to get rid of so powerful a statesman if he could.

The sultan's fears were undoubtedly fanned by Damad Mahmud Paşa and others with palace connections. They may well have accused Midhat of subversion, of republicanism, of wanting to be a dictator, as is often reported. Abdülhamid believed such stories. When Midhat objected to the sultan's naming Galib Paşa a senator before the confusion in finances had been straightened out, a matter which the chamber of deputies might look into, the sultan was told, "He threatens you with the deputies."[149] But probably the sultan's chief fear was always that he himself might be deposed. Such fear was nourished by

[146] A. H. Midhat, *Life*, pp. 122-127; *idem, Tabsıra-i ibret*, pp. 396-398; Y. A., *Midhat-Pacha*, pp. 9-10; Mahmud Celaleddin, *Mirât-ı hakikat*, I, 268. On Cassape see Gallenga, *Two Years*, II, 350-352; Fesch, *Constantinople*, pp. 37-38; Kératry, *Mourad V*, pp. 288-289.

[147] A. H. Midhat, *Life*, pp. 121-122, 138-141; Mahmud Celaleddin, *Mirât-ı hakikat*, I, 267-268.

[148] A. H. Midhat, *Life*, pp. 141-143; *idem, Tabsıra-i ibret*, pp. 330-331; Y. A., *Midhat-Pacha*, p. 12.

[149] İnal, *Son sadrıâzamlar*, p. 357.

the discovery in the locker of a military academy student, Ali Nazmi, known as an admirer of Namık Kemal, of a paper saying that the caliphate properly belonged not to the house of Osman, but to the *şerif* of Mecca.[150] Murad, of course, was still alive, and there had already been in late November or early December 1876 one hare-brained plot, the so-called "Stavrides affair," to rescue him from internment.[151] Maybe there would be other plots, with Midhat's backing. The sultan's suspicion affected even their unimportant relationships. "Pasha, you don't like me at all," said Abdülhamid one day because Midhat, disliking diamonds, did not wear the diamond cuff links given him by the sultan.[152]

The other element of incompatibility revolved around the conception held by each man of his own place in the government. Abdülhamid was intent on maintaining his supreme authority. One way of expressing this, in addition to controlling all appointments and public acts, was to insist that he was the author of the constitution. As the semiofficial *La Turquie* put it after Midhat's dismissal, Abdülhamid alone had the right to conceive it and to grant it to his subjects. Midhat simply had the honor of being the interpreter of the august will.[153] Midhat, for his part, was trying to act like a European prime minister, despite the fact that the constitution had not created this role. This involved downgrading the sultan's authority. Ziya partially expressed Midhat's view in most unpolitic fashion when, en route to his Syrian governorship, he stopped off at İzmir and made remarks to the effect that, under the constitution, the sultan is the servant of the state.[154] The same view was fully expressed in a letter to the sultan dated January 30, 1877, which is often attributed to Midhat. It put his thoughts almost brutally: that the constitution was aimed at abolish-

---

[150] Mahmud Celaleddin, *Mirât-ı hakikat*, I, 267; Story, *Ismail Kemal*, pp. 146-147; Kératry, *Mourad V*, pp. 229-231.

[151] Elliot to Derby, #1336, 6 December 1876, and #1342, 7 December 1876, FO 78/2467. Cf. İ. H. Uzunçarşılı, "Beşinci Murad ile oğlu Salâhaddin Efendiyi kaçırmak için kadın kıyafetinde Çırağana girmek istiyen şahıslar," *Belleten*, 8:32 (1944), 589-597.

[152] A. H. Midhat, *Hâtıralarım*, pp. 10-11. Cf., on the sultan's fears, İnal, *Son sadrıâzamlar*, pp. 360-362.

[153] *La Turquie*, 8 February 1877. This emphasis on Abdülhamid as the true father of the constitution appears also in Ahmed Midhat's *Üss-i inkılâb*, written for the sultan: II, 177, 189-193.

[154] Fesch, *Constantinople*, pp. 49-50; Mordtmann, *Stambul*, I, 239; Osman Nuri, *Abdülhamid-i Sani*, I, 181. Cf. Abdolonyme Ubicini, *La constitution ottomane* (Paris, 1877), p. 15, n.2.

ing absolutism and defining the sultan's rights and duties, as well as those of the ministers; that the sultan is responsible to the nation; that the grand vezir, by the ordinances of the şeriat, must refuse obedience to imperial commands which do not coincide with the national interest; that the state is organized on the basis of consultation. Midhat offers to accept dismissal if the sultan disagrees.[155] Whether or not this letter was ever sent to the palace, it indicated Midhat's stand, and for some days at the beginning of February he kept to his house, having in effect broken direct relations with the sultan until matters on which he had requested action should be cleared up. Undoubtedly Midhat overestimated his position vis-à-vis the sultan, both as constitutional grand vezir and as popular leader. It was in this period that Midhat expressed the view that the people would uphold him. "I will not resign," he said. "If the sultan dismiss me, let him. But my dismissal this time will not be comparable to former ones. The people will come to take me from my house and place me in the grand vezirate." But since this would create difficulties, he said he was prepared to go to live on the island of Midilli (Mitylene) instead.[156]

When after some days Midhat was asked to come to the palace, on

---

[155] A. H. Midhat, Midhat Paşa's son, published this letter in four books: *Tabsıra-i ibret*, pp. 394-396; *Life*, pp. 143-144; *Midhat Pacha*, pp. 117-118; *Hâtıralarım*, pp. 26-27. The English translation in *Life* is loose in places. In *Hâtıralarım*, p. 25, the son says that the opinion that someone other than Midhat wrote this letter is groundless. Midhat, however, is reported to have denied the authenticity of the letter, saying, "Those are my ideas, but I have never spoken so impertinently to the Sultan." *Stamboul*, 1 March 1877. Devereux, *First Ottoman Constitutional Period*, p. 96 and n.5, records that Midhat also denied the authenticity to Léouzon le Duc. İnal, *Son sadrıâzamlar*, pp. 358-359, says the letter was undoubtedly a fabrication and that Midhat denied its authenticity. M. T. Gökbilgin in *İslâm ansiklopedisi*, VIII, 279, s.v. Midhat, thinks it conceivable that Midhat sent such a letter. Baykal, "93 meşrutiyeti," p. 66, raises no question as to the authenticity of the letter. *Levant Herald*, 6 February 1877, seems to refer to this letter as a fact.

The first publication of the document, so far as the author knows, was in the *Manchester Guardian*, 16 February 1877, in telegraphic summary datelined Pera via Giurgevo, 13 February. A full version appeared in *The* (London) *Times*, 20 February 1877, taken from the *République Française* of unnamed date, and also in the *Journal des débats* of 20 February 1877, taken from an unnamed English paper! All these versions date the letter as 4 February, not 30 January. Denials of the authenticity followed swiftly. Midhat is quoted as declaring it to the *Neue Freie Presse* a "fabrication composed by his adversaries," and to a Naples newspaper as "apocryphal," which the *Augsburger Allgemeine Zeitung* also reported: *Manchester Guardian*, 24 and 26 February 1877; *Journal des débats*, 25 and 27 February 1877. The appearance of the letter in the European press remains unexplained.

[156] Mahmud Celaleddin, *Mirât-ı hakikat*, I, 268. Cevdet says Midhat thought he was immune from dismissal under the constitution: Mardin, *Cevdet*, p. 139, n.118.

the pretext that all his recommendations had been accepted, it was only to be told to give up the seal of office. He was dismissed as grand vezir on February 5, 1877, and immediately packed off to the imperial yacht, without being allowed to return to his house. The yacht took him to Brindisi, and to exile. The sultan had presumably acted under the exile power clause of article 113 of the constitution, having been furnished some short police reports, as required by that clause, showing that Midhat was dangerous to the state. Certainly Abdül-hamid had the right to dismiss the grand vezir from office. But the legality of the exile, under the constitution, was dubious, since the clause was a part of the article on a state of siege, which did not then exist.[157] The constitution, further, in guarantee of individual liberty, forbade punishment except according to the procedures prescribed by law. The real reason for the exile was not that Midhat was a danger to the state, but that he was a danger to the sultan's concept of his own role in the government. The truth was hinted at in the *hat* of February 5 appointing Edhem Paşa as Midhat's successor; it said that officials must not exceed their competence.[158] More of the truth appeared between the lines of the official communiqué published in the press two days later, which said that Midhat was trying to resurrect the absolutism which Abdülhamid, by issuing the constitution, had suppressed. Midhat, further, had not stopped plots against the sultan's prerogatives. Therefore, to preserve the constitution, the sultan was obliged to get rid of Midhat.[159] Further semiofficial comment was less guarded in following the same line. Midhat did not stay within bounds in upholding the sovereign prestige, said *La Turquie*. The sultan, therefore, had to appoint another vezir who really understood the constitution. To insinuate that Midhat's dismissal was a move against the constitution was more than an evil thought; it was an evil act. As for exile instead of trial, Abdülhamid chose this in order to spare the country more domestic confusion.[160]

The most candid explanation of Midhat's fall and exile was given in confidence to the British Government by the Ottoman under-secretary for justice, Vahan Efendi, who was charged personally by

[157] It first existed in İstanbul in late May 1877 when the fall of Ardahan led to a softa invasion of the chamber of deputies.
[158] *Staatsarchiv*, 32 (1877), #5997.
[159] *Stamboul*, 7 February 1877. A similar proclamation was posted in İstanbul; text in Story, *Ismail Kemal*, pp. 150-151.
[160] *La Turquie*, 8 February 1877, quoted in *Levant Herald*, 10 February.

Abdülhamid to do just this. Midhat, said the sultan's emissary, had assumed a position which was incompatible with the sultan's authority, "took all power into his own hands, seemed disposed to allow the sultan no voice in public affairs," and kept appointments under his own control. He used unbecoming language about the sultan's ideas, "and was surrounded by a party whose language was not such as any Minister ought to countenance." Persons connected with Midhat talked about unnecessary palace expenditures and of replacing Abdül-hamid with some other member of the family. Midhat did not suppress such talk, saying that "he could not interfere with the free expression of opinion." And Midhat allowed people to think that the constitution was his own work, "extorted" from Abdülhamid against the latter's will.[161] Like the parting of Bismarck and Kaiser Wilhelm II in 1890, the parting of Midhat and Abdülhamid II came about because the government was not big enough to hold both the young self-assertive ruler and the older self-assertive statesman.[162] This, despite rumors that Midhat's fall was due to Russian intrigue, to a plot to restore Murad, to Midhat's opposition to the employment of British experts, and other similar concoctions, seems to be the essential truth.[163]

There was some danger that Midhat's exile might provoke a popular demonstration that could embarrass the sultan, for in the capital Midhat was undoubtedly more popular than Abdülhamid. As a precaution the imperial yacht was ordered to wait twenty-four hours in the Sea of Marmara before proceeding, so that a signal for Midhat's return might be sent if necessary. But the exile was so sudden, and opinion about it among officials so divided, that there was no significant demonstration, and probably no leadership for it. Some newspapers suspended themselves voluntarily for a few days, some individuals made their feelings known by writing to newspapers or posting placards demanding Midhat's return, but this was all. And Midhat himself had acquiesced without resistance. A good many among the officials seem to have been happy over the exile, the bulk of the İstanbul population depressed, the press rather divided. Ali Suavi proclaimed joyfully that now equality was achieved, since a grand vezir was exiled where formerly that was the fate only of defenseless

---

[161] *Staatsarchiv,* 32 (1877), #6327.

[162] On the dismissal and exile: A. H. Midhat, *Tabsıra-i ibret,* pp. 195-198; *idem, Life,* pp. 145-146; *idem, Hâtıralarım,* p. 28; Story, *Ismail Kemal,* pp. 147-149.

[163] On rumors see Gallenga, *Two Years,* II, 304-306; ABCFM, Western Turkey Mission II, #488, 8 February 1877; *Levant Herald,* 6, 8, 19, 22, 26 February 1877.

individuals.[164] Ahmed Midhat, Midhat Paşa's old protégé who had just been made director of the imperial printing office, turned against his mentor in his journal *İttihad* and praised the sultan.[165] The division of opinion ensured that Edhem Paşa could take up office as grand vezir without fear of Midhat's immediate return.[166]

The immediate significance of Midhat's exile was that Abdülhamid had proved to himself he could violate the spirit, if not the letter, of the new constitution and get away with it. He was, of course, careful still to pose as a defender of the constitution. But he began immediately to strengthen his grip on the government. The imperial *hat* which named Edhem grand vezir also, in unusual fashion, made more than a dozen other official appointments, as if to indicate that now appointments were in the sultan's own hands.[167] Cevdet, Midhat's opponent, was significantly made minister of the interior, an office in abeyance since Âli's death, and he at once began to keep a file of dossiers on all Porte officials.[168] Ahmed Vefik, also an opponent of Midhat, was, in contradiction to the provisions of the constitution, named president of the chamber of deputies, which was supposed to elect its own slate of candidates. Then various friends of Midhat were arrested, including Namık Kemal, on trumped-up charges. Namık Kemal, acquitted by a tribunal, was nevertheless exiled to Midilli, while Abdülhamid fired the courageous chief judge of the court involved.[169]

Seen in broader perspective, Midhat's exile meant that the Tanzimat period was drawing to a close. This was not for want of further reform decrees, but for want of the driving spirit that Midhat and his associates might have provided. Abdülhamid, not so bad a

---

[164] *Stamboul*, 8, 9, and 10 February 1877. Ali Suavi was now growing incoherent; some of his writing here is nonsense.

[165] *Stamboul*, 8 February and 1 March 1877.

[166] On reactions to the exile: ABCFM, Western Turkey Mission II, #623, 7 February 1877, and #488, 8 February 1877; Kératry, *Mourad V*, pp. 245-251; Gallenga, *Two Years*, II, 342-346; Raschdau, "Die Botschafterkonferenz," pp. 25-26, 28; A. H. Midhat, *Hâtıralarım*, p. 29; *Stamboul*, 10, 22, 28 February and 2 March 1877. In reward Ahmed Midhat was made director of the official gazette, the *Takvim-i vekayi*, and Ali Suavi named head of the Galatasaray *lycée*.

[167] *Levant Herald*, 6 February 1877; Ahmed Midhat, *Üss-i inkılâb*, II, 385-389.

[168] Mardin, *Cevdet*, p. 139, n.118.

[169] *Stamboul*, 10, 12, and 15 February 1877; *Levant Herald*, 16 February 1877; Gallenga, *Two Years*, II, 352-354; İhsan Sungu, *Namık Kemal* (İstanbul, 1941), p. 23.

sultan as he has often been painted, was in his own way a reformer. Like the statesmen of the Tanzimat, he meant to strengthen, improve, and save the Ottoman Empire, but he meant to do it himself. The locus of power was to be in the Palace, not the Porte or the parliament. Abdülhamid had begun by approving the constitution, to help counteract European diplomacy. As soon as he could, he shook off the influence of Midhat and the constitutional reformers who would have checked his power, as his ancestor Mahmud had done away with the Janissary and *derebeyi* controls. It may have been a political mistake for the sultan to get rid of Midhat, for the latter might have controlled opinion and officials in the empire sufficiently to avoid the Russo-Turkish War of 1877-1878 that brought a disastrous defeat to the Turks and complete independence to the provinces of Serbia, Montenegro, and Roumania.[170] Nevertheless, Abdülhamid persisted in his quest for power. When, a year later, he felt that it was safe, he dissolved the second session of the chamber of deputies and called no other for thirty years. The two sessions of March to June 1877 and December 1877 to February 1878 had proven that the deputies had sufficient intelligence and independence of mind to criticize constructively the actions of the administration. The constitutionalists of 1876 were vindicated by the deputies' performance.

In a final explosion to a committee of senators and deputies, one of whom dared to blame the administration for the bad situation at the end of the Russo-Turkish War, and to castigate it for not taking the chamber's advice, Abdülhamid said: "I made a mistake when I wished to imitate my father Abdülmecid, who sought reforms by permission and by liberal institutions. I shall follow in the footsteps of my grandfather, Sultan Mahmud. Like him I now understand that it is only by force that one can move the people with whose protection God has entrusted me."[171] Five years later Abdülhamid expanded on these views to a European journalist: "People are wrong in representing me as opposed to liberty. I know that a country must keep up with the times, but the excess of a liberty to which one is un-

---

[170] This was İzzet's opinion later: *Denkwürdigkeiten*, p. 81.

[171] Hakkı Tarık Us, *Meclis-i Meb'usân, 1293/1877, zabıt ceridesi* (İstanbul, 1940-1954), II, 401, quoted by Robert Devereux, *A Study of the First Ottoman Parliament* (Washington, George Washington University, unpublished M.A. thesis, 1956), p. 179. In this thesis by Devereux, and in his *First Ottoman Constitutional Period*, is the best analysis of the organization and work of the Ottoman parliament, based on the two volumes of reconstructed proceedings by Us, cited above, and other sources.

accustomed is as dangerous as the absence of all liberty." He would, instead, prepare the country for liberty by increasing educational opportunities, he said. But his real objection followed thereafter. "When it was seen that this country could not support a Constitution, and a Parliament which did not entirely represent the country, but only part of the country, people came to me and began to talk about responsibilities. It was another way of reorganizing a Constitution. I refused this. Those who spoke of responsibilities only saw in this a means of substituting their will for mine at the expense of others, and the great mass of the country would only have changed from the will of one to that of another."[172] In an easier situation Abdülhamid might have dismissed the constitutional commission without letting it finish the job, as Friedrich Wilhelm IV of Prussia dissolved the constituent assembly in 1848; or he might simply never have applied the constitution, as Schwarzenberg, acting for his emperor, Franz Joseph of Austria, managed never to apply the Kremsier constitution of 1849. But in the crisis of 1876 to 1878 Abdülhamid felt his way gradually —first weakening the constitutional draft, then getting rid of the chief supporters of the constitution, then proroguing the chamber sine die, but never abolishing the constitution. From his viewpoint, he did well. Palace controlled Porte, and parliament was no more.

From the viewpoint of the constitutionalists, of course, the strangulation of the infant constitution was a disaster. At some point before his death in 1880, while he was in provincial exile, Ziya penned this refrain to what has been called "probably the saddest poem in the Turkish language":

> "Naught but sorrows on the loyal to this Empire ever wait;
> Sheerest madness is devotion to this People and this State."[173]

With the strengthening of Abdülhamid's personal rule, liberal political reform was driven underground or to foreign countries.

Later generations of Turks have often castigated the men of the Tanzimat not so much for their failure to oppose Abdülhamid and to keep the constitution in working order as for their half measures, their superficiality, and their lack of understanding of the fundamental

---

[172] H. de Blowitz, *My Memoirs* (London, 1903), p. 290.
[173] E. J. W. Gibb, *A History of Ottoman Poetry* (London, 1900-1909), V, 68-69.

necessities of Turkish development. The Tanzimat statesmen, it is sometimes said, attempted to import alien institutions and graft them onto Turkish society. They were ignorant of Islamic culture. They should have developed Muslim law, *vakıf*, and the medrese to meet the needs of the age. Instead, they created a fatal dualism of European and Ottoman institutions side by side. They were usually concerned with matters of form only, not of substance. The forms and slogans with which they bemused themselves found no popular following. They introduced institutions of representative government into a society unprepared to receive them. They rejected the absolutism of the sultan only to impose their own absolutism. Or again, critics have said that the Tanzimat reformers were not radical enough. They kept outworn snippets of Islamic culture. They should have abandoned these relics of a dead age and gone more rapidly toward secularism.[174]

Obviously the critics are not in agreement on what was wrong with the Tanzimat. Yet, considered separately and *in vacuo*, each of the criticisms has merit. Considered in the context of the times, however, most of the criticisms appear irrelevant, because they disregard the necessity for both change and continuity in history, for doing what is possible, for grafting the new on the old. Because of the failures of the Tanzimat period, it is easy to make such criticisms. Hayreddin Paşa had voiced some similar opinions in a memorandum of 1882 to Sultan Abdülhamid: "It is impossible to transplant the institutions of one country to another where the temperament of men, their customs and their education as well as climatological conditions are different." He went on to say that the efforts of the past forty years had failed because the Tanzimat statesmen had not been willing to undertake radical reform fitted to the needs of the country.[175] But temperament, customs, and education, of course, disposed the Ottomans to resist any radical reform. Despite the truth of other portions of his memorandum, the critic destroyed himself.

It is more to the point to inquire whether the Tanzimat statesmen

---

[174] For examples of such twentieth-century criticism, see Niyazi Berkes, ed., *Turkish Nationalism and Western Civilization: Selected Essays of Ziya Gökalp* (New York, 1959), pp. 133, 146, 223, 237, 249, 260, 262, 270, 276, 286-290, 307-308; Okandan, *Umumî âmme hukukumuz*, pp. 111-112, 203-204; Onar, "Transformations," pp. 779-780; Mehmed Fuad Köprülü, "L'institution du Vakouf," *Vakıflar dergisi*, II (1942), 3-48; Âfet İnan, "*Aperçu général sur l'histoire économique de l'Empire turc-ottoman* (İstanbul, 1941), p. 16.

[175] A. Demeerseman, "Idéal politique de Khéréddine: Sa valeur morale," *IBLA*, 20:79 (3ème trimestre, 1957), 205-206.

achieved what they sought. Their main objective was to preserve the Ottoman Empire by reinvigorating it. This involved reforming the central administration, creating flexible provincial administration which would combine central control with a local voice in government, and maintaining the allegiance of all peoples of the empire. Only thus could the intervention of foreign powers be warded off, separatist drives of the minorities be blunted, and the empire again be made a going concern. The many reform decrees aimed at these objectives introduced into the empire in varying degrees western political and administrative forms, some western law, some western educational concepts and institutions, and the concept of equal rights for all subjects of whatever race or creed. It became fashionable in Europe to regard these reform decrees as so many varieties of waste paper, designed simply to deceive the powers and to postpone their effective intervention to improve the state of affairs in the empire. Up to a point, this was a valid judgment. Certainly many of the decrees had served a diplomatic purpose. None, furthermore, was applied with complete success. Good men were lacking in sufficient numbers to administer good measures. Popular education and understanding were not yet equal to accepting the needed changes. The base of economic reform for a vigorous empire was lacking. The Tanzimat represented the views of a small bureaucratic and intellectual elite, and not even of all that elite. Such reform from the top down is less likely to achieve success than reform that has vigorous popular support. One can go further, to acknowledge that the critics were frequently right in saying that external forms were changed while the substance was not. In addition to coming from the top down and the outside in, reform also sometimes came backward: for instance, parliamentary procedure was introduced into the central government in the Supreme Council in 1839, the principle of representation in the same body in 1856, but actual election of representatives —and then only indirect—first with the constitution of 1876.

When all this is admitted, it is still possible to maintain that the condition of the empire, aside from the public debt, was better by the time of the constitution of 1876 than it had been in 1839, or even in 1856. Though like all governments the Porte was more successful in making plans than in putting them into effect, something had been accomplished. Administration was a little more efficient. The organs both of central and of provincial government were better adapted to the demands of the age, though good men to fill the offices were still in short supply. Justice was a little better. The westernized codes were enforced in part. Where in 1839 the emphasis was primarily on security of life and property, enough had been achieved in this regard so that by 1876 the emphasis was on equality. The educational system was improved. An active press had developed, partly with government encouragement and partly despite government. The non-Muslim millets were better administered despite the many flaws still present. The principle of Osmanlılık had made some progress, though it had aroused much opposition. The representative principle had become established in government, both local and national. The constitution of 1876—developing out of the Tanzimat decrees since 1839, the vilayet and millet reforms, and the New Ottoman program—was the culmination of the reform movement. Given the temper of the times, and the psychological resistance to change, the achievement was considerable. It by no means measured up to the standards set by the reform decrees themselves, but perhaps this is a false standard. It is as fair or as unfair to compare Ottoman performance to promise as it is to compare the performance of elected western governments to their campaign platforms. The important fact is that the tone of public life had by 1876 changed perceptibly. The Ottoman Empire was now irrevocably committed to the path of modernization and westernization. Some progress had been made. The creeping fact was more significant than the sweeping promise.

In the long run, the most signal failure of the Tanzimat period was the attempt to hold the empire together with the doctrine of Osmanlılık. Though equality was increased, and though the 1876 constitution gave promise of furthering it, the effort was probably both too little and too late. Yet it had to be made. The Ottoman statesmen could not have been expected to prepare the empire for partition. They were simply unable to meet the challenge of the new nationalism among minority peoples, supported as it was by great power action. It is worth pointing out that in the Tanzimat period the Ottoman Empire lost definitively not one bit of territory, and even gained a little through the Crimean War and through conquest in Arabia. But the bonds of control over Serbia, Montenegro, Roumania, and Egypt had been loosened; Crete and the Lebanon had new special status; and the Bulgars were going rapidly in the same direction. Probably nothing that the Tanzimat statesmen could have done would have kept the empire as it was. Many Christians moved out of a separate millet consciousness into a nationalist consciousness without ever having wholly accepted Osmanlılık. The Turks found in the Tanzimat period, through the patriotic Islamic reaction to Europe and the writings of the New Ottomans, the seeds of their own future nationalism, without ever having wholly accepted Osmanlılık in its Tanzimat connotation. Even the Tanzimat statesmen believed, for the most part, in a Turkish-colored Osmanlılık. The equality finally attained, years after the Tanzimat, was that of competing independent national sovereignties, instead of the equality of a brotherhood of different races and creeds within one empire.

But these results came after 1876. In its day the Tanzimat may be considered either a qualified success or a qualified failure. Whichever view one adopts, it is a period significant for many beginnings in administration, law, education and the like, which carried on through Abdülhamid's reign into the Young Turk period and the era of the present-day republic. The Tanzimat period was a seedtime. These beginnings, usually western-inspired, did sometimes create new institutions alongside old. This was not necessarily a fatal dualism, as critics have said, but may, on the contrary, be viewed as a part of the normal process of growth. No sweeping reforms like Atatürk's could have been effected in the years 1856 to 1876; but his reforms could not have been effected in his own time without the preparation that the Tanzimat gave. The comparatively cautious steps of Âli and Fuad, and the still reasonably cautious moves of Midhat, were of fundamental importance. These men were not, as has often been charged, reckless westernizers, but went only as fast as possible without causing a fatal reaction, and as the way opened. The preparation of the Tanzimat period was not only of new or reformed institutions, and of men with experience in them, but of minds—a greater emphasis on individual liberties, on the importance of the people, on government by representation and consultation, on public opinion, on the concept of territorial sovereignty as opposed to monarchical sovereignty. The constitution of 1876, which epitomized these concepts, was suspended by Abdülhamid, but he could not snuff out the new mentality. Cevdet Paşa, in 1892, saw fit to warn the sultan about the power of public opinion.[176] The constitution remained a symbol to which men would again rally in 1908.

[176] Mardin, *Cevdet*, p. 10, n.7.

GLOSSARY

berat - a patent or warrant

bid'at - innovation, in a pejorative sense

çorbacı - a notable in a Christian community

derebeyi - "lord of the valley," a local semi-autonomous ruler

efendi - a title used after the name, like "Mr."; also the usual designation for a government clerk or other educated person

esnaf - artisans; artisan or trade gild

evkaf - plural of vakıf; also the government office in charge of these religious trusts

eyalet - province; the term commonly used before 1867

ferman - an edict or decree of the sultan

fetva - a formal opinion on a question of religious law by a müfti

gâvur - a non-Muslim, infidel; an uncomplimentary term

hat - a writing; in the forms hatt-ı hümayun and hatt-ı şerif an edict of the sultan to his grand vezir (see Chapt. 1, n.61)

irade - a decree (usually of the sultan)

kadı - a judge

kaime - paper money; treasury obligations

kariye - a commune or town quarter in the vilayet organization

kaymakam - governor of a kaza, in the vilayet organization

kaza - subdivision of a sancak, in the vilayet organization

kocabaşı - elected headman of a community

mazbata - a protocol, minute, or written report

mecelle - the codified Muslim civil law, done by Cevdet's commission

meclis - an assembly, council (used in many combinations)

meclis-i umumî - a general assembly; as of notables in the capital, or in the vilayet capital under the 1867 organization

medrese - the higher Muslim school

mekteb - school, particularly primary or grammar school

millet - religious community; in later usage, "nation"

mirî - belonging to the state; especially, state-owned land

muhtar - headman of a village or commune

mutasarrıf - governor of a sancak

müdür - governor of a nahiye

müfettiş - inspector; commissioner on inspection

müfti - Muslim jurist or juriconsult

mülk - property held in fee simple; freehold property

nahiye - a group of hamlets or farms, subdivision of the kaza in the vilayet organization

Osmanlılık - "Ottomanism," the concept of equality and brotherhood of all Ottoman subjects

rüşdiye - the higher level of state primary school

sancak - formerly a province; in the vilayet organization, a subdivision of a vilayet

softa - a Muslim theological student

şeriat - the religious law of Islam

şeyh - leader of a tribe; or a head of a Muslim religious order

şeyhülislâm - chief müfti of the capital and chief Muslim official of the empire, ranking just after the grand vezir

tekke - a dervish convent

tımar - formerly, a fief

ulema - the body of learned men of Islam

vakıf - a pious foundation or charitable trust

vali - governor of a vilayet, and earlier of an eyalet

valide sultan - mother of the reigning sultan; sultan-mother

vatan - fatherland, in the later nineteenth-century meaning

vezir - the highest rank classification in Ottoman officialdom; the grand vezir was the sultan's chief official

vilayet - the term for a province after 1867

APPENDICES

APPENDIX A

Foreign Intervention in Ottoman Affairs
Under the Paris Treaty

Article 9 of the Treaty of Paris of March 30, 1856, said that the communication of the Hatt-ı Hümayun to the signatories of the treaty "cannot in any case, give to the said powers the right to interfere, either collectively or separately, in the relations of His Majesty the Sultan with his subjects nor in the internal administration of his empire."[1] But the mere fact that the *hat* was officially recognized in the treaty thrust it into the area of diplomatic concern, and damaged the prestige of the Ottoman government, as did also the phrase in the same article that Abdülmecid's ferman "records his generous intentions toward the Christian population of his empire." Reşid argued, in effect, that the mere mention of the *hat* in the Paris treaty, in whatever phraseology, made it an integral part of the treaty and would give the powers a right of intervention and supervision over reforms.[2] This was an extreme interpretation. It could be argued also that the nonintervention pledge should be taken at its face value, as some Turks did in later crisis periods.[3]

It soon became obvious that the powers did not regard the nonintervention pledge as binding, and in the next twenty years they made frequent representations, based on the Hatt-ı Hümayun's promises, to the Porte. Stratford deplored the prohibition on intervention,[4] and soon was proposing to Abdülmecid that he put teeth in the Hatt-ı Hümayun by calling to İstanbul an Anglo-Turkish contingent of twenty thousand, all of whose superior officers were English.[5] By 1876 Stratford argued that the nonintervention pledge was "limited and conditional" and, further, that article 9 said only that the

---

[1] Treaty text in Gabriel Noradounghian, *Recueil d'actes internationaux de l'Empire ottoman* (Paris, 1897-1903), III, 70-79.

[2] Cevdet Paşa, *Tezâkir 1-12*, ed. by Cavid Baysun (Ankara, 1953), pp. 72, 82.

[3] Cf. Mehmed Memduh, *Mirât-ı şuûnat* (İzmir, 1328), p. 58, in discussing the Andrassy Note of 1875.

[4] Stratford to Clarendon, 19 March 1856, in Stanley Lane-Poole, *The Life of the Right Hon. Stratford Canning* (London, 1888), II, 442.

[5] Prokesch to Buol #37B Réservé, 8 May 1856, HHS, XII/56.

communication of the edict to the powers did not warrant intervention, but that there were certainly many other grounds justifying interference.[6]

Likewise the treaty of April 15, 1856, in which Britain, France, and Austria guaranteed the integrity of the Ottoman Empire was destined to remain a dead letter. Cevdet argued that this treaty also, though advantageous, damaged Ottoman independence and sovereignty because the empire was not a signatory.[7]

APPENDIX B

Population of the Ottoman Empire

There are no trustworthy figures on the population of the empire. Reasonably accurate statistical methods have not existed in Turkey until very recent years, under the republic. Not only have the census methods been defective, but eastern peoples generally have resisted being counted, since this meant to them only that taxation and military conscription would follow. The census has generally been in bad odor.[1] This reluctance to be counted also led to a reluctance to vote when elections for the first Ottoman parliament were held in 1877, again for fear of taxation.[2] The first "modern" census taken in the Ottoman Empire under Mahmud II was, as a matter of fact, primarily for conscription purposes.[3] Karal explains the methods used. One general method of estimating the population was to count houses and multiply by the estimated average number of a family under one roof.[4]

The figure for mid-century which has found greatest acceptance is between 35,000,000 and 36,000,000. This total is derived from a census taken in 1844 for military service.[5] Midhat Paşa in 1877 accepted the

---

[6] Stratford's letter to *The* (London) *Times*, 3 January 1876.
[7] Cevdet, *Tezâkir*, p. 88.

~~~~~~~~~~

[1] Cf. II Sam. 24: 1-15.
[2] Abdurrahman Şeref, *Tarih musahabeleri* (İstanbul, 1339), p. 213.
[3] Enver Ziya Karal, *Nizam-ı cedit ve Tanzimat devirleri* (Ankara, 1947), pp. 159-160.
[4] Cf. Henry J. Van Lennep, *Travels in Little-Known Parts of Asia Minor* (London, 1870), I, 4-5; ABCFM, Armenian Mission V, #166, 3 April 1857. See, further, on census difficulties and errors, H. F. B. Lynch, *Armenia* (London, 1901), II, 414-415.
[5] Great Britain, *Parliamentary Papers*, 1857-1858, vol. 58, *Accounts and Papers*,

APPENDIX C

figure of 36,000,000.[6] Other estimates have ranged as high as 56,000,000 (in 1874).[7] A semiofficial tabulation of 1867 placed the total population at an even 40,000,000.[8] Every writer on the Ottoman Empire selected whatever figures seemed to him most reliable, or else those which he wanted to prove a point about minorities. Often these figures were given on the authority of others; sometimes they were based partly on investigations conducted on the spot.[9]

APPENDIX C

Âli Paşa's Political Testament

Mehmed Emin Âli Paşa is supposed to have written a political testament which was published in the newspapers of the time after

---

vol. 26, Foreign Countries, p. 162; Abdolonyme Ubicini, *Letters on Turkey*, tr. by Lady Easthope (London, 1856), I, 18-25. İbrahim Hakkı Aykol describes the deficiencies of the 1844 census in *Tanzimat*, I (İstanbul, 1940), 548-550, but calls it the first census in the whole empire on modern principles.

[6] Ali Haydar Midhat, *Life of Midhat Pasha* (London, 1903), p. 167, Midhat to Kâmil Bey, November 1877.

[7] Edouard Scrosoppi, *L'empire ottoman au point de vue politique* (Florence, 1874), I, 257-277.

[8] Salaheddin Bey, *La Turquie à l'exposition universelle de 1867* (Paris, 1867), pp. 210-214.

[9] Population estimates may be found in: Aykol, *Tanzimat*, I, 549, n.2; Ami Boué, *La Turquie d'Europe* (Paris, 1840), II, 32; E. H. Michelsen, *The Ottoman Empire and its Resources* (London, 1853), pp. 139-140; Alfred de Bessé, *The Turkish Empire* (Philadelphia, 1854), pp. 184-185; ABCFM, Armenian Mission VIII, #59, April 1857; Edmond Chertier, *Réformes en Turquie* (Paris, 1858), pp. 10-11; B. C. Collas, *La Turquie en 1864* (Paris, 1864), pp. 38-40; A. Synvet, *Traité de géographie générale de l'Empire ottoman* (Constantinople, 1872), pp. 214-215; Ali Suavi, *A propos de l'Herzégovine* (Paris, 1875), pp. 69-74; Ubicini and Pavet de Courteille, *État présent de l'Empire ottoman* (Paris, 1876), pp. 17-70; James L. Farley, *Turks and Christians* (London, 1876), pp. 96-97; G. G. B. St. Clair and C. A. Brophy, *Twelve Years' Study of the Eastern Question* (London, 1877), p. 245; Vital Cuinet, *La Turquie d'Asie* (Paris, 1890), I, preface; Karl Süssheim, *Der Zusammenbruch des türkischen Reiches in Europa* (Munich, 1914), p. 78; Halil İnalcık, *Tanzimat ve Bulgar meselesi* (Ankara, 1943), p. 1, n.1; Friedrich Wilhelm von Reden, *Die Türkei und Griechenland* (Frankfurt a.M., 1856), pp. 66-71; F. Bianconi, *La question d'Orient dévoilée* (Paris, 1876), pp. 12-13; idem, *Ethnographie et statistique de la Turquie d'Europe* (Paris, 1877).

Isidore Loeb, *La situation des israélites en Turquie* (Paris, 1877), p. 2, gives figures for Jewish populations of various Ottoman cities; Sarkis Atamian, *The Armenian Community* (New York, 1955), pp. 43-44, appraises figures for the Armenian population; A. Synvet, *Les Grecs de l'Empire ottoman* (Constantinople, 1878), pp. 8-9, gives figures for Greeks, which fail to add correctly; Lorenz Rigler, *Die Türkei und deren Bewohner* (Vienna, 1852), I, 141, gives 1846 census figures for İstanbul.

415

his death.[1] I have not seen a copy of the document in Turkish, though presumably it has been published in that language.[2]

I have found only the French version of Âli's testament, which appeared in 1910.[3] The only reference to this French edition in other works that I have noticed is by Edouard Driault and Michel Lhéritier, who list the testament under "published documents" in their bibliography and apparently accept it as genuine.[4] The document is addressed to Sultan Abdülaziz, its first paragraph states explicitly that the author is writing a political testament, and it is provided with Âli's name at the end and dated "Bebek, September 1871." There is no indication of the original language of the testament, and no editor or translator is named. Âli could have written in French, but it is more likely that he would have written in Turkish. For Abdülaziz, Turkish would have been necessary, since his French was scanty. The date offers no clew to authenticity, since it was public knowledge that Âli died in his house at Bebek (a suburb of İstanbul on the Bosporus) on September 6, 1871. A brief review of Âli's life prefixed to this French version states that Âli died in 1872, an error which is insufficient to impugn the genuineness of the document.

The testament is interesting as a review of the previous decade of Turkish history, and as a summary of the supposed views held by Âli on foreign and domestic political matters. It would be possible to conclude from internal evidence that the document is genuinely Âli's, since almost everything in it accords with his known views, and some parts echo his famous 1867 memorandum on reforms. The testament recommends that Christians be taken into the Ottoman army, which Âli really may have opposed, though he had in his 1867 memorandum adumbrated this opinion also. One sentence

[1] Mehmed Gâlib, "Tarihten bir sahife—Âli ve Fuad Paşaların vasiyetnameleri," *Tarih-i osmanî encümeni mecmuası*, 1:2 (1329), 70. The author does not specify the newspapers, their date or place of publication, or the language in which the testament appeared.

[2] The late Walter L. Wright, Jr., in letters to the author of May 23 and October 28, 1939, stated that he was sure that "Âli . . . left a sort of political testament" and that it has been printed in Turkish. The bibliography of *Tanzimat*, I (İstanbul, 1940), 982, lists *Âli Paşanın vasiyetnamesi* (İstanbul, no date) as a separate publication; but the late J. K. Birge, in a letter to the author of October 21, 1948, says that although the testament is listed in this volume he is told that it never actually appeared in print.

[3] [Aali Pacha], "Testament politique," *La Revue de Paris* 17:7 (1 April 1910), 505-524; 17:9 (1 May 1910), 105-124. A separate offprint of the same was published as Aali-Pacha, *Testament politique* (Coulommiers, 1910).

[4] *Histoire diplomatique de la Grèce* (Paris, 1925-1926), III, ix.

may indicate that the document was composed or altered by an unknown hand: a direct quotation attributed to Abdülaziz, who asks why Napoleon III did not open his veins with scissors rather than submit to defeat by the Prussian armies in 1870. Such a quotation may be genuine, particularly if the testament originally appeared at the time of Âli's death in 1871, although it sounds like a later justification for the claim that Abdülaziz committed suicide by that method in 1876 and was not murdered.

Mehmed Gâlib, in the article above referred to, conjectures that Âli's testament was written by a Persian, Melküm Han (usually called Malkom Khan in the West), and that Melküm did this to gain revenge on Âli because the latter had refused to appoint Melküm to a post in the Ottoman government despite Fuad's sponsorship.[5] But this is only conjecture, not proof. Since the testament did castigate Abdülaziz for excessive expenditures, its publication would turn the sultan against the memory of Âli; but this is small revenge, and the testament does not attempt the greater revenge of grossly distorting Âli's political views. It is theoretically possible that Melküm could have written Âli's testament. Melküm was a curious character, the son of an Armenian convert to Islam, educated at least partly in France, and the founder of a Freemasonic lodge in Tehran. Melküm could easily have written in French, and may have known Âli as a brother Mason. He was acquainted with Âli, and was in İstanbul after having fled Iran and the shah's displeasure. The year after Âli's death, Melküm was appointed Persian minister to London.[6]

Mehmed Gâlib, in his attempted proof that the testament is not Âli's, fails to argue that it was not customary for Ottoman statesmen to write political testaments. Yet this is true.[7] Âli, however, was sick for several months before his death, and might have used the occasion of his illness to write a testament.

None of these considerations is sufficient either to prove or disprove the authenticity of the testament, or to prove who wrote it if Âli did not. My own feeling is that Âli would not have done this sort of thing, but this is again conjecture. Whoever did write the testament

[5] Mehmed Gâlib, "Tarihten bir sahife," pp. 73-74.
[6] On Melküm see *ibid.*; Percy Sykes, *A History of Persia* (London, 1930), I, 397-399; Charles Mismer, *Souvenirs du monde musulman* (Paris, 1892), pp. 132-143.
[7] The late Dr. Abdülhak Adnan-Adıvar gave great weight to this argument: interview with the author, March 29, 1947.

had a good knowledge of the state of the Ottoman Empire and of Âli's political views. Although this verisimilitude seems to indicate that the testament may be used with caution, I have actually placed no reliance on it.

APPENDIX D

Was Sultan Abdülaziz Murdered?

In 1881 Midhat was arrested, interrogated, and tried for implication in the murder of Abdülaziz. A complete theory of conspiracy to depose Abdülaziz, and to assassinate him thereafter, was worked out by Abdülhamid and his henchmen. Confessions, probably paid for, were obtained from several servants who said they had held Abdülaziz while one slit his arms with a knife. Other evidence, probably also contrived, was introduced to prove that not only Murad, his mother, some other palace functionaries, and two imperial brothers-in-law were involved, but also a "directing commission" of Mehmed Rüşdi, Hüseyin Avni, Midhat, and Hayrullah, which controlled the government at that time. Midhat was given a rather farcical, though public, trial. He was then convicted and sentenced to death. This was changed to life imprisonment and exile to Taif, in Arabia, where Midhat was strangled in 1884. A. H. Midhat, *The Life of Midhat Pasha* (London, 1903) and *idem, Mirât-ı hayret* (İstanbul, 1325) give extensive accounts of much of this. In İsmail Hakkı Uzunçarşılı, *Midhat ve Rüştü Paşaların tevkiflerine dair vesikalar* (Ankara, 1946) appears most clearly the charge of complicity in murder, with the outline of the supposed plot, in the report on the 1881 interrogation of Mehmed Rüşdi; see especially pp. 135-137, 147-148. Mehmed Rüşdi's answer to this, p. 148, was, "This is an open lie." At the end of his interrogation the inquisitors asked what his defense was against their proof that Abdülaziz had died by another hand, and their demonstration of those involved in the murder. He replied: "I have no defense. What shall I defend? If the causes were thus may Allah and the Prophet and the whole world be damned" (p. 167). Midhat also disclaimed all knowledge of the alleged murder by hired servants (pp. 90-99). Midhat's comment on the indictment drawn up against him for his trial was that it was correct in just two places: the *besmele* ("invocation") at the start and the date at the end (A. H. Midhat,

Mirât-ı hayret, p. 217). The whole charge of conspiracy and murder betrays a pathological fear on the part of Abdülhamid II that he might be deposed like his uncle or might be assassinated, and a fear of those who had twice carried through depositions of his predecessors. The denials of Midhat and Mehmed Rüşdi, though they were interested parties, are more convincing than the charges, however detailed and circumstantial and supported by confessions.

Cevdet Paşa, often associated with Midhat although a personal antagonist in 1876, severely tarnished his otherwise good name by lending his support to Abdülhamid's charges and the inquisition of Midhat. Cevdet further, and evidently not honestly, altered slightly his original account of the events of the day of Abdülaziz's death, to replace his original statement of suicide with a more ambiguous one allowing the possibility of murder: Ebül'ulâ Mardin, *Medenî hukuk cephesinden Ahmet Cevdet Paşa* (İstanbul, 1946), pp. 258-259.

APPENDIX E

Did Abdülhamid Sign a Pledge to Abdicate?

Sir Edwin Pears, writing in about 1916, said that "the belief almost universally entertained among the Turks is that there was such a document."[1] What became of it is a mystery, for which he offers two rumored solutions, one of which was that Midhat sent it to London. Others have testified to belief in the same document. Georges Dorys, a Greek journalist in İstanbul, and said to have been close to the Palace, wrote in 1901 that Midhat Paşa had obliged Abdülhamid to give him such a written pledge, which Midhat then placed in good hands in London.[2] Albert Fua, a prominent Young Turk exile and writer of the 1890's, goes so far as to say that Midhat got the document from Abdülhamid (on August 31, the wrong date) at the ceremony of girding at Eyüb, when the Mevlevi *şeyh* of Konya refused on legal grounds to proceed with the ceremony since Murad was not yet legally deposed.[3] This sort of story sounds like wishful thinking on the part of later Young Turks who wanted to depose Abdülhamid.

---

[1] Edwin Pears, *The Life of Abdul Hamid* (New York, 1917), pp. 42-43.
[2] Georges Dorys, *Abdul Hamid intime* (Paris, 1901), p. 42.
[3] Albert Fua, *Abdul Hamid II et Mourad V* (Paris, 1909), pp. 33-34.

The fact that some later scholars have tended to accept the story of a promise, written or unwritten, to abdicate proves nothing.[4]

But there are some who believed in an abdication pledge whose word carries more weight. Midhat's personal secretary, who served him in 1876, wrote that on August 31, 1876, the day of his accession, Abdülhamid signed such a promise, which was then sealed and kept by Midhat.[5] But it is not clear that Vasıf ever saw the document. He is not always trustworthy in his recollections, as other evidence in his book makes plain. The major source for the story of the signed abdication pledge is, however, Midhat's own son, Ali Haydar Midhat. When he published his *Life of Midhat Pasha* (London, 1903) he made no mention of such a document. But in the rather different French biography of his father he explains that since 1903 he has found among his father's papers proof that at the Musluoğlu interview Abdülhamid promised to quit the throne if Murad regained his health. Now he can document the rumor. But the "proof" he gives is the translation of a note written by Midhat to his wife in 1881, when he was arrested by Abdülhamid in İzmir.[6] The original Turkish text of the note is given in three other works published by the son.[7] Its brief text says that inside a black portfolio, in a blue envelope, is a document on the imperial accession, which should be given to whoever will be the heir of the sultanate. Send it to M. Mayer the banker at 6 East India Avenue in London. If this can't be done, it should be destroyed, so as not to fall into the hands of officials.

This, of course, is proof of nothing, since the document to which Midhat's note refers is not adequately described. Ali Haydar Midhat refers to it as a pact or written agreement (*mukavelename*) between Midhat and the heir Hamid Efendi, but this is his term, not his father's. And, according to the son, Midhat's wife destroyed the document, having no chance to send it to London.[8] The son of Süleyman Paşa also believed in the existence of such a document, called

[4] Riza Izzet, *La Turquie réformatrice et Midhat Pacha* (Lille, 1913), pp. 65, 68; Harold Temperley, "British Policy towards Parliamentary Rule and Constitutionalism in Turkey (1830-1914)," *Cambridge Historical Journal*, IV (1933), 173.

[5] Clician Vassif, *Son Altesse Midhat-Pacha* (Paris, 1909), p. 75.

[6] A. H. Midhat, *Midhat Pacha. Sa vie—son oeuvre* (Paris, 1908), p. 65. This was published before the 1908 revolution.

[7] *Midhat Paşa, Hayat-ı siyâsiyesi*, I: *Tabsira-i ibret* (İstanbul, 1325), 394; *Midhat Paşa* (Cairo, 1322), p. 469; *Hâtıralarım* (İstanbul, 1946), p. 135.

[8] *Ibid.*

by him a *sened* ("written agreement," "convention"). His evidence comes, however, entirely from two of Ali Haydar Midhat's works.[9] Osman Nuri also relies on the same evidence, although, unlike Süleyman's son, he quotes the note inaccurately.[10] All this then goes back to the note that Ali Haydar Midhat found in his father's papers some twenty-five years after the arrest of 1881.

The nearest thing to a contemporary statement by one of the principals is contained in a document from Midhat's interrogation in 1881. His questioners alleged that his private secretary, Vasıf, had said in various circles that Abdülhamid signed a pledge containing conditions concerning his accession and that Midhat later sent it to England. Midhat's answer, as recorded, was that he had never said such a thing, the charge was false, and that his secretary, a truthful man, should be questioned directly.[11]

It may be argued, as some have, that the existence of such a signed abdication pledge, or Abdülhamid's belief in its existence, was a fundamental reason for the arrest, trial, exile, and murder of Midhat. But Abdülhamid had reason enough to fear Midhat, who had been instrumental in deposing two sultans and in promulgating a constitution that limited the sovereign powers. And it seems unlikely that Abdülhamid, in view of his patent opposition to any sort of conditional rule, would have signed such a paper. In any case, no documents seem now to remain from the confrontation of Midhat and the heir Abdülhamid.[12]

[9] Süleyman Paşa zade Sami, ed., *Süleyman Paşa muhakemesi* (İstanbul, 1328), p. 52 and n.2.

[10] Osman Nuri, *Abdülhamid-i Sani ve devr-i saltanatı* (İstanbul, 1327), I, 98.

[11] İbnülemin Mahmud Kemal İnal, *Osmanlı devrinde son sadrıâzamlar* (İstanbul, 1940-1953), p. 411.

[12] Bekir Sıtkı Baykal, "93 meşrutiyeti," *Belleten*, 9:21/22 (January-April 1942), 51, n.12.

BIBLIOGRAPHY

NOTE

The titles listed hereafter represent perhaps three quarters of the works used. Some of the less important are not given where a reference in a footnote or two is sufficient. A few works which have little to contribute to the subject are, however, included where their range of subject, general standard reputation, or their authorship would lead one to expect better treatment of the Tanzimat period; the comments will indicate which these titles are. Most of the general bibliographies which give a starting point for research into this period have been omitted. They may be found by following the leads given in sections M and s of the American Historical Association's *Guide to Historical Literature* (New York, 1961). A few bibliographies, because of their obscurity or their special usefulness or both, are inserted in the alphabetized listing of books and periodical articles.

UNPUBLISHED DOCUMENTS

American Board of Commissioners for Foreign Missions, Archives (cited as ABCFM). On deposit in the Houghton Library, Harvard University, Cambridge, Mass.

A valuable source, especially on provincial conditions. These are volumes of manuscript reports by missionaries of the Congregational Church scattered all over the Ottoman Empire. Volumes are grouped under heads of Armenian Mission, Assyrian Mission, Syrian Mission, Western Turkey Mission, Central Turkey Mission, Eastern Turkey Mission, and are numbered within each series. Within each volume, arrangement of reports is alphabetical by missionaries, and chronological under each name. Largely concerned with mission problems, the reports inevitably include much information on political, social, and economic conditions in the empire. Used for the years 1854-1877.

Austria, Haus- Hof- und Staatsarchiv, Politisches Archiv (cited as HHS). Vienna.

Volumes of reports from Constan-tinople contain a wealth of information on Ottoman internal conditions as well as on diplomatic affairs. Prokesch-Osten was a seasoned observer. Volumes XII/56, XII/57, and XII/58 used, for 1856.

France, Archives des Affaires Etrangères, Correspondance Politique (cited as AEE). Paris.

Used Turquie 341 (July-September 1859), 371 (May-June 1867), 404 (May-June 1876). In general, not so informative as the British reports.

Great Britain, Public Record Office, Foreign Office Archives (cited as FO). London.

Selected volumes of dispatches from the embassy in Constantinople used, 1856 to 1876, from volume FO 78/-1173 to volume FO 78/2468, especially for the years 1856, 1859, 1867, 1871-1873, 1875-1876. Also several volumes of the Constantinople embassy archives, in the FO 195 series, for 1867. Though diplomatic business is paramount, there is much reporting on internal politics and conditions in the Ottoman Empire, together with enclosures which are often valuable.

Sweden, Svenska Riksarkivet, Diplomatica Samlingen (cited as SRA). Stockholm.
Beskickningen i Konstantinopels (Legation in Constantinople) dispatches used for occasional periods of crisis: 1856, 1859, 1867. Detailed information.

Trowbridge, Tillman C., *Notes of a Tour in Armenia, 1858*. Holograph, in ABCFM, Armenian Mission VIII, #291.
Deserves special mention because of fine account of conditions around Van, Bitlis, Muş, and Erzurum in 1858-1859.

United States National Archives, Department of State (cited as USNA). Washington.
Legation dispatches 1853 to 1877 in eighteen volumes, Turkey 14 to Turkey 31. Spotty in value, depending on the minister. Contain occasional dispatches of great value, and enclosures of articles, proclamations, et cetera.
Consular dispatches of less value. Used: Egypt V (1868-1870), Egypt VI (1870-1872), Egypt XX (1876), Constantinople XI (1874-1876), Smyrna VII (1863-1870), Smyrna VIII (1870-1875), Smyrna IX (1875-1880), Tripoli IX (1873-1880), Tunis XI (1872-1877), Beirut V (1864-1867), Beirut XIV (1875-1880).

PUBLISHED OFFICIAL DOCUMENTS

Archives Diplomatiques. Paris, 1861 ff.
Annual volumes reproducing official documents of all sorts.

Aristarchi Bey, Grégoire, *Législation ottomane, ou recueil des lois, règlements, ordonnances, traités, capitulations et autres documents officiels de l'Empire ottoman*. 7 vols. Constantinople, 1873-1888.
Title varies after vol. IV. First four volumes include laws and ordinances to 1874; vol. V covers 1874-1878; vols. VI and VII translate the *Mecelle*. Sometimes catalogued under name of Demetrius Nicolaides, the publisher, and vols. VI-VII sometimes under name of Takvor Baghtchebanoglou, the translator, who was in the Tercüme odası. George Young, *Corps de droit*, I, xiii, notes flaws in this work, but for Tanzimat period documents it is preferable to Young, because earlier and more complete; occasionally also preferable to *Düstur* for the same reasons, as well as that some official documents were originally in French.

Austria, Auswärtige Angelegenheiten, *Correspondenzen des Kaiserlichköniglichen Ministeriums des Äussern*. 8 fasc. in 2 vols. Vienna, 1866-1874.
Largely on diplomacy, but occasional reflections on internal affairs in Turkey.

Belin, [François Alphonse], "Charte des Turcs," *Journal asiatique*, Series III:9 (January 1840), 5-29.
A more literal translation of the 1839 Hatt-ı Şerif of Gülhane than the official French text. Annotated, with Turkish text on facing pages.

Bianchi, Thomas Xavier, *Khaththy Humaïoun, ou Charte impériale ottomane du 18 février 1856, en français et en turc; suivie de . . . notes et d'explications. . . .* Paris, 1856.
Texts in Turkish and French, with valuable comments.

————, *Le nouveau guide de la conversation en français et en turc . . . suivi . . . du Khaththi chérif . . . du 3 novembre 1839 . . .* , 2nd ed. Paris, 1852.
Gives Osmanli as well as French text.

Constitution ottomane promulguée le 7 Zilhidjé 1294 (11/23 Décembre 1876). Constantinople, 1876.
Official version. Gives also Abdülhamid's *hat* of proclamation.

Fisher, Stanley, *Ottoman Land Laws, Containing the Ottoman Land Code and Later Legislation Affecting Land. . . .* London, 1919.
Gives the 1858 code in English. Annotated. A handbook made for use in Cyprus.

BIBLIOGRAPHY

Giacometti, G., *Russia's Work in Turkey: a revelation.* Edgar Whitaker, trans. London, 1877.

A small volume of purported documents of Ignatyev and Russian agents in the Balkans, covering 1871-1873. Published in January 1877 in İstanbul as *Les responsabilités*, and in Turkish as *Mes'uliyet*. For comment on authenticity see *Levant Herald*, 8 February 1877; Sumner, *Russia and the Balkans*, p. 681; Langer, *European Alliances*, p. 68; Harris, *Diplomatic History*, p. 42, n.147. If not authentic, the documents have verisimilitude.

Gözübüyük, A. Şeref, and Suna Kili, *Türk anayasa metinleri, Tanzimattan bügüne kadar.* [Turkish constitution texts, from the Tanzimat to the present.] Ankara, 1957.

Reproduces without commentary the decrees of 1839 and 1856, and the 1876 constitution, in new Turkish characters.

Great Britain, *Parliamentary Papers.* London, various dates.

The later volumes of the series for each year, with the subtitle *Accounts and Papers*, carry many command papers on Turkey which provide detailed information not only on diplomatic events, but on political, financial, economic, and social conditions within the Ottoman Empire. Those particularly used were 1856, vol. 61; 1861, vol. 67; 1862, vol. 64; 1870, vol. 66; 1871, vol. 68; 1875, vol. 83.

Grigsby, William E., trans., *The Medjelle or Ottoman Civil Law.* London, 1895.

From the authorized Greek edition, by an English judge in Cyprus.

Hertslet, Edward, *The Map of Europe by Treaty*, IV, 1875-1891. London, 1891.

Reprints a number of Turkish state papers.

Holland, Thomas E., *The European Concert in the Eastern Question: A Collection of Treaties and Other Public Acts.* Oxford, 1885.

Useful compilation, from other published collections.

Hurewitz, J[acob] C[oleman], *Diplomacy in the Near and Middle East.* 2 vols. Princeton, 1956.

A well-annotated collection of documents, 1535 to 1914 in vol I. All are translated into English.

Jorga, Nicholas, ed., *Correspondance diplomatique roumaine sous le roi Charles Ier (1866-1880).* Paris, 1923.

Includes some reports from Roumanian agents in Belgrade and İstanbul.

Kaynar, Reşat, *Mustafa Reşit Paşa ve Tanzimat* [Mustafa Reşid Paşa and the Tanzimat]. Ankara, 1954.

A collection of documents, to the year 1845, heaviest on 1838 to 1841, from archives and published works. Much on foreign affairs.

Kraelitz-Greifenhorst, Friedrich von, *Die Verfassungsgesetze des Osmanischen Reiches, aus dem Osmanisch-türkischen übersetzt und zusammengestellt.* Leipzig, 1909, and Vienna, 1919.

Chiefly texts. Contains 1839 and 1856 *hat*'s, and 1876 constitution.

Mehmed Selaheddin, *Bir Türk diplomatının evrak-ı siyasiyesi* [The political papers of a Turkish diplomat]. İstanbul, 1306.

Principally a rather unscientific though useful collection of Reşid Paşa's diplomatic documents, largely pre-1856, preceded by a sketch of his life.

Noradounghian, Gabriel, *Recueil d'actes internationaux de l'Empire ottoman.* 4 vols. Paris, 1897-1903.

Volume III covers 1856 to 1876.

Nord, Erich, *Das türkische Strafgesetzbuch vom 28. Zilhidje 1274 (9 August 1858)* .... Berlin, 1912.

The text of the penal code, with an introduction.

"The Ottoman Constitution, Promulgated the 7th Zilbridje [sic] 1293 (11/23 December, 1876)," *American Journal of International Law*, Supplement, II (1908), 367-387.

Text of an English translation made in İstanbul at the time of promulgation.

427

Petit, L., "Règlements généraux de l'église orthodoxe en Turquie," *Revue de l'Orient Chrétien,* III (1898), 393-424, and IV (1899), 227-246.

By an Augustinian of Istanbul. Translates the Greek texts of the 1860-1862 millet organic laws, better than the incomplete translation in Young's *Corps de droit.* Some historical explanation attached.

Rodkey, Frederick Stanley, "Reshid Pasha's Memorandum of August 12, 1839," *Journal of Modern History,* II:2 (June 1930), 251-257.

An important reflection of Reşid's views, taken from the British Foreign Office archives.

Schopoff, A., *Les réformes et la protection des chrétiens en Turquie, 1673-1904: firmans, bérats, protocoles . . . lois, memorandums, etc.* Paris, 1904.

Compiled chiefly from Aristarchi, Noradounghian, and Testa. Incomplete and not always accurate.

Das Staatsarchiv. Sammlung der officiellen Actenstücke zur Geschichte der Gegenwart. Leipzig, several volumes annually, 1861 ff.

Fine collection, printing many Turkish documents arranged by subject, often retrospectively. Used especially vols. 30-32, for 1875-1876.

Testa, I. de, *et al., Recueil des traités de la Porte ottomane avec les puissances étrangères depuis . . . 1536 jusqu'à nos jours.* 11 vols. Paris, 1864-1911.

Contains also much diplomatic correspondence, and some Ottoman laws, especially in vol. VII.

[Turkey], [Ministry of Justice], *Düstur* [Code of Laws]. İstanbul, various dates.

The volumes under this title are badly organized, contain errors, but are essential as collections of laws and regulations of the Tanzimat. The one-volume collection published in 1279, very poorly printed, was re-edited in another better-printed single volume in 1282, with additions. A new series under the same title was begun with volume I in 1289, volume II in 1289/-1290, and others thereafter to a total of four, plus four appendix volumes in the 1880's. This series does not repeat all earlier regulations. Cf. comments in Young, *Corps de droit,* I, xiii, and Jäschke, "Türkische Gesetzsammlungen" (q.v.).

[Turkey] Sublime Porte. Ministère des Affaires Etrangères. *Instructions relatives à l'administration générale des vilayets (traduction).* Constantinople, 1876.

Tute, R. C., *The Ottoman Land Laws with a Commentary on the Ottoman Land Code of 7th Ramadan 1274.* [Jerusalem, 1927].

A handbook for working lawyers by the president of the land court in Jerusalem. Much of the annotation concerns later amendments to the law and conditions in Palestine.

Tyser, C. R., trans., with D. G. Demetriades and Ismail Haqqi Effendi, *The Mejelle.* Nicosia, 1901.

Fairly literal translation from Turkish, following the *Düstur,* with glossary and notes.

Ubicini, [Jean Henri] A[bdolonyme], *La Constitution ottomane du 7 zilhidjé 1293 (23 décembre 1876) expliquée et annotée.* Paris, 1877.

Gives also a number of related documents, and a brief background of the making of the constitution, some of it erroneous.

Uzunçarşılı, İsmail Hakkı, *Midhat ve Rüştü Paşaların tevkiflerine dair vesikalar* [Documents concerning the arrests of Midhat and Rüşdi Paşas]. Ankara, 1946.

Mostly documents of 1881, with some explanatory text. The interrogation of Mehmed Rüşdi is the most revealing portion, together with the official summary of Midhat's interrogation.

Walpole, Charles G., *The Ottoman Penal Code 28 Zilhijeh 1274.* London, 1888.

Translated from the French text.

Young, George, *Corps de droit ottoman;*

BIBLIOGRAPHY

recueil des codes, lois, règlements, ordonnances et actes les plus importants du droit intérieur, et d'études sur le droit coutumier de l'Empire ottoman. 7 vols. Oxford, 1905-1906.

A very useful collection of translations, but often defective from the historical viewpoint, as articles or laws later superseded are omitted; also errors in dates and references.

BOOKS AND ARTICLES

Aali [Âli] Pacha, "Testament politique," *La Revue de Paris,* 17:7 and 17:9 (1 April and 1 May 1910), 505-524, 105-124.
Of dubious authenticity.

Abdurrahman Şeref, "Ahmed Midhat Efendi," *Tarih-i osmanî encümeni mecmuası,* III:18 (1 February 1328), 1113-1119.
A brief survey of his life.

————, *Tarih musahabeleri* [Causeries on history]. İstanbul, 1339.
Delightful sketches of leading nineteenth-century figures, and discussions of historical questions, which originally appeared as newspaper articles. Anecdotal, sometimes based on personal knowledge.

Adams, Charles C., *Islam and Modernism in Egypt. A Study of the modern reform movement inaugurated by Muhammad 'Abduh.* London, 1933.
A solid study, with an introductory chapter on Jemaleddin el Afghani.

Adnan-Adıvar, Abdülhak, *Osmanlı Türklerinde ilim* [Science among the Ottoman Turks]. İstanbul, 1943.
A scholarly study, using Turkish and western sources; largely on mathematics, astronomy, geography, and medicine. This is a revised and enlarged edition of the following title.

————, *La science chez les Turcs ottomans.* Paris, 1939.

Ahmed Midhat, *Üss-i inkılâb* [The basis of revolution]. 2 vols. in 1. İstanbul, 1294-1295.
Written on Sultan Abdülhamid II's order, by Midhat Paşa's former protégé. Covers events from 1856; detailed on 1876-1877. Rather anti-Midhat; flatters Abdülhamid. Documentary appendices.

Ahmed Rasim, *İlk büyük muharrirlerden Şinasi* [Şinasi, (one of) the first great writers]. İstanbul, 1928.
A survey of his career, with a good deal of undigested evidence in the notes, and samples of his writing.

————, *İstibdaddan hakimiyeti milliyeye* [From absolutism to sovereignty of the people]. 2 vols. İstanbul, 1342.
Covers reign of Selim III to Murad V. Somewhat superficial, though drawing on both Turkish and French published sources, because of effort to see constitutional development over a long period.

————, *Resimli ve haritalı osmanlı tarihi* [Illustrated Ottoman history with maps], IV. İstanbul, 1328-1330.
Largely political history from Mahmud II to 1876, based on Turkish and French published works.

Ahmed Refik, "Türkiyede ıslahat fermanı," [The reform decree (of 1856) in Turkey] *Tarih-i osmanî encümeni mecmuası,* 14:81 (1 July 1340), 193-215.
The unpublished documents here presented are largely verbatim from some of Cevdet Paşa's *Tezâkir,* since published (q.v.).

Ahmed Saib, *Tarih-i Sultan Murad-ı Hamis* [History of Sultan Murad V]. Cairo, n.d. [190?].
————, *Vaka-i Sultan Abdülaziz* [The episode of Sultan Abdülaziz]. Cairo, 1320.
Popular, unscientific histories by a Young Turk in exile who uses Kératry, Ahmed Midhat, and various newspapers as sources. The former is largely on 1876; one third of the latter concerns 1875-1876.

Akçura, Yusuf, *Osmanlı devletinin dağıl-*

429

ma devri (XVIII. ve XIX. asırlarda) [The period of dissolution of the Ottoman state in the 18th and 19th centuries]. İstanbul, 1940.
Misleading title; deals mostly with Selim III's reign. The author died before completing the work.

Aktchoura Oglou Youssouf Bey [Yusuf Akçura], "L'oeuvre historique de Mustapha Djelalettin Pacha et ses points de vue sur l'histoire des Turcs," 7ᵉ Congrès des Sciences Historiques, *Résumés*, II (1933), 233-236.

Alboyajian, Arshag, "Azkayin Sahmanaterouthiune," *Entartzag ....Oratzoytz sourp Perkechian Hivantonotzy Hayotz* ["The national constitution," Comprehensive calendar of the Armenian Holy Savior's hospital], (1910), 76-528.
A factual and rather detailed account of the Armenian millet constitution, using the files of the Armenian newspaper *Massis* extensively.

Alderson, A. D., *The Structure of the Ottoman Dynasty*. Oxford, 1956.
Contains detailed genealogical tables, along with much information on succession, marriages, et cetera.

Ali Fuad, *Rical-i mühimme-i siyasiye* [Important political personages]. İstanbul, 1928.
Informative essays, reprinted from supplements of the *Servet-i fünun*, on Reşid, Âli, and Fuad Paşas. Based on oral information as well as on French and Turkish works.

Ali Suavi, *A propos de l'Herzégovine*. Paris, 1875.
One of his polemics, campaigning for Ottomanism.

Allen, W. E. D., and Paul Muratoff, *Caucasian Battlefields: A History of the Wars on the Turco-Caucasian Border, 1828-1921*. Cambridge, 1953.
Gives considerable information on the Ottoman armies; sometimes useful for political and social as well as military matters.

Arnold, R. Arthur, *From the Levant, the Black Sea, and the Danube*. 2 vols. London, 1871.
Intelligent travel letters of an 1867-1868 trip to Greece, İstanbul, the Crimea, and up the Danube to Vienna.

Arnold, Thomas W., *The Caliphate*. Oxford, 1924.
Well-integrated work on the Sunni caliphate to Abdülhamid II, and its relation to Muslim princes.

Arpee, Leon, *The Armenian Awakening; a history of the Armenian Church, 1820-1860*. Chicago, 1909.
Based on Armenian sources. Gives a factual, concise account of the origins of the 1860 constitution.

———, *A History of Armenian Christianity from the Beginning to Our Own Time*. New York, 1946.
Gives little detail on the nineteenth century.

Aspirations et agissements révolutionnaires des comités arméniens avant et après la proclamation de la constitution ottomane. Constantinople, 1917.
Evidently a Turk wartime publication to justify the Armenian massacres. Biased, but informative, reaching back to 1870 Armenian nationalists.

Auriant, "Un émir afghan, adversaire de l'Angleterre en Orient, Djemmal ed Dine, ténébreux agitateur," *Mercure de France*, 288 (1 December 1938), 316-330.
A short, informative history, especially on Jemaleddin in India and Egypt, and on his stay in Paris.

———, "Un Grec au service des pachas d'Egypte: Draneht Bey," *Acropole*, VIII (1933), 161-176.
Reflects on Ismail's relations with Mustafa Fazıl.

Aus dem Leben König Karls von Rumänien: Aufzeichnungen eines Augenzeugen. 4 vols. in 3. Stuttgart, 1894-1900.
Based on diary of Jehan de Witte, personal secretary to Karl, including letters by the prince-king. First three volumes cover 1866-1878.

[Azimzade Hakkı], *Türkiyede meclis-i meb'usan* [The chamber of deputies in Turkey]. Cairo, 1907.
This is labelled vol. 1; I have seen no second. A compilation of documents related to the 1877 parliament's creation, opening, and meetings of the first session. Much taken directly from newspapers, fall 1876 on, especially *Vakit* and *Basiret*.

Babinger, Franz, *Die Geschichtsschreiber der Osmanen und ihre Werke*. Leipzig, 1927.
Descriptions of Turkish histories and brief authors' lives.

Bailey, Frank Edgar, *British Policy and the Turkish Reform Movement: A Study in Anglo-Turkish Relations, 1826-1853*. Cambridge, Mass., 1942.
Useful, but more so on British policy than on Ottoman developments.

Bailleux de Marisy, "Moeurs financières de la France; IV - Les valeurs orientales, les finances de la Turquie et de l'Egypte," *Revue des deux mondes*, 3rd period, v (1 October 1874), 650-678.
A fair brief summary, foreseeing no disaster.

Baker, James, *Turkey*. New York, 1877.
By a farm owner near Salonika. Attempt at general description of European Turkey not too good, but contains firsthand information on local taxes and agriculture.

Bamberg, Felix, *Geschichte der orientalischen Angelegenheiten im Zeitraume des Pariser und des Berliner Friedens*. Berlin, 1892.
Out of date, but gives information on internal events.

Barbier de Meynard, "Lehdjè-i-osmani, Dictionnaire ottoman," *Journal asiatique*, Series VII:8 (August-September 1876), 275-280.
Description and praise of Ahmed Vefik's Turkish-based work.

Barbiera, Raffaello, *La Principessa Belgiojoso, i suoi amici e nemici*. Milan, 1902.
The princess lived in inner Anatolia for a number of years.

Barker, John, *Syria and Egypt under the last five Sultans of Turkey, being experiences during fifty years*. E. B. B. Barker, ed. 2 vols. London, 1876.
From the consul's letters and journals, edited by his son. Covers only first half of nineteenth century.

Barth, H., "Beschreibung einer Reise quer durch das Innere der Europäischen Türkei . . . im Herbst 1862," *Zeitschrift für Allgemeine Erdkunde*, Neue Folge 15 (1863), 301-358, 457-538, and 16 (1864), 117-208.
Details on routes, monuments, villages, with a little on officials and general conditions, Ruschuk to Salonika.

Basmadjian, K. J., *Histoire moderne des arméniens depuis la chute du royaume jusqu'à nos jours (1375-1916)*. Paris, 1917.
Sketchy, though useful in spots.

Baykal, Bekir Sıtkı, "93 meşrutiyeti," [The constitution of (12)93], *Belleten*, VI:21/22 (January-April 1942), 45-83.
Good brief survey of the making of the constitution of 1876, from end of Abdülaziz's reign to 1877 chamber session. Uses some unpublished documents. Strongly pro-Midhat.

———, "Midhat paşa'nın gizli bir siyasî teşebbüsü," [A secret diplomatic attempt by Midhat Paşa], pp. 470-477 in Türk Tarih Kurumu, III. *Türk Tarih Kongresi, Ankara 15-20 Kasım 1943*. Ankara, 1948.
On Odian Efendi's mission to London and Paris, December 1876-February 1877, using Odian-Midhat telegrams.

Behrnauer, W. F. A., "Die türkische Akademie der Wissenschaften zu Constantinopel," *Zeitschrift der Deutschen Morgenländischen Gesellschaft*, VI:2 (1852), 273-285.
Gives a translation of the statutes of the Encümen-i Daniş and the original membership list.

Belgiojoso, Christine, *Asie Mineure et Syrie; souvenirs de voyages*. Paris, 1858.

431

Good descriptions of native life and conditions by an Italian political exile who lived near Ankara at the time of the Crimean War. Originally articles in *Revue des deux mondes*, 1855.

Belin, [François Alphonse], "Bibliographie ottomane . . . ," *Journal asiatique*, Series VI: 11 (April-May 1868), 465-491; 14 (August-September 1869), 65-95; 18 (August-September 1871), 125-157; series VII: 1 (May-June 1873), 522-563; 9 (February-March 1877), 122-146.
    Valuable lists and brief descriptions of works published in Turkish, mainly in İstanbul but sometimes in Egypt. These continue earlier lists by Bianchi (q.v.). *See also* Schlechta-Wssehrd.

————, "Essais sur l'histoire économique de la Turquie," *Journal asiatique*, Series VI:5 (January-February 1865), 127-167.
    Covers 1789-1863, chiefly on money, loans, and debts.

————, *Etude sur la propriété foncière en pays musulman et spécialement en Turquie (rite Hanéfite)*. Paris, 1862.
    Reprinted from *Journal asiatique*, Series V:18-19 (1861-1862). On historic principles of forms of land tenure, and 1858 land code. Cevdet Paşa aided the author.

————, "Tableau de la presse périodique et quotidienne à Constantinople en 1864," *Journal asiatique*, Series VI:5 (January-February 1865), 170-174.
    With brief descriptions. Based on the 1864 *Salname*.

Bellew, H. W., *Kashmir and Kashghar, A Narrative of the Journey of the Embassy to Kashghar in 1873-1874*. London, 1875.
    By the doctor of Forsyth's mission, who knew Persian and some Turki. Some notes on Ottoman-Yakub relations.

Berkes, Niyazi, "Historical Background of Turkish Secularism," pp. 41-67 in Richard N. Frye, ed., *Islam and the West*. The Hague, 1957.
    Concentrated before 1839; critical of Tanzimat dualism.

Beth, Karl, *Die orientalische Christenheit der Mittelmeerländer. Reisestudien zur Statistik und Symbolik der griechischen, armenischen und koptischen Kirche*. Berlin, 1902.
    Concise, on history and organization of the churches, as well as dogma and symbolism.

Bianchi, [Thomas Xavier], "Bibliographie ottomane . . . ," *Journal asiatique*, Series V:13 (June 1859), 519-555; 14 (October-November 1859), 287-298; 16 (October-November 1860), 323-346; Series VI:2 (August-September 1863), 217-271.
    See comment under Belin, "Bibliographie ottomane." These lists by Bianchi start with late 1856.

————, "Notice sur le premier annuaire (. . . salname) impérial de l'Empire ottoman . . . (1847)," *Journal asiatique*, Series IV:10 (September 1847), 177-207; 11 (January and April-May 1848), 293-333.
    Really a reproduction of the yearbook, outlining the Ottoman government, listing officials and statistics. Gives also a brief account of progress since 1800.

Bianconi, F., *Ethnographie et statistique de la Turquie d'Europe et de la Grèce*. Paris, 1877.
    By a Turcophobe French engineer employed on Balkan railways in the 1870's. Critical of Ubicini's figures.

————, *La question d'Orient dévoilée*. Paris, 1876.
    Firsthand information on peoples and conditions.

Birge, J. Kingsley, *The Bektashi Order of Dervishes*. London, 1937.
    Based on Turkish sources, and personal interviews, with short review of Bektashi history, and more on tenets and rites.

Blaisdell, Donald C., *European Financial Control in the Ottoman Empire: a study of the establishment, activities, and significance of the Ottoman Public Debt*. New York, 1929.
    Up to 1881 relies on DuVelay and Morawitz, is poor on historical context.

For later period uses Public Debt archives.

Blancard, Théodore, *Les Mavroyéni. Histoire d'Orient (de 1700 à nos jours).* 2 vols. Paris, 1909.
A massive hodgepodge of information, largely on the eighteenth century, with some on the nineteenth.

Blau, O., "Nachrichten über kurdische Stämme," *Zeitschrift der Deutschen Morgenländischen Gesellschaft,* 16:4 (1862), 607-627.
Contains some information on orthographic reform.

Blerzy, H., "Les révolutions de l'Asie centrale—les conquêtes de la Russie," *Revue des deux mondes,* 3rd period, v (1 September 1874), 127-154.
A concise account of Russian advances to 1871, with notes on Muslim feeling and embassies to the Porte.

Blowitz, H. G. S. A. O. de, *My Memoirs.* London, 1883.
————, *Une course à Constantinople,* 2nd ed. Paris, 1884.
He travelled to İstanbul in 1883, describes a number of personalities. Interview with Abdülhamid in both books.

Bobčev, S. S., "Notes comparées sur les čorbajis chez les peuples balkaniques et en particulier chez les Bulgares," *Revue internationale des études balkaniques,* III (1937-1938), 428-445.
Contains praise for Midhat's work at Tirnovo in 1857.

[Bodrumlu], Abraham Galanté, *Histoire des Juifs d'Istanbul depuis . . . 1453 . . . jusqu'à nos jours,* I. İstanbul, 1941.
Disordered and occasionally quite informative.
————, *Turcs et Juifs: étude historique, politique.* Stamboul, 1932.
A translation, with some additions, of the İstanbul professor's *Türkler ve Yahudiler* of 1928.

[Bodrumlu], Avram Galanti, *Türkler ve Yahudiler: tarihî, siyasî tetkik* [Turks and Jews: a historical and political

study], 2nd enlarged ed. İstanbul, 1947.
An enlarged edition of the preceding title. Chaotic, aimed at showing Jewish services to Turkey, full of miscellaneous information.

Bolander, Knud Graah, *Förspelet till Balkankrisen på 1870-talet. En Studie i Europeisk Politik, efter otryckta aktstycken i det Nyöppnade Statsarkivet i Wien.* Göteborg, 1925.
Concentrates on 1875-1876. Useful for information from Haus- Hof- und Staatsarchiv.

[Bolayır], Ali Ekrem, *Namık Kemal.* İstanbul, 1930.
A disjointed account by Namık Kemal's son, not very full on the political aspects.

Boué, Ami, *La Turquie d'Europe, ou observations sur la géographie, la géologie, l'histoire naturelle, la statistique, les moeurs, les coutumes, l'archéologie, l'agriculture, l'industrie, le commerce, les gouvernemens divers, le clergé, l'histoire et l'état politique de cet empire.* 4 vols. Paris, 1840.

Boulger, Demetrius C., *The Life of Yakoob Beg; Athalik Ghazi, and Badaulet; Ameer of Kashgar.* London, 1878.
Scholarly, using accounts of men on Forsyth's mission.

Bradley, Edward S., *George Henry Boker, Poet and Patriot.* Philadelphia, 1927.
Based on Boker's papers, more literary than political, sometimes useful. Boker was United States minister to the Porte in 1871-1875.

Braun, Julius, *Gemälde der mohammedanischen Welt.* Leipzig, 1870.
A work of compilation, sketching the various sects of the Near East, very poor on political matters.

Braun-Wiesbaden, Karl, *Eine türkische Reise.* 2 vols. Stuttgart, 1876.
By an intelligent Reichstag member, who talked to many people who knew the country well.

Brockelman, Carl, *Geschichte der islam-*

ischen Völker und Staaten. Munich, 1939.

Based on standard works, of necessity brief on nineteenth-century Turkey, but fair within that compass. Editions in English 1947 and 1960.

Brown, John P., *The Dervishes, or Oriental Spiritualism.* London, 1868.

By the American dragoman at İstanbul. Poorly organized, repetitious, but full of information from oriental manuscripts, personal knowledge, and European works.

——, "The Sublime Porte," *Knickerbocker,* 38:1 (July 1851), 34-41.

On Turkish government, by a good orientalist.

Browne, Edward G., *The Persian Revolution of 1905-1909.* Cambridge, 1910.

An excellent account, using many Persian sources. Centers on post-1890, but has substantial information on Jemaleddin el Afghani.

——, "Some Remarks on the Babi Texts edited by Baron Victor Rosen . . . ," *Journal of the Royal Asiatic Society,* 24, n.s., (April 1892), 259-335.

Contains a letter by Beha to Abdülaziz, and a celebration of Fuad's death.

Brunswik, Benoît, *La crise financière de la Turquie.* Paris, 1874.

A mixture of criticism and suggestion for reform.

——, *Etudes pratiques sur la question d'Orient: réformes et capitulations.* Paris, 1869.

Brunswik lived in Turkey 1854 on. Depicts governmental conditions with a western impatience for reform.

——, *La réforme et les garanties, mémoire présenté à la conférence de Constantinople,* 2nd ed. Paris, 1877.

A polemic against Midhat's reforms and constitution.

——, *La succession au trône de la Turquie,* 2nd ed. Paris, 1872.

A diatribe against Abdülaziz's plans for Yusuf İzzeddin.

——, *La Turquie, ses créanciers, et la diplomatie.* Paris, 1877.

On the 1875 default, its causes,

possible remedies. Argues for European experts, concessionaires, tax farmers.

——, *La vérité sur Midhat Pacha.* Paris, 1877.

A tirade against Midhat as a dictator.

Burks, Richard Voyles, *The Diplomacy of the Romanian War for Independence (1875-1878).* Chicago, 1939.

Useful summary of a solid Chicago University thesis.

Burnaby, Frederick G., *On Horseback through Asia Minor.* 2 vols. 6th ed. London, 1877.

An intelligent account from notes taken on the spot in winter of 1876-1877 by an English officer who knew some Turkish.

——, *A Ride to Khiva: travels and adventures in Central Asia.* New York, 1877.

Anecdotal, on 1875-1876 ride from Orenburg to Khiva. Mostly on English-Russian relations, but some information on Muslim peoples.

Burnouf, Emile, "La Turquie en 1869," *Revue des deux mondes,* 2nd period, 84 (15 December 1869), 962-986.

An intelligent discussion of Ottoman external and internal strengths and weaknesses, and reforms, using Fuad's testament as basis for argument.

Busch, "Schreiben des Hrn. Dr. Busch an Prof. Brockhaus," *Zeitschrift der Deutschen Morgenländischen Gesellschaft,* 17:3/4 (1863), 711-714.

On the periodical press of İstanbul, especially a description of the first seven issues of the *Mecmua-i fünun.*

Butler-Johnstone, H. A. Munro, *The Eastern Question.* London, 1875.

By a conservative Turcophile who knew Turkey.

——, *The Turks: their character, manners and institutions as bearing on the Eastern Question.* London, 1876. Turcophile defense of simple Turkish morals and theocracy as a "constitutional system."

Cahun, Léon, "Le monde islamique de 1840 à 1870," pp. 527-560 in Ernest

Lavisse and Alfred Rambaud, *Histoire générale*, XI. Paris, 1899.

————, "Le monde islamique de 1870 à nos jours," pp. 479-503 in *ibid.*, XII. Paris, 1901.
Not good history, confusing New Ottomans with Young Turks, but containing a little firsthand information on the former.

Campbell, Sir George, *A Handy Book on the Eastern Question, being a very recent view of Turkey*. London, 1876.
By a sane M.P. and former Bengal official who went to Bulgaria and İstanbul in the fall of 1876.

[Canini], Marco Antonio, *Vingt ans d'exil*. Paris, 1868.
By an Italian revolutionary exile who travelled and lived in Greece, Bulgaria, Roumania, İstanbul. Sketchy.

Capoléone, Dr. L., *Une réponse à M. de Kératry à propos de son ouvrage intitulé Mourad V: prince-sultan-prisonnier d'état*. Padua, 1878.
A self-justification by Murad's physician, fairly good.

Çark, Y. G., *Türk devleti hizmetinde Ermeniler, 1453-1953* [Armenians in the service of the Turkish state, 1453-1953]. İstanbul, 1953.
A disjointed but useful account with many biographical sketches. Fullest on period 1753 to 1913.

Carra de Vaux, Baron [Bernhard], *Les penseurs de l'Islam*. 5 vols. Paris, 1921-1926.
The section on Midhat is poor, and has important errors of fact.

Castille, [Charles] Hippolyte, *Réchid-pacha*. Paris, 1857.
Favorable to Reşid, but a balanced judgment on Ottoman reforms.

Caston, Vicomte Alfred de, *Musulmans et chrétiens: la Turquie en 1873*, II. Constantinople, 1874.
Evidently by a Frenchman resident in Turkey. Disjointed chronicle of events from 1861 to 1869 fully, almost day by day, and 1869 to 1874 sketchily.

Catalogue de la bibliothèque du feu Ahmed Véfyk Pacha. Constantinople, 1893.
Some 3,800 items, an index to his broad interests.

Cevdet Paşa, [Ahmed], *Tezâkir 1 - 12* [Memoranda 1-12]. Cavid Baysun, ed. Ankara, 1953.
A well-edited volume of some of Cevdet's historical memoranda written for the historian Lûtfi, based here on drafts in the İstanbul municipal library. Cevdet wrote these, largely on the Crimean War period, twenty years after the event, and was not entirely objective, but this is a most useful historical source. Well annotated, indexed.

Challemel-Lacour, P., "Les hommes d'état de la Turquie; Aali-Pacha et Fuad-Pacha," *Revue des deux mondes*, 2nd period, 73 (15 February 1868), 886-925.
Based on interviews by an unnamed Frenchman.

Charikles [Aristarchi Bey?], "Türkische Skizzen in Briefen an eine Freundin, 1876," *Deutsche Zeit- und Streit-fragen*, VI: 83/84 (1877), 85-154.
Author either a Greek or German who knew Turkey. Letters dated from İstanbul and suburbs between May 29, 1876 and October 10, 1876. Obviously edited, probably genuine base.

Charmes, Gabriel, *L'avenir de la Turquie; le panislamisme*. Paris, 1883.
Mostly post-1878, but contains an estimate of Midhat's work.

Chatelier, A. Le, "Révolutions d'Orient," *Revue politique et littéraire, Revue bleue*, Series V:10 (15 August 1908), 193-199.
Mostly on 1908 revolutions, but some on New Ottoman origins.

[Cherbuliez], "L'Angleterre et la Russie en Orient; une page d'histoire contemporaine, 1876-1877," *Revue d'histoire diplomatique*, X (1896), 56-118, 171-222.
By an unidentified diplomat, written in 1877, betrays an intimate knowledge of events in Turkey.

Chertier, Edmond, *Réformes en Turquie*. Paris, 1858.
Lightweight, on reforms past and pending.

Chiha, Habib K., *La province de Bagdad. Son passé, son présent, son avenir.* . . . Cairo, 1908.
A handbook, with historical background, and a good deal on nomadic tribes.

Chirol, Sir Valentine, *Fifty Years in a Changing World*. London, 1927.
Retrospective essays. Chirol was in Turkey in 1876.

Clician Vassif Effendi, A. [Vasıf Kiliçyan, or Clician zade Antoine Vassif], *Son Altesse Midhat-Pacha, grand vizir*. Paris, 1909.
A very laudatory and rather incomplete biography by Midhat's personal secretary, a Croat whom he took into his service at Ruschuk, and who followed Midhat into exile. Though not completely trustworthy as an account, and slim on the period before 1875, it is useful.

Cobham, Claude Delaval, *The Patriarchs of Constantinople*. Cambridge, 1911.
General description and lists of patriarchs.

Coke, Richard, *Bagdad, the City of Peace*. London, 1927.
———, *Heart of the Middle East*. New York, 1926.
Both reflect something of Midhat's work as vali.

Collas, B. C., *La Turquie en 1861*. Paris, 1861.
———, *La Turquie en 1864*. Paris, 1864.
Quite similar handbooks, based on the best information available to a resident of Turkey who used western-language sources.

Colombe, Marcel, "Une lettre d'un prince égyptien du XIXᵉ siècle au Sultan ottoman Abd al-Aziz," *Orient*, v (1st quarter 1958), 23-38.
Reproduces the text of Mustafa Fazıl's letter of 1867, from an unidentified source, with a useful introduction based on French diplomatic and consular reports.

Crabitès, Pierre, *Ismail the Maligned Khedive*. London, 1933.
A defense of Ismail, sometimes exaggerated. Uses Abdin Palace Archives of Cairo, adduces evidence of Ismail's bribery in İstanbul.

Creasy, Edward S., *History of the Ottoman Turks: from the beginning of their empire to the present time*, rev. ed. London, 1877.
Very weak on post-1839, based on standard sources, emphasizing battles and diplomacy.

Cuinet, Vital, *La Turquie d'Asie; géographie administrative, statistique descriptive et raisonnée de chaque province de l'Asie Mineure*. 4 vols. Paris, 1890.

Dadian, le Prince Mek.-b., *La société arménienne contemporaine; les Arméniens de l'Empire ottoman*. Paris, 1867.
On press, culture, education, and quarrels preceding 1860 constitution. Not so detailed as Arpee.

al-Damlūji, Ṣiddiq, *Midḥat Bāshā*. Baghdad, 1952-1953.
A somewhat flowery biography, favorable to Midhat, using his memoirs and some western sources, as well as local knowledge.

Danişmend, İsmail Hami, *Ali Suâvi'nin türkçülügü* [Ali Suavi's advocacy of Turkish national culture]. İstanbul, 1942.
A somewhat overdrawn pamphlet, seemingly trying to link Ali Suavi to some of the principles of the Republican Peoples Party, but a useful sketch of his ideas, especially Turkist ideas.

———, *İzahlı osmanlı tarihi kronolojisi* [Explanatory chronology of Ottoman history], IV. İstanbul, 1955.
Useful not only for dates, but for excerpts from, and summaries of, Turkish historical writers. This volume covers 1703 to 1924. Some articles strongly biased.

Davison, Roderic H., "The Question of Fuad Paşa's 'Political Testament,' "

Belleten, 23:89 (January 1959), 119-136.

Investigates the possible authenticity, and the publication history, of this document.

————, "Turkish Attitudes Concerning Christian-Muslim Equality in the Nineteenth Century," *American Historical Review*, 59:4 (July 1954), 844-864.

"The Death of the ex-Sultan," *The Lancet*, 10 June 1876, pp. 872-873.

English medical journal discounts the suicide thesis. See also "The murder of the ex-Sultan," *The Lancet*, 2 July 1881, pp. 17-18.

Debelak, Julius, "Die central-asiatische Frage," *Streffleur's Oesterreichische Militärische Zeitschrift*, 16:3 (1875), 117-148, 189-220; 16:4 (1875), 33-48, 85-107.

A good synthesis from respectable sources; largely military, with something on Yakub Beg and the Porte.

De Leon, Edwin, "The Old Ottoman and the Young Turk," *Harper's*, 44] (March 1872), 606-612.

Has nothing to do with New Ottomans. De Leon describes Reşid and Âli, whom he knew, and Mustafa Fazıl.

Demeerseman, A., "Au berceau des premières réformes démocratiques en Tunisie," *IBLA*, 20:77 (1st quarter 1957), 1-12.

————, "Doctrine de Khéréddine en matière de politique extérieure," *IBLA*, 21:81 (1st quarter 1958), 13-29.

————, "Un grand témoin des premières idées modernisantes en Tunisie," *IBLA*, 19:76 (4th quarter 1956), 349-373.

————, "Idéal politique de Khéréddine: Sa valeur morale," *IBLA*, 20:79 (3rd quarter 1957), 179-215.

————, "Indépendance de la Tunisie et politique extérieure de Khéréddine," *IBLA*, 21:83 (3rd quarter 1958), 229-277.

Useful though sometimes wordy analyses of Hayreddin's life, his work in Tunis as a statesman, his reform ideas, and his concepts of Tunis-Ottoman relationships.

Denton, William, *The Christians in Turkey*. London, 1863.

Special pleading by an Anglican cleric resident for some time in Bosnia. Based on highly selected portions of Senior, MacFarlane, and the 1861 consular reports.

De Salve, "L'enseignement en Turquie: le lycée impérial de Galata-Seraï," *Revue des deux mondes*, 3rd period, v (15 October 1874), 836-853.

By the first Galatasaray director. Good brief summary of Turkish education, and of his school.

Desjardin (Paul de Régla), *Au pays de l'espionnage; les sultans Mourad V et Abd-ul-Hamid II*. Paris, n.d. (ca. 1902).

Journalistic. Desjardin claims to be an intimate friend of Dr. Mavroyeni, Abdul Hamid's physician. Needs constant checking.

Destrilhes, M., *Confidences sur la Turquie*, 2nd ed. Paris, 1855.

Slight, useful for sketches of leading Turks, but needs checking. Pro-French, anti-English, anti-Reşid.

Devereux, Robert, *The First Ottoman Constitutional Period: A Study of the Midhat Constitution and Parliament*. Washington, D.C., unpublished doctoral thesis for the School of Advanced International Studies of the Johns Hopkins University, 1961. (Published under the same title, Baltimore, 1963.)

————, *A Study of the First Ottoman Parliament, 1877-1878*. Washington, D.C., unpublished master's thesis for the George Washington University, 1956.

The later study incorporates most of the earlier, and expands it. Best study of the 1877-1878 parliaments.

Djelaleddin, Moustapha [Konstanty Polkozic-Borzęcki], *L'Europe et le touro-aryanisme*. n.p., n.d.

Contains some wild linguistic theories on Turkish as a western language and possibly the father of them all. Reproduces last section of the following work.

————, *Les Turcs anciens et modernes.* Constantinople, 1869; Paris, 1870.
By a Polish exile turned Muslim, officer in Ottoman army. A curious Turcophile, Russophobe defense of Turks, with suggestions for representative government.

Djemaleddin Bey, *Sultan Murad V. The Turkish Dynastic Mystery, 1876-1895.* London, 1895.
Supposedly by an eyewitness, perhaps an Ottoman Christian, perhaps a New Ottoman. Novelized, light.

Dorys, Georges, *Abdul-Hamid intime.* Paris, 1901.
Presumably by an Ottoman Greek, son of Samos prince, and an İstanbul newspaper correspondent and New Ottoman. Very little on pre-1876.

"Douglas Forsyth's Gesandschaftsreise nach Kaschgar," *Globus*, 25:18 (1874), 282-284, 298-302.
From Forsyth's Reports.

Douin, G., *Histoire du règne du Khédive Ismail*, I, *1863-1867*; II, *1867-1873.* Rome, 1933-1934.
A very detailed work, not well integrated, but supplying copious information out of French, British, and Egyptian documents. Most of vol. II concerns Ismail's relations with the Porte.

Dowson, Ernest, *An Inquiry into Land Tenure and Related Questions.* Letchworth, England, for the 'Iraqi Government, [1931?].
Contains some information on the Ottoman period.

Driault, Edouard, *La question d'Orient depuis ses origines jusqu'à la paix de Sèvres (1920)*, 8th ed. Paris, 1921.
Unsatisfactory. Turcophobe and Francophile.

Dumont, [Charles] Albert A. E., *Le Balkan et l'Adriatique.* Paris, 1874.
A good travel book, based on residence in and intimate knowledge of Edirne, Tekirdağ (Rodosto), Epirus, and Albania, 1868-1871.

Durand de Fontmagne, La Baronne (Drummond de Melfort), *Un séjour à l'ambassade de France à Constantinople sous le Second Empire.* Paris, 1902.
By a relative of Thouvenel who lived at the embassy from 1856 to 1858. Some information, but fails as another Lady Montagu.

Du Velay, A., *Essai sur l'histoire financière de la Turquie depuis le règne du Sultan Mahmoud II jusqu'à nos jours.* Paris, 1903.
By an Ottoman Bank official. Easily the best financial history. Translated into Turkish as *Türkiye malî tarihi* in *Maliye mecmuası* 12 (April-June 1939) ff.

Dwight, H. G. O., *Christianity Revived in the East; or, a narrative of the work of God among the Armenians of Turkey.* New York, 1850.
Strong evangelical viewpoint of one of the original Congregational missionaries in İstanbul. Some information on Armenian church problems.

Dwight, Henry O., "Some Peculiarities of Turkish Politics," *Harper's*, 61 (October 1880), 745-753.
Good observations, with a criticism of Midhat's Ottoman brotherhood plans.

Eckardt, J. T., "Islamitische Reformbestrebungen der letzten hundert Jahre," *Deutsche Rundschau*, 104:10 (July 1900), 39-60.
On the contrast between Wahhabis, Babis, and "Young Turk" Islam on one hand, and the general obscurantism prevailing in the nineteenth century on the other.

Edmonds, William A., "Language Reform in Turkey and its Relevance to Other Areas," *Muslim World*, 45:1 (January 1955), 53-60.
Includes discussion of nineteenth-century alphabet reform proposals. Largely a translation of an article by Agâh Sırrı Levend in *Ulus*, 9 August 1953.

Edwards, H. Sutherland, *Sir William White, for Six Years Ambassador at*

Constantinople: his life and correspondence. London, 1902.
Fairly thin. White was in Belgrade from 1875 to 1878, and in İstanbul for the 1876-1877 conference.

Eichmann, F., *Die Reformen des osmanischen Reiches, mit besonderer Berücksichtigung des Verhältnisses der Christen des Orients zur türkischen Herrschaft.* Berlin 1858.
By the Prussian minister to the Porte, 1853-1856. Solid work on Hatt-ı Hümayun's origins, provisions, implications.

Elliot, Gertrude, "Turkey in 1876. A Retrospect," *Nineteenth Century,* 64: 380 (October 1908), 552-566.
By the ambassador's daughter. Informative, pro-Midhat, covers end 1875 to start 1877, includes several letters.

Elliot, Sir Henry G., "The Death of Abdul Aziz and of Turkish Reform," *Nineteenth Century,* 23:132 (February 1888), 276-296.
An account of 1875-1877 by the British ambassador; a vindication of Midhat.

————, *Some Revolutions and other Diplomatic Experiences.* London, 1922.
Edited by his daughter, based on diaries and letters. Elliot was ambassador in İstanbul from 1867 to 1876.

Emin, Ahmed—*see* Yalman.

The Encyclopaedia of Islam. London and Leyden, 1913-1938.
Invaluable, both for scholarly articles and for bibliographies.

The Encyclopaedia of Islam, new ed. Leiden and London, 1954-
Excellent articles, much superior in many cases to the first edition. Those on Turkish subjects often draw liberally from *İslâm ansiklopedisi* (q.v.). Now in letter *D*.

Engelhardt, Edouard, *La Turquie et le Tanzimat, ou histoire des réformes dans l'Empire ottoman depuis 1826 jusqu'à nos jours.* 2 vols. Paris, 1882-1884.

By a French consul at Belgrade. A unique book, the only connected reform history, very useful despite many lacunae. Based on documents and his own notes on conditions, though sources not always specified. Quite a few factual errors.

Ergin, Osman, *Türkiye maarif tarihi* [History of education in Turkey]. 5 vols. in 2. İstanbul, 1939-1943.
Full of useful information, based on published works and some unpublished documents, especially for nineteenth century. Organized topically, not historically. Last two volumes are post-1908. Dates given are not always accurate.

Esad Efendi, *Hükûmet-i meşrute* [Constitutional government]. İstanbul, 1293.
Pamphlet of 26 October 1876 supporting constitution, reprinted in Süleyman Paşa zade, *Süleyman Paşa muhakemesi* (q.v.).

Eversley, Lord, *The Turkish Empire from 1288 to 1914, and from 1914 to 1922 by Sir Valentine Chirol.* New York, 1923.
Pedestrian, slight, rather Turcophobe.

Farley, J[ames] Lewis, *The Decline of Turkey, financially and politically,* 2nd ed. London, 1875.
————, *Egypt, Cyprus, and Asiatic Turkey.* London, 1878.
————, *Modern Turkey.* London, 1872.
————, *Turkey.* London, 1866.
————, *Turks and Christians, a solution of the Eastern Question.* London, 1876.
————, *Two Years in Syria.* London, 1858.
Farley was employed in the Ottoman Bank in Turkey, and then became Ottoman consul in Bristol. His earlier books are all favorable to Turkey, aiming to show its economic potential and to attract capital and settlers. He himself was involved in financial development schemes. After 1872 his books are more critical of the Turks, and are pro-Slav after 1875, perhaps because the Porte's economies stopped his salary as consul. The above are the most informative of his works on

439

Turkey; several others exist. He claimed to know Âli and Fuad well. His books of 1875 and 1876 are very anti-Mahmud Nedim. Three of the works publish Fuad's testament.

Fatma Aliye, *Ahmed Cevdet Paşa ve zamanı* [Ahmed Cevdet Paşa and his time]. İstanbul, 1332.
A life of the jurist and statesman by his daughter, based on his *Tezâkir*, especially #6 and #40. Goes only to the Crimean War period, but has valuable reflections on other Ottoman statesmen.

Fehmi, Youssouf, *Histoire de la Turquie*. Paris, 1909.
By a 1908 Young Turk, slightly apologist for Turks, brief, with rare indication of sources.

Fesch, Paul, *Constantinople aux derniers jours d'Abdul-Hamid*. Paris, [1907].
Contains a wealth of information on Turkey under Abdülhamid II, with some retrospective sections.

Forsyth, Douglas, *Autobiography and Reminiscences*. Edited by his daughter. London, 1887.
This Indian civil servant travelled to Kashgar in 1870 and 1873. Account from his letters, reports, and *The* (London) *Times*. Centered on English-Turkestan relations, but deals with İstanbul as factor also.

Franco, Gad, *Développements constitutionnels en Turquie*. Paris, 1925.
A better-than-average law thesis, using some Ottoman historians, though giving neither footnotes nor bibliography. Fair on 1876.

Franco, M., *Essai sur l'histoire des israélites de l'Empire ottoman depuis les origines jusqu'à nos jours*. Paris, 1897.
By an İstanbul notable, sketchy, but informative on religion, press, books. Good deal on nineteenth century.

Frechtling, Louis E., "Anglo-Russian Rivalry in Eastern Turkistan, 1863-1881," *Royal Central Asian Journal*, 26:3 (July 1939), 471-489.

Based on Foreign Office and other British documents.

Freeman, Edward A., *The Ottoman Power in Europe, its nature, its growth, and its decline*. London, 1877.
Pure invective against the criminal Turk, almost racist in its concepts.

Fua, Albert, *Abdul-Hamid II et Mourad V, masque de fer*. Paris, 1909.
By a Young Turk editor in exile. Upholds Murad's sanity, condemns Abdülhamid. No documentation.

Fuad, Muhammad—Paşa, and Ahmed Jawdat [Mehmed Fuad and Ahmed Cevdet], *Grammatik der osmanischen Sprache*. Kellgren, trans. Helsingfors, 1855.
Translation of this significant early grammar.

Gallenga, Antonio, *Two Years of the Eastern Question*. 2 vols. London, 1877.
Valuable account of events in İstanbul by the *Times* correspondent there, November 1875 to April 1877. Some inaccuracies, especially on provincial matters. Somewhat pro-Russian and anti-Elliot.

Gambier, J. W., "The Life of Midhat Pasha," *Nineteenth Century*, ..III:11 (January 1878), 71-96.
Pro-Midhat, but fairly sane and matter-of-fact, by an Englishman in İstanbul in 1877.

Ganem, Halil, *Les Sultans ottomans*. 2 vols. Paris, 1902.
By a Syrian, a delegate to the 1877 parliament, later exile in Paris. Poor history, not documented.

Geary, Grattan, *Through Asiatic Turkey. Narrative of a Journey from Bombay to the Bosphorus*. 2 vols. London, 1878.
By the editor of the *Times of India*, who rode horseback across Iraq and Syria, March-June 1878. Acute observations.

Gelzer, Heinrich, *Geistliches und Weltliches aus dem türkisch-griechischen Orient*. Leipzig, 1900.
Poor on Turks, better on Greek and

Armenian churches in the Ottoman Empire, chiefly under Abdülhamid II.

[Gerçek], Selim Nüzhet, *Türk gazeteciliği, yüzüncü yıl dönömü vesilesile* [Turkish journalism, on the occasion of its hundredth anniversary]. İstanbul, 1931.
Useful survey of the Turkish press in the Ottoman Empire (not exile papers) from 1831 to 1880, preceded by an account of the French language press there since 1790.

Gibb, E. J. W., *A History of Ottoman Poetry.* 6 vols. London, 1900-1909.
Excellent, ranges into politics and general culture. Vol. IV on 1700-1850; vol. V on Şinasi and Ziya, but never completed. See adverse criticism in Martin Hartmann, *Der Islamische Orient* (Leipzig, 1902), I, 140, 144-145.

Gibb, H. A. R., and Harold Bowen, *Islamic Society and the West: A Study of the Impact of Western Civilization on Moslem Culture in the Near East,* I: *Islamic Society in the Eighteenth Century.* 2 parts. London, 1950-1957.
A detailed examination of the structure of government and society in the eighteenth-century Ottoman Empire, with some historical background. Uses Turkish and Arabic sources, as well as western.

Giese, Friedrich, "Das Seniorat in osmanischen Herrscherhause," *Mitteilungen zur osmanischen Geschichte,* II (1923-1926), 248-256.
On the question of succession in the dynasty.

"A Glimpse of the Yemen Insurrection," *Chambers's Journal,* I:407 and II:408 (14 and 21 October 1871), 641-644, 659-662.
An Englishman who travelled on a Turk transport describes inefficiency and deplorable army conditions.

Gobineau, C. S. de, ed., *Correspondance entre le Comte de Gobineau et le Comte de Prokesch-Osten (1854-1876).* Paris, 1933.
Prokesch was Austrian ambassador in İstanbul during most of these years; Gobineau, French envoy in Tehran, Athens, and elsewhere. Valuable information on Babis and some other Eastern matters.

Gökalp, Ziya, *Turkish Nationalism and Western Civilization: Selected Essays of Ziya Gökalp.* Niyazi Berkes, trans. and ed. New York, 1959.
Careful translation with scholarly annotations. Gökalp made many comments on the Tanzimat period, some acute and some born of ignorance.

Gövsa, İbrahim Alâettin, *Türk meşhurları ansiklopedisi* [Encyclopedia of Turkish notables]. İstanbul, n.d. [1946?].
Useful brief biographies, fairly full for nineteenth-century men.

Goldziher, Ignaz, *Vorlesungen über den Islam.* Heidelberg, 1910.
Scholarly, excellent. Chiefly on older times, but comes down to 1908, on law, dogma, asceticism, sects.

Gordon, Leland J., *American Relations with Turkey, 1830-1930; an economic interpretation.* Philadelphia, 1932.
Concentrates on 1900-1930, earlier part slighter and in places inaccurate.

Greppi, Comte, "Souvenirs d'un diplomate italien à Constantinople, 1861-1866," *Revue d'histoire diplomatique,* 24 (July 1910), 372-387.
By a first secretary of the legation. Chiefly useful for description of Abdülaziz.

Hachtmann, Otto, "Türkische Übersetzungen aus europäischen Literaturen. Ein bibliographischer Versuch," *Die Welt des Islams,* VI:1 (1918), 1-23.
Starts with Şinasi; chiefly 1890 on.

Haim, Sylvia G., "Islam and the Theory of Arab Nationalism," *Die Welt des Islams,* n.s., IV:2/3 (1955), 124-149.
Useful for the development of nationalist terminology.

Hajek, Alois, *Bulgarien unter der Türkenherrschaft.* Stuttgart, 1925.
The best on this subject, using Bulgarian sources, fuller as it approaches

1876. Some reflections also on the Turkish side of the question.

Halid, Halil, *The Diary of a Turk.* London, 1903.
Light, short, but honest, by a Turk who fled in 1894. Gives some information on New Ottomans and Abdülhamid.

Hamdy Bey, *Les costumes populaires de la Turquie en 1873.* Constantinople, 1873.
Photographs and comments, done for the Vienna Exposition of 1873.

Hamid, Mustafa, "Das Fremdenrecht in der Türkei. Mit einer geschichtlichen Darstellung über das türkische Recht und die Kapitulationen," *Die Welt des Islams,* VII:1/2 (1919), 1-96.
Good brief historical summary.

Hamlin, Cyrus, *Among the Turks.* New York, 1878.
——, *My Life and Times.* Boston, 1893.
The first contains far more of general interest and acute observation; the second is more personal. Hamlin was first president of Robert College, knew Turkey well.

Hammer-Purgstall, Joseph von, *Des osmanischen Reichs Staatsverfassung und Staatsverwaltung.* 2 vols. Vienna, 1815.
Description of central and provincial government, with translation of many laws and ordinances.
——, *Geschichte des osmanischen Reiches.* 10 vols. Pest, 1827-1835.
Often more of a source book than an integrated history. Stops at the beginning of the nineteenth century. Vol. x deals with some of Mahmud II's reforms.

Harris, David, *Britain and the Bulgarian Horrors of 1876.* Chicago, 1939.
Useful for account of Turkish opinion and statements.
——, *A Diplomatic History of the Balkan Crisis of 1875-1878. The First Year.* Stanford, 1936.

Immensely detailed, using British and Austrian archives.

Hasluck, F. W., *Christianity and Islam under the Sultans.* Margaret M. M. Hasluck, ed. 2 vols. Oxford, 1929.
Essays and information, copious, not integrated. On religious lore, folklore, mixtures and survivals, chiefly in Anatolia, but also Balkans and Egypt.

Heidborn, A., *Manuel de droit public et administratif de l'Empire ottoman.* 2 vols. Vienna, 1908-1912.
On land, justice, administration, kinds of laws, and public finance.

L'Hellénisme contemporain. Second series, VII, extra fascicle. *1453-1953. Le cinq-centième anniversaire de la prise de Constantinople.* Athens, 1953.
A spotty collection of sixteen articles, half on 1453, the rest on Greeks under Ottoman rule.

Hellwald, Friedrich, *Der Islam. Türken und Slaven.* Augsburg, 1877.
Intelligent essays, despite anti-Turk bias. Sees no hope for reform.

Heuschling, Xavier, *L'empire de Turquie.* Brussels, 1860.
A survey and handbook.

Hidden, Alexander, *The Ottoman Dynasty; a history of the Sultans of Turkey from the earliest authentic record to the present time.* New York, 1912.
By a Robert College graduate, son of an employee of the Ottoman mint. Anecdotal, uneven, of little value.

Hilaire, P.—de Barenton, *La France catholique en Orient durant les trois derniers siècles d'après des documents inédits.* Paris, 1902.
By a Capucin, using documents of his order; also on Jesuits, Augustinians, Lazarists, et cetera.

Hill, George [Francis], *A History of Cyprus,* IV: *The Ottoman Province. The British Colony, 1571-1948.* Cambridge, 1952.
Poorly written, but excellent for information on events and administration

in Cyprus. Uses French and British consular reports, many Greek sources, a few Turkish.

Hobart Pasha, Admiral [Augustus Charles Hobart-Hampden], *Sketches from my Life*. New York, 1887.
Disappointingly slight and breezy, by an Englishman in the Turkish navy from 1867 through 1878.

Holborn, Hajo, ed., *Aufzeichnungen und Erinnerungen aus dem Leben des Botschafters Joseph Maria von Radowitz*. 2 vols. Berlin, 1925.
Frequently useful. Written by Radowitz for his family. He was in İstanbul in 1861-1862 and 1871-1872, and in Bucharest in 1870-1871.

Horn, Paul, *Geschichte der türkischen Moderne*. Leipzig, 1902.
Convenient work summarizing writings of moderns since Şinasi. Some excerpts given, no political information, occasional errors. Curiously omits Ziya.

Hornby, Edmund, *Autobiography*. London, 1928.
Hornby was judge of the British consular court in İstanbul in 1856-1865. A sound observer.

Hornby, Lady [Emilia B. Maceroni H.], *Constantinople During the Crimean War*. London, 1863.
Letters from fall 1855 to January 1858 by the wife of the British consular judge in İstanbul. Light, occasionally informative. An enlarged edition of *In and Around Stamboul* (1858).

Hoskiær, V., *Et Besøg i Grækenland, Ægypten og Tyrkiet*. Copenhagen, 1879.
Mostly on Turkey; he was in İstanbul in 1872-1873. A good observer.

Huszar, Emmerich von, "Die Memoiren des Grafen N. P. Ignatew," *Oesterreichische Rundschau*, 41:4 (15 November 1914), 166-174.
Valuable. Excerpts from Ignatyev's memoirs in *Istoricheskii Viestnik* (January 1914), on his activities 1861-1876.

İğdemir, Uluğ, *Kuleli vak'ası hakkında bir araştırma* [An investigation of the Kuleli incident]. Ankara, 1937.
A scholarly examination of the 1859 conspiracy and its motivation, based on contemporary documents.

Ignatyev, N. P., "Zapiski Grapha N. P. Ignatyeva (1864-1874)," [Memoirs of Count N. P. Ignatyev], *Izvestiia Ministerstva Inostrannykh Diel* [Ministry of Foreign Affairs News], 1914, I, 93-135; 1914, II, 66-105; 1914, III, 92-121; 1914, IV, 75-103; 1914, V, 129-148; 1914, VI, 147-168; 1915, I, 142-174; 1915, II, 164-189; 1915, III, 160-175; 1915, IV, 222-236; 1915, VI, 109-127.
Contains valuable information, despite Ignatyev's justification of his policies as Russian ambassador to the Porte.

İnal, İbnülemin Mahmud Kemal, *Osmanlı devrinde son sadrıâzamlar* [The last grand vezirs in the Ottoman period]. 14 fascicles paged continuously. İstanbul, 1940-1953.
Rather old-fashioned biographies of grand vezirs from Âli Paşa (1852) on, atomistic, not seeing history whole, yet of great value for information from a wide range of sources, some unpublished, which are often quoted at length, and for occasional shrewd observations. Oral information also used. Many citations are woefully incomplete.

——, *Son asır türk şairleri* [Turkish poets of the last century]. 3 vols. or 12 fascicles, paged continuously. İstanbul, 1930-1942.
Similar in structure to the foregoing. Gives political as well as literary information.

İnalcık, Halil, "Land Problems in Turkish History," *Muslim World*, 45:3 (July 1955), 221-228.
Concise review of the original tenure system, its breakdown, and later reform efforts.

——, "Tanzimat nedir?" [What is the Tanzimat?], pp. 237-263 in *Tarih araştırmaları, 1940-1941* [Investigations in history, 1940-1941]. İstanbul, 1941.

443

Argues that the land problem was a basic question.

———, *Tanzimat ve Bulgar meselesi* [The Tanzimat and the Bulgar question]. Ankara, 1943.
A good doctoral thesis, using Turkish archival sources and some Bulgar and western materials. Concentrates on the land problem. Summary in French.

İskit, Server Rifat, *Türkiyede matbuat idareleri ve politikaları* [Press administrations and policies in Turkey]. İstanbul, 1943.

———, *Türkiyede matbuat rejimleri* [Regimes of the press in Turkey]. İstanbul, 1939.

———, *Türkiyede neşriyat hareketleri tarihine bir bakış* [A survey of the history of publication activities in Turkey]. İstanbul, 1939.
All useful, sometimes repetitious of one another. Dates given need checking. Press, regulation, censorship generally covered.

İslâm ansiklopedisi. İstanbul, 1940-
Based on *The Encyclopaedia of Islam* (q.v.), with rewritten and often vastly enlarged and improved articles on Turkish subjects, as, for instance, the articles on Âli, Fuad, Cevdet, Midhat. A valuable reference work, now in the letter Ö.

İsmail Habib—*see* Sevük.

İstanbul Üniversitesi, *Hukuk Fakültesī öğretim üyeleri ve yardımcılarının yayınları, 1933-1947* [Publications of the staff of instruction and assistants of the law faculty, 1933-1947]. İstanbul, 1948.
A useful bibliography, listings by author and by subject, with summaries of each work.

———, Université de Stamboul, *Université de Stamboul; historique, organisation, et administration actuelles.* Stamboul, 1925.
A slight pamphlet, half on the historical aspect.

Izzet, Riza, *La Turquie réformatrice et Midhat Pacha.* Lille, 1913.
A poor thesis without critical apparatus; contributes nothing new, though lists Turkish sources in bibliography.

Jäschke, Gotthard, "Die Entwicklung des osmanischen Verfassungsstaates von den Anfängen bis zur Gegenwart," *Die Welt des Islams*, V: 1/2 (1917), 5-56.
Good pioneer account, chiefly on 1876 and 1908 constitutions, using Turkish sources. Errors on 1876.

———, "Türkische Gesetzsammlungen," *Die Welt des Islams*, n.s., III:3/4 (1954), 225-234.
Information on laws, codes, and translations since 1839.

Jánossy, Dénes, "Die ungarische Emigration und der Krieg im Orient," *Archivum Europae Centro-Orientalis*, V:1-4 (1939), 113-275.
Covering 1850-1856, and fullest on 1853, showing Kossuth's efforts to use the Crimean War crisis, and reproducing a list of Magyars in the Ottoman Empire.

Jelavich, Barbara, "The British Traveller in the Balkans: the abuses of Ottoman administration in the Slavonic provinces," *Slavonic and East European Review*, 33:81 (June 1955), 396-413.
On the status of Christians, from travel accounts.

Jenks, Leland H., *The Migration of British Capital to 1875.* New York, 1938.
Treats British investments from 1800 to 1875, fairly well linked to political history. Brief chapter on Near East.

Jerrold, W. Blanchard, *Egypt under Ismail Pasha, being Some Chapters of Contemporary History.* London, 1879.
Principally a political treatment, sketchy to 1863. Gives some information on Halim and Mustafa Fazıl.

Jessup, Henry Harris, *Fifty-Three Years in Syria.* 2 vols. New York, 1910.
Based on a diary from 1855 on, and letters; covers Syria from 1856 to 1909, centers largely on Beirut missions, but adds other items, though in typical missionary style.

444

————, *The Women of the Arabs*. New York, 1873.
Contains reflections on cultural conditions.

Jonquière, le Vicomte de la, *Histoire de l'Empire ottoman depuis les origines jusqu'à nos jours*, rev. ed. 2 vols. Paris, 1914.
Spread thin, and not scholarly.

Jorga, Nicholas, *Geschichte des osmanischen Reiches*. 5 vols. Gotha, 1908-1913.
Fairly good. Vol. v covers 1774-1912.

Jwaideh, Albertine, *Municipal Government in Baghdad and Basra from 1869 to 1914*. Oxford, unpublished B.Litt. thesis, 1953.
Based on interviews, Arabic and Turkish works, and the vilayet newspaper. Some reflections on Midhat as vali.

Kanitz, [Philipp] Felix, *Donau-Bulgarien und der Balkan. Historisch-geographisch-ethnographische Reisestudien aus den Jahren 1860-1878*. 3 vols. Leipzig, 1875-1879.
Pedestrian account of seventeen trips in this region. Kanitz's chief interest is geography, but he includes many comments on Turkish government. The chapter promised in vol. ii on Turkish provincial administration did not appear in vol. iii.

Kaplan, Mehmed, *Namık Kemal, hayatı ve eserleri* [Namık Kemal, his life and works]. İstanbul, 1948.
A good doctoral thesis, relying on published sources, summarizing his life and analyzing his views topically.

Karal, Enver Ziya, *Osmanlı tarihi*, v: *Nizam-ı cedit ve Tanzimat devirleri (1789-1856)* [Ottoman history, v: the periods of the Nizam-i cedid and the Tanzimat]. Ankara, 1947.
A general account, much based on European works, half concerned with military and diplomatic aspects.

————, *Osmanlı tarihi*, vi: *Islahat fermanı devri, 1856-1861* [The period of the reform decree (of 1856), 1856-1861]. Ankara, 1954.
Also general, topical rather than chronological in approach, reaching back at times to Mahmud II or Selim III. Mostly on revolts, administrative organs, and economy.

————, *Osmanlı tarihi*, vii: *Islahat fermanı devri, 1861-1876* [The period of the reform decree (of 1856), 1861-1876]. Ankara, 1956.
Constructed like the preceding volume. Best parts on description of governmental institutions.

Kératry, E[mile] de, *Mourad V: prince - sultan - prisonnier d'état (1840-1878), d'après des témoins de sa vie*. Paris, 1878.
Well-informed, though inaccurate at times, and needs checking. Kératry was in İstanbul and the Balkans about 1877, but omits documentation except for reference to Murad's friend Alexander Holinski.

Khadduri, Majid, and Herbert J. Liebesny, eds., *Law in the Middle East*, i: *Origin and Development of Islamic Law*. Washington, 1955.
Uneven work; chapters on şeriat and *mecelle* in the Ottoman Empire are not up to the level of some others.

Khérédine, Le Général [Hayreddin], *Réformes nécessaires aux états musulmans*. Paris, 1868.
An essay written in 1867 by the Tunisian statesman, as an introduction to a larger work (in Arabic) on the state.

Kissling, Hans J., "Die türkische Sprachreform," *Leipziger Vierteljahrschrift für Südosteuropa*, 1:3 (October 1937), 69-81.
Outlines progress from the Arab-Persian style to Atatürk's reforms.

Köprülü, Fuad, "L'institution du Vakouf: Sa nature juridique et son évolution historique," *Vakıflar dergisi*, ii (1942), partie française, 3-48.
Excellent article, explaining and defending the worth of the institution.

445

Koetschet, Josef, *Aus Bosniens letzter Türkenzeit.* Vienna, 1905.
Essentially memoirs by a Swiss physician in the Ottoman official service, covering 1875-1878. Most of this time Koetschet was in Bosnia, but in March-April 1876 he was in İstanbul.

[————], K., Dr., *Erinnerungen aus dem Leben des Serdar Ekrem Omer Pascha (Michael Lattas).* . . . Sarajevo, 1885.
By Ömer's physician, with him 1856 on, valuable on military aspect and Ömer as vali of Baghdad, 1857-1859.

————, *Osman Pascha, der letzte grosse Wesier Bosniens, und seine Nachfolger.* Sarajevo, 1909.
By the same, covering 1864-1874, mostly on civil government under Osman, who was vali to 1869. Informed and honest account.

Koray, Enver, *Türkiye tarih yayınları bibliyografyası, 1729-1950* [Bibliography of historical publications in Turkey]. Ankara, 1952.
Uncritical list, but most useful, including articles as well as books in old letters and new, with index. The major sections are on Ottoman and Turkish history. Second ed., 1959, includes works to 1955.

Kukiel, M., *Czartoryski and European Unity, 1770-1861.* Princeton, 1955.
Based on Handelsman's biography, plus some archival materials. Reflects Polish exile concerns with Ottoman Empire.

Kuntay, Mithat Cemal, *Namık Kemal, devrinin insanları ve olayları arasında* [Namık Kemal, among the men and events of his time]. 2 vols. in 3. İstanbul, 1944-1956.
A mine of information, badly organized, using and reproducing many unpublished documents.

————, *Sarıklı ihtilâlci Ali Suavi* [The turbaned revolutionary Ali Suavi]. İstanbul, 1946.
A biography based on Ali Suavi's writings, Ebüzziya's account of the New Ottomans, and some unpublished documents.

Kuran, Ahmed Bedevî, *Osmanlı İmparatorluğunda inkılâp hareketleri ve millî mücadele* [Revolutionary movements and the national struggle in the Ottoman empire]. İstanbul, 1956.
Repeats and expands his 1948 *İnkılâp tarihimiz ve İttihad ve Terakki* [Our history of revolution and (the committee of) union and progress]. Thin on events to 1877.

Kyriakos, A. Diomedes, *Geschichte der Orientalischen Kirchen von 1453-1898.* Erwin Rausch, trans. Leipzig, 1902.
A part of the Athens professor's three-volume history of the Christian church. Very pro-Orthodox. Chapters on millets and Greek church in Turkey.

Lamouche, Léon, *Histoire de la Turquie depuis les origines jusqu'à nos jours.* Paris, 1934.
Of little use for the Tanzimat period.

————, *L'organisation militaire de l'Empire ottoman.* Paris, 1895.
Factual, sensible, on the Turkish army of about 1890, by a captain of engineers and an oriental scholar. Curiously omits the 1869 reforms of Hüseyin Avni.

Landau, Jacob M., *Parliaments and Parties in Egypt.* Tel-Aviv, 1953.
Has information from the 1860's on.

Lane-Poole, Stanley, *The Life of the Right Hon. Stratford Canning, Viscount Stratford de Redcliffe.* 2 vols. London, 1888.
Includes long quotations from Stratford. Somewhat eulogistic.

————, *Turkey.* New York, 1899.
Brief, and very poor on nineteenth century.

Langer, William L., *European Alliances and Alignments,* 2nd ed. New York, 1950.
Standard for European diplomacy, 1871-1890, and introduces pertinent material on internal Ottoman affairs.

Layard, Austen Henry, *Discoveries in the Ruins of Nineveh and Babylon, with Travels in Armenia, Kurdistan and the Desert.* . . . New York, 1853.

Contains observations on conditions in 1849-1850.

———, "The Eastern Question and the Conference," *Quarterly Review*, 143 (January 1877), 276-320.
In support of Turkey, by the newly arrived British ambassador.

Lee, Dwight Erwin, *Great Britain and the Cyprus Convention Policy of 1878*. Cambridge, Mass., 1934.
Based largely on unpublished British documents, covering 1875-1880.

———, "The Origins of Pan-Islamism," *American Historical Review*, 47:2 (January 1942), 278-287.
Based on western sources; raises problem of origins, suggesting possible answers. Finds term first used in 1876.

Léouzon, le Duc Louis Antoine, *Midhat Pacha*. Paris, 1877.
Very poorly documented, and eulogistic, but factual statements seem largely true. Disappointing on 1876.

Leroy-Beaulieu, Anatole, "Les réformes de la Turquie; la politique russe et le panslavisme," *Revue des deux mondes*, 3rd period, 18 (1 December 1876), 508-537.
Distrusts constitution, campaigns for local reforms and local autonomies in Balkans.

Levend, Agâh Sırrı, *Türk dilinde gelişme ve sadeleşme safhaları* [Aspects of development and simplification in the Turkish language]. Ankara, 1949.
Concerned with style, vocabulary, alphabet, and grammar in the nineteenth and twentieth centuries.

Lewak, Adam, *Dzieje emigracji polskiej w Turcji (1831-1878)* [Account of the Polish emigration in Turkey (1831-1878)]. Warsaw, 1935.
A scholarly study based on archival materials in Poland, France, and Hungary, showing Polish influence in the Ottoman Empire and connections with the New Ottomans. Value now enhanced because the Polish documents were destroyed in World War II.

Lewis, Bernard, "The Concept of an Islamic Republic," *Die Welt des Islams*, n.s., IV:1 (1955), 1-9.
Discusses the term "cumhuriyet," and whether the caliphate embodied elective or republican principles.

———, *The Emergence of Modern Turkey*. London, 1961.
The best account of political and cultural development since the eighteenth century, based on a wide variety of sources.

———, "The Impact of the French Revolution on Turkey," *Journal of World History*, 1:1 (July 1953), 105-125.
A perceptive essay on the infiltration of new ideas.

Lewis, Geoffrey, *Turkey*. New York, 1955.
Contains brief sections on the nineteenth century.

Loeb, Isidore, *La situation des Israélites en Turquie, en Serbie et en Roumanie*. Paris, 1877.
Misleading title. Almost all on Serbia and Roumania; documents showing Jewish struggles for equality.

Longrigg, Stephen H., *Four Centuries of Modern Iraq*. Oxford, 1925.
Gives some attention to Midhat.

Lybyer, Albert H., *The Government of the Ottoman Empire in the Time of Suleiman the Magnificent*. Cambridge, Mass., 1913.
Pioneer study. Provides background for decline and reform.

———, "The Turkish Parliament," *Proceedings of the American Political Science Association*, 1910, pp. 65-77.
On the 1908 parliament, citing precedents.

Lynch, H. F. B., *Armenia: Travels and Studies*, II: *The Turkish Provinces*. London, 1901.
A thorough descriptive work. Armenian millet constitution printed as an appendix.

MacColl, Malcolm, *The Eastern Question: its facts and fallacies*. London, 1877.

447

Righteous indignation against the Turks, by one in İstanbul in 1876.

———, "Midhat Pasha on Turkish History and Reform," *Gentleman's Magazine*, 243 (July 1878), 31-49.
A bitter and ignorant reply to Midhat's article of 1878 (q.v.).

Mackenzie, G. Muir, and A. P. Irby, *Travels in the Slavonic Provinces of Turkey-in-Europe*. London, 1866.
Good reporting by two doughty women who carried their zinc-lined bathtub on an extensive Balkan trip in 1863. Basically sympathetic to Slav freedom.

Macler, Frédéric, "Les Arméniens en Turquie," *Revue du monde musulman*, 24 (September 1913), 115-173.
Deals in part with the Armenian millet constitution. This article is reprinted in the following title.

———, *Autour de l'Arménie*. Paris, 1917.
By a first-rate Armenian scholar. A collection of articles, frequently overlapping, as in three accounts of the Armenian constitution. Useful for condensations from Armenian works, especially the revolutionary *Haykakan Charmjan Nakhapalmouthiun* [Origins of the Armenian movement] (Geneva, 1912-1914) of Varandian.

Mahmud Celaleddin, *Mirât-ı hakikat. Tarih-i Mahmud Celaleddin Paşa* [The mirror of truth. History of Mahmud Celaleddin Paşa]. 3 vols. İstanbul, 1326-1327.
Valuable work, much of it based on firsthand information, by a competent observer who was head of the office in the Porte charged with palace communications. Begins with 1839, but concentrates almost entirely on 1875-1878.

Malcolm-Smith, E. F., *The Life of Lord Stratford Canning (Lord Stratford de Redcliffe)*. London, 1935.
A better biography than Lane-Poole's, though not so full.

Mardin, Ebül'ulâ, *Medenî hukuk cephesinden Ahmet Cevdet Paşa (1822-1895)* [Ahmed Cevdet Paşa from the viewpoint of civil law]. İstanbul, 1946.
His life and an analysis of his work, using many documents, some unpublished, including pieces of Cevdet's historical notes or memoirs on his own time (*Tezâkir* and *Mâruzat*).

Mardin, Şerif, *The Genesis of Young Ottoman Thought: A Study in the Modernization of Turkish Political Ideas*. Princeton, 1962.
Scholarly analysis of political thought of the leading New Ottomans, and their intellectual background.

Mehmed Gâlib, "Tarihten bir sahife—Âli ve Fuad Paşaların vasiyetnameleri" [A page of history—the testaments of Âli and Fuad Paşas], *Tarih-i osmanî encümeni mecmuası*, 1:2 (1329), 70-84.
Gives text of Fuad's testament, with an introduction on the authenticity and possible authorship of the documents.

Mehmed Memduh, *Mirât-ı şuûnat* [Mirror of events]. İzmir, 1328.
Firsthand account, written originally in 1876, by a Palace official. Mostly on court and ministerial politics, sometimes trivial.

Mehmed Süreyya, *Sicilli Osmanî* [Ottoman register]. 4 vols. İstanbul, 1308-1311.
One of the best biographical dictionaries.

Melek-Hanum, *Six Years in Europe. . . .* L. A. Chamarovzow, ed. London, 1873.
Largely personal and lightweight. Melek was in this period, 1866-1872, already divorced from Kıbrıslı Mehmed.

———, *Thirty Years in the Harem: or, the Autobiography of Melek-Hanum, wife of H. H. Kibrizli-Mehemet-Pasha*. London, 1872.
Though probably this French-Greek-Armenian wife of Dr. Millingen and Kıbrıslı Mehmed had help in writing her memoirs, the naïve quality is often quite revealing. Covers her life to 1866.

448

BIBLIOGRAPHY

Midhat, [Ahmed Şefik], "The Past, Present, and Future of Turkey," *Nineteenth Century*, III:18 (June 1878), 981-993.

The French original is printed immediately following, pp. 993-1000. It appeared also in the *Revue scientifique de la France*, 2nd series, VII:49 (8 June 1878), 1149-1154; also in pamphlet form with an introduction by A. H. Midhat as *La Turquie, son passé, son avenir* (Paris, 1901), slightly edited but not materially altered. Turkish translations appeared in pamphlet form in 1295, 1324, and 1326, and an Arabic translation in Beirut in 1879. Midhat wrote in exile, for Turkey and against Russia. It is a reasonably good exposé of his views, but not profound.

[———], *Question d'Orient. Adresse des positivistes à Midhat-Pacha . . . (26 août 1877) [Réponse de Midhat-Pacha]*. Paris, 1877.

Midhat's brief reply echoes others of his statements.

Midhat, Ali Haydar, "English and Russian Politics in the East," *Nineteenth Century*, 53:311 (January 1903), 67-78.

Brief review of reform by Midhat's son, reproducing some of his father's letters of 1876-1877. Some factual errors.

———, *Hâtıralarım, 1872-1946* [My memoirs, 1872-1946]. İstanbul, 1946.

Somewhat disordered. Almost one half is on his father, Midhat Paşa, though the portions to 1877 are scantier than in his English *Life of Midhat Pasha* (q.v.).

———, *The Life of Midhat Pasha, a record of his services, political reforms, banishment, and judicial murder, derived from private documents and reminiscences*. London, 1903.

A most useful biography by the son, but with many inaccuracies and garbled dates, and somewhat tailored to the English-reading public. Reproduces quite a few documents. The son must have had good editorial assistance in writing.

———, *Midhat-Pacha. Sa vie—son oeuvre, par son fils. . . .* Paris, 1908.

Subject to the same criticisms as the *Life* in English, but also useful because it often presents different information or documents.

———, ed., *Midhat Paşa: Hayat-ı siyâsiyesi, hidematı, menfa hayatı. . . .* [Midhat Paşa: his political life, services, life in exile], I: *Tabsıra-i ibret* [Demonstration of warning]. II: *Mir'ât-ı hayret* [Mirror of amazement]. İstanbul, 1325.

These are Midhat Paşa's "memoirs," though actually they seem to be based on memoranda and incomplete memoirs by Midhat, and documents preserved by him, the whole edited by his son. See A. H. Midhat, *Hâtıralarım*, pp. 83, 137-138. Volume I is a biography of Midhat, corresponding exactly neither to the life in French nor to that in English, though with many duplications. Volume II is essentially on Abdülaziz's death and Midhat's trial for alleged complicity in his murder.

———, *Midhat Paşanın hayat-ı siyâsiyesi, hidematı, şehadeti. . . .* [Midhat Pasha's political life, services, martyrdom]. Cairo, 1322.

Essentially a translation of the 1903 English *Life*, indicating that the first third was written by Midhat Paşa while exiled in Taif, and the rest compiled by his son from various papers.

———, *Souvenir de mon exil volontaire.* Geneva, 1905.

A collection of articles and documents, half of them reviews of his English biography of Midhat. Others on Abdülhamid's rule and on Young Turks.

Milev, Nicholas, "Réchid pacha et la réforme ottomane," *Zeitschrift für Osteuropäische Geschichte*, II (1912), 382-398.

Chiefly a résumé of a memorandum by Reşid for Metternich, of 10 March 1841. Deals with the Hatt-ı Şerif of 1839 among other things.

449

Miller, William, *The Ottoman Empire and its Successors*. Cambridge, 1927.
Concerned chiefly with the Balkan successor states and diplomatic problems; very little on internal Ottoman affairs.

[Millingen, Frederick], Major Vladimir Andrejevich Osman-Bey, *Les Anglais en Orient, 1830-1876*. Paris, 1877.
Remarkable book, Millingen's defense of his mother, who was married to Byron's doctor, then to Kıbrıslı Mehmed Paşa. Some information on New Ottomans.

[———],Vladimir Andrejevitch Osman-Bey, *Les imams et les derviches; pratiques, superstitions, et moeurs des Turcs*. Paris, 1881.
Sections on ulema, softas, superstitions, and the succession problem.

[———], Osman-Seify Bey, *La Turquie sous le règne d'Abdul Aziz, 1862-1867*. Paris, 1868.
Millingen served in the Turkish army from 1853 to 1864, and then fell out with Fuad. This dispute colors the book strongly, but it is of value.

———, *Wild Life among the Koords*. London, 1870.
Some resemblance to the above. Concerns eastern Anatolian conditions about 1862.

Mismer, Charles, *Souvenirs du monde musulman*. Paris, 1892.
By a Frenchman, editor of *La Turquie* in İstanbul from 1867 to 1871, very close to Âli, and for a time Âli's "French secretary." Useful, but must be checked, since written twenty years after.

Moltke, Helmuth von, *Briefe über Zustände und Begebenheiten in der Türkei aus den Jahren 1835 bis 1839*, 2nd ed. Berlin, 1876.
Written 1841 or before. Moltke covered a good deal of the empire and had official entrée as military adviser.

Morawitz, Charles, *Die Türkei im Spiegel ihrer Finanzen*. George Schweitzer, trans. Berlin, 1903.
Largely a description of receipts and expenses as of date of writing; historically adds little to Du Velay.

Mordtmann, Andreas David, *Anatolien, Skizzen und Reisebriefe (1850-1859)*. Franz Babinger, ed. Hannover, 1925.
On geography, place names, ruins, as well as political, social, and economic conditions. Appeared as fifty articles in *Das Ausland*, 1855-1863. By a Hamburger, good orientalist, and at this time chargé d'affaires of Hanseatic legation in İstanbul.

[———], *Stambul und das moderne Türkenthum: politische, sociale und biographische Bilder, von einem Osmanen*. 2 vols. Leipzig, 1877-1878.
An invaluable source. Mordtmann was in İstanbul from 1846 to 1879, as Hanseatic diplomat, judge of a Turkish commercial court, editor, and professor. Book composed largely of dispatches written to *Augsburger Allgemeine Zeitung* and *Hamburger Nachrichten* right after the event. Some are reworked. The book is unorganized, repetitious, in spots exaggerated, but full of information.

———, "Ueber das Studium des Türkischen," *Zeitschrift der Deutschen Morgenländischen Gesellschaft*, III (1849), 351-358.
On grammars, difficulties, and the various types of spoken and written language.

Morris, Robert, *Freemasonry in the Holy Land*. Chicago, 1880.
By a naïve enthusiast of LaGrange, Kentucky, who travelled in the Near East in 1868. Useful for some information on Muslim Masons in Turkey.

Mosse, W. E., "The Return of Reschid Pasha: An Incident in the Career of Lord Stratford de Redcliffe," *English Historical Review*, 68:269 (October 1953), 546-573.
Uses British, French, and Austrian archival reports to elucidate Reşid's return to power in 1856; critical of Temperley's "Last Phase of Stratford de Redcliffe" (q.v.).

Moüy, Charles de, *Lettres du Bosphore: Bucarest-Constantinople-Athènes*. Paris, 1879.

By the French chargé d'affaires, in İstanbul from 1875 to 1878. This is a fairly ordinary travel book.

———, "Souvenirs d'un diplomate: un essai du régime parlementaire en Turquie (1876-1878)," *Revue des deux mondes*, 4th period, 157 (1 February 1900), 616-652.
A spiritual reconstruction of these years. Moüy was secretary of the Constantinople Conference, 1876-1877.

al Mudarris, Fahmi, "Al-mathal al-ʿalā wa Midḥat Bāshā" [The ideal and Midhat Paşa], pp. 52-65 in *Maqālāt siyāsiyya, tārikhiyya, ijtimāʿiyya* [Political, historical, and social articles], I. Baghdad, 1349/1931.
Praise of Midhat's achievements used as a springboard for criticism of later developments.

Mülinen, Eberhard Graf von, *Die Lateinische Kirche im türkischen Reiche*, 2nd ed. Berlin, 1903.
Slight, concise.

[Murray, E. C. Grenville], *Turkey. Being sketches from life by the Roving Englishman*, rev. ed. London, 1877.
A reprint of articles written from 1851 to 1856; delightful sketches of Ottoman peoples and customs.

[Mustafa Fazıl], *Lettre adressée à Sa Majesté le Sultan par S. A. le Prince Mustapha-Fazil-Pacha*. Paris, n.d. [1867].
The famous letter of the Egyptian to Abdülaziz. For a list and discussion of other editions see chapter VI, notes 109 and 111.

[Namık] Kemal Bey, *Heimat oder Silistria*. Leopold Pekotsch, trans. Vienna, 1887.
His 1873 play, *Vatan*, in German translation.

Nelidow, "Souvenirs d'avant et d'après la guerre de 1877-1878," *Revue des deux mondes*, 6th period, 27 (15 May 1915), 302-339, and 28 (15 July 1915), 241-277.
Valuable. Nelidov was counsellor of the Russian embassy in İstanbul. Fairly impartial; covers years 1875-1877; some mistakes in dates.

Newton, Charles Thomas, *Travels and Discoveries in the Levant*. 2 vols. London, 1865.
Letters by the British vice-consul in Mytilene, 1852-1859, also in Rhodes. Chiefly antiquarian in interest, but some political side lights.

Newton, Lord [Thomas W. Legh], *Lord Lyons: A Record of British Diplomacy*. 2 vols. London, 1913.
Lyons was ambassador to the Porte from 1865 to 1867. Fairly thin on this period.

Nicolaïdy, B., *Les Turcs et la Turquie contemporaine: itinéraire et compte rendu de voyages dans les provinces ottomanes*. 2 vols. Paris, 1859.
By a Greek army engineer; Turcophobe account of a trip in Macedonia and Thessaly c. 1858-1859.

Nour, Riza, "Namik Kemal, grand poète turc," *Revue de Turcologie*, II (1932), 1-25.

Noury, Soubhy, *Le régime représentatif en Turquie*. Paris, 1914.
Of some value, though depends largely on Engelhardt.

Østrup, J., *Islam under der Nittonde Århundradet* [Islam in the nineteenth century]. Axel Nihlen, trans. Stockholm, 1924.
A concise review of religion, politics, literature, society in Near and Middle East.

———, "Den moderne, literaere bevaegelse i Tyrkiet" [The modern literary movement in Turkey], *Nordisk Tidskrift för Vetenskap, Konst och Industri* (1900), 206-222.
A good general article on Şinasi, Namık Kemal, Ahmed Midhat, and a few others.

[Özön], Mustafa Nihat, *Metinlerle muasır türk edebiyatı tarihi* [History of modern Turkish literature with texts]. İstanbul, 1934.
A textbook covering the period since 1800, with biographical sketches and bibliographies as well as extracts.

————, *Namık Kemal ve İbret gazetesi* [Namık Kemal and the Newspaper *İbret*]. İstanbul, 1938.

A useful selection of Namık Kemal's articles in this paper in 1872-1873, with some explanatory comment on the times and the Turkish press.

————, *Son asır türk edebiyatı tarihi* [History of Turkish literature of the last century]. İstanbul, 1941.

A *lycée* text, much like his 1934 book.

Okandan, Recai G., *Âmme hukukumuzda Tanzimat ve birinci meşrutiyet devirleri* [The Tanzimat and first constitutional periods in our public law]. İstanbul, 1946.

Incorporated into the next work.

————, *Umumî âmme hukukumuzun ana hatları* [Outline of our general public law]. 1: *Osmanlı devletinin kuruluşundan inkırazına kadar* [From the founding of the Ottoman state until its collapse]. İstanbul, 1948.

A useful scholarly work with detailed, somewhat harsh, examination of the constitution of 1876; the latter half is on the period of the 1908 constitution.

Omer [Ömer] Hilmi, *A Treatise on the Laws of Evkaf*, C. R. Tyser and D. G. Demetriades, trans. Nicosia, 1899.

A technical discussion, with references to the *Mecelle* where appropriate.

Onar, Sıddık Sami, *İdare hukukunun umumî esasları* [The general bases of administrative law]. İstanbul, 1952.

Includes local and provincial administration. Mostly on the Republic, but some historical sections.

————, "Les transformations de la structure administrative et juridique de la Turquie et son état actuel," *Revue internationale des sciences administratives*, IV (1955), 741-786.

Large parts derived from the preceding work. Useful summary.

Onou, Alexander, "The Memoirs of Count N. Ignatyev," *Slavonic Review*, X:29, 30 (December 1931, April 1932), 386-407, 627-640; and XI:31 (July 1932), 108-125.

Ignatyev's memoirs digested and discussed by the son of his dragoman.

Ormanian, Malachia, *L'Eglise arménienne; son histoire, sa doctrine, son régime, sa discipline, sa liturgie, sa littérature, son présent*. Paris, 1910.

Gives a sketchy history of the church. Ormanian was an ex-patriarch of İstanbul. English translation, *The Church of Armenia*, London, 1955.

Osman Nuri, *Abdülhamid-i Sani ve devr-i saltanatı* [Abdülhamid II and the period of his rule]. 3 vols. in 1. İstanbul, 1327.

A popular history, not always reliable, with an irritating lack of reference to sources.

Ostrorog, Leon, *The Angora Reform*. London, 1927.

Three brilliant lectures; on the roots of the law, Turkish psychology and nineteenth-century reforms, and the 1922-1926 reforms.

Ost-Turkestan und das Pamir-Plateau nach den Forschungen der Britischen Gesandschaft unter Sir T. D. Forsyth 1873 und 1874 (Petermann's Mittheilungen, Ergänzungsheft 52). Gotha, 1877.

From the English report published in 1875 in Calcutta. Petermann treats geography more, excluding most of the political elements.

Padel, W. and L. Steeg, *De la législation foncière ottomane*. Paris, 1904.

A straightforward textbook by the German embassy dragoman and the French consul in Salonika.

Pâkalın, Mehmed Zeki, *Tanzimat maliye nazırları* [Ministers of Finance in the Tanzimat]. 2 vols. İstanbul, 1939-1940.

Disordered biographies with much useful information.

Palgrave, William Gifford, *Essays on Eastern Questions*. London, 1872.

A collection of articles published in English magazines, 1867-1872. Palgrave knew the East, lived in Anatolia, but was an eccentric not always reliable.

Palmieri, Aurelio, *L'Associazione commerciale artigiana di pietà in Costantinopoli. Cenni storici, 1837-1902.* Naples, 1902.
Concerned with Catholic charitable foundations; gives occasional light on the Latin community in İstanbul.

Papadopoullos, Theodore H., "Prologomena to the History of the Greek Church under Turkish Domination (1450-1800)," pp. 1-158 in *Studies and Documents relating to the History of the Greek Church and People under Turkish Domination.* Brussels, 1952.
Deals in scholarly fashion with Greek church organization, weaknesses, and reform.

Pears, Edwin, *Forty Years in Constantinople.* New York, 1916.
Anecdotal reminiscences written without notes by an English barrister in İstanbul, 1873-1915. Somewhat Turcophobe; a number of factual errors.

————, *Life of Abdul Hamid.* New York, 1917.
A poor biography, duplicates Pears' *Forty Years* in spots, but is more accurate. Leans on Midhat's biography and Elliot's article, damns Abdülhamid.

Pelissié du Rausas, G., *Le régime des capitulations dans l'Empire ottoman.* 2 vols. Paris, 1902-1905.
Most of vol. II is on Egypt.

Perrot, Georges, *Souvenirs d'un voyage en Asie Mineure.* Paris, 1864.
By a classical archaeologist who travelled in central and western Anatolia. This incorporates and expands a series of four articles in the March and April 1863 issues of the *Revue des deux mondes.*

Petrosian, IUriı Ashotovich, "*Novye Osmany*" *i bor'ba za konstitutsiiu 1876 g. v Turtsii* [The "New Ottomans" and the struggle for the 1876 constitution in Turkey]. Moscow, 1958.
A good study, based on Turkish and western sources, but disappointing because of lack of thorough use of Russian archives, and because of attempt to fit New Ottomans and polit-

ical events into a straitjacket of Marxist economic-political terminology.

[Piazzi, Mme. Adriana Delcembre] Leila Hanoum, *Le Harem impérial et les sultanes aux xixe siècle, souvenirs . . . ,* 2nd ed. Paris, 1925.
Unpretentious memoirs dealing with the years 1854 to 1876 and beyond, possibly by a Frenchwoman married to a Turkish official or possibly, as is claimed, by the daughter of a prominent Turk.

Pitzipios-Bey, J. G., *L'Orient. Les réformes de l'Empire byzantin.* Paris, 1858.
Apparently a Greek, writing in exile. Criticizes Turkey, proposes that the sultan turn Christian!

"The Political Testament of Fuad Pasha," *Nineteenth Century*, 53:312 (February 1903), 190-197.
Editor's note claims this was translated from an authentic copy and is its first appearance in English. See R. H. Davison in *Belleten*, 1959.

Poujade, Eugène, *Chrétiens et Turcs; scènes et souvenirs de la vie politique, militaire et religieuse en Orient.* Paris, 1859.
By a French consul. All pre-1854.

Prime, E. D. G., *Forty Years in the Turkish Empire, or Memoirs of Rev. William Goodell,* 4th ed. New York, 1877.
Goodell was a Congregational missionary in Beirut from 1822 to 1831, and in İstanbul from 1831 to 1865. Book based on his letters and journal. Very little on nonmission affairs.

Prokesch-Osten, Anton Graf, "Ein Beitrag zur Geschichte der orientalischen Frage, aus dem Nachlass des Grafen Prokesch-Osten, k. k. Österr. Feldzeugmeisters und Botschafters," *Deutsche Revue*, IV:1 (October-December 1879), 6-19, 171-188.

————, "Erinnerungen aus Konstantinopel, aus dem Nachlass des Grafen Prokesch-Osten, k. k. Botschafter und Feldzeugmeister," *Deutsche Revue*, IV:2 (January-March 1880), 61-74.

————, "Erinnerungen aus den Jahren 1870 und 1871. Aus den hinterlassenen Papieren des k. k. Botschafters Grafen von Prokesch-Osten," *Deutsche Revue*, IV:3 (April-June 1880), 11-21.

Three extracts from Prokesch's unpublished memoirs on his years as ambassador in İstanbul. The first covers 1855-1858, the second 1860-1861, the third 1870-1871.

"Provincial Turkey," *Quarterly Review*, 137 (October 1874), 313-354.

Based on Slade, Van Lennep, and consular reports. Sees *derebeyi*'s as better than reforms.

Ramsay, William M., "The Intermixture of Races in Asia Minor: some of its causes and effects," *Proceedings of the British Academy 1915-1916*, pp. 359-422.

A historical explanation of the mixture, increases, and decreases, with chief attention to late nineteenth century.

Ranke, Leopold von, *The Ottoman and Spanish Empires in the Sixteenth and Seventeenth Centuries*. Walter K. Kelly, trans. Philadelphia, 1845.

The first part is a perceptive essay, based on Venetian archives and western published sources, on the Ottoman system and its decline to Murad IV's time.

Raschdau, L[udwig], ed., "Aus dem politischen Nachlass des Unterstaatssekretärs Dr. Busch," *Deutsche Rundschau*, 137 (December 1908), 368-405.

————, "Die Botschafterkonferenz in Konstantinopel und der russisch-türkische Krieg (1877-1878), aus dem literarischen Nachlass des Unterstaatssekretärs Dr. Busch," *Deutsche Rundschau*, 141 (October-December 1909), 12-28, 207-222, 361-379.

————, "Diplomatenleben am Bosporus. Aus dem literarischen Nachlass des Unterstaatssekretärs Dr. Busch," *Deutsche Rundschau*, 138 (January-March 1909), 203-222, 380-405.

Articles from memoirs and diaries of the German dragoman in İstanbul from 1861 to 1868, and early in 1877,

who was an acute observer and good Turkish scholar. The third deals with 1861-1868, the first chiefly with 1875-1876, the second with 1877-1878.

Raschdau, Ludwig, *Ein sinkendes Reich; Erlebnisse eines deutschen Diplomaten im Orient 1877-1879*. Berlin, 1934.

By a German consular official who arrived in İstanbul at the end of April 1877.

Reden, Freiherr F. W. von, *Die Türkei und Griechenland in ihrer Entwicklungsfähigkeit; eine geschichtlich-statistische Skizze*. Frankfurt a. M., 1856.

Written in 1855. Chiefly on Turkey. Treats finance, army, population questions, et cetera.

Redjai, Omer, *L'évolution constitutionnelle en Turquie et l'organisation politique actuelle*. Strasbourg, 1934.

Chiefly on the Ankara government. Very weak on period to 1877.

Reed, Howard A., *The Destruction of the Janissaries by Mahmud II in June, 1826*. Princeton University, unpublished Ph.D. thesis, 1951.

Uses both Turkish and western published sources; a detailed examination.

Riker, Thad Weed, *The Making of Roumania: A Study of an International Problem, 1856-1866*. London, 1931.

Chiefly on great-power diplomacy, but detailed use of British, French, and Austrian archives casts light on Ottoman situation and policies also.

————, "Michael of Serbia and the Turkish Occupation," *Slavonic and East European Review*, 12:34-36 (July 1933), 133-154, (January 1934), 409-429, (April 1934), 646-658.

Similar in character to the foregoing.

Risal, P., *La ville convoitée—Salonique*. Paris, 1914.

A general history of Salonika from ancient times to 1914. Pro-Jewish. Small section on Tanzimat era.

Rodkey, F[rederick] S[tanley], "Ottoman Concern about Western Economic Penetration in the Levant, 1849-1856,"

Journal of Modern History, 30:4 (December 1958), 348-353.
Based entirely on British Foreign Office archives, and deals almost entirely with loan proposals.

Rosen, Georg, *Geschichte der Türkei von dem Siege der Reform im Jahre 1826 bis zum Pariser Tractat vom Jahre 1856.* 2 vols. Leipzig, 1866-1867.
With Temperley, the best on this period. Draws on Prussian archives and his own experience in İstanbul and Syria.

Rouvière, Franck, *Essai sur l'évolution des idées constitutionnelles en Turquie.* Montpellier, 1910.
Better than most theses, with a fair discussion of the 1876 constitution, though inadequate sources.

Rumbold, Sir Horace, *Recollections of a Diplomatist.* 2 vols. London, 1902.
Breezy and anecdotal, by a chargé under Elliot in İstanbul from 1871 to 1873.

Sabry, M., *L'empire égyptien sous Ismail et l'ingérence anglo-française (1863-1879).* Paris, 1933.
Uses London and Paris archives, principally on finance, Suez, Sudan, and intervention. Little on relations with the Porte. Large portions verbatim from his 1924 Paris thesis.

Said Paşa, [Mehmed], *Said Paşanın hâtıratı* [Said Paşa's memoirs]. 3 vols. İstanbul, 1328.
Said was Abdülhamid's secretary from 1876 to 1877, but says almost nothing about these years.

St. Clair, G. G. B., and C. A. Brophy, *Twelve Years' Study of the Eastern Question in Bulgaria.* London, 1877.
A revised edition of their *A Residence in Bulgaria* (1869). By an English ex-captain and an ex-consul, who also had Polish relatives, lived near Edirne, and knew Turkish. Very pro-Muslim, anti-Christian, with some errors of fact, but has a good deal of information.

Salaheddin Bey, *La Turquie à l'exposition universelle de 1867.* Paris, 1867.
By Âli's son-in-law. A review of the Turkish exhibits, together with a section of statistics on Turkey, which appear to be from the 1865-1866 *Salname* (Almanac), but which Ubicini (*Etat présent*, p. vi) claims were lifted from his *Lettres* via Viquesnel.

Salname [Almanac]. İstanbul, 1263 (1846-1847) ff.
The yearbook of the Ottoman government, useful chiefly for lists of central and provincial offices and officials. Used #24 (1869-1870), #27 (1872-1873), #29 (1874-1875).

Sammarco, Angelo, *Histoire de l'Egypte moderne, depuis Mohammed Ali jusqu'à l'occupation britannique (1801-1882), d'après les documents égyptiens et étrangers,* III: *Le règne du Khédive Ismail, de 1863 à 1875.* Cairo, 1937.
Based on Egyptian, English, French, Italian, Austrian, and American archives, thorough, unimaginative. Some information on relations with the Porte, much as in his following work, but not so good as Douin.

————, *Les règnes de ʿAbbas, de Saʿid et d'Ismaʿil (1848-1879) avec un aperçu de l'histoire du Canal de Suez.* Rome, 1935.
Quite like the preceding in sources and treatment.

Sarkiss, Harry Jewell, "The Armenian Renaissance, 1500-1863," *Journal of Modern History,* IX:4 (December 1937), 433-448.
Cultural in its approach.

Sarkissian, A. O., *History of the Armenian Question to 1885.* Urbana, Illinois, 1938.
Full of information from Armenian sources.

Sassoon, David Solomon, *A History of the Jews in Baghdad.* Letchworth, Eng., 1949.
Portions on the nineteenth century are not detailed.

Sax, Carl Ritter von, *Geschichte des Machtverfalls der Türkei bis Ende des 19. Jahrhunderts und die Phasen der "orientalischen Frage" bis auf die*

Gegenwart, 2nd ed. Vienna, 1913.
Based on good sources, including some Turkish. Entirely political in its approach.

Scheltema, J. F., ed., *The Lebanon in Turmoil. Syria and the Powers in 1860.* New Haven, 1920.
A translation of the chronicle of Iskander ibn Yaqʻūb Abkāriyūs, with notes, introduction, and conclusion. Deals in part with Fuad's work as special commissioner.

Schlechta-Wssehrd, O. Freiherr von, "Bibliographische Anzeigen. Bericht über die in Constantinopel erschienen neuesten orientalischen Druckwerke," *Zeitschrift der Deutschen Morgenländischen Gesellschaft,* 20:2/3 (1866), 448-455.
Like the lists of Bianchi and Belin. Continues Wssehrd's earlier lists in the *Sitzungsberichte der Wiener Akademie der Wissenschaften.*

———, "Ueber den neugestifteten türkischen Gelehrter-Verein," *Zeitschrift der Deutschen Morgenländischen Gesellschaft,* 17:3/4 (1863), 682-684.
A report on the Cemiyet-i ilmiye-i osmaniye.

Schmeidler, W. F. Carl, *Geschichte des osmanischen Reiches im letzten Jahrzehnt.* Leipzig, 1875.
Sketchy, but accurate as far as it goes. Not an integrated history, but a review of the empire by sections.

Schuyler, Eugene, *Selected Essays. With a memoir by Evelyn Schuyler Schaeffer.* New York, 1901.
The memoir, pp. 1-204, is a biography by his sister, quoting a number of his letters. Schuyler came to the United States legation in İstanbul in June 1876.

———, *Turkistan. Notes of a Journey in Russian Turkistan, Khokand, Bukhara, and Kuldja.* 2 vols. New York, 1876.
Intelligent travel account, by a Russian scholar and American diplomat. Some references to Ottoman-Turkestan relations.

Schweiger-Lerchenfeld, Amand Freiherr von, *Bosnien, das Land und seine Bewohner,* 2nd rev. ed. Vienna, 1879.
A good general description, with information on the vilayet system.

———, "Ingenieur Josef Černik's Technische Studien-Expedition durch die Gebiete des Euphrat und Tigris . . . ," *Petermann's Mittheilungen,* Ergänzungshefte, 44 and 45 (1875-1876).
From diaries and personal accounts. Cernik was sent out to study Baghdad railway routes by Pressel, in Syria and Iraq. Largely technical, but observations on people, government, and Midhat's reputation in Baghdad.

[———], *Serail und Hohe Pforte, Enthüllungen über die jüngsten Ereignisse in Stambul, nach Original-Aufzeichnungen und Documenten.* Vienna, 1879.
Author apparently knew Turkey well, and New Ottomans, perhaps in their exile. He may have been an İstanbul Mason. At one point he used Midhat's notes.

———, *Unter dem Halbmonde: ein Bild des ottomanischen Reiches und seiner Völker nach eigener Anschauung und Erfahrung.* Jena, 1876.
Really a long essay on Ottoman corruption, tantalizing in lack of detail despite evident knowledge.

Schweitzer, Georg, *Emin Pascha, eine Darstellung seines Lebens und Wirkens mit Benutzung seiner Tagebücher, Briefe, und Wissenschaftlichen Aufzeichnungen.* Berlin, 1898.
Story of Eduard Schnitzer, a doctor in Turkish service around Antivari (Bar), 1864-1874. Copious letters.

Şehsuvaroğlu, Halûk Y., *Sultan Aziz: hususî, siyasî hayatı, devri ve ölümü* [Sultan Aziz: his private and political life, his period, and his death]. İstanbul, 1949.
A popular book, based on some of the best published sources and some manuscripts, though documentation is incomplete. A good deal on 1876.

Selim Nüzhet—*see* Gerçek.

Senior, Nassau W., *A Journal Kept in Turkey and Greece in the Autumn of*

1857 and the Beginning of 1858. London, 1859.

Verbatim reports of conversations with foreign and native residents in İstanbul, İzmir, and Dardanelles region.

Seton-Watson, R. W., *Disraeli, Gladstone, and the Eastern Question: a study in diplomacy and party politics*. London, 1935.

Based largely on British sources, with a few French and German. Slavophile, Turcophobe, but informative.

[Sevük], İsmail Habib, *Avrupa edebiyatı ve biz. Garpten tercümeler* [European literature and ourselves. Translations from the West]. İstanbul, 1940-1941.

Chronological survey, divided topically by period and country, from ancient Greek to the twentieth century.

Shaw, Stanford J., "Archival Sources for Ottoman History: The Archives of Turkey," *Journal of the American Oriental Society*, 80:1 (January-March 1960), 1-12.

A scholarly, methodical survey of resources in the Başvekâlet, Top Kapı, and other official archives, plus some private *fonds*. Shows how much needs yet to be worked for monographic studies.

Sidarouss, Sésostris, *Des patriarcats. Les patriarcats dans l'Empire ottoman et spécialement en Egypte*. Paris, 1906.

A reasonably good law thesis, dealing with Orthodox, Armenian, and Catholic patriarchates and sectarian divisions.

Silbernagl, Dr. Isidor, *Verfassung und gegenwärtiger Bestand sämtlicher Kirchen des Orients. Eine kanonistisch-statistische Abhandlung*, 2nd ed., rev. by Joseph Schnitzer. Regensburg, 1904.

Good factual descriptions of Roman, Orthodox, and Gregorian churches, and lesser Christian churches.

Sousa, Nasim, *The Capitulatory Regime of Turkey: Its History, Origin, and Nature*. Baltimore, 1933.

The most detailed of recent treatments, from a legal viewpoint.

Sperling, E., "Ein Ausflug in die isaurischen Berge im Herbst 1862," *Zeitschrift für Allgemeine Erdkunde*, Neue Folge, 15 (1863), 418-438; 16 (1864), 1-69.

By the Prussian dragoman. His chief interest was cartography, but some acute observations on provincial government are included.

Spuler, Bertold, *Die Minderheitenschulen der europäischen Türkei von der Reformzeit bis zum Weltkrieg (mit einer Einleitung über das türkische [mohammedanische] Schulwesen)*. Breslau, 1936.

Outlines Turkish education from 1800 to 1877, then treats minorities.

Stavrianos, L[eften] S[tavros], *Balkan Federation: A History of the Movement Toward Balkan Unity in Modern Times*. Northampton, Mass., 1944.

Covers 1770-1941, including detailed treatment of the 1860-1878 alliance system.

Steen de Jehay, le Comte F. van den, *De la situation légale des sujets ottomans non-musulmans*. Brussels, 1906.

By a Belgian minister. Summarizes millet organizations. Good bibliography.

Stern, Bernhard, *Jungtürken und Verschwörer, Die innere Lage der Türkei unter Abdul Hamid II. Nach eigenen Ermittelungen und Mittheilungen osmanischer Parteiführer*, 2nd ed. Leipzig, 1901.

First edition suppressed by Abdülhamid. Well-informed, though sources not given. Chiefly on post-1876. Section on pre-1876 probably represents views of later Young Turks. Stern knew Midhat's doctor.

Story, Sommerville, ed., *The Memoirs of Ismail Kemal Bey*. London, 1920.

By a Muslim Albanian, aide to Midhat. Dictated in Paris when he was seventy. A little confused in spots, but useful.

Stratford de Redcliffe, "Turkey," *Nineteenth Century*, 1:4 (June 1877), 707-728, and 5 (July 1877), 729-752.

457

Observations written in 1861, with some notes as of 1877. An analysis of the need for, and possibilities of, reform.

Süleyman Paşa, *Hiss-i inkılâb, yahud Sultan Abdülazizin hal'i ile Sultan Murad-ı Hamisin cülusu* [The feeling of the revolution, or Sultan Abdülaziz's deposition and Murad V's accession]. İstanbul, 1326.
Valuable small volume of memoirs, giving a firsthand account by a participant in these events. Written probably immediately afterwards, in the summer and fall of 1876. Stops abruptly in the first days of Murad's reign.

Süleyman Paşa zade Sami, ed., *Süleyman Paşa muhakemesi . . .* [Süleyman Pasha's trial]. İstanbul, 1328.
A biography and defense of his constitutionalist father by the son, with large portions on his interrogation and trial arising from his generalship in the Russo-Turkish War of 1877. Includes part of an unfinished memoir by Süleyman on the events of December 1876 and January 1877 connected with the constitution.

Süssheim, Karl, "Der Zusammenbruch des türkischen Reiches in Europa," pp. 67-104 in *Die Balkanfrage*, vol. III of the *Veröffentlichungen der Handelshochschule München*. Munich, 1914.
Covers 1566-1913, concentrating on post-1826.

Sumner, B[enedict] H[umphrey], "Ignatyev at Constantinople," *Slavonic Review*, 11:32 (January 1933), 341-353, and 33 (April 1933), 556-571.
A concise summary of Ignatyev's memoirs from the *Istoricheskii Viestnik* and the *Izvestiia Ministerstva Inostrannykh Diel.*

———, *Russia and the Balkans, 1870-1880.* Oxford, 1937.
Wide use of printed Russian sources, which throw occasional light on Ottoman affairs. Excellent study.

Sungu, İhsan, "Galatasaray Lisesinin kuruluşu," [The founding of the Galatasaray *lycée*], *Belleten*, VII:28 (October 1943), 315-347.

Uses documents and press comments of the time.

———, *Namık Kemal, 21 Birincikânun 1840—2 Birincikânun 1888* [Namık Kemal, 21 December 1840—2 December 1888]. İstanbul, 1941.
A laudatory pamphlet life of the writer, with fairly extensive quotations from him.

Synvet, A., *Les Grecs de l'Empire ottoman. Etude statistique et ethnographique*, 2nd rev. ed. Constantinople, 1878.
Based on Ottoman government and Orthodox church statistics plus private information. Fuller on Europe than Asia.

———, *Traité de géographie générale de l'Empire ottoman.* Constantinople, 1872.
A text by a Galatasaray teacher with French training.

Tanpınar, Ahmed Hamdi, *XIX. asır türk edebiyatı tarihi* [History of nineteenth century Turkish literature], I, 2nd rev. ed. İstanbul, 1956.
On the westernizing movement generally; fairly full on the New Ottoman writers.

Tansel, Fevziye Abdullah, "Arap harflerinin ıslahı ve değiştirilmesi hakkında ilk teşebbüsler ve neticeleri (1862-1884)" [The initial efforts at reform and alteration of the Arabic characters and the results], *Belleten*, 17:66 (April 1953), 223-249.
The views and proposals of Münif Paşa, Ahundzade Feth-Ali, and other writers of the period.

———, *Namık Kemal ve Abdülhak Hâmid, hususî mektuplarına göre* [Namık Kemal and Abdülhak Hamid as seen in their private correspondence]. Ankara, 1949.
Covers 1875-1885, including reflections on political life and figures as well as on literature.

Tanzimat, Yüzüncü yıldönömü münasebetile [The Tanzimat, on the occasion of its hundredth anniversary], I. İstanbul, 1940.
A huge work of some thirty uneven essays on various aspects of the period,

unintegrated, but valuable, though much of it is narrowly legal in viewpoint. İhsan Sungu's long essay on the New Ottomans is practically a source collection of writings taken from their newspapers.

Taylor, J. G., "Journal of a Tour in Armenia, Kurdistan, and Upper Mesopotamia . . . in 1866," *Journal of the Royal Geographical Society*, 38 (1868), 281-361.
Chiefly on geography and antiquities, with some information on the Kızılbaşı's. Taylor was British consul in Kurdistan.

Temperley, Harold, "British Policy towards Parliamentary Rule and Constitutionalism in Turkey (1830-1914)," *Cambridge Historical Journal*, IV:2 (1933), 156-191.
———, "The Last Phase of Stratford de Redcliffe, 1855-1858," *English Historical Review*, 47:186 (April 1932), 216-259.
———, "The Treaty of Paris of 1856 and its Execution," *Journal of Modern History*, IV:3 (September 1932), 387-414, and 4 (December 1932), 523-543.
Three articles, chiefly on diplomacy, but also reflecting on internal Ottoman conditions. Based largely on British and Austrian archives.
———, *England and the Near East. The Crimea.* London, 1936.
Story of Anglo-Turkish relations from 1808 to 1853, with considerable sections on Turkish government and reform based on British, Dutch, and French archives.

Thielmann, Max von, *Streifzüge im Kaukasus, in Persien, und in der asiatischen Türkei.* Leipzig, 1875.
Interesting account of a trip in 1872-1873: Poti-Tiflis-Tabriz-Baghdad-Damascus-Beirut.

[Thornbury, George Walter], "The Late Insurrection in Turkey," *Chambers's Journal*, 13:326 (31 March 1860), 193-197.
Chatty account of the abortive 1859

revolt by an Englishman who was in İstanbul at the time.
———, *Turkish Life and Character.* 2 vols. London, 1860.
A chatty, overdramatized account of a trip to İstanbul and Bursa in 1859, mostly on externals. The chapter on the Kuleli incident of 1859 reproduces the above article.

Thouvenel, L., *Trois années de la Question d'Orient, 1856-1859.* Paris, 1897.
Largely composed of letters by Thouvenel, French ambassador to the Porte during these years. Centers on diplomatic problems.

Tischendorf, Paul Andreas von, *Das Lehnswesen in den moslemischen Staaten insbesondere im osmanischen Reiche.* Leipzig, 1872.
By the German embassy dragoman. A solid work on feudal holdings, summarizing land problems to 1858. Reprints Ayni Ali's work on fiefs.

Treitschke, Heinrich von, "Die Türkei und die Grossmächte," *Preussische Jahrbücher*, 37:6 (1876), 671-712.
Sees Ottoman strength in strict Islam and absolute sultan, and westernizing reform as a sin against nature.

Tschihatscheff, P. von, *Reisen in Kleinasien und Armenien, 1847-1863.* Petermann's Mittheilungen, Ergänzungsheft 20, (1867).
His notebooks on eight trips, 1848-1863, edited by Kiepert, oriented toward cartography, but containing political observations also.

Türkiye Cumhuriyeti, Maarif Vekilliği. *Türkiye bibliyoğrafyası.* [Bibliography (of publications) in Turkey], I: *Resmî neşriyat, 1928-1938* [Official publications]; II: *Hususî neşriyat, 1928-1938* [Private publications]. İstanbul, 1939.
———, Millî Eğitim (or Kultur) Bakanlığı, *Türkiye bibliyoğrafyası.* İstanbul, 1935 ff.
Together these volumes list publications since the alphabet change, including historical works, though there is no selective or critical principle.

459

Books, offprints, newspapers, and periodicals intermingled. The second series has appeared with varying numbers of fascicles yearly.

Tunaya, Tarık Z., *Türkiyede siyasî partiler, 1859-1952* [Political parties in Turkey, 1859-1952]. İstanbul, 1952.
A disjointed but very useful survey of parties and programs, including groups that were not genuine political parties. Though mostly on the period since 1908, deals also with the Tanzimat period.

Les Turcs et la Bulgarie. Paris, 1869.
An anonymous Bulgarophile pamphlet, not too violent, with criticism of Midhat and the vilayet law.

La Turquie après la Conférence. Constantinople, 1877.
Possibly Midhat's work. Apparently a governmental exposition of Turkey's position, dated 29 January 1877.

Tutundjian, Télémaque, *Du pacte politique entre l'Etat ottoman et les nations non musulmanes de la Turquie.* Lausanne, 1904.
Contains a detailed description of the 1863 Armenian millet constitution and organization.

Tyser, C. R., F. Ongley, and M[ehmed] Izzet, *The Laws Relating to Immoveable* [sic] *Property Made Vaqf.* Nicosia, 1904.
Treatise based on the *Düstur* and various İstanbul treatises.

Ubicini, J. H. Abdolonyme, *Letters on Turkey: an account of the religious, political, social, and commercial conditions of the Ottoman Empire; the reformed institutions, army, navy, etc.* Lady Easthope, trans. 2 vols. London, 1856.
Excellent descriptions, somewhat Turcophile. Written for the *Moniteur Universel*, 1850-1853. Ubicini was a Lombard born and educated in France who had been secretary of the provincial government of Wallachia.

————, *La Turquie actuelle.* Paris, 1855.
Also good; descriptions of places, peoples, institutions.

————, and Pavet de Courteille, *Etat présent de l'Empire ottoman, statistique, gouvernement, administration, finances, armée, communautés non-musulmanes, etc.* Paris, 1876.
Slighter than the *Letters*, but most useful. Based largely on the official *Salname*'s (*Yearbooks*). Written before the 1876 revolutions.

Uras, Esat, *Tarihte Ermeniler ve ermeni meselesi* [The Armenians in history and the Armenian question]. Ankara, 1950.
Pro-Turkish and badly organized, but useful for quotation of documents. Uses Armenian published sources. Deals with Armenian millet constitution of 1863, though most is post-1878.

Urquhart, David (?), *Fragments on Politeness.* London, 1870.
Extols the dignity of the Turks. Quite Turcophile.

Us, Hakkı Tarik, ed., *Meclis-i meb'usan, 1293/1877 zabıt ceridesi* [Journal of the proceedings of the 1293/1877 chamber of deputies]. 2 vols. İstanbul, 1940-1954.
Not the actual minutes, but proceedings reconstructed from the reports in contemporary newspapers.

Uzunçarşılı, İsmail Hakkı, "Beşinci Sultan Murad'ın tedâvisine ve ölümüne ait rapor ve mektuplar, 1876-1905" [Reports and letters on the treatment and death of Sultan Murad V, 1876-1905], *Belleten*, x:38 (April 1946), 317-367.
Chiefly documents, including several physicians' reports from the summer and early fall of 1876.

————, "Tunus'un 1881'de Fransa tarafından işgaline kadar burada valilik eden Hüseyni âilesi" [The Hüseyni family in the governorship of Tunis until its occupation by France in 1881], *Belleten*, 18:72 (October 1954), 545-580.
A short history of the beys of Tunis from the early eighteenth century, with accounts written by Hayreddin Paşa on the period 1862-1877.

Valmy, le Duc de [F. C. E. Kellermann],

La Turquie et l'Europe en 1867. Paris, 1867.
Supports Ottoman integrity and progress, intelligently, but often without enough substantiation.

Vambéry, Arminius, [or Hermann], *Central Asia and the Anglo-Russian Frontier Question: a series of political papers.* F. E. Bunnett, trans. London, 1874.
From 1867-1873 articles in *Unsere Zeit*, including two on Yakub Beg, one on Persian-Turkish relations.

————, "Erinnerungen an Midhat Pascha," *Deutsche Rundschau*, 11:8 (May 1878), 186-195.
In 1858 Vambéry lived in İstanbul at the house of Afif Bey, whose secretary was Midhat.

————, "Freiheitliche Bestrebungen im moslemischen Asien," *Deutsche Rundschau*, 77:1 (October 1893), 63-75.
On Turkey, Persia, and India, chiefly in 1890's, but includes firsthand information on "Young Turks" presumably in 1864.

————, *His Life and Adventures, written by himself.* New York, 1883?
Autobiography of the orientalist's early life. Vambéry was in İstanbul from 1856 to 1860, went to Bokhara in 1862-1863.

————, *Der Islam im neunzehnten Jahrhundert: eine culturgeschichtliche Studie.* Leipzig, 1875.
A general review of Islam and its relations to western progress. Anglophile bias.

————, "Jugendwanderungen," *Globus*, 25:11, 13, 14 (1874), 171-173, 201-204, 218-221.
Egoistic. On his start from İstanbul to Bokhara.

————, *Sittenbilder aus dem Morgenlande.* Berlin, 1876.
Essays on family, women, tobacco, schools, dervishes, et cetera, in Persia, Afghanistan, Central Asia, and above all in Turkey. Reprints Şinasi's play *Şair Evlenmesi* [*A Poet's Marriage*].

————, *Sketches of Central Asia.* Philadelphia, 1868.
Chapters on literature, dress, life, Islam, et cetera.

————, *Travels in Central Asia; being the account of a journey from Teheran across the Turkoman desert on the eastern shore of the Caspian to Khiva, Bokhara, and Samarcand.* New York, 1865.
Observations on the three khanates. Vambéry posed as a dervish. Some information on Ottoman relations with Central Asia. Excellent and deprecatory review by Mordtmann in *Augsburger Allgemeine Zeitung*, 14 July 1865.

————, *Das Türkenvolk in seinen ethnologischen und ethnographischen Beziehungen.* Leipzig, 1885.
On all Turks of Asia, with small section on the Ottoman mixture.

————, *La Turquie d'aujourd'hui et d'avant quarante ans.* Georges Tirard, trans. Paris, 1898.
A reply to Argyll's condemnation of Turkey. Vambéry sees progress comparing his 1856-1860 experiences to a visit c. 1897.

————, *Ueber die Reformfähigkeit der Türkei.* (Separat-Abdruck aus dem *Pester Lloyd*). Budapest, 1877.
Sane, friendly to Turks, sees some reform achieved.

Van Lennep, Henry J., *Travels in Little-Known Parts of Asia Minor.* 2 vols. London, 1870.
By a Congregational missionary resident thirty years in İstanbul, İzmir, and Tokat. Very little missionary bias, acute observation, intimate knowledge of Turkey.

Vassif, Clician—*see* Clician Vassif.

"Vefyk Pasha on Asia and Europe," *Littell's Living Age*, Series V:23 (20 July 1878), 185-188.
Based on an interview with him in Paris.

Verney, Noël, and George Dambmann, *Les puissances étrangères dans le Levant en Syrie et Palestine.* Paris, 1900.
A ponderous compendium of facts about the powers' political, educational,

religious, and economic interests, largely from 1880 to 1900, but often retrospective.

Viquesnel, Auguste, *Voyage dans la Turquie d'Europe, description physique et géologique de la Thrace.* 2 vols. Paris, 1868.
Volume I is a general survey of the Ottoman Empire as of approximately 1850.

Vucinich, Wayne S., "The Yugoslav Lands in the Ottoman Period: Postwar Marxist Interpretations of Indigenous and Ottoman Institutions," *Journal of Modern History*, 27:3 (September 1955), 287-305.
Describes a good many articles dealing with the nineteenth century.

Wachenhusen, Hans, *Ein Besuch im Türkischen Lager.* Leipzig, 1855.
Chatty, intelligent account of the Ottoman army and administration by a Prussian who was in the Balkans.

Wanda, *Souvenirs anecdotiques sur la Turquie (1820-1870).* Paris, 1884.
Rambling recollections of a Slav who was for thirty years an Ottoman army officer.

Washburn, George, *Fifty Years in Constantinople and Recollections of Robert College.* Boston, 1909.
By Robert College's second president, 1872-1903, who had lived in İstanbul since 1856. Largely on the college. Sane, pro-Bulgar, but not anti-Turk.

Wassa Effendi, *The Truth on Albania and the Albanians, historical and critical.* Edward St. J. Fairman, trans. London, 1879.
By a Christian Albanian official. Contains a section on Ottoman government.

[Werner, Franz von], Murad Efendi, *Türkische Skizzen.* 2 vols. Leipzig, 1877.
Werner left the Austrian army to serve Turkey in the Crimean War, and was later in Turkish government service.

White, Wilbur W., *The Process of Change in the Ottoman Empire.* Chicago, 1937.
Misleading title, lightweight in history, centers on international law.

Widerszal, Ludwik, *Sprawy Kaukaskie w polityce europejskiej w latach 1831-1864* [The Caucasian question in European politics in the years 1831-1864]. Warsaw, 1934.
Reflects on the Polish exiles in Turkey and their efforts to use the Caucasian question. Based on Polish, British, French archives.

Wolff, Sir Henry Drummond, *Rambling Recollections.* 2 vols. London, 1908.
Wolff was sent on various Foreign Office missions to the Near East, knew Fuad well.

"A Word for Turkey," *Knickerbocker*, 58:6 (December 1861), 476-486.
A friendly appraisal of Turkey, reflecting the hopes placed in Abdülaziz at his accession.

Y. A., *Midhat-Pacha, la constitution ottomane et l'Europe. Extrait du "Mechveret."* Paris, 1903.
Well-informed and sober pamphlet review of the New Ottomans and Midhat, using some correspondence between Midhat and Said Paşa.

[Yalman], Ahmed Emin, *The Development of Modern Turkey as Measured by its Press.* New York, 1914.
Sketchy, but full of useful information, though with some factual errors. First half is pre-1908.

Ydlibi, Abdoullah, *Why Turkey is in its Present State; an exposition of diplomatic interference.* Manchester, 1861.
By the Ottoman consul in Manchester, against capitulations and interference.

Zboinski, H., *Armée ottomane. Son organisation actuelle telle qu'elle résulte de l'exécution de la loi de 1869. . . .* Paris, 1877.
Objective and statistical description

of Ottoman military and naval strength and organization by a Belgian artillery officer who taught at the İstanbul military academy.

Zinkeisen, Johann W., *Geschichte des osmanischen Reiches in Europa.* 8 vols. Hamburg, 1840-1863.

Stops with 1812; fairly thorough to that point; uses western sources; concentrates on Europe and foreign relations.

MISCELLANEOUS PERIODICALS

Augsburger Allgemeine Zeitung.

Carries fairly full Ottoman news. Used for 1856-1877 passim, especially 1876. Mordtmann was its İstanbul correspondent. It reprinted other news, and also carried frequent İzmir dispatches.

The Diplomatic Review.

Apparently an organ for views of Urquhart, Butler-Johnstone, and their friends. Unsigned Turcophile articles. Used from January 1874 to January 1877, vols. 22-25.

Journal des débats. Paris.

Carries telegrams and occasional correspondence from İstanbul and Beirut. Used for parts of 1867.

The Levant Herald. İstanbul.

Daily edition used from 1873 to 1 March 1877, plus scattered earlier issues, and the weekly edition of 5 July 1876 (which appeared after an eight-week suspension).

The Levant Times and Shipping Gazette. İstanbul.

Used from first issue, 16 November 1868, to 30 June 1874. Daily, half English and half French, the two sections not always identical. In addition to economic news, carries official news and considerable provincial correspondence and minorities news.

Le Nord. Brussels and Paris.

Used for January to June 1867. Near East news rather anti-Turkish, and paper known as a Russian organ.

Smyrna Mail. İzmir.

Used 23 September 1862 to 1 October 1863, and 23 April to 21 May 1864. Weekly; monthly after August 1863; distinctly an organ of the local British colony and commercial interests.

Stamboul. İstanbul.

Used from its first issue, 16 August 1875, to 5 March 1877. Contains a good deal of news.

La Turquie. İstanbul.

Used for 7-13 March 1867, 1870 (after 16 August), 1871, 1873, 1875 (to 30 September). Often considered a semiofficial paper, it gives official news, and usually defends the ministry in office.

INDEX

NOTE: Names of Turkish persons are usually listed under the first component of the personal name, where the two components are ordinarily used. Some individuals commonly known by the last component only are listed under that name. For a number of important persons there are cross references. Titles such as Efendi and Paşa which in Turkish come after the name are not treated as part of the name.

aziz's European trip, 236-37; likes Midhat, 160; feud with Mustafa Fazıl, 198-99; opposed by New Ottomans, 175, 193, 219, 222, 225; and Council of State creation, 240-42; and educational reform, 244-50; and civil law reform, 253; and land reform, 256, 258-60; attacks capitulations, 260-62; death, 234; "political testament," 91-92; grammar, 178-79

Galata, 74 n75, 111, 112, 160 n63, 355, 383
Galatasaray lycée, 246-48, 250, 277, 370, 402 n166
Galib Paşa, 397
Gambetta, Léon, 320, 363
Ganesco, Gregory, 102 n108, 215 n152
Gazette du Levant, 195 n89
Gedik Paşa theatre, 297-300
Gelibolu, 297
general assembly, *see meclis-i umumî*
Germany, 74, 290. *See also* Prussia
gerontes, 127-29
gilds, 63, 120-21, 127
Gorchakov, Alexander M., 348 n177
grand council, *see meclis-i umumî*
grand rabbi, 3, 13, 383 n107. *See also* Jews
grand vezir, office of, 11, 12, 16, 28, 29, 35, 232, 292-93, 372, 399; rank of, 200
Granville, Earl, 320
Great Britain, 4, 25, 38, 290, 329, 349, 414; influence and example, 38, 52-54, 71, 74, 75, 82, 92, 112, 122, 172, 225, 235-38, 283, 293, 309, 337, 344, 353, 367; and Central Asian Turks, 272-75; and pan-Islamic sentiment, 275; and 1876 Balkan crisis, 358-59; and Constantinople Conference, 383, 391-93. *See also* Stratford de Redcliffe
Greece, 26, 50, 86, 87, 116, 133, 143, 158
Greek revolt, 25, 29
Greeks (Orthodox millet), 3, 12, 18 and n12, 21-22, 29, 43, 58-59, 61-62, 95, 106, 114-20, 222, 247, 262, 310, 316, 347, 359, 383, 385, 394, 415 n9; millet reform, 126-29, 365
Greek uniates, 119 n17
Gueron, Yakir, 130
Güllü Agop, *see* Vartovian

Hadika, 296

hahambaşı, *see* grand rabbi
Hakikat, 278, 367 n41
Halet Bey, İbrahim, 298
Halil Efendi, Kara, 343-45, 354
Halil Ganem, 345 n163
Halil Hamid Paşa, 21
Halil Şerif Paşa, 206, 268, 279, 284-85, 297, 319 n41, 326, 328, 340, 344, 366; foreign minister 1872-73, 288-91; and federalism plans, 290-91
Halim (fils), 93
Halim, Egyptian Prince, 197-98, 284, 394
Hamlin, Cyrus, 75, 78, 117 n9, 292
haraç, 53, 94 n43. *See also bedel, cizye*
Harput, 139 n8, 302, 303
Hasan Bey, *see* O'Reilly
Hasan, Çerkez, 346, 352
Hasan, Fehmi Efendi, 271, 325-26
Hasköy dockyards, 75
Hassunist controversy, 119 n17, 133
hatt-ı hümayun, 38 n61
Hatt-ı Hümayun of 1856, 54 n10, 127, 130, 222, 230, 239, 245, 260; origin, 53-54; proclamation, 3-4, 103; content, 54-57; style, 178; in Paris treaty, 4; and foreign intervention, 413-14; reaction to, 57-60, 78-79; powers' 1859 memorandum on, 105; execution of, 92-99, 114-33, 142ff, 172
hatt-ı şerif, 38 n61
Hatt-ı Şerif of Gülhane, 19, 54-55, 222, 230, 239, 360, 376, 378; proclamation, 36-38; content, 39-41; reception, 42-44; execution, 44-45, 48-50
Hayreddin Paşa, Tunuslu, 172, 228-30, 275, 364, 366, 405
Hayrullah Efendi (historian), 178 n21, 180
Hayrullah Efendi, Hasan, 322, 327-28, 330, 331, 333, 336, 339, 342 n152, 354, 364, 418
Herzegovina, 80, 104, 110, 168, 270, 307-10, 311-12, 348 n177, 369, 392. *See also* Balkans, Bosnia
Hijaz, 261, 288
Hobart Paşa, 266
Hungarians in Ottoman Empire, 76-77, 90, 100 n67, 188 n61
Hünkâr İskelesi, treaty of, 25
Hürriyet, 213 n144, 217-18, 220, 224, 296
Hurşid Paşa, 285
Hüseyin Avni Paşa, 287 n62, 292-95,

INDEX

45, 370-71; on constitutional commission, 370

Sultan, position of, 10, 15-16, 19, 353, 372; in Hatt-ı Şerif of Gülhane, 41-42; question of prerogatives in constitution, 373, 376-80, 386-87; concept of Ziya and Midhat, 398-99; in Abdülhamid II's view, 400-01, 403-04

Supreme Council of Judicial Ordinances, 28, 30, 32, 35, 43, 44, 45, 57, 82, 142-43 and n18, 239, 332, 365; parliamentary procedure in, 41; non-Muslims appointed, 93-94

Şura-yı devlet, see Council of State

Syria, 44, 75, 108, 145, 158, 172, 302

Szechenyi, Count, 355

Tahsin Efendi, Hoca, 249

Takvim-i vekayi, 27, 184, 402 n166

Talas, 303

Tanzimat, 5-9, 40, 42, 50; criticism and assessment of, 404-08. See also reform (cross-references)

Tanzimat Council, 52-53, 83-84, 86-87, 140, 143 n18, 239, 251

tariffs, 112-13, 304

Tashkent, 272

Tasvir-i efkâr, 185-86, 196, 207, 208-09

Tatars, 80, 151, 350

taxes, 11, 13, 40, 47, 73, 99-100, 104, 118, 125, 127, 131, 148, 158 n53, 162-63, 226-27, 259, 301-05, 329, 387, 414; farming of, 24, 44, 55, 107, 111, 116, 137, 141, 303; military exemption, 45, 53, 94-95. See also bedel, finances

telegraph, 9, 69, 77-78, 98, 154, 288

Télémaque, 181-82

Tercüman-ı ahval, 185-86, 191, 194 n86

Tercüme odası, 28-30, 179, 185, 188-89, 207, 297

theatre, Ottoman, see literature, drama, Gedik Paşa

Thessaly, 76

Thiers, Adolphe, 320

Thouvenel, Antoine Edouard, 53, 82, 86

Three Emperors' League, 329

Times (London), 371

Tokat, 141

Topkapı palace, 336, 341, 354

Tott, Baron de, 21

Trabzon, 359 and n5

Translation Bureau, see Tercüme odası

Treaty, see Carlowitz, Hünkâr İskelesi, Küçük Kaynarca, Paris

Treaty of guarantee (Paris, 1856), 4-5, 414

Treitschke, Heinrich von, 389

Tripoli in Africa, 80, 158, 383-84

Tuna, 153-54

Tuna vilayet, 160 n63; under Midhat, 151-58, 236, 246, 320

Tunis, 61, 158 n57, 160 n63, 204, 228, 275, 345, 350, 364 n27, 365

Turkestan, 272-76, 347

Turkish language, 63-64, 84, 247, 250, 372, 388. See also drama, literature, schools

Turkomans, 273, 359

La Turquie, 90, 102 n108, 168, 263, 269, 275, 282, 306, 398, 400

Ubicini, J. H. Abdolonyme, 67, 173

ulema, 12, 22, 24, 25, 27, 34, 42, 45, 67-69, 101, 174, 245-46, 249-50, 258-59, 320, 326, 329, 331, 344, 361, 368, 369, 373; and constitutional discussion 1876, 348 and n176; oppose constitution, 373-74. See also softas

Ulûm, 218, 220, 225 n189

United States, 74, 158, 261 n111, 285, 306

university, 45, 245, 249-50, 271, 375

Utujian, Garabed, 121-22

Uzunçarşılı, İ. H., 418

Vahan Efendi, 370, 400

vakıf, 18, 86, 99, 111 and n88, 142, 241, 256-58, 304; reform of, 236, 258-60

Vakit, 367, 384

vali, 147. See also vilayet law

Van, 385 n114

Van Lennep, Henry J., 174

Varna, 152, 153

Vartovian, Agop, 298-99

Vasıf Efendi, Kiliçyan, 154, 420-21

vatan, 56 n15, 194 and n86, 221, 298. See also nationalism (Turkish), patriotism

Vatan yahut Silistre, 298-301, 347, 395-96

Vefik, Ahmed, see Ahmed Vefik

Veli Efendi plot, 211-12

Veysi, 20

Victoria, Queen, 236, 237 and n11, 238

Vidin, 105, 138 n6, 145, 151, 301

vilayet law, 48, 106, 108, 135, 157, 232,

478